Lecture Notes in Artificial Intellige

Subseries of Lecture Notes in Computer Scienc
Edited by J. G. Carbonell and J. Siekmann

Lecture Notes in Computer Science

Edited by G. Goos, J. Hartmanis and J. van Leeuwen

Springer
Berlin
Heidelberg
New York
Barcelona
Hong Kong
London
Milan
Paris
Singapore
Tokyo

Philippe de Groote Glyn Morrill
Christian Retoré (Eds.)

Logical Aspects of Computational Linguistics

4th International Conference, LACL 2001
Le Croisic, France, June 27-29, 2001
Proceedings

Springer

Series Editors

Jaime G. Carbonell, Carnegie Mellon University, Pittsburgh, PA, USA
Jörg Siekmann, University of Saarland, Saabrücken, Germany

Volume Editor

Philippe de Groote
INRIA Lorraine
615 rue du Jardin Botanique, B.P. 101
54602 Villers-lès-Nancy Cedex, France
E-mail: Philippe.deGroote@loria.fr

Glyn Morrill
Universitat Politècnica de Catalunya
Jordi Girona Salgado, 1-3, 08028 Barcelona, Spain
E-mail: morrill@lsi.upc.es

Christian Retoré
Institut de recherche en Informatique de Nantes (IRIN), Faculté des Sciences
2, rue de la Houssinière, B.P. 92208, 44322 Nantes Cedex 03, France
E-mail: retore@irisa.fr

Cataloging-in-Publication Data applied for

Die Deutsche Bibliothek - CIP-Einheitsaufnahme

Logical aspects of computational linguistics : 4th international conference ; proceedings / LACL 2001, LeCroisic, France, June 27 - 29, 2001. Philippe de Groote ... (ed.). - Berlin ; Heidelberg ; New York ; Barcelona ; Hong Kong ; London ; Milan ; Paris ; Singapore ; Tokyo : Springer, 2001
(Lecture notes in computer science ; Vol. 2099 : Lecture notes in artificial intelligence)
ISBN 3-540-42273-0

CR Subject Classification (1998): I.2, F.4.1

ISBN 3-540-42273-0 Springer-Verlag Berlin Heidelberg New York

Springer-Verlag Berlin Heidelberg New York
a member of BertelsmannSpringer Science+Business Media GmbH

http://www.springer.de

Typesetting: Camera-ready by author, data conversion by Boller Mediendesign
Printed on acid-free paper SPIN: 10839469 06/3142 5 4 3 2 1 0

Preface

This volume contains the proceedings of the 4th International Conference on Logical Aspects of Computational Linguistics, held June 27–29, 2001 in Le Croisic, France. The LACL conferences aim to provide a forum for the presentation and discussion of current research in all the formal and logical aspects of computational linguistics.

The program committee selected 16 papers from submissions of overall high quality. The papers cover a wide range of topics, including categorial grammars, dependency grammars, formal language theory, grammatical inference, hyperintensional semantics, minimalism, and type-logical semantics, by authors from Australia, Canada, Denmark, France, Germany, Italy, The Netherlands, Poland, Spain, Sweden, United Kingdom, and USA.

M. Moortgat (Universiteit Utrecht), G. K. Pullum (University of California, Santa Cruz), and M. Steedman (University of Edinburgh) presented invited talks, on "Structural Equations in Language Learning", "On the Distinction between Model-Theoretic and Generative-Enumerative Syntactic Frameworks", and "Reconciling Type-Logical and Combinatory Extensions of Categorial Grammar" respectively.

We would like to thank all the people who made this 4th LACL possible: the program committee, the external reviewers, the organization committee, and the LACL sponsors.

April 2001

Philippe de Groote
& Glyn Morrill

Organization

Program Committee

W. Buszkowski (Poznan)
R. Crouch, (Palo Alto)
A. Dikovsky (Nantes)
M. Dymetman (Grenoble)
C. Gardent (Nancy)
Ph. de Groote, co-chair (Nancy)
M. Kanazawa (Tokyo)
G. Morrill, co-chair (Barcelona)
R. Muskens (Tilburg)
F. Pfenning (Pittsburgh)
B. Rounds, (Ann Arbor)
E. Stabler (Los Angeles)

Organizing Committee

B. Daille (Nantes)
A. Dikovsky (Nantes)
A. Foret (Rennes)
E. Lebret (Rennes)
C. Piliere, publicity chair (Nancy)
C. Retoré, chair (Rennes)
P. Sebillot (Rennes)

Additional Referees

J.-M. Andreoli
P. Blackburn
C. Brun
T. Holloway King
M. Kandulski
F. Lamarche
J. Marciniec
J.-Y. Marion
G. Perrier

Table of Contents

Structural Equations in Language Learning

Michael Moortgat

Utrecht Institute of Linguistics — OTS
Trans 10, 3512 JK Utrecht, The Netherlands
Michael.Moortgat@let.uu.nl

Abstract. In categorial systems with a fixed structural component, the learning problem comes down to finding the solution for a set of type-assignment equations. A hard-wired structural component is problematic if one want to address issues of structural variation. Our starting point is a type-logical architecture with separate modules for the logical and the structural components of the computational system. The logical component expresses *invariants* of grammatical composition; the structural component captures variation in the realization of the correspondence between form and meaning. Learning in this setting involves finding the solution to both the type-assignment equations and the structural equations of the language at hand. We develop a view on these two subtasks which pictures learning as a process moving through a two-stage cycle. In the first phase of the cycle, type assignments are computed statically from structures. In the second phase, the lexicon is enhanced with facilities for structural reasoning. These make it possible to dynamically relate structures during on-line computation, or to establish off-line lexical generalizations. We report on the initial experiments in [15] to apply this method in the context of the Spoken Dutch Corpus.
For the general type-logical background, we refer to [12]; §1 has a brief recap of some key features.

1 Constants and Variation

One can think of type-logical grammar as a functional programming language with some special purpose features to customize it for natural language processing tasks. Basic constructs are demonstrations of the form $\Gamma \vdash A$, stating that a structure Γ is a well-formed expression of type A. These statements are the outcome of a process of computation. Our programming language has a built-in vocabulary of logical constants to construct the type formulas over some set of atomic formulas in terms of the indexed unary and binary operations of (1a). Parallel to the formula language, we have the structure-building operations of (1b) with $(\cdot \circ_i \cdot)$ and $\langle \cdot \rangle^j$ as counterparts of $\bullet_i$ and $\Diamond_j$ respectively. The indices i and j are taken from given, finite sets I, J which we refer to as composition *modes*.

(1) *a.* $\mathsf{Typ} ::= \mathsf{Atom} \mid \Diamond_j \mathsf{Typ} \mid \Box_j \mathsf{Typ} \mid \mathsf{Typ} \bullet_i \mathsf{Typ} \mid \mathsf{Typ} /_i \mathsf{Typ} \mid \mathsf{Typ} \backslash_i \mathsf{Typ}$

b. $\mathsf{Struc} ::= \mathsf{Typ} \mid \langle \mathsf{Struc} \rangle^j \mid \mathsf{Struc} \circ_i \mathsf{Struc}$

P. de Groote, G. Morrill, C. Retoré (Eds.): LACL 2001, LNAI 2099, pp. 1–16, 2001.

In presenting the rules of computation characterizing the derivability relation, we keep logical and structural aspects apart. The different composition modes all have the same *logical rules*. But we can key access to different *structural rules* by means of the mode distinctions.

Let us consider the logical component first. For each type-forming operation in (1a) there is a *constructor* rule (rule of use, assembly) and a *destructor* rule (rule of proof, disassembly). These rules can be presented in a number of equivalent ways: algebraically, in Gentzen or natural deduction format, or in a proof net presentation. The assembly/disassembly duality comes out particulary clearly in the algebraic presentation, where we have the *residuation laws* of (2). In the natural deduction format, these laws will turn up as Introduction/Elimination rules; in the Gentzen format as Left/Right introduction rules.

(2)
$$\Diamond_j A \vdash B \quad \text{iff} \quad A \vdash \Box_j B$$
$$A \vdash C/_i B \quad \text{iff} \quad A \bullet_i B \vdash C \quad \text{iff} \quad B \vdash A\backslash_i C$$

The composition of natural language *meaning* proceeds along the lines of the Curry-Howard interpretation of derivations, which reads off the meaning assembly from the logical inference steps that make up a computation. In this sense, the composition of meaning is *invariant* across languages — it is fully determined by the elimination/introduction rules for the grammatical constants. Languages show variation in the structural realization of the correspondence between form and meaning. Such variation is captured by the structural component of the computational system. Structural rules have the status of *non-logical axioms* (or postulates). The structural rules we consider in this paper are *linear transformations*:[1] they reassemble grammatical material, but they cannot duplicate or waste it. The familiar rules of Associativity and Commutativity in (3) can serve as illustrations. In a global form, these rules destroy essential grammatical information. But we will see in §2.2 how they can be tamed.

(3)
$$A \bullet B \vdash B \bullet A$$
$$(A \bullet B) \bullet C \dashv\vdash A \bullet (B \bullet C)$$

To obtain a type-logical grammar over a terminal vocabulary Σ, we have to specify a lexicon $\mathsf{Lex} \subseteq \Sigma \times \mathsf{Type}$, assigning each vocabulary item a finite number of types. A grammar, then, is a structure $G = \langle \mathsf{Lex}, \mathsf{Op} \rangle$, where Op is the union of the logical and the structural rules. Let $L(G, B)$ be the set of strings of type B generated by G, and let $\mathsf{Struc}(A_1, \ldots, A_n)$ be the set of structure trees with yield $A_1, \ldots, A_n$. For a string $\sigma = w_1 \cdot \ldots \cdot w_n \in \Sigma^+$, we say that $\sigma \in L(G, B)$ iff there are $A_1, \ldots, A_n$ and $\Gamma \in \mathsf{Struc}(A_1, \ldots, A_n)$ such that for $1 \leq i \leq n$, $\langle w_i, A_i \rangle \in \mathsf{Lex}$, and $\Gamma \vdash B$. To obtain $L(G)$, the language generated by the type-logical grammar G, we compute $L(G, B)$ for some fixed (finite set of) goal type(s)/start symbol(s) B.

[1] That is, we do not address multiple-use issues like parasitic gaps here, which might require (a controlled form of) Contraction.

2 Structural Reasoning in Learning

The modular treatment of logical and structural reasoning naturally suggests that we break up the learning problem in two subtasks. One task consists in finding appropriate categorization for the words in Σ as the elementary building blocks for meaning composition. This is essentially the problem of computing type-assignments as we know it from classical categorial learning theory. The second subtask addresses the question: What is the dynamic potential of words in syntax? Answering this question amounts to solving structural equations within a space set by universal grammar.

In tackling the second subtask, we will rely heavily on the unary constant $\Diamond$ and its residual $\Box$. As we have seen in §1, the binary product $\bullet$ captures the composition of grammatical parts, while the residual implications / and \ express incompleteness with respect to the composition relation. Extending the vocabulary with the unary constants $\Diamond, \Box$ substantially increases the analytical power of the categorial type language. This can be seen already in *the base logic* (i.e. the pure residuation logic, with empty structural module): the unary operators make it possible to refine type-assignments that would be overgenerating without the unary decoration. Moreover, in systems with a non-empty structural component, the unary operators can provide lexically anchored control over structural reasoning. We discuss these two aspects in turn.

In the base logic, the fundamental derivability pattern created by the unary operators is $\Diamond\Box A \vdash A \vdash \Box\Diamond A$. One can exploit this pattern to obtain the agreement configurations of (4).

$$(4)\quad \Diamond\Box A \bullet \begin{cases} \Diamond\Box A\backslash B \vdash B \\ A\backslash B \vdash B \\ \Box\Diamond A\backslash B \vdash B \end{cases} \qquad A \bullet \begin{cases} \Diamond\Box A\backslash B \not\vdash B \\ A\backslash B \vdash B \\ \Box\Diamond A\backslash B \vdash B \end{cases} \qquad \Box\Diamond A \bullet \begin{cases} \Diamond\Box A\backslash B \not\vdash B \\ A\backslash B \not\vdash B \\ \Box\Diamond A\backslash B \vdash B \end{cases}$$

The treatment of polarity sensitive items in [2] illustrates this use of modal decoration. Consider the contrast between 'Nobody left yet' with the negative polarity item 'yet' and '*Somebody left yet'. The negative polarity trigger 'nobody' is assigned the type $s/(np\backslash\Box\Diamond s)$, whereas 'somebody' has the undecorated type $s/(np\backslash s)$. The negative polarity item 'yet' is typed as $\Box\Diamond s\backslash\Box\Diamond s$ — it requires a trigger such as 'nobody' to check the $\Box\Diamond$ decoration in its result subtype. In the base logic, we have $s/(np\backslash\Box\Diamond s) \vdash s/(np\backslash s)$, i.e. the $\Box\Diamond$ decoration on argument subtypes can be simplified away, allowing a derivation of e.g. 'Nobody left' where there is no polarity item to be checked. This strategy of unary decoration is extended in [3] to lexically enforce constraints on the scopal possibilities of generalized quantifier expressions such as discussed in [1].

For the use of unary type decoration to provide controlled access to structural reasoning, we can rely on the results of [11]. In that paper, we present embedding translations $\cdot^\natural$ from source logics $\mathcal{L}$ to target logics $\mathcal{L}'\Diamond$, in the sense that $A \vdash B$ is derivable in $\mathcal{L}$ iff $A^\natural \vdash B^\natural$ is derivable in $\mathcal{L}'\Diamond$. The translations $\cdot^\natural$ decorate the type assignments of the source logic with the unary operators $\Diamond, \Box$ in such a way that they licence access to restricted versions of the structural rules.

In the following sections, we use this modalization strategy to develop our two-stage view on the learning process. The first stage consists of learning from structures in the base logic. Because the base logic has no facilities for structural reasoning, the lexical ambiguity load in this phase soon becomes prohibitive. In the second stage, the lexicon is optimized by shifting to modalized ($\Diamond, \Box$) type assignments. The modal decoration is designed in such a way that lexical ambiguity is reduced to derivational polymorphism. We will assume that the learning process cycles through these two stages. To carry out this program, a number of questions have to be answered:

- What kind of MODAL DECORATION do we envisage?
- What is the STRUCTURAL PACKAGE which delimits the space for variation?

We discuss these questions in §2.2. First, we address the problem of learning from structures in the base logic.

2.1 Solving Type Equations by Hypothetical Reasoning

The unification perspective on learning type assignments from structures is well understood — we refer the reader to the seminal work of [5], and to [9]. Here we present the problem of solving type assignment equations from a Logic Programming perspective in order to highlight the role of hypothetical reasoning in the process.

Consider the standard abstract interpreter for logic programs (see for example [16]). The resolution algorithm takes as input a program P and a goal G and initializes the resolvent to be the input goal G. While the resolvent is non-empty, the algorithm chooses a goal A from the resolvent and a matching program clause $A' \leftarrow B_1, \ldots, B_n$ $(n \geq 0)$ from P such that A and A' unify with mgu θ. A is removed from the resolvent and $B_1, \ldots, B_n$ added instead, with θ applied to the resolvent and to G. As output, the algorithm produces $G\theta$, if the resolvent is empty, or failure, if the empty clause cannot be derived.

[6] presents a variant on this refutation algorithm which does not return failure for an incomplete derivation, but instead extracts information from the non-empty resolvent which provides the *conditional answer* that would make the goal G derivable. In [6] the conditional answer approach is illustrated with the polymorphic type inference problem from lambda calculus. This illustration can be straightforwardly adapted to our categorial type inference problem. Writing $\Gamma \triangleleft \Delta$ for functor-argument structures with the functor as the left component and $\Gamma \triangleright \Delta$ for such structures with the functor as the right component, the 'program clauses' for categorial type assignment appear as (5).

(5) $\Gamma \triangleleft \Delta \vdash A$ *if* $\Gamma \vdash A/B$ *and* $\Delta \vdash B$ $\qquad$ $\Gamma \triangleright \Delta \vdash A$ *if* $\Gamma \vdash B$ *and* $\Delta \vdash B\backslash A$

In order to derive the empty clause, the program would need a lexicon of type assignment facts. In the absence of such a lexicon (or in the case of an incomplete lexicon), the conditional answer derivation returns the resolvent with the type assignment goals that would be needed for a successful refutation. The conditional answer is optimized by *factoring*, i.e. by the contraction of unifiable type assignment goals. A sample run of the algorithm is given below.

input Alice $\triangleright$ dreams, Lewis $\triangleright$ dreams, (the $\triangleleft$ girl) $\triangleright$ dreams, Alice $\triangleright$ (knows $\triangleleft$ Lewis), Lewis $\triangleright$ (knows $\triangleleft$ Alice), (the $\triangleleft$ mathematician) $\triangleright$ (knows $\triangleleft$ Alice), Alice $\triangleright$ (knows $\triangleleft$ (the $\triangleleft$ mathematician)), Alice $\triangleright$ (irritates $\triangleleft$ (the $\triangleleft$ mathematician)), (the $\triangleleft$ mathematician) $\triangleright$ (irritates $\triangleleft$ Alice), Alice $\triangleright$ (dreams $\triangleright$ (about $\triangleleft$ Lewis)), Lewis $\triangleright$ (wrote $\triangleleft$ (the $\triangleleft$ book)), Lewis $\triangleright$ (knows $\triangleleft$ (the $\triangleleft$ girl)), Lewis $\triangleright$ (wrote $\triangleleft$ (the $\triangleleft$ (nice $\triangleleft$ book))), (the $\triangleleft$ girl) $\triangleright$ (knows $\triangleleft$ (the $\triangleleft$ book)), (the $\triangleleft$ girl) $\triangleright$ (knows $\triangleleft$ (the $\triangleleft$ (book $\triangleright$ (which $\triangleleft$ (irritates $\triangleleft$ (the $\triangleleft$ mathematician)))))), (the $\triangleleft$ girl) $\triangleright$ (knows $\triangleleft$ (the $\triangleleft$ (book $\triangleright$ ((which $\triangleleft$ (the $\triangleleft$ mathematician)) $\triangleleft$ wrote)))), ...

output The term assignments of (6). With the gloss $A = n$, $B = np$, $C = s$ for the type variables, these will look familiar enough.

(6)

Alice $\vdash B$	Lewis $\vdash B$
dreams $\vdash B\backslash C$	the $\vdash B/A$
girl $\vdash A$	mathematician $\vdash A$
book $\vdash A$	nice $\vdash A/A$
about $\vdash ((B\backslash C)\backslash(B\backslash C))/B$	irritates $\vdash (B\backslash C)/B$
knows $\vdash (B\backslash C)/B$	wrote $\vdash (B\backslash C)/B$
which $\vdash (A\backslash A)/(B\backslash C)$	which $\vdash ((A\backslash A)/((B\backslash C)/B))/B$

The interesting point of this run is the two type assignments for 'which': one for subject relativization (obtained from '...which irritates Alice'), the other for object relativization (from '...which Lewis wrote') — and, of course, many others for different structural contexts. Factoring (unification) cannot relate these assignments: this would require structural reasoning. To see that the learning algorithm is missing a generalization here, consider the meaning assembly for these two type assignments to the relative pronoun. The lambda program of (7a), expressing property intersection, would be adequate for the subject relativization type. To obtain appropriate meaning assembly for the object relativization assignment, one would need the lambda program of (7b).

(7) *a.* which $\vdash (n\backslash n)/(np\backslash s)$ $\lambda x\lambda y\lambda z.(x\ z) \wedge (y\ z)$ (= **wh**)
b. which $\vdash ((n\backslash n)/((np\backslash s)/np))/np$ $\lambda x'\lambda y'\lambda y\lambda z.((y'\ z)\ x') \wedge (y\ z)$

The point is that these two meaning programs are not unrelated. We can see this by analysing them from the perspective of **LP** (or Multiplicative Linear Logic) — a system which removes all structural obstacles to meaning composition in the sense that free restructuring and reordering under Associativity and Commutativity are available. In **LP**, the different type assignments are simply structural realizations of one and the same meaning. See the derivation of Figure 1, which produces the proof term of (8). Unfortunately, **LP** is of little use as a framework for natural language analysis: apart from the required meaning assembly of (8), there is a second derivation for the type transition of Figure 1 producing the proof term $\lambda y_1.\lambda x_2.(\mathbf{wh}\ (x_2\ y_1))$, which gets the thematic roles of subject and object wrong. Can we find a way of controlling structural reasoning, so that we can do with a single type assignment to the relative pronoun, while keeping the thematic structure intact?

$$
\cfrac{
  \cfrac{
    \text{which}
  }{
    (n\backslash n)/(np\backslash s)
  }
  \quad
  \cfrac{
    \cfrac{
      \cfrac{
        [p_1 \vdash np]^2 \quad
        \cfrac{
          [r_1 \vdash (np\backslash s)/np]^3 \quad [r_0 \vdash np]^1
        }{
          r_1 \circ r_0 \vdash np\backslash s
        }\ [/E]
      }{
        p_1 \circ (r_1 \circ r_0) \vdash s
      }\ [\backslash E]
    }{
      \cfrac{
        \cfrac{
          \cfrac{
            \cfrac{
              (p_1 \circ r_1) \circ r_0 \vdash s
            }{}
          }{
            r_0 \circ (p_1 \circ r_1) \vdash s
          }\ [\text{Comm}]
        }{
          p_1 \circ r_1 \vdash np\backslash s
        }\ [\backslash I]^1
      }{
        \text{which} \circ (p_1 \circ r_1) \vdash n\backslash n
      }\ [/E]
    }\ [\text{Ass}]
  }
}{}
$$

$$
\cfrac{
  [p_2 \vdash n]^4 \quad
  \cfrac{
    \cfrac{
      \cfrac{
        \cfrac{
          \cfrac{
            \text{which} \circ (p_1 \circ r_1) \vdash n\backslash n
          }{
            p_2 \circ (\text{which} \circ (p_1 \circ r_1)) \vdash n
          }\ [\backslash E]
        }{
          p_2 \circ ((\text{which} \circ p_1) \circ r_1) \vdash n
        }\ [\text{Ass}]
      }{
        (\text{which} \circ p_1) \circ r_1 \vdash n\backslash n
      }\ [\backslash I]^4
    }{
      \text{which} \circ p_1 \vdash (n\backslash n)/((np\backslash s)/np)
    }\ [/I]^3
  }{
    \text{which} \vdash ((n\backslash n)/((np\backslash s)/np))/np
  }\ [/I]^2
}{}
$$

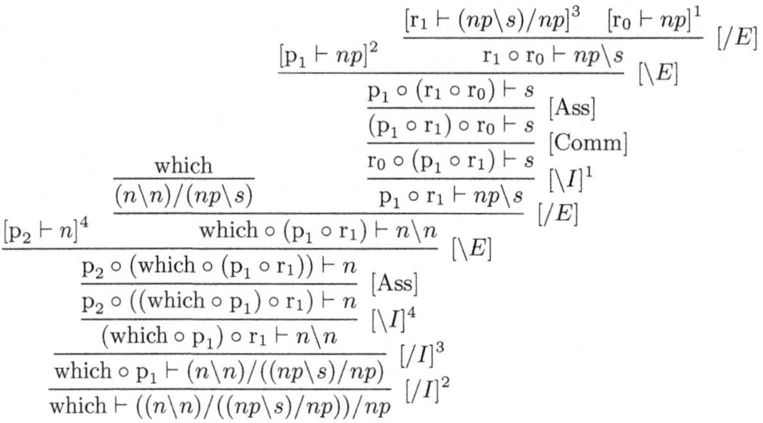

Fig. 1. Relating subject and object relativization in **LP**.

$$
(8) \qquad \mathbf{wh} \vdash_{\mathbf{LP}} \lambda y_1.\lambda x_2.(\mathbf{wh}\ \lambda z_0.((x_2\ z_0)\ y_1)) \qquad =_\beta
$$
$$
\lambda y_1.\lambda x_2.\lambda z_3.\lambda x_4.(((x_2\ x_4)\ y_1) \wedge (z_3\ x_4))
$$

2.2   Modal Decorations for Solving Structural Equations

To answer this question, we turn to the second phase of the learning process. Let $\mathsf{type}(w)$ be the set of types which the algorithm of §2.1 associates with a word w in the base logic lexicon: $\mathsf{type}(w) = \{A \mid \langle w, A\rangle \in \mathsf{Lex}\}$. The type assignments found in §2.1 are built up in terms of the binary connectives $/$ and $\backslash$: they do not exploit the full type language, and they do not appeal to structural reasoning. In the second phase of the learning cycle, these limitations are lifted. We translate the question at the end of the previous section as follows: Can we find a modal decoration $\cdot^\natural$ and an associated structural package $\mathcal{R}$ which would allow the learner to identify a $B \in \mathsf{type}(w)$ such that $B^\natural \vdash A$ for all $A \in \mathsf{type}(w)$? Or, if we opt for a weaker package $\mathcal{R}$ that makes unique type-assignment unattainable, can we at least reduce the cardinality of $\mathsf{type}(w)$ by removing some derivable type assignments from the type-set? In what follows, we consider various options for $\cdot^\natural$ and for $\mathcal{R}$.

Consider first the decorations $\lfloor\cdot\rfloor, \lceil\cdot\rceil : \mathbf{B} \mapsto \mathbf{B}\Diamond$ of (9) for *input* and *output* polarities respectively.[2]

(9)
$$\begin{array}{rclrcl} \lfloor p \rfloor &=& p & \lceil p \rceil &=& p \\ \lfloor A \bullet B \rfloor &=& \Diamond\Box\lfloor A\rfloor \bullet \Diamond\Box\lfloor B\rfloor & \lceil A\bullet B\rceil &=& \lceil B\rceil \bullet \lceil A\rceil \\ \lfloor A/B\rfloor &=& \Diamond\Box\lfloor A\rfloor/\lceil B\rceil & \lceil A/B\rceil &=& \lceil A\rceil/\Diamond\Box\lfloor B\rfloor \\ \lfloor B\backslash A\rfloor &=& \lceil B\rceil\backslash\Diamond\Box\lfloor A\rfloor & \lceil B\backslash A\rceil &=& \Diamond\Box\lfloor B\rfloor\backslash\lceil A\rceil \end{array}$$

The effect of $\lfloor\cdot\rfloor, \lceil\cdot\rceil$ is to prefix all input subformulas with $\Diamond\Box$. In the absence of structural rules, this modal marking would indeed be a pure embellishment, in the sense that $\mathbf{B} \vdash \bullet\Gamma \Rightarrow A$ iff $\mathbf{B}\Diamond \vdash \lfloor\bullet\Gamma\rfloor \Rightarrow \lceil A\rceil$. But we are interested in the situation where the $\Diamond\Box$ decoration gives access to structural reasoning. As a crude first attempt, consider the postulate package (10) which would be the modal analogue of (3), i.e. it allows full restructuring and reordering under $\Diamond$ control. In the Associativity postulates, one of the factors A_i $(1 \leq i \leq 3)$ is of the form $\Diamond A'$, with the rule label indexed accordingly.

(10)
$$\begin{array}{lr} A_1 \bullet (A_2 \bullet A_3) \vdash (A_1 \bullet A_2) \bullet A_3 & [A_i] \\ (A_1 \bullet A_2) \bullet A_3 \vdash A_1 \bullet (A_2 \bullet A_3) & [A_i^{-1}] \\ \\ B \bullet \Diamond A \vdash \Diamond A \bullet B & [C] \\ \Diamond B \bullet A \vdash A \bullet \Diamond B & [C^{-1}] \end{array}$$

With the package (10), we again have the embedding

$$\mathbf{LP} \vdash \bullet\Gamma \Rightarrow A \quad \text{iff} \quad \mathbf{B}\Diamond + (10) \vdash \lfloor\bullet\Gamma\rfloor \Rightarrow \lceil A\rceil$$

Consider again the type assignments we computed in (6) for the relative pronoun:

$$\begin{array}{rl} \mathsf{type}(\text{which}) = & \{(n\backslash n)/(np\backslash s), \\ & ((n\backslash n)/((np\backslash s)/np))/np, \\ & \ldots\} \end{array}$$

Calculating $\lfloor\cdot\rfloor$ for the first of these, we obtain (11)

(11)
$$\begin{array}{rl} \lfloor (n\backslash n)/(np\backslash s)\rfloor & = \Diamond\Box\lfloor n\backslash n\rfloor/\lceil np\backslash s\rceil \\ & = \Diamond\Box(\lceil n\rceil\backslash\Diamond\Box\lfloor n\rfloor)/(\Diamond\Box\lfloor np\rfloor\backslash\lceil s\rceil) \\ & = \Diamond\Box(n\backslash\Diamond\Box n)/(\Diamond\Box np\backslash s) \end{array}$$

which indeed gives the type transformation

$$\Diamond\Box(n\backslash\Diamond\Box n)/(\Diamond\Box np\backslash s) \vdash ((n\backslash n)/((np\backslash s)/np))/np$$

In Figure 2, we give an example derived from the modalized type assignment to the relative pronoun. We concentrate on the subderivation that realizes non-peripheral extraction via $\Diamond$ controlled structural reasoning. The modal decoration implements the 'key and lock' strategy of [14]. For a constituent of type

---

[2] $\mathbf{B}$ is the base logic for the binary connectives: the pure residuation logic for $/, \bullet, \backslash$, with no structural postulates at all. $\mathbf{B}\Diamond$ is the extended system with the unary connectives $\Diamond, \Box$.

$\Diamond\Box A$, the $\Diamond$ component provides access to the structural postulates in (10). At the point where such a marked constituent has found the structural position where it can be used by the logical rules, the $\Diamond$ key unlocks the $\Box$ lock: the control feature is cancelled through the basic law $\Diamond\Box A \vdash A$.

$$\dfrac{\dfrac{\text{dedicated}}{((np\backslash s)/pp)/np} \quad \dfrac{[\mathrm{p}_2 \vdash \Box np]^5}{\langle \mathrm{p}_2\rangle \vdash np}\,[\Box E]}{\text{dedicated} \circ \langle \mathrm{p}_2\rangle \vdash (np\backslash s)/pp}\,[/E] \qquad \dfrac{\dfrac{\text{to}}{pp/np} \quad \dfrac{\text{Alice}}{np}}{\text{to} \circ \text{Alice} \vdash pp}\,[/E]$$

$$\dfrac{\dfrac{\text{Lewis}}{np} \quad \dfrac{\text{dedicated} \circ \langle \mathrm{p}_2\rangle \vdash (np\backslash s)/pp \quad \text{to} \circ \text{Alice} \vdash pp}{(\text{dedicated} \circ \langle \mathrm{p}_2\rangle) \circ (\text{to} \circ \text{Alice}) \vdash np\backslash s}\,[/E]}{\text{Lewis} \circ ((\text{dedicated} \circ \langle \mathrm{p}_2\rangle) \circ (\text{to} \circ \text{Alice})) \vdash s}\,[\backslash E]$$

$$\dfrac{\text{Lewis} \circ ((\text{dedicated} \circ \langle \mathrm{p}_2\rangle) \circ (\text{to} \circ \text{Alice})) \vdash s}{\text{Lewis} \circ (\text{dedicated} \circ (\langle \mathrm{p}_2\rangle \circ (\text{to} \circ \text{Alice}))) \vdash s}\,[A_2]$$

$$\dfrac{}{\text{Lewis} \circ (\text{dedicated} \circ ((\text{to} \circ \text{Alice}) \circ \langle \mathrm{p}_2\rangle)) \vdash s}\,[C]$$

$$\dfrac{}{\text{Lewis} \circ ((\text{dedicated} \circ (\text{to} \circ \text{Alice})) \circ \langle \mathrm{p}_2\rangle) \vdash s}\,[A_3^{-1}]$$

$$\dfrac{}{(\text{Lewis} \circ (\text{dedicated} \circ (\text{to} \circ \text{Alice}))) \circ \langle \mathrm{p}_2\rangle \vdash s}\,[A_3^{-1}] \quad \dagger$$

$$\dfrac{}{\langle \mathrm{p}_2\rangle \circ (\text{Lewis} \circ (\text{dedicated} \circ (\text{to} \circ \text{Alice}))) \vdash s}\,[C^{-1}]$$

$$\dfrac{[\mathrm{r}_1 \vdash \Diamond\Box np]^4 \qquad \langle \mathrm{p}_2\rangle \circ (\text{Lewis} \circ (\text{dedicated} \circ (\text{to} \circ \text{Alice}))) \vdash s}{\dfrac{\mathrm{r}_1 \circ (\text{Lewis} \circ (\text{dedicated} \circ (\text{to} \circ \text{Alice}))) \vdash s}{\text{Lewis} \circ (\text{dedicated} \circ (\text{to} \circ \text{Alice})) \vdash \Diamond\Box np\backslash s}\,[\backslash I]^4}\,[\Diamond E]^5$$

Fig. 2. Non-peripheral extraction under $\Diamond$ control: '(the book which) Lewis dedicated to Alice'. The (†) sign marks the entry point for an alternative derivation, driven from an assignment $(n\backslash n)/(s/\Diamond\Box np)$ for the relative pronoun. See the discussion in §2.3.

2.3 Calibration

The situation we have obtained is a crude first approximation in two respects. First, the *modal decoration* is overly rich in the sense that every input subformula is given a chance to engage in structural reasoning. Second, the structural package (10) is not much better that the global structural reasoning of §1 in that it allows full reordering and restructuring, this time under $\Diamond$ control. The task here is to find the proper trade-off between the degree of lexical ambiguity one is prepared to tolerate, and the expressivity of the structural package. We discuss these two considerations in turn.

STRUCTURAL REASONING Consider first the structural component. The package in (12) seems to have a pleasant balance between expressivity and structural constraint. We refer the reader to the discussion of extraction asymmetries between head-initial and head-final languages in [14], Dutch verb-raising in [13], and the analysis of French cliticization in [10], all of which are based essentially on the structural features of (12). In this section, we discuss the postulates in their schematic form — further fine-tuning in terms of mode distinctions for the $\bullet$ and $\Diamond$ operations is straightforward and will be taken into consideration in §3.

(12)

$$\begin{array}{lr} \Diamond A \bullet (B \bullet C) \dashv\vdash (\Diamond A \bullet B) \bullet C & (Pl1) \\ \Diamond A \bullet (B \bullet C) \dashv\vdash B \bullet (\Diamond A \bullet C) & (Pl2) \end{array}$$

$$\begin{array}{lr} (A \bullet B) \bullet \Diamond C \dashv\vdash (A \bullet \Diamond C) \bullet B & (Pr2) \\ (A \bullet B) \bullet \Diamond C \dashv\vdash A \bullet (B \bullet \Diamond C) & (Pr1) \end{array}$$

The postulates can be read in two directions. In the $\vdash$ direction, they have the effect of *revealing* a $\Diamond$ marked constituent, by promoting it from an embedded position to a position where it is visible for the logical rules: the immediate left or right daughter of the structural root node.[3] In the $\dashv$ direction, they *hide* a marked constituent, pushing it from a visible position to an embedded position. Apart from the $\dashv\vdash$ asymmetry, the postulates preserve the left-right asymmetry of the primitive operations / and \: the *Pl* postulates have a bias for left branches; for the *Pr* postulates only right branches are accessible.

We highlight some properties of this package.

Linearity The postulates rearrange a structural configuration; they cannot duplicate or waste grammatical material.

Control The postulates operate under $\Diamond$ control. Because the logic doesn't allow the control features to enter a derivation out of the blue, this means they have to be lexically anchored.

Locality The window for structural reasoning is strictly local: postulates can only see two products in construction with each other (with one of the factors bearing the licensing $\Diamond$ feature).

Recursion Non-local effects of structural reasoning arise through recursion.

In comparison with universal package (10), the postulates of (12) represent a move towards *more specific* forms of structural reasoning. One can see this in the deconstruction of $Pr2$ (similarly, $Pl2$) as the compilation of a sequence of structural inferences in (10). The postulate C of (10) is removed from (12) as an independent structural inference; instead, a restricted use of it is *encapsulated* in $Pr2$ (or $Pl2$).

$$(A \bullet B) \bullet \Diamond C \vdash (A \bullet \Diamond C) \bullet B \qquad (Pr2)$$

$$\text{Combinator:} \quad Pr2 = \gamma^{-1}(\gamma(A_2) \circ C) \circ A_3^{-1}$$

$$(A \bullet B) \bullet \Diamond C \overset{A_3^{-1}}{\vdash} A \bullet (B \bullet \Diamond C) \overset{C}{\vdash} A \bullet (\Diamond C \bullet B) \overset{A_2}{\vdash} (A \bullet \Diamond C) \bullet B$$

The careful reader may have noticed that the package (12) is too weak to allow the derivation of the extraction example in Figure 2. The modalized type

[3] The reader should keep in mind that, as a result of the cut rule, it is the pattern to the *left* of $\vdash$ that shows up in the conclusion of the natural deduction inferences we have given.

assignment for the relative pronoun in (11) has $(\Diamond\Box np\backslash s)$ as the subtype for the relative clause body: the $\Diamond\Box np$ hypothesis is withdrawn to the left. But this means that complement positions on right branches are inaccessible for the $\Diamond\Box np$ gap hypothesis, if we want to stay within the limits of (12). Accessing a right branch position from the launching point of $\Diamond\Box np$ would require the extra postulate $Pl3$ (and by symmetry $Pr3$), establishing communication between the left- and right-biased options. Again, these are forms of structural reasoning encapsulating a controlled amount of C.

(13)
$$\Diamond A \bullet (B \bullet C) \dashv\vdash B \bullet (C \bullet \Diamond A) \quad (Pl3)?$$
$$(A \bullet B) \bullet \Diamond C \dashv\vdash (\Diamond C \bullet A) \bullet B \quad (Pr3)?$$

$$\dfrac{\dfrac{\text{dedicated}}{((np\backslash s)/pp)/np} \quad \dfrac{[\mathrm{s}_1 \vdash \Box np]^2}{\langle \mathrm{s}_1\rangle \vdash np}[\Box E]}{\text{dedicated} \circ \langle \mathrm{s}_1\rangle \vdash (np\backslash s)/pp}[/E] \qquad \dfrac{\dfrac{\text{to}}{pp/np} \quad \dfrac{\text{Alice}}{np}}{\text{to} \circ \text{Alice} \vdash pp}[/E]$$

$$\dfrac{\dfrac{\text{Lewis}}{np} \quad \dfrac{\text{dedicated} \circ \langle \mathrm{s}_1\rangle \vdash (np\backslash s)/pp \quad \text{to} \circ \text{Alice} \vdash pp}{(\text{dedicated} \circ \langle \mathrm{s}_1\rangle) \circ (\text{to} \circ \text{Alice}) \vdash np\backslash s}[/E]}{\text{Lewis} \circ ((\text{dedicated} \circ \langle \mathrm{s}_1\rangle) \circ (\text{to} \circ \text{Alice})) \vdash s}[\backslash E]$$

$$\dfrac{\text{Lewis} \circ ((\text{dedicated} \circ \langle \mathrm{s}_1\rangle) \circ (\text{to} \circ \text{Alice})) \vdash s}{\dfrac{\text{Lewis} \circ ((\text{dedicated} \circ (\text{to} \circ \text{Alice})) \circ \langle \mathrm{s}_1\rangle) \vdash s}{(\text{Lewis} \circ (\text{dedicated} \circ (\text{to} \circ \text{Alice}))) \circ \langle \mathrm{s}_1\rangle \vdash s}[Pr1]}[Pr2]$$

$$\dfrac{\dfrac{[\mathrm{q}_1 \vdash \Diamond\Box np]^1 \quad (\text{Lewis} \circ (\text{dedicated} \circ (\text{to} \circ \text{Alice}))) \circ \langle \mathrm{s}_1\rangle \vdash s}{(\text{Lewis} \circ (\text{dedicated} \circ (\text{to} \circ \text{Alice}))) \circ \mathrm{q}_1 \vdash s}[\Diamond E]^2}{\text{Lewis} \circ (\text{dedicated} \circ (\text{to} \circ \text{Alice})) \vdash s/\Diamond\Box np}[/I]^1$$

Fig. 3. Non-peripheral extraction in terms of the package (12). Compare with the derivation in Figure 2.

There is a lexical alternative to strengthening the postulate package which is obtained from a directional variant of the type assignment to the relative pronoun, with $(s/\Diamond\Box np)$ as the subtype for the relative clause body. Under this alternative, the lexicon assigns two types to 'which': one for subject relativization, one for non-subject cases. See the derivation in Figure 3. Notice the trade-off here between increasing the size of the lexicon (storage) versus simplification of the on-line computation (the structural package). Different learners could make different choices with respect to this trade-off: we do not want to assume that the solution for the lexicon and the structural module has to be unique. Individual solutions can count as equally adequate as long as they associate the same forms with the same meaning. As we have noticed in §1, meaning composition is fully determined by the logical introduction/elimination rules for the type-logical constants modulo directionality (i.e. / and \ are indentified).

The two alternatives above make different choices with respect to the distribution of grammatical complexity over the lexicon and the structural module. For an example of alternative solutions that are essentially of the same complexity, we refer to the analysis of Dutch verb raising (VR) in [13], where a leftwing and a rightwing solution to the verb raising puzzle are presented. A schematic comparison is given in Figure 4. We use mode 0 for the composition of the lexical cluster, and mode 1 for phrasal composition. The leftwing approach treats VR-triggers (modals/auxiliaries) as $\Box_0(vp/_0 inf)$, and relates the surface order to the configuration required for meaning assembly in terms of $Pl2$. The rightwing solution assigns VR-triggers a type $\Box_0(inf\backslash_0 vp)$, and obtains the phrasal reconfiguration in terms of $Pr1$. The first step, in the two derivations, is a feature percolation postulate checking lexicality of the verb cluster — we do not go into this aspect of the analysis here.

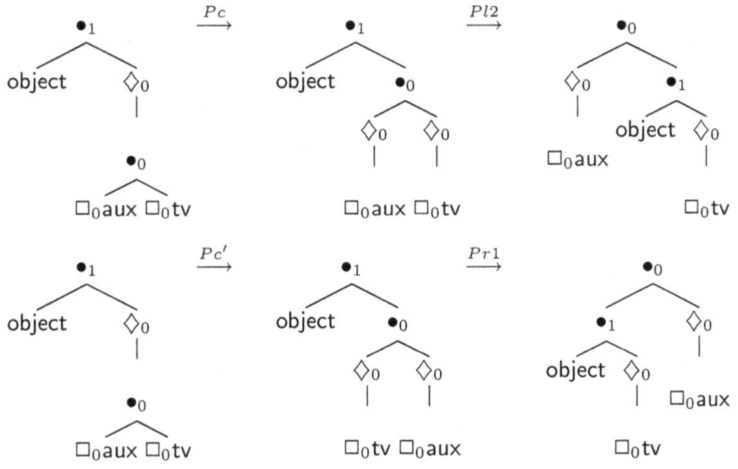

Fig. 4. Two views on Dutch VR. Surface order on the left. Meaning composition on the right. Phrasal composition: $\bullet_1$, lexical cluster formation: $\bullet_0$.

MODAL DECORATION The decoration of (9) marks every input subtype of a type formula. These subtypes will become active, in some stage of the derivation, in the structural part (antecedent) of a sequent, where they have the potential to trigger structural reasoning. Various options for a sparser style of modal decoration present themselves. One could choose to mark only *terminal* input formulae, i.e. lexical and hypothetical assumptions. Compare the full decoration for the relative pronoun type in (11) $\Diamond\Box(\Diamond\Box(n\backslash\Diamond\Box n)/(\Diamond\Box np\backslash s))$ with the terminal-inputs-only marking $\Diamond\Box((n\backslash n)/(\Diamond\Box np\backslash s))$. Or one could mark subtypes that one wants to consider as 'major phrases' — atomic types, and maybe some others, such as the relative clause type $n\backslash n$ in our example which, with a modal prefix, could be extraposed via the Pr family. In the next section, we compare some of these options in a concrete application.

A second aspect of the modal decoration strategy has to do with the dynamics of the learning process, as it goes through its two-phase cycle. In fine-tuning the lexicon, a reasonable strategy would be to go for the *most general* type compatible with the data. Modal decoration that turns out to be non-functional, in this sense, 'dies off' in the course of the learning process. In our relative pronoun example, if all $\Diamond\Box$ marks remain inert, except for the $\Diamond\Box np$ gap hypothesis, the learner at a certain point is justified in applying the following pruning type transformation.

$$\Diamond\Box(\Diamond\Box(n\backslash\Diamond\Box n)/(\Diamond\Box np\backslash s)) \vdash (n\backslash n)/(\Diamond\Box np\backslash s)$$

3 Testcase: The Spoken Dutch Corpus

In the previous section, we have sketched some options for the structural package and for the modal decoration that gives access to this package. We are currently exploring these options in the context of the Spoken Dutch Corpus project (CGN) — our initial experiments are reported in [15], on which this section is based.

The CGN project is a Dutch-Flemish collaborative effort to put together an annotated Dutch speech corpus of 10 million words — some 1000 hours of audio. Upon its completion in 2003 the CGN corpus will be a major resource for R&D in language and speech technology. A rich part-of-speech annotation is provided for the complete corpus. In addition, a core corpus of one million words is annotated syntactically (cf. [8]). The annotation is designed in such a way that it can be easily translated into the analysis formats of the various theoretical frameworks that want to use the CGN treebank to train and test computational grammars.

The CGN annotation provides information on two levels: syntactic constituent structure and the semantic dependencies between them. Because these two dimensions often do not run in parallel, the annotation format has to be rich enough to naturally represent dependency relations also where they are at odds with surface constituency. The DAG (directed acyclic graphs) data structure has the required expressivity.

Figure 5 is an example of a CGN annotation graph for the sentence 'Wat gaan we doen het komend uur?' ('What shall we do the next hour?'). The nodes of the graph are labeled with syntactic category information (circled in Figure 5) — part-of-speech labels for the leaves, phrasal category labels for the internal nodes. The edges carry dependency labels (boxed in the picture), indicating the grammatical function of the immediate subconstituents of a phrase. In the dependency dimension, the basic distinctions are between the head of a phrase, its complements, and its modifiers.

The annotation graph of Figure 5 illustrates how the specific features of DAG's (as compared to trees) are exploited. In the example, we want to express the fact that the interrogative pronoun 'wat' ('what') serves as direct object of the transitive infinitive 'doen' ('do'). This is a discontinuous dependency, which leads to *crossing branches* in the annotation graph. At the same time, we want to indicate that the question word is responsible for projecting the top node WHQ

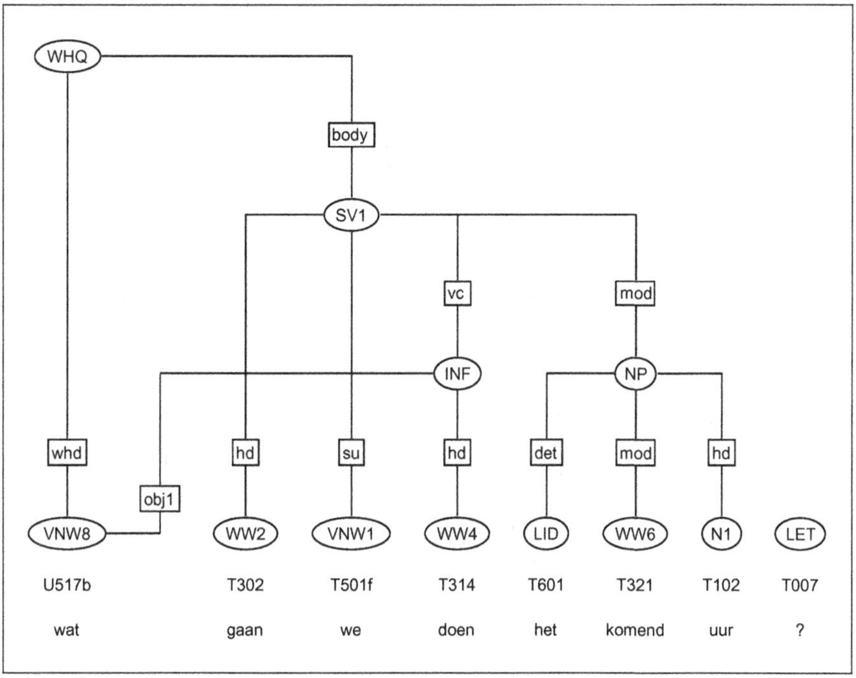

Fig. 5. A CGN annotation graph.

(constituent question) and in this sense is acting as the head of the WHQ phrase. This means that a constituent can carry *multiple dependency roles*. Finally, an annotation DAG can consist of disconnected parts. This makes it possible to accommodate a number of phenomena that are very frequent in spontaneous speech: discourse fragments, interjections, etc.

The algorithm for the extraction of a type-logical lexicon out of the CGN annotation graphs is set up in such a way that one can easily experiment with the options we have discussed in the previous sections. The following parameters can be manipulated.

- Node labels. The choice here is which of the category labels are to be maintained as atomic types in the categorial lexicon.
- Edge labels. The dependency labels provide a rich source of information for mode distinctions. A 'light' translation implements the dependency labels as mode indices on the binary composition operation $\bullet$. One can furthermore keep the head component implicit by starting from a basic distinction between leftheaded and rightheaded products. An intransitive main clause verb, for example, is typed $np\backslash_{r(su)}s$: it creates a rightheaded configuration, where the np complement bears the subject role with respect to the head.
- Thematic hierarchy. One can fix the canonical order of complements within a dependency domain in terms of the degree of coherence with the head.

- Head position. For the various clausal types, one can determine the directional orientation of the head with respect to its complements.
- Licensing structural reasoning. Targets for $\Diamond\Box$ decoration.

In (14) the reader sees the effect of some of these settings on the lexicon that is extracted out of the annotation graph of Figure 5.

(14)
$$\begin{array}{l} \text{doen} : \Diamond_{hd}\Box_{hd}(np\backslash_{r(obj1)}inf) \\ \text{gaan} : \Diamond_{hd}\Box_{hd}((s1/_{l(vc)}inf)/_{l(su)}np) \\ \text{het} : \Diamond_{det}\Box_{det}(\Diamond_{mod}\Box_{mod}(s1\backslash s1)/_{l(hd)}np) \\ \text{komend} : \Diamond_{mod}\Box_{mod}(\Diamond_{mod}\Box_{mod}(s1\backslash s1)/\Diamond_{mod}\Box_{mod}(s1\backslash s1)) \\ \text{uur} : np \\ \text{wat} : \Diamond_{whd}\Box_{whd}(whq/_{l(body)}(\Diamond_{se}\Box_{se}np\backslash_{r(obj1)}s1)) \\ \text{we} : np \end{array}$$

The np hypothesis in the type assignment to the question word 'wat' (the gap hypothesis) gains access to structural reasoning by means of its *se* (for secondary edge) decoration. Relating the hypothesis to the direct object complement for the transitive infinitive 'doen' ('do') requires the mode-instantiated form of $Pl1$ in (15). We present a derivation in Figure 6. Note the structural move in step 20, which establishes the required configuration for the logical introduction/elimination steps.

(15)
$$\Diamond_{se}A \bullet_{r(obj1)} (B \bullet_{l(vc)} C) \vdash B \bullet_{l(vc)} (\Diamond_{se}A \bullet_{r(obj1)} C) \ (Pl1)$$

At the point of writing, the first set of syntactically annotated CGN data has been released, for some 50,000 words. We hope to report on the effect of different choices for the structural module and the parameters for the lexicon extraction algorithm in future work.

4 Conclusion

This paper represents an attempt to decompose the learning problem into a two-phase cycle, in line with the architecture of multimodal type-logical grammar. The first phase computes type-assignments from structured input, unifying type-assignment solutions in structurally similar contexts. The second phase enhances the lexicon with control features licencing structural reasoning. Lexical ambiguity is reduced by dynamically relating structural environments.

Needless to say, the ideas in this paper are in a stage of initial exploration. The only work we are aware of which also attributes a role to the unary connectives in learning is [7]. This author gives lambda terms as input to the learning algorithm, as a form of 'semantic bootstrapping'. Although we agree that semantics cannot be ignored in learning, we think the lambda term input is too rich — it gives away too much of the learning puzzle. We mention some areas for future investigation that naturally suggest themselves. As we remarked in the Introduction, classical Gold-style categorial learning theory does not address issues of structural variation. Could one recast the two-stage learning cycle of

1.	$\mathrm{wat} : \Diamond_{whd}\Box_{whd}(whq/_{l(body)}(\Diamond_{se}\Box_{se}np\backslash_{r(obj1)}s1))$	*Lex*
2.	$\mathrm{r}_0 : \Box_{whd}(whq/_{l(body)}(\Diamond_{se}\Box_{se}np\backslash_{r(obj1)}s1))$	*Hyp*
3.	$\langle \mathrm{r}_0\rangle^{whd} : whq/_{l(body)}(\Diamond_{se}\Box_{se}np\backslash_{r(obj1)}s1)$	$\Box E$ (2)
4.	$\mathrm{wat} : whq/_{l(body)}(\Diamond_{se}\Box_{se}np\backslash_{r(obj1)}s1)$	$\Diamond E$ (1, 2, 3)
5.	$\mathrm{s}_0 : \Diamond_{se}\Box_{se}np$	*Hyp*
6.	$\mathrm{doen} : \Diamond_{hd}\Box_{hd}(np\backslash_{r(obj1)}inf)$	*Lex*
7.	$\mathrm{gaan} : \Diamond_{hd}\Box_{hd}((s1/_{l(vc)}inf)/_{l(su)}np)$	*Lex*
8.	$\mathrm{s}_1 : \Box_{hd}((s1/_{l(vc)}inf)/_{l(su)}np)$	*Hyp*
9.	$\langle \mathrm{s}_1\rangle^{hd} : (s1/_{l(vc)}inf)/_{l(su)}np$	$\Box E$ (8)
10.	$\mathrm{we} : np$	*Lex*
11.	$\langle \mathrm{s}_1\rangle^{hd} \circ_{l(su)} \mathrm{we} : s1/_{l(vc)}inf$	$/E$ (9, 10)
12.	$\mathrm{q}_1 : \Box_{se}np$	*Hyp*
13.	$\langle \mathrm{q}_1\rangle^{se} : np$	$\Box E$ (12)
14.	$\mathrm{r}_2 : \Box_{hd}(np\backslash_{r(obj1)}inf)$	*Hyp*
15.	$\langle \mathrm{r}_2\rangle^{hd} : np\backslash_{r(obj1)}inf$	$\Box E$ (14)
16.	$\langle \mathrm{q}_1\rangle^{se} \circ_{r(obj1)} \langle \mathrm{r}_2\rangle^{hd} : inf$	$\backslash E$ (13, 15)
17.	$(\langle \mathrm{s}_1\rangle^{hd} \circ_{l(su)} \mathrm{we}) \circ_{l(vc)} (\langle \mathrm{q}_1\rangle^{se} \circ_{r(obj1)} \langle \mathrm{r}_2\rangle^{hd}) : s1$	$/E$ (11, 16)
18.	$(\mathrm{gaan} \circ_{l(su)} \mathrm{we}) \circ_{l(vc)} (\langle \mathrm{q}_1\rangle^{se} \circ_{r(obj1)} \langle \mathrm{r}_2\rangle^{hd}) : s1$	$\Diamond E$ (7, 8, 17)
19.	$(\mathrm{gaan} \circ_{l(su)} \mathrm{we}) \circ_{l(vc)} (\langle \mathrm{q}_1\rangle^{se} \circ_{r(obj1)} \mathrm{doen}) : s1$	$\Diamond E$ (6, 14, 18)
20.	$\langle \mathrm{q}_1\rangle^{se} \circ_{r(obj1)} ((\mathrm{gaan} \circ_{l(su)} \mathrm{we}) \circ_{l(vc)} \mathrm{doen}) : s1$	*Pl*1 (19)
21.	$\mathrm{s}_0 \circ_{r(obj1)} ((\mathrm{gaan} \circ_{l(su)} \mathrm{we}) \circ_{l(vc)} \mathrm{doen}) : s1$	$\Diamond E$ (5, 12, 20)
22.	$(\mathrm{gaan} \circ_{l(su)} \mathrm{we}) \circ_{l(vc)} \mathrm{doen} : \Diamond_{se}\Box_{se}np\backslash_{r(obj1)}s1$	$\backslash I$ (5, 21)
23.	$\mathrm{wat} \circ_{l(body)} ((\mathrm{gaan} \circ_{l(su)} \mathrm{we}) \circ_{l(vc)} \mathrm{doen}) : whq$	$/E$ (4, 22)

Proof term:(**wat** λx_1.((**gaan we**) (**doen** x_1)))

Fig. 6. Extraction in terms of (15).

this paper in terms of the identification-in-the-limit paradigm? A second area worth exploring is the relation between the deductive view on learning in this paper and results in the field of (human) language acquisition. The test case in §3 takes the machine learning perspective of grammar induction from an annotated corpus. But of course, we are interested in this test case because it opens a window on the effect of parameters that find their motivation in the cognitive setting of language acquisition. There is an affinity here between the proposals in this paper and the work on language acquisition and co-evolution in [4]. Briscoe's approach is formulated in terms of a rule-based categorial framework. The connection with our logic-based approach needs further investigation.

References

1. Beghelli F. and T. Stowell, 'Distributivity and Negation: The syntax of each and every'. In Szabolcsi (ed.) *Ways of Scope Taking*, Kluwer, 1997, pp. 72–107.
2. Bernardi, R., 'Polarity items in resource logics. A comparison'. Proceedings Student Session, ESSLLI2000, Birmingham.
3. Bernardi, R. and R. Moot, 'Generalized quantifiers in declarative and interrogative sentences'. Proceedings ICoS2.

4. Briscoe, E.J., 'Grammatical Acquisition: Inductive Bias and Coevolution of Language and the Language Acquisition Device', Language 76.2, 2000.
5. Buszkowski, W. & G. Penn, 'Categorial grammars determined from linguistic data by unification'.
Studia Logica **49**, 431–454.
6. Emden, M.H. van, 'Conditional answers for polymorphic type inference'. In Kowalski and Bowen (eds.) *Proceedings 5th International Conference on Logic Programming*, 1988.
7. Fulop, S., *On the Logic and Learning of Language.* PhD Thesis, UCLA.
8. Heleen Hoekstra, Michael Moortgat, Ineke Schuurman, Ton van der Wouden, Syntactic Annotation for the Spoken Dutch Corpus Project (CGN). Proceedings CLIN2000.
9. Kanazawa, M., *Learnable classes of categorial grammars.* PhD Dissertation, Stanford, 1994.
10. Kraak, E., 'A deductive account of French object clitics'. In Hinrichs, Kathol & Nakazawa (eds.) *Complex Predicates in Nonderivational Syntax.*
Syntax and Semantics, Vol 30. Academic Press.
11. Kurtonina, N. and M. Moortgat, 'Structural control'. In Blackburn and de Rijke (eds.) *Specifying Syntactic Structures.* CSLI Publications, 1997.
12. Moortgat, M., 'Categorial type logics'. Chapter 2 in Van Benthem and ter Meulen (eds.) *Handbook of Logic and Language.* Elsevier, 1997, pp. 93–177.
13. Moortgat, M., 'Meaningful patterns'. In Gerbrandy, Marx, de Rijke and Venema (eds.) *JFAK. Essays dedicated to Johan van Benthem on the occasion of his 50th birthday,* UAP, Amsterdam.
14. Moortgat, M., 'Constants of grammatical reasoning'. In Bouma, Hinrichs, Kruijff and Oehrle (eds.) *Constraints and Resources in Natural Language Syntax and Semantics,* CSLI, Stanford, 1999.
15. Moortgat, M. and R. Moot, CGN to Grail. Extracting a type-logical lexicon from the CGN Annotation. Proceedings CLIN2000.
16. Sterling, L. and E. Shapiro, *The Art of Prolog.* MIT Press, Cambridge, MA.

On the Distinction between Model-Theoretic and Generative-Enumerative Syntactic Frameworks*

Geoffrey K. Pullum[1] and Barbara C. Scholz[2]

[1] Department of Linguistics, University of California, Santa Cruz, California 95064, USA
(pullum@ling.ucsc.edu)
[2] Department of Philosophy, San José State University, San José, California 95192, USA
(scholz@ling.ucsc.edu)

Abstract. Two kinds of framework for stating grammars of natural languages emerged during the 20th century. Here we call them generative-enumerative syntax (GES) and model-theoretic syntax (MTS). They are based on very different mathematics. GES developed in the 1950s out of Post's work on the syntactic side of logic. MTS arose somewhat later out of the semantic side of logic. We identify some distinguishing theoretical features of these frameworks, relating to cardinality of the set of expressions, size of individual expressions, and 'transderivational constraints'. We then turn to three kinds of linguistic phenomena: partial grammaticality, the syntactic properties of expression fragments, and the fact that the lexicon of any natural language is in constant flux, and conclude that MTS has some major advantages for linguistic description that have been overlooked. We briefly consider the issue of what natural languages in MTS terms, and touch on implications for parsing and acquisition.

1 Introduction

The second half of the 20th century saw the emergence of two quite different types of frameworks for theorizing about the syntax of natural languages. One sprang from the syntactic side of mathematical logic, the other from the semantic side. They are more different than has been recognized hitherto. This paper contrasts them and highlights some of their theoretical and empirical differences.

* Early versions of some of this material were presented to the Chicago Linguistic Society, the Ohio State University, and the Australasian Association for Philosophy. We thank John Goldsmith, Lloyd Humberstone, Phokion Kolaitis, Paul Postal, Frank Richter, Jim Rogers, Arnold Zwicky for advice, comments, and assistance. We particularly thank Patrick Davidson, Line Mikkelsen, Glyn Morrill, Chris Potts, and Michael Wescoat for comments on the first draft of this paper. It should not, of course, be assumed that any of these people agree with what we say here; some of them definitely do not.

P. de Groote, G. Morrill, C. Retoré (Eds.): LACL 2001, LNAI 2099, pp. 17–43, 2001.

We begin by briefly sketching the two types of framework. In section 2 we survey three theoretical differences between them. Section 3 then points out the implications of three relevant types of linguistic phenomena that have been hitherto very largely ignored. Section 4 briefly touches on the issue of what natural languages are. Section 5 summarizes and concludes.

We should note that we use the term EXPRESSION throughout with a twofold ambiguity. First, it refers to both types and tokens of items in natural languages like words, phrases, and clauses. Second, it is used both for linguistic items and for idealized representations of their structures. When necessary, we disambiguate.

1.1 Generative-Enumerative Syntax

The first framework type we consider was developed in the 1950s on the basis of Emil Post's work on formalizing logical inference rules. Post's concern was the properties of rule systems for mechanically deriving inferences from an initial axiomatic sentence variable (Post 1943). His formalization was general enough to provide a new characterization of the recursively enumerable (henceforth, r.e.) sets. Chomsky (1959) applied Post's work on inference systems to the description of sets of strings more generally, defining a grammar is a finite device that generates a set of strings or other structures ('generates' in the sense of Post 1944, synonymous with 'recursively enumerates').

Chomsky's work defined the first framework for grammatical description of the type that we will call GENERATIVE-ENUMERATIVE SYNTAX (henceforth GES). It laid the foundation for the syntactic study of programming languages, and launched the subfield of formal language theory within computer science. But his application of Post's work to natural languages (Chomsky 1957) had even greater influence. Within natural language syntax, GES has been overwhelmingly dominant since 1957. Frameworks of the GES type include:

- all the types of phrase structure grammar in the Chomsky Hierarchy;
- transformational grammar in almost all its varieties, including those that used 'filters' as an overlay on a GES base to rule out some of the generated structures – as in Perlmutter (1971), or the government-binding (GB) theory of the 1980s;
- generalized phrase structure grammar as presented in Gazdar et al. (1985), which despite some components framed in terms of constraints on trees (e.g. the feature instantiation principles), still clearly falls within the GES frameworks;
- all forms of categorial grammar, which generate sets by providing a general rule for composing primitives (categorized lexical items) to construct larger units of structure;
- tree-adjoining grammars (Joshi 1987), which generate structure through combinatory operations on a finite set of primitives (known as 'initial trees');
- Chomsky's post-1990 'minimalist' work (e.g. Chomsky (1995);

- the abstract syntax of Keenan and Stabler (1996), under which a set of structures is generated by closing a set of lexical items under certain combinatory operations;

and many more frameworks that we do not have space to list. Notice that not all GES frameworks are formalized; the recursive definitions of formation rules for wffs given in logic textbooks – 'if A is a wff then $\neg A$ is a wff', and so on – can be seen as informal GES descriptions.

It is the dominance of GES within linguistics that has led to dynamic and procedural metaphors being endemic within natural language syntax today: GES naturally engenders such metaphors, since the steps in the process of generating structures are so easily visualized as operations taking place in real time.

1.2 Model-Theoretic Syntax

The second approach we consider emerged some time later, from developments on the semantic rather than the syntactic side of logic. It applies model theory rather than proof theory to natural language syntax. The work in computer science that it parallels lies in descriptive complexity theory (Ebbinghaus and Flum 1999; Immerman 1998) rather than formal language theory, its mathematical concepts and methods being typically set-theoretic rather than combinatory.

The idea is to state a grammar as a finite set of axioms in a formal logic with a model-theoretic interpretation. We refer to these axioms as CONSTRAINTS. The models of the constraints are the expressions that are described by the grammar. An expression is well formed only if it is a model of the theory. We refer to this approach to grammar as MODEL-THEORETIC SYNTAX (MTS).

Notice (since it will be important below) that expressions, not sets of expressions, are the models for an MTS grammar: an individual expression either satisfies or does not satisfy a grammar. An MTS grammar does NOT recursively define a set of expressions; it merely states necessary conditions on the syntactic structure of individual expressions.

There have been few developments within linguistics so far that could be described as fully and explicitly representative of the MTS approach; compared to GES, it has had very little influence. But among the kinds of work we would cite as exhibiting the seeds of MTS are:

- the non-procedural recasting of transformational grammar in terms of conditions on tree sequences that can be found (albeit not very explicitly) in Lakoff (1971);
- the pioneering but mostly ignored work on formalizing relational grammar by Johnson and Postal (1980), a work that (especially in chapter 14) makes several key points we mention below;
- Gerald Gazdar's reformulation of generalized phrase structure grammar in terms of conditions satisfied or not satisfied by individual trees, presented in unpublished lectures at Nijmegen and Stanford during 1987; and

- the effort in Gazdar et al. (1988), particularly the Appendix (pp. 15–17), to describe finite labeled trees by directly imposing conditions on them using a modal logic; and
- head-driven phrase structure grammar in its more recent forms, as discussed by Sag and Wasow (1999, ch. 16), King (1999), and Pollard (1999).[1]

Some other frameworks might be added; for example, the construction grammar of Fillmore and Kay (1999), which is informally presented but appears to contain no GES elements, and perhaps recent lexical-functional grammar and some varieties of optimality-theoretic syntax (though the latter is by no means fully clear; we return to the matter briefly in section 3.1).

These separate lines of research in linguistics reveal gradual convergence on one idea: that grammars might be framed as sets of direct constraints on expression structure rather than devices for recursively enumerating sets of expressions. Nonetheless, MTS did not really begin to take explicit form until the 1990s, when the idea of natural language expression structures as models of grammars framed as statements in a logic really began to coalesce in the work of Marcus Kracht (1993, 2001), Patrick Blackburn and his colleagues (Blackburn, Gardent and Meyer-Viol 1993, Blackburn and Meyer-Viol 1997, Blackburn and Gardent 1995), and James Rogers (1996, 1997, 1998, 1999).

However, in a sense even the work of these researchers has been done in the shadow of GES. It has largely focused on comparing MTS and GES. Kracht (1993) attempts to clarify the content of GB; Blackburn and Gardent (1997) proposes a way to give an MTS account of the lexical functional grammar of Bresnan and Kaplan (1982); and Rogers develops an MTS characterization of the tree-sets that are generable by context-free grammars (henceforth, CFGs), using it to give an MTS restatement of the linguistic content of two theories couched in GES terms, mid-1980s GPSG (Rogers 1997) and mid-1980s GB (1998).

Given the enormous influence of GES frameworks, early advocates of MTS needed to show that sets of expressions could be defined, because in GES frameworks sets of expressions are identified with the object of study, i.e., the natural language being described. But the concentration on how MTS can simulate GES has led to certain differences between the two kinds of framework going unnoticed. The main aim of this paper is to consider MTS on its own terms, highlighting some of its overlooked features.

2 Theoretical Divergences

2.1 Cardinality of the Set of Expressions

Any grammar of the GES type generates a set, with a fixed, definite number of expressions as elements. No grammar of the MTS type entails that the grammatical expressions form a set of some definite cardinality.

[1] Note in particular Sag and Wasow's remark (1999: 382) that a grammar is "nothing more than a set of descriptions of typed objects ... the constructs of the grammar are no longer clauses in a recursive definition of linguistic structures."

For GES the matter is purely definitional. A GES grammar states the characteristic function of a specific set of expressions. In the formal language theory literature the set in question is notated $L(G)$ for a grammar G.[2] To say that G generates a specific set means that for each element x of the set, G licenses a derivation, i.e. a finite set of steps that amounts to a proof that x is grammatical according to the rules of G.

Under certain conditions $L(G)$ will be denumerably infinite. For example, let $G = \langle V_N, V_T, S, P\rangle$ be an e-free CFG in which no nonterminals are useless (i.e. every nonterminal is accessible from S and has some positive yield). If for some $\alpha \in V_N$ we have $\alpha \stackrel{+}{\Longrightarrow} \psi_1\alpha\psi_2$ (where $\psi_1\psi_2 \neq e$), then $L(G)$ is infinite, and in all other cases $L(G)$ is finite.

The property of licensing derivations that allow a constituent labeled α as a proper subconstituent of another such constituent – which we will henceforth call the α-within-α property – is decidable for CFGs (though not, by an application of Rice's theorem, for context-sensitive grammars or URSs).[3]

If the conditions for generating an infinite language are not met, on the other hand, there will be just a finite number of expressions generated (and at least in the case of CFGs, the number will be computable from G).

Turning to MTS, we find some significant differences, though they are subtle and have been generally overlooked. MTS grammars are in effect statements in a logic, and although such statements can determine an upper bound on the number of their models, it takes a rather special kind of statement to do it. As an example, consider the MTS grammar Γ_1 over a node-label vocabulary $\{B, S\}$ and terminal vocabulary $\{a, b\}$, consisting of the union of the usual axioms for trees (for concreteness, those in Rogers 1998: 15–16)[4] conjoined with (1).

(1) $\exists x \exists y[S(x) \wedge a(y) \wedge x \lhd y \wedge \forall z[z \neq x \rightarrow z = y]]$

(where $S(x)$ means 'x is labeled by the nonterminal symbol S' and $a(y)$ means 'y is labeled by the terminal symbol a'). There is only one tree that models it, the tree with S-labeled root and one a-labeled daughter. But most MTS grammars do not determine a bound on the number of their models in this way. If we remove the constraint '$\forall z[z \neq x \rightarrow z = y]$' from Γ_1 we get a much more permissive grammar, namely the tree axioms plus (2):

(2) $\exists x \exists y[S(x) \wedge a(y) \wedge x \lhd y]$

This grammar, which we will call Γ_2, has arbitrarily many models, since it requires only that there be SOME S-labeled node with an a-labeled daughter.

---

[2] In what follows we adopt the convention of using G as a variable over GES grammars but Γ for MTS grammars.

[3] To see this, consider the relation 'feeds' that holds between a rule $R_1 = \alpha \rightarrow \ldots \beta \ldots$ and a rule $R_2 = \beta \rightarrow \ldots$, for some $\alpha, \beta \in V_N$. We can construct a finite graph of the 'feeds' relation for any CFG, labeling the vertices with rules and adding an edge from the R_i vertex to the R_j vertex whenever R_i feeds R_j. G has the α-within-α property, and hence $L(G)$ is infinite, iff the graph of the 'feeds' relation contains a cycle, and this can be determined straightforwardly by inspection of the graph.

[4] Rogers' axiom $A4$ should read: $(\forall x, y)[x \lhd^+ y \leftrightarrow (x \lhd^* y \wedge x \not\approx y)]$.

But while a grammar like Γ_2 is COMPATIBLE with there being infinitely many expressions, it is also compatible with there being only some finite number of expressions, or even none. In all but the rather peculiar case of grammars like Γ_1, the issue of how many expressions there really are is a question to be settled independently of the grammar.

Some logicians may object at this point that there certainly is an answer to how many models Γ_2 has: it demonstrably has $\aleph_0$ models, since the set of finite labeled trees that satisfy it can be enumerated in lexicographical order and put into one-to-one correspondence with the natural numbers.

The response to this objection is as follows. We grant that if $\mathcal{T}$ is the set of all finite labeled trees over a given finite vocabulary of labels, then the set $\mathcal{T}_{\Gamma_2}$ defined by (3) is denumerably infinite.

(3) $\mathcal{T}_{\Gamma_2} \stackrel{\text{def}}{=} \{\tau : \tau \in \mathcal{T} \wedge \tau \models \Gamma_2\}$

However, notice that the cardinalities of the sets $\mathcal{T}$ and $\mathcal{T}_{\Gamma_2}$ are not determined by Γ_2. These sets are specified in the metatheory. Indeed, not only are they not defined by Γ_2, neither of them can be defined by ANY grammar written in the same metalanguage: Γ_2 is a first-order statement, and the property of finiteness is not first-order expressible (by an easy corollary of Trakhtenbrot's theorem for arbitrary first-order structures).

Natural language syntax must (at least) describe the shared structural properties of an indefinite number of distinct expressions. What is important is that there is no definite upper bound on how many expressions are described. GES satisfies this desideratum on grammars by generating a denumerably infinite set of expressions, and MTS satisfies it by NOT EXCLUDING the possibility of there being indefinitely many models for the grammar.

2.2 Finite and Infinite Expressions

We now turn to a point distinct from the previous one but intimately related to it: in a GES framework, a grammar always fixes a finite size for each grammatical expression, while for grammars in an MTS framework this is not the case.

Again, in GES frameworks this is a trivial consequence of the definition of a grammar. For an expression x to be in $L(G)$ for some GES grammar G, it must be possible to derive x in a finite number of steps using the rules of the grammar, and each rule either introduces at most a finite number of new symbols (in a top-down grammar) or combines a finite number of symbols (in a bottom-up grammar).

Again, with MTS things are quite different. Given an MTS grammar Γ with trees as models, there may be infinite objects satisfying Γ. In fact, if an MTS grammar is given in a first order language and there are finite trees of arbitrary size that are models of the grammar, there MUST be an infinite model – this is a corollary of compactness. The grammar Γ_2 considered above, for example, clearly has infinite models.

No absolute advantage or disadvantage accrues to MTS, or to GES, in virtue of this observation.[5] GES grammars can in principle be modified to permit generation of infinite strings with infinite parse trees (see Thomas 1990). And the issue of whether an MTS grammar can exclude the possibility of expressions of infinite size depends on the choice of the metalanguage for stating grammars: using a second-order logic for stating constraints it is possible to restrict models to the finite by statements in an MTS grammar. It is likewise possible using modal logic: **S4Grz** (which is in effect the logic used by Gazdar et al. 1988 to describe feature trees: Kracht 1989 proves the equivalence) is a modal logic that exactly characterizes the set of finite trees, as noted by Hughes and Cresswell (1984: 162–3, n. 5).

The point is not about absolute advantage but about tradeoffs in capability. GES grammars, by definition, generate r.e. sets and fix cardinalities for them. MTS grammars do not: defining a specific set containing all intended models of a certain sort for an MTS grammar must be done in the metatheory. It follows that GES in its classic form blocks the inclusion of any infinite expression in the generated set, whereas MTS by default allows infinite models to satisfy a grammar.

2.3 Optionality and Transderivationality

A much more important difference emerges when we focus on a key feature of MTS grammars, namely that their models are individual expression structures. This feature of MTS has implications for universal syntactic theory. No MTS grammar quantifies over whole expression structures. For example, if trees are the intended models, quantifiers in the statements of an MTS grammar range over a set of nodes, not over a set of trees. A rather striking consequence of this emerges when we re-examine the principles of X-bar theory.

We review the principles very informally first. X-bar theory takes the nonterminal vocabulary (those with which internal nodes are labeled) to be partitioned into several sets known as bar levels. 'X' is used as a variable over the atomic symbols or feature complexes needed for lexical category distinctions ('finite transitive verb', 'singular proper noun', etc.). Node labels can be represented in the form X^i, where for each $i \geq 0$ the category label X^i belongs to bar level i. (Intuitively, a phrase of bar level i is a phrase i levels of inclusiveness up from the lexical category constituent of X^0 that is its ultimate lexical head.) A maximum bar level m is a constant fixed by the specific theory. The full nonterminal vocabulary V_N is the union of all X^i for $0 \leq i \leq m$. A constituent labeled X^m for some X is referred to as a *maximal projection*, or simply as *maximal*. The principles of the theory can be stated very informally thus:

[5] The argument of Langendoen and Postal (1984), to the effect that GES grammars are falsified by their failure to describe infinite expressions, seems to us completely misguided.

(4) PRINCIPLES OF X-BAR THEORY

Lexicality:	for every X^i ($i \geq 0$) there is an X^0;
Uniformity:	for every X^0 there is an X^m;
Succession:	every node X^i node ($i \geq 1$) has an X^{i-1} head daughter;
Centrality:	the root node label is X^m for some X;
Maximality:	non-head daughters are maximal;
Optionality:	non-head daughters are optional.

Kornai and Pullum (1990) state these principles entirely in terms of a GES framework (specifically, in terms of statements about sets of CFG rules). However, it is actually impossible to make all of the above principles precise in an MTS framework. We can show this by contrasting Maximality with Optionality.

The apparent similarity between the statements 'non-heads are maximal' and 'non-heads are optional', using English adjectives, disguises a fundamental difference. Maximality can be defined on trees considered individually. Optionality cannot. The property of a node that makes it maximal is that its category label X^i is such that $i = m$. There is no property of a node, or relation between nodes, that makes it optional. Whether a constituent in a tree is optional depends on properties of other trees.

Specifically, optionality of a constituent can be defined only by quantifying over the trees belonging to some set. Let τ be a local subtree of some tree in a tree-set $\mathcal{T}$. Then a daughter α in τ is optional w.r.t. $\mathcal{T}$ iff erasing α from τ yields a local tree τ' that occurs in some tree in $\mathcal{T}$. Optionality is not a property of nodes in a tree at all, but a quantificationally complex property involving a different universe of discourse, namely a set of trees. Only by allowing quantification over trees can we express its content at all.

It should not be a surprise, then, that in the account of X-bar theory set forth in Rogers (1998) there is no mention of Optionality. This is not an oversight: Rogers' framework, like any MTS framework, simply does not permit it to be stated: his models are trees.

Whether this is an advantage or a major problem turns on whether Optionality is a sound principle of universal grammar. In actuality, it seems not to be. Though it is announced as a general principle in a number of works (for clear examples see e.g. Emonds 1976: 16, Base Restriction III, and Jackendoff 1977: 36, 43), it turns out to be incompatible with numerous uncontroversial facts about syntactic structure in natural languages (see Kornai and Pullum 1990: 34–35).

If this is correct – if it is a deep fact about natural languages that they do NOT respect the Optionality principle – then the absolute impossibility of expressing that principle in MTS terms may be seen as a virtue of MTS frameworks.

Related to this point is a more general one. Some GES theories in the 1970s posited TRANSDERIVATIONAL CONSTRAINTS, which excluded transformational derivations (i.e. finite tree sequences) on the basis of comparison with other derivations, e.g. by saying 'a structure with property π is well formed only if a structure $f(\pi)$ is well formed', or 'a structure with property π is well formed only if a structure $f(\pi)$ is not well formed', where f is a function from properties of derivations to properties of derivations.

For example, it has occasionally been claimed that certain natural languages permit constituent order inversions up to, but not beyond, the point where ambiguity would arise. Russian is a case in point. Its basic constituent order is Subject-Verb-Object (SVO), but stylistic inversion yielding Object-Verb-Subject (OVS) constituent order is often found. Hetzron (1972: 252–3), citing an earlier claim by Roman Jakobson, claims that in exactly those cases where the sequence of constituents $N_a\ V_b\ N_c$ in the clause has a corresponding SVO clause $N_c\ V_b\ N_a$ that is also grammatical, so that ambiguity arises between SVO and OVS interpretations of the same string, Russian syntax forbids inversion to OVS. For example, he claims that (5a) cannot be expressed in the form (5b).

(5) a. *mat'* *rodila* *doč*
mother gave-birth-to daughter
'The mother gave birth to the daughter.'
b. *doč* *rodila* *mat'*
daughter gave-birth-to mother

Intuitively this is because neither case-marking on the nouns *mat'* and *doč* nor gender-marking agreement on the verb *rodila* differentiates (5b) from the SVO clause that would have identical form.

Such a constraint is unstatable in an MTS grammar. Again this is because the models are individual expression structures. A question therefore arises about whether ambiguity-avoidance constraints are ever required in grammars. We think not. There are certainly functional considerations that (sometimes) militate against ambiguous use of a language by its speakers: people do sometimes attempt to make sure they choose expressions with forms that convey their intended meaning unambiguously. But it has repeatedly been found that building such functional pressures into syntactic constraints is a mistake. Both theoretical and empirical considerations suggest that grammars of natural languages do not ban ambiguity.

In the case of Hetzron's claims, one suspicious aspect of his analysis of Russian is that his description calls for a syntactic constraint to be sensitive to various aspects of phonological and phonetic realization of morphosyntactic feature (not just, e.g., whether a given noun is accusative, but whether its form contains a distinct accusative marker). There is a compelling weight of evidence against describing natural languages in such terms (see Miller et al. 1997 for references on the Principle of Phonology-Free Syntax, and discussion of some instructive examples). But there is also direct empirical evidence: Hetzron's (and Jakobson's) claims about Russian are just not true. OVS clauses in which neither NP case nor verb agreement disambiguate OVS from SVO are found in texts. There is syntactically wrong with Majakovskij's line in (6), where the allegedly forbidden ambiguous OVS appears twice.

(6) *Teplo daet peč, peč piaet ugol'*
warmth gives stove stove feeds coal
'The stove gives warmth, coal feeds the stove.'

Such examples appear in all kinds of text; Buttke (1969: 57) notes that up to 3% of cases of O before S in Russian prose are ambiguous in this way.[6]

If it is true that ambiguity-avoidance constraints do not figure in the syntactic constraints of the grammars of natural languages, then it may be seen as a positive virtue for a framework to be unable to express them.

3 Phenomena

In this section we argue that there are three related kinds of linguistic phenomena that are better described in MTS frameworks than in GES. In these domains at least, MTS frameworks have both broader scope and greater accuracy in describing the phenomena.

3.1 Gradient Ungrammaticality

Anyone who knows a natural language knows that some utterances are not completely well formed. Speakers produce utterances that even they would agree are grammatically imperfect – not by some external authority's standard but by their own. But experienced users of a language are also aware that some ungrammatical utterances are much closer to being grammatical than others.

We take this feature of utterances to be also a feature of expressions – or rather (since it may be better to limit the term 'expression' to what is fully grammatical) those objects that are like expressions except that they are only partially well-formed; let us call these QUASI-EXPRESSIONS. What we are saying is that some quasi-expressions are closer to being grammatical than others. In consequence, any framework for describing syntactic structure that can also describe degrees of ungrammaticality for quasi-expressions is to be preferred to one that cannot.

Some take a different view. For example, Schütze (1996) assumes that no GES grammar should generate any quasi-expression, of any degree of ungrammaticality. Rather, any perceived degree of ungrammaticality is a property to be described by performance processing mechanisms, not by the grammar. We believe this is the wrong view of partial ungrammaticality, and is probably an artifact of the difficulty GES frameworks have in describing that phenomenon.

MTS states grammars in a way that offers an elegant and heuristically suggestive starting point for thinking about the comparative ungrammaticality of quasi-expressions. Recall that an MTS grammar $\Gamma = \{\varphi_1, \ldots, \varphi_n\}$ is a finite set of statements in which each φ_i must be satisfied by any expression if the expression is to count as (fully) well formed. Γ may also be satisfied by various

[6] Thanks to Bernard Comrie for the Russian references.

quasi-expressions. Given any arbitrary set of expression structures and quasi-expression structures, we can use an MTS grammar Γ to define on that set a partial order that, intuitively, holds between two structures when one is, according to Γ and relative to the specified set, AT LEAST AS CLOSE TO BEING GRAMMATICAL as the other.

Let $\mathcal{U}$ be some universe of labeled trees, and let Γ be an MTS grammar with trees as models. Then there is a partial ordering $\trianglelefteq^{\mathcal{U}}_{\Gamma}$ defined on $\mathcal{U}$ by

$$(7) \quad \trianglelefteq^{\mathcal{U}}_{\Gamma} \stackrel{\text{def}}{=} \{\langle\tau_1,\tau_2\rangle : \tau_1,\tau_2 \in \mathcal{U} \;\wedge\; |\{\varphi : \tau_1 \models \varphi\}| \geq |\{\varphi : \tau_2 \models \varphi\}|\}$$

That is, $\tau_1 \trianglelefteq^{\mathcal{U}}_{\Gamma} \tau_2$ (for τ_1 and τ_2 in $\mathcal{U}$) iff τ_1 satisfies at least as many of the constraints of Γ as τ_2.

Clearly, a plausible starting point for describing degrees of ungrammaticality would be to assume that, other things being equal, a quasi-expression with structure τ_1 will be ungrammatical to a greater degree than a quasi-expression with structure τ_2 if and only if $\tau_1 \trianglelefteq^{\mathcal{U}}_{\Gamma} \tau_2$ for all suitable $\mathcal{U}$.

This is the most basic version, but various ways of refining the proposal immediately suggest themselves: the constraints of the grammar might fall into different classes determining the strength of their influence on ungrammaticality: constraints governing the inflection of words might be outranked by constraints applying to the composition of phrasal constituents in terms of the major categories of their daughters, and so on. (Ranking of constraints is, of course, a central idea of optimality theory, which we discuss further below.)

Notice that no extra machinery is called for: the suggested analysis of degrees of ungrammaticality simply exploits the content of the MTS grammar that is constructed to describe the fully grammatical expressions: on any set $\mathcal{U}$, there is a relation $\trianglelefteq^{\mathcal{U}}_{\Gamma}$ for MTS grammar Γ.

GES contrasts sharply in the extent of its failure to provide resources to define gradient ungrammaticality. A GES grammar G simply defines a set $L(G)$. It defines no ordering on the complement of that set, or for that matter on any set at all. The elements of $L(G)$ are perfectly grammatical, by definition, and where $\mathcal{Z}$ is any set, no element of $\mathcal{Z} - L(G)$ is described by a GES grammar for $L(G)$ as sharing any grammatical properties with any elements of $L(G)$. Arbitrary supplementary devices can be developed ad hoc to describe facts about degrees of ungrammaticality for non-members of $L(G)$, but the GES grammar G will contribute nothing to the project; all the work must be done by the extra machinery.

Three suggestions about accounting for gradient ungrammaticality deserve some brief discussion at this point. We will therefore digress to make a few remarks about (a) an early proposal of Chomsky's (1955, 1961), which provides a good illustration of what we mean about adding ad hoc machinery to a GES grammar; (b) the possible relevance of the optimality theory framework in this context; and (c) the implications of stochastic or probabilistic grammars.

Digression (a): Chomsky's Proposal. The failure of early GES grammars to represent degrees of ungrammaticality was noted quite soon after the publication of Chomsky (1957) by Archibald Hill (1961). Responding to the criticism, Chomsky (1961) published a proposed solution to the problem taken from a then unpublished work (Chomsky 1955), but the solution is not adequate. It involves, in effect, a function that maps members of the complement of the generated set to numbers representing the degree of their ungrammaticality. Given a language over a vocabulary V_T, Chomsky proposes defining a function $f : V_T^* - L(G) \mapsto \{1, 2, 3\}$ such that for any sequence $w \in V_T^* - L(G)$, the value of $f(w)$ gives a degree of ungrammaticality for w by comparing it with the expressions in $L(G)$ that it most closely matches in the sequence of lexical categories it instantiates.

The function f will be defined as follows. Let G be a transformational grammar with a lexicon that assigns the words (terminal symbols) to a set $K = \{\kappa_1, \ldots, \kappa_n\}$ of n lexical (bar-level 0) categories. Let λ be the binary relation holding between a word and a lexical (bar-level 0) category that it can realize according to the lexicon of G; that is, $\lambda(w_i, \kappa_j)$ for some $j \leq n$) means that word w_i is a permissible realization of lexical category κ_j. For a word sequence $w = w_1 \ldots w_m$ and a lexical category sequence $\kappa = \kappa_1 \ldots \kappa_m$, define $\lambda(w, \kappa)$ to mean $\forall i \leq m[\lambda(w_i, \kappa_i)]$. (From now on κ and κ' will be used as variables over lexical category sequences.) Then for a word sequence $w \notin L(G)$ and $i \in \{1, 2, 3\}$:

(8) $$f(w) = i \stackrel{\text{def}}{\Longleftrightarrow} \exists\kappa\, \exists\kappa'\, \exists w'\ [w' \in L(G) \wedge \lambda(w, \kappa) \wedge \lambda(w', \kappa') \wedge \kappa \approx_i \kappa']$$

Crucial here are the relations $\approx_i$ of similarity between lexical category sequences, and these are as follows:

- $\approx_1$ is a relation of similarity among lexical category sequences that allows selection restriction features to be ignored (thus f(*Golf plays people*) $= 1$ because its lexical category sequence matches the sequence of a grammatical expression like *Golf amuses people* if we ignore the selection restrictions of *plays*: 'inanimate noun + transitive verb taking animate subject and inanimate object + animate noun' $\approx_1$ 'inanimate noun + transitive verb taking inanimate subject and animate object + animate noun');
- $\approx_2$ is a relation of similarity among lexical category sequences that allows strict subcategorization features to be ignored (thus f(*Golf elapses people*) $= 2$ because its lexical category sequence matches the sequence of a grammatical expression like *Golf amuses people* if we ignore the transitive subcategorization of *plays*: 'noun + transitive verb + noun' $\approx_2$ 'noun + intransitive verb + noun'); and
- $\approx_3$ is a relation of similarity among lexical category sequences that allows lexical category to be ignored altogether (i.e. it is the universal relation on K^*, relating every sequence to every other); thus f(*Elapses golf entertains*) $= 3$ because its lexical category sequence matches the sequence of a grammatical expression like *Golf amuses people* if we ignore the difference between nouns and verbs completely: 'noun + verb + noun' $\approx_3$ 'verb + noun + verb').

We see at least three difficulties with this proposal. The first is that it is not sufficiently fine-grained: there are in fact far more than three degrees of ungrammaticality. Consider:

(9) a. *I am the chair of my department.*
b. **I are the chair of my department.*
c. **Me are the chair of my department.*
d. **Me are the chair of me's department.*
e. **Me are chair the of me's department.*
f. **Me are chair the me's department of.*

Example (9a) is fully grammatical; (9b) is worse in virtue of one grammatical error; (9c) is worse than that (with two errors); (9d) is worse yet; (9e) is even worse; (9f) is worse still; and we could go on like this through arbitrarily many degrees of grammatical deviance. None of the degrees of difference in ungrammaticality in these examples is described under Chomsky's proposal (it does not cover deviance resulting from violations of constraints on inflection at all, as far as we can see).

The second difficulty is that the lack of any relationship between the proposed degrees of ungrammaticality and any specific violations of grammatical constraints leads to cases that intuitively involve multiple violations of constraints being represented as not differing in grammaticality from cases that intuitively involve only single constraint violations. For example, consider (10).

(10) **The car is in the the garage.*
D N V P D D N

This is just one incorrectly repeated determinative away from being fully grammatical.[7] Yet under Chomsky's proposal it is treated no differently from strings of complete gibberish like (11).

(10) **Of the and a but through or.*
P D Crd D Crd P Crd

Neither (10) nor (11) has a lexical category sequence matching that of any grammatical sentence of English, hence f maps both (10) and (11) to 3.

A third difficulty is that the whole proposal is nonconstructive and nonlocal. Instead of identifying the local sources of grammatical deviance (e.g., relating the ill-formedness of **They am here* to a failure of verb agreement), the proposal relates the status of a word sequence of a quasi-expression to the truth value of a statement that quantifies over the entire set of well-formed expressions. No algorithm for determining the status of an arbitrary word sequence is suggested, and for a transformational grammar there could not be one: because of the Turing-equivalence of transformational grammar, for a transformational grammar G, a word sequence $w \notin L(G)$, and a lexical category sequence κ such that $\lambda(w, \kappa)$, the question in (12) is undecidable:

[7] The category labels shown in (10) and (11) are as in Huddleston and Pullum (forthcoming): 'Crd' = Coordinator, 'D' = Determinative, 'N' = Noun, 'Nom' = Nominal, 'P' = Preposition, 'V' = Verb.

(12) $\exists w', \kappa' \, [w' \in L(G) \wedge \lambda(w', \kappa')]$?

Digression (b): Optimality-Theoretic Syntax. It might seem that optimality theory (OT) syntax would be highly relevant to the gradience of ungrammaticality: The central idea is that a grammar consists of a ranked (i.e. well-ordered) set of (putatively universal) constraints on structures called CANDIDATES relative to a given structure called the INPUT. (As we said above, it seems quite plausible to suppose that some constraints in natural language are of greater importance than others.) But in OT the constraint set is typically not consistent, so complete satisfaction of all the constraints is an impossibility. The expression structures defined as well formed are therefore not those that satisfy all the constraints. Whether a structure is defined as well formed is determined by a competition between candidate expressions regarding which does best at satisfying higher-ranked constraints.

To put it more precisely, an optimal candidate is chosen by finding the candidate α that in every pairwise competition with some other candidate β satisfies (or comes closer to satisfying, i.e. violates at fewer points) the highest-ranking constraint that distinguishes between α and β.

OT is distinguished, then, not by anything about the semantics of constraints, but by the semantics for a SET of constraints, which in OT is not the same as the semantics for the logical conjunction of those constraints.

The brief account given above of how degrees of ungrammaticality can be described by an MTS grammar may have seemed highly reminiscent of the way an OT grammar structures the set of candidates. Our view, however, is that although future research could vindicate such a view, it cannot be said to be borne out by the mainstream of the OT literature so far.

Much will turn on details of how OT grammars are interpreted. In most of the current literature a set of 'inputs' is assumed (what these are is highly obscure to us, but they may be something like representations of lexical items and semantically relevant grammatical relations including phrase membership). The grammar defines the optimal 'output' (some kind of more superficial representation of structure) for each, picking that optimal structure from a set defined by a (universal) function called `Gen`, which associates each input with a (generally infinite) set of candidates $\mathtt{Gen}(I)$. The grammar defines the set of all pairs $\langle I, O \rangle$ such that I is an input and O is its optimal output – the candidate that wins when I is submitted to the algorithm that runs the pairwise competition with all the other candidates in $\mathtt{Gen}(I)$.

In other words, the grammar determines a set just as a GES grammar does. Although in each competition there is a set of losing candidates, and that set is ordered (perhaps well-ordered) by the grammar, the order is not normally referred to in OT discussions of syntax, and for a given I no ordering is defined for any structures outside $\mathtt{Gen}(I)$. Details of `Gen` are not normally supplied (OT researchers generally restrict attention to a handful of interesting alternatives for O for which membership in $\mathtt{Gen}(I)$ is assumed to be obvious), so it is not possible to say how inclusive $\mathtt{Gen}(I)$ is in a given case.

This is not a criticism of OT. We are merely pointing out that there is no simple relationship between OT and the MTS treatment of gradient ungrammaticality, since for the most part OT has not attempted to describe ungrammatical structures at all.[8]

Digression (c): Stochastic Grammars. Stochastic grammars have been the subject of increasing interest and attention within computational linguistics over the last decade. It has been suggested to us that they offer an effective defense of GES frameworks as regards the treatment of gradient ungrammaticality. We have pointed out that GES grammars simply define a set of perfectly well-formed expressions and do not say anything about degrees of approach to full grammaticality. Stochastic grammars differ from other GES grammars in that they associate probabilities with both rules and expressions, and describe some kinds of expression structures as having dramatically lower probability than others.

We see no basis for the suggestion that stochastic grammars have something to do with the topic of degrees of ungrammaticality, however. It seems to us that they do not address the issue at all. What a stochastic grammar does is to assign probabilities to the members of the set of generated expressions. For example, *You did it* can be represented as more probable than *I know you did it*, which in turn is more probable than *I know she knows you did it*, which in turn is more probable than *I know she knows I know you did it*, and so on down to vanishingly small (but still finite) probabilities. This is all very well – expressions with 37 degrees of subordinate clause embedding are indeed astronomically less likely to be encountered than those with 2 or 1 degrees of embedding. But (and this is the crucial point) an expression that is not generated by the grammar gets no probability assignment whatsoever.

Of course, a stochastic grammar that does not generate a given expression could always be revised to generate it and assign it a very low probability. But proceeding in that direction leads ultimately to a grammar that generates EVERY string over the terminal vocabulary; the probability assignments do all the work of defining what we commonly think of as well-formedness. This is a major departure from defining measures of relative probability for the grammatical expressions the grammar generates. It amounts to conflating the notion of ungrammaticality with the notion of extreme improbability. Some seem to have proposed such a conflation in the past (e.g. Hockett 1955: 10; Dixon 1963: 83–84), but the criticism by Chomsky (1957: 15–17) seems fully appropriate.

What MTS grammars can give an account of is the fact that quasi-expressions which everyone would agree are NOT grammatical nonetheless have syntactic structure. And this is something that stochastic grammars say absolutely nothing about.

---

[8] We note at least one exception: Keller (1998, 2000) has a very interesting treatment of the topic, in which selective re-ranking of constraints is used to shed light on degrees of well-formedness as assessed by acceptability judgments.

3.2 The Structure of Expression Fragments

Linguistic phenomena include not only complete expressions but also EXPRESSION FRAGMENTS. A fragment like *and of the* is certainly not generated by any GES grammar of English, and thus no GES grammar for English will describe its structure. It will be treated no differently from a random word string, like *the of and*, which does not share syntactic structure with any expression. Yet *and of the* has quite a bit of syntactic structure. We can represent part of it as in (13).

(13) THE STRUCTURE OF AN EXPRESSION FRAGMENT

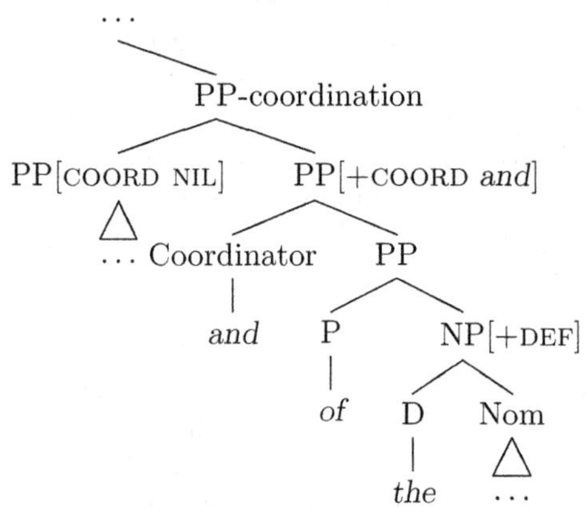

The incomplete structure shown here is a syndetic coordination of prepositional phrases. The right coordinate daughter is marked [COORD *and*] (the '[CONJ NIL]' of Gazdar et al. 1985), and thus must have the Coordinator *and* as left branch. (The left coordinate daughter has no COORD value; either [COORD NIL] or [COORD *and*] would be grammatically possible.) The right sister of the Coordinator is a PP which has the preposition *of* as its head (left branch) and an NP object (right branch). This object NP is definite, and has as its left daughter a Determinative (D), namely *the*, the Determiner of the NP. The right branch is a Nominal (Nom), the head of the NP. The fragment would be seen in the context of full expressions like (14).

(14) *That cat is afraid of the dog and of the parrot.*

Our point is simply that while a GES grammar for English cannot describe the structure of any expression fragment, an MTS grammar will describe an expression fragment as satisfying all the relevant constraints on its structure. The absent left coordinate in the structure considered above satisfies every constraint of English (vacuously). Constraints like the one requiring a Preposition as head daughter of a PP, and the one requiring the Preposition *of* to have an NP object, are non-vacuously satisfied. The words that are present have their usual grammatical properties, and are combined as they ordinarily are. An MTS grammar does not require that an expression be complete in order to be described as having grammatical structure; the subparts of an expression have just the same structure as they do in fuller syntactic contexts.

The point just made is essentially the one made by Bresnan and Kaplan (1982: xlv–xlvii) under the heading of 'order-free composition', though there it is presented as a psychological claim. Bresnan and Kaplan point out (p. xlv) that "complete representations of local grammatical relations are effortlessly, fluently, and reliably constructed for arbitrary segments of sentences" by competent native speakers. We are pointing to a non-psychological analog of their claim: expression fragments have grammatical (and semantic) properties, but GES grammars do not describe them.

3.3 Lexical Flux

The third phenomenon we draw attention to is that the lexicons of natural languages are constantly in flux. No natural language has a fixed word stock. Each day and each hour new words are being added by creative recombination of combining forms (*Internet*, *Ebonics*, *futurology*), recategorizations (*Don't start Clintoning on me*), trade name coinages (*Celica*, *Camry*, *Elantra*), technical term creation (*bioinformatics*, *genomics*, *quark*), the invention of unprecedented personal names like *DeShonna* for girls (a familiar feature of African-American culture), spontaneous dubbings (*I will call him 'Mini-Me'!*), nonce uses (*Suppose we have a file called 'arglebargle'*), jocular coinages (*You bet your bippy!*), conventionalization of abbreviations (*MTV*, *IBM*, *CIA*), creation of acronyms (*NAFTA*, *AIDS*, *UNESCO*), onomatopoetic invention (*It went 'gadda-ga-DACK!' and stopped*), and so on.

Indeed, as noted by Harris (1968: 11), spoken expressions can even incorporate random vocal noises (of which there is arguably a nondenumerable infinity). Familiar utterances such as (15) suggest that the variety of material that can fill a categorized slot in a linguistic expression is in a sense not even bounded by the combinatory possibilities of some finite phonetic alphabet.

(15) *My car goes 'ehhrgh!' when I go over a bump.*

This is not an new observation. But it presents a serious difficulty for GES grammars, which enumerate sequences over a fixed terminal vocabulary. No sequence containing an element that is not in that fixed vocabulary is generated, and if a sequence is not generated, its structure is not described. It follows that the syntactic structure of any expression of English containing a novel lexical item goes undescribed by a GES grammar.

The point here is not that there would be some difficulty in modifying a GES grammar to make a new one that accommodated some novel lexical item. Our point is about the failure of a fixed GES grammar to describe phenomena correctly. Take a GES grammar for English over a vocabulary not including a word of the form *dibble* (for example). Such a grammar does not describe the structure of an expression like (16).

(16) *Do you have any of those little dibbles you had yesterday?*

Clearly it has the structure of an English expression despite the fact that *dibble* is not (as far as we know) in any dictionaries and has no meaning. The expression is a clause of closed interrogative type, with second person subject, plural direct object with an attributive adjective, bare relative clause containing a preterite verb, and so on and so on. Even *dibbles* has properties: it is inflected for plural number, it has a regular inflectional paradigm, and so on. A GES grammar over a vocabulary not including *dibble* does not generate the string at all and thus does not describe its syntax.

Bottom-up types of GES grammar, like categorial grammars or 'minimalism', exhibit this problem of not covering the phenomena in a particularly acute way: if *dibble* is not a lexical item, then it has no category; if it has no category, then it cannot be combined with *little* to make *little dibbles*; and that means there is no phrase of that form to combine with *you had yesterday* to make a phrase *little dibbles you had yesterday*; and so on. Absolutely no grammatical structure is built at all for an expression containing a nonexistent word.

The right claim to make about this word sequence is not that its structure cannot be described but that it is perfectly grammatical. Its oddness resides solely in the fact that since there are no lexical semantic constraints on *dibble*, the expression has a singularly large range of possible meanings. Novel lexical items do not by themselves make the syntactic structure of expressions containing them indescribable. Nor do they obliterate the structure of the expressions in which they occur.

This point is essentially the one made by Johnson and Postal (1980: 675–7), and they draw the same conclusion: MTS grammars make the right claims about expressions containing novel lexical items, and GES grammars make strikingly incorrect claims about them. And since the lexicon of any natural language is continuously in flux, the phenomena cannot be overlooked. Grammars should describe syntactic structure in a way that is not tied to the existence of any particular set of words in a lexicon. GES grammars conspicuously fail to do this.

4 Languages

So far in this paper we have not used the word 'language' without qualification. We use phrases like 'natural language', 'programming language', 'formal language theory', 'first-order language' and so on, but we avoid the use of the word 'language' in technical senses like those current in mathematical linguistics and GES frameworks, e.g. the sense 'set of strings'. In this section we argue that the use of the word 'language' for both the object of study in linguistics and the set defined by a GES grammar, has led to the mistaken view that a trivial consequence of GES frameworks is a deep discovery about natural languages. We propose a different view of what natural languages are.

4.1 The Supposed Infiniteness of Natural Languages

The claim that natural languages are infinite is not just dogma subscribed to by those who work within GES frameworks, but a shibboleth for the linguistics profession: failure to endorse it signals non-membership in the community of generative grammarians. Hardly any introductory text or course on generative linguistics fails to affirm it. The following three distinct claims are all made on the same page of Lasnik (2000: 3):

(i) "We need to find a way of representing structure that allows for infinity—in other words, that allows for a sentence inside a sentence inside a sentence, and so on."
(ii) "Infinity is one of the most fundamental properties of human languages, maybe the most fundamental one. People debate what the true linguistic universals are, but indisputably, infinity is central."
(iii) "Once we have some notion of structure, we are in a position to address the old question of the creative aspect of language use... The ability to produce and understand new sentences is intuitively related to the notion of infinity."

These claims are not elaborations of the same point; they are respectively about (i) the recursive structure of natural language syntax, (ii) the size of the sets generated by GES grammars, and (iii) the native speaker's ability to understand novel expressions.

The first claims that linguistic structure is sometimes recursive, and this is clearly correct: expressions as simple as *See Spot run* uncontroversially exhibit α-within-α structure – that is, constituents of some category α properly contained within larger constituents of category α. (*Run* is a verb phrase, and so is *see Spot run*, which properly contains it in *See Spot run*.) We fully accept that some natural language expressions exhibit α-within-α structure, of course.

Lasnik's second claim concerns something different: the existence of a denumerably infinite collection of expressions defined by a GES grammar. This is not a claim about the structure of expressions. It is supposed to be a claim about the size of natural languages. But in fact it is simply a trivial point about GES frameworks: basically, the set generated by a GES grammar G is countably infinite just in case G describes α-within-α structure. As we noted in section 2.1 (see footnote 3), this is a decidable property for some types of GES grammar, such as CFGs. And as we have just agreed, English has α-within-α structure: even a cursory examination of plausible structures for a few expressions of English reveals that VPs occur within VPs, NPs occur within NPs, and so on. Hence IF WE ASSUME THAT A NATURAL LANGUAGE CAN ONLY BE CORRECTLY DESCRIBED BY A GES GRAMMAR, it immediately follows that the set generated by a grammar for English contains infinitely many expressions.

But this is not a fact about natural languages. It is purely a fact about the properties of (a certain class of) GES grammars. Under an MTS framework it does NOT follow that the set generated by a grammar for English contains infinitely many expressions. From the fact that a grammar for a natural language should never specify that expressions have an upper bound on their length, and that some of their structures are α-within-α structures, no conclusion follows about how many expressions there are.

Notice that when applied to cultural products, inferences to infinity from lack of an upper bound clearly fail: there is no upper bound on the length of poems, but it does not follow that there are infinitely many poems. Similar reasoning also fails in biological domains: there is no set upper bound on length of lineage for an organism in generations, but it does not follow that there are, or could be, organisms with infinitely many descendants. To suppose an inference is valid in the case of expressions of a natural language is to confuse a property of GES grammars with a substantive claim about natural languages.

Turning now to the claim in (iii), we note that this is not a claim about either the structure of expressions or the size of a set of expressions, but about human linguistic capacities. To get the claim about capacities to follow from the claim about sets we need to assume not only that grammars generate sets but also that grammars describe speakers' linguistic capacities. We only get the conclusion that human linguistic capacities are infinite (in the sense that a speaker can in principle understand any of an infinite range of expressions) if we accept both. So a case for saying that human linguistic capacities are infinite must be made on the basis of two assumptions: (i) the assumption that GES grammars best describe languages, and (ii) the assumption that GES grammars best describe linguistic knowledge. Since the first assumption rests on a confusion, the second does too.

If instead we assume that natural languages are best described by MTS grammars, and that human linguistic capacities are too, we get the result that those capacities are creative and productive without any commitment to the existence of a determinate set containing all possible expressions. As Gareth Evans (1981) insightfully pointed out, creative and productive language use has nothing to do with infinity, and can even be realized (through the ability to recombine expression parts) within a finite language.

Moreover, other things are not equal in this case: since GES grammars do not cover the linguistic phenomena discussed in section 3, it is increasingly doubtful that natural languages are best described in GES terms.

4.2 Some Caveats and Clarifications

It should be stressed that we are NOT making the claim that an appropriate MTS grammar for natural language has only finitely many models. Given that any adequate grammar will describe α-within-α structure, the set $\mathbf{Mod}(\Gamma)$ of all models for an MTS grammar Γ is infinite. But that is a fact about what is true in the metatheory of the logic in which Γ is stated. By itself, Γ does not entail that there are infinitely many expressions, because an MTS grammar states only necessary conditions on the structure of expressions considered individually.

Note also that we do not deny that infinite sets of expressions are crucial in some areas of mathematical logic, computer science, formal learning theory, etc. Without reference to infinite sets of expressions in mathematically defined languages

- we cannot even talk about the compactness theorem for first-order logic in its usual form (if every finite subset of an infinite set of formulae has a model then the entire set has a model);
- we cannot construct complete theories about integer arithmetic because the truths about integers will outnumber the expressions of our language;
- computational complexity theory is trivialized because without an infinite set of algorithmic problem presentations in some language we can solve every problem in constant time by table look-up;
- formal learning theory is trivialized because the interesting problems of learning theory arise only with infinite classes of decidable languages (every class of finite languages is identifiable in the limit from text).

For these reasons and many others, the definition of infinite sets of expressions within various fields of logic and applied mathematics is essential.

But that is not the same as saying that it is appropriate for the framework linguists use in stating grammars to stipulate how many expressions there are in a natural language. Doubtless, it is sensible to ensure that the metalanguage in which we write MTS grammars for natural languages is NOT one in which every formula is guaranteed to have only finitely many models (see Thomas 1986, for example, where a class of logics with boundedly many variables is studied and shown to be of this sort). And if we adopt a grammar-statement metalanguage that allows a formula to have infinitely many models, it will probably be possible to define an infinite set $\mathcal{E}$ such that $\forall x[x \in \mathcal{E} \rightarrow x \models \Gamma_E]$, where Γ_E is a suitable MTS grammar for English. But English itself is not thereby equated with $\mathcal{E}$. To make that equation is to commit the error Lasnik commits concerning the alleged infiniteness of languages: it confuses a property of GES grammars with properties of natural languages and of human abilities.

An adequate MTS account of the syntax of a natural language will first and foremost accurately describe the structural properties of some large finite set of attested expressions. Uncontroversially, this will involve describing α-within-α structure. The 'creative aspect of language use' under this view is described by the way MTS grammars not only represent the structure of attested expressions correctly but also predict the structure of as yet unattested novel expressions, expression fragments, and quasi-expressions.

No statement about the size of the set of unattested expressions of a natural language plays any role in describing or explaining any linguistic data. Different views about the ontology of linguistics force different answers to how many expressions there are. Clearly, a thoroughgoing nominalist might accept that there are only finitely many expressions. And a platonist might claim that there are uncountably many of them (Langendoen and Postal 1984). A framework for syntax does not, and should not, decide such issues. Indeed, we have argued elsewhere that no framework or theory should rule out any purely ontological theory about what natural languages are (see Pullum and Scholz 1997 for some discussion of this point).

4.3 What Languages Are

We address one other issue, more tentatively, before concluding. It concerns the ordinary, common-sense notion of a language under which we can say that *The Times* in the UK, *The New York Times* in the USA, *The Sydney Morning Herald* in Australia, and other newspapers around the world, all publish in the same language – though of course we would not deny that there may be local differences concerning which expressions are judged grammatical by the relevant editors.

Generative grammar makes no attempt to reconstruct this notion. Indeed, Chomsky applauds the way GES frameworks have replaced the common-sense notion of a language with a stipulated technical concept: in ordinary parlance, he says,

> We speak of Chinese as "a language," although the various "Chinese dialects" are as diverse as Romance languages. We speak of Dutch and German as two separate languages, although some dialects of German are very close to dialects that we call "Dutch"... That any coherent account can be given of "language" in this sense is doubtful; surely none has been offered or even seriously attempted. Rather all scientific approaches have abandoned these elements of what is called "language" in common usage. (Chomsky, 1986: 15)

The idea seems to be that advances in theoretical linguistics may and should replace our ordinary concept of 'a language' with a theoretical one. Under GES, the commonsense notion of an expression being 'in English' is not conserved, and is not intended to be; it is replaced by the notion of belonging to a certain r.e. set. In ordinary parlance, the phrase 'in English' means something like 'structured in the English manner' ('in English' has manner adjunct function, and certainly does not mean 'in the r.e. set known as English'). The ordinary understanding of 'She spoke in English', for example, is fairly well captured by 'She spoke in the English manner.' An MTS grammar for English plausibly reconstructs this common-sense idea: the grammar is a set of statements that state conditions for being an expression that is structured in the English manner.

MTS frameworks therefore provide a better basis for a conservative reconstruction of the common-sense concept of a language, the one under which millions of different people may be correctly described as speakers of the same language. And contra GES advocates, we regard this as no bad thing. It may be that a select set of constraints can provide a useful description of the linguistic structure that is shared between the differing idiolects of the hundreds of millions of people around the world who can, in their different ways, be said to use Standard English. GES frameworks appear to have no chance of capturing such a notion.

5 Conclusions and Prospects

We have distinguished two types of framework for describing natural language syntax: GES, under which grammars enumerate sets of expressions, and MTS, under which grammars place necessary conditions on the structure of individual expressions. We noted three differences between them.

- GES grammars define sets of expressions with definition cardinalities, while MTS grammars do not.
- MTS grammars give structural descriptions that are (in some cases) satisfied by expressions of infinite size, while to do the same thing in GES terms would require redefining the fundamental notions of the framework such as 'derivation'.
- MTS frameworks, because their models are individual expression structures, are entirely unable to state any kind of generalization of the sort that was called 'transderivational' in 1970s generative grammar, or to express principles such as the putative Optionality principle of X-bar theory, while ways of doing both can be and have been explored within GES frameworks.

We have argued that there are well known linguistic phenomena that are more accurately and elegantly described by MTS. These same phenomena have been largely ignored by advocates of GES frameworks, perhaps because of the difficulty such frameworks have in describing them.

More questions at this point remain than have been answered. We need to explore which kind of logic will best describe natural languages:

- Are there PAROCHIAL syntactic properties that need second-order quantification, or is all such second-order quantification needed only in defining concepts of universal grammar?
- Is there a suitable description language that never commits to whether the class of all models is finite, denumerable, or nondenumerably infinite?
- Is there a suitable logic that guarantees that checking satisfaction of a grammar by an arbitrary model will be not just decidable but tractable?

And the familiar problems of processing and learning take on some new aspects. Given a solution to the segmentation problem of figuring out the sequence of words in an utterance as phonetically presented, the computational problem of processing can be informally stated, under MTS assumptions, like this:

(17) **The Parsing Problem:** Given a word sequence, find an expression structure that satisfies the grammar and has that word sequence as its frontier.

The point of parsing is to provide part of the basis for solving a much more difficult computational problem:

(18) **The Conveyed Meaning Problem:** Given an expression presented in some context of utterance, find the conveyed meaning of the expression in that context.

We need to know more about the complexity of these problems in terms that are not based entirely in GES assumptions about grammar. The 'dynamic syntax' of Kempson, Gabbay and Meyer-Viol (2001) is a welcome development in this regard, since its dynamic account of how meaning representations might be constructed in real time as a word sequence is presented word by word is in fact based on an MTS approach to syntactic description using a modal logic.

Ultimately, the hardest of all the problems in the language sciences awaits us: the problem of language acquisition. Learners of a natural language in effect accomplish, in MTS terms, something like a solution to the following computational problem:

(19) **The Acquisition Problem:** Given a sequence of expression structures paired with the contexts in which the expressions were uttered, devise a set of constraints on the structure and meaning of expressions that will permit success in parsing future unconsidered utterances.

This is an enormously hard problem: the primary linguistic data underdetermines every MTS grammar. But we close by pointing out one piece of good news that emerges from taking an MTS approach to syntax. The theorems presented by Gold (1967), which are often cited as proof that language learning from presented examples is impossible, will not be applicable. What Gold proves is often stated rather loosely, e.g. as that it is impossible to learn a grammar from nothing but exposure to a finite sequence of presentations of examples of grammatical expressions. More precisely, the result is this:

(20) *Theorem* (Gold): Let $\mathcal{L}$ be a class of string-sets containing all finite string-sets over a finite vocabulary V and at least some infinite string-sets over V. Then there is no algorithm that solves the following problem for all string-sets in $\mathcal{L}$: given a continuing sequence of presentations of elements taken from some member of $\mathcal{L}$, guess a GES grammar after each presentation, arriving after some finite number of presentations at a correct guess that is never subsequently changed.

What concerns us here is that Gold's results are entirely about algorithms for successful guessing of exact definitions of sets in the form of GES grammars (or equivalent recognition automata). The exact cardinalities of these sets are crucially relevant: a learning algorithm that is unable to determine from the presented data whether the right grammar generates an infinite set or not is defined as having failed.

Under the MTS view THERE IS NO SET DEFINITION TO BE GUESSED. The problem of devising a suitable constraint set on the basis of exposure to utterances in normal contexts of use remains apparently very hard, and the answer to whether the learner's cognitive system has innate linguistic priming is by no means settled (see Pullum and Scholz forthcoming for further discussion). But at least under MTS we do not start out under the cloud of a proof that the task is in principle impossible.

References

[1995]Backofen, Rolf; James Rogers; and K. Vijay-shanker (1995): A first-order axiomatization of the theory of finite trees. *Journal of Logic, Language, and Information* **4**: 5–39.

[1995]Blackburn, Patrick and Claire Gardent (1995): A specification language for lexical functional grammars. *Proceedings of the 7th EACL*, 39–44. European Association for Computational Linguistics.

[1993]Blackburn, Patrick, Claire Gardent, and Wilfried Meyer-Viol (1993): Talking about trees. *Proceedings of the 1993 Meeting of the European Chapter of the Association for Computational Linguistics*, 21–29.

[1997]Blackburn, Patrick and Wilfried Meyer-Viol (1997): Modal logic and model-theoretic syntax. In M. de Rijke (ed.), *Advances in Intensional Logic*, 29–60. Dordrecht: Kluwer Academic.

[1982]Bresnan, Joan and Ronald M. Kaplan (1982): Introduction: grammars as mental representations of language. In *The Mental Representation of Grammatical Relations*, ed. by Joan Bresnan, xvii–lii. Cambridge, MA: MIT Press.

[1969]Buttke, Kurt (1969): *Gesetzmässigkeiten der Wortfolge im Russischen.* Halle: Max Niemeyer.

[1955]Chomsky, Noam (1955): *The Logical Structure of Linguistic Theory.* Unpublished dittograph, MIT. Published in slightly revised form by Plenum, New York, 1975.

[1957]Chomsky, Noam (1957): *Syntactic Structures.* The Hague: Mouton.

[1959]Chomsky, Noam (1959): On certain formal properties of grammars. *Information and Control* **2** (1959) 137–167.

[1961]Chomsky, Noam (1961): Some methodological remarks on generative grammar. *Word* **17**, 219–239. Section 5 republished as 'Degrees of grammaticalness' in Fodor and Katz (1964), 384–389.

[1964]Chomsky, Noam (1964): *Current Issues in Linguistic Theory.* The Hague: Mouton. Page reference to reprinting in Fodor and Katz, eds.

[1986]Chomsky, Noam (1986): *Knowledge of Language: Its Origins, Nature, and Use.* New York: Praeger.

[1995]Chomsky, Noam (1995): *The Minimalist Program.* Cambridge, MA: MIT Press.

[1963]Dixon, Robert W. (1963): *Linguistic Science and Logic.* The Hague: Mouton.

[1999]Ebbinghaus, Heinz-Dieter, and Jorg Flum (1999): *Finite Model Theory.* Second edition. Berlin: Springer.

[1976]Emonds, Joseph E. (1976): *A Transformational Approach to English Syntax.* New York: Academic Press.

[1981]Evans, Gareth (1981): Reply: syntactic theory and tacit knowledge. In S. H. Holtzman and C. M. Leich (eds.), *Wittgenstein: To Follow a Rule*, 118–137. London: Routledge and Kegan Paul.

[1999]Fillmore, Charles W. and Paul Kay (1999) Grammatical constructions and linguistic generalizations: The What's X doing Y? construction. *Language* **75**: 1-33.

[1964]Fodor, Jerry A. and Jerrold J. Katz, eds. (1964): *The Structure of Language: Readings in the Philosophy of Language.* Englewood Cliffs, NJ: Prentice-Hall.

[1985]Gazdar, Gerald; Ewan Klein; Geoffrey K. Pullum; and Ivan A. Sag (1985): *Generalized Phrase Structure Grammar.* Oxford: Basil Blackwell; Cambridge, MA: Harvard University Press.

[1988]Gazdar, Gerald; Geoffrey K. Pullum; Bob Carpenter; Ewan Klein; Thomas E. Hukari; and Robert D. Levine (1988): Category structures. *Computational Linguistics* **14**: 1–19.

[1967]Gold, E. Mark (1967): Language identification in the limit. *Information and Control* **10**: 441–474.

[1968]Harris, Zellig S. (1968): *Mathematical Structures of Language* (Interscience Tracts in Pure and Applied Mathematics, 21). New York: Interscience Publishers.

[1972]Hetzron, Robert (1972): Phonology in syntax. *Journal of Linguistics* **8**, 251–265.

[1961]Hill, Archibald A. (1961): Grammaticality. *Word* **17**, 1–10.

[1955]Hockett, Charles F. (1955): *A Manual of Phonology*. Baltimore, MD: Waverly Press.

[forthcoming]Huddleston, Rodney and Geoffrey K. Pullum (forthcoming): *The Cambridge Grammar of the English Language*. Cambridge: Cambridge University Press.

[1984]Hughes, G. E. and M. J. Cresswell (1984): *A Companion to Modal Logic*. London: Methuen.

[1998]Immerman, Neil (1998): *Descriptive Complexity*. Berlin: Springer, 1998.

[1977]Jackendoff, Ray S. (1977): *$\bar{X}$ Syntax*. Cambridge, MA: MIT Press.

[1980]Johnson, David E., and Paul M. Postal (1980): *Arc Pair Grammar*. Princeton: Princeton University Press.

[1987]Joshi, Aravind (1987): An introduction to tree adjoining grammars. In Alexis Manaster-Ramer (ed.), *Mathematics of Language*, 87–114. Amsterdam: John Benjamins.

[1996]Keenan, Edward L. and Edward Stabler (1996): Abstract syntax. In *Configurations: Essays on Structure and Interpretation*, ed. by Anna-Maria Di Sciullo (ed.), 329–344. Somerville, MA: Cascadilla Press.

[1998]Keller, Frank (1998): Gradient grammaticality as an effect of selective constraint re-ranking. In M. Catherine Gruber, Derrick Higgins, Kenneth S. Olson, and Tamra Wysocki, eds., *Papers from the 34th Meeting of the Chicago Linguistic Society; Vol. 2: The Panels*, 95–109. Chicago: Chicago Linguistic Society.

[2000]Keller, Frank (2000): *Gradience in Grammar: Experimental and Computational Aspects of Degrees of Grammaticality*. PhD Thesis, University of Edinburgh.

[2001]Kempson, Ruth; Wilfried Meyer-Viol; and Dov Gabbay (2001): *Dynamic Syntax: The Flow of Language Understanding*. Oxford: Basil Blackwell.

[1999]King, Paul John (1999): Towards truth in head-driven phrase structure grammar. Bericht Nr. 132, Arbeitspapiere des Sonderforschungsbereich 340, Seminar für Sprachwissenschaft, Eberhard-Karls-Universität, Tübingen.

[1990]Kornai, Andràs and Geoffrey K. Pullum (1990): The X-bar theory of phrase structure. *Language* **66**: 24–50.

[1989]Kracht, Marcus (1989): On the logic of category definitions. *Computational Linguistics* **15**: 111–113.

[1993]Kracht, Marcus (1993): Syntactic codes and grammar refinement. *Journal of Logic, Language and Information* **4**: 41–60.

[2001]Kracht, Marcus (2001): Logic and syntax: a personal view. In Michael Zhakharyaschev, Krister Segerberg, Maarten de Rijke and Heinrich Wansing (eds.), *Advances in Modal Logic 2*. Stanford: CSLI Publications.

[1971]Lakoff, George (1971): On generative semantics. In Danny D. Steinberg and Leon A. Jakobovitz (eds.), *Semantics: An Interdisciplinary Reader in Philosophy, Linguistics and Psychology*, 232–296. Cambridge: Cambridge University Press, 1971.

[1984]Langendoen, Terry and Paul M. Postal (1984): *The Vastness of Natural Languages*. Oxford: Basil Blackwell.

[2000]Lasnik, Howard (2000): Syntactic Structures *Revisited: Contemporary Lectures on Classic Transformational Theory*. Cambridge, MA: MIT Press.

[1997]Miller, Philip, Geoffrey K. Pullum, and Arnold M. Zwicky (1997): The Principle of Phonology-Free Syntax: Four apparent counterexamples from French. *Journal of Linguistics* **33**: 67–90.

[1971]Perlmutter, David M. (1971): *Deep and Surface Structure Constraints in Syntax.* New York: Holt Rinehart and Winston.

[1994]Pollard, Carl and Ivan A. Sag (1994): *Head-driven Phrase Structure Grammar.* Stanford, CA: CSLI Publications.

[1999]Pollard, Carl (1999): Strong generative capacity in HPSG. In Gert Webelhuth, Jean-Pierre Koenig, and Andreas Kathol (eds.), *Lexical and Constructional Aspects of Linguistic Explanation*, 281–297. Stanford, CA: CSLI Publications.

[1943]Post, Emil (1943): Formal reductions of the general combinatory decision problem. *American Journal of Mathematics* **65** (1943) 197–215.

[1944]Post, Emil (1944): Recursively enumerable sets of positive integers and their decision problems. *Bulletin of the American Mathematical Society* **50** (1944) 284–316.

[1993]Prince, Alan and Paul Smolensky (1993): *Optimality Theory* (Technical Report RuCCS TR–2, Rutgers University Center for Cognitive Science). Piscataway, NJ: Rutgers University.

[1997]Pullum, Geoffrey K. and Barbara C. Scholz (1997): Theoretical linguistics and the ontology of linguistic structure. In *1997 Yearbook of the Linguistic Association of Finland*, 25–47. Turku: Linguistic Association of Finland.

[forthcoming]Pullum, Geoffrey K. and Barbara C. Scholz (forthcoming): Empirical assessment of stimulus poverty arguments. *The Linguistic Review*, in press.

[1996]Rogers, James (1996): A model-theoretic framework for theories of syntax. In *34th Annual Meeting of the Assocation for Computational Linguistics: Proceedings of the Conference*, 10–16. San Francisco, CA: Morgan Kaufmann.

[1997]Rogers, James (1997): "Grammarless" phrase structure grammar. *Linguistics and Philosophy* **20**: 721–746.

[1998]Rogers, James (1998): *A Descriptive Approach to Language-Theoretic Complexity.* Stanford, CA: CSLI Publications.

[1999]Rogers, James (1999): The descriptive complexity of generalized local sets. In Hans-Peter Kolb and Uwe Mönnich (eds.), *The Mathematics of Syntactic Structure: Trees and their Logics*, (Studies in Generative Grammar, 44), 21–40. Berlin: Mouton de Gruyter.

[1985]Sag, Ivan A.; Gerald Gazdar; Thomas Wasow; and Stephen Weisler (1985): Coordination and how to distinguish categories. *Natural Language and Linguistic Theory* **3**: 117–171.

[1999]Sag, Ivan A. and Thomas Wasow (1999): *Syntactic Theory: A Formal Introduction.* Stanford, CA: CSLI Publications.

[1996]Schütze, Carson (1996): *The Empirical Base of Linguistics: Grammaticality Judgments and Linguistic Methodology.* Chicago: University of Chicago Press.

[1986]Thomas, Simon (1986): Theories with finitely many models. *Journal of Symbolic Logic* **51**: 374-376.

[1990]Thomas, Wolfgang (1990): Automata on infinite objects. In J. van Leeuwen (ed.), *Handbook of Theoretical Computer Science*, 135–191. New York: Elsevier Science.

A Formal Definition of Bottom-Up Embedded Push-Down Automata and Their Tabulation Technique

Miguel A. Alonso[1], Eric de la Clergerie[2], and Manuel Vilares[3]

[1] Departamento de Computación, Universidad de La Coruña
Campus de Elviña s/n, 15071 La Coruña, Spain
alonso@dc.fi.udc.es, vilares@dc.fi.udc.es
http://coleweb.dc.fi.udc.es/

[2] Institut National de Recherche en Informatique et en Automatique
Domaine de Voluceau, Rocquecourt, B.P. 105, 78153 Le Chesnay Cedex, France
Eric.De_La_Clergerie@inria.fr
http://atoll.inria.fr/

Abstract. The task of designing parsing algorithms for tree adjoining grammars could be simplified by providing a separation between the description of the parsing strategy and the execution of the parser. This can be accomplished through the use of Bottom-up Embedded Push-Down Automata. Towards this aim, we provide a formal and consistent definition of this class of automata and, by removing the finite-state control, we obtain an alternative definition which is adequate to define a tabulation framework for this model of automata and to show the equivalence with respect to other kinds of automata accepting tree adjoining languages.

1 Introduction

Tree Adjoining Languages (TAL) belong to the class of mildly context-sensitive languages, placed between context-free languages and context-sensitive languages. They can be described by Tree Adjoining Grammars (TAG) [12] and several grammar formalisms which have been shown to be equivalent to TAG with respect to their weak generative capacity [23]: Linear Indexed Grammars [10], Head Grammars [17], Combinatory Categorial Grammars [21], Context-Free Recursive Matrix Systems of index 2 [5], Positive Range Concatenation Grammars of arity 2 [6], Coupled Context-Free Grammars of range 2 [16], and Control Grammars of level 2 [24]. Several parsing algorithms have been proposed for all of them, but the design of correct and efficient parsing algorithms is a difficult task that could be simplified by providing a separation between the description of the parsing strategy and the execution of the parser. This can be accomplished through the use of automata: the actual parsing strategy can be described by means of the construction of a non-deterministic pushdown automaton, and tabulation can be introduced by means of some generic mechanism such as memoization. The construction of parsers in this way allows more straightforward proofs

P. de Groote, G. Morrill, C. Retoré (Eds.): LACL 2001, LNAI 2099, pp. 44–61, 2001.

of correctness and makes parsing strategies easier to understand and cheaper to implement [4].

Bottom-up embedded push-down automata (BEPDA) have been described in [19] as an extension of push-down automata adequate to implement parsing strategies for TAG in which adjunctions are recognized in a bottom-up way. In fact, BEPDA are the dual version of embedded push-down automata (EPDA) [22,2], a model of automata in which adjunctions must be recognized in a top-down way. A less informal presentation of BEPDA has been shown in [18], with some inconsistencies between the set of allowed transitions and the set of configurations attainable.

Right-oriented linear indexed automata [14] and bottom-up 2–stack automata [8] can be used to implement parsing strategies similar to those of BEPDA. Both models of automata have associated a tabulation framework allowing their execution in polynomial time with respect to the size of the input string.

This article is outlined as follows. The rest of this section is devoted to introduce tree adjoining grammars. Section 2 provides a formal and consistent definition of classic BEPDA. In Sect. 3 the finite-state control is removed to obtain an alternative definition. Section 4 shows how this new definition is useful to implement parsers by defining a compilation schema from TAG into BEPDA. The relation between right-oriented linear indexed automata, bottom-up 2–stack automata and BEPDA is considered in Sect. 5. Derivations of bottom-up embedded push-down automata are studied in Sect. 6 in order to define a tabular technique allowing them to be executed efficiently. Section 7 presents final conclusions.

1.1 Tree Adjoining Grammars

Tree adjoining grammars (TAG) [12] are an extension of context-free grammars that use trees instead of productions as the primary representing structure. Formally, a TAG is a 5-tuple $\mathcal{G} = (V_N, V_T, S, \boldsymbol{I}, \boldsymbol{A})$, where V_N is a finite set of non-terminal symbols, V_T a finite set of terminal symbols, $S \in V_N$ is the axiom of the grammar, $\boldsymbol{I}$ a finite set of *initial trees* and $\boldsymbol{A}$ a finite set of *auxiliary trees*. $\boldsymbol{I} \cup \boldsymbol{A}$ is the set of *elementary trees*. Internal nodes are labeled by non-terminals and leaf nodes by terminals or ε, except for just one leaf per auxiliary tree (the *foot*) which is labeled by the same non-terminal used as the label of its root node. The path in an elementary tree from the root node to the foot node is called the *spine* of the tree.

New trees are derived by *adjoining*: let α be a tree containing a node N^α labeled by A and let β be an auxiliary tree whose root and foot nodes are also labeled by A. Then, the adjoining of β at the *adjunction node* N^α is obtained by excising the subtree of α with root N^α, attaching β to N^α and attaching the excised subtree to the foot of β.

The operation of *substitution* does not increase the generative power of the formalism but it is usually considered when we are dealing with lexicalized tree adjoining grammars. In this case, non-terminals can also label leaf nodes (called substitution nodes) of elementary trees. An initial tree can be substituted at a substitution node if its root is labeled by the same non-terminal that labels the substitution node.

2 A Formal Definition of BEPDA

Bottom-up embedded push-down automata are an extension of push-down automata (PDA), so we first introduce this last model of automata, the operational device for parsing context-free grammars. A push-down automata [11] consists of a finite-state control, an input tape and a stack made up of stack symbols. Formally, a PDA can be defined as a tuple $(Q, V_T, V_S, \delta', q_0, Q_F, \$_f)$ where:

- Q is a finite set of states.
- V_T is a finite set of terminal symbols.
- V_S is a finite set of stack symbols.
- $q_0 \in Q$ is the initial state.
- $Q_F \subseteq Q$ is the set of final states.
- $\$_f \in V_S$ is the final stack symbol.
- δ' is a mapping from $Q \times V_T \cup \{\epsilon\} \times V_S$ into finite subsets of $Q \times V_S^*$.

In the case of bottom-up embedded push-down automata, the stack (that we call the main stack) is made up of non-empty stacks containing stack symbols. Formally, a BEPDA is defined by a tuple $(Q, V_T, V_S, \delta, q_0, Q_F, \$_f)$ where Q, V_T, V_S, $q_0 \in Q$, $Q_F \subseteq Q$ and $\$_f \in V_S$ are defined as before, but δ is now defined as a mapping from $Q \times V_T \cup \{\epsilon\} \times ([V_S^+)^* \times V_S^* \times ([V_S^+)^*$ into finite subsets of $Q \times V_S \cup \{[V_S\}$, where $[\notin V_S$ is a new symbol used as stack separator.

An *instantaneous configuration* is a triple (q, Υ, w), where q is the current state, $\Upsilon \in ([V_S^+)^*$ represents the contents of the automaton stack and w is the part of the input string that is yet to be read. It is important to remark that every individual stack contained in the main stack must store at least one stack symbol. The main stack will be empty only in the initial configuration (q_0, ϵ, w).

Transitions in δ allow an automaton to derive a new configuration (q', Υ', w) from a configuration (q, Υ, aw), which is denoted $(q, \Upsilon, aw) \vdash (q', \Upsilon', w)$. The reflexive and transitive closure of $\vdash$ is denoted by $\overset{*}{\vdash}$. There exist two different types of transitions:

1. Transitions of the first type are of the form

$$(q', [Z) \in \delta(q, a, \epsilon, \epsilon, \epsilon)$$

and they can be applied to a configuration (q, Υ, aw) to yield a configuration $(q', \Upsilon[Z, w)$.

2. Transitions of the second type are of the form

$$(q', Z) \in \delta(q,\ a,\ [\alpha_k \ldots [\alpha_{i+1},\ Z_m \ldots Z_1,\ [\alpha_i \ldots [\alpha_1)$$

(a) $(q_0, [D) \in \delta(q_0, a, \epsilon, \epsilon, \epsilon)$
(b) $(q_1, [C) \in \delta(q_0, b, \epsilon, \epsilon, \epsilon)$
(c) $(q_1, [C) \in \delta(q_1, b, \epsilon, \epsilon, \epsilon)$
(d) $(q_2, B) \in \delta(q_1, c, \epsilon, C, \epsilon)$
(e) $(q_2, B) \in \delta(q_2, c, [C, \epsilon, \epsilon)$
(f) $(q_3, B) \in \delta(q_2, d, [D, BB, \epsilon)$
(g) $(q_3, B) \in \delta(q_3, d, [D, BB, \epsilon)$
(h) $(q_3, \$_f) \in \delta(q_3, d, [D, B, \epsilon)$
(i) $(q_0, [\$_f) \in \delta(q_0, a, \epsilon, \epsilon, \epsilon)$

	q_0		$aabbccdd$
(a)	q_0	$[D$	$abbccdd$
(a)	q_0	$[D[D$	$bbccdd$
(b)	q_1	$[D[D[C$	$bccdd$
(c)	q_1	$[D[D[C[C$	$ccdd$
(d)	q_2	$[D[D[C[B$	cdd
(e)	q_2	$[D[D[BB$	dd
(f)	q_3	$[D[B$	d
(h)	q_3	$[\$_f$	

Fig. 1. BEPDA accepting $\{a^n b^n c^n d^n \mid n > 0\}$ and configurations for *aabbccdd*

where $m \geq 0$ and $k \geq i \geq 0$. They can be applied to a configuration

$$(q,\ \Upsilon[\alpha_k \ldots [\alpha_{i+1}[\alpha Z_m \ldots Z_1[\alpha_i \ldots [\alpha_1,\ aw)$$

to yield a configuration

$$(q', \Upsilon[\alpha Z, w)$$

The *language accepted by final state* by a BEPDA is the set $w \in V_T^*$ of input strings such that $(q_0, \epsilon, w) \vdash {}^*(p, \Upsilon, \epsilon)$, where $p \in Q_F$ and $\Upsilon \in ([V_S^+)^*$.

The *language accepted by empty stack* by a BEPDA is the set $w \in V_T^*$ of input strings such that $(q_0, \epsilon, w) \vdash {}^*(q, [\$_f, \epsilon)$ for any $q \in Q$. At this point it is interesting to observe the duality with respect to embedded push-down automata: computations in EPDA start with a stack $[\$_0$ to finish with an empty stack while computations in BEPDA start with an empty stack to finish with a stack $[\$_f$.

It can be proved that for any BEPDA accepting a language L by final state there exists a BEPDA accepting the same language by empty stack and vice versa[1].

Example 1. The bottom-up embedded push-down automaton defined by the tuple $(\{q_0, q_1, q_2, q_3\}, \{a, b, c, d\}, \{B, C, D\}, \delta, q_0, \emptyset, \$_f)$, with δ containing the transitions shown in Fig. 1 (left box), accepts the language $\{a^n b^n c^n d^n \mid n \geq 0\}$ by empty stack. The sequence of configurations for the recognition of the input

[1] The proof is analogous to the proof of equivalence of acceptance by final state and empty stack in the case of push-down automata [11].

string *aabbccdd* is shown in Fig. 1 (right box), where the first column shows the transition applied, the second one the current state, the third one the contents of the stack and the fourth column shows the part of the input string to be read.

3 BEPDA without States

Finite-state control is not a fundamental component of push-down automata, as the current state in a configuration can be stored in the top element of the stack of the automaton [13]. Thus, we can obtain an alternative definition that considers a PDA as a tuple $(V_T, V_S, \Theta', \$_0, \$_f)$ where:

- V_T is a finite set of terminal symbols.
- V_S is a finite set of stack symbols.
- $\$_0 \in V_S$ is the initial stack symbol.
- $\$_f \in V_S$ is the final stack symbol.
- Θ' is a finite set of three types of transition:
  SWAP: Transitions of the form $C \overset{a}{\longmapsto} F$ that replace the top element of the stack while scanning a. The application of such a transition on a stack ξC returns the stack ξF.
  PUSH: Transitions of the form $C \overset{a}{\longmapsto} C\ F$ that push F onto C. The application of such a transition on a stack ξC returns the stack $\xi C F$.
  POP: Transitions of the form $C\ F \overset{a}{\longmapsto} G$ that replace C and F by G. The application of such a transition on $\xi C F$ returns the stack ξG.
  where $C, F, G \in V_S$, $\xi \in V_S^*$ and $a \in V_T \cup \{\epsilon\}$.

Finite-state control can also be eliminated from bottom-up embedded push-down automata, obtaining a new definition that considers a BEPDA as a tuple $(V_T, V_S, \Theta, \$_0, \$_f)$ where V_T, V_S, $\$_0 \in V_S$ and $\$_f \in V_S$ are defined as before but Θ is now defined as a finite set of six types of transition:

SWAP: Transitions of the form $C \overset{a}{\longmapsto} F$ that replace the top element of the top stack while scanning a. The application of such a transition on a stack $\Upsilon[\alpha C$ returns the stack $\Upsilon[\alpha F$.

PUSH: Transitions of the form $C \overset{a}{\longmapsto} C\ F$ that push F onto C. The application of such a transition on a stack $\Upsilon[\alpha C$ returns the stack $\Upsilon[\alpha C F$.

POP: Transitions of the form $C\ F \overset{a}{\longmapsto} G$ that replace C and F by G. The application of such a transition on $\Upsilon[\alpha C F$ returns the stack $\Upsilon[\alpha G$.

WRAP: Transitions of the form $C \overset{a}{\longmapsto} C, [F$ that push a new stack $[F$ on the top of the main stack. The application of such a transition on a stack $\Upsilon[\alpha C$ returns the stack $\Upsilon[\alpha C[F$.

UNWRAP-A: Transitions *unwrap-above* of the form $C, [F \overset{a}{\longmapsto} G$ that delete the top stack $[F$ and replace the new top element by G. The application of such a transition on a stack $\Upsilon[\alpha C[F$ returns the stack $\Upsilon[\alpha G$.

UNWRAP-B: Transitions *unwrap-below* of the form $[C, F \overset{a}{\longmapsto} G$ that delete the stack $[C$ placed just below the top stack and replace the top element by G. The application of such a transition on a stack $\Upsilon[C[\alpha F$ returns the stack $\Upsilon[\alpha G$.

where $C, F, G \in V_S$, $\Upsilon \in ([V_S^*)^*$, $\alpha \in V_S^*$ and $a \in V_T \cup \{\epsilon\}$.

$(a)\ \$_0 \overset{a}{\longmapsto} \$_0, [D$
$(b)\ D \overset{a}{\longmapsto} D, [D$
$(c)\ D \longmapsto D, [C$
$(d)\ C \overset{b}{\longmapsto} C, [C$
$(e)\ C \longmapsto B$
$(f)\ B \longmapsto BE$
$(g)\ [C, E \overset{c}{\longmapsto} C$
$(h)\ BC \longmapsto B$
$(i)\ [D, B \overset{d}{\longmapsto} D$
$(j)\ BD \longmapsto B$
$(k)\ \$_0, [D \longmapsto \$_f$

	$[\$_0$	$aabbccdd$
(a)	$[\$_0[D$	$aabbccdd$
(b)	$[\$_0[D[D$	$abbccdd$
(c)	$[\$_0[D[D[C$	$bbccdd$
(d)	$[\$_0[D[D[C[C$	$bccdd$
(d)	$[\$_0[D[D[C[C[C$	$ccdd$
(e)	$[\$_0[D[D[C[C[B$	$ccdd$
(f)	$[\$_0[D[D[C[C[BE$	$ccdd$
(g)	$[\$_0[D[D[C[BC$	cdd
(e)	$[\$_0[D[D[C[BB$	cdd
(f)	$[\$_0[D[D[C[BBE$	cdd
(g)	$[\$_0[D[D[BBC$	dd
(h)	$[\$_0[D[D[BB$	dd
(i)	$[\$_0[D[BD$	d
(j)	$[\$_0[D[B$	d
(i)	$[\$_0[D$	
(k)	$[\$_f$	

Fig. 2. BEPDA without finite-state control for $\{a^n b^n c^n d^n \mid n > 0\}$

An *instantaneous configuration* is a pair (Υ, w), where Υ represents the contents of the automaton stack and w is the part of the input string that is yet to be read. A configuration (Υ, aw) derives a configuration (Υ', w), denoted $(\Upsilon, aw) \vdash (\Upsilon', w)$, if and only if there exist a transition that applied to Υ gives Υ' and scans a from the input string. We use $\vdash^*$ to denote the reflexive and transitive closure of $\vdash$. An input string is accepted by an BEPDA if $([\$_0, w) \vdash^* ([\$_f, \epsilon)$. The language accepted by an BEPDA is the set of $w \in V_T^*$ such that $([\$_0, w) \vdash^* ([\$_f, \epsilon)$.

Example 2. The bottom-up embedded push-down automaton without states defined by the tuple $(\{a, b, c, d\}, \{B, C, D, E, F, \$_0, \$_f\}, \Theta, \$_0, \$_f)$, with Θ containing the transitions shown in Fig. 2 (left box), accepts the language $\{a^n b^n c^n d^n \mid n \geq 0\}$. The sequence of configurations to recognize the input string $aabbccdd$ is also shown in Fig. 2 (right-box), where the first column shows the transition applied in each step, the second one shows the contents of the stack and the third column shows the part of the input string to be read.

It can be proved that transitions of a BEPDA with states can be emulated by transitions a BEPDA without states and vice versa.

Sketch of the proof: As a first step, we must consider a normalized version of transitions for BEPDA with states. These transitions are of the form:

$$(q', [Z) \in \delta(q, a, \epsilon, \epsilon, \epsilon)$$

$$(q', Z) \in \delta(q,\ a,\ [Z'_k \ldots [Z'_{i+1},\ Z_m \ldots Z_1,\ [Z'_i \ldots [Z'_1)$$

where $q, q' \in Q$, $a \in V_T \cup \{\epsilon\}$, $Z, Z_1, \ldots, Z_m \in V_S$, $Z'_1, \ldots, Z'_k \in V_S$, $0 \leq i \leq k$ and $0 \leq m \leq 2$. Then, we show these transitions can be emulated by a set of SWAP, PUSH, POP, WRAP, UNWRAP-A and UNWRAP-B transitions, and vice versa, with the help of a kind of complex transitions of the form

$$[F_k \ldots [F_{i+1}, DC_1 \ldots C_m, [F_i \ldots [F_1 \stackrel{a}{\longmapsto} DB$$

created by the application of a sequence of simple transitions, where $a \in V_T \cup \{\epsilon\}$; $0 \leq m \leq 2$; $B, C_1, \ldots, C_m, F_1, \ldots, F_k, \in V_S$; and if $m = 0$ then $D \in V_S$ else $D = \epsilon$. □

[INIT]	$\$_0 \longmapsto \$_0\ [\overrightarrow{\top^\alpha}$	$\alpha \in \boldsymbol{I},\ S = \text{label}(\mathbf{R}^\alpha)$
[FINAL]	$\$_0\ [\overleftarrow{\top^\alpha} \longmapsto \$_f$	$\alpha \in \boldsymbol{I},\ S = \text{label}(\mathbf{R}^\alpha)$
[CALL]	$\nabla^\gamma_{r,s} \longmapsto \nabla^\gamma_{r,s},\ [\overrightarrow{N^\gamma_{r,s+1}}$	$N^\gamma_{r,s+1} \notin \text{spine}(\gamma),\ \mathbf{nil} \in \text{adj}(N_{r,s+1})$
[SCALL]	$\nabla^\beta_{r,s} \longmapsto \nabla^\beta_{r,s}\ [\overrightarrow{N^\beta_{r,s+1}}$	$N^\beta_{r,s+1} \in \text{spine}(\beta),\ \mathbf{nil} \in \text{adj}(N^\beta_{r,s+1})$
[SEL]	$\overrightarrow{N^\gamma_{r,0}} \longmapsto \nabla^\gamma_{r,0}$	
[PUB]	$\nabla^\gamma_{r,n_r} \longmapsto \overleftarrow{N^\gamma_{r,0}}$	
[RET]	$\nabla^\gamma_{r,s},\ [\overleftarrow{N^\gamma_{r,s+1}} \longmapsto \nabla^\gamma_{r,s+1}$	$N^\gamma_{r,s+1} \notin \text{spine}(\gamma),\ \mathbf{nil} \in \text{adj}(N_{r,s+1})$
[SRET]	$[\nabla^\beta_{r,s},\ \overleftarrow{N^\beta_{r,s+1}} \longmapsto \nabla^\beta_{r,s+1}$	$N^\beta_{r,s+1} \in \text{spine}(\beta),\ \mathbf{nil} \in \text{adj}(N^\beta_{r,s+1})$
[SCAN]	$\overrightarrow{N^\gamma_{r,0}} \stackrel{a}{\longmapsto} \overleftarrow{N^\gamma_{r,0}}$	$N^\gamma_{r,0} \rightarrow a$
[AdjCALL]	$\nabla^\gamma_{r,s} \longmapsto \nabla^\gamma_{r,s},\ [\overrightarrow{\top^\beta}$	$\beta \in \text{adj}(N^\gamma_{r,s+1})$
[AdjRET-a]	$[\nabla^\gamma_{r,s},\ \overleftarrow{\top^\beta} \longmapsto \top$	$\beta \in \text{adj}(N^\gamma_{r,s+1})$
[AdjRET-b]	$\Delta^\gamma_{r,s}\ \top \longmapsto \nabla^\gamma_{r,s+1}$	
[FootCALL]	$\nabla^\beta_{f,0} \longmapsto \nabla^\beta_{f,0},\ [\overrightarrow{N^\gamma_{r,s+1}}$	$N^\beta_{f,0} = \mathbf{F}^\beta,\ \ \beta \in \text{adj}(N^\gamma_{r,s+1})$
[FootRET-a]	$[\nabla^\beta_{f,0},\ \overleftarrow{N^\gamma_{r,s+1}} \longmapsto \Delta^\gamma_{r,s}$	$N^\beta_{f,0} = \mathbf{F}^\beta,\ \ \beta \in \text{adj}(N^\gamma_{r,s+1})$
[FootRET-b]	$\Delta^\gamma_{r,s} \longmapsto \Delta^\gamma_{r,s}\ \nabla^\beta_{f,1}$	$N^\beta_{f,0} = \mathbf{F}^\beta,\ \ \beta \in \text{adj}(N^\gamma_{r,s+1})$
[SubsCALL]	$\nabla^\gamma_{r,s} \longmapsto \nabla^\gamma_{r,s},\ [\overrightarrow{\top^\alpha}$	$\alpha \in \text{subs}(N_{r,s+1})$
[SubsRET]	$\nabla^\gamma_{r,s},\ [\overleftarrow{\top^\alpha} \longmapsto \nabla^\gamma_{r,s+1}$	$\alpha \in \text{subs}(N_{r,s+1})$

Fig. 3. Generic compilation schema for TAG

4 Compiling TAG into BEPDA

Automata are interesting for parsing because they allow us to separate two different problems that arise during the definition of parsing algorithms: the description of the parsing strategy and the execution of the parser. By means of automata, a parsing strategy for a given grammar can be translated into a set of transitions defining a (possibly non deterministic) automaton and then the automaton can be executed using some standard technique.

In this section we define a generic compilation schema for tree adjoining grammars based on a call/return model [9]. We consider each elementary tree γ of a TAG as formed by a set of context-free productions $\mathcal{P}(\gamma)$: a node N^γ and its g children $N_1^\gamma \dots N_g^\gamma$ are represented by a production $N^\gamma \rightarrow N_1^\gamma \dots N_g^\gamma$. The elements of the productions are the nodes of the tree, except for the case of elements belonging to $V_T \cup \{\varepsilon\}$ in the right-hand side of production. Those elements may not have children and are not candidates to be adjunction nodes, so we identify such nodes labeled by a terminal with that terminal. We use $\beta \in \text{adj}(N^\gamma)$ to denote that a tree $\beta \in \boldsymbol{A}$ may be adjoined at node N^γ. If adjunction is not mandatory at N^γ, then $\mathbf{nil} \in \text{adj}(N^\gamma)$. If a tree $\alpha \in \boldsymbol{I}$ may be substituted at node N^γ, then $\alpha \in \text{subs}(N^\gamma)$. We consider the additional productions $\top^\alpha \rightarrow \mathbf{R}^\alpha$, $\top^\beta \rightarrow \mathbf{R}^\beta$ and $\mathbf{F}^\beta \rightarrow \bot$ for each initial tree α and each auxiliary tree β, where $\mathbf{R}^\alpha$ is the root node of α and $\mathbf{R}^\beta$ and $\mathbf{F}^\beta$ are the root node and foot node of β, respectively.

Fig. 3 shows the compilation rules from TAG to BEPDA, where symbols $\nabla_{r,s}^\gamma$ has been introduced to denote dotted productions

$$N_{r,0}^\gamma \rightarrow N_{r,1}^\gamma \dots N_{r,s}^\gamma \bullet N_{r,s+1}^\gamma \dots N_{r,n_r}^\gamma$$

where n_r is the length of the right hand side of the production. The meaning of each compilation rule is graphically shown in Fig. 4. This schema is parameterized by $\overrightarrow{N^\gamma}$, the information propagated top-down with respect to the node N^γ, and by $\overleftarrow{N^\gamma}$, the information propagated bottom-up. When the schema is used to implement a top-down traversal of elementary trees $\overrightarrow{N^\gamma} = N^\gamma$ and $\overleftarrow{N^\gamma} = \Box$, where $\Box$ is a fresh stack symbol. A bottom-up traversal requires $\overrightarrow{N^\gamma} = \Box$ and $\overleftarrow{N^\gamma} = N^\gamma$. For a mixed traversal of elementary trees, $\overrightarrow{N^\gamma} = \overline{N^\gamma}$ and $\overleftarrow{N^\gamma} = \overline{\overline{N^\gamma}}$, where $\overline{N^\gamma}$ and $\overline{\overline{N^\gamma}}$ are used to distinguish the top-down prediction from the bottom-up propagation of a node.

With respect to adjunctions, we can observe in Fig. 3 that each stack stores pending adjunctions with respect to the node placed on the top of the stack in a bottom-up treatment of adjunctions: when a foot node is reached, the adjunction node is stored on the top of the stack ([**FootCALL-a**]); the traversal of the elementary tree is suspended to continue with the traversal of the adjoined auxiliary tree ([**FootCALL-b**]); the adjunction stack is propagated through the spine ([**SRET**]) up to the root node ([**AdjRET-a**]); and then the stack element corresponding to the auxiliary tree is eliminated to resume the traversal of the elementary tree ([**AdjRET-b**]). To avoid confusion, we store $\Delta_{r,s}^\gamma$ instead of $\nabla_{r,s}^\gamma$ to indicate that an adjunction was started at node $N_{r,s+1}^\gamma$. A symbol Δ can be seen as a symbol ∇ waiting an adjunction to be completed.

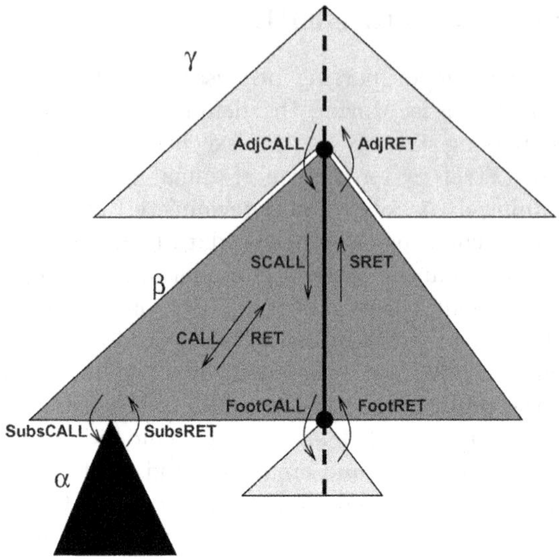

Fig. 4. Meaning of compilation rules

Substitution is managed trough transitions generated by compilation rules [**SubsCALL**], which start the traversal of the substituted trees, and [**SubsRET**], which resume the traversal of the tree containing the substitution node once the substituted tree has been completely traversed.

5 BEPDA and Other Automata for TAG

5.1 Right-Oriented Linear Indexed Automata

Linear indexed automata (LIA) [4] are an extension of push-down automata in which each stack symbol has been associated to a list of indices. Right-oriented linear indexed automata (R-LIA) [14,15] are a subclass of linear indexed automata that can be used to implement parsing strategies for TAG in which adjunctions are recognized in a bottom-up way. BEPDA and R–LIA are equivalent classes of automata. Given a BEPDA, the equivalent R-LIA is obtained by means of a simple change in the notation: the top element of a stack is considered a stack symbol, and the rest of the stack is considered the indices list associated to it, as is shown in Fig. 5. The same procedure also serves to obtain the BEPDA equivalent to a given R–LIA.

5.2 Bottom-Up 2–Stack Automata

Strongly-driven 2-stack automata (SD–2SA) [7] are an extension of push-down automata working on a pair of asymmetric stacks, a master stack and an auxiliary stack. These stacks are partitioned into sessions. Computations in each session

Transition	BEPDA	R-LIA
SWAP	$C \overset{a}{\longmapsto} F$	$C[\circ\circ] \overset{a}{\longmapsto} F[\circ\circ]$
PUSH	$C \overset{a}{\longmapsto} CF$	$C[\circ\circ] \overset{a}{\longmapsto} F[\circ\circ C]$
POP	$CF \overset{a}{\longmapsto} G$	$F[\circ\circ C] \overset{a}{\longmapsto} G[\circ\circ]$
UNWRAP-A	$C, [F \overset{a}{\longmapsto} G$	$C[\circ\circ]\ F[\,] \overset{a}{\longmapsto} G[\circ\circ]$
UNWRAP-B	$[C, F \overset{a}{\longmapsto} G$	$C[\,]\ F[\circ\circ] \overset{a}{\longmapsto} G[\circ\circ]$
WRAP	$C \overset{a}{\longmapsto} C, [F$	$C[\circ\circ] \overset{a}{\longmapsto} C[\circ\circ]\ F[\,]$

Fig. 5. Equivalence between BEPDA and R-LIA

are performed in one of two modes *write* and *erase*. A session starts in mode write and switches at some point to mode erase. In mode write (resp. erase), no element can be popped from (resp. pushed to) the master stack. Switching back from erase to write mode is not allowed. Bottom-up 2–stack automata (BU–2SA) [8] are a projection of SD–2SA requiring the emptiness of the auxiliary stack during computations in mode write. When a new session is created in a BU–2SA, a mark $\models$ is left on the master stack, other movements performed in write mode leaving a mark $\triangleright$. These marks are popped in erase mode.

The full set of BU–2SA transitions is shown in Fig. 6. Transitions of type **SWAP2** are equivalent to $[C \overset{a}{\longmapsto} [F$ in BEPDA, compound transitions obtained from the consecutive application of $C \longmapsto C, [F'$ and $[C, F' \overset{a}{\longmapsto} F$, where F' is a fresh stack symbol. In a similar way, transitions of type $\nearrow$**ERASE** are translated into compound transitions formed by an UNWRAP-B and a POP transition, and transitions of type $\searrow$**ERASE** are translated into the composition of UNWRAP-B and PUSH transitions. Slightly different is the case for transitions of type $\triangleright$**WRITE**, equivalent to $[C \overset{a}{\longmapsto} [C, [F$ transitions in BEPDA, which are obtained as the consecutive application of $[C \overset{a}{\longmapsto} [C'$ and $C' \longmapsto C', [F$, an additional transition $C', [G \overset{b}{\longmapsto} K$ for each transition $C, [G \overset{b}{\longmapsto} K$ in the automaton, and an additional transition $[C', G \overset{b}{\longmapsto} K$ for each transition $[C, G \overset{b}{\longmapsto} K$, where C' is a fresh stack symbol.

As a consequence, it is possible to build a BEPDA for any given BU–2SA. However, the reverse is not always true: PUSH and POP transitions can only be translated into BU–2SA if they are merged with an UNWRAP-B transition. So, a BEPDA implementing a shift-reduce strategy (requiring the use of PUSH and POP transitions in combination with UNWRAP-A transitions[2]) can not be translated into a BU–2SA.

[2] A linear indexed automata implementing a LR-like strategy for linear indexed grammars using this kind of transitions is described in [1].

BEPDA transition		BU–2SA transition	
SWAP	$C \overset{a}{\longmapsto} F$	$(m, C, \epsilon) \overset{a}{\longmapsto} (m, F, \epsilon)$	**SWAP1**
	$[C \overset{a}{\longmapsto} [F$	$(\mathbf{w}, C, \models^m) \overset{a}{\longmapsto} (\mathbf{e}, F, \models^m)$	**SWAP2**
WRAP	$C \overset{a}{\longmapsto} C, [F$	$(m, C, \epsilon) \overset{a}{\longmapsto} (\mathbf{w}, C \models^m F, \models^m)$	$\models$**WRITE**
	$[C \overset{a}{\longmapsto} [C, [F$	$(\mathbf{w}, C, \epsilon) \overset{a}{\longmapsto} (\mathbf{w}, C \rhd F, \epsilon)$	$\rhd$**WRITE**
UNWRAP-A	$C, [F \overset{a}{\longmapsto} G$	$(\mathbf{e}, C \models^m F, \models^m) \overset{a}{\longmapsto} (m, G, \epsilon)$	$\models$**ERASE**
UNWRAP-B	$[C, F \overset{a}{\longmapsto} G$	$(\mathbf{e}, C \rhd F, \epsilon) \overset{a}{\longmapsto} (\mathbf{e}, G, \epsilon)$	$\rightarrow$**ERASE**
	$[C, XF \overset{a}{\longmapsto} G$	$(\mathbf{e}, C \rhd F, X) \overset{a}{\longmapsto} (\mathbf{e}, G, \epsilon)$	$\nearrow$**ERASE**
	$[C, F \overset{a}{\longmapsto} XG$	$(\mathbf{e}, C \rhd F, \epsilon) \overset{a}{\longmapsto} (\mathbf{e}, G, X)$	$\searrow$**ERASE**

Fig. 6. Correspondence between BEPDA and BU–2SA

6 Tabulation

The direct execution of (bottom-up embedded) push-down automata may be exponential with respect to the length of the input string and may even loop. To get polynomial complexity, we must avoid duplicating stack contents when several transitions may be applied to a given configuration. Instead of storing all the information about a configuration, we must determine the information we need to trace to retrieve that configuration. This information is stored into a table of *items*.

6.1 Tabulation of PDA

In a context-free grammar, if $B \overset{*}{\Rightarrow} \delta$ then $\alpha B \beta \overset{*}{\Rightarrow} \alpha \delta \beta$ for all $\alpha, \beta \in (V_N \cup V_T)^*$. This context-freeness property can be translated into push-down automata: given a derivation

$$(B, a_{i+1} \dots a_{j+1} \dots a_n) \overset{*}{\vdash} (C, a_{j+1} \dots a_n)$$

for all $\xi \in V_S^*$ we also have

$$(\xi B, a_{i+1} \dots a_{j+1} \dots a_n) \overset{*}{\vdash} (\xi C, a_{j+1} \dots a_n)$$

Thus, the only information we need to store about this last derivation are the stack elements B and C and the input positions i and j. We store this information in the form of an item $[B, i, C, j]$. New items[3] are derived from existing items by means of inference rules of the form $\frac{\textit{antecedents}}{\textit{consequent}}$ *conditions* similar to those used in grammatical deduction systems [20], meaning that if all antecedents are

[3] In this article we are considering items based on SWAP transitions, as in [15], but items can be also defined based on PUSH transitions, as in [13].

present and conditions are satisfied then the consequent item should be generated. Conditions usually refer to transitions of the automaton and to terminals from the input string.

In the case of PDA we have three inference rules, one for each type of transition:

- The inference rule for SWAP transitions

$$\frac{[B,i,C,j]}{[B,i,F,k]} \quad C \overset{a}{\longmapsto} F$$

means that given a derivation $(\xi B, a_{i+1}\ldots a_n) \overset{*}{\vdash} (\xi C, a_{j+1}\ldots a_n)$, the application a a transition $C \overset{a}{\longmapsto} F$ yields a derivation $(\xi B, a_{i+1}\ldots a_n) \overset{*}{\vdash} (\xi F, a_{k+1}\ldots a_n)$, where $k = j + |a|$.
- In the case of a PUSH transition, the inference rule

$$\frac{[B,i,C,j]}{[F,k,F,k]} \quad C \overset{a}{\longmapsto} CF$$

means that given an derivation $(\xi B, a_{i+1}\ldots a_n) \overset{*}{\vdash} (\xi C, a_{j+1}\ldots a_n)$, the application of a transition $C \overset{a}{\longmapsto} CF$ yields a derivation $(\xi F, a_{k+1}\ldots a_n) \overset{0}{\vdash} (\xi F, a_{k+1}\ldots a_n)$, where $k = j + |a|$.
- In the case of POP transition, the following inference rule

$$\frac{\begin{array}{l}[F',k',F,k]\\ [B,i,C,j]\end{array}}{[B,i,G,l]} \quad \begin{array}{l} C \overset{b}{\longmapsto} CF' \\ CF \overset{a}{\longmapsto} G\end{array}$$

is applied to indicate that given a derivation $(\xi B, a_{i+1}\ldots a_n) \overset{*}{\vdash} (\xi C, a_{j+1}\ldots a_n)$, a PUSH transition $C \overset{b}{\longmapsto} CF'$ that yields a derivation $(\xi C, a_{j+1}\ldots a_n) \vdash (\xi CF', a_{k'+1}\ldots a_n)$ and a derivation $(\xi F', a_{k'+1}\ldots a_n) \overset{*}{\vdash} (\xi F, a_{k+1}\ldots a_n)$, the application of a POP transition $CF \overset{a}{\longmapsto} G$ yields a derivation $(\xi CF, a_{k+1}\ldots a_n) \vdash (\xi G, a_{l+1}\ldots a_n)$, where $k' = j + |b|$ and $l = k + |a|$.

A PDA computation starts with the initial item $[\$_0, 0, \$_0, 0]$. An input string $a_1 \ldots a_n$ has been recognized if the final item $[\$_0, 0, \$_f, n]$ is generated indicating that a derivation $(\$_0, a_1\ldots a_n) \overset{*}{\vdash} (\$_f, \epsilon)$ has been attained.

6.2 Tabulation of BEPDA

For BEPDA, we extend the technique proposed for push-down automata in the previous subsection. We must take into account that the push-down in BEPDA is made up of stacks instead of single stack elements. So, an item $[B, i, C, j]$ can only

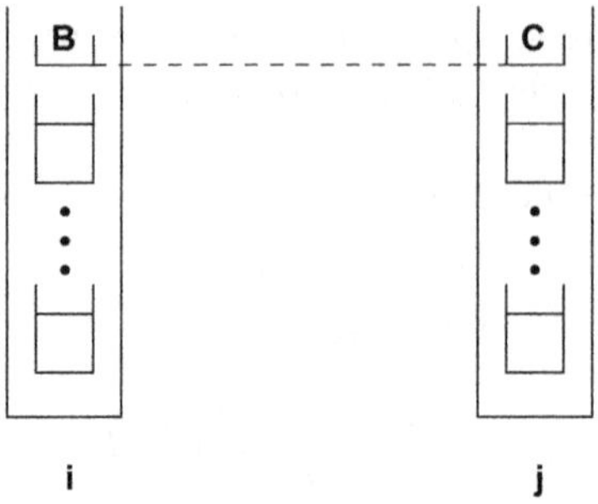

Fig. 7. Call derivations

be used to represent derivations of the form $([B, a_{i+1} \dots a_n) \vdash^* ([C, a_{j+1} \dots a_n)$. We can generalize this result by considering items of the form $[B, i, \alpha C, j]$ in order to represent derivations $([B, a_{i+1} \dots a_n) \vdash^* ([\alpha C, a_{j+1} \dots a_n)$. However, the size of α is not bounded and so the complexity of inference rules is not polynomial. To get polynomial complexity we must study in detail the form of derivations. We can observe that two different kinds of derivation can be attained in BEPDA:

Call derivations. Correspond to the placement of an unitary stack onto the top of the main stack, typically by means of a WRAP transition:

$$([B, a_{i+1} \dots a_n) \vdash^* ([C, a_{j+1} \dots a_n)$$

where $B, C \in V_S$. These derivations are context-freeness in the sense that for any $\Upsilon \in ([V_S^*)^*$ we have

$$(\Upsilon\ [B, a_{i+1} \dots a_n) \vdash^* (\Upsilon\ [C, a_{j+1} \dots a_n)$$

Thus, they can be represented by call items of the form

$$[B, i, C, j, - \mid -, -, -, -]$$

A graphical representation of call derivations and items is shown in figure 7.

Return derivations. Correspond to the placement of a non-unitary stack onto the top of the main stack:

$$\begin{aligned}
&([B, a_{i+1} \dots a_n) \\
&\vdash^* ([B\ \Upsilon_1\ [D, a_{p+1} \dots a_n) \\
&\vdash^* ([B\ \Upsilon_1\ [\alpha E, a_{q+1} \dots a_n) \\
&\vdash^* ([\alpha X C, a_{j+1} \dots a_n)
\end{aligned}$$

where $B, C, D, E, X \in V_S$ and $\alpha \in V_S^*$. The two occurrences of α denote the same stack in the sense that α is neither consulted nor modified through

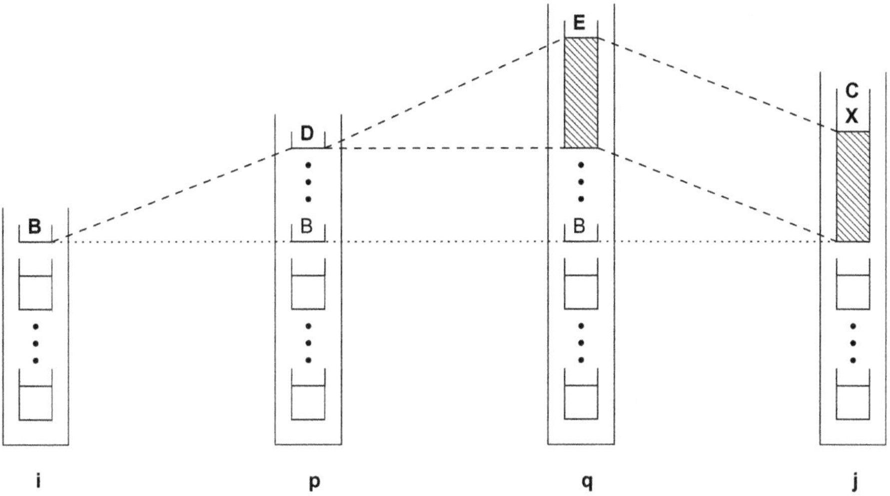

Fig. 8. Return derivations

derivation. These derivations are context-free with respect to the low part of the main stack and so, for any $\Upsilon, \Upsilon_1 \in ([V_S^*)^*$ we have

$$\begin{array}{l}(\Upsilon\ [B, a_{i+1} \ldots a_n) \\ \vdash {}^*(\Upsilon\ [B\ \ \Upsilon_1\ [D, a_{p+1} \ldots a_n) \\ \vdash {}^*(\Upsilon\ [B\ \ \Upsilon_1\ [\alpha E, a_{q+1} \ldots a_n) \\ \vdash {}^*(\Upsilon\ [\alpha X C, a_{j+1} \ldots a_n)\end{array}$$

but they are not independent with respect to the subderivation

$$([D, a_{p+1} \ldots a_n) \vdash {}^*([\alpha E, a_{q+1} \ldots a_n)$$

We can not store a entire subderivation into items if we want to get polynomial complexity. To solve this problem, we need to consider an item as formed by two different parts, a *head* storing some information about the top elements of the initial and final configurations of the derivation we are representing, and a *tail* that store information about a subderivation. The tail acts like a pointer to another configuration. Following the tail pointers we can retrieve the whole contents of a given stack. Therefore, for return derivations we are considering return items of the form

$$[B, i, C, j, X \mid D, p, E, q]$$

where (B, i, C, j, X) is the head and (D, p, E, q) is the tail. A graphical representation of call derivations and items is shown in figure 8.

Call and return items are combined by means of the following set of inference rules:

$$\frac{[B,i,C,j,-\mid -,-,-,-]}{[B,i,F,k,-\mid -,-,-,-]}\ C \overset{a}{\longmapsto} F$$

$$\frac{[B,i,C,j,X\mid D,p,E,q]}{[B,i,F,k,X\mid D,p,E,q]}\ C \overset{a}{\longmapsto} F$$

$$\frac{[B,i,C,j,-\mid -,-,-,-]}{[B,i,F,k,C\mid B,i,C,j]}\ C \overset{a}{\longmapsto} CF$$

$$\frac{[B,i,C,j,X\mid D,p,E,q]}{[B,i,F,k,C\mid B,i,C,j]}\ C \overset{a}{\longmapsto} CF$$

$$\frac{\begin{array}{c}[B,i,F,j,C\mid D,p,E,q]\\ [D,p,E,q,-\mid -,-,-,-]\end{array}}{[B,i,G,k,-\mid -,-,-,-]}\ CF \overset{a}{\longmapsto} G$$

$$\frac{\begin{array}{c}[B,i,F,j,C\mid D,p,E,q]\\ [D,p,E,q,X'\mid O,u,P,v]\end{array}}{[B,i,G,k,X'\mid O,u,P,v]}\ CF \overset{a}{\longmapsto} G$$

$$\frac{[B,i,C,j,-\mid -,-,-,-]}{[F,k,F,k,-\mid -,-,-,-]}\ C \overset{a}{\longmapsto} C,[F$$

$$\frac{[B,i,C,j,X\mid D,p,E,q]}{[F,k,F,k,-\mid -,-,-,-]}\ C \overset{a}{\longmapsto} C,[F$$

$$\frac{\begin{array}{c}[F,k,F',k',-\mid -,-,-,-]\\ [B,i,C,j,-\mid -,-,-,-]\end{array}}{[B,i,G,l,-\mid -,-,-,-]}\ \begin{array}{c}C \overset{a}{\longmapsto} C,[F\\ C,[F' \overset{b}{\longmapsto} G\end{array}$$

$$\frac{\begin{array}{c}[F,k,F',k',-\mid -,-,-,-]\\ [B,i,C,j,X\mid D,p,E,q]\end{array}}{[B,i,G,l,X\mid D,p,E,q]}\ \begin{array}{c}C \overset{a}{\longmapsto} C,[F\\ C,[F' \overset{b}{\longmapsto} G\end{array}$$

$$\frac{\begin{array}{c}[F,k,F',k',-\mid -,-,-,-]\\ [B,i,C,j,-\mid -,-,-,-]\end{array}}{[B,i,G,l,-\mid -,-,-,-]}\ \begin{array}{c}C \overset{a}{\longmapsto} C,[F\\ [C,F' \overset{b}{\longmapsto} G\end{array}$$

$$\frac{\begin{array}{c}[F,k,F',k',X\mid D,p,E,q]\\ [B,i,C,j,-\mid -,-,-,-]\end{array}}{[B,i,G,l,X\mid D,p,E,q]}\ \begin{array}{c}C \overset{a}{\longmapsto} C,[F\\ [C,F' \overset{b}{\longmapsto} G\end{array}$$

where $k = j$ if $a = \epsilon$, $k = j + 1$ if $a = a_{j+1}$, $l = k'$ if $b = \epsilon$ and $l = k' + 1$ if $b = a_{k'+1}$.

Computations start with the initial item $[\$_0, 0, \$_0, 0, - \mid -, -, -, -]$. An input string $a_1 \dots a_n$ has been recognized if the final item $[\$_0, 0, \$_f, n, - \mid -, -, -, -]$ is present. It can be proved that handling items with the inference rules is equivalent to applying the transitions on the whole stacks.

Sketch of the proof: We show that each item represents a derivation and that any derivation is represented by an item. Taking as base case the item and derivation corresponding to the initial configuration, we must apply induction on the length of the derivations. We can observe that given the set of antecedents items (each of them representing a derivation, by induction hypothesis) and the transitions specified by an inference rule, we obtain an item representing a derivation when this rule is applied. We can also observe that, given an item, it can be decomposed by some inference rule into a set of antecedent items (representing derivations by induction hypothesis) and a set of transitions, such that the application of the rule gives as a result this item representing a derivation. The proof is tedious but not difficult. The important point is to consider the exhaustive list of all kinds of derivation that can be involved in the application of each inference rule. □

The space complexity of the proposed tabulation technique with respect to the length of the input string is $\mathcal{O}(n^4)$, due to every item stores four positions of the input string. The worst case time complexity is $\mathcal{O}(n^6)$ due to the inference rule

$$\frac{\begin{array}{c}[B, i, F, j, C \mid D, p, E, q] \\ [D, p, E, q, X' \mid O, u, P, v]\end{array}}{[B, i, G, k, X' \mid O, u, P, v]} \quad CF \overset{a}{\longmapsto} G$$

that stores 6 independent input positions i, j, p, q, u and v.

7 Conclusion

We have provided a formal definition of bottom-up embedded push-down automata. We have also shown that finite-state control can be eliminated, obtaining a new definition in which transitions are in a form useful to describe compilation schemata for TAG and suitable for tabulation. The resulting definition has been shown to be equivalent to right-oriented linear indexed automata and a superset of bottom-up 2–stack automata with respect to the parsing strategies that can be described in both models of automata.

Acknowledgments

A previous and shorter version of this article was presented at the *Second International Workshop on Parsing and Deduction (TAPD'2000)*[4] held in Vigo

[4] `http://coleweb.dc.fi.udc.es/tapd2000/`

(Spain) in September 2000 [3]. We are grateful to the participants in this workshop for their comments and suggestions. The research reported in this article has been partially supported by Plan Nacional de Investigación Científica, Desarrollo e Innovación Tecnológica (Grant TIC2000-0370-C02-01), FEDER of EU (Grant 1FD97-0047-C04-02) and Xunta de Galicia (Grant PGIDT99XI10502B).

References

1. Miguel A. Alonso, Eric de la Clergerie, and Manuel Vilares. Automata-based parsing in dynamic programming for Linear Indexed Grammars. In A. S. Narin'yani, editor, *Proc. of DIALOGUE'97 Computational Linguistics and its Applications International Workshop*, pages 22–27, Moscow, Russia, June 1997.
2. Miguel A. Alonso, Eric de la Clergerie, and Manuel Vilares. A redefinition of Embedded Push-Down Automata. In *Proc. of 5th International Workshop on Tree Adjoining Grammars and Related Formalisms (TAG+5)*, pages 19–26, Paris, France, May 2000.
3. Miguel A. Alonso, Eric de la Clergerie, and Manuel Vilares. A formal definition of Bottom-up Embedded Push-Down Automata and their tabulation technique. In David S. Warren, Manuel Vilares, Leandro Rodríguez Liñares and Miguel A. Alonso (eds.), *Proc. of Second International Workshop on Tabulation in Parsing and Deduction (TAPD 2000)*, pp. 101-112, Vigo, Spain, September 2000.
4. Miguel A. Alonso, Mark-Jan Nederhof, and Eric de la Clergerie. Tabulation of automata for tree adjoining languages. *Grammars* **3** (2000) 89–110.
5. Tilman Becker and Dominik Heckmann. Recursive matrix systems (RMS) and TAG. In *Proc. of Fourth International Workshop on Tree Adjoining Grammars and Related Frameworks (TAG+4)*, pages 9–12, Philadelphia, PA, USA, August 1998.
6. Pierre Boullier. A generalization of mildly context-sensitive formalisms. In *Proc. of Fourth International Workshop on Tree Adjoining Grammars and Related Frameworks (TAG+4)*, pages 17–20, Philadelphia, PA, USA, August 1998.
7. Eric de la Clergerie and Miguel A. Alonso. A tabular interpretation of a class of 2-Stack Automata. In *COLING-ACL'98, 36th Annual Meeting of the Association for Computational Linguistics and 17th International Conference on Computational Linguistics, Proceedings of the Conference*, volume II, pages 1333–1339, Montreal, Quebec, Canada, August 1998. ACL.
8. Eric de la Clergerie, Miguel A. Alonso, and David Cabrero. A tabular interpretation of bottom-up automata for TAG. In *Proc. of Fourth International Workshop on Tree-Adjoining Grammars and Related Frameworks (TAG+4)*, pages 42–45, Philadelphia, PA, USA, August 1998.
9. Eric de la Clergerie and François Barthélemy. Information flow in tabular interpretations for generalized Push-Down Automata. *Theoretical Computer Science*, 199(1–2):167–198, 1998.
10. Gerald Gazdar. Applicability of indexed grammars to natural languages. In U. Reyle and C. Rohrer, editors, *Natural Language Parsing and Linguistic Theories*, pages 69–94. D. Reidel Publishing Company, 1987.
11. John E. Hopcroft and Jeffrey D. Ullman. *Introduction to Automata Theory, Languages and Computation.* Series in Computer Science. Addison-Wesley Publishing Company, Reading, Massachussetts, USA, 1979.

12. Aravind K. Joshi and Yves Schabes. Tree-adjoining grammars. In Grzegorz Rozenberg and Arto Salomaa, editors, *Handbook of Formal Languages. Vol 3: Beyond Words*, chapter 2, pages 69–123. Springer-Verlag, Berlin/Heidelberg/New York, 1997.
13. Bernard Lang. Towards a uniform formal framework for parsing. In Masaru Tomita, editor, *Current Issues in Parsing Technology*, pages 153–171. Kluwer Academic Publishers, Norwell, MA, USA, 1991.
14. Mark-Jan Nederhof. Linear indexed automata and tabulation of TAG parsing. In *Proc. of First International Workshop on Tabulation in Parsing and Deduction (TAPD'98)*, pages 1–9, Paris, France, April 1998.
15. Mark-Jan Nederhof. Models of tabulation for TAG parsing. In *Proc. of the Sixth Meeting on Mathematics of Language (MOL 6)*, pages 143–158, Orlando, Florida, USA, July 1999.
16. Gisela Pitsch. $LL(k)$ parsing of coupled-context-free grammars. *Computational Intelligence* **10** (1994) 563–578.
17. C. Pollard. *Generalized Phrase Structure Grammars, Head Grammars and Natural Language*. PhD thesis, Stanford University, 1984.
18. Owen Rambow. *Formal and Computational Aspects of Natural Language Syntax*. PhD thesis, University of Pennsylvania, 1994. Available as IRCS Report 94-08 of the Institute of Research in Cognitive Science, University of Pennsylvania.
19. Yves Schabes and K. Vijay-Shanker. Deterministic left to right parsing of tree adjoining languages. In *Proc. of 28th Annual Meeting of the Association for Computational Linguistics*, pages 276–283, Pittsburgh, Pennsylvania, USA, June 1990. ACL.
20. Stuart M. Shieber, Yves Schabes, and Fernando C. N. Pereira. Principles and implementation of deductive parsing. *Journal of Logic Programming* **24** (1995) 3–36.
21. M. Steedman. Combinators and grammars. In R. Oehrle, E. Bach, and D Wheeler, editors, *Categorial Grammars and Natural Language Structures*, pages 417–442. Foris, Dordrecht, 1986.
22. K. Vijay-Shanker. *A Study of Tree Adjoining Grammars*. PhD thesis, University of Pennsylvania, January 1988. Available as Technical Report MS-CIS-88-03 LINC LAB 95 of the Department of Computer and Information Science, University of Pennsylvania.
23. K. Vijay-Shanker and David J. Weir. The equivalence of four extensions of context-free grammars. *Mathematical Systems Theory* **27** (1994) 511–545.
24. K. Vijay-Shanker, David J. Weir, and Aravind K. Joshi. On the progression from context-free to tree adjoining languages. In Alexis Manaster-Ramer, editor, *Mathematics of Language*, pages 389–401. John Benjamins Publishing Company, Amsterdam/Philadelphia, 1987.

An Algebraic Approach to French Sentence Structure

Daniele Bargelli and Joachim Lambek*

McGill University, Montreal

Abstract. We propose to investigate the structure of French sentences with the help of a minimal algebraic technique based on the assignment of types to words. Mathematically speaking, the types are elements of the free "pregroup" (a generalization of a partially ordered group) generated by a partially ordered set of basic types. In particular, this partial order is carefully adjusted to account for the order of preverbal clitic pronouns in a sentence.

1 Types

The main idea is this: to each French word there are assigned one or more types so that the sentencehood of a string of French words can be checked by a simple calculation. To begin with, there are a number of *basic types* such as the following:

$\mathbf{s}_1$ for direct statements, that is, declarative sentences, in the present tense;
$\mathbf{s}_2$ for direct statements in the past (imperfect) tense;
$\mathbf{s}$ for direct statements when the tense does not matter;
$\overline{\mathbf{s}}$ for indirect statements.

The set of basic types is *partially ordered* by a relation $\rightarrow$. By this is meant a binary relation satisfying the following axioms and rules of inference:

$$a \rightarrow a \qquad \frac{a \rightarrow b \;\; b \rightarrow c}{a \rightarrow c} \qquad \frac{a \rightarrow b \;\; b \rightarrow a}{a = b}.$$

Furthermore we shall postulate that e.g.

$$\mathbf{s}_1 \rightarrow \mathbf{s}, \quad \mathbf{s}_2 \rightarrow \mathbf{s}, \quad \mathbf{s} \rightarrow \overline{\mathbf{s}}.$$

In fact, we shall adopt the convention that $a \rightarrow \overline{a} \rightarrow \overline{\overline{a}}$ for any basic type a. The bar here plays a rôle similar to that in the $\overline{X}$-theory of Chomsky and Jackendoff [1977]; but for us it is merely a notational device, not driven by their theory.

---

* The authors acknowledge support from the Social Sciences and Humanities Research Council of Canada.

P. de Groote, G. Morrill, C. Retoré (Eds.): LACL 2001, LNAI 2099, pp. 62–78, 2001.

From the basic types we construct *simple types*: if a is a simple type, then so are a^ℓ and a^r, called the *left* and *right adjoint* respectively. Thus, if a is a basic type then

$$a,\ a^\ell,\ a^{\ell\ell}, \cdots, a^r,\ a^{rr}, \cdots$$

are simple types.

By a *type* we shall mean a string of simple types $a_1 a_2 \cdots a_n$. In particular, if $n = 1$, this implies that a simple type is a type; and, if $n = 0$, according to the usual mathematical convention, the empty string 1 is a type, it being understood that

$$a1 = a = 1a.$$

The partial order $\rightarrow$ may be extended by the rule

$$\frac{a \rightarrow a' \quad b \rightarrow b'}{ab \rightarrow a'b'}$$

to the monoid of all types. Moreover, we postulate the following *contraction rules*:

$$a^\ell a \rightarrow 1, \quad aa^r \rightarrow 1.$$

For the purpose of sentence verification these suffice; but mathematicians will also require the *expansion rules*:

$$1 \rightarrow aa^\ell, \quad 1 \rightarrow a^r a,$$

which will assure the uniqueness of the adjoints. For example, one can then prove that

$$a^{r\ell} = a, \quad a^{\ell r} = a,$$

but neither $a^{\ell\ell} = a$ nor $a^{rr} = a$. The adjoints may easily be extended to all types, that is, strings of simple types, by defining

$$1^\ell = 1,\ 1^r = 1,\ (ab)^\ell = b^\ell a^\ell,\ (ab)^r = b^r a^r.$$

2 Infinitives

Crucial to all sentences are the verbs, usually represented by their infinitives. For example, we have

dormir of type $\mathbf{i}$
prendre of type $\mathbf{io}^\ell$
manger of type $\mathbf{i}$ or $\mathbf{io}^\ell$.

Here $\mathbf{i}$ and $\mathbf{o}$ are basic types:

$\mathbf{i}$ for infinitives of intransitive verbs,
$\mathbf{o}$ for direct objects (COD).

For example,

$$\underset{(\mathbf{i}\mathbf{o}^{\ell})}{\textit{manger}}\ \underbrace{\textit{une pomme}}_{\mathbf{o}}$$

is an expression of type

$$(\mathbf{i}\mathbf{o}^{\ell})\mathbf{o} = \mathbf{i}(\mathbf{o}^{\ell}\mathbf{o}) \to \mathbf{i}1 = \mathbf{i}.$$

Direct objects are only one kind of verb complements. Others are indirect objects (CID) and locatives, as in

$$\underset{(\mathbf{i}\omega^{\ell})}{\textit{obéir}}\ \underbrace{\textit{à Jean}}_{\omega}$$

and

$$\underset{(\mathbf{i}\lambda^{\ell})}{\textit{habiter}}\ \underbrace{\textit{à Paris}}_{\lambda}.$$

We have used types ω and λ as follows:

ω for indirect objects,
λ for locatives.

3 Noun-Phrases

If separate types for *une, pomme, Jean, Paris* and *à* are required, we introduce new basic types:

$\mathbf{c}$ for count nouns, e.g. *pomme,*
$\mathbf{n}_s$ for singular noun-phrases, e.g. *Jean, Paris.*

Hence we are led to assign

$\mathbf{n}_s\mathbf{c}^{\ell}$ to the article *une,*
$\omega\mathbf{o}^{\ell}$ and $\lambda\ \mathbf{o}^{\ell}$ to the preposition *à.*

We postulate $\mathbf{n}_s \to \mathbf{o}$ to indicate that singular noun-phrases may be direct objects. Thus, we may calculate the types of *une pomme, à Jean* and *à Paris* as follows:

$$(\mathbf{n}_s\mathbf{c}^{\ell})\mathbf{c} = \mathbf{n}_s(\mathbf{c}^{\ell}\mathbf{c}) \to \mathbf{n}_s1 = \mathbf{n}_s,$$
$$(\omega\mathbf{o}^{\ell})\mathbf{n}_s \to \omega(\mathbf{o}^{\ell}\mathbf{o}) \to \omega1 = \omega,$$
$$(\lambda\mathbf{o}^{\ell})\mathbf{n}_s \to \lambda(\mathbf{o}^{\ell}\mathbf{o}) \to \lambda1 = \lambda.$$

For the last two calculations we recall that $n_s \to \mathbf{o}$.

For later use we also mention the following basic types:

$\mathbf{m}$ for mass nouns, e.g. *pain,*
$\mathbf{p}$ for plurals (usually of count nouns), e.g. *pommes,*
$\mathbf{n}_p$ for plural noun-phrases.

We postulate $\mathbf{n}_p \to \mathbf{o}$ to indicate that plural noun-phrases can also occur as direct objects. We can now account for such noun-phrases as *du pain* and *des pommes* with the help of the indefinite articles

$$\begin{aligned} &\textit{du} \text{ of type } \mathbf{n}_s\mathbf{m}^\ell, \\ &\textit{des} \text{ of type } \mathbf{n}_p\mathbf{p}^\ell. \end{aligned}$$

We have ignored here one essential fact of French grammar, namely that *pomme* and *une* are both feminine and that their genders must agree. But, in this first attempt to apply our algebraic technique to French grammar, we choose to ignore some complications, just as Galileo, in his first attempt to analyze motion mathematically, chose to ignore friction.

4 Extended Infinitives

In English, the noun phrase *an apple* can be replaced by the pronoun *it* in the same position. In French, the situation is more complicated: the clitic pronoun *la* appears before the verb, as in *la + manger.* We want this expression to be treated like an infinitive of an intransitive verb, so we should assign to it the type $\mathbf{i}$. For reasons that will become clear later, we assign to it the type $\bar{\mathbf{i}}$ instead, subject of course to the rule $\mathbf{i} \to \bar{\mathbf{i}}$. We accomplish this by assigning to the clitic pronoun *la* the type $\bar{\mathbf{i}}\mathbf{o}^{\ell\ell}\bar{\mathbf{i}}^\ell$, where, for reasons that will be discussed later, we have put a bar on the second $\mathbf{i}$ as well, so *la + manger* has type

$$\begin{aligned} (\bar{\mathbf{i}}\mathbf{o}^{\ell\ell}\bar{\mathbf{i}}^\ell) &= \bar{\mathbf{i}}(\mathbf{o}^{\ell\ell}(\bar{\mathbf{i}}^\ell\mathbf{i})\mathbf{o}^\ell) \\ &\to \bar{\mathbf{i}}(\mathbf{o}^{\ell\ell}\mathbf{o}^\ell) && \text{since } \bar{\mathbf{i}}^\ell\mathbf{i} \to \bar{\mathbf{i}}^\ell\bar{\mathbf{i}} \to 1 \\ &\to \bar{\mathbf{i}} && \text{since } \mathbf{o}^{\ell\ell}\mathbf{o}^\ell \to 1 \end{aligned}$$

We represent this calculation diagramatically, by a method that goes back to Z. Harris [1966], as follows:

$$\begin{array}{cc} \textit{la} \;+ & \textit{manger} \\ (\bar{\mathbf{i}}\mathbf{o}^{\ell\ell}\bar{\mathbf{i}}^\ell) & (\mathbf{i}\mathbf{o}^\ell) \end{array}$$

Note that we have inserted the symbol + to prepare the reader for our claim that *la + manger* is to be treated like a single word, we shall call it an extended infinitive of type $\bar{\mathbf{i}}$.

We recall that there are other kinds of direct objects, constructed from mass nouns or plurals, such as *du pain* of type $\mathbf{n}_s \to \mathbf{o}$ and *des pommes* of type $\mathbf{n}_p \to \mathbf{o}$, with the help of the indefinite articles *du* and *des*. They are represented by another preverbal clitic pronoun *en*, as in *en + manger*, another extended infinitive, this time of type $\mathbf{i}$. We accomplish this by assigning to *en* the type $\mathbf{i}\mathbf{o}^{\ell\ell}\mathbf{i}^\ell$ without bars.

Consider now a verb, such as *donner*, which requires two objects, a direct one and an indirect one, as in *donner une pomme à Jean,*

donner à Jean une pomme.

The second of these two sentences is less common, but it is permitted for emphasis. Recalling that the indirect object has type ω, we require that *donner* has two types, namely $\mathbf{i}\omega^{\ell}\mathbf{o}^{\ell}$ and $\mathbf{i}\mathbf{o}^{\ell}\omega^{\ell}$. For example, we have

$$\textit{donner}\ \underbrace{\textit{une pomme}}\ \underbrace{\textit{à Jean}}$$
$$(\mathbf{i}\omega^{\ell}\mathbf{o}^{\ell})\quad \mathbf{o}\quad \omega$$

The indirect object *à Jean* may be replaced by the preverbal pronoun *lui* of type $\bar{\mathbf{i}}\omega^{\ell\ell}\mathbf{i}^{\ell}$, to justify the following:

$$\textit{lui} + \textit{donner}\ \underbrace{\textit{la pomme}},$$
$$(\bar{\mathbf{i}}\omega^{\ell\ell}\mathbf{i}^{\ell})(\mathbf{i}\omega^{\ell}\mathbf{o}^{\ell})\mathbf{o}$$

$$\textit{la} + \textit{donner}\ \underbrace{\textit{à Jean}},$$
$$(\bar{\mathbf{i}}\mathbf{o}^{\ell\ell}\bar{\mathbf{i}}^{\ell})(\mathbf{i}\mathbf{o}^{\ell}\omega^{\ell})\omega$$

$$\textit{en} + \textit{donner}\ \underbrace{\textit{à Jean}},$$
$$(\mathbf{i}\mathbf{o}^{\ell\ell}\mathbf{i}^{\ell})(\mathbf{i}\mathbf{o}^{\ell}\omega^{\ell})\omega$$

$$\textit{la} + \textit{lui} + \textit{donner},$$
$$(\bar{\mathbf{i}}\mathbf{o}^{\ell\ell}\bar{\mathbf{i}}^{\ell})(\bar{\mathbf{i}}\omega^{\ell\ell}\mathbf{i}^{\ell})(\mathbf{i}\omega^{\ell}\mathbf{o}^{\ell})$$

$$\textit{lui} + \textit{en} + \textit{donner},$$
$$(\bar{\mathbf{i}}\omega^{\ell\ell}\mathbf{i}^{\ell})(\mathbf{i}\mathbf{o}^{\ell\ell}\mathbf{i}^{\ell})(\mathbf{i}\mathbf{o}^{\ell}\omega^{\ell})$$

However, we are forbidden to say

$$*\ \textit{lui} + \textit{la} + \textit{donner}, \qquad\qquad *\ \textit{en} + \textit{lui} + \textit{donner},$$
$$(\bar{\mathbf{i}}\omega^{\ell\ell}\mathbf{i}^{\ell})(\bar{\mathbf{i}}\mathbf{o}^{\ell\ell}\bar{\mathbf{i}}^{\ell})(\mathbf{i}\mathbf{o}^{\ell}\omega^{\ell}) \qquad\qquad (\mathbf{i}\mathbf{o}^{\ell\ell}\mathbf{i}^{\ell})(\bar{\mathbf{i}}\omega^{\ell\ell}\mathbf{i}^{\ell})(\mathbf{i}\omega^{\ell}\mathbf{o}^{\ell})$$

In fact, it was to avoid these contractions that the bars were introduced. Note that $a^{\ell}\overline{a} \not\to 1$, but

$$\overline{a}^{\ell}a \to \overline{a}^{\ell}\overline{a} \to 1.$$

5 Other Clitic Pronouns

The clitic pronouns *la, lui* and *en* are not the only ones:

the accusative pronouns *le, la, les* have type $\bar{\mathbf{i}}\mathbf{o}^{\ell\ell}\bar{\mathbf{i}}^{\ell}$;
the dative pronouns *lui, leur* have type $\bar{\mathbf{i}}\omega^{\ell\ell}\mathbf{i}^{\ell}$;
the partitive pronoun *en* has type $\mathbf{i}\mathbf{o}^{\ell\ell}\mathbf{i}^{\ell}$
the personal pronouns *me, te, se, nous* and *vous* can be either accusative of type $\bar{\bar{\mathbf{i}}}\,\mathbf{o}^{\ell\ell}\mathbf{i}^{\ell}$ or dative of type $\bar{\bar{\mathbf{i}}}\,\omega^{\ell\ell}\bar{\mathbf{i}}^{\ell}$. (The last two are not strictly speaking clitics, but they should be treated the same way.) Why the bars?

We want to admit

$$vous + les + offrir,$$
$$(\bar{\bar{\mathbf{i}}}\,\omega^{\ell\ell}\bar{\mathbf{i}}^{\ell})(\bar{\mathbf{i}}\mathbf{o}^{\ell\ell}\bar{\mathbf{i}}^{\ell})(\mathbf{i}\mathbf{o}^{\ell}\omega^{\ell})$$

but not

$${}^{*}les + vous + offrir,$$
$$(\bar{\mathbf{i}}\mathbf{o}^{\ell\ell}\mathbf{i}^{\ell})(\bar{\bar{\mathbf{i}}}^{\ell}\omega^{\ell\ell}\bar{\mathbf{i}}^{\ell})(\mathbf{i}\omega^{\ell}\mathbf{o}^{\ell})$$

We also want to avoid the following combinations:

$${}^{*}vous + lui, \quad * \; lui + vous,$$
$$(\bar{\bar{\mathbf{i}}}\mathbf{o}^{\ell\ell}\mathbf{i}^{\ell})(\bar{\mathbf{i}}\omega^{\ell\ell}\mathbf{i}^{\ell}) \quad (\bar{\mathbf{i}}\omega^{\ell\ell}\mathbf{i}^{\ell})(\bar{\bar{\mathbf{i}}}\mathbf{o}^{\ell\ell}\mathbf{i}^{\ell})$$

$${}^{*}vous + nous, \; * \; vous + nous,$$
$$(\bar{\bar{\mathbf{i}}}\mathbf{o}^{\ell\ell}\mathbf{i}^{\ell})(\bar{\bar{\mathbf{i}}}\omega^{\ell\ell}\mathbf{i}^{\ell}) \quad (\bar{\bar{\mathbf{i}}}\omega^{\ell\ell}\bar{\mathbf{i}}^{\ell})(\bar{\bar{\mathbf{i}}}\mathbf{o}^{\ell\ell}\mathbf{i}^{\ell})$$

Finally, there is also the locative clitic *y* of type $\bar{\mathbf{i}}\lambda^{\ell\ell}\mathbf{i}^{\ell}$. Consider

$$aller \; \underbrace{\grave{a} \;\; Paris}$$
$$(\mathbf{i}\lambda^{\ell}) \quad \lambda$$

where λ is the type of a locative expression, and

$$y \; + \; aller$$
$$(\bar{\mathbf{i}}\lambda^{\ell\ell}\mathbf{i}^{\ell})\,(\mathbf{i}\lambda^{\ell})$$

The first bar on the type of *y* will be justified later. Consider next *mettre* of type $\mathbf{i}\lambda^{\ell}\mathbf{o}^{\ell}$ or $\mathbf{i}\mathbf{o}^{\ell}\lambda^{\ell}$ as exemplified by

$$mettre \; \underbrace{une\ pomme} \; \underbrace{sur\ la\ table}$$
$$(\mathbf{i}\lambda^{\ell}\mathbf{o}^{\ell}) \qquad \mathbf{o} \qquad \lambda$$

or, for emphasis, by

$$\textit{mettre}\ \underbrace{\textit{sur la table}}\ \underbrace{\textit{une pomme}}$$
$$(\mathbf{i}\mathbf{o}^{\ell}\lambda^{\ell})\quad \lambda \quad \mathbf{o}$$

The clitic y then appears in

$$y + \textit{mettre}\ \underbrace{\textit{une pomme}},$$
$$(\bar{\mathbf{i}}\lambda^{\ell\ell}\mathbf{i}^{\ell})(\mathbf{i}\lambda^{\ell}\mathbf{o}^{\ell})\mathbf{o}$$

$$\textit{la} + y + \textit{mettre},$$
$$(\bar{\mathbf{i}}\mathbf{o}^{\ell\ell}\bar{\mathbf{i}}^{\ell})(\bar{\mathbf{i}}\lambda^{\ell\ell}\mathbf{i}^{\ell})(\mathbf{i}\lambda^{\ell}\mathbf{o}^{\ell})$$

$$y + \textit{en} + \textit{mettre},$$
$$(\bar{\mathbf{i}}\lambda^{\ell\ell}\mathbf{i}^{\ell})(\mathbf{i}\mathbf{o}^{\ell\ell}\mathbf{i}^{\ell})(\mathbf{i}\mathbf{o}^{\ell}\lambda^{\ell})$$

but not in

$$* \textit{en} + y + \textit{mettre},$$
$$(\mathbf{i}\mathbf{o}^{\ell\ell}\mathbf{i}^{\ell})(\bar{\mathbf{i}}\lambda^{\ell\ell}\mathbf{i}^{\ell})(\mathbf{i}\lambda^{\ell}\mathbf{o}^{\ell})$$

We shall list a few verbs together with some of their types and past participles. However, we will ignore the gender and the number of the latter, so that *dormi* represents *dormi(e)(s)*. A more complete list could be elaborated from Gross [1969], [Boons et al, 1972] and [Guillet and Leclere 1992]. We distinguish between past participles of type $\mathbf{p}_2$ and those of type $\mathbf{p}_2'$. The former require the auxiliary verb *avoir*, the latter *être*. We also use $\mathbf{a}$ for the type of adjectives.

dormir: $\mathbf{i}$	*dormi*: $\mathbf{p}_2$
venir: $\mathbf{i}$	*venu*: $\mathbf{p}_2'$
prendre: $\mathbf{i}\mathbf{o}^{\ell}$	*pris*: $\mathbf{p}_2\mathbf{o}^{\ell}$
manger: $\mathbf{i}, \mathbf{i}\mathbf{o}^{\ell}$	*mangé*: $\mathbf{p}_2, \mathbf{p}_2\mathbf{o}^{\ell}$
obéir: $\mathbf{i}\omega^{\ell}$	*obéi*: $\mathbf{p}_2\omega^{\ell}$
aller: $\mathbf{i}\lambda^{\ell}$	*allé*: $\mathbf{p}_2\lambda^{\ell}$
donner: $\mathbf{i}\omega^{\ell}\mathbf{o}^{\ell},\ \mathbf{i}\mathbf{o}^{\ell}\omega^{\ell}$	*donné*: $\mathbf{p}_2\omega^{\ell}\mathbf{o}^{\ell},\ \mathbf{p}_2\mathbf{o}^{\ell}\omega^{\ell}$

mettre: $\mathbf{i}\lambda^{\ell}\mathbf{o}^{\ell}$, $\mathbf{i}\mathbf{o}^{\ell}\lambda^{\ell}$ *mis*: $\mathbf{p}_2\lambda^{\ell}\mathbf{o}^{\ell}$, $\mathbf{p}_2\mathbf{o}^{\ell}\lambda^{\ell}$

vouloir: $\bar{\bar{\mathbf{i}}}\,\bar{\bar{\mathbf{i}}}^{\ell}$ *voulu*: $\mathbf{p}_2\,\bar{\bar{\mathbf{i}}}^{\ell}$

avoir: $\mathbf{i}\mathbf{o}^{\ell}$, $\mathbf{i}\mathbf{p}_2^{\ell}$ *eu*: $\mathbf{p}_2\mathbf{o}^{\ell}$, $\mathbf{p}_2\mathbf{p}_2^{\ell}$

être: $\mathbf{i}\mathbf{a}^{\ell}$, $\mathbf{i}\mathbf{p}_2'^{\ell}$, $\mathbf{i}\mathbf{o}^{\ell\ell}\mathbf{p}_2^{\ell}$ *été*: $\mathbf{p}_2\mathbf{a}^{\ell}$, ${}^*\mathbf{p}_2\mathbf{p}_2'^{\ell}$, $\mathbf{p}_2\mathbf{o}^{\ell\ell}\mathbf{p}_2^{\ell}$.

6 Modal and Auxiliary Verbs

The last three verbs in the above list require some discussion. The modal verb *vouloir*, like *pouvoir* and *devoir*, has been given type $\bar{\bar{\mathbf{i}}}\,\bar{\bar{\mathbf{i}}}^{\ell}$ to avoid

$$\begin{array}{c}{}^*\textit{la} + \textit{vouloir prendre},\\ (\bar{\mathbf{i}}\mathbf{o}^{\ell\ell}\bar{\bar{\mathbf{i}}}^{\ell})(\bar{\bar{\mathbf{i}}}\,\bar{\bar{\mathbf{i}}}^{\ell})(\mathbf{i}\mathbf{o}^{\ell})\end{array}$$

but to admit

$$\begin{array}{c}\textit{vouloir la} + \textit{prendre}\\ (\bar{\bar{\mathbf{i}}}\,\bar{\bar{\mathbf{i}}}^{\ell})\ (\bar{\mathbf{i}}\mathbf{o}^{\ell\ell}\bar{\bar{\mathbf{i}}}^{\ell})(\mathbf{i}\mathbf{o}^{\ell})\end{array}$$

and

$$\begin{array}{c}\textit{vouloir pouvoir venir}\\ (\bar{\bar{\mathbf{i}}}\,\bar{\bar{\mathbf{i}}}^{\ell})\ (\bar{\bar{\mathbf{i}}}\,\bar{\bar{\mathbf{i}}}^{\ell})\quad \mathbf{i}\end{array}$$

even

vouloir vouloir venir.

The verb *avoir* may occur as an ordinary transitive verb, as in

$$\begin{array}{c}\textit{avoir}\ \underbrace{\textit{une pomme}}\\ \mathbf{i}\mathbf{o}^{\ell}\quad \mathbf{o}\end{array}$$

but we are here interested in its rôle as an auxiliary verb to form the composite past, as in

$$\begin{array}{c}\textit{avoir}\quad \textit{dormi}\\ (\mathbf{i}\mathbf{p}_2^{\ell})\qquad \mathbf{p}_2\end{array}$$

or even in

$$\begin{array}{c}\textit{avoir eu dormi},\\ (\mathbf{i}\mathbf{p}_2^{\ell})\ (\mathbf{p}_2\mathbf{p}_2^{\ell})\ \mathbf{p}_2\end{array}$$

the so-called super-composite past, supposedly common in French Switzerland. Unfortunately, this type assignment also allows

$$\begin{array}{c}\textit{avoir eu eu dormi},\\ (\mathbf{i}\mathbf{p}_2^{\ell})\ (\mathbf{p}_2\mathbf{p}_2^{\ell})\ (\mathbf{p}_2\mathbf{p}_2^{\ell})\ \mathbf{p}_2\end{array}$$

which should perhaps be ruled out on other grounds.

Care should be taken in analyzing

$$\begin{array}{ccc} la + & avoir & mangée, \\ (\bar{\mathbf{i}}\mathbf{o}^{\ell\ell}\bar{\mathbf{i}}^{\ell}) & (\mathbf{i}\mathbf{p}_2^{\ell}) & (\mathbf{p}_2\mathbf{o}^{\ell}). \end{array}$$

The past participle here should not be formed from the extended infinitive *la* + *manger* of type $\bar{\mathbf{i}}$, instead the extended infinitive of the auxiliary verb has type $\bar{\mathbf{i}}\mathbf{o}^{\ell\ell}\mathbf{p}_2^{\ell}$.

The verb *être* allows many kinds of complements, e.g. adjectives of type $\mathbf{a}$, as in

$$\begin{array}{cc} être & heureux \\ (\mathbf{i}\mathbf{a}^{\ell}) & \mathbf{a} \end{array}$$

in which case its past participle has type $\mathbf{p}_2\mathbf{a}^{\ell}$, as in

$$\begin{array}{ccc} avoir & été & heureux \\ (\mathbf{i}\mathbf{p}_2^{\ell}) & (\mathbf{p}_2\mathbf{a}^{\ell}) & \mathbf{a} \end{array}$$

It can also serve as an auxiliary verb to form the composite part of certain intransitive verbs as well as the passive of transitive verbs:

$$\begin{array}{cc} être & venu, \\ (\mathbf{i}\mathbf{p}_2'^{\ell}) & \mathbf{p}_2' \end{array} \qquad \begin{array}{cc} être & pris \\ (\mathbf{i}\mathbf{o}^{\ell\ell}\mathbf{p}_2^{\ell}) & (\mathbf{p}_2\mathbf{o}^{\ell}) \end{array} \qquad \begin{array}{ccc} lui + & être & donné \\ (\bar{\mathbf{i}}\omega^{\ell\ell}\bar{\mathbf{i}}^{\ell}) & (\mathbf{i}\mathbf{o}^{\ell\ell}\mathbf{p}_2^{\ell}) & (\mathbf{p}_2\mathbf{o}^{\ell}\omega^{\ell}) \end{array}$$

As far as we know, a past participle *été* of type $^*\ \mathbf{p}_2\mathbf{p}_2'^{\ell}$ does not exist, since

$$\begin{array}{ccc} {}^*avoir & été & venu \\ (\mathbf{i}\mathbf{p}_2^{\ell}) & (\mathbf{p}_2\mathbf{p}_2'^{\ell}) & \mathbf{p}_2' \end{array}$$

seems to be inadmissible. However, the following is allowed:

$$\begin{array}{ccc} avoir & été & mangé \\ (\mathbf{i}\mathbf{p}_2^{\ell}) & (\mathbf{p}_2\mathbf{o}^{\ell\ell}\mathbf{p}_2^{\ell}) & (\mathbf{p}_2\mathbf{o}^{\ell}) \end{array}$$

The types of past participles are covered by the following:

METARULE I. If the infinitive of the (non-extended) verb V has type $\mathbf{i}x^{\ell}$, then its past participle has type $\mathbf{p}_2x^{\ell}$ for most verbs, including all transitive verbs, and type $\mathbf{p}_2'x^{\ell}$ for a select group of intransitive verbs and for all reflexive verbs. The composite past of the former is formed with *avoir* of type $\mathbf{i}\mathbf{p}_2^{\ell}$, that of the latter with *être* of type $\mathbf{i}\mathbf{p}_2'^{\ell}$.

We shall look at a few examples:

$$\begin{array}{ccc} avoir & mangé & \underbrace{une\ pomme}, \\ (\mathbf{i}\mathbf{p}_2^{\ell}) & (\mathbf{p}_2\mathbf{o}^{\ell}) & \mathbf{o} \end{array}$$

la + avoir mangée,

$$(\bar{\mathbf{i}}\mathbf{o}^{\ell\ell}\bar{\mathbf{i}}^{\ell})(\mathbf{i}\mathbf{p}_2^{\ell})\ (\mathbf{p}_2\mathbf{o}^{\ell})$$

être mangé(e)(s),

$$(\mathbf{i}\mathbf{o}^{\ell\ell}\mathbf{p}_2^{\ell})\ (\mathbf{p}_2\mathbf{o}^{\ell})$$

nous + avoir donné une pomme,

$$(\bar{\bar{\mathbf{i}}}\,\omega^{\ell\ell}\bar{\mathbf{i}}^{\ell})\ (\mathbf{i}\mathbf{p}_2^{\ell})\ (\mathbf{p}_2\,\omega^{\ell}\mathbf{o}^{\ell})\ \mathbf{o}$$

nous + la + avoir donnée,

$$(\bar{\bar{\mathbf{i}}}\,\omega^{\ell\ell}\mathbf{i}^{\ell})\ (\bar{\mathbf{i}}\mathbf{o}^{\ell\ell}\bar{\mathbf{i}}^{\ell})(\mathbf{i}\mathbf{p}_2^{\ell})\ (\mathbf{p}_2\,\mathbf{o}^{\ell}\omega^{\ell})$$

la + avoir donnée à Jean,

$$(\bar{\mathbf{i}}\mathbf{o}^{\ell\ell}\bar{\mathbf{i}}^{\ell})\ (\mathbf{i}\mathbf{p}_2^{\ell})\ (\mathbf{p}_2\,\mathbf{o}^{\ell}\omega^{\ell})\quad \omega$$

la + lui + avoir donnée,

$$(\bar{\mathbf{i}}\mathbf{o}^{\ell\ell}\bar{\mathbf{i}}^{\ell})\ (\bar{\mathbf{i}}\omega^{\ell\ell}\mathbf{i}^{\ell})\ (\mathbf{i}\mathbf{p}_2^{\ell})\ (\mathbf{p}_2\,\omega^{\ell}\mathbf{o}^{\ell})$$

y + être allé(e)(s),

$$(\bar{\mathbf{i}}\lambda^{\ell\ell}\mathbf{i}^{\ell})\ (\mathbf{i}\mathbf{p}_2'^{\ell})\ (\mathbf{p}_2'\lambda^{\ell})$$

être mis(e)(s) sur la table,

$$(\mathbf{i}\mathbf{o}^{\ell\ell}\mathbf{p}_2^{\ell})\ (\mathbf{p}_2\,\mathbf{o}^{\ell}\lambda^{\ell})\qquad \lambda$$

y + être mis(e)(s),

$$(\bar{\mathbf{i}}\lambda^{\ell\ell}\mathbf{i}^{\ell})\ (\mathbf{i}\mathbf{o}^{\ell\ell}\mathbf{p}_2^{\ell})\ (\mathbf{p}_2\,\mathbf{o}^{\ell}\lambda^{\ell})$$

y + avoir été mis(e)(s).

$$(\bar{\mathbf{i}}\lambda^{\ell\ell}\mathbf{i}^{\ell})\ (\mathbf{i}\mathbf{p}_2^{\ell})\ (\mathbf{p}_2\,\mathbf{o}^{\ell\ell}\mathbf{p}_2^{\ell})\ (\mathbf{p}_2\,\mathbf{o}^{\ell}\lambda^{\ell})$$

7 Finite Verb Forms

To form a sentence we require the finite form of a verb. With any verb V in colloquial French there are associated $5 \times 6 = 30$ finite forms V_{jk}, where j ranges from 1 to 5 representing four simple tenses and the subjunctive mode:

present,	imperfect,	future,	conditional,	subjunctive,
1	2	3	4	5

and k ranges from 1 to 6 representing three persons singular followed by three persons plural. In literary French there are two additional tenses:

$$\begin{array}{cc} \text{simple past,} & \text{past subjunctive} \\ 6 & 7 \end{array}$$

For expository purposes, we shall ignore the last two, although they could be treated in the same way as the first five.

In this article, we shall assume the 30 finite forms as given, but the interested reader can look them up in [Bescherelle 1, 1998] or calculate them by the method of [Lambek 1976]. (Warning: the arrow there points in the opposite direction.)

Here, for example are the 30 finite forms of the verb *devoir*:

dois	*dois*	*doit*	*devons*	*devez*	*doivent*
devais	*devais*	*devait*	*devions*	*deviez*	*devaient*
devrai	*devras*	*devra*	*devrons*	*devrez*	*devront*
devrais	*devrais*	*devrait*	*devrions*	*devriez*	*devraient*
doive	*doives*	*doive*	*devions*	*deviez*	*doivent*

It is shown [loc.cit.] how these forms can be calculated from the following stems:

doi/s, *dev/ons*, *doiv/ent*, *dev/r/ai*,

the stems appearing before the /. Similar calculations apply to all other verbs, the only exceptions being 10 frequently occurring verbs such as *aller, avoir, être, vouloir* and *pouvoir*.

What are the types of the finite forms? We assign the type $\mathbf{s}_j$ to a declarative sentence in the j-th tense ($j = 1$ to 4) and $\mathbf{s}_5$ to an incomplete subjunctive clause before the *que*. We assign the type π_k ($k = 1$ to 6) to the k-th personal subject pronoun:

$$\begin{array}{cccccc} \textit{je,} & \textit{tu,} & \textit{il/elle/on,} & \textit{nous,} & \textit{vous,} & \textit{ils/elles.} \\ \pi_1 & \pi_2 & \pi_3 & \pi_4 & \pi_5 & \pi_6 \end{array}$$

We assign type $\overline{\pi}_k^r \mathbf{s}_j \bar{\mathbf{i}}^\ell$ to $(devoir)_{jk}$. The reason for the two bars will become clear later. For example, we have

$$\begin{array}{ccc} \textit{il} & \textit{devait} & \textit{dormir,} \\ \pi_5 & (\overline{\pi}_3^r\ \mathbf{s}_2\ \bar{\mathbf{i}}^\ell) & \mathbf{i} \end{array}$$

a statement in the imperfect tense of type $\mathbf{s}_2$.

We expect to be able to type all finite forms of all verbs with extended infinitives of type $\mathbf{i}x^\ell$, $\bar{\mathbf{i}}x^\ell$ or $\bar{\bar{\mathbf{i}}}x^\ell$.

For example, we should be able to handle

dormir	of type $\mathbf{i} = \mathbf{i1} = \mathbf{i1}^\ell$	$(x = 1)$
manger	of type $\mathbf{io}^\ell$	(x=$\mathbf{o}$)
en + manger	of type i	$(x = 1)$
la + manger	of type i	$(x = 1)$
donner	of type $\mathbf{i}\omega^\ell\mathbf{o}^\ell = \mathbf{i}(\mathbf{o}\omega)^\ell$	$(x = \mathbf{o}\omega)$
	or $\mathbf{io}^\ell\omega^\ell = \mathbf{i}(\omega\mathbf{o})^\ell$	$(x = \omega\mathbf{o})$
lui + donner	of type $\bar{\mathbf{i}}\overline{\mathbf{o}}^\ell$	$(x = \mathbf{o})$
la + donner	of type $\bar{\mathbf{i}}\omega^\ell$	$(x = \omega)$
en + donner	of type $\mathbf{i}\omega^\ell$	$(x = \omega)$
la + lui + donner	of type $\bar{\mathbf{i}}$	$(x = 1)$
lui + en + donner	of type $\bar{\mathbf{i}}$	$(x = 1)$

8 Direct Sentences

We can now state the following:

METARULE II. If the extended verb V has type $\mathbf{i}x^\ell$, $\bar{\mathbf{i}}x^\ell$ or $\bar{\bar{\mathbf{i}}}\,x^\ell$, its finite form V_{jk} has type $\overline{\pi}_k^r\mathbf{s}_j x^\ell$ in a direct declarative sentence.

To extend the metarule to direct questions, we introduce the following basic types:

$\mathbf{q}_j$ for direct questions in the j-th tense ($j = 1$ to 4) subject to the following ordering:

$$\mathbf{q}_j \longrightarrow \mathbf{q} \longrightarrow \overline{\mathbf{q}}.$$

METARULE II (continued). $V_{jk}(j = 1$ to $4)$ has type $\mathbf{q}_j x^\ell \pi_k^\ell$ in inverted direct questions.

Direct questions can also be formed without inversion from a declarative sentence by prefixing *est-ce que* of type $\mathbf{qs}^\ell$.

Both direct statements and inverted direct questions are formed from the extended infinitive. Here are some examples:

From *lui + en + donner* of type $\bar{\mathbf{i}}$ we form

$$\underset{\pi_4}{\textit{nous}}\quad \underset{(\pi_4^r\,\mathbf{s}_1)}{\textit{lui + en + donnons}}$$

and

$$\underset{(\mathbf{q}_1\pi_4^\ell)}{\textit{lui + en + donnons}} - \underset{\pi_4}{\textit{nous}}?$$

From *manger* of type $\mathbf{io}^\ell$ we form

$$\underset{\pi_3}{\textit{il}}\ \underset{(\overline{\pi}_3^r\,\mathbf{s}_1\mathbf{o}^\ell))}{\textit{mange}}\ \underbrace{\textit{une pomme}}_{\mathbf{o}}$$

and

$$\begin{array}{cc} \textit{mange} - t - \textit{il} & \underbrace{\textit{une pomme}}? \\ (\mathbf{q}_1\mathbf{o}^\ell\pi_3^\ell) & \pi_3 \end{array}$$

We must blame the Académie Française for not insisting that *mange* be spelled with a silent t at the end. We are told that

$$\begin{array}{ccc} \textit{mangé-je} & \multicolumn{2}{c}{\underbrace{\textit{une pomme}}?} \\ (\mathbf{q}_1\mathbf{o}^\ell\pi_1^\ell) & \pi & \mathbf{o} \end{array}$$

while acceptable, with the unusual spelling $e\acute{}$, is better avoided.

We postulate $\mathbf{n}_s \to \overline{\pi}_3$, $\mathbf{n}_p \to \overline{\pi}_6$, so

$$\begin{array}{ccc} \textit{Jean} & \textit{mange} & \underbrace{\textit{une pomme}}, \\ \mathbf{n}_3 & (\overline{\pi}^\ell\mathbf{s}_1\mathbf{o}^\ell) & \mathbf{o} \end{array}$$

and

$$\begin{array}{cc} \underbrace{\textit{des professeurs}} & \textit{en} + \textit{mangent} \\ \overline{\pi}_6 & (\overline{\pi}^r\mathbf{s}_1) \end{array}$$

are acceptable. Finally, the bar on $\overline{\pi}_k$ guards against

$$\begin{array}{ccc} {}^*\textit{mange} & \textit{Jean} & \underbrace{\textit{une pomme}}? \\ (\mathbf{q}_1\mathbf{o}^\ell\pi_3^\ell) & \overline{\pi} & \mathbf{o} \end{array}$$

and

$$\begin{array}{cc} {}^*\textit{en} + \textit{mangent} & \underbrace{\textit{les professeurs}}? \\ (\mathbf{q}_1\pi_6^\ell) & \overline{\pi} \end{array}$$

There are other ways of asking direct questions with the help of special question words such as *pourquoi* and *qui*. We shall assign the type $\overline{\mathbf{q}}$ to such questions, hence $\overline{\mathbf{q}}\mathbf{q}^\ell$ to *pourquoi*, as in

$$\begin{array}{cc} \textit{pourquoi} & \textit{vient} - \textit{il}? \\ (\overline{\mathbf{q}}\mathbf{q}^\ell) & (\mathbf{q}\ \pi_3^\ell)\ \pi \end{array}$$

The bar is required to avoid

$$\begin{array}{cc} {}^*\textit{pourquoi} & \textit{pourquoi} \\ (\overline{\mathbf{q}}\mathbf{q}^\ell) & (\overline{\mathbf{q}}\mathbf{q}^\ell) \end{array}$$

The word *qui* can ask either for the subject or for the object. In the former case it has type $\overline{\mathbf{q}}\mathbf{s}^\ell\pi_3$, in the latter case type $\overline{\mathbf{q}}\mathbf{o}^{\ell\ell}\mathbf{q}^\ell$:

$$\begin{array}{ccc} \textit{qui} & \textit{aime} & \textit{Jeanne}? \\ (\overline{\mathbf{q}}\mathbf{s}^\ell\pi_3) & (\overline{\pi}^r\mathbf{s}\ \mathbf{o}^\ell) & \mathbf{o} \end{array} \qquad \begin{array}{cc} \textit{qui} & \textit{aime} - t - \textit{il}? \\ (\overline{\mathbf{q}}\mathbf{o}^{\ell\ell}\mathbf{q}^\ell) & (\mathbf{q}\ \mathbf{o}^\ell\pi_3^\ell)\ \pi \end{array}$$

These two occurrences of *qui* have distinct translations into German (*wer*/*wen*) or into pedantic English (*who*/*whom*).

9 Indirect Sentences

The word *que* of type $\bar{\mathbf{s}}\mathbf{s}^\ell$ is widely used to convert direct statements of type s into indirect ones of type $\bar{\mathbf{s}}$. These occur after such verbs as

$$\textit{dire, penser, croire}, \cdots \quad \text{of type } \mathbf{i}\bar{\mathbf{s}}^\ell.$$

Thus we may say:

$$\begin{array}{c}\textit{je pense qu'il viendra}\\ \pi_1\ (\bar{\pi}^r\mathbf{s}_1\bar{\mathbf{s}}^\ell)(\bar{\mathbf{s}}\mathbf{s}^\ell)\pi_3\ (\bar{\pi}^r\mathbf{s}_3)\cdot\end{array}$$

The fact that $\mathbf{s} \longrightarrow \bar{\mathbf{s}}$ can be exploited to say instead:

$$\begin{array}{c}\textit{je pense : il viendra}\\ \pi_1\ (\bar{\pi}_1^r\mathbf{s}_1\mathbf{s}^\ell)\ \pi_3\ (\bar{\pi}_3^r\mathbf{s}_3)\end{array}$$

We shall adopt the basic type σ for complete subjunctive clauses. The word *que* of type $\sigma\mathbf{s}_5^\ell$ can then be used to convert an incomplete subjunctive clause into a complete one. Certain verbs such as

$$\textit{vouloir, aimer, souhaiter, douter}, \cdots \text{ of type } \mathbf{i}\sigma^\ell$$

take a complement of type σ. For example,

$$\begin{array}{c}\textit{j'aimerais que tu viennes}\\ \pi_1\ (\bar{\pi}^r\mathbf{s}_4\sigma^\ell)\ (\sigma\mathbf{s}_5^\ell)\pi_2\ (\bar{\pi}^r\mathbf{s}_5)\end{array}$$

We shall assign the type $\bar{\bar{\mathbf{q}}}$ to indirect questions, to be distinguished from the type $\bar{\mathbf{q}}$ for certain direct ones. For example, the verbs

$$\textit{savoir, se + demander} \text{ have type } \mathbf{i}\,\bar{\bar{\mathbf{q}}}^\ell \text{ and type } \bar{\bar{\mathbf{i}}}\,\bar{\bar{\mathbf{q}}}^\ell \text{ respectively.}$$

We might ensure the latter by asserting that

$$\textit{demander} \text{ has type } \mathbf{i}\omega^\ell\,\bar{\bar{\mathbf{q}}}^\ell \text{ or } \mathbf{i}\,\bar{\bar{\mathbf{q}}}^\ell\,\omega^\ell.$$

Thus we may say, using *si* and *pourquoi* of type $\bar{\bar{\mathbf{q}}}\mathbf{s}^\ell$:

$$\begin{array}{c}\textit{je saurai si tu venais,}\\ \pi_1\ (\bar{\pi}_1^r\mathbf{s}_3\ \bar{\bar{\mathbf{q}}}^\ell)(\bar{\bar{\mathbf{q}}}\mathbf{s}^\ell)\pi_2\ (\bar{\pi}_2^r\mathbf{s}_2)\end{array}$$

$$\begin{array}{c}\textit{je me + demande pourquoi tu viendras,}\\ \pi_1\ (\bar{\pi}_1^r\mathbf{s}_1\,\bar{\bar{\mathbf{q}}}^\ell)\quad(\bar{\bar{\mathbf{q}}}\mathbf{s}^\ell)\ \pi_2\ (\bar{\pi}_2^r\mathbf{s}_3)\end{array}$$

il a demandé à Robert s'il avait une voiture,

$$\pi_3(\bar\pi_3^r\mathbf{s}_1\mathbf{p}_2^\ell)(\mathbf{p}_2\,\bar{\bar{\mathbf{q}}}^\ell\,\omega^\ell)\;\omega\;(\bar{\bar{\mathbf{q}}}\mathbf{s}^\ell)\pi_3\;(\bar\pi_3^r\mathbf{s}_2\mathbf{o}^\ell)\;\mathbf{o}$$

je voudrais savoir si tu habites à Paris.

$$\pi_1\;(\bar\pi_1^r\mathbf{s}_4\mathbf{i}^\ell)\;(\mathbf{i}\,\bar{\bar{\mathbf{q}}}^\ell)(\bar{\bar{\mathbf{q}}}\mathbf{s}^\ell)\pi_2\;(\bar\pi_2^r\mathbf{s}_1\lambda^\ell)\;\lambda$$

In the following examples we use the conjunction *où* of type $\bar{\bar{\mathbf{q}}}\,\lambda^{\ell\ell}\bar{\mathbf{s}}^\ell$ and the expression *ce que* of type $\bar{\mathbf{s}}\mathbf{o}^{\ell\ell}\mathbf{s}^\ell$:

elle voulait savoir où Marie a mis la montre,

$$\pi_3\;(\bar\pi_3^r\mathbf{s}_2\mathbf{i}^\ell)\;(\mathbf{i}\,\bar{\bar{\mathbf{q}}}^\ell)(\bar{\bar{\mathbf{q}}}\lambda^{\ell\ell}\bar{\mathbf{s}}^\ell)\bar\pi_3\;(\bar\pi_3^r\mathbf{s}_1\mathbf{p}_2^\ell)(\mathbf{p}_2\,\lambda^\ell\mathbf{o}^\ell)\mathbf{o}$$

je sais ce que tu aime,

$$\pi_1\;(\bar\pi_1^r\mathbf{s}\bar{\mathbf{s}}^\ell)(\bar{\mathbf{s}}\mathbf{o}^{\ell\ell}\mathbf{s}^\ell)\;\pi_2\;(\bar\pi_2^r\mathbf{s}_1\mathbf{o}^\ell)$$

and even

je sais ce que tu dis que tu aime.

$$\pi_1(\bar\pi_1^r\mathbf{s}_1\bar{\mathbf{s}}^\ell)\;(\bar{\mathbf{s}}\mathbf{o}^{\ell\ell}\mathbf{s}^\ell)\pi_2(\bar\pi_2^r\mathbf{s}_1\bar{\mathbf{s}}^\ell)(\bar{\mathbf{s}}\mathbf{s}^\ell)\pi_2(\bar\pi_2^r\mathbf{s}_1\mathbf{o}^\ell)$$

10 Some Final Words

In this provisional attempt to describe French sentence structure by computations on types, we have necessarily confined ourselves to a small part of French grammar, and it goes without saying that some of our type assignments may have to be revised when further work is done. In particular, we have not yet looked at any but the most rudimentary noun-phrases and we have completely omitted from our investigation adverbs, relative clauses, negatives and imperatives. While many of these topics can be included in our framework, more serious problems may arise if we try to incorporate essential distinctions between masculine and feminine, between singular and plural and between persons and things. These distinctions often require semantic and pragmatic considerations outside our scope.

To look at only one example, in

la + avoir mangée

$$(\bar{\mathbf{i}}\mathbf{o}^{\ell\ell}\bar{\mathbf{i}}^\ell)(\mathbf{i}\mathbf{p}_2^\ell)\qquad(\mathbf{p}_2\,\mathbf{o}^\ell)$$

the silent *e* at the end of the past participle is not audible and could be ignored in analyzing spoken French. However, this excuse won't work with

la + avoir prise.

Conceivably, we could extend our treatment to account for this gender mark, but in

j'ai été heureuse

we cannot account for the ending of the adjective on syntactic grounds at all: we must know the sex of the speaker.

The mathematical analysis underlying our approach was first explored in [Lambek 1999] and its history has been discussed in [Casadio and Lambek, to appear].

11 Response to Referees' Comments

Not everybody will be happy about our proposal. Referee 1 objects to our attempt to lump syntactic categories, morphological features and grammatical functions under the single heading of what we call "types". On the other hand, he or she criticizes us for not incorporating semantics.

Of course, *lexical* semantics has to be stored in the dictionary; but *functional* semantics, as in Montague grammar, could in principle be derived from the structure of compound types. For example, ab^{ℓ} and $b^r a$ could be interpreted as denoting functions from the set of entities of type b to the set of entities of type a. However, to fully justify such an interpretation, one should adopt a more elaborate algebraic system, namely "classical bilinear logic", as proposed by Claudia Casadio, but at the cost of making computations more difficult. For a more thorough discussion of this question, see the article "A tale of four grammars", to appear in Studia Logica.

The referee also raises the question of how to block such sentences as "*to eat an apple on one foot sleeps*". This could be blocked by suitable type assignments if one took the trouble; but it seems more reasonable to regard it as acceptable *syntactically*. Indeed, attempts to block it might also block "*to eat an apple on one foot makes one's foot fall asleep*" and even Chomsky's "*colourless green ideas sleep furiously*".

Referee 2 wants to know the limitations of our approach and whether it also applies to other languages. The approach has been applied to English, German and Italian. Admittedly, these are all Indo-European languages, but first steps are being taken to look at some non-Indo-European languages as well, e.g. Arabic.

There are of course serious limitations to our approach, even for English. For example, if the word "*whom*" is omitted in "*people (whom) John likes like him*", there is no word left to which the type of "*whom*" can be attached. Indeed, it becomes necessary to admit some grammatical rules other than those encoded in the types stored in the dictionary.

Referee 3 wants to know whether we can predict the correct order of preverbal clitic pronouns, which is well-known to all teachers of French. This is precisely what we have been trying to do, by carefully choosing appropriate type assignments and by fine-tuning the partial order in the set of basic types.

References

Bescherelle 1, *L'Art de conjuger*, Éditions Hurtubise, Montréal 1998.

Bescherelle 3, *La grammaire pour tous*, Éditions Hurtubise, Montréal 1998.

J.-P. Boons, A. Guillet and C. Leclerc. *La structure des phrases simples en français, Constructions intransitives*, Librairie Droz, Genève-Paris 1976.

C. Casadio and J. Lambek. A tale of four grammars, *Studia Logica* (to appear).

M. Gross. *Grammaire transformationelle du français, Syntaxe du verbe*, Librairie Larousse, Paris 1968.

M. Gross. *Table des verbes entrant dans des constructions complètives*, Éditions du CNRS, Paris 1969.

A. Guillet and C. Leclerc. *La structure des phrases simples en français, Constructions transitives locatives*, Librairie Droz, Genève Paris 1992.

Z. Harris, A cycling cancellation-automaton for sentence well-formedness, *International Computation Center Bulletin* 5 (1966), 69-94.

R. Jackendoff, $\overline{X}$ *Syntax: A Study of Phrase Structure*, The MIT Press, Cambridge, Mass., 1977.

J. Lambek, A mathematician looks at French conjugation, *Linguistic Analysis* 2 (1976), 203-214.

J. Lambek, Type grammar revisited, in: A. Lecomte, F. Lamarche and G. Perrier (eds). *Logical aspects of computational linguistics*, Springer LNAI 1582(1999), 1-27.

Deductive Parsing of Visual Languages*

Paolo Bottoni[1], Bernd Meyer[2**], Kim Marriott[2], and Francesco Parisi Presicce[1]

[1] Dipartimento di Scienze dell'Informazione
Università La Sapienza di Roma
[bottoni | parisi]@dsi.uniroma1.it
[2] School of Computer Science & Software Engineering
Monash University, Australia
[berndm | marriott]@csse.monash.edu.au

Abstract. Computational linguistics has largely focussed on written and spoken textual languages. However, humans use many other kinds of symbolic notations for communication, in particular, two-dimensional graphical notations such as mathematical notation, choreography notation, organizational charts and electrical circuit diagrams. We can term such multi-dimensional symbolic notations, *visual languages*. Like textual languages, many of these notations have a well defined syntax and semantics. The standard approach to computer interpretation of visual languages is to utilize parsing technologies based on multi-dimensional grammars. In this paper we investigate a new approach to parsing visual languages based on linear logic. The advantages of this logic-based approach are threefold: It provides a more adequate level for modelling the semantics of visual languages; it allows us to implement them based on automated deduction and it provides a good basis for the investigation of their formal properties. We show how attributed multiset grammars, one of the most widely used methods for multi-dimensional parsing, can be embedded into linear logic, demonstrate how parsing corresponds to linear proofs and prove the soundness and correctness of this embedding. Importantly, our embedding is into a subset of a linear logic programming language. Thus, we also demonstrate how multi-dimensional parsing can be implemented as a directly executable linear logic program.

1 Introduction

While computational linguistics has been (almost) exclusively concerned with the use of spoken textual languages and their written equivalents, many other types of symbolic notations can also be regarded as languages. In particular, visual languages such as organizational charts, dance notation, electrical circuit diagrams and mathematical notations. Such diagrammatic notations differ

* Work partially supported by the European Community TMR network GETGRATS and by the Australian Research Council.

** Part of the research reported was done while the author was affiliated with Università La Sapienza di Roma.

P. de Groote, G. Morrill, C. Retoré (Eds.): LACL 2001, LNAI 2099, pp. 79–94, 2001.

from textual language in that they are inherently two- or three-dimensional in nature rather than linear, so that different structures are required for their representation. Some other non-diagrammatic visual languages, such as American Sign Languages, are non-static and consist of dynamic multi-dimensional arrangements of symbols. Diagrammatic languages cover the whole spectrum from highly informal means of communication, such as draft sketches in architecture and design, to rigidly formalized systems, such as category diagrams in mathematics or digital circuit diagrams. Just like conventional textual languages, many diagram notations have a well defined syntax and semantics.

The research field "diagrammatic reasoning" investigates the question of how we understand and use such diagram languages [GNC95]. A particularly interesting aspect of this field is how we employ diagrammatic languages as aids in reasoning processes. To illustrate this, a simple example is given in Figure 1 which provides a visualisation of a step in the analysis of a string by a deterministic finite state automaton: The current state is identified by placing the residual input string under it and the automaton's behaviour can diagrammatically be simulated by truncating and moving this residual input string.

Obviously, one of the most fundamental questions to be answered is, how the process of diagram *interpretation* can be understood. From the perspective of computer science, we are particularly interested in how this process can be performed automatically on the basis of a *formal specification* of a visual or diagrammatic language.

The majority of computational methods for the automatic interpretation of diagrams takes a syntax-based approach, i.e. interpretation is split into two parts: *parsing* and *interpretation* proper [MMA00]. The methods that are employed are in essence mostly generalizations of methods found in computational linguistics for textual languages. In particular the parsing phase of diagram interpretation is most commonly built on multi-dimensional grammars, which can be considered as extensions of standard grammars. Grammar-based parsing of diagrammatic languages is now relatively well-understood, having been investigated for over 35 years [MMW98].

Fig. 1. State Transition Diagram

However, a purely grammar based approach has two significant disadvantages. First, grammars do not provide adequate support for specifying semantic information. Thus, although well-suited for parsing they are not suited to interpretation proper. Furthermore, it is of importance that diagrams are rarely understood or used in isolation, but rather in combination with textual language. In a grammar-based approach, the integration of such contextual information into the parsing process is difficult. Second, the theory of multi-dimensional grammars is not well developed, meaning that it is difficult, for instance, to prove formal properties, such as the equivalence of grammars. A formalization in terms of logic would be on a more adequate level and could lead to a deductive calculus for diagrammatic languages. For these reasons, embeddings of multi-dimensional grammars into logic formalisms have been investigated.

Previous logic-based approaches to diagram parsing have only considered classical first-order logic.[1] However, first-order logic is less than ideal. The most direct approach to modelling diagrams in first-order logic is to model diagram elements directly as predicates themselves. This is very appealing because implication can be used to encode recognition directly. Unfortunately, this approach is unsatisfactory, because of the monotonicity of classical first-order logic. The second approach, similar to how sequential grammatical formalisms such as Definite Clause Grammars [PW80] are coded into logic, is to model the diagram and its components as terms [MMW98]. The disadvantage of this approach is that it is complex and that it does not really leverage from the underlying logical implication.

In this paper, we therefore investigate an alternative approach to deductive diagram parsing, based on a non-standard logic that is more suitable for these tasks, namely linear logic [Gir87]. Its chief advantage is that it is a resource-oriented logic, which renders the embedding of grammars straight-forward. We show how to map attributed multiset grammars to linear logic so that diagram parsing can be understood as linear proof search.

While we have introduced the idea of using linear logic for diagram interpretation in an earlier paper [MM00], this paper presents a new embedding that, in contrast to the earlier version, is suitable for automated deduction.

The main technical contribution of the present paper is the proof that this new embedding is sound and complete, which gives us a provably correct deductive theory for diagrammatic syntax. Since the linear logic fragment used is a subset of the fragment used for linear logic programming, the new embedding turns diagram grammars into directly executable parsers.

The paper is structured as follows: In Section 2, we present the formalism of Attributed Multiset Grammars and its application to diagram interpretation, while in Section 3, we discuss alternative logical embeddings of this formalism. Section 4 presents the linear logic embedding and proofs its soundness and completeness. Finally, Section 5 draws some conclusions and discusses related work both in the diagrammatic and textual areas.

2 Diagram Parsing with Attributed Multiset Grammars

As mentioned above, most approaches to diagram interpretation and more particularly to diagram parsing are based on various forms of multi-dimensional grammars. The main differences between these grammars and more standard grammars for textual languages are that the grammar must allow us to define more complex geometric relationships between symbols instead of just sequential concatenation. As a consequence, sets or multisets of symbols are rewritten rather than sequences of symbols.

[1] Whenever we mention first-order logic in the remainder of the paper we are referring to *classical* first-order logic.

Here we review a particular type of attributed multiset grammars, termed constraint multiset grammars (CMGs) [HMO91], which have been used by a number of researchers for reasonably complex tasks such as the interpretation of state diagrams and mathematical equations. In [Mar94] a precise formal treatment of CMGs is given, and we review only the basic notions required to understand their mapping to linear logic.

A diagrammatic sentence to be parsed by a CMG is just an attributed multiset of graphical tokens. CMG productions rewrite multisets of attributed tokens and have the form

$$U ::= U_1, \ldots, U_n \; where \; (C) \; \{E\}$$

indicating that the non-terminal symbol U can be recognized from the symbols $U_1, \ldots, U_n$ whenever the attributes of $U_1, \ldots, U_n$ satisfy the constraints C. The attributes of U are computed using the assignment expression E. The constraints C restrict the applicability of the production to particular spatial arrangements of the symbols $U_1, \ldots, U_n$. For an example, see Production (1) below.

The terms *terminal* and *non-terminal* are used analogously to the case in linear languages. The only difference lies in the fact that terminal types in CMGs refer to graphic primitives, such as *line* and *circle*, instead of textual tokens and each of these *symbol types* has a set of one or more attributes, typically used to describe its geometric properties. A *symbol* is an instance of a symbol type. In each grammar, there is a distinguished non-terminal symbol type called the *start* type.

Additional semantic attributes can be associated with tokens. As productions are applied in the parsing process, semantic functions can compute the attribute values for the generated non terminal, up to the construction of a global interpretation in a designated attribute of the start symbol. Semantic attributes are computed using the $\{E\}$ part of the production.

As a running example for diagram interpretation, consider the language of state transition diagrams. If we draw these in the same way as the example diagrams on the left hand side and the right hand side of the transformation arrow in Figure 1, the following terminal symbol types and their associated attributes can be used: *arrow(start:point,mid:point,end:point)*, *text(mid:point,label:string)*, *circle(mid:point,radius:real)*. The non-terminal symbol types for these diagrams are *std(ss:states,ts:transitions)*, *arc(start:point,mid:point,end:point,label:string)*, *state(mid:point,radius:real,label:string,kind:string)* and *transition(start:string, tran:string,end:string)* where *std* is the start type.

As an example of a production in a CMG consider that for recognizing a final state. This is made up of two circles *C1* and *C2* and text *T* satisfying three geometric relationships: the mid-points of the circle *C1* and the circle *C2* are the same; the mid-points of the circle *C1* and the text *T* are the same; and *C2* is the outermost circle. Note the additional attributes *kind* and *label* used to construct an "interpretation". The production is:

(1)
$$\begin{array}{l} \textit{S:state ::= C1:circle,C2:circle,T:text where (} \\ \quad \textit{C1.mid = C2.mid and C1.mid = T.mid and C1.radius} \leq \textit{C2.radius) \{} \\ \quad \textit{S.mid = C1.mid and S.radius = C2.radius and} \\ \quad \textit{S.label = T.label and S.kind = final \}} \end{array}$$

Using similar productions we can define normal states and start states as well as an *arc* which is an arrow with text above its midpoint. CMGs also include context-sensitive productions. Context symbols are denoted by existential quantification. The following context-sensitive production recognizes a transition:

```
T:transition ::= A:arc
   exist S1:state,S2:state where (
      OnCircle(A.start,S1.mid,S1.radius) and OnCircle(A.end,S2.mid,S2.radius))
   {T.start = S1.label and T.tran = A.label and T.end = S2.label }
```

A parsing algorithm for attributed multiset grammars was presented in [Mar94].

3 Logic Approaches to Multiset Grammars

Embeddings of attributed multiset grammars into logic have been investigated before, but only for first-order logic and logic programming based on first-order logic. There have been two main approaches: The first approach encodes a diagram as a single term modelling a hierarchical collection of the graphical objects in the diagram. This is closely related to the way linear sentences are modelled in DCGs [PW80] and, in fact, one of the first approaches to use this modelling was a straight forward extension of DCGs by set structures, called Definite Clause Set Grammars or DCSGs [Tan91]. Various other forms of such encodings have been demonstrated in [HMO91, Mey97, MMW98]. The idea is to model a diagram as a single hierarchical term. The key predicate is $reduce(D, D')$ which holds if diagram D can be reduced to D' using one of the productions in the grammar. To handle spatial conditions, we assume a first-order theory C which models the relevant aspects of geometry. C is assumed to be an additional set of axioms in our inferences.

For the state transition diagram grammar we can define $reduce_{fs}(D, D')$ which holds if D' can be obtained from D by recognizing a final state:

$$\begin{array}{l} reduce_{fs}(D, D') \leftrightarrow \widetilde{\exists\{D, D'\}}. \\ \quad circle(C^1_{mid}, C^1_{radius}) \in D \wedge circle(C^2_{mid}, C^2_{radius}) \in D \wedge \\ \quad text(T_{mid}, T_{label}) \in D \wedge \\ \quad C^1_{mid} = C^2_{mid} \wedge C^1_{mid} = T_{mid} \wedge C^1_{radius} \leq C^2_{radius} \wedge \\ \quad S_{mid} = C^1_{mid} \wedge S_{radius} = C^2_{radius} \wedge S_{label} = T_{label} \wedge S_{kind} = final \wedge \\ \quad D' = D \setminus \{circle(C^1_{mid}, C^1_{radius}), circle(C^2_{mid}, C^2_{radius}), text(T_{mid}, T_{label})\} \\ \qquad \uplus \{state(S_{mid}, S_{radius}, S_{label}, S_{kind})\} \end{array}$$

where we use the Prolog convention of using identifiers starting with an uppercase letter for variables and those starting with a lowercase letter for predicates and functions, the functions $\uplus$, $\setminus$ and $\in$ work on multisets, and $\widetilde{\exists\{D, D'\}}$ indicates existential closure over all variables but D and D'.

This encoding, of course, allows a faithful modelling of diagram parsing—it exactly captures rewriting with a CMG production. However, it does not greatly leverage from first-order logic. In contrast, the second approach encodes the graphical objects directly as predicates, rather than terms. Modellings based on classical first order logic using this approach have been demonstrated in [HM91, Mar94, Mey00].

In such an embedding we map, for example, the production for the (final) *state* type from the state transition diagram grammar to the predicate *state*:

$$\begin{aligned} state(S_{mid}, S_{radius}, S_{label}, S_{kind}) \leftrightarrow \widetilde{\exists}\overline{\{S_{mid}, S_{radius}, S_{label}, S_{kind}\}}.\\ circle(C1_{mid}, C1_{radius}) \wedge circle(C2_{mid}, C2_{radius}) \wedge text(T_{mid}, T_{label}) \wedge \\ C1_{mid} = C2_{mid} \wedge C1_{mid} = T_{mid} \wedge C1_{radius} \leq C2_{radius} \wedge \\ S_{mid} = C1_{mid} \wedge S_{radius} = C2_{radius} \wedge S_{label} = T_{label} \wedge S_{kind} = final \end{aligned}$$

where $\widetilde{\exists}$ denotes existential quantification.

The advantage of this embedding is that implication directly corresponds to reduction. The disadvantage is that there is a fundamental mismatch between implication in first-order logic and grammatical reduction: Because first-order logic is monotonic there is no way of determining if an element in the diagram has already been reduced; in particular there is no way to determine whether all elements in the original diagram have been reduced to the start symbol. Thus parsing cannot truthfully be captured in such a modelling if it is based on classical first-order logic.

This problem is even more significant in the broader context of diagrammatic reasoning. Parsing and interpreting diagrams are only first steps towards using them in reasoning processes. It would be advantageous if parsing formalisms could be integrated or even unified with more general formalisms for diagrammatic reasoning. Above we have outlined how reasoning with diagrams can often be understood as transformation of diagram configurations. In our example (Figure 1) the transformation that simulates a single execution step in the FSA consists of truncating the input marker and moving it from below the current state to the next state. Such an execution step can be easily expressed with an attributed multiset grammar if we use context-sensitive (type-0) forms [MM97b]:

T:transition, S1:state, S2:state, L1:text ::=
T:transition, S1:state, S2:state, L0:text where (
  first(L0.label)=T.tran and L0.mid=S1.mid – (0,S1.radius) and
  T.start=S1.label and T.end=S2.label) {
  L1.mid=S2.mid – (0,S2.radius) and L1.label=rest(L0.label) }

Unfortunately, a predicate-based embedding of type-0 grammars into classical first-order logic is impossible because of the monotonicity constraint: An execution step requires *removing* the input marker from the current state which is impossible to model in monotonic logic.

For these reasons, we have to look at alternative logical systems that can be used as the basis of diagram parsing with deductive systems.

4 Diagram Parsing as Linear Logic Programming

Linear logic [Gir87] is a suitable candidate for an alternative logic-based approach, because it is resource-oriented. Essentially a linear implication captures exactly a rewrite step in a multiset grammar. Intuitively, it is therefore clear that a CMG can be modelled as a set of linear implications and that a successful parse consists of rewriting the original multi-set of terminal symbols into a multiset that only contains the single non-terminal symbol which is the start symbol.

Earlier [MM00] we have advocated the most straight forward mapping of CMG productions into linear implications by concatenating all tokens with multiplicative conjunction. For example, consider the CMG production P for recognizing a final state. One linear logic encoding of this production is

$$\tilde{\forall}(S \otimes A \multimap T \otimes C_1 \otimes C_2 \otimes R)$$

- T is $text(T_{mid}, T_{label})$;
- C_i is $circle(C^i_{mid}, C^i_{radius})$, for $i = 1, 2$;
- S is $state(S_{mid}, S_{radius}, S_{label}, S_{kind})$,
- R is $(C^1_{mid} = C^2_{mid}) \otimes (C^1_{mid} = T_{mid}) \otimes (C^1_{radius} \leq C^2_{radius})$, and
- A is $!(S_{mid} = C^1_{mid}) \otimes !(S_{radius} = C^2_{radius}) \otimes$
  $!(S_{label} = T_{label}) \otimes !(S_{kind} = final)$.

This mapping is a natural and conceptually correct choice. However, we are not interested in modelling diagram parsing in linear logic for its theoretical properties alone, but we are also interested in linear logic as a well-founded theoretical framework for declarative computational implementations of diagram parsing. Therefore, it is crucial that the fragment of linear logic we choose is adequate for automated deduction.

Multiplicative connectives express the simultaneous existence of elements in the multiset of diagram elements and linear implication is adequate to express the rewriting as such. Since *all* the elements in a multiset of objects representing a diagram have to exist simultaneously, the natural choice made above is to use multiplicative conjunction ($\otimes$) to model their union in a multiset.

Unfortunately, current linear logic programming languages [Mil95] do not allow the use of multiplicative conjunction in the rule head. While this would not be a problem for the embedding of context-free CMGS, it has been shown in [MM97a] that the definition of most diagram languages requires some form of context-sensitive grammar formalism. With the above mapping, such grammars cannot be encoded directly as linear logic programs. Therefore we have to find a different fragment of linear logic that directly corresponds to a linear logic programming language and allows us to embed context-sensitive CMGs.

The fragment we introduce in this paper is a subset of the linear logic programming language Lygon [HPW96, Win96]. Alternatively it can also be viewed as a minor extension of the linear logic programming language LO [AP91].[2]

[2] The extension to LO is that we allow limited use of the linear goal **1**, which terminates an agent if and only if this agent does not have any resources left (i.e. **1** succeeds if and only if the linear proof context is empty).

The revised mapping uses linear disjunction instead of conjunction to concatenate tokens, but it still uses (additive) conjunction to express (spatial) constraints that limit the applicability of a rule: For a CMG production

$$(2) \qquad U ::= U_1, \ldots, U_n \ \textit{exists}\ U_{n+1}, \ldots, U_m \ \textit{where}\ (C)\ \{E\}$$

we use the equivalent linear rule:

$$\tau(u_1) \parr \ldots \parr \tau(u_m) \multimapinv \{C\} \& \{E\} \& \tau(u) \parr \tau(u_{n+1}) \parr \ldots \parr \tau(u_m)$$

where τ is a mapping of grammatical types to first-order terms.

To provide some intuition, we note that additive disjunction, although technically classified as a disjunctive operator, has strong conjunctive properties. The reader is referred to the Appendix A for the proof rules for additive disjunction and is encouraged to compare them with those for multiplicative disjunction. To quote the father of linear logic, J.-Y. Girard, "$\parr$ [...] is technically a disjunction, but has prominent conjunctive features [...] The meaning of $\parr$ is not that easy [...]; in some sense $\parr$ is the constructive content of classical disjunction" [Gir95]. The use of additive conjunction for the constraints and attribute computations is motivated by the theory of *focusing proofs* in LO [And92].

Each CMG terminal and non-terminal object u_i will be represented by a first order term $\tau(u_i)$ which has the token type of u_i as the main functor and contains the attributes in some fixed order. We extend this mapping function canonically so that we use $\tau(u_1, \ldots, u_n)$ to denote $\tau(u_1) \parr \ldots \parr \tau(u_n)$. In the same way, $\tau(p)$, for a CMG production p, will denote its mapping to a linear rule and $\tau(G) = \{\tau(p) \mid p \in P\}$ denotes the complete mapping of a CMG G to a linear program.

The linear logic mapping $\tau(p)$ of a production p is an exponential universal closure:

$$(3) \qquad !\,\widetilde{\forall}\ \tau(u_1) \parr \ldots \parr \tau(u_m) \multimapinv \{C\} \& \{E\} \& \tau(u) \parr \tau(u_{n+1}) \parr \ldots \parr \tau(u_m)$$

The complete translation of a grammar is the set of all rules obtained from the individual mappings of all its productions.

As a concrete example consider the CMG production for *transition* which was given earlier and the definitions of the token types it uses. The linear mapping of this production is:

$$\begin{array}{l} !\,\widetilde{\forall}\ state(mid_{s1}, radius_{s1}, label_{s1}, kind_{s1}) \parr state(mid_{s2}, radius_{s2}, label_{s2}, kind_{s2}) \\ \quad \parr arc(start_a, mid_a, end_a, label_a) \multimapinv \\ \qquad OnCircle(start_a, mid_{s1}, radius_{s1}) \& \\ \qquad OnCircle(end_a, mid_{s2}, radius_{s2}) \& \\ \qquad start_t = label_{s1} \& tran_t = label_a \& \\ \qquad end_t = label_{s2} \& \\ \qquad state(mid_{s1}, radius_{s1}, label_{s1}, kind_{s1}) \parr \\ \qquad state(mid_{s2}, radius_{s2}, label_{s2}, kind_{s2}) \parr \\ \qquad transition(start_t, tran_t, end_t) \end{array}$$

To evaluate the constraints in the grammar and to compute the attribute assignments we assume that the geometric (arithmetic) theory is available as a first-order theory Γ_g in linear logic.

Each rule $\tau(p)$ emulates exactly one production p. To emulate parsing fully, we also need a rule which declares that a parse is successful if and only if the initial diagram is reduced to the start symbol and no other symbols are left. For a CMG G with start symbol s, we can do this in linear logic by adding $\tau(s) \circ\!\!- \mathbf{1}$ as an axiom to $\tau(G)$ using the linear goal $\mathbf{1}$, which succeeds if and only if the linear proof context is empty.[3] The complete set of linear rules that implement a grammar G is: $\Pi = \tau(G) \cup \{(\tau(s) \circ\!\!- \mathbf{1})\}$

A successful parse of a diagram D now corresponds to a proof of $\Gamma_g, \Pi \vdash \tau(D)$.

Our new embedding maps CMGs to proper linear logic programs so that we directly obtain an executable deductive theory for diagram parsing. Therefore the following theorem states the correctness of our embedding as well as the correctness of the linear programs that we obtain: The linear logic embedding of CMGs is sound and complete.

Theorem 1. *$D \in \mathcal{L}(G) \Leftrightarrow \Gamma_g, \Pi \vdash \tau(D)$.*

Proof: Due to space restrictions we can only give a limited amount of detail here. The reader can consult Appendix A for a description of the inference rules. We first show the "only if" direction. An accepting derivation in G has the following structure: $D \rightarrow_{p_{i_1}} D_1 \rightarrow_{p_{i_2}} \rightarrow \ldots \rightarrow_{p_{i_n}} \{s\}$ In which $\rightarrow_{p_{i_j}}$ indicates the application of production p_{i_j} in step j. We show that each derivation step j corresponds to a valid sequent in linear logic. We can consider each derivation step in isolation. Let p_{i_j} have the form (2). Then derivation step j has the form: $\{V, u_1, \ldots, u_m\} \rightarrow_{p_{i_j}} \{V, u, u_{n+1}, \ldots, u_m\}$ where V is the application context, i.e. the sub-multiset which is not modified by the rule application, $u_{n+1}, \ldots, u_m$ is the rule context and there is a ground substitution θ for C and E such that $\Gamma_g \vdash (C \wedge E)\theta$ where Γ_g is the geometric/arithmetic theory. Let $\Upsilon = \tau(V)$, $v = \tau(u)$, $v_i = \tau(u_i)$.

Now, the linear equivalent of p_{i_j} is the exponential universal closure of $\tau(p_{i_j})$ which has the form (3). Therefore the following sequent can be constructed:

---

[3] In fact, this use of **1** is the only extension to the original LO calculus that is required for our mapping. In LO, our treatment of spatial constraints as arithmetic evaluations corresponds to encapsulating an arithmetic evaluator as a "geometry machine" in a separate agent and give evaluation requests to this agent. Our usage of "with" (&) corresponds in LO to spawning an additional agent for such computations. The LO semantics of such agent calls is given by "focusing proofs" in linear logic [And92].

$$\dfrac{\dfrac{\dfrac{\dfrac{\dfrac{\dfrac{\dfrac{\dfrac{\dfrac{\dfrac{}{\Gamma_g \vdash \top, \Upsilon}\,(\top - R)}{\vdots}}{\Gamma_g \vdash (C\&E)\theta, \Upsilon} \qquad \Gamma_g, \Pi \vdash \upsilon\theta \parr \upsilon_{n+1} \parr \ldots \parr \upsilon_m, \Upsilon}{\Gamma_g, \Gamma_g, \Pi \vdash (C\&E)\theta \& \upsilon\theta \parr \upsilon_{n+1} \parr \ldots \parr \upsilon_m, \Upsilon}\,(\&-R)}{\vdots}}{\Gamma_g, \Pi \vdash (C\&E)\theta \& \upsilon\theta \parr \upsilon_{n+1} \parr \ldots \parr \upsilon_m, \Upsilon}\,(C! - L) \qquad *_1}{\Gamma_g, \Pi, \tau(p_{i_j})\theta \vdash \upsilon_1, \ldots, \upsilon_m, \Upsilon}\,(\multimap - L)}{\Gamma_g, \Pi, \widetilde{\forall}\tau(p_{i_j}) \vdash \upsilon_1, \ldots, \upsilon_m, \Upsilon}\,(\forall - L)}{\Gamma_g, \Pi \vdash \upsilon_1, \ldots, \upsilon_m, \Upsilon}\,(C! - L); (! - L)}{\vdots}}{\Gamma_g, \Pi \vdash \upsilon_1 \parr \ldots \parr \upsilon_m, \Upsilon}\,(\parr - R)$$

$$\dfrac{\dfrac{\dfrac{}{\upsilon_1 \vdash \upsilon_1}\,(ax) \quad \ldots \quad \dfrac{}{\upsilon_m \vdash \upsilon_m}\,(ax)}{\vdots}}{\dfrac{\upsilon_1 \parr \ldots \parr \upsilon_m \vdash \upsilon_1 \parr \ldots \parr \upsilon_m}{*_1}}\,(\parr - L)$$

Therefore, to prove that $\Gamma_g, \Pi \vdash D_i$ it suffices to show that $\Gamma_g, \Pi \vdash D_{i+1}$. So all that remains to show is that $\Gamma_G, \Pi \vdash \tau(s)$. This is trivial, since we have included the appropriate rule $\tau(s) \circ\!\!- \mathbf{1}$ explicitly in Π:

$$\dfrac{\dfrac{\dfrac{\dfrac{}{\vdash \mathbf{1}}\,(1 - R)}{\vdots}}{\Gamma_g, \Pi \vdash \mathbf{1}}\,(W! - L) \qquad \dfrac{}{\tau(s) \vdash \tau(s)}\,(ax)}{\Gamma_g, \Pi \vdash \tau(s)}\,(\multimap - L)$$

In the opposite direction ("if") the proof proceeds by induction on the number of derivation steps in the linear proof. We first have to note that every linear representation of a sentential form has a special syntactic form:[4] In $\Gamma \vdash \Delta$, the linear sentential form representation Δ on the right hand side must be of a form corresponding to some $\tau(D)$. This is the case if and only if $\Delta = \Upsilon$ or $\Delta = C\&\upsilon_0 \parr \Upsilon$, where υ_0 is a token corresponding to a terminal or non-terminal symbol, $\Upsilon = \upsilon_1 \parr \ldots \parr \upsilon_n$ is a multiplicative disjunction of tokens and $C = C_0 \& \ldots \& C_m$ is an additive conjunction of arithmetic/geometric constraints, i.e. C does not contain any tokens. Υ can also take the form $\Upsilon = \upsilon_1, \ldots, \upsilon_n$ which we consider as an alternative linear representation for the sentential form $\upsilon_1 \parr \ldots \parr \upsilon_n$.

[4] Note that subsequently we will use the terms *sentential form* and *linear representation of a sentential form* interchangeably where the intended meaning is evident from the context.

We will show that every proof that ultimately leads to a conclusion $\Gamma \vdash \Delta$, in which Δ is in this form, contains only sequents of the forms

$$\frac{}{\Gamma \vdash \Delta} \tag{4}$$

$$\frac{\Gamma_1 \vdash \Delta_1 \quad \Gamma_2 \vdash \Delta_2}{\Gamma \vdash \Delta} \tag{5}$$

in which the left hand side can be decomposed as $\Gamma = \Gamma_g, \Pi, \Sigma$ into arithmetic axioms Γ_g, the grammar rules Π and a multiset of tokens Σ and Δ is a sentential form that can be derived from Σ according to Π under the theory Γ_g. Note that we consider $\Delta = C_1 \& \ldots \& C_k$ with $\Gamma_g \vdash \Delta$ as a sentential form for an empty diagram and that the empty diagram is implicitly always contained in the language.

Throughout the proof, the left hand side Γ of any sequent can only be augmented except for the application of $(\multimap -L)$. But $(\multimap -L)$ introduces a form $\phi \multimap \psi$ into Γ which must be the representation of a grammar rule, since no other implications may ultimately exist on the left hand side. Therefore ψ must be of the form $\Sigma = \psi_1 \parr \ldots \parr \psi_m$.

This means that only axioms of the geometric theory and rules for the grammar productions or elements of the form of Σ may be introduced into Γ in any sequent for the proof to finally arrive at the form $\Gamma_g, \Pi \vdash \tau(D)$ where $\Pi = \{\tau(G), \tau(s) \circ\!\!- \mathbf{1}\}$. It follows that the left hand side of any sequent in the proof can be decomposed as $\Gamma = \Gamma_g, \Pi, \Sigma$ into arithmetic axioms Γ_g, the grammar Π and a multiset of tokens Σ.

W.l.o.g. we assume that the arithmetic/geometric theory Γ_g contains all arithmetic truths as facts, i.e. contains no implications.

According to the syntactic structure of our rules, we can only have sequents of the following types in the proof after the elimination of cuts: $(ax), (X-L), (X-R), (\&-R), (\parr-L), (\parr-R), (\multimap -L), (!-L), (W!-L), (C!-L), (\forall-L)$.

Therefore any production of form (4) is of type (ax) so that Δ is a sentential form. If the proof contains only a single sequent, it must be of the form (4). Therefore Δ is a sentential form.

If the proof contains $n+1$ sequents, the last sequent can have any of the forms $(X-L), (X-R), (\&-R), (\parr-L), (\parr-R), (\multimap -L), (!-L), (W!-L), (C!-L), (\forall-L)$

The induction is trivial for $(X-L), (X-R)$, because only the order of elements in the grammar and axiom set (sentential form, respectively) is changed. The induction is also trivial for $(!-L), (W!-L), (C!-L)$ since only axioms and grammar rules are exponential. For $(\parr-R)$ it is trivial, because we consider ϕ, ψ, Δ and $\phi \parr \psi, \Delta$ as equivalent representations of the same sentential form. Thus we need only show that the induction holds for $(\&-R), (\parr-L), (\multimap -L)$.

In the case of

$$\frac{\Gamma \vdash \phi, \Delta \quad \Gamma \vdash \psi, \Delta}{\Gamma \vdash \phi \& \psi, \Delta} \ (\&-R)$$

we can observe that either ϕ or ψ must be an arithmetic/geometric truth, because otherwise $\Gamma \vdash \phi \& \psi, \Delta$ could never reach the syntactical structure required for a sentential form. Let this be ϕ. Then ψ must either be a token or an arithmetic/geometric truth and Δ must be a sentential form. So $\tau^{-1}(\psi, \Delta)$ is a sentential form that can be derived from Σ with the grammar $\tau^{-1}(\Pi)$ and $\Gamma_g \vdash \phi$, i.e. ϕ can be derived from the arithmetic theory. Therefore $\tau^{-1}(\phi \& \psi, \Delta)$ is a sentential form that can be derived from Σ with the grammar $\tau^{-1}(\Pi)$ under the axiom set Γ_g. This proves the induction for $(\&-R)$.

The form

$$\frac{\Gamma, \phi \vdash \Delta \quad \Gamma', \phi' \vdash \Delta'}{\Gamma, \Gamma', \phi \parr \phi' \vdash \Delta, \Delta'} \ (\parr - L)$$

is explained by the concatenation of two grammars: As above, we can decompose the left hand sides into arithmetic axioms Γ_g, the grammar Π and a multiset of tokens Σ (Γ'_g, Π', Σ', respectively). Thus the grammar $\tau^{-1}(\Pi)$ allows the derivation of $\tau^{-1}(\Delta)$ from $\tau^{-1}(\Sigma)$ under Γ_g and the grammar $\tau^{-1}(\Pi')$ allows to derive $\tau^{-1}(\Delta')$ from $\tau^{-1}(\Sigma')$ under Γ'_g. We can concatenate these grammars into a grammar G and the arithmetic theories into a theory T such that G allows to derive $\tau^{-1}(\Delta') \cup \tau^{-1}(\Delta)$ from $\tau^{-1}(\Sigma') \cup \tau^{-1}(\Sigma)$ under T. This proves the induction for $(\parr - L)$.

For the case of

$$\frac{\Gamma \vdash \phi, \Delta \quad \Gamma', \phi' \vdash \Delta'}{\Gamma, \Gamma', \phi \multimap \phi' \vdash \Delta, \Delta'} \ (\multimap -L)$$

we can decompose Γ, Γ' as above.

The grammar $\tau^{-1}(\Pi)$ allows to derive $\tau^{-1}(\phi, \Delta)$ from $\tau^{-1}(\Sigma)$ under Γ_g and the grammar $\tau^{-1}(\Pi')$ allows to derive $\tau^{-1}(\Delta')$ from $\tau^{-1}(\Sigma', \phi')$ under Γ'_g. We can concatenate these grammars into a grammar G and the arithmetic theories into a theory T such that G allows to derive $\tau^{-1}(\Delta') \cup \tau^{-1}(\Delta)$ from $\tau^{-1}(\Sigma), \tau^{-1}(\Sigma')$ under T, if we add the production $\tau^{-1}(\phi) ::= \tau^{-1}(\phi')$ to G. Exactly the linear representation of this production is added to the axiom set by $(\multimap -L)$.

This concludes the proof. □

5 Related Work and Conclusions

We have demonstrated the embedding of multi-dimensional grammars into linear logic and have shown that multi-dimensional parsing can be considered as a linear proof search.

Our initial motivation for investigating such embeddings was the wish to find a theory combining a rigorous formalization of multi-dimensional parsing with a semantically adequate level of modelling. These aims have been achieved in the linear framework: The syntactic theory has been faithfully captured, while the logical level offers an adequate semantic treatment. Based on our new embedding we were additionally able to show how visual language parsers can directly be implemented as linear logic programs.

We have also argued that the linear embedding continues to be adequate in the broader context of diagrammatic reasoning where the transformation of diagram configuration is the fundamental operation. For a more thorough discussion of this aspect see [BMPP00].

Various researchers have previously formalized approaches to diagram interpretation directly in classical first-order logic, see e.g. [RM89, HM91, Mey97]. In [Haa98] description logic [WS92] is used as the formal basis, while [GC96] is based on a specialized spatial logic. Explicit embeddings for multi-dimensional grammars into first-order logic are given in [Tan91, HMO91, Mar94, MMW98, Mey00].

However, as discussed such approaches are inherently limited by the structural properties of classical first-order logic. Thus, as first suggested in our earlier paper [MM00] linear logic provides a better basis for diagram interpretation. The current paper extends this idea by giving a new embedding of multi-dimensional parsing into linear logic that is suitable for automated deduction since it uses a subset of a linear logic programming language. Furthermore, we have provided a proof of the soundness and correctness of the embedding.

Various forms of constraint-based grammars have been used in approaches to textual language parsing. Several studies, originating from the work on unification grammars [AD89], have used constraint solving for parsing. For example, Range Concatenation Grammars [Bou00] associate predicates with non terminals and use strings as arguments of these predicates. Other studies have aimed at modelling the whole task of parsing as a constraint satisfaction problem, where the state of the constraint solver at the end of the analysis is viewed as the result of the parse [Bla00]. Chart parsing has been formulated as a constraint solving process in [Mor00]. Diagram parsing as a constraint problem has been described for the first time by one of the authors in [Mey00].

A relation between Applicative Universal Grammar (AUG) and linear logic is likely to exist. In [SH99] a functional logic programming approach to AUG was described and interpretations of functional programming in intuitionistic linear logic are well known. This connection is interesting, since some principles on which AUG is based, such as the inseparability of syntax and semantics (*contensiveness*), appear to be particularly relevant in diagrammatic languages.

One of the most interesting applications of linear logic programming to computational linguistics is presented in [Hod99], where the problem of unbounded dependencies is tackled with intuitionistic linear logic elaborating on previous work by Pareschi and Miller [PM90]. One of the core ideas is to create specialized rules for managing gaps "on the fly". The connective $\&$ is used to coordinate uses of a filler in different gaps. It is interesting to note that languages with unbounded dependencies can in some sense also be considered as deviating from strict sequential order. Visual languages, of course, depart from sequential structure in a much more radical way. It is therefore not surprising that our modelling is substantially different from augmented DCG formalisms such as [Hod99]. However, a generalized mechanism of creating rules on the fly in intuitionistic linear logic may turn out to have very useful applications to the interpretation of more complex types of diagram languages, where instances of grammar rules have to be modified when applied to particular parts of a diagram. This idea could have particularly exciting applications in the coordination between text parsing and diagram parsing. As we have pointed out above, diagrams are rarely used on their own, but usually in conjunction with (explicative) texts; in this case it is obvious that the interpretation of the text should influence and direct the interpretation of the diagram. This could be achieved by augmenting the diagram grammar "on the fly" while parsing the corresponding explicative text.

We plan to investigate the integration of heterogeneous notations in which diagrams and text are used side by side in future work.

References

[AD89] H. Abramson and V. Dahl. *Logic Grammars.* Springer, 1989.

[And92] J.-M. Andreoli. Logic programming with focusing proofs in linear logic. *Journal of Logic and Computation*, 2(3), 1992.

[AP91] J.-M. Andreoli and R. Pareschi. Linear objects: Logical processes with built-in inheritance. *New Generation Computing*, 9:445–473, 1991.

[Bla00] P. Blache. Property grammars: A solution for parsing with constraints. In *6th Int. Wks. on Parsing Technologies*, pages 295–296. ITC-irst, Trento, February 2000.

[BMPP00] P. Bottoni, B. Meyer, and F. Parisi-Presicce. Visual multiset rewriting. In *Pre-proceedings of the Workshop on Multiset Processing*, pages 35–50. Centre for Discrete Mathematics and Theoretical Computer Science, Univ. of Auckland, August 2000.

[Bou00] P. Boullier. Range concatenation grammars. In *6th Int. Wks. on Parsing Technologies*, pages 53–64. ITC-irst, Trento, February 2000.

[GC96] J.M. Gooday and A.G. Cohn. Using spatial logic to describe visual programming languages. *Artificial Intelligence Review*, 10:171–186, 1996.

[Gir87] J.-Y. Girard. Linear logic. *Theoretical Computer Science*, 50:1–102, 1987.

[Gir95] J.-Y. Girard. Linear logic, its syntax and semantics. In Regnier Girard, Lafont, editor, *Advances in Linear Logic*, London Mathematical Society Lecture Notes Series 222. Cambridge University Press, 1995.

[GNC95] J. Glasgow, N.H. Narayanan, and B. Chandrasekaran, editors. *Diagrammatic Reasoning.* AAAI Press and MIT Press, 1995.

[Haa98] V. Haarslev. A fully formalized theory for describing visual notations. In K. Marriott and B. Meyer, editors, *Visual Language Theory*, pages 261–292. Springer, New York, 1998.

[HM91] R. Helm and K. Marriott. A declarative specification and semantics for visual languages. *Journal of Visual Languages and Computing*, 2:311–331, 1991.

[HMO91] R. Helm, K. Marriott, and M. Odersky. Building visual language parsers. In *ACM Conf. Human Factors in Computing*, pages 118–125, 1991.

[Hod99] J.S̃. Hodas. A linear logic treatment of phrase -structure grammars for unbounded dependencies. In *Logical Aspects of Computational Linguistics*, LNAI 1582, pages 160–179. Springer, 1999.

[HP94] J. Harland and D. Pym. A uniform proof-theoretic investigation of linear logic programming. *Journal of Logic and Computation*, 4(2):175–207, April 1994.

[HPW96] J. Harland, D. Pym, and M. Winikoff. Programming in Lygon: An overview. In *Algebraic Methodology and Software Technology*, LNCS 1101, pages 391–405. Springer, July 1996.

[Mar94] K. Marriott. Constraint multiset grammars. In *IEEE Symposium on Visual Languages*, pages 118–125. IEEE Computer Society Press, 1994.

[Mey97] B. Meyer. Formalization of visual mathematical notations. In M. Anderson, editor, *AAAI Symposium on Diagrammatic Reasoning (DR-II)*, pages 58–68, Boston/MA, November 1997. AAAI Press.

[Mey00] B. Meyer. A constraint-based framework for diagrammatic reasoning. *Applied Artificial Intelligence: An International Journal. Special Issue on Constraint Handling Rules*, 4(14):327–344, 2000.

[Mil95] D. Miller. A survey of linear logic programming. *Computational Logic*, 2(2):63–67, December 1995.

[MM97a] K. Marriott and B. Meyer. On the classification of visual languages by grammar hierarchies. *Journal of Visual Languages and Computing*, 8(4):374–402, 1997.

[MM97b] B. Meyer and K. Marriott. Specifying diagram animation with rewrite systems. In *International Workshop on Theory of Visual Languages (TVL'97)*, pages 85–96, Capri, Italy, September 1997.

[MM00] K. Marriott and B. Meyer. Non-standard logics for diagram interpretation. In *Diagrams 2000: International Conference on Theory and Application of Diagrams*, Edinburgh, Scotland, September 2000. Springer. To appear.

[MMA00] B. Meyer, K. Marriott, and G. Allwein. Intelligent diagrammatic interfaces: State of the art. In P. Olivier, M. Anderson, and B. Meyer, editors, *Diagrammatic Representation and Reasoning.* Springer, London, 2000. To appear.

[MMW98] K. Marriott, B. Meyer, and K. Wittenburg. A survey of visual language specification and recognition. In K. Marriott and B. Meyer, editors, *Visual Language Theory*, pages 5–85. Springer, New York, 1998.

[Mor00] F. Morawietz. Chart parsing as constraint propagation. In *6th Int. Wks. on Parsing Technologies*, pages 315–316. ITC-irst, Trento, February 2000.

[PM90] R. Pareschi and D. Miller. Extending definite clause grammars with scoping constructs. In *1990 International Conference in Logic Programming*, pages 373–389. MIT Press, 1990.

[PW80] F.C.N. Pereira and David H.D. Warren. Definite clause grammars for language analysis - a survey of the formalism and a comparison with augmented transition networks. *Artificial Intelligence*, 13:231–278, 1980.

[RM89] R. Reiter and A.K. Mackworth. A logical framework for depiction and image interpretation. *Artificial Intelligence*, 41:125–155, 1989.

[SH99] S. Shaumyan and P. Hudak. Linguistic, philosophical and pragmatic aspects of type-directed natural language parsing. In *Logical Aspects of Computational Linguistics*, LNAI 1582, pages 70–91. Springer, 1999.

[Tan91] T. Tanaka. Definite clause set grammars: A formalism for problem solving. *Journal of Logic Programming*, 10:1–17, 1991.

[Win96] M. Winikoff. Hitch Hiker's Guide to Lygon 0.7. Technical Report TR 96/36, University of Melbourne, Dept. of Computer Science, 1996.

[WS92] W.A. Woods and J.G. Schmolze. The KL-ONE family. In F. Lehmann, editor, *Semantic Networks in Artificial Intelligence*, pages 133–177. Pergamon Press, Oxford, 1992.

Appendix A: Linear Sequent Calculus

This appendix shows the relevant rules of the sequent calculus presented in [HP94].

$$\frac{}{\phi \vdash \phi}\ (ax) \qquad \frac{\Gamma \vdash \phi, \Delta \quad \Gamma', \phi \vdash \Delta'}{\Gamma, \Gamma' \vdash \Delta, \Delta'}\ (cut)$$

$$\frac{\Gamma, \phi, \psi, \Gamma' \vdash \Delta}{\Gamma, \psi, \phi, \Gamma' \vdash \Delta}\ (X - L) \qquad \frac{\Gamma \vdash \Delta, \phi, \psi, \Delta'}{\Gamma \vdash \Delta, \psi, \phi, \Delta'}\ (X - R)$$

$$\frac{\Gamma, \phi \vdash \Delta}{\Gamma, \psi \& \phi \vdash \Delta} \qquad \frac{\Gamma, \psi \vdash \Delta}{\Gamma, \psi \& \phi \vdash \Delta}\ (\& - L) \qquad \frac{\Gamma \vdash \phi, \Delta \quad \Gamma \vdash \psi, \Delta}{\Gamma \vdash \phi \& \psi, \Delta}\ (\& - R)$$

$$\frac{\Gamma, \phi \vdash \Delta \quad \Gamma', \psi \vdash \Delta'}{\Gamma, \Gamma', \psi ⅋ \phi \vdash \Delta, \Delta'}\ (⅋ - L) \qquad \frac{\Gamma \vdash \phi, \psi, \Delta}{\Gamma \vdash \phi ⅋ \psi, \Delta}\ (⅋ - R)$$

$$\frac{\Gamma \vdash \phi, \Delta \quad \Gamma', \psi \vdash \Delta'}{\Gamma, \Gamma', \phi \multimap \psi \vdash \Delta, \Delta'}\ (\multimap - L) \qquad \frac{\Gamma, \phi[t/x] \vdash \Delta}{\Gamma, \forall x.\phi \vdash \Delta}\ (\forall - L)$$

$$\frac{\Gamma \vdash \Delta}{\Gamma, !\phi \vdash \Delta}\ (W! - L) \qquad \frac{\Gamma, !\phi, !\phi \vdash \Delta}{\Gamma, !\phi \vdash \Delta}\ (C! - L)$$

$$\frac{\Gamma, \phi \vdash \Delta}{\Gamma, !\phi \vdash \Delta}\ (! - L) \qquad \frac{}{\vdash \mathbf{1}}\ (\mathbf{1} - R)$$

$$\frac{\Gamma, \phi \vdash \Delta \quad \Gamma, \psi \vdash \Delta}{\Gamma, \phi \oplus \psi \vdash \Delta}\ (\oplus - L) \qquad \frac{\Gamma \vdash \phi, \Delta}{\Gamma \vdash \phi \oplus \psi, \Delta} \qquad \frac{\Gamma \vdash \psi, \Delta}{\Gamma \vdash \phi \oplus \psi, \Delta}\ (\oplus - R)$$

Lambek Grammars Based on Pregroups

Wojciech Buszkowski

Faculty of Mathematics and Computer Science
Adam Mickiewicz University
Poznań Poland
buszko@amu.edu.pl

Abstract. Lambek [14] introduces pregroups as a new framework for syntactic structure. In this paper we prove some new theorems on pregroups and study grammars based on the calculus of free pregroups. We prove that these grammars are equivalent to context-free grammars. We also discuss the relation of pregroups to the Lambek calculus.

1 Introduction and Preliminaries

A pregroup is a structure $\mathcal{G} = (G, \leq, \cdot, l, r, 1)$ such that $(G, \leq, \cdot, 1)$ is a partially ordered monoid, and l, r are unary operations on G, satisfying the inequalities:

$$\text{(PRE) } a^l a \leq 1 \leq a a^l \text{ and } a a^r \leq 1 \leq a^r a,$$

for all $a \in G$. The elements a^l and a^r are called *the left adjoint* and *the right adjoint*, respectively, of a. Recall that a partially ordered (p.o.) monoid is a monoid (i.e. a semigroup with unit), satisfying the monotony conditions with respect to the partial ordering $\leq$: if $a \leq b$, then $ca \leq cb$ and $ac \leq bc$, for all elements a, b, c.

The notion of a pregroup, introduced in Lambek [14], is related to the notion of a residuated monoid, known from the theory of partially ordered algebraic systems [9]. *A residuated monoid* is a structure $\mathcal{G} = (G, \leq, \cdot, \backslash, /, 1)$ such that $(G, \leq, \cdot, 1)$ is a p.o. monoid, and $\backslash, /$ are binary operations on G, fulfilling the equivalences:

$$\text{(RES) } ab \leq c \text{ iff } b \leq a\backslash c \text{ iff } a \leq c/b,$$

for all $a, b, c \in G$. It suffices to assume that $(G, \leq)$ is a poset, and $(G, \cdot, 1)$ is a monoid, since the monotony conditions can be

derived, using (RES). Residuated monoids are most general algebraic frames for the Lambek calculus with empty antecedents: the sequents provable in this calculus express precisely the inequalities valid in all frames of that kind [4].

Now, in any pregroup one can define $a\backslash b = a^r b$ and $a/b = ab^l$, and the defined operations satisfy (RES). Accordingly, every pregroup can be expanded (by definitions) to a residuated monoid. Then, all sequents provable in the Lambek calculus with empty antecedents are valid in all pregroups. As observed by Lambek, the converse does not hold: $(a \cdot b)/c = a \cdot (b/c)$ is true in all pregroups but not all residuated monoids.

P. de Groote, G. Morrill, C. Retoré (Eds.): LACL 2001, LNAI 2099, pp. 95–109, 2001.

First examples of pregroups are partially ordered groups, i.e. structures of the form $(G, \leq, \cdot, ()^{-1}, 1)$ such that $(G, \leq, \cdot, 1)$ is a p.o. monoid, and $()^{-1}$ is a unary operation on G, satisfying $a^{-1}a = 1 = aa^{-1}$, for all $a \in G$. In a partially ordered group one defines $a^l = a^r = a^{-1}$, and inequalities (PRE) hold true. Conversely, if $a^l = a^r$, for all $a \in G$, then one can define $a^{-1} = a^l$, and the resulting structure is a partially ordered group. We say that a pregroup $\mathcal{G}$ is *proper*, if it is not a group, that means, $a^l \neq a^r$, for some $a \in G$. If $\cdot$ is commutative ($ab = ba$, for all a, b), then the pregroup is not proper (in a group, the converse element a^{-1} is uniquely determined by a). Consequently, proper pregroups must be noncommutative.

Lambek [14] provides only one natural example of a proper pregroup. It consists of all unbounded, monotone functions from the set
of integers into itself with the monoid structure defined by composition (see section 2). For $f(n) = 2n$, one obtains $f^l(n) = [(n+1)/2]$ and $f^r = [n/2]$, hence $f^l \neq f^r$; here $[x]$ denotes the greatest integer $m \leq x$. This example will be further discussed in section 2. This pregroup will be referred to as *the Lambek pregroup*.

Lambek's approach to syntactic structure is based on the notion of a free pregroup, generated by a poset $(P, \leq)$. A precise definition of this notion will be given in section 3. Roughly speaking, elements of P are treated as atomic types in categorial grammars. For $p \in P$, one forms iterated adjoints $p^{l\dots l}$, $p^{r\dots r}$. Types assigned to expressions are strings $a_1 \dots a_n$ such that $a_1, \dots, a_n$ are atomic types or iterated adjoints. If A, B are types, then $A \leq B$ holds, if this inequality can be derived by (PRE) and the presupposed ordering $\leq$ on P together with antimonotony conditions: if $A \leq B$, then $B^l \leq A^l$ and $B^r \leq A^r$, which are true in all pregroups.

Let us illustrate the matter by simple examples, after Lambek [14]. Atomic types π_1, π_2, π_3 are assigned to personal pronouns: π_1 to *I*, π_2 to *you, we ,they*, π_3 to *he, she, it.* Types s_1 and s_2 correspond to declarative sentences in the present tense and in the past tense, respectively.

Types of conjugated verb forms are as follows: *go* - types $\pi_1^r s_1$ and $\pi_2^r s_1$, *goes* - type $\pi_3^r s_1$,
went - types $\pi_k^r s_2$, for $k = 1, 2, 3$. We obtain the following parsing forms:

(1) *he goes* - $\pi_3(\pi_3^r s_1) \leq s_1$,
(2) *I went* - $\pi_1(\pi_1^r s_2) \leq s_2$.

Type i is assigned to infinitives. The auxiliary verb *do* in conjugated forms is given types $\pi_k^r s_l i^l$, for $k = 1, 2, 3$ and $l = 1, 2$, which yields:

(3) *he does go* - $\pi_3(\pi_3^r s_1 i^l)i \leq s_1$.

Adverbs (*quietly*) are of type $i^r i$. Lambek proposes to analyse conjugated forms of verbs as modifications of infinitives: *goes* as C_{31}*go*, *going* as Part*go*, *gone* as Perf*go*, where: $C_{kl} = \pi_k^r s_l i^l$, Part= $p_1 i^l$, Perf= $p_2 i^l$. Then, p_1 and p_2 are types of present participle and past participle, respectively, since $p_l i^l i \leq i$, for $l = 1, 2$. Conjugated forms of *be* can be given types $\pi_k^r s_l p_1^l$, for $k = 1, 2, 3$, $l = 1, 2$; so, *am* is of type $\pi_1^r s_1 p_1^l$. We obtain:

(4) *she goes quietly* - $\pi_3(\pi_3^r s_1 i^l)i(i^r i) \leq s_1$,
(5) *I was going quietly* - $\pi_1(\pi_1^r s_2 p_1^l)(p_1 i^l)i(i^r i) \leq s_2$.

To account for transitive verbs Lambek introduces type o of objects (also accusative forms of pronouns) and assigns types $\pi_k^r s_l o^l$, for $k = 1, 2, 3$ and $l = 1, 2$ to conjugated forms of transitive verbs.

(6) *I saw you* - $\pi_1(\pi_1^r s_2 o^l)o \leq s_2$.

Since plural forms of verbs are independent of Person, one can introduce a common type π of personal pronouns together with inequalities $\pi_k \leq \pi$, for $k = 1, 2, 3$. Then, transitive verbs in past tense can be given a common type $\pi^r s_2 o^l$, and the latter example admits another parsing:

(7) *I saw you* - $\pi_1(\pi^r s_2 o^l)o \leq \pi(\pi^r s_2 o^l)o \leq s_2$.

Modal verbs are given types: $\pi^r s_1 j^l$ for *may, can, will, shall* and $\pi^r s_2 j^l$ for *might, could, would, should.* Here, j is the type of infinitival intransitive verb phrases, and one supposes $i \leq j$.

(8) *I may go* - $\pi_1(\pi^r s_1 j^l)i \leq s_1$,
(9) *I should have loved him* - $\pi_1(\pi^r s_2 j^l)(i p_2^l)(p_2 o^l)o \leq s_2$,

Lambek uses types q_1, q_2 for interrogatives in present tense and past tense, respectively, and a common type q with postulates $q_l \leq q$.

(10) *does he go?* - $(q_1 i^l \pi_3^l)\pi_3 i \leq q_1$.

Type q' is a common type of interrogatives and wh-questions, and one stipulates $q \leq q'$.

(11) *whom does he see?* - $(q' o^{ll} q_1^l)(q_1 i^l \pi_3^l)\pi_3(i o^l) \leq q'$.

The above examples may be enough to give the reader an idea of Lambek's approach. It is interesting to compare this method with the earlier one, based on the Lambek calculus, introduced in Lambek [13]. First, we recall basic notions.

Syntactic types (shortly: types) are formed out of atomic types by means of operation symbols $\cdot$ (product), \ (left residuation) and / (right residuation). A, B, C will denote types and Γ, Δ finite (possibly empty) strings of types. *Sequents* are of the form $\Gamma \vdash A$. The calculus **L1** (the Lambek calculus with empty antecedents) admits the following axioms and inference rules:

$$\text{(Ax) } A \vdash A,$$

$$\text{(L}\cdot\text{)}\ \frac{\Gamma, A, B, \Gamma' \vdash C}{\Gamma, A \cdot B, \Gamma' \vdash C}, \quad \text{(R}\cdot\text{)}\ \frac{\Gamma \vdash A;\ \Delta \vdash B}{\Gamma, \Delta \vdash A \cdot B},$$

$$\text{(L}\backslash\text{)}\ \frac{\Gamma, B, \Gamma' \vdash C;\ \Delta \vdash A}{\Gamma, \Delta, A\backslash B, \Gamma' \vdash C}, \quad \text{(R}\backslash\text{)}\ \frac{A, \Gamma \vdash B}{\Gamma \vdash A\backslash B},$$

$$\text{(L/)}\ \frac{\Gamma, A, \Gamma' \vdash C;\ \Delta \vdash B}{\Gamma, A/B, \Delta, \Gamma' \vdash C}, \quad \text{(R/)}\ \frac{\Gamma, B \vdash A}{\Gamma \vdash A/B},$$

$$\text{(CUT)}\ \frac{\Gamma, A, \Gamma' \vdash B;\ \Delta \vdash A}{\Gamma, \Delta, \Gamma' \vdash B}.$$

The original calculus **L** (from [13]) results from restricting (R\) and (R/) to nonempty Γ. **L1** is a natural strengthening of the original calculus. As shown by Abrusci [1], **L1** is a conservative fragment of two systems of classical noncommutative linear logic: Cyclic MALL and Noncommutative MALL. Both calculi admit cut elimination, but (CUT) is necessary for axiomatic extensions of these systems. In models, $\vdash$ is interpreted by $\leq$, and $\vdash A$ is true iff $1 \leq \mu(A)$ ($\mu(A)$ is the element of the model which interprets type A).

Let R be a calculus of types. *An R-grammar* is a quadruple (V, I, s, R) such that V is a nonempty, finite lexicon (alphabet), I is a mapping which assigns a finite set of types to each word from V, and s is a distinguished atomic type. Different calculi R determine different classes of categorial grammars. **L**-grammars and **L1**-grammars are two kinds of Lambek categorial grammars. Classical categorial grammars are based on the calculus **AB**, of Ajdukiewicz [2] and Bar-Hillel [3], which admits product-free types only and can be axiomatized by (Ax), (L\) and (L/). Then, **AB** is a subsystem of **L**. One says that the R-grammar *assigns* type A to string $v_1 \ldots v_n$, for $v_i \in V$, if there exist types $A_i \in I(v_i)$, for $i = 1, \ldots, n$, such that sequent $A_1 \ldots A_n \vdash A$ is provable in R. *The language* of this grammar is defined as the set of all nonempty strings on V which are assigned type s. As shown by Pentus [15], the languages of **L**-grammars are precisely the context-free languages (not containing the empty string), and the same is true for **L1**-grammars [6] and **AB**-grammars [3].

It has been observed by Kiślak [12] that parsing examples provided in Lambek [14] can also be accomplished in **L**-grammars; precisely, in some cases one must add to **L** postulates $A \vdash B$, for some atomic A, B. Actually, the types assigned by Lambek are translations of syntactic types according to the rules: $A\backslash B = A^r B$, $A/B = AB^l$, using equalities $(AB)^l = B^l A^l$ and $(AB)^r = B^r A^r$, which are valid in pregroups (see section 2). For (1)-(11), we obtain the following sequents, derivable in **L** ((1)-(10) are even derivable in **AB**!).

(1') $\pi_3, \pi_3\backslash s_1 \vdash s_1$,
(2') $\pi_1, \pi_1\backslash s_2 \vdash s_2$,
(3') $\pi_3, (\pi_3\backslash s_1)/i, i \vdash s_1$,
(4') $\pi_3, (\pi_3\backslash s_1)/i, i, i\backslash i \vdash s_1$,
(5') $\pi_1, (\pi_1\backslash s_2)/p_1, p_1/i, i, i\backslash i \vdash s_2$,
(6') $\pi_1, (\pi_1\backslash s_2)/o, o \vdash s_2$,
(7') $\pi_1, (\pi\backslash s_2)/o, o \vdash s_2$ assuming $\pi_1 \vdash \pi$,
(8') $\pi_1, (\pi\backslash s_1)/j, i \vdash s_1$ assuming $i \vdash j$,
(9') $\pi_1, (\pi\backslash s_2)/j, i/p_2, p_2/o, o \vdash s_2$ under assumptions from (7'), (8'),
(10') $(q_1/i)/\pi_3, \pi_3, i \vdash q_1$,
(11') $q'/(q_1/o), (q_1/i)/\pi_3, \pi_3, i/o \vdash q'$.

This observation might suggest that **L1** is equivalent to the calculus of pregroups for sequents $A_1 \ldots A_n \vdash A$ such that $A_1, \ldots, A_n$ are product-free and A is atomic. This conjecture is false. The sequent $(p/((p/p)/p))/p \vdash p$ with p

atomic, is not provable in **L1** (use cut-free derivations and the fact that $\vdash p$ is not provable), but its translation $pp^{ll}p^{ll}p^{l}p^{l} \leq p$ is valid in pregroups. In section 3, we show that the calculus of pregroups is equivalent to **AB**, hence also to **L** and **L1**, for sequents $A_1, \ldots, A_n \vdash A$ such that $A_1, \ldots, A_n$ are product-free types of order not greater than 1 and A is atomic. Recall that *the order* of a product-free type A ($o(A)$) is defined as follows: (i) $o(A) = 0$, for atomic A, (ii) $o(A/B) = o(B\backslash A) = \max(o(A), o(B)+1)$ (see [7]). Sequents (1')-(10') are of that form, whereas in (11') the left-most type is of order 2. Yet, the latter sequent is provable in **L**. This leads us to the open question: are there any 'linguistic constructions' which can be parsed by means of pregroups but

not the Lambek calculus? In other words: do any syntactic structures in natural language require types of order greater than 1 such that the resulting sequents are valid in pregroups but not provable in **L1**? Evidently, this problem cannot be solved by purely mathematical methods.

We briefly describe further contents. In section 2, we prove some theorems on pregroups. In particular, we prove: (i) no totally ordered pregroup is

proper, (ii) no finite pregroup is proper, (iii) every pregroup of all unbounded, monotone functions on a totally ordered set $(P, \leq)$, P infinite, is isomorphic to the Lambek pregroup. In section 3, we define grammars based on the calculus of free pregroups and prove that the languages of these grammars are precisely the context-free languages. It is noteworthy that this proof is easier than the proofs of analogous theorems for **L** and **L1** as well as the nonassociative Lambek calculus [5,11]. In general, pregroups are definitely easier to handle than residuated semigroups and monoids. On the other hand, the latter are abundant in natural language models, which is not the case for the former. One cannot define a pregroup structure on the powerset of a free monoid or the family of all binary relations on a set, which are typical examples of residuated monoids, significant for linguistic and logical applications.

2 Pregroups

The aim of this section is to throw more light on the notion of a pregroup by establishing some basic properties of these structures. We are motivated by Lambek's confession that he does not know any 'natural model' except for the pregroup of unbounded, monotone functions on the set of integers (and p.o. groups, of course). Our results can help to understand the reasons.

Many properties of pregroups, mentioned in this section, are variants of well-known properties of other partially ordered algebraic systems or poset variants of standard category-theoretic facts (e.g. propositions 1 and 2, lemmas 2 and 3). They are included here for the completeness of exposition.

The following conditions are valid in pregroups:

$$1^l = 1 = 1^r,\ a^{lr} = a = a^{rl},\ (ab)^l = b^l a^l,\ (ab)^r = b^r a^r,$$

$$aa^l a = a,\ aa^r a = a,\ \text{if } a \leq b \text{ then } b^l \leq a^l \text{ and } b^r \leq a^r.$$

Proofs are elementary. We consider one case. By (PRE),

$$a \leq a^{lr}a^{l}a \leq a^{lr} \text{ and } a^{lr} \leq aa^{l}a^{lr} \leq a,$$

which yields $a^{lr} = a$. One can also use:

Proposition 1 *In any p.o. monoid, for every element a, there exists at most one element b such that $ba \leq 1 \leq ab$, and there exists at most one element c such that $ac \leq 1 \leq ca$.*

PROOF. If $ba \leq 1 \leq ab$ and $b'a \leq 1 \leq ab'$, then $b \leq bab' \leq b'$ and $b' \leq b'ab \leq b$, hence $b = b'$. □

Let $(P, \leq)$ be a poset. A function $f : P \mapsto P$ is said to be *monotone*, if $x \leq y$ entails $f(x) \leq f(y)$. For functions f, g, one defines $(f \circ g)(x) = f(g(x))$, and $f \leq g$ iff, for all $x \in P$, $f(x) \leq g(x)$. I denotes the identity function: $I(x) = x$. The set $M(P)$, of all monotone functions from P into P with $\leq$, $\circ$ and I is a p.o. monoid. A pregroup is called *a pregroup of functions*, if it is a substructure (as a p.o. monoid) of the p.o. monoid $M(P)$, for some poset $(P, \leq)$.

Proposition 2 *Every pregroup is isomorphic to a pregroup of functions.*

PROOF. Let $(G, \leq, \cdot, l, r, 1)$ be a pregroup. We consider the poset $(G, \leq)$. For $a \in G$, we define $f_a(x) = ax$. Clearly, f_a is a monotone function from G into G. Further, $f_{ab} = f_a \circ f_b$, $f_1 = I$, and $a \leq b$ iff $f_a \leq f_b$. Then, the mapping $h(a) = f_a$ is an isomorphic embedding of $(G, \leq, \cdot, 1)$ into $M(G)$. We define adjoints: $f_a^l = f_{a^l}$ and $f_a^r = f_{a^r}$. Then, (PRE) hold, and h is the required isomorphism. □

The above proposition does not pretend to originality, since it exploits a routine representation of monoids in monoids of functions. However, for pregroups this representation seems to be quite useful. The next proposition establishes nice characterizations of adjoints in pregroups of functions.

Proposition 3 *Let F be a pregroup of functions on a poset $(P, \leq)$. For every $f \in F$, the following equalities are true:*

$$f^l(x) = min\{y \in P : x \leq f(y)\}, \text{ for all } x \in P,$$

$$f^r(x) = max\{y \in P : f(y) \leq x\}, \text{ for all } x \in P.$$

PROOF. Since $f^l(f(x)) \leq x \leq f(f^l(x))$, for all x, then $f^l(x)$ belongs to the set of all y such that $x \leq f(y)$. Let z also belong to this set. Then, $x \leq f(z)$, and consequently, $f^l(x) \leq f^l(f(z)) \leq z$. This proves the first equality. The second one is dual. □

Conversely, if F is a substructure of $M(P)$, and for every $f \in F$, the functions f^l, f^r, defined above, exist and belong to F, then F is a pregroup of functions. For $f^l(f(x))$ =min$\{y : f(x) \leq f(y)\} \leq x$ and $x \leq f(f^l(x))$. The second part of (PRE) can be proved in a similar way.

Corollary 1 *If F is a pregroup of functions on a poset $(P, \leq)$, then all functions in F are unbounded, that is: $\forall x \exists y (x \leq f(y))$ and $\forall x \exists y (f(y) \leq x)$.*

PROOF. The sets on the right hand side of equalities from proposition 3 must be nonempty. □

Accordingly, pregroups of functions must consist of unbounded, monotone functions on a poset. The Lambek pregroup F_L consists of all unbounded, monotone functions on $(\mathbf{Z}, \leq)$, where $(\mathbf{Z}, \leq)$ is the set of integers with the natural ordering. Since the composition of two unbounded functions is unbounded, then the Lambek pregroup is a substructure of $M(\mathbf{Z})$, hence it is a p.o. monoid. For every $f \in F_L$, functions f^l, f^r, defined (!) as in proposition 3, exist and are monotone. We show that f^l is unbounded. Since $f^l(f(x)) \leq x$, then f^l is unbounded in the negative direction. If f^l were bounded in the positive direction, then $f \circ f^l$ would also be bounded, against $x \leq f(f^l(x))$. For f^r, the reasoning is dual. Consequently, $f^l, f^r \in F_L$, hence F_L is a pregroup. For $f(x) = 2x$, one obtains:

$$f^l(x) = \min\{y : x \leq 2y\} = [(x+1)/2],\ f^r(x) = \max\{y : 2y \leq x\} = [x/2];$$

which yields $f^l \neq f^r$. Thus, the Lambek pregroup is proper.

Lemma 1 *Let F be a pregroup of functions on a poset $(P, \leq)$, and let a be the first or the last element of $(P, \leq)$. Then, for all $f \in F$ and $x \in P$, $f(x) = a$ iff $x = a$.*

PROOF. We only consider the case that a is the first element. Let $f \in F$. Since f is unbounded, then $f(y) = a$, for some $y \in P$, and consequently, $f(a) = a$, by monotony. Assume $f(x) = a$. Then, $f^r(a) \geq x$, by proposition 3, hence $x = a$ due to the fact $f^r(a) = a$. □

We prove that the Lambek pregroup is (up to isomorphism) the only pregroup of all unbounded, monotone functions on an infinite, totally ordered set.

Theorem 1 *Let $(P, \leq)$ be a totally ordered set of cardinality greater than 2 such that the family of all unbounded, monotone functions on $(P, \leq)$ is a pregroup. Then, $(P, \leq)$ is isomorphic to $(\mathbf{Z}, \leq)$.*

PROOF. First, we show that $(P, \leq)$ has no endpoints. Suppose a to be the first element of $(P, \leq)$. By the cardinality assumption, there exist $b, c \in P$ such that $a < b < c$. We define $f(x) = a$, for all $x \leq b$, $f(x) = x$, for all $x > b$. Clearly, f is monotone and unbounded, which contradicts lemma 1, since $f(b) = a$, $b \neq a$. If a is the last element, the reasoning is similar.

Consequently, P is infinite. It suffices to show that, for all $a, b \in P$, if $a < b$, then $\{x \in P : a < x < b\}$ is a finite set. Suppose this set to be infinite, for some $a < b$. We consider two cases.

(I) $\{x : a < x < b\}$ is well-ordered by $\leq$. Then, there exists an infinite chain (x_n) such that $a < x_n < b$ and $x_n < x_{n+1}$, for all $n \geq 0$. We define a function

$f : P \mapsto P$ by setting: $f(x) = x$, if $x < a$ or $x > x_n$, for all $n \geq 0$, and $f(x) = a$, otherwise. Clearly, f is unbounded and monotone. On the other hand, $\{y : f(y) \leq a\}$ is cofinal with (x_n), hence it contains no maximal element. Then, $f^r(a)$ does not exist, which contradicts the assumptions of the theorem.

(II) $\{x : a < x < b\}$ is not well-ordered by $\leq$. Then, there exists an infinite chain (x_n) such that $a < x_n < b$ and $x_{n+1} < x_n$, for all $n \geq 0$. We define a function $f : P \mapsto P$ by setting: $f(x) = x$, if $x > b$ or $x < x_n$, for all $n \geq 0$, and $f(x) = b$, otherwise. Again, f is unbounded and monotone. The set $\{y : b \leq f(y)\}$ is cofinal with (x_n), hence it contains no minimal element. Then, $f^l(b)$ does not exist. □

Pregroups are closed under direct products. Thus, from the Lambek pregroup one can construct other proper pregroups. The simplest one is $F_L \times F_L$. It is easy to see that $F_L \times F_L$ is isomorphic to the following pregroup of functions on a totally ordered set. This set is the union $Z_1 \cup Z_2$ of two copies of $\mathbf{Z}$ with the natural ordering on Z_1 and Z_2 and, additionally, $x < y$, for all $x \in Z_1, y \in Z_2$. $F_L \times F_L$ can be represented as the family of all functions on this poset whose restrictions to Z_i are unbounded and monotone mappings on Z_i, for $i = 1, 2$. Clearly, this new pregroup consists of some but not all unbounded, monotone mappings from $Z_1 \cup Z_2$ into itself. Other interesting pregroups are countable substructures of the Lambek pregroup (not considered here).

Lemma 2 *For every element a of a pregroup, the following conditions are equivalent: (i) $a^l \leq a^r$, (ii) $aa^l = 1$, (iii) $aa^r = 1$.*

Lemma 3 *For every element a of a pregroup, the following conditions are equivalent: (i) $a^r \leq a^l$, (ii) $a^l a = 1$, (iii) $a^r a = 1$.*

PROOF. We only prove lemma 2. Assume (i). Then, $1 \leq aa^l \leq aa^r \leq 1$, hence (ii) and (iii) hold. Assume (ii). Then, $a^r = a^r aa^l \geq a^l$, hence (i) holds. (iii) entails (i), by a similar argument. □

An element a fulfilling conditions of lemma 2 (resp. lemma 3) is called *surjective* (resp. *injective*); it is called *bijective* if $a^l = a^r$. In pregroups of functions, f is surjective (resp. injective) in the sense of pregroups iff f is surjective (resp. injective) as a mapping. For assume $f \circ f^l = I$. Then, $f \circ f^l$ is a surjective mapping, hence f must be a surjective mapping. Assume f be a surjective mapping. Then, $f \circ f^l \circ f = f$ yields $(f \circ f^l)(f(x)) = f(x)$, for all x, and consequently, $f \circ f^l = I$. The second claim is proved in a similar way. Consequently, a pregroup of functions is proper iff not all functions in it are bijective mappings. We have got another form of evidence that the Lambek pregroup is proper.

Using the above observations and proposition 2, one obtains the following facts, true for every pregroup: (1) if ab is injective, then b is injective, (2) if ab is surjective, then a is surjective, (3) if a is injective (resp. surjective), then a^l and a^r are surjective (resp. injective).

Lemma 4 *If every element of a pregroup is injective or surjective, then every element*
of this pregroup is bijective.

PROOF. Assume the antecedent. Suppose a to be not injective. Then, $a^l a$ is not injective, by (1), hence $a^l a$ is surjective, and consequently, a^l is surjective, by (2). Then, a is injective, by (3). Accordingly, all elements are injective. By (3), all elements are surjective. □

Theorem 2 *No totally ordered pregroup is proper.*

PROOF. In a totally ordered pregroup, $a^l \leq a^r$ or $a^r \leq a^l$, for all elements a. Use lemma 4. □

Theorem 3 *No finite pregroup is proper.*

PROOF. We prove more: if $(G, \leq, \cdot, l, r, 1)$ is a finite pregroup, then $\leq$ is the identity relation, and consequently, this pregroup must be a group. It is known that there are no finite p.o. groups with a nontrivial ordering [9], but the proof for pregroups is different.

In pregroups, $aa^r b \leq b$ and $ba^r a \geq b$. Consequently, for all a, b, there exist x, y such that $ax \leq b$ and $ya \geq b$. Now, let a be a minimal and b be a maximal element of $(G, \leq)$. There exists x such that $bx \leq a$, hence there exists a minimal element x such that $bx = a$. Let $x_1, \ldots, x_n$ be all minimal elements. Then, the set $\{bx_1, \ldots, bx_n\}$ must contain all elements $x_1, \ldots, x_n$, hence this set equals $\{x_1, \ldots, x_n\}$. As a consequence, bx is minimal, for every minimal element x. A dual argument yields: if x is minimal, and y is maximal, then yx is maximal. Since b is maximal, then all elements bx_i are maximal. Accordingly, all minimal elements are maximal, which proves the theorem. □

Finally, we show that there exist no proper pregroups of functions on a dense, totally ordered set, as e.g. the set of real numbers or the set of rational numbers. First, we observe that every pregroup of functions on a totally ordered set must consist of continuous functions only. The function $f : P \mapsto P$ is *continuous*, if it satisfies the conditions: (i) if $x = \sup\{y : y < x\}$, then $f(x) = \sup\{f(y) : y < x\}$, (ii) if $x = \inf\{y : y > x\}$, then $f(x) = \inf\{f(y) : y > x\}$. Assume f to be not continuous. Let $x \in P$ be such that it does not fulfil (i). Since f is monotone, then $f(x)$ is an upper bound of $\{f(y) : y < x\}$. Since $f(x)$ is not the least upper bound, then there exists another upper bound $z < f(x)$. Yet, $f^r(z) = \max\{y : f(y) \leq z\} = \max\{y : y < x\}$ does not exist. If x does not fulfil (ii), the reasoning is similar.

Let $(P, \leq)$ be a dense, totally ordered set. Let F be a pregroup of functions on $(P, \leq)$. We show that all functions in F are injective; so, they are also bijective, by lemma 4. Suppose $f \in F$ to be not injective. Then, there are $x, y \in P$ such that $x < y$ and $f(x) = f(y)$. Set $a = f(x)$. By lemma 1, a is not an endpoint of

P. Since P is dense, $a = \sup\{z : z < a\}$. We have $f^r(a) \geq y$, but $f^r(z) < x$, for all $z < a$.

Consequently, f^r is not continuous, which contradicts the above paragraph.

In a forthcoming paper [8], other representations of pregroups are discussed. Representations in monoids of relations (with composition and inclusion) are shown to be reducible to pregroups of functions on a poset. There exist no proper pregroups of functions on a tree. We also discuss left and right pregroups; they are defined as pregroups with dropping right (left) adjoints. Theorems 2 and 3 remain true for left (right) pregroups, but theorem 1 does not. Also, there exist proper left (not right!) pregroups of functions on infinite trees (the root is treated as the least element of the tree).

3 Free Pregroups and Grammars

For any element a of a pregroup, one defines an element $a^{(n)}$, for $n \in \mathbf{Z}$: $a^{(0)} = a$, $a^{(n+1)} = (a^n)^r$, for $n \geq 0$, $a^{(n-1)} = (a^{(n)})^l$, for $n \leq 0$. Then, the equalities $a^{(n+1)} = (a^{(n)})^r$ and $a^{(n-1)} = (a^n)^l$ hold true, for all $n \in \mathbf{Z}$. As a consequence of (PRE) and antimonotony conditions, we obtain:

$$a^{(n)}a^{(n+1)} \leq 1 \leq a^{(n+1)}a^{(n)}, \text{ for all } n \in \mathbf{Z}.$$

$$\text{if } a \leq b \text{ then } a^{(2n)} \leq b^{(2n)} \text{ and } b^{(2n+1)} \leq a^{(2n+1)}, \text{ for all } n \in \mathbf{Z}.$$

This motivates the construction of a free pregroup, due to Lambek [14]. Let $(P, \leq)$ be a poset. Elements of P are treated as constant symbols. *Terms* are expressions $a^{(n)}$, for $a \in P$, $n \in \mathbf{Z}$; $a^{(0)}$ is identified with a. *Types* are finite strings of terms.

Quasi-pregroups are defined as pregroups except that $\leq$ need not be antisymmetrical, that means, $\leq$ is a quasi-ordering. If $\leq$ is a quasi-ordering on X, then one defines $x \sim y$ iff $x \leq y$ and $y \leq x$, for $x, y \in X$. Then, $\sim$ is an equivalence relation, and the quotient relation $[x] \leq [y]$ iff $x \leq y$ is a partial ordering on the quotient set $X/\sim$. If $(G, \leq, \cdot, l, r, 1)$ is a quasi-pregroup, then $\sim$ is a congruence on this structure (use monotony conditions for $\cdot$ and antimonotony conditions for l, r). We can construct the quotient-structure on $G/\sim$, by setting: $[x] \cdot [y] = [xy]$, $[x]^l = [x^l]$, $[x]^r = [x^r]$, for $x \in G$. The quotient-structure is a pregroup whose unit element equals $[1]$.

First, we define a quasi-pregroup whose elements are types. For types x, y, $x \cdot y$ is the concatenation of strings x, y, and 1 is the empty string. The adjoints are defined as follows:

$$(a_1^{(n_1)} \ldots a_k^{(n_k)})^l = a_k^{(n_k-1)} \ldots a_1^{(n_1-1)}, \; (a_1^{(n_1)} \ldots a_k^{(n_k)})^r = a_k^{(n_k+1)} \ldots a_1^{(n_1+1)},$$

The quasi-ordering $\leq$ is the reflexive and transitive closure of the relation defined by the following clauses:

(CON) $xa^{(n)}a^{(n+1)}y \leq xy$ (contraction),
(EXP) $xy \leq xa^{(n+1)}a^{(n)}y$ (expansion),

(IND) $xa^{(2n)}y \leq xb^{(2n)}y$ and $xb^{(2n+1)}y \leq xa^{(2n+1)}y$ if $a \leq b$ in P (induced steps),

for all types x, y, $n \in \mathbf{Z}$, and $a, b \in P$,

It is easy to check that this structure is a quasi-pregroup. It is not a pregroup, since $aa^{(1)}a \sim a$ but $aa^{(1)}a \neq a$. The quotient-structure, defined as above, is a pregroup. It is called *the free pregroup* generated by $(P, \leq)$ and denoted $F((P, \leq))$ or $F(P)$, for short.

In what follows, we are mainly concerned with inequalities $x \leq y$ which hold in the quasi-pregroup underlying $F(P)$. Following Lambek, we distinguish two special cases:

(GCON) $xa^{(n)}b^{(n+1)}y \leq xy$ if either n is even and $a \leq b$ in P, or n is odd and $b \leq a$ in P (generalized contraction),
(GEXP) $xy \leq xa^{(n+1)}b^{(n)}y$ if either n is even and $a \leq b$ in P, or n is odd and $b \leq a$ in P (generalized expansion).

Clearly, (GCON) can be obtained as (IND) followed by (CON), and (GEXP) as

(EXP) followed by (IND). Clearly, (CON) and (EXP) are special cases of (GCON) and (GEXP), respectively. Thus, if $x \leq y$ in the quasi-pregroup, then there exists a derivation $x = x_0 \leq x_1 \leq \ldots \leq x_m = y$, $m \geq 0$ such that $x_k \leq x_{k+1}$ is (GEXP), (GCON) or (IND), for all $0 \leq k < m$. The number m is called *the length* of this derivation.

Lemma 5 *(Lambek switching lemma) If $x \leq y$ has a derivation of length m, then there exist types z, z' such that $x \leq z$ by generalized contractions or $x = z$, $z \leq z'$ by induced steps or $z = z'$, and $z' \leq y$ by generalized expansions or $z' = y$, and the sum of lengths of these three derivations is not greater than m.*

PROOF. ([14]) The key observation is that two adjacent steps of the form (IND)-(GCON) or (GEXP)-(IND) can be interchanged, if the relevant terms do not overlap, and reduced to a single (GCON) or (GEXP), otherwise; also, two adjacent steps of the form (GEXP)-(GCON) can be interchanged, if the relevant terms do not overlap, and reduced to a single induced step, otherwise. Let us demonstrate the latter reduction. There are two possibilities.

(I) $va^{(n)}w \leq va^{(n)}b^{(n+1)}c^{(n)}w \leq vc^{(n)}w$, by (GEXP) and (GCON). Assume n to be even. Then, $b \leq c$ and $a \leq b$, which yields $a \leq c$. Clearly, $va^{(n)}w \leq vc^{(n)}w$ is an induced step. Assume n to be odd. Then, $c \leq b$ and $b \leq a$, which yields $c \leq a$. Again, these two steps can be reduced to a single induced step.

(II) $vc^{(n+1)}w \leq va^{(n+1)}b^{(n)}c^{(n+1)}w \leq va^{(n+1)}w$, by (GEXP) and (GCON). Assume n to be even. Then, $a \leq b$ and $b \leq c$, hence $a \leq c$, and we reason as above. Assume n to be odd. Then, $b \leq a$ and $c \leq b$, hence $c \leq a$, and we reason as above.

Now, the lemma can easily be proved by induction on m. In the initial derivation of length m one moves all generalized contractions to the left. If the move is blocked, then the derivation can be replaced by a shorter one, and we apply the induction hypothesis. Next, one moves all generalized expansions to the right.

□

It follows from the lemma that if $x \leq t$ holds in the quasi-pregroup, and t is a term, then there is a derivation of $x \leq t$ which does not apply (GEXP). Consequently, inequalities $x \leq t$ can be derived by (CON) and (IND) only.

Let $(P, \leq)$ be a finite poset. *A pregroup grammar* based on this poset is defined as a triple (V, I, s) such that V is a finite lexicon (alphabet), I is a mapping which assigns a finite set of types (in the sense of this section) to every $v \in V$, and $s \in P$. We say that this grammar assigns a type x to a string $v_1 \dots v_n$, $v_i \in V$, if there exist types $x_i \in I(v_i)$, $i = 1, \dots, n$, such that $x_1 \dots x_n \leq x$ in the quasi-pregroup underlying $F(P)$. *The language* of this grammar consists of all nonempty strings on V which are assigned type s. Evidently, these notions are analogous to basic notions for categorial grammars (see section 1).

As a consequence of lemma 5, we show that the language of each pregroup grammar must be a context-free language. Fix a pregroup grammar (V, I, s) based on a finite poset $(P, \leq)$. Let X denote the set of all terms appearing in types assigned by I to words from V. We define:

$$p = \max\{n \geq 0 : (\exists a \in P)(a^{(n)} \in X \vee a^{(-n)} \in X)\}.$$

By N we denote the set of all terms $a^{(n)}$ such that $a \in P$ and $-p \leq n \leq p$. We show that the set L of all types $t_1 \dots t_n$ such that $n > 0$, $t_i \in N$, for $i = 1, \dots, n$, and $t_1 \dots t_n \leq s$ in the quasi-pregroup underlying $F(P)$ is a context-free language. The context-free grammar which generates L is defined as follows. Both terminal and nonterminal symbols are all terms from N. By lemma 5, $t_1 \dots t_n \leq s$ iff it can be derived by (CON) and (IND) only. Clearly, if $t_1, \dots, t_n \in N$, then all terms in such a derivation are elements of N. Accordingly, production rules of the context-free grammar are of the following form: (i) all rules $t \to tuv$ such that $t, u, v \in N$ and $tuv \leq t$ is a contraction, (ii) all rules $t \to uvt$ such that $t, u, v \in N$ and $uvt \leq t$ is a contraction, (iii) all rules $t \to u$ such that $t, u \in N$ and $u \leq t$ is an induced step.

For any $v \in V$ and any $x \in I(v)$, we create a new symbol v_x. Let V' denote the set of all new symbols. We define a homomorphism f from V' into the set of types, by setting: $f(v_x) = x$. The coimage of L under f is the set:

$$f^{-1}[L] = \{v^1_{x_1} \dots v^n_{x_n} : n > 0,\ x_1 \dots x_n \in L\}.$$

Since context-free languages are closed under homomorphic coimages [10], then $f^{-1}[L]$ is a context-free language. We define a homomorphism g from V' into the set of strings on V, by setting: $g(v_x) = v$. Clearly, the language of the pregroup grammar (V, I, s) equals $g[f^{-1}[L]]$. Since context-free languages are also closed under homomorphic images, then the latter language is context-free.

We also prove the converse: every context-free language, not containing the empty string, is the language of some pregroup grammar. We use the classical theorem of Gaifman [3]: every context-free language, not containing the empty string, is the language of an **AB**-grammar whose mapping I uses types of the form p, p/q, $(p/q)/r$ only, where p, q, r are atomic types. These types are of order not greater than 1.

Lemma 6 *Let $A_1, \ldots, A_n \vdash p$ be a sequent such that p is atomic, and $o(A_i) \leq 1$, for all $1 \leq i \leq n$. Then, this sequent is derivable in* **AB** *iff it is derivable in* **L1**.

PROOF. One direction is straightforward, since **AB** is a subsystem of **L1**. We prove the converse direction. Assume the sequent is derivable in **L1**. Then, it has a cut-free derivation in **L1**. By induction on the height of this derivation, we show that it is derivable in **AB**. If it is the axiom $p \vdash p$, the thesis is true. Otherwise, it must be a conclusion of (L\) or (L/). In both cases, the premises are sequents $\Gamma \vdash q$ such that q is atomic and all types in Γ are of order not greater than 1; Γ cannot be empty, since $\vdash q$ has no derivation. By the induction hypothesis, both premises are derivable in **AB**. Since **AB** admits (L\) and (L/), then the conclusion is derivable in **AB**. □

For every product-free type A, we define a pregroup type $T(A)$, by the following recursion: $T(p) = p$, $T(A\backslash B) = T(A)^r T(B)$, $T(A/B) = T(A)T(B)^l$. Here, we identify atomic types with members of P.

Lemma 7 *Under the assumptions of lemma 6, $A_1 \ldots A_n \vdash p$ is derivable in* **AB** *iff $T(A_1) \ldots T(A_n) \leq p$ has a derivation in the sense of free pregroups, by contractions only.*

PROOF. It is well know that $\Gamma \vdash p$ is derivable in **AB** iff Γ can be reduced to p by a finite number of Ajdukiewicz contractions $A, A\backslash B \to B$ and $A/B, B \to A$. By (CON), we derive $T(A)T(A\backslash B) \leq T(B)$ and $T(A/B)T(B) \leq T(A)$. Consequently, the implication ($\Rightarrow$) holds true.

The converse implication is proved by induction on n. Let $n = 1$. Assume $T(A_1) \leq p$ to be derivable in free pregroups by contractions. It is easy to see that, if $o(A) \leq 1$, then $T(A)$ is of the form $q_k^r \ldots q_1^r p r_1^l \ldots r_m^l$, for $k, m \geq 0$ and p, q_i, r_j atomic. Clearly, no contraction can be executed within $T(A)$. So, $T(A_1) \leq p$ must be the trivial case $T(A_1) = A_1 = p$, and $p \vdash p$ is derivable in **AB**. Let $n > 0$. Assume $T(A_1) \ldots T(A_n) \leq p$ to be derivable in free pregroups by contractions. Consider the first contraction. By the above observation, this contraction cannot be executed

within some $T(A_i)$. So, for some $0 \leq i < n$, the relevant terms must be the right-most term of $T(A_i)$ and the left-most term of $T(A_{i+1})$. Assume this contraction is $r^l r \leq 1$. Then, $T(A_i) = q_k^r \ldots q_1^r p r_1^l \ldots r_m^l r^l$ and $T(A_{i+1}) = r s_1^l \ldots s_j^l$. We can represent A_i and A_{i+1} as:

$$A_i = q_k\backslash \cdots \backslash q_1\backslash p/r_1/ \cdots /r_m/r,$$

$$A_{i+1} = r/s_1/ \cdots /s_j.$$

In A_{i+1} parentheses are associated to the left, and in A_i they are associated to the middle p in any way, since the laws:

$$(A\backslash B)/C \vdash A\backslash(B/C),\ A\backslash(B/C) \vdash (A\backslash B)/C$$

are derivable in **L1**. We construct the type:

$$B = q_k\backslash \cdots \backslash q_1\backslash p/r_1/\cdots/r_m/s_1/\cdots/s_j.$$

Now, $T(B)$ results from $T(A_i)T(A_{i+1})$ by the contraction, and $A_iA_{i+1} \vdash B$ is derivable in **L1**. The inequality:

$$T(A_1)\dots T(A_{i-1})T(B)T(A_{i+2})\dots T(A_n) \leq p$$

is derivable by contractions in free pregroups, hence the sequent:

$$A_1 \dots A_{i-1}, B, A_{i+2} \dots A_n \vdash p$$

is derivable in **AB**, by the induction hypothesis. Consequently, the sequent $A_1 \dots A_n \vdash p$ (i.e. our starting sequent) is derivable in **L1**, hence also in **AB**, by lemma 6. If the first contraction is $qq^r \leq 1$, then the reasoning is similar. □

Let L be a context-free language, not containing the empty string. By the Gaifman theorem, there is an **AB**-grammar (V, I, s), using types of order not greater than 1, which generates this language. We consider the poset $(P, =)$ such that P is the set of atomic types used by this grammar. We define a pregroup grammar (V, I', s) based on this poset, by setting $I'(v) = \{T(A) : A \in I(v)\}$. Now, $v_1 \dots v_n \in L$ iff there exist types $A_i \in I(v_i)$, for $i = 1, \dots, n$, such that $A_1 \dots A_n \vdash s$ is derivable in **AB** iff there exist pregroup types $T(A_i) \in I'(v_i)$ such that $T(A_1)\dots T(A_n) \leq s$ in free pregroups (lemmas 5, 7) iff $v_1 \dots v_n$ belongs to the language of (V, I', s). Consequently, L equals the language of the pregroup grammar. We have proved the following theorem.

Theorem 4 *The languages of pregroup grammars are precisely the context-free languages, not containing the empty string.*

An analogous theorem can be proved for grammars based on free left (right) pregroups [8].

References

1. V.M. Abrusci, Lambek Calculus, Cyclic Multiplicative-Additive Linear Logic, Noncommutative Multiplicative-Additive Linear Logic: language and sequent calculus, in: V.M. Abrusci and C. Casadio (eds.), *Proofs and Linguistic Categories*, Proc. 1996 Roma Workshop, Bologna, 1996, 21-48.
2. K. Ajdukiewicz, Die syntaktische Konnexität, *Studia Philosophica* 1 (1935), 1-27.
3. Y. Bar-Hillel, C. Gaifman and E. Shamir, On categorial and phrase structure grammars, *Bull. Res. Council Israel* F 9 (1960), 155-166.
4. W. Buszkowski, Completeness results for Lambek Syntactic Calculus, *Zeitschrift für mathematische Logik und Grundlagen der Mathematik* 32 (1986), 13-28.
5. W. Buszkowski, Generative capacity of nonassociative Lambek calculus, *Bull. Polish Academy Scie. Math.* 34 (1986), 507-516.

6. W. Buszkowski, Extending Lambek grammars to basic categorial grammars, *Journal of Logic, Language and Information* 5 (1996), 279-295.
7. W. Buszkowski, Mathematical linguistics and proof theory, in: J. van Benthem and A. ter Meulen (eds.), *Handbook of Logic and Language*, Elsevier, Amsterdam, MIT Press, Cambridge Mass., 1997, 683-736.
8. W. Buszkowski, Pregroups and grammars, *Proc. 6th Roma Workshop*, to appear.
9. L. Fuchs, *Partially Ordered Algebraic Systems*, Pergamon Press, Oxford, 1963.
10. S. Ginsburg, *The Mathematical Theory of Context-Free Languages*, McGraw-Hill, New York, 1966.
11. M. Kandulski, The equivalence of nonassociative Lambek categorial grammars and context-free grammars, *Zeitschrift für mathematische Logik und Grundlagen der Mathematik* 34 (1988), 41-52.
12. A. Kiślak, Parsing based on pre-groups. Comments on the new Lambek theory of syntactic structure, in: Y. Hamamatsu, W. Kosiński, L. Polkowski, M. Toho and T. Yonekura (eds.), *Formal Methods and Intelligent Techniques in Control, Decision Making, Multimedia, and Robotics*, Polish-Japanese Institute of Information Technology, Warsaw, 2000, 41-49.
13. J. Lambek, The mathematics of sentence structure, *American Mathematical Monthly* 65 (1958), 154-170.
14. J. Lambek, Type grammars revisited, in: A. Lecomte, F. Lamarche and G. Perrier (eds.), *Logical Aspects of Computational Linguistics*, LNAI 1582, Springer, Berlin, 1999, 1-27.
15. M. Pentus, Lambek grammars are context-free. *Prepublication Series: Mathematical Logic and Theoretical Computer Science* 8, Steklov Mathematical Institute, Moscow, 1992.

An Algebraic Analysis of Clitic Pronouns in Italian

Claudia Casadio[1] and Joachim Lambek[2]

[1] Dipartimento di Filosofia, Università di Bologna
Via Zamboni 38, 40126 Bologna, Italy
casadio@philo.unibo.it

[2] Dept. of Mathematics and Statistics, McGill University
805 Sherbrooke St. West, Montreal QC Canada H3A 2K6
lambek@math.mcgill.ca

Abstract. We[1] analyze both pre- and post-verbal clitics in Italian in the context of infinitival phrases and declarative sentences, using a new form of categorial grammar in which one assigns to each morpheme a type, an element of the free "pregroup" generated by a partially ordered set of basic types.

1 Introduction

Clitic pronouns in French have been analyzed in [1], with the help of a technique known as "compact bilinear logic", essentially by performing calculations in a partially ordered monoid, not quite a group, elsewhere ([6], [7]) called a "pregroup". Like other Romance languages, Italian has clitic pronouns. Unlike French, it has not only preverbal clitics but, like Spanish and Portuguese, also postverbal ones in declarative sentences[2].

The main idea, which is shared with other categorial grammars, is this: we assign to each word of the language a compound type and hope that a calculation on the types associated with a string of words will recognize whether the latter is a well formed sentence. While one of the authors has written a book [2] on cliticization in Italian, the other does not speak Italian and is completely dependent on such computations.

Here is how the compound types are constructed: we begin with a partially ordered set (A, $\rightarrow$) of *basic types*, the partial order being denoted by the arrow. We form the *free pregroup* generated by A, whose elements are products of *simple types*. Each simple type has the form:

$$\ldots, a^{\ell\ell}, a^{\ell}, a, a^{r}, a^{rr}, \ldots$$

where $a \in$A is a basic type. The only computations required are *contractions*

[1] The first author acknowledges support from Italian CNR and the second author from the Social Sciences and Humanities Research Council of Canada.

[2] French differs in this respect from the other Romance languages.

P. de Groote, G. Morrill, C. Retoré (Eds.): LACL 2001, LNAI 2099, pp. 110–124, 2001.

$$x^\ell x \to 1 \,,\; x\,x^r \to 1 \,,$$

and *expansions*

$$1 \to x\,x^\ell \,,\; 1 \to x^r x \,,$$

where x is a simple type. Fortunately, for the purpose of sentence verification the expansions are not needed, but only the contractions, combined with some rewriting induced by the partial order of A, as we proved in [6]. Still, for theoretical purposes, the expansions are useful, for example to prove

$$x^{r\ell} = x = x^{\ell r} \,,$$
$$x \to y \Rightarrow (y^\ell \to x^\ell \wedge y^r \to x^r).$$

One can also extend the operation $(\dots)^\ell$ and $(\dots)^r$ to compound types, by defining

$$1^\ell = 1 = 1^r \,,$$
$$(x \cdot y)^\ell = y^\ell \cdot x^\ell \,,$$
$$(x \cdot y)^r = y^r \cdot x^r \,.$$

The symbol 1 here stands for the empty string of types in the free pregroup and will usually be omitted, as will be the dot that stands for multiplication.

2 Verbs and Their Types

We start introducing the following basic types:

i, i^*	for complete infinitive or infinitival verb phrase ,
o	for direct object ,
ω	for indirect object ,
λ	for locative phrase .

The following basic and compound types will be assigned to a few representative verbs [3]:

vedere :	i , $i\,\mathrm{o}^\ell$;
obbedire :	i , $i\,\omega^\ell$;
dare :	$i\,\omega^\ell \mathrm{o}^\ell$, $i\,\mathrm{o}^\ell \omega^\ell$;
mettere :	$i\,\lambda^\ell \mathrm{o}^\ell$, $i\,\mathrm{o}^\ell \lambda^\ell$;
arrivare :	i^* , $i^* \lambda^\ell$.

The star on i^* will act as a reminder that the perfect tense is to be formed with the auxiliary *essere* rather than *avere* (see Sect. 6).

[3] See the Appendix for English translations of the Italian expressions and sentences considered in this paper.

These type assignments will justify the derivation of the following infinitival phrases of type i or i^* :

vedere , *vedere* (*un libro*) ;
$$i \qquad (i\,o^\ell)\ o \to i$$

obbedire , *obbedire* (*a Mario*) ;
$$i \qquad (i\,\omega^\ell)\ \omega \to i$$

dare (*un libro*) (*a Mario*) , *dare* (*a Mario*) (*un libro*) ;
$$(i\,\omega^\ell o^\ell)\ o\ \omega \to i \qquad (i\,o^\ell \omega^\ell)\ \omega\ o \to i$$

mettere (*un libro*) (*sul tavolo*) , *mettere* (*sul tavolo*) (*un libro*) ;
$$(i\,\lambda^\ell o^\ell)\ o\ \lambda \to i \qquad (i\,o^\ell \lambda^\ell)\ \lambda\ o \to i$$

arrivare , *arrivare* (*a Roma*) ;
$$i^* \qquad (i^*\,\lambda^\ell)\ \lambda \to i^*$$

We note that each of the above verbs has more than one type. For example, *vedere* can be used intransitively as an item of type i and transitively as an item of type $i\,o^\ell$. The two types for *dare* are required to allow for the less common but admissible expression *dare a Mario un libro.*

We have not analyzed the direct object phrase *un libro*, the indirect object phrase *a Mario* and the locative prepositional phrase *sul tavolo.* In principle, types can also be assigned to the separate words *un*, *libro*, *a*, *Mario*, *sul* and *tavolo*; but we desist from doing so in the present paper, since our main concern is the analysis of verb phrases and their subcategorization properties within the context of cliticization.

When combined with a postverbal clitic, the final letter of the infinitive is dropped and the type is changed as follows:

veder : $\bar{\imath}\,\bar{o}^{\,\ell}$;
obbedir : $\bar{\imath}\,\bar{\omega}^{\,\ell}$;
dar : $\bar{\imath}\,\omega^\ell\,\bar{o}^{\,\ell}$, $\bar{\imath}\,o^\ell\,\bar{\omega}^{\,\ell}$;
metter : $\bar{\imath}\,\lambda^\ell\,\bar{o}^{\,\ell}$, $\bar{\imath}\,o^\ell\,\bar{\lambda}^\ell$;
arrivar : $\overline{i^*}\,\bar{\lambda}^\ell$.

The purpose of the *bar* will become clear later, but it is inspired by the standard conventions of $\overline{X}$-theory; we postulate in the partially ordered set of basic types

$$i \to \bar{\imath}\ ,\ o \to \bar{o}\ ,\ \omega \to \bar{\omega}\ ,\ \lambda \to \bar{\lambda}\ ,\ i^* \to \overline{i^*}\ .$$

We do not postulate $\bar{x} \to x$, and here we assume $\bar{x} \not\to x$.

3 Postverbal Clitics

Italian has both preverbal and postverbal clitic pronouns. Here is a list of the clitic pronouns together with their types when they are used postverbally:

Accusative	*mi, ti, ci, vi, si* : $\bar{o}$
	lo, la, li, le : $\widehat{o}$
Dative	*mi, ti, ci, vi, si, gli, le* : $\overline{\omega}$
	me, te, ce, ve, se, glie : $\overline{\omega}\ \mathrm{o}\ \widehat{o}^{\,\ell}$
Locative	*ci, vi* : $\overline{\lambda}$
	ce, ve : $\overline{\lambda}\ \mathrm{o}\ \widehat{o}^{\,\ell}$

We shall ignore the partitive clitic *ne* in this article (see [2]). We have introduced a new basic type $\widehat{o}$ for the clitics *lo, etc.*, which require special treatment, and we postulate $\widehat{o} \to \bar{o}$, but $\bar{o} \not\to \widehat{o}$. We illustrate these type assignments with a representative set of infinitival phrases of type $\bar{\imath}$ or $\overline{\imath^*}$:

veder . lo ,
$$(\bar{\imath}\,\bar{o}^{\ell})\ \widehat{o} \to \bar{\imath}$$

obbedir . mi ,
$$(\bar{\imath}\,\overline{\omega}^{\ell})\ \overline{\omega} \to \bar{\imath}$$

dar . mi (un libro) ,
$$(\bar{\imath}\,\mathrm{o}^{\ell}\,\overline{\omega}^{\ell})\ \overline{\omega}\quad \mathrm{o} \to \bar{\imath}$$

dar . lo (a Mario) ,
$$(\bar{\imath}\,\omega^{\ell}\,\bar{o}^{\ell})\ \widehat{o}\quad \omega \to \bar{\imath}$$

dar . me . lo ,
$$(\bar{\imath}\,\mathrm{o}^{\ell}\,\overline{\omega}^{\ell})\ (\overline{\omega}\ \mathrm{o}\ \widehat{o}^{\,\ell})\ \widehat{o} \to \bar{\imath}$$

arrivar . ci ,
$$(\overline{\imath^*}\,\overline{\lambda}^{\ell})\ \overline{\lambda} \to \overline{\imath^*}$$

Note that $\bar{o}^{\ell}\ \hat{o} \rightarrow \bar{o}^{\ell}\ \bar{o} \rightarrow 1$. The dots were introduced to separate the morphemes, but the usual spelling is *darmelo*, *etc.* . We observe that two consecutive clitics only contract when the first is a dative such as *me* or a locative such as *ce* and the second is an accusative such as *lo* :

$$\begin{array}{ccc} me\ .\ lo & , & ce\ .\ lo \\ (\bar{\omega}\ o\ \underbrace{\hat{o}^{\ell})\ \hat{o}} & & (\bar{\lambda}\ o\ \underbrace{\hat{o}^{\ell})\ \hat{o}} \end{array} .$$

However, no contraction takes place with

$$\begin{array}{ccccc} mi\ .\ lo & , & lo\ .\ mi & , & lo\ .\ me\ , \\ \bar{\omega}\ \ \hat{o} & & \hat{o}\ \ \bar{\omega} & & \hat{o}\ (\bar{\omega}\ o\ \hat{o}^{\ell}) \end{array}$$

$$\begin{array}{ccccccc} mi\ .\ ti & , & mi\ .\ lo & , & mi\ .\ ti & , & me\ .\ ti\ , \\ \bar{\omega}\ \ \bar{o} & & \bar{o}\ \ \hat{o} & & \bar{o}\ \ \bar{\omega} & & (\bar{\omega}\ o\ \hat{o}^{\ell})\ \bar{o} \\ & & & & & & \hat{o}^{\ell} \not\rightarrow \bar{o} \end{array}$$

the last because $\bar{o} \not\rightarrow \hat{o}$, and similarly with λ in place of ω. The following ungrammatical examples show why such pairings are useless:

$$\begin{array}{ccccc} {}^{*}dar\ .\ mi\ .\ lo & , & {}^{*}dar\ .\ lo\ .\ mi & , & \\ \underbrace{(\bar{\imath}\ o^{\ell}\ \underbrace{\bar{\omega}^{\ell})\ \bar{\omega}}\ \hat{o}} & & \underbrace{(\bar{\imath}\ \omega^{\ell}\ \underbrace{\bar{o}^{\ell})\ \hat{o}}\ \bar{\omega}} & & (\hat{o} \not\rightarrow o\ ,\ \bar{\omega} \not\rightarrow \omega) \end{array}$$

The bar on the initial i or i^{*} of the short infinitives will ensure that these cannot be preceded by clitics (see Sect. 4).

4 Preverbal Clitics

We now list the types of the same clitics when used preverbally:

Accusative	*mi, ti, ci, vi* : $\bar{\jmath}\, o^{\ell\ell}\, i^{\ell}$ *si* : $\bar{\jmath}^{*}\, o^{\ell\ell}\, i^{\ell}$ *lo, la, li, le* : $\jmath\, o^{\ell\ell}\, i^{\ell}$
Dative	*mi, ti, ci, vi, gli, le* : $\bar{\jmath}\, \omega^{\ell\ell}\, i^{\ell}$, $\bar{\jmath}^{*}\, \omega^{\ell\ell}\, i^{*\ell}$ *si* : $\bar{\jmath}^{*}\, \omega^{\ell\ell}\, i^{\ell}$ *me, te, ce, ve, se, glie* : $\bar{\jmath}\, \omega^{\ell\ell}\, j^{\ell}$ *se* : $\bar{\jmath}^{*}\, \omega^{\ell\ell}\, j^{\ell}$
Locative	*ci, vi* : $\bar{\jmath}\, \lambda^{\ell\ell}\, i^{\ell}$, $\bar{\jmath}^{*}\, \lambda^{\ell\ell}\, i^{*\ell}$ *ce, ve* : $\bar{\jmath}\, \lambda^{\ell\ell}\, j^{\ell}$

We have introduced four new basic types j , j^*, $\bar{j}$ and $\bar{j}^*$ for infinitives and we postulate $j \to \bar{j}$, $j^* \to \bar{j}^*$, but $i \not\to j \not\to \bar{i}$ *etc.* . It follows that infinitives of type $\bar{j}$ cannot be preceded by any clitics and infinitives of type j only by clitics such as *me* and *ce*. We have double clitics such as

$$\begin{array}{llll} \textit{me} \quad . & \textit{lo} \;, & & \\ (\bar{j}\ \omega^{\ell\ell}\ j^{\ell}) & (j\ \mathrm{o}^{\ell\ell}\ i^{\ell}) & \to & \bar{j}\ \omega^{\ell\ell}\ \mathrm{o}^{\ell\ell}\ i^{\ell} \end{array}$$

$$\begin{array}{llll} \textit{me} \;.\; \textit{lo} & \textit{dare} \;, & & \\ (\bar{j}\ \omega^{\ell\ell}\ \mathrm{o}^{\ell\ell}\ i^{\ell}) & (i\ \mathrm{o}^{\ell}\omega^{\ell}) & \to & \bar{j} \end{array}$$

$$\begin{array}{llll} \textit{ce} \;.\; \textit{lo} & \textit{mettere} \;, & & \\ (\bar{j}\ \lambda^{\ell\ell}\ \mathrm{o}^{\ell\ell}\ i^{\ell}) & (i\ \mathrm{o}^{\ell}\lambda^{\ell}) & \to & \bar{j} \end{array}$$

Other pairs of clitics will not contract. Here are some illustrations of preverbal clitics:

$$\begin{array}{llll} \textit{lo} & \textit{vedere} \;, & & \\ (j\ \mathrm{o}^{\ell\ell}\ i^{\ell}) & (i\ \mathrm{o}^{\ell}) & \to & j \end{array} \qquad \begin{array}{llll} \textit{ci} & \textit{arrivare} \;, & & \\ (\bar{j}^*\ \lambda^{\ell\ell}\ i^{*\ell}) & (i^*\lambda^{\ell}) & \to & \bar{j}^* \end{array}$$

$$\begin{array}{lllll} \textit{mi} & \textit{dare} & \textit{(un libro)} \;, & & \\ (\bar{j}\ \omega^{\ell\ell}\ i^{\ell}) & (i\ \omega^{\ell}\mathrm{o}^{\ell}) & \mathrm{o} & \to & \bar{j} \end{array} \qquad \begin{array}{lllll} \textit{lo} & \textit{dare} & \textit{(a Mario)} \;, & & \\ (j\ \mathrm{o}^{\ell\ell}\ i^{\ell}) & (i\ \mathrm{o}^{\ell}\omega^{\ell}) & \omega & \to & j \end{array}$$

but

$$\begin{array}{lll} {}^*\textit{mi} & \textit{dar} \;.\; \textit{lo} \;, & \\ (\bar{j}\ \omega^{\ell\ell}\ i^{\ell}) & (\bar{i}\ \omega^{\ell}\ \bar{o}^{\ell})\ \hat{o} & \end{array} \qquad \begin{array}{lll} {}^*\textit{mi} & \textit{dare} & \textit{lo} \;. \\ (\bar{j}\ \omega^{\ell\ell}\ i^{\ell}) & (i\ \omega^{\ell}\mathrm{o}^{\ell})\ \hat{o} & \end{array}$$

These results follow from the assumptions $\bar{i} \not\to i$, $\hat{o} \to \bar{o}$, $\hat{o} \not\to \mathrm{o}$. Therefore our type assignments never allow preverbal and postverbal clitics to occur together, expressing a fundamental property of Italian pronominal cliticization.

5 The Perfect Tense with *avere*

The perfect infinitive, corresponding to Latin *amavisse*, is formed in Italian from the past participle with the help of the auxiliary verbs *avere* or *essere*. The latter applies only to a set of intransitive verbs and in this section we shall concentrate on the former. We adopt the type assignments

$$avere \ : \ i p_2^{\ell} \ , \quad aver \ : \ \bar{\imath}\, \overline{p}_2^{\ell}$$

where p_2 is the type of the past participle of a verb with infinitive of type i, *e.g.* the type of *visto* when *vedere* is used intransitively. The role of the bar on p_2 will become clear later.

We shall construct the past participle of a verb with the help of a so-called "inflector" (see [6]). Here we use the inflector Perf of type $p_2 i^{\ell}$ so that

$$\begin{array}{lll} \mathrm{Perf}\,(vedere) & = & visto \\ (p_2 i^{\ell}) \quad i & & \quad p_2 \end{array}$$

and

$$\begin{array}{lll} \mathrm{Perf}\,(vedere) & = & visto \\ (p_2 i^{\ell})\ (i\ o^{\ell}) & & p_2\, o^{\ell} \end{array}$$

In the following examples, we require a preliminary analysis of the past participles before the types are assigned:

$$\begin{array}{llllll} & avere & visto & un\ libro\ , & & \\ = & avere & \mathrm{Perf}\,(vedere) & (un\ libro) & & \\ & (i p_2^{\ell}) & (p_2 i^{\ell})\ (i\ o^{\ell}) & o & \rightarrow & i \end{array}$$

$$\begin{array}{lllllll} & avere & dato & un\ libro & a\ Mario\ , & & \\ = & avere & \mathrm{Perf}\,(dare) & (un\ libro) & (a\ Mario) & & \\ & (i p_2^{\ell}) & (p_2 i^{\ell})\ (i \omega^{\ell} o^{\ell}) & o & \omega & \rightarrow & i \end{array}$$

It must be pointed out that *visto* and *dato* may change the final vowel *o* to *a*, *i* or *e*, depending on the gender and number of any preceding accusative clitic pronoun. This is something that we shall ignore in our preliminary type theoretic analysis.

In general, the inflector Perf is used in connection with "extended infinitives" (see [1] for this notion for French). By an *extended infinitive* we shall mean the infinitive of a verb together with all the preverbal clitics that happen to precede it. In the presence of preverbal clitics the type of Perf should be $\overline{p}_2 \overline{\jmath}^{\ell}$, as in the following examples:

$$\begin{array}{lllll} & \textit{aver.lo} & \textit{visto} & , & \\ = & \textit{aver} & \mathrm{Perf} & (\textit{lo} & \textit{vedere}) \\ & (\bar{\imath}\,\bar{p}_2^{\ell}) & (\bar{p}_2\,\bar{\jmath}^{\ell}) & (j\,\mathrm{o}^{\ell\ell}\,i^{\ell}) & (i\,\mathrm{o}^{\ell}) \rightarrow \bar{\imath} \end{array}$$

where Perf (*lo vedere*) gives *lo visto* which combined with *aver* becomes *aver.lo visto*[4]. The verb *avere* can also be a transitive verb like *vedere*, so we must allow

$$\begin{array}{lllll} & \textit{avere} & \textit{avuto} & \textit{un libro} \; , & \\ = & \textit{avere} & \mathrm{Perf}(\textit{avere}) & (\textit{un libro}) & \\ & (i p_2^{\ell}) & (p_2\, i^{\ell})\,(i\,\mathrm{o}^{\ell}) & \mathrm{o} & \rightarrow i \end{array}$$

where *avuto* has type $p_2\,\mathrm{o}^{\ell}$. Unfortunately, our analysis also admits the ungrammatical string

$$\begin{array}{llllll} * & \textit{avere} & \textit{avuto} & \textit{visto} & \textit{un libro} & \\ = & \textit{avere} & \mathrm{Perf}(\textit{avere}) & \mathrm{Perf}(\textit{vedere}) & (\textit{un libro}) & \\ & (i p_2^{\ell}) & (p_2\, i^{\ell})\,(i\, p_2^{\ell}) & (p_2\, i^{\ell})\,(i\,\mathrm{o}^{\ell}) & \mathrm{o} & \rightarrow i \end{array}$$

To avoid this, we would have to modify our type assignments in such a way as to prevent *avuto* = Perf (*avere*) from receiving the type $p_2 p_2^{\ell}$, or we could stipulate that the *auxiliary* verb *avere* does not possess a past participle.

6 The Auxiliary Verb *essere*

A number of intransitive verbs require the auxiliary verb *essere* for forming the perfect infinitive, *e.g.* the verb of motion *arrivare* of type i^* or $i^*\lambda^{\ell}$. We account for this by judicious applications of the star, assigning types as follows:

$$\textit{essere} \; : \; i^* p_2^{*\ell} \; , \quad \textit{esser} \; : \; \bar{\imath}^* \, \bar{p}_2^{*\ell} \; ,$$

$p_2^* \rightarrow \bar{p}_2^*$ being new basic types, and by giving two new types to the inflector Perf, in summary:

$$\mathrm{Perf} \; : \; p_2\, i^{\ell} \; , \; \bar{p}_2\, \bar{\jmath}^{\ell} \; , \; p_2^*\, i^{*\ell} \; , \; \bar{p}_2^*\, \bar{\jmath}^{*\ell} \; .$$

[4] The alternative infinitives *aver.la vista, aver.li visti, aver.le viste* are not explained by the uniform type $j\,\mathrm{o}^{\ell\ell}\,i^{\ell}$ for the preverbal clitics *lo, la, li* and *le*. A possible way out would be to replace the basic type o by o_n, where n = 1, 2, 3 and 4 in the four cases respectively. If this strategy were adopted, *mi* and *ti* would require n = 1 or 2, *ci* and *vi* would require n = 3 or 4, but *si* would go with any n.

The following examples will illustrate how the perfect infinitive of the starred verbs is formed:

$$\begin{array}{lll} & \textit{essere} & \textit{arrivato}\ , \\ = & \textit{essere} & \mathrm{Perf}(\textit{arrivare}) \\ & (i^* p_2^{*\ell}) & (p_2^* i^{*\ell})\ i^* \ \rightarrow\ i^* \end{array}$$

$$\begin{array}{lll} & \textit{esser}\ .\ \textit{ci} & \textit{arrivato}\ , \\ = & \textit{esser} & \mathrm{Perf}(\ \textit{ci}\ \ \textit{arrivare}\ ) \\ & (\bar{\imath}^*\ \bar{p}_2^{*\ell}) & (\bar{p}_2^* \bar{\jmath}^{*\ell})(\bar{\jmath}^* \lambda^{\ell\ell}\ i^{*\ell})(i^* \lambda^{\ell}) \ \rightarrow\ \bar{\imath}^* \end{array}$$

$$\begin{array}{llll} & \textit{ci} & \textit{essere} & \textit{arrivato}\ , \\ = & \textit{ci} & \textit{essere} & \mathrm{Perf}(\textit{arrivare}) \\ & (\bar{\jmath}^* \lambda^{\ell\ell} i^{*\ell}) & (i^* p_2^{*\ell}) & (p_2^* i^{*\ell})(i^* \lambda^{\ell}) \ \rightarrow\ \bar{\jmath}^* \end{array}$$

Unfortunately, our analysis also allows the ungrammatical string

$$\begin{array}{llll} & {}^*\ \textit{essere} & \textit{stato} & \textit{arrivato}\ , \\ = & \textit{essere} & \mathrm{Perf}(\textit{essere}) & \mathrm{Perf}(\textit{arrivare}) \\ & (i^* p_2^{*\ell}) & (p_2^* i^{*\ell})(i^* p_2^{*\ell}) & (p_2^* i^{*\ell})\ i^* \ \rightarrow\ i^* \end{array}$$

To avoid this, as remarked at the end of Section 5, we would have to modify our type assignments in such a way as to prevent *stato* = Perf(*essere*) from receiving the type $p_2 p_2^{\ell}$, or to stipulate that the *auxiliary* verb *essere* does not possess a past participle.

The auxiliary verb *essere* can also be used to form the passive infinitive, corresponding to Latin *amari*, again from the past participle; but it has a different type:

$$\textit{essere}\ :\ i^* \mathrm{o}^{\ell\ell} p_2^{\ell}\ ,\quad \textit{esser}\ :\ \bar{\imath}^* \mathrm{o}^{\ell\ell} \bar{p}_2^{\ell}$$

as illustrated by the following examples:

$$\begin{array}{lll} & \textit{essere} & \textit{visto}\ , \\ = & \textit{essere} & \mathrm{Perf}(\textit{vedere}) \\ & (i^* \mathrm{o}^{\ell\ell} p_2^{\ell}) & (p_2\, i^{\ell})(i\mathrm{o}^{\ell}) \ \rightarrow\ i^* \end{array}$$

$$\begin{array}{llll} & \textit{essere} & \textit{stato} & \textit{visto}\ , \\ = & \textit{essere} & \mathrm{Perf}(\textit{essere}) & \mathrm{Perf}(\textit{vedere}) \\ & (i^* p_2^{*\ell}) & (p_2^* i^{*\ell})(i^* \mathrm{o}^{\ell\ell} p_2^{\ell}) & (p_2\, i^{\ell})(i\mathrm{o}^{\ell}) \ \rightarrow\ i^* \end{array}$$

$$\begin{array}{ll} \textit{esser . mi dato ,} & \textit{mi essere dato ,} \\ = \textit{esser}\ \mathrm{Perf}(\textit{mi dare}) & = \textit{mi essere}\ \mathrm{Perf}(\textit{dare}) \\ (\bar{\imath}^* o^{\ell\ell}\bar{p}_2^{\ell})(\bar{p}_2\bar{\jmath}^{\ell})(\bar{\jmath}\omega^{\ell\ell}i^{\ell})(i\omega^{\ell}o^{\ell}) \to \bar{\imath}^* & (\bar{\jmath}^*\omega^{\ell\ell}i^{*\ell})(i^* o^{\ell\ell}p_2^{\ell})(p_2 i^{\ell})(io^{\ell}\omega^{\ell}) \to \bar{\jmath}^* \end{array}$$

7 The Modal Verbs

We now consider the modal verbs *potere*, *volere*, *dovere* with types as follows:

$$\textit{potere} : i\,\bar{\imath}^{\ell}\,,\ i^*\,\bar{\imath}^{*\ell} \quad ; \quad \textit{poter} : \bar{\imath}\bar{\jmath}^{\ell}\,,\ \bar{\imath}^*\bar{\jmath}^{*\ell}$$

and here are a few illustrative examples:

$$\begin{array}{ll} \textit{potere obbedire (a Mario) ,} & \textit{poter . mi obbedire ,} \\ (i\,\bar{\imath}^{\ell})\ (i\,\omega^{\ell})\quad \omega \to i & (\bar{\imath}\bar{\jmath}^{\ell})\ (\bar{\jmath}\omega^{\ell\ell}i^{\ell})\ (i\,\omega^{\ell}) \to \bar{\imath} \end{array}$$

$$\begin{array}{ll} \textit{mi potere obbedire ,} & \textit{potere dar . me . lo ,} \\ (\bar{\jmath}\,\omega^{\ell\ell}\,i^{\ell})\ (i\,\bar{\imath}^{\ell})\ (i\,\omega^{\ell}) \to \bar{\jmath} & (i\,\bar{\imath}^{\ell})\ (\bar{\imath}\,o^{\ell}\,\bar{\omega}^{\ell})\ (\bar{\omega}\,o\,\hat{o}^{\ell})\ \hat{o} \to i \\ \textit{poter . me . lo dare ,} & \textit{me . lo potere dare ,} \\ (\bar{\imath}\bar{\jmath}^{\ell})\ (\bar{\jmath}\,\omega^{\ell\ell}o^{\ell\ell}\,i^{\ell})\ (i\,o^{\ell}\omega^{\ell}) \to \bar{\imath} & (\bar{\jmath}\,\omega^{\ell\ell}o^{\ell\ell}\,i^{\ell})\ (i\,\bar{\imath}^{\ell})\ (i\,o^{\ell}\omega^{\ell}) \to \bar{\jmath} \\ \textit{potere arrivar . ci ,} & \textit{poter . ci arrivare ,} \\ (i^*\,\bar{\imath}^{*\ell})\ (\bar{\imath}^*\,\bar{\lambda}^{\ell})\ (\bar{\lambda}) \to i^* & (\bar{\imath}^*\bar{\jmath}^{*\ell})\ (\bar{\jmath}^*\lambda^{\ell\ell}i^{*\ell})\ (i^*\lambda^{\ell}) \to \bar{\imath}^* \\ \textit{ci potere arrivare ,} & \\ (\bar{\jmath}^*\lambda^{\ell\ell}i^{*\ell})\ (i^*\,\bar{\imath}^{*\ell})\ (i^*\lambda^{\ell}) \to \bar{\jmath}^*\,. & \end{array}$$

Modal verbs allow repetition, not only

$$\begin{array}{llllll} \textit{potere volere ,} & \text{but even} & \textit{potere potere ,} & \text{and} & \textit{potere poter,} \\ (i\,\bar{\imath}^{\ell})(i\,\bar{\imath}^{\ell}) \to i\,\bar{\imath}^{\ell} & & (i\,\bar{\imath}^{\ell})(i\,\bar{\imath}^{\ell}) \to i\,\bar{\imath}^{\ell} & & (i\,\bar{\imath}^{\ell})(\bar{\imath}\bar{\jmath}^{\ell}) \to i\,\bar{\jmath}^{\ell}\,. \end{array}$$

In the last three examples we can replace i by i^* and j by j^*. How do the modal verbs interact with the auxiliary verbs *avere* and *essere*? The following examples will answer the question.

$$\begin{array}{ll} & \textit{potere avere visto un libro ,} \\ = & \textit{potere avere}\ \mathrm{Perf}(\textit{vedere})\ (\textit{un libro}) \\ & (i\,\bar{\imath}^{\ell})\ (ip_2^{\ell})\ (p_2 i^{\ell})\ (i\,o^{\ell})\quad o \to i \end{array}$$

avere potuto vedere un libro ,

= *avere* Perf (*potere*) *vedere* (*un libro*)

$$(i p_2^{\ell})\,(p_2 i^{\ell})\,(i\,\bar{\imath}^{\ell})\,(i\,\mathrm{o}^{\ell})\quad \mathrm{o} \;\rightarrow\; i$$

potere esser . ci arrivato

= *potere esser* Perf (*ci arrivare*)

$$(i^{*}\,\bar{\imath}^{*\ell})\;(\bar{\imath}^{*}\,\bar{p}_2^{*\ell})\;(\bar{p}_2^{*}\,\bar{\jmath}^{*\ell})(\bar{\jmath}^{*}\lambda^{\ell\ell} i^{*\ell})(i^{*}\lambda^{\ell}) \;\rightarrow\; i^{*}$$

essere potuto arrivar . ci

= *essere* Perf (*potere*) *arrivar . ci*

$$(i^{*} p_2^{*\ell})\,(p_2^{*}\, i^{*\ell})\,(i^{*}\,\bar{\imath}^{*\ell})\,(\overline{i^{*}}\;\bar{\lambda}^{\ell})\;\;\bar{\lambda} \;\rightarrow\; i^{*}$$

esser . ci potuto arrivare

= *esser* Perf(*ci potere*) *arrivare*

$$(\bar{\imath}^{*}\,\bar{p}_2^{*\ell})(\bar{p}_2^{*}\,\bar{\jmath}^{*\ell})(\bar{\jmath}^{*}\lambda^{\ell\ell} i^{*\ell})\quad (i^{*}\,\bar{\imath}^{*\ell})(i^{*}\lambda^{\ell}) \;\rightarrow\; i^{*}$$

Up to now we have introduced eight different basic types

$$i \rightarrow \bar{\imath}\,,\; j \rightarrow \bar{\jmath}\,,\; i^{*} \rightarrow \overline{i^{*}}\,,\; j^{*} \rightarrow \bar{\jmath}^{*}$$

all representing *complete* infinitival phrases, that is, infinitival phrases that do not require a direct or indirect object or a locative phrase for their completion. It would be convenient to subsume all of them under a single basic type $\bar{\bar{\imath}}$, by postulating

$$\bar{\imath}\,,\; \bar{\jmath}\,,\; \overline{i^{*}}\,,\; \bar{\jmath}^{*} \;\rightarrow\; \bar{\bar{\imath}}$$

8 Finite Verb-Forms and Declarative Sentences

So far we have looked only at infinitives and infinitival verb phrases, but sentences are constituted from *finite* verb-forms. To each Italian verb V there is associated a matrix V_{jk} of 7 × 6 = 42 finite verb-forms, where j = 1, ... ,7 denotes tenses (including moods) and k = 1, 2, 3 denotes the three persons singular, while k = 4, 5, 6 denotes the three persons plural. We shall use the types

s_j for declarative sentences in j-th tense ,
π_k for k-th person subject .

For purpose of illustration, we shall confine our attention to the cases j = 1 (present tense) and k = 1 (first person) or k = 3 (third person). For example, the present tense sentence

$$\begin{array}{llll} (io) & vedo & (un\ libro)\ , & \\ \pi_1 & (\pi_1^r\ \mathrm{s}_1\ \mathrm{o}^\ell) & \mathrm{o} & \rightarrow \mathrm{s}_1 \end{array}$$

where the optional pronoun *io* has type π_1, leads us to assign to the first verb-form *vedo* the type $(\pi_1^r\ \mathrm{s}_1\ \mathrm{o}^\ell)$. We shall assume that Italian speakers are familiar with the whole conjugation matrix V_{jk} and we shall not discuss rules for constructing this matrix, although there certainly are such rules. For our purposes V_{jk} is obtained from the infinitive V by an inflector C_{jk} such that

$$\mathrm{C}_{jk}(\mathrm{V}) = \mathrm{V}_{jk}\ .$$

We intend to apply C_{jk} not only to plain infinitives such as *vedere*, but also to extended infinitives, following the procedure adopted for French in [1]. We assign the following types to this inflector:

$$\mathrm{C}_{jk} : \pi_k^r\ \mathrm{s}_j\ \bar{\bar{\imath}}^\ell\ ,\ \ \mathrm{s}_j\ \bar{\bar{\imath}}^\ell\ ,$$

the former if the optional subject is present, as we shall assume from now on.

We conclude by looking at some examples of declarative sentences in the present tense involving pre- or post-verbal cliticization.

$$\begin{array}{l} (io)\quad te\ .\ lo\quad do\ , \\ =\ io\quad \mathrm{C}_{11}(\ te\ .\ lo\quad dare) \\ \quad \pi_1\ (\pi_1^r\ \mathrm{s}_1\ \bar{\bar{\imath}}^\ell)\ (\bar{\jmath}\ \omega^{\ell\ell}\mathrm{o}^{\ell\ell}\ i^\ell)\ (i\ \mathrm{o}^\ell\omega^\ell) \rightarrow \mathrm{s}_1 \qquad (\bar{\jmath} \rightarrow \bar{\bar{\imath}}) \end{array}$$

$$\begin{array}{l} Mario\quad lo\ vuole\ vedere\ , \\ =\ Mario\ \ \mathrm{C}_{13}(\ lo\quad volere\ )\ \ vedere \\ \quad \pi_3\ \ (\pi_3^r\ \mathrm{s}_1\ \bar{\bar{\imath}}^\ell)\ (j\ \mathrm{o}^{\ell\ell}\ i^\ell)\ (i\,\bar{\imath}^\ell)(i\ \mathrm{o}^\ell) \rightarrow \mathrm{s}_1 \qquad (j \rightarrow \bar{\jmath} \rightarrow \bar{\bar{\imath}}) \end{array}$$

$$\begin{array}{l} Mario\quad vuole\ vedere\ lui\ , \\ =\ Mario\ \ \mathrm{C}_{13}(\ volere\ )\ vedere\ \ lui \\ \quad \pi_3\ \ (\pi_3^r\ \mathrm{s}_1\ \bar{\bar{\imath}}^\ell)\ (i\,\bar{\imath}^\ell)\ (i\ \mathrm{o}^\ell)\ \ \mathrm{o}\ \rightarrow \mathrm{s}_1 \end{array}$$

$$\begin{array}{l} (io)\quad devo\quad dar\ .\ te\ .\ lo\ , \\ =\ io\quad \mathrm{C}_{11}(\ dovere\ )\quad dar\ .\quad te\ \ .\ \ lo \\ \quad \pi_1\ \ (\pi_1^r\ \mathrm{s}_1\ \bar{\bar{\imath}}^\ell)\ (i\,\bar{\imath}^\ell)(\bar{\imath}\ \mathrm{o}^\ell\,\overline{\omega}^\ell)\ (\overline{\omega}\ \mathrm{o}\ \widehat{o}^\ell)\ \ \widehat{o}\ \rightarrow \mathrm{s}_1 \end{array}$$

$$(\textit{io}) \quad \textit{te . lo} \quad \textit{devo} \quad \textit{dare} \;,$$
$$= \textit{io} \quad C_{11}(\; \textit{te . lo} \quad \textit{dovere} \;) \quad \textit{dare}$$
$$\pi_1 \;\; (\pi_1^r\, s_1\, \bar{\bar{i}}^\ell)\; (\bar{j}\, \omega^{\ell\ell} o^{\ell\ell}\, i^\ell)(i\,\bar{i}^\ell)\; (i\; o^\ell \omega^\ell) \;\rightarrow\; s_1 \qquad (\,\bar{j} \rightarrow \bar{\bar{i}}\,)$$

$$*\; (\textit{io}) \quad \textit{devo} \quad \textit{te . lo} \quad \textit{dare} \;,$$
$$= \textit{io} \quad C_{11}(\; \textit{dovere} \;) \quad \textit{te . lo} \quad \textit{dare}$$
$$\pi_1 \;\; (\pi_1^r\, s_1\, \bar{\bar{i}}^\ell)\; (i\,\bar{i}^\ell)(\bar{j}\, \omega^{\ell\ell} o^{\ell\ell}\, i^\ell)\; (i\; o^\ell \omega^\ell) \qquad (\,\bar{j} \not\rightarrow \bar{i}\,)$$

$$(\textit{io}) \quad \textit{lo} \quad \textit{ho} \quad \textit{visto} \;,$$
$$= \textit{io} \quad C_{11}(\; \textit{lo} \quad \textit{avere} \;) \quad \mathrm{Perf}(\textit{vedere})$$
$$\pi_1 \;\; (\pi_1^r\, s_1\, \bar{\bar{i}}^\ell)\; (j\; o^{\ell\ell}\, i^\ell)(i p_2^\ell)(p_2\, i^\ell)(i\; o^\ell) \;\rightarrow\; s_1 \qquad (\, j \rightarrow \bar{j} \rightarrow \bar{\bar{i}}\,)$$

$$*\; (\textit{io}) \quad \textit{ho} \quad \textit{lo} \quad \textit{visto} \;,$$
$$= \textit{io} \quad C_{11}(\; \textit{avere} \;) \quad \mathrm{Perf}(\textit{lo} \quad \textit{vedere})$$
$$\pi_1 \;\; (\pi_1^r\, s_1\, \bar{\bar{i}}^\ell)\; (i p_2^\ell)(p_2\, i^\ell)(j\; o^{\ell\ell}\, i^\ell)(i\; o^\ell) \qquad (j \not\rightarrow i)$$

(Had we picked Perf : $\overline{p}_2\, \bar{j}^\ell$, we would have been led to $p_2^\ell\, \overline{p}_2 \not\rightarrow 1$.)

$$(\textit{io}) \quad \textit{ci} \quad \textit{metto} \quad \textit{un libro} \;,$$
$$= \textit{io} \quad C_{11}(\; \textit{ci} \quad \textit{mettere} \;) \quad (\textit{un libro})$$
$$\pi_1 \;\; (\pi_1^r\, s_1\, \bar{\bar{i}}^\ell)\; (\bar{j}\; \lambda^{\ell\ell}\, i^\ell)(i\; \lambda^\ell o^\ell)\;\; o \;\rightarrow\; s_1 \qquad (\,\bar{j} \rightarrow \bar{\bar{i}}\,)$$

$$(\textit{io}) \quad \textit{lo} \quad \textit{metto} \quad \textit{sul tavolo} \;,$$
$$= \textit{io} \quad C_{11}(\; \textit{lo mettere} \;) \quad (\textit{sul tavolo})$$
$$\pi_1 \;\; (\pi_1^r\, s_1\, \bar{\bar{i}}^\ell)\; (j\; o^{\ell\ell}\, i^\ell)(i\; o^\ell \lambda^\ell)\;\; \lambda \;\rightarrow\; s_1 \qquad (\, j \rightarrow \bar{j} \rightarrow \bar{\bar{i}}\,)$$

$$(\textit{io}) \quad \textit{ce} \quad \textit{lo} \quad \textit{metto} \;,$$
$$= \textit{io} \quad C_{11}(\; \textit{ce} \quad \textit{lo} \quad \textit{mettere} \;)$$
$$\pi_1 \;\; (\pi_1^r\, s_1\, \bar{\bar{i}}^\ell)\; (\bar{j}\; \lambda^{\ell\ell}\, o^{\ell\ell}\, i^\ell)(i\; o^\ell \lambda^\ell) \;\rightarrow\; s_1 \qquad (\,\bar{j} \rightarrow \bar{\bar{i}}\,)$$

9 Appendix

vedere	:	to see	*avere*	:	to have
obbedire	:	to obey	*essere*	:	to be
dare	:	to give	*potere*	:	may, can
mettere	:	to put	*volere*	:	shall, will
arrivare	:	to arrive	*dovere*	:	must

vedere un libro	:	to see a book
obbedire a Mario	:	to obey Mario
dare un libro a Mario	:	to give a book to Mario
mettere un libro sul tavolo	:	to put a book on the table
arrivare a Roma	:	to arrive at Rome

10 Concluding Remarks

As far as we know, this is the first attempt to give an accurate account of Italian clitics by means of an algebraic formalism. The advantages of the approach via pregroups as compared with earlier forms of categorial grammars have been discussed elsewhere, e.g. in [4]. Still, the following remarks should help the present reader [5].

In analyzing a sentence, we go from left to right and mimic the way a human hearer might proceed: recognizing the type of each word as it is received and rapidly calculating the type of the string of words up to that point, never overburdening the temporary storage capacity of the human mind beyond Miller's [8] seven chunks of information. (This simplified account neglects the necessity of parallel computation.)

Earlier kinds of categorial grammar, in spite of their mathematical elegance, require much more complicated calculations, such as Gentzen-style proofs in tree-form. While these can be carried out on paper or on the blackboard, it is hard to imagine that they lend themselves to rapid mental computations.

Proof nets of linear logic provide a nice visual representation of the kind of deductions or derivations that are required; but again it is not likely (at least in the opinion of one of us) that they correspond to anything in the human mind. Nonetheless, we have not ignored them: in the compact bilinear logic we employ here, the proof nets are just the links indicating contractions, expansions having been shown to be unnecessary for sentence recognition in [6]. We are indebted to A. K. Joshi for pointing out that such links were first introduced by Z. Harris [5] in a different context.

[5] We are grateful to Mario Fadda for his careful reading of the manuscript and for spotting a couple of mistakes. He also pointed out that the symbol j^* never actually occurs as a type in the present fragment.

Some readers may wonder why we need so many basic types, where the earliest categorial grammars used only two (**s** for sentences and **n** for names). We introduced the smallest number of basic types which allowed us to account for the linguistic data, recognizing all and only grammatically well-formed sentences. Moreover, many of such basic types are related, e.g. the types for infinitives

$$\bar{\imath}\,,\,\bar{\jmath}\,,\,\overline{\imath^*}\,,\,\bar{\jmath}^{\,*}\ \rightarrow\ \bar{\bar{\imath}}\,.$$

We hope that our grammar, with the finely tuned order on the set of basic types, will not accept non-grammatical strings as sentences; if it does, we must revise it by introducing yet more basic types. In selecting basic types, we are primarily interested in their algebraic effectiveness and not so much in whether they correspond to traditional grammatical categories.

References

1. Bargelli, D., Lambek, J.: An algebraic approach to French sentence structure (In this volume).
2. Casadio, C.: *A Categorial Approach to Cliticization and Agreement in Italian*, Saggi di Filosofia del Linguaggio e della Scienza, CLUEB Editrice, Bologna, (1993).
3. Casadio, C.: Non-commutative linear logic in linguistics, submitted to *Grammar*.
4. Casadio, C., Lambek, J.: A tale of four grammars, to appear in *Studia Logica*.
5. Harris, Z.: A cyclic cancellation-automaton for sentence well-formedness, *International Computation Centre Bulletin* 5 (1966), 69-94.
6. Lambek, J.: Type grammars revisited, in A. Lecomte, F. Lamarche and G. Perrier (eds.), *Logical Aspects of Computational Linguistics*, Springer LNAI 1582, (1999) 1-27.
7. Lambek, J.: Pregroups: a new algebraic approach to sentence structure, in C. Martin-Vide and G. Paun (eds), *Recent Topics in Mathematical and Computational Linguistics*, Editura Academici Române, Bucharest (2000).
8. Miller, G.A.: The magical number seven plus or minus two: some limits on our capacity for processing information, *Psychological Review* 63 (1956), 81-97.
9. Ragusa, O.: *Essential Italian Grammar*, Dover Publications, New York 1963.

Consistent Identification in the Limit of Any of the Classes k-Valued Is NP-hard*

Christophe Costa Florêncio

UiL OTS (Utrecht University)
Trans 10, 3512 JK Utrecht, Netherlands
Tel.: +31.30.253.6178, Fax: +31.30.253.6000
costa@let.uu.nl

Abstract. In [Bus87], [BP90] 'discovery procedures' for CCGs were defined that accept a sequence of structures as input and yield a set of grammars.
In [Kan98] it was shown that some of the classes based on these procedures are learnable (in the technical sense of [Gol67]). In [CF00] it was shown that learning some of these classes by means of a consistent learning function is NP-hard.
The complexity of learning classes from one particular family, $\mathcal{G}_{k\text{-valued}}$, was still left open. In this paper it is shown that learning any (except one) class from this family by means of a consistent learning function is NP-hard as well.

Keywords: Categorial grammars, Formal language theory, Grammatical inference, Learning theory.

1 Identification in the Limit

In [Gol67] a model of learning called identification in the limit was introduced. In this model a learning function receives an endless stream of sentences from the target language, called a *text*, and hypothesizes a grammar for the target language at each time-step.

A *class* of languages is called *learnable* if and only if there exists a learning function such that after a finite number of presented sentences it guesses the right language on every text for every language from that class and does not deviate from this hypothesis. Research within this framework is known as *formal learning theory*.

In this paper only those aspects of formal learning theory that are relevant to the proof of NP-hardness will be discussed. See [OdJMW96] and [JORS99] for a comprehensive overview of the field.

Let the set Ω denote the hypothesis space, which can be any class of finitary objects. Members of Ω are called *grammars*.

* I would like to thank an anonymous referee whose comments helped to greatly simplify the proof of Lemma 9.

P. de Groote, G. Morrill, C. Retoré (Eds.): LACL 2001, LNAI 2099, pp. 125–138, 2001.

The set **S** denotes the sample space, a recursive subset of Σ^* for some fixed finite alphabet Σ. Elements of **S** are called *sentences*, subsets of **S** are called *languages*.

The *naming function* L maps elements of Ω to subsets of **S**. If G is a grammar in Ω, then $\mathrm{L}(G)$ is called the *language generated by (associated with)* G. The question whether a sentence belongs to a language generated by a grammar is called the *universal membership problem.* A triple $\langle \Omega, \mathbf{S}, \mathrm{L} \rangle$ satisfying the above conditions is called a *grammar system.* A class of grammars is denoted $\mathcal{G}$, a class of languages is denoted $\mathcal{L}$.

I will adopt notation from [Kan98][1] and let $\mathcal{FL}$ denote a class of *structure languages*, to be defined in Section 3. The corresponding naming function is $\mathrm{FL}(G)$. Learning functions are written as φ, their input sequences as σ or τ.

1.1 Constraints on Learning Functions

The behaviour of learning functions can be constrained in a number of ways, such a constraint is called *restrictive* if it restricts the space of learnable classes.

Only some important constraints relevant to this discussion will be defined here:

Definition 1. ***Consistent Learning***

A learning function φ *is* consistent *on* $\mathcal{G}$ *if for any* $L \in \mathrm{L}(\mathcal{G})$ *and for any finite sequence* $\langle s_0, \ldots, s_i \rangle$ *of elements of* L*, either* $\varphi(\langle s_0, \ldots, s_i \rangle)$ *is undefined or* $\{s_0, \ldots, s_i\} \subseteq \mathrm{L}(\varphi(\langle s_0, \ldots, s_i \rangle))$.

Informally, consistency requires that the learning function explains with its conjecture all the data it has seen.

Definition 2. ***Prudent Learning***
A learning function φ *learns* $\mathcal{G}$ prudently *if* φ *learns* $\mathcal{G}$ *and* $\mathrm{content}(\varphi) \subseteq \mathcal{G}$.

Prudent learners only hypothesize grammars that are in their class, i.e. that they are willing to converge on.

Definition 3. ***Responsive Learning***
A learning function φ *is* responsive *on* $\mathcal{G}$ *if for any* $L \in \mathrm{L}(\mathcal{G})$ *and for any finite sequence* $\langle s_0, \ldots, s_i \rangle$ *of elements of* L $(\{s_0, \ldots, s_i\} \subseteq L)$, $\varphi(\langle s_0, \ldots, s_i \rangle)$ *is defined.*

A responsive learning function is always defined, as long as the text is consistent with some language from its class. Neither prudence nor responsiveness are by itself restrictive, and are often implicitly assumed.

None of these constraints are restrictive for the classes under discussion.

[1] In formal learning theory, recursion theoretic notation is the norm. However, since the issues addressed here have more to do with formal language theory and complexity, hence the choice of notation.

1.2 Time Complexity of Learning Functions

In formal learning theory there are no a priori constraints on the computational resources required by the learning function. It turns out that giving a usable definition of the complexity of learning functions is not exactly easy. In this subsection some proposals and their problems will be discussed, and the choice for one particular definition will be motivated.

Let the complexity of the update-time of some (computable) learning function φ be defined as the number of computing steps it takes to learn a language, with respect to $|\sigma|$, the size of the input sequence. In [Pit89] it was first noted that requiring the function to run in a time polynomial with respect to $|\sigma|$ does not constitute a significant constraint, since one can always define a learning function φ' that combines φ with a clock so that its amount of computing time is bounded by a polynomial over $|\sigma|$.

Obviously, φ' learns the same class as φ, and it does so in polynomial update-time[2].

The problem is that without additional constraints on φ the 'burden of computation' can be shifted from the number of computations the function needs to perform to the amount of input data considered by the function. Requiring the function to be consistent already constitutes a significant constraint when used in combination with a complexity restriction (see [Bar74]).

There does not seem to be any generally accepted definition of what constitutes a tractable learning function. I will therefore apply only the restrictions of consistency and polynomial update-time, since this seems to be the weakest combination of constraints that is not trivial and has an intuitive relation with standard notions of computational complexity. This definition has at least one drawback: not all learnable classes can be learned by a learning function that is consistent on its class, so even this complexity measure cannot be generally applied.

There is also no guarantee that for a class that is learnable by a function consistent on that class characteristic samples (i.e. samples that justify convergence to the right grammar) can be given that are uniformly of a size polynomial in the size of their associated grammar.

See [Ste98, WZ95] for discussions of the relation between the consistency constraint and complexity of learning functions.

2 Classical Categorial Grammar and Structure Languages

The classes defined in [Bus87, BP90] are based on a formalism for (ϵ-free) context-free languages called classical categorial grammar (CCG)[3]. In this section the relevant concepts of CCG will be defined. I will adopt notation from [Kan98].

[2] To be more precise: in [DS86] it was shown that any unbounded monotone increasing update boundary is not by itself restrictive.

[3] Also known as *AB languages*.

In CCG each symbol in the alphabet Σ gets assigned a finite number of *types*. Types are constructed from *primitive types* by the operators $\backslash$ and $/$. We let Pr denote the (countably infinite) set of primitive types. The set of types Tp is defined as follows:

Definition 4. *The set of types* Tp *is the smallest set satisfying the following conditions:*

1. $Pr \subseteq \mathrm{Tp}$,
2. *if* $A \in \mathrm{Tp}$ *and* $B \in \mathrm{Tp}$, *then* $A\backslash B \in \mathrm{Tp}$.
3. *if* $A \in \mathrm{Tp}$ *and* $B \in \mathrm{Tp}$, *then* $B/A \in \mathrm{Tp}$.

Definition 5. *The* degree *of a type is defined as follows:*
$\mathrm{degree}(A) = 0$, *if* $A \in Pr$,
$\mathrm{degree}(A/B) = 1 + \mathrm{degree}(A) + \mathrm{degree}(B)$,
$\mathrm{degree}(B\backslash A) = 1 + \mathrm{degree}(A) + \mathrm{degree}(B)$.

One member t of Pr is called the *distinguished type*. In CCG there are only two modes of type combination, *backward application*, $A, A\backslash B \Rightarrow B$, and *forward application*, $B/A, A \Rightarrow B$. In both cases, type A is an *argument*, the complex type is a *functor*. *Grammars* consist of type assignments to symbols, i.e. `symbol`$\mapsto T$, where `symbol` $\in \Sigma$, and $T \in \mathrm{Tp}$.

Definition 6. *A* derivation *of* B *from* $A_1, \ldots, A_n$ *is a binary branching tree that encodes a proof of* $A_1, \ldots, A_n \Rightarrow B$.

Through the notion of derivation the association between grammar and language is defined. All structures contained in some given structure language correspond to a derivation of type t based solely on the type assignments contained in a given grammar. The *string language* associated with G consists of the strings corresponding to all the structures in its structure language, where the string corresponding to some derivation consists just of the leaves of that derivation.

The class of all categorial grammars is denoted CatG, the grammar system under discussion is $\langle \mathrm{CatG}, \Sigma^{\mathrm{F}}, \mathrm{FL} \rangle$. The symbol FL is an abbreviation of functor-argument language, which is a structure language for CCG. Structures are of the form `symbol`, `fa(s1,s2)` or `ba(s1,s2)`, where `symbol` $\in$ Pr, `fa` stands for forward application, `ba` for backward application and `s1` and `s2` are also structures.

We will only be concerned with structure languages in the remainder of this article. The definition of identification in the limit (Section 1) can be applied in a straightforward way by replacing 'language' with 'structure language', from a formal point of view this makes no difference. Note that, even though structure languages contain more information than string languages, learning a class of structure languages is not necessarily easier than learning the corresponding class of string languages. This is because the *identification criterion* for structure languages is stronger than that for string languages: when learning structure languages, a learner must identify grammars that produce the same *derivations*, not just the same strings. This makes learning such classes hard, from the perspective of both learnability and complexity.

All learning functions in [Kan98] are based on the function GF. This function receives a sample of structures D as input and yields a set of assignments (i.e. a grammar) called the *general form* as output. It is a homomorphism and runs in linear time. It assigns t to each root node, assigns distinct variables to the argument nodes, and computes types for the functor nodes: if $\mathtt{s1} \mapsto A$, given $\mathtt{ba(s1,s2)} \Rightarrow B$, $\mathtt{s2} \mapsto A \backslash B$. If $\mathtt{s1} \mapsto A$, given $\mathtt{fa(s2,s1)} \Rightarrow B$, $\mathtt{s2} \mapsto B/A$.

Categorial types can be treated as terms, so natural definitions of substitution and unification apply. A substitution over a grammar is just a substitution over all of the types contained in its assignments. We state without proof that for any substitution Θ, $\mathrm{FL}(G) \subseteq \mathrm{FL}(\Theta[G])$, see [Kan98] for details.

3 The Classes of Grammars

In the following paragraphs definitions for the relevant classes will be given:

Rigid Grammars: A *rigid grammar* is a partial function from Σ to Tp. It assigns either zero or one type to each symbol in the alphabet.

We write $\mathcal{G}_{\text{rigid}}$ to denote the class of rigid grammars over Σ. The class $\{\mathrm{FL}(G) \mid G \in \mathcal{G}_{\text{rigid}}\}$ is denoted $\mathcal{FL}_{\text{rigid}}$.

This class is learnable with polynomial update-time, by simply unifying all types assigned to the same symbol in the general form. The other classes defined in [Bus87] and [BP90] are generalizations of this class.

k-Valued Grammars: A *k-valued* grammar is a partial function from Σ to Tp. It assigns at most k types to each symbol in the alphabet.

We write $\mathcal{G}_{k\text{-valued}}$ to denote the class of k-valued grammars over Σ. The class $\{\mathrm{FL}(G) \mid G \in \mathcal{G}_{k\text{-valued}}\}$ is denoted $\mathcal{FL}_{k\text{-valued}}$.

Note that in the special case $k = 1$, $\mathcal{G}_{k\text{-valued}}$ is equivalent to $\mathcal{G}_{\text{rigid}}$.

The learning function φ_{VG_k}[4] learns $\mathcal{G}_{k\text{-valued}}$ from structures.

4 Why Learning $\mathcal{G}_{2\text{-valued}}$ by Means of a Function Consistent on That Class Is NP-hard

From here on it will be assumed that φ is responsive and consistent on $\mathcal{G}_{2\text{-valued}}$ and learns that class prudently. The following is a useful corollary taken from [CF00]:

Lemma 7. *For every consistent learning function φ learning a subclass of* CatG *(from structures) and every sequence σ for a language from that subclass there exists a substitution Θ such that $\Theta[\mathrm{GF}(\sigma)] \subseteq \varphi(\sigma)$, if $\varphi(\sigma)$ is defined.*

[4] With this function, and the functions defined for the other classes, we will denote arbitrary learning functions that learn these classes, not necessarily the particular functions defined in [Kan98].

Thus, if GF(σ) assigns x different types to the same symbol that are pairwise not unifiable, the consistent learning function $\varphi(\sigma)$ hypothesizes a grammar that assigns at least x different types to that same symbol.

Definition 8. *Let* $\text{or}(p_1, p_2)$ *be the function that, given the two propositions* p_1 *and* p_2*, yields the following sample* D_{or} *for a language in* $\mathcal{L}_{\text{2-valued}}$:

$$D_{or} = \left\{ \begin{array}{l} \texttt{fa(fa(fa(d,fa(a,a)),fa(b,b)),c)} \\ \texttt{fa(fa(fa(d,fa(c,c)),c),fa(c,c))} \\ \texttt{fa(fa(fa(d,c),fa(c,c)),fa(r,r))} \\ \texttt{c} \\ \texttt{fa(c,c)} \\ \texttt{fa(fa(r,r),r)} \\ \texttt{a} \\ \texttt{b} \\ \texttt{c} \\ \texttt{r} \end{array} \right\}$$

Lemma 9. *Let* p *and* q *be two propositions. Then* $p \vee q$ *if and only if the following holds:*

For any learning function φ *that is responsive and consistent on* $\mathcal{G}_{\text{2-valued}}$ *and learns that class prudently (from structures) there exists a substitution* Θ *such that* $\Theta[\text{GF}(\text{or}(p,q))] \subseteq \varphi(\text{or}(p,q))$.

`Proof:` The general form for D_{or} from Definition 8 is :

$$\text{GF}(D_{or}): \quad \begin{array}{rl} \texttt{a} \mapsto & A/A_2, A_2, t \\ \texttt{b} \mapsto & B/B_2, B_2, t \\ \texttt{c} \mapsto & C, \\ & D/D_2, D_2, \\ & E, \\ & F/F_2, F_2, \\ & G, \\ & H/H_2, H_2, \\ & t, \\ & t/J, J \\ \texttt{d} \mapsto & ((t/A)/B)/C, \\ & ((t/D)/E)/F, \\ & ((t/G)/H)/I \\ \texttt{r} \mapsto & t, \\ & I/I_2, \\ & I_2, \\ & (t/K)/L, \\ & K, \\ & L \end{array}$$

The symbol r has t and some complex types assigned to it. Since a constant and a complex term cannot be unified, the complex terms have to be unified. Since I_2, K and L occur in these complex types they have to unify with t. The same reasoning can be applied to the types assigned to symbols a, b and c, thus G' is obtained:

$$
G' : \begin{array}{l}
\mathtt{a} \mapsto A/t, t \\
\mathtt{b} \mapsto B/t, t \\
\mathtt{c} \mapsto C, E, G, \\
\qquad t, t/t \\
\mathtt{d} \mapsto ((t/A)/B)/C, \\
\qquad ((t/t)/E)/t, \\
\qquad ((t/G)/t)/(t/t) \\
\mathtt{r} \mapsto t, \\
\qquad (t/t)/t
\end{array}
$$

Depending on p_1 being true or false, let $\mathtt{a} \mapsto t/t$ or $\mathtt{a} \mapsto (t/t)/t$, respectively. Depending on p_2 being true or false, let $\mathtt{b} \mapsto t/t$ or $\mathtt{b} \mapsto (t/t)/t$, respectively. If both p_1 and p_2 are false, A and B have to be substituted by (t/t), resulting in G'':

$$
G'' : \begin{array}{l}
\mathtt{a} \mapsto (t/t)/t, t \\
\mathtt{b} \mapsto (t/t)/t, t \\
\mathtt{c} \mapsto C, E, G, \\
\qquad t, t/t \\
\mathtt{d} \mapsto ((t/(t/t))/(t/t))/C, \\
\qquad ((t/t)/E)/t, \\
\qquad ((t/G)/t)/(t/t) \\
\mathtt{r} \mapsto t, \\
\qquad (t/t)/t
\end{array}
$$

One glance at the three types assigned to d will show that none of them can be unified with any of the others, so there is no Θ such that $\Theta[G''] \in \mathcal{G}_{\text{2-valued}}$. Thus $\neg(p_1 \vee p_2)$ implies that there is no Θ such that $\Theta[\mathrm{GF}(\mathrm{or}(p_1, p_2))] \subseteq \varphi(\mathrm{or}(p, q))$, for any learning function φ that is responsive and consistent on $\mathcal{G}_{\text{2-valued}}$ and learns that class prudently (from structures).

In the other cases – i.e. either p_1 or p_2 or both are true – the required substitution exists, this can easily be checked by the reader. □

In order to prove NP-hardness of an algorithmic problem L, it suffices to show that there exists a polynomial-time reduction from an NP-complete problem L' to L. We will present such a reduction using the vertex-cover problem, an NP-hard optimization problem.

Definition 10. *Let $G = (V, E)$ be an undirected graph, where V is a set of vertices and E is a set of edges, represented as tuples of vertices. A* vertex cover *of G is a subset $V' \subseteq V$ such that if $(u, v) \in E$,*

then $u \in V'$ or $v \in V'$ (or both). That is, each vertex 'covers' its incident edges, and a vertex cover for G is a set of vertices that covers all the edges in E. The size *of a vertex cover is the number of vertices in it.*

The vertex-cover problem *is the problem of finding a vertex cover of minimum size (called an* optimal vertex cover*) in a given graph.*

The vertex cover problem can be restated as a decision problem: *does a vertex cover of given size k exist for some given graph? Related to this is the* production problem *variant: given a graph, produce a cover of given size k, if it exists.*

Proposition 11. *The vertex-cover problem is* NP*-hard, the decision problem related to the vertex-cover problem is* NP*-complete, and the production problem is* NP*-hard.*

Note that the proof of both Lemma 9 and the following theorem use the right slash / exclusively. The subclass of $\mathcal{G}_{\text{2-valued}}$ with this property will be denoted as $\mathcal{G}_{\text{2-valued}} \restriction \{/\}$.[5]

Theorem 12. *Learning $\mathcal{G}_{\text{2-valued}} \restriction \{/\}$ from structures by means of a function that is responsive and consistent on its class and learns its class prudently is* NP*-hard in the size of the alphabet.* [6]

`Proof`: It will be shown that the production version of the vertex-cover problem can be reduced in polynomial time to a learning problem for the class $\mathcal{G}_{\text{2-valued}} \restriction \{/\}$, thus showing NP-hardness. We proceed by demonstrating a procedure for rewriting a graph as a sample for this class and interpreting the output of a learning function as a vertex-cover.

Let $e = |E|, v = |V|$. The coding defined in Definition 8 can be used to enforce the constraint that, for every edge in the graph, at least one of the vertices incident on that edge is included in the cover. Doing this for every edge in the graph requires e versions of the sample in Definition 8, each with its own unique symbols (for convenience, these will be written as indexed versions of the original symbols). Since detailing this sample will unnecessarily clutter the proof it will simply be assumed that e2or -a function from E to sample D_{or} based on the function or - has the required properties.

What remains to be shown is how a bound on the size of the cover can be translated to the problem of learning a 2-valued grammar. Let b be this bound, and $size = v - b$.

---

[5] Unidirectional *rigid* grammars that only use / generate a subclass of the class of *simple languages*, which is a subclass of deterministic context-free languages.

[6] Note that the notion of NP-hardness does not apply to *functions* but to *problems*. The problem here is *learning a specific class* under certain restrictions.

Let D_v be the following sample:

$$
\left\{
\begin{array}{l}
\texttt{x}_1 \\
\texttt{fa(fa(s1,fa(g,f)),fa(e,f))} \\
\texttt{fa(s1,fa(e,f))} \\
\texttt{fa(x}_1\texttt{,fa(s1,fa(v}_1\texttt{,f)))} \\
\\
\text{For every } v_i \in V, v > 1: \\
\texttt{x}_i \\
\texttt{fa(x}_i\texttt{(fa(fa(s}_i\texttt{,fa(g,f)),fa(e,f)))} \\
\texttt{fa(x}_{i-1}\texttt{,fa(s}_i\texttt{,fa(e,f)))} \\
\texttt{fa(x}_i\texttt{,fa(s}_i\texttt{,fa(v}_i\texttt{,f)))} \\
\\
\texttt{e} \\
\texttt{fa(e,f)} \\
\texttt{fa(x}_v\texttt{,fa(t,f))} \\
\texttt{fa(fa(}\underbrace{\texttt{...fa(fa(t,fa(e,f)),fa(e,f)), ...}}_{size\ \text{times}}\texttt{),f)} \\
\texttt{t} \\
\texttt{fa(fa(g,fa(e,f)),fa(e,f))}
\end{array}
\right\}
$$

Note that this sample does not have symbols in common with D_{or}, which allows us to consider their general forms in isolation from one another. Eventually a relation between the two has to be established, so for this purpose certain symbols occurring in the two samples will be identified later.

Let $G = \mathrm{GF}(D_v)$:

$$
G: \quad
\begin{array}{rlrl}
\texttt{s1} \mapsto & (t/E_0)/A_1, & \texttt{t} \mapsto & T/G, \\
& t/E_1, & & \underbrace{((t/\ldots)/t)}_{size\ \text{times}}/I, \\
& X_{1,3}/V_1 & & t \\
\texttt{s2} \mapsto & (X_{2,1}/E_2)/A_2, & \texttt{e} \mapsto & t, \\
& X_{2,2}/E_3, & & t/F, \\
& X_{2,3}/V_2 & & J_1/L_1, \\
\ldots & & & J_2/L_2, \\
\texttt{s}_v \mapsto & (X_{v,1}/E_v)/A_v, & & E_0/H_0, \\
& X_{v,2}/E_{v+1}, & & E_1/H_1, \\
& X_{v,3}/V_v & & E_2/H_2, \\
& & & \ldots \\
\texttt{x}_1 \mapsto & t, & \texttt{v}_1 \mapsto & V_1/N_1 \\
& t/X_{1,3}, & \texttt{v}_2 \mapsto & V_2/N_2 \\
& t/X_{2,1}, & \ldots & \\
& t/X_{2,2} & \texttt{v}_v \mapsto & V_v/N_v \\
\texttt{x}_2 \mapsto & t, & \texttt{f} \mapsto & F, G, I, L_1, L_2, \\
& t/X_{2,3} & & H_0, H_1, H_2, \ldots, \\
\ldots & & & M_1, M_2, \ldots, \\
\texttt{x}_{v-1} \mapsto & t, & & N_1, N_2, \ldots \\
& t/X_{v-1,3}, & \texttt{g} \mapsto & (t/J_1)/J_2, \\
& t/X_{v,1}, & & A_1/M_1, \\
& t/X_{v,2} & & A_2/M_2, \\
\texttt{x}_v \mapsto & t, & & \ldots \\
& t/X_{v,3}, & & \\
& t/T & &
\end{array}
$$

Unifying all complex types assigned to $\mathtt{x}_i$, for any $1 \le i \le v$ yields grammar G':

$$
G' : \begin{array}{rl@{\qquad}rl}
\mathtt{s1} \mapsto & (t/E_0)/A_1, & \mathtt{t} \mapsto & T/G, \\
 & t/E_1, & & \underbrace{((t/\ldots)/t)}_{size \text{ times}}/I, \\
 & X_1/V_1 & & t \\
\mathtt{s2} \mapsto & (X_1/t)/A_2, & \mathtt{e} \mapsto & t, \\
 & X_1/E_2, & & t/F, \\
 & X_2/V_2 & & J_1/L_1, \\
\ldots & & & J_2/L_2, \\
\mathtt{s}_v \mapsto & (X_{v-1}/t)/A_v, & & E_0/H_0, \\
 & X_{v-1}/E_v, & & \ldots \\
 & X_v/V_v & \mathtt{v}_1 \mapsto & V_1/N_1 \\
 & & \ldots & \\
\mathtt{x}_1 \mapsto & t, & \mathtt{v}_v \mapsto & V_v/N_v \\
 & t/X_1 & \mathtt{f} \mapsto & F, G, I, L_1, L_2, \\
\ldots & & & H_0, H_1, \ldots, \\
\mathtt{x}_{v-1} \mapsto & t, & & M_1, M_2, \ldots, \\
 & t/X_{v-1} & & N_1, N_2, \ldots \\
\mathtt{x}_v \mapsto & t, & \mathtt{g} \mapsto & (t/J_1)/J_2, \\
 & t/X_v & & A_1/M_1, \\
 & t/T & & A_2/M_2, \\
 & & & \ldots
\end{array}
$$

Unifying all complex types assigned to $\mathtt{e}$, $\mathtt{g}$ and $\mathtt{t}$ respectively yields G'':

$$
G'' : \begin{array}{rl@{\qquad}rl}
\mathtt{s1} \mapsto & (t/t)/(t/t), & \mathtt{t} \mapsto & \underbrace{((t/\ldots)/t)}_{size \text{ times}}/G, \\
 & t/t, & & t \\
 & X_1/V_1 & \mathtt{e} \mapsto & t, \\
\mathtt{s2} \mapsto & (X_1/t)/(t/t), & & t/F \\
 & X_1/t, & \mathtt{v}_1 \mapsto & V_1/N_1 \\
 & X_2/V_2 & \ldots & \\
\ldots & & \mathtt{v}_v \mapsto & V_v/N_v \\
\mathtt{s}_v \mapsto & (X_{v-1}/t)/(t/t), & \mathtt{f} \mapsto & F, G, t, \\
 & X_{v-1}/t, & & N_1, N_2, \ldots \\
 & X_v/V_v & \mathtt{g} \mapsto & (t/t)/t \\
\mathtt{x}_1 \mapsto & t, & & \\
 & t/X_1 & & \\
\ldots & & & \\
\mathtt{x}_v \mapsto & t, & & \\
 & t/X_v, & & \\
 & t/\underbrace{(t/\ldots)/t}_{size \text{ times}} & &
\end{array}
$$

Since D_v is a sample for a language in $\mathcal{L}_{\text{2-valued}}$, for all $1 \leq i \leq v$, the type X_i/V_i assigned to $\mathtt{s}_i$ has to be unified with one of the two other types assigned to $\mathtt{s}_i$. Thus for any $G''' = \varphi(D_v)$, $G''' = \Theta[G'']$, where Θ unifies the type X_i assigned to symbol $\mathtt{x}i$ with either X_{i-1}/t or X_{i-1} (in the case $i = 1$, with either t/t or t). Thus $\Theta[X_v]$ will have a minimum degree of 0 and a maximum degree of v, and this degree is exactly the number of types X_i unified with types X_{i-1}/t.

The assignments to $\mathtt{x}_v$ necessitate the unification of t/X_v with $t/\underbrace{(t/\ldots)/t}_{size\ \text{times}}$. This implies that X_v must have degree $size$, so exactly $size$ X_i types must have been unified with X_{i-1}/t types in the assignments to $\mathtt{s}i$. This implies that Θ has to unify a total number of $size$ V_i-types with t/t, and $v - size$ V_i-types with t. So $\Theta[GF(D_v)]$ will be defined if and only if the vertex-cover is of size b.

What remains to be shown is how D_{or} and D_v can be related to one another. As mentioned earlier certain symbols will be identified for this purpose.

Let $fe(i, a)$ and $fe(i, b)$ give indices for the two vertices incident on edge i. Recall that $G = \varphi(D_{or})$ contains for every $e_i \in E$ the following assignments:

$$\mathsf{a}_i \mapsto A_i/t, t$$
$$\mathsf{b}_i \mapsto B_i/t, t$$

Here A_i and B_i indicate (non)inclusion in the vertex-cover of vertices $v_{fe(i,a)}$ and $v_{fe(i,b)}$, respectively. Simply identifying the symbols a_i and b_i with the right symbols $\mathtt{v}_{fe(i,a)}$ and $\mathtt{v}_{fe(i,b)}$ will ensure that every variable $V_j, 1 \leq j \leq v$ is identified with all the A- and B-variables in $\mathrm{GF}(D_{or})$ that it should be identified with, given the graph. Since, given the constraints on the learning function and class, D_{or} only allows for assignments of t ('true', or 'assigned to cover') or t/t ('false', or 'not assigned to cover') to variables A_i and B_i, by this identification, the same is true for the V-variables.

Since the sample D_{or} ensures that all edges in E are covered, and D_v ensures that the cover contains only a given number of vertices, a learning function for the class $\mathcal{G}_{\text{2-valued}}$ that is responsive and consistent on its class and learns its class prudently can solve *any* (production version of the) vertex-cover problem, which is NP-hard.

The computation time needed for the reduction from graph to sample is linear in e and v, as is the size of the alphabet, and the solution can be read from the assignments in G''' to symbols $\mathtt{v}_1 \ldots \mathtt{v}_v$ in linear time. Thus, updating the hypothesis for such a learning function is NP-hard in the size of the alphabet. □

Since the direction of the slash is immaterial for the proof of Theorem 12, it follows immediately that

Corollary 13. *Learning $\mathcal{G}_{\text{2-valued}} \upharpoonright \{\backslash\}$ from structures by means of a function that is responsive and consistent on its class and learns its class prudently is* NP*-hard in the size of the alphabet.*

The proof of Theorem 12 can easily be adapted to the class $\mathcal{G}_{k\text{-valued}}$, for any given $k > 2$, by extending the sample with structures that result in the assignment to all $symbol \in \Sigma$ of extra types that are pairwise not unifiable. This can be done using one slash exclusively, by including the following structure in the sample for all symbols $symbol$, and for as many different x's as needed: $\mathtt{fa(}\underbrace{\ldots\mathtt{fa(fa(}symbol\mathtt{,fa(e,f)),fa(e,f)),}\ldots}_{x\text{ times}}\mathtt{)}$. This will result in the assignment $symbol \mapsto \underbrace{((t/\ldots)/t)}_{x\text{ times}}$ being included in any $G = \varphi(\mathrm{GF}(D)), G \in \mathcal{G}_{2\text{-valued}}$. Thus:

Corollary 14. *Learning any class* $\mathcal{G}_{k\text{-valued}} \restriction \{/\}, k \geq 2$ *from structures by means of a function that is responsive and consistent on its class and learns its class prudently is* NP*-hard in the size of the alphabet.*

And since the direction of the slash is immaterial with respect to complexity, we also get:

Corollary 15. *Learning any class* $\mathcal{G}_{k\text{-valued}} \restriction \{\backslash\}, k \geq 2$ *from structures by means of a function that is responsive and consistent on its class and learns its class prudently is* NP*-hard in the size of the alphabet.*

In general, proving NP-hardness of learning class $\mathcal{L}$ under a set of constraints C does not imply that the result holds for learning a class $\mathcal{L}', \mathcal{L} \subset \mathcal{L}'$ under C, since a learning function for $\mathcal{L}'$ would not in general be prudent with respect to $\mathcal{L}$. The function could therefore be able to 'postpone' certain conjectures by hypothesizing languages in $\mathcal{L}' - \mathcal{L}$, thus invalidating our type of proof. Given Lemma 7 however it should be clear that allowing slashes in both directions does not affect our proof at all, thus it follows that

Theorem 16. *Learning any class* $\mathcal{G}_{k\text{-valued}}, k \geq 2$ *from structures by means of a function that is responsive and consistent on its class and learns its class prudently is* NP*-hard in the size of the alphabet.*

Considering these results it is natural to ask whether these problems are also NP-*complete*. In order to prove this it has to be

shown that the problem is in NP, for example by showing that verification of solutions is in P. In this case the complexity of the verification problem would be related with the complexity of problems like deciding consistency of the conjecture with the input and membership of the conjecture in the class. However, the question whether the conjecture is *justified* given the input is problematic, since this notion is based on the concept of identification in the limit. It is not clear how this constraint can be expressed in terms of computational complexity. (Cf Section 1.2.)

5 Conclusion and Further Research

In [CF00] it has been shown that learning any of the classes $\mathcal{G}_{\text{least-valued}}$, $\mathcal{G}_{\text{least-card}}$, and $\mathcal{G}_{\text{minimal}}$ from structures by means of a learning function that is consistent on its class is NP-hard in the size of the sample. The result for the classes $\mathcal{G}_{k\text{-valued}}$ was weaker: one function that can learn these classes *for each* k and is consistent on its class is NP-hard in the size of the sample. It was still an open question whether there exist polynomial-time learning functions for $\mathcal{G}_{k\text{-valued}}$ for each k separately. In this paper it has been shown that learning any class in $\mathcal{G}_{k\text{-valued}}, k \geq 2$ from structures by means of a learning function that is consistent on its class is NP-hard in the size of the *alphabet*. Complexity with respect to the size of the *sample* is still open, but in the light of our result this question seems of academic interest only. The problem does not scale well with the size of the alphabet (lexicon), which makes the problem intractable in practice.

It is a well-known fact that learning functions for any learnable class without consistency- and monotonicity constraints can be transformed to trivial learning functions that have polynomial update-time (see Subsection 1.2). It is an open question whether there exist 'intelligent' inconsistent learning functions that have polynomial update-time for the classes under discussion. In [LW91] an example of such a function can be found that learns the class of all pattern languages ([Ang79]) and is computationally well-behaved given certain assumption about the distribution of the input.

References

[Ang79] D. Angluin. Finding common patterns to a set of strings. In *Proceedings of the 11th Annual Symposium on Theory of Computing*, pages 130–141, 1979.

[Bar74] J. Barzdin. Inductive inference of automata, functions and programs. In *Proceedings International Congress of Math.*, pages 455–460, Vancouver, 1974.

[BP90] W. Buszkowski and G. Penn. Categorial grammars determined from linguistic data by unification. *Studia Logica*, 49:431–454, 1990.

[Bus87] W. Buszkowski. Discovery procedures for categorial grammars. In E. Klein and J. van Benthem, editors, *Categories, Polymorphism and Unification.* University of Amsterdam, 1987.

[CF00] C. Costa Florêncio. On the complexity of consistent identification of some classes of structure languages. In Arlindo L. Oliveira, editor, *Grammatical Inference: Algorithms and Applications*, volume 1891 of *Lecture Notes in Artificial Intelligence*, pages 89–102. Springer-Verlag, 2000.

[DS86] R. Daley and C. Smith. On the complexity of inductive inference. *Information and Control*, 69:12–40, 1986.

[Gol67] E. M. Gold. Language identification in the limit. *Information and Control*, 10:447–474, 1967.

[JORS99] Sanjay Jain, Daniel Osherson, James Royer, and Arun Sharma. *Systems that Learn: An Introduction to Learning Theory.* The MIT Press, Cambridge, MA., second edition, 1999.

[Kan98] M. Kanazawa. *Learnable Classes of Categorial Grammars.* CSLI Publications, Stanford University, 1998.

[LW91] Steffen Lange and Rolf Wiehagen. Polynomial time inference of arbitrary pattern languages. *New Generation Computing*, 8:361–370, 1991.

[OdJMW96] D. N. Osherson, D. de Jongh, E. Martin, and S. Weinstein. Formal learning theory. In J. van Benthem and A. ter Meulen, editors, *Handbook of Logic and Language.* Elsevier Science Publishing, 1996.

[Pit89] L. Pitt. Inductive inference, dfas, and computational complexity. In K. P. Jantke, editor, *Proceedings of International Workshop on Analogical and Inductive Inference*, number 397 in Lecture Notes in Computer Science, pages 18–44, 1989.

[Ste98] Werner Stein. Consistent polynominal identification in the limit. In *Algorithmic Learning Theory (ALT)*, volume 1501 of *Lecture Notes in Computer Science*, pages 424–438, Berlin, 1998. Springer-Verlag.

[WZ95] R. Wiehagen and T. Zeugmann. Learning and consistency. In K. P. Jantke and S. Lange, editors, *Algorithmic Learning for Knowledge-Based Systems*, number 961 in Lecture Notes in Artificial Intelligence, pages 1–24. Springer-Verlag, 1995.

Polarized Non-projective Dependency Grammars

Alexander Dikovsky

Université de Nantes, IRIN, 2, rue de la Houssinière
BP 92208 F 44322 Nantes cedex 3 France
Alexandre.Dikovsky@irin.univ-nantes.fr
http://www.sciences.univ-nantes.fr/info/perso/permanents/dikovsky/

Abstract. *Dependency tree grammars* are proposed in which unbounded discontinuity is resolved through the first available valency saturation. In general, they are expressive enough to generate non-semilinear context sensitive languages, but in the practical situation where the number of non saturated valencies is bounded by a constant, they are weakly equivalent to cf-grammars, are parsable in cubic time, and are stronger than non-projective dependency grammars without long dependencies.

1 Introduction

Dependency based theories of surface syntax are well suited for treating discontinuity, which corresponds in dependency terms to non-projectivity. In contrast to phrase structure, the word order is separated from dependency structure. So one should describe syntactic relations between words explicitly in terms of *precedence* and *dependency* or its transitive closure : *dominance*. Being more flexible, the dependency syntax allows one to express some properties of syntactic structure which are hardly ever expressible in terms of phrase structure. The *projectivity* is one of such properties. It requires that any word occurring between a word g and a word d dependent on g were dominated by g. In first dependency grammars [4] and in some more recent grammars : link grammars [19], projective dependency grammars [10] the projectivity is implied by definition. In some other theories, e.g. in word grammar [6], it is included into the axioms defining acceptable surface structures. In presence of this property, D-trees are in a sense equivalent to phrase structures with head selection. For this reason, D-trees determined by grammars of Robinson [18], categorial grammars [1], and some other formalisms are projective. Projectivity affects the complexity of parsing: as a rule, it allows dynamic programming techniques which lead to polynomial time algorithms (cf. Earley-type algorithm for link grammars in [19]). Meanwhile, till the early 80ies, the search is continued of formalisms treating various non-projective constructions such as pronoun or WH-word extraction in Romance or Germanic languages, interrogative sentences, relative clauses, topicalization, paired conjunctions or prepositions, discontinuous negation, French pronominal clitics, etc. In a sense, non-projectivity and parsing efficiency are

P. de Groote, G. Morrill, C. Retoré (Eds.): LACL 2001, LNAI 2099, pp. 139–157, 2001.

mutually exclusive. It is not surprising then, that to find a formalism which would be acceptable from both expressivity and effectiveness points of view is a difficult problem.

There are various formal dependency based approaches to this problem. Most liberal are the dependency grammars in the framework of Meaning-Text Theory [12], where dependencies are defined by independent rules, whose applicability to a pair of word-forms is determined by local constraints. The cost of this liberty is theoretically non-tractable parsing (the NP-hardness argument of Neuhaus and Bröker [17] applies to them). More recent versions of dependency grammars (see e.g.[8,11,2]) impose on non-projective D-trees some constraints weaker than projectivity (cf. meta-projectivity [16] or pseudo-projectivity [8]), sufficient for existence of a polynomial time parsing algorithm. Still another approach is developed in the context of intuitionistic resource-dependent logics, where D-trees are constructed from derivations (cf. e.g. a method in [9] for Lambek calculus). In this context, non-projective D-trees are determined with the use of hypothetical reasoning, structural rules such as commutativity and associativity, and multi-modality (see e.g. [14,15,5]).

An approach to non-projective dependencies proposed in this paper is combining the polarity idea of resource-dependent logics and a tree composition mechanism of dependency tree grammars [13,3], which brings the benefit of effective parsing. The *dependency tree (DT-) grammars* we define here are analyzing in the same sense as categorial grammars: they reduce phrases to types and simultaneously compose the corresponding dependency structures. These structures (we call them *DV-structures*) are discontinuous and polarized in the sense that some their nodes may have valencies (positive for potential governors and negative for potential dependents). Saturating a pair of corresponding valencies introduces a *long dependency.* We impose on dependencies no projectivity-like constraints. Instead, we use a simple discipline of saturating valencies, so called first-available (FA) saturation and we keep track of valencies non-saturated in a DV-structure in its *integral valency.* "First available" means "closest not yet saturated". This natural discipline was already used in the literature (cf. [20]). The polarities are controlled in such a way that a cycle-free DV-structure becomes a D-tree if its integral valency is empty. So a DT-grammar determines D-trees FA-saturating DV-structures of reducible strings.

The first result of this paper is that when the integral valency is bounded by a constant and the FA-saturation causes no cycles, DT-grammars are weakly equivalent to cf-grammars and have a $\boldsymbol{O}(n^3)$-time parsing algorithm. The second result is that they are stronger than non-projective dependency grammars without long dependencies. The weak equivalence to cf-grammars doesn't prevent to express structural discontinuity in terms of dependencies. In presence of FA-saturation, long dependencies represent such phenomena as unbounded raising and extraction. Bounded integral valency doesn't mean that the nesting of discontinuous structures is bounded. It means that before nesting a new discontinuous construction the valencies of the current one should be saturated. In Fig. 1(a) we show a sentence with integral valency 2 (extraction from extracted phrase), which is maybe most complex in French. It contrasts with lifting to a host word in the case of French pronominal clitics (see D-tree (b) in Fig. 1), which is described by a local non-projective dependency.

The paper is organized as follows. Dependency structures and their properties are described in Section 2, dependency grammars and main results are in Section 3. All proofs are moved to the Appendix.

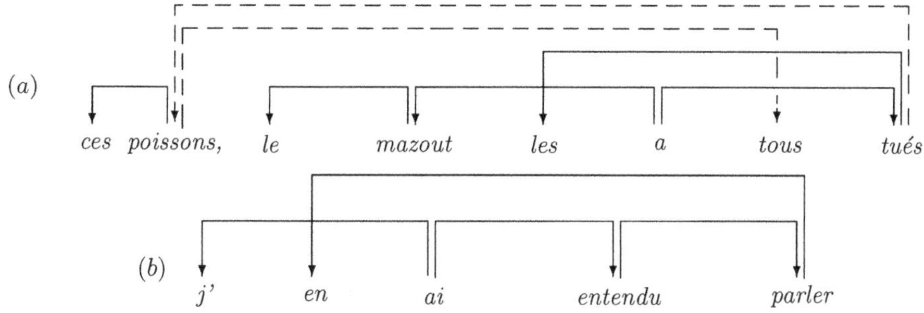

Fig. 1.

2 Dependency Structures

We fix alphabets W of *terminals* (words), C of *nonterminals* (syntactic types or classes), and N of *dependency names*. For a string $x \in (W \cup C)^+$, we denote by $\mu(x)$ the list of occurrences of symbols in x.

Definition 1 *Let $x \in (W \cup C)^+$ be a string. A set $\pi = \{d_1, ..., d_n\}$ of trees covering $\mu(x)$ (called* components *of π), which have no nodes in common and whose arcs are labeled by names in N, is a* dependency (D-) structure *on x if one component d_t of π is selected as its* head [1]. *We use the notation $x = w(\pi)$. If x belongs to W^+, π is said to be* terminal. *When π has only one component, it is a* dependency (D-) tree *on x.*

Composition of D-structures is defined as follows.

Definition 2 *Let $\pi_1 = \{d_1, ..., d_k\}$ be a D-structure, n be its node, $w(\pi_1) = w_1 n w_2$, and $\pi_2 = \{d'_1, ..., \underline{d'_t}, ..., d'_l\}$ be a D-structure with the head component d'_t. Then the result of the composition of π_2 into π_1 in n is the D-structure $\pi_1[n\backslash\pi_2]$, in which π_2 is substituted for n (i.e. $w(\pi_1[n\backslash\pi_2]) = w_1 w(\pi_2) w_2$), the root of d'_t inherits all dependencies of n in π_1, and the head component is that of π_1 (changed respectively if touched on by composition)* [2].

Composition of D-trees is a special case of this definition. For example, in Fig. 2, $\pi_3 = \pi_1[A\backslash\pi_2]$ and $d_3 = d_1[A\backslash d_2]$.

[1] We visualize d_t underlining it or its root, when there are some other components.

[2] This composition generalizes the substitution used in TAGs [7] and is not like the adjunction.

We will consider *long* the dependencies implicitly specified by *valencies* of nodes in D-structures. A valency indicates that a dependency r is expected at this node with some sign and in some direction. For example, the intuitive sense of a positive valency $+R : r$ of a node n is that a long dependency r would go from n somewhere on its right. Respectively, a negative valency $-L : r$ of m means that a long dependency r would enter m from somewhere on its left. Assigning to terminal nodes of D-structures their valencies, we obtain a new kind of D-structures: *DV-structures.* The explicit dependencies of DV-structures are considered *local.*

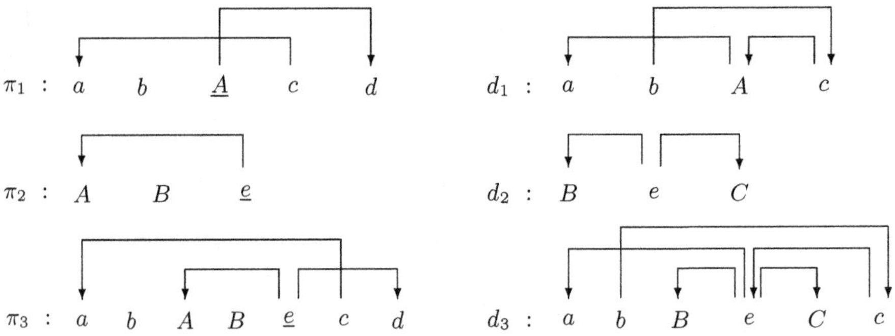

π_1 and π_2 are respectively 3- and 2-component D-structures (e.g., in π_1, the head component is the D-tree with the root A and dependent d), whereas π_3 is a four-component D-structure; d_1, d_2 and d_3 are D-trees (d_2 is projective, d_1, d_3 are non-projective).

Fig. 2.

Definition 3 *A* valency *is an expression of one of the forms* $+L : r, +R : r$ *(a* positive *valency), or* $-L : r, -R : r$ *(a* negative *valency),* r *being a dependency name*[3]. *A terminal* n *is* polarized *if a finite list of valencies* $V(n)$ *(its* valency list*) is assigned to it.* n *is* positive, *if* $V(n)$ *does not contain negative valencies, otherwise it is* negative. *As it concerns nonterminals, we presume that* C *is decomposed into two classes : of* positive $(C^{(+)})$ *and* negative $(C^{(-)})$ *nonterminals respectively. A D-tree with polarized nodes is* positive *if its root is* positive, *otherwise it is* negative.

A D-structure π *on a string* x *of polarized symbols is a* D-structure with valencies *(a* DV-structure*) on* x, *if the following conditions are satisfied :*

(v1) if a terminal node n *of* π *is negative, then* $V_\pi(n)$ *(or* $V(n)$ *when clear) contains exactly one negative valency,*

(v2) if a dependency of π *enters a node* n, *then* n *is positive,*

(v3) the non-head components of π *(if any) are all negative.*

The polarity of a DV structure *is that of its head.*

---

[3] We denote the valencies by dashed arcs in braces entering from or going to the indicated direction.

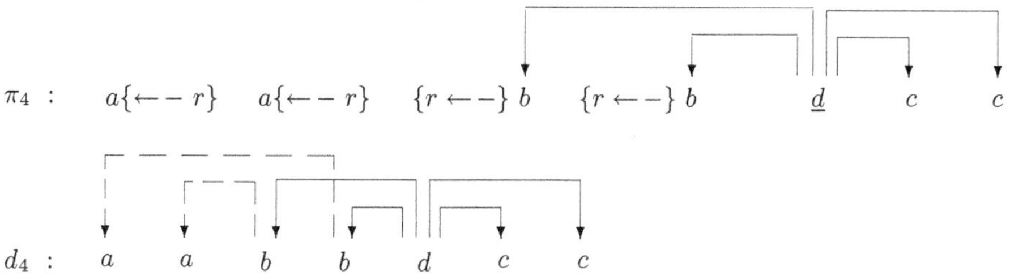

Fig. 3.

For example, π_4 in Fig. 3 is a DV-structure, in which two occurrences of a with $V(a) = \{-R : r\}$ are two negative non-head components, two occurrences of b with $V(b) = \{+L : r\}$ belong to the head component, and V is empty for the other three occurrences.

Valencies are *saturated* by *long dependencies*, eventually completing terminal DV-structures so that they become D-trees.

Definition 4 *Let π be a terminal DV-structure. A triplet $l =< n_1, n_2, r >$, where n_1, n_2 are nodes of π and $r \in N$, is a* long dependency *with the name r, directed from n_1 to n_2 (notation: $n_1 \overset{r}{- - >} n_2$), if there are valencies $v_1 \in V(n_1), v_2 \in V(n_2)$ such that :*

(v4) either $n_1 < n_2$ (n_1 precedes *n_2), $v_1 = +R : r$, and $v_2 = -L : r$, or*

(v5) $n_2 < n_1$, $v_1 = +L : r$, and $v_2 = -R : r$.

We will say that v_1 saturates *v_2 by long dependency l.*

The set of valencies in π is totally ordered by the order of nodes and the orders in their valency lists: $v_1 < v_2$ if

(o1) either $v_1 \in V_\pi(n_1), v_2 \in V_\pi(n_2)$ and $n_1 < n_2$,

(o2) or $v_1, v_2 \in V_\pi(n)$ and $v_1 < v_2$, in $V_\pi(n)$.

Let π_1 be the structure resulting from π by adding the long dependency l and replacing $V_\pi(n_1)$ by $V_{\pi_1}(n_1) = V_\pi(n_1) \setminus \{v_1\}$ and $V_\pi(n_2)$ by $V_{\pi_1}(n_2) = V_\pi(n_2) \setminus \{v_2\}$. We will say that π_1 is a saturation *of π by l and denote it by $\pi \prec \pi_1$. Among all possible saturations of π we will select the following particular one :*

Let $v_1 \in V_\pi(n_1)$ be the first non saturated positive valency in π, and $v_2 \in V_\pi(n_2)$ be the closest corresponding[4] *non saturated negative valency in π. Then the long dependency $l = \left(n_1 \overset{r}{- - >} n_2\right)$ saturating v_2 by v_1 is* first available (FA) *in π. The resulting saturation of π by l is* first available *or* FA-saturation *(notation : $\pi \prec^{FA} \pi_1$).*

We transform the relations $\prec, \prec^{FA}$ into partial orders closing them by transitivity.

---

[4] *Corresponding* means :

(c1) $n_2 < n_1$ and $v_2 = -R : r$ if $v_1 = +L : r$, and

(c2) $n_1 < n_2$ and $v_2 = -L : r$ if $v_1 = +R : r$.

Lemma 1 *Let π be a terminal DV-structure and $\pi \prec \pi_1$ for some structure π_1. Then either π_1 has a cycle, or it is a DV-structure.*

As it follows from Definition 4, all saturations of a terminal DV-structure π have the same set of nodes, but strictly narrower sets of valencies. This implies that any terminal DV-structure has *maximal saturations* with respect to the order relations $\prec$, $\prec^{FA}$. Very importantly, *there is a single maximal FA-saturation* of a terminal DV-structure π denoted $MS^1(\pi)$. For example, the saturation d_4 of π_4 in Fig. 3 is first available.

Eventually, all valencies in a DV-structure should be saturated. In order to keep track of those valencies which are not yet saturated we use the following notion of *integral valency.*

Definition 5 *Let π be a terminal DV-structure. If its maximal FA-saturation $MS^1(\pi)$ is a d-tree, we say that this D-tree* saturates *π and call π* saturable. *The* integral valency $\sum\limits_{FA}\pi$ *of π is the list $\bigcup\limits_{n\in\mu(w(\pi))} V_{MS^1(\pi)}(n)$ ordered by the order of valencies in π.*

By this definition, $\sum\limits_{FA} MS^1(\pi) = \sum\limits_{FA}\pi$.

Saturability is easily expressed in terms of integral valency.

Lemma 2 *Let π be a terminal DV-structure. Then :*
(1) $MS^1(\pi)$ is a D-tree iff it is cycle-free and $\sum\limits_{FA}\pi = \emptyset$,
(2) π has at most one saturating D-tree.

Nonterminals in DV-structures represent types of substructures. The types are realized through composition of DV-structures which extends that of D-structures.

Definition 6 *Let π_0 be a DV-structure, A be some its nonterminal node, and π_1 be some DV-structure* of the same polarity as A. *Then the* composition *of π_1 into π_0 in the place of A is the structure $\pi = \pi_0[A\backslash\pi_1]$, in which valency sets of terminal nodes and polarities of nonterminal nodes $B \neq A$ are the same as in π_0 and π_1.*

This composition has the following natural properties.

Lemma 3 *(1) If $\pi = \pi_0[A\backslash\pi_1]$ is defined for DV-structures π_0 and π_1, then it is also a DV-structure.*
(2) $\pi_0[A\backslash\pi_1]$ has the same polarity as π_0.

Lemma 4 *Let π_1, π_2 be terminal DV-structures and π_0 a DV-structure such that the compositions $\pi_0[A\backslash\pi_1]$, $\pi_0[A\backslash\pi_2]$ are both defined, and $\sum\limits_{FA}\pi_1 = \sum\limits_{FA}\pi_2$. Then $\sum\limits_{FA}\pi_0[A\backslash MS^1(\pi_1)] = \sum\limits_{FA}\pi_0[A\backslash MS^1(\pi_2)]$.*

Composition may be used to project some DV-structures onto shallow DV-structures representing the same non saturated valencies.

Definition 7 *Let us fix a set* $\bar{A} = \{\bar{A} \mid A \in C\}$ *of* terminal doubles *of nonterminals in* C*. Let* π_0 *be a DV-structure with* k *occurrences of nonterminals* $A_1, ..., A_k$*, and* $\pi_1, ..., \pi_k$ *be some terminal DV-structures with the corresponding polarities. Then the DV-structure* $\pi = \pi_0[A_1\backslash\bar{A}_1, ..., A_k\backslash\bar{A}_k]$ *with the valencies defined by assignments:* $V_\pi(\bar{A}_i) = \sum_{FA} \pi_i,\ 1 \le i \le k,$ *is a* projection *of the structure* $\pi_0[A_1\backslash\pi_1, ..., A_k\backslash\pi_k]$ *on* π_0*. We denote it by* $\pi_0\{A_1[\sum_{FA}\pi_1], ..., A_k[\sum_{FA}\pi_k]\}$.

Clearly, the so defined projection is unique. It also captures the integral valency of the projected structure when this structure results by composition from maximal FA-saturated structures.

Lemma 5 *If the DV-structure* $\pi_0[A_1\backslash\pi_1, ..., A_k\backslash\pi_k]$ *is defined for some* π_0, π_1, ..., π_k*, then*

$$\sum_{FA} \pi_0\{A_1[\sum_{FA}\pi_1], ..., A_k[\sum_{FA}\pi_k]\} = \sum_{FA} \pi_0[A_1\backslash MS^1(\pi_1), ..., A_k\backslash MS^1(\pi_k)].$$

This Lemma follows directly from Lemma 4 because the unit terminal structures $\bar{A}_i$ with valency sets $V_\pi(\bar{A}_i)$, $1 \le i \le k$, are maximally FA-saturated.

Adding long dependencies to DV-structures may in general cause cycles. For example, the structure π_5' in Fig. 4 is the result of adding long dependencies $b \overset{1}{--\!>} e$ and $g \overset{2}{--\!>} b$ into the four-component DV-structure π_5.

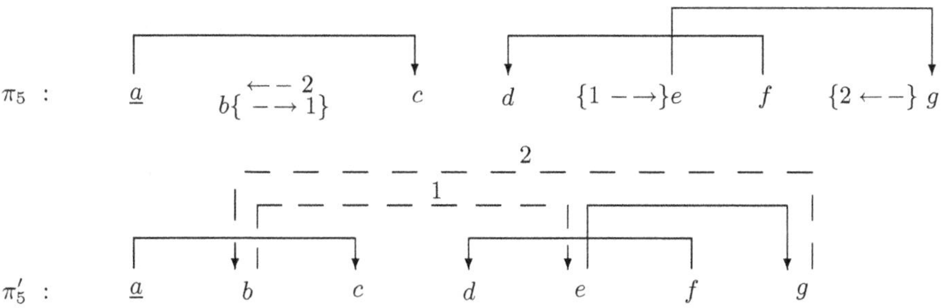

Fig. 4.

Projections capture the existence of cycles in maximal saturations of terminal DV-structures.

Lemma 6 *Let* $\pi_0[A_1\backslash\pi_1, ..., A_k\backslash\pi_k]$ *be defined for some terminal DV-structures* π_0, π_1, ..., π_k*, and* $\hat{\pi}$ *be the projection of the structure* $\pi = \pi_0[A_1\backslash MS^1(\pi_1), ..., A_k\backslash MS^1(\pi_k)]$ *on* π_0*. If* $MS^1(\pi)$ *has a cycle, whereas all* $MS^1(\pi_1), ..., MS^1(\pi_k)$ *are cycle-free, then* $MS^1(\hat{\pi})$ *also has a cycle.*

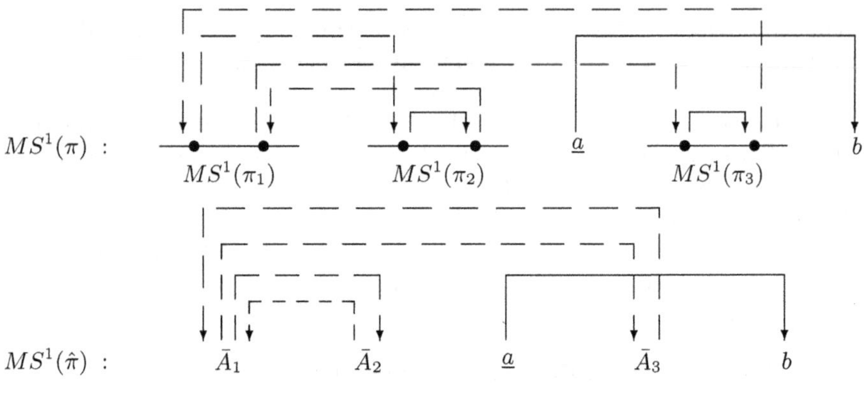

Fig. 5.

Fig. 5 presents an example of a correspondence between the maximal FA-saturation $MS^1(\pi)$ of a composition $\pi = \pi_0[A_1\backslash MS^1(\pi_1), A_2\backslash MS^1(\pi_2), A_3\backslash MS^1(\pi_3)]$ and the maximal FA-saturation of its projection $\hat{\pi}$.

3 Dependency Tree Grammars

Dependency tree grammars determine DV-structures in the bottom-up manner: they reduce DV-structures to their types. The reduction step is a composition of DV-structures followed by FA-saturation. The yield of a successful reduction is a D-tree.

Definition 8 Syntax. *A* dependency tree (DT-) grammar *is a system* $G = (W, C, N, I, R)$, *where* $I \in C^{(+)}$ *is the axiom (which is a positive nonterminal), and R is a set of reduction rules of the form* $\pi \rightarrow A$, *where* $A \in C$ *and* π *is a DV-structure of the same polarity as A. In the special case, where the DV-structures in the rules are D-trees, the DT-grammar is* local (LDT-grammar) [5].
Semantics. *1. A terminal rule* $r = (\pi \rightarrow A)$ *is a* reduction *of the structure* $MS^1(\pi)$ *to its type A (notation* $MS^1(\pi) \vdash^r A$*).*
[*The* integral valency *of* $MS^1(\pi)$ via r *is* $\sum\limits_{r} = \sum\limits_{FA} \pi$, π *is the* projection *of this reduction, and* r *has the* reduction rank $rr(r) = 1$.] [6]
2. Let $r = (\pi \rightarrow A)$ *be a reduction rule with k nonterminals occurrences* $A_1, ..., A_k$ *in* π, $k > 0$, *and* $\pi_1 \vdash^{\rho_1} A_1$, ..., $\pi_k \vdash^{\rho_k} A_k$ *be some reductions. Then* $\rho = (\rho_1 ... \rho_k; r)$ *is a reduction of the structure* $\pi_0 = MS^1(\pi[A_1\backslash\pi_1, ..., A_k\backslash\pi_k])$ *to its type A (notation* $\pi_0 \vdash^\rho A$*).* $\rho_1, ..., \rho_k$ *as well as* ρ *itself are* subreductions *of* ρ.

---

[5] LDT-grammars are strongly equivalent to dependency tree grammars of [13,3] which are generating and not analysing as here.

[6] We put into square brackets the notions used for technical needs.

[*The* integral valency *of* π_0 via ρ *is* $\sum_{\rho} \pi_0 = \sum_{FA} \pi[A_1\backslash\pi_1, ..., A_k\backslash\pi_k] = \sum_{FA} \pi_0$, $\pi\{A_1[\sum_{\rho_1} \pi_1], ..., A_k[\sum_{\rho_k} \pi_k]\}$ *is the* projection *of this reduction, and* ρ *has the* reduction rank $rr(\rho) = 1 + max\{rr(\rho_1), ..., rr(\rho_k)\}$.]
A D-tree d *is* determined *by* G *if there is a reduction* $d \vdash^{\rho} I$. *The* DT-language determined by G *is the set* $D(G)$ *of all D-trees it determines.* $L(G) = \{w(d) \mid d \in D(G)\}$ *is the* language determined by G. $\mathcal{L}(DTG)$ *and* $\mathcal{L}(LDTG)$ *denote the classes of languages determined by DT-grammars and LDT-grammars respectively.*

Remark. In this definition, the DT-grammars are devoid of various features indispensable for their application in practice, but unnecessary for purely theoretical analysis. In fact, as the categorial grammars, they should have a set of elementary types $E \subset C$. The valencies should be assigned to elementary types (and not to words). The DV-structures should be defined on E^+. There should be a *lexical interpretation* $\lambda \subseteq W \times E$ propagated to phrases by: $a_1...a_n\lambda e_1...e_n$, where $a_i\lambda e_i$, $1 \leq i \leq n$. Respectively, $L(G) = \{x \in W^+ \mid \exists\pi \in D(G)\ (x\lambda w(\pi))\}$. In Fig. 6, we show several rules of the kind.

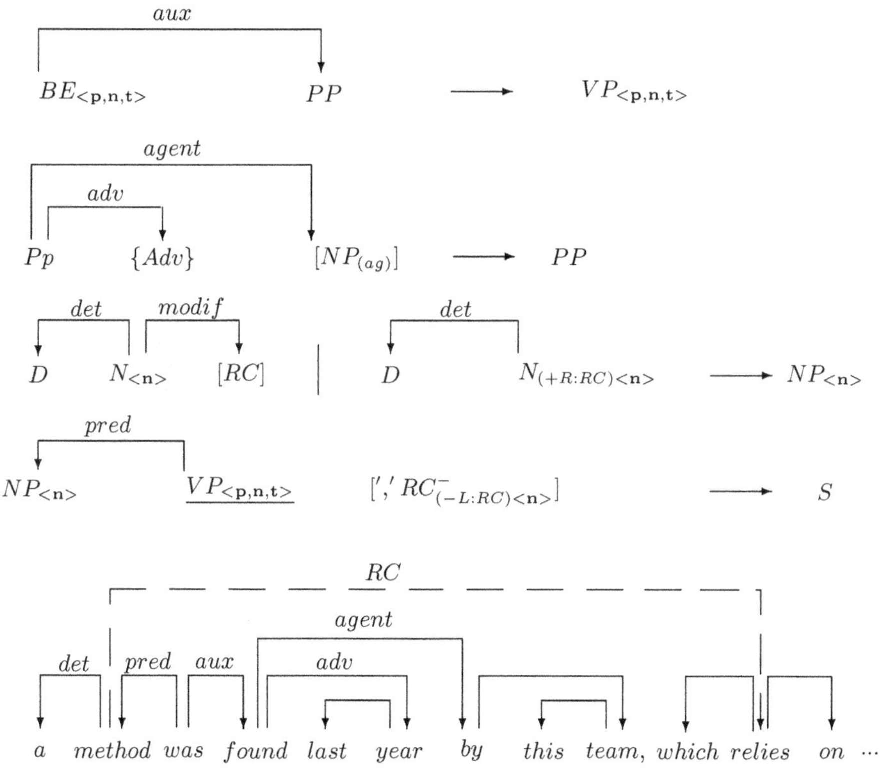

Fig. 6.

In a type $A_{(\gamma)<\tau>}$, γ is a list of grammatical dictionary features (valencies included) and τ is a list of morphological features. In the rules, $\{A\}$ means that A is iterable,

$[A]$ means that A is optional. The D-tree in this figure becomes reducible if we use the two polarized rules, which reduce respectively to $NP_{<n>}$ and S.

LDT-grammars are weakly equivalent to cf-grammars. The weak generative capacity of DT-grammars is stronger than that of cf-grammars. For example, the DT-grammar G_1 in Fig. 7 (a) determines a non-cf language $\{w(n) \mid w(n) = a^n b^n dc^n, \ n \geq 0\}$. D-tree d_4 in Fig. 3 is determined by G_1 on $w(2)$. Its reduction tree combined with the diagram of local and long dependencies (*reduction diagram*) is presented in Fig. 7(b). So weak generative capacity of DT-grammars is higher than that of LDT-grammars.

There is a trivial linear space decision procedure (hence, a cs-grammar) for languages determined by DT-grammars.

Proposition 1 $\mathcal{L}(CFG) = \mathcal{L}(LDTG) \subset \mathcal{L}(DTG) \subseteq \mathcal{L}(CSG)$.

As it concerns the strong generative capacity, even LDT-grammars simulate the projective dependency grammars of [10,8] and are stronger because they can generate non-projective D-trees.

Proposition 2 $\mathcal{D}(P-DG) \subset \mathcal{D}(LDTG) \subset \mathcal{D}(DTG)$ [7].

$$G_1 : \quad a\{\leftarrow - r\} \quad \underline{I} \quad | \quad A \quad \longrightarrow \quad I$$

$$\{r \leftarrow - \}b \quad A \quad c \quad | \quad d \quad \longrightarrow \quad A$$

(a)

(b)

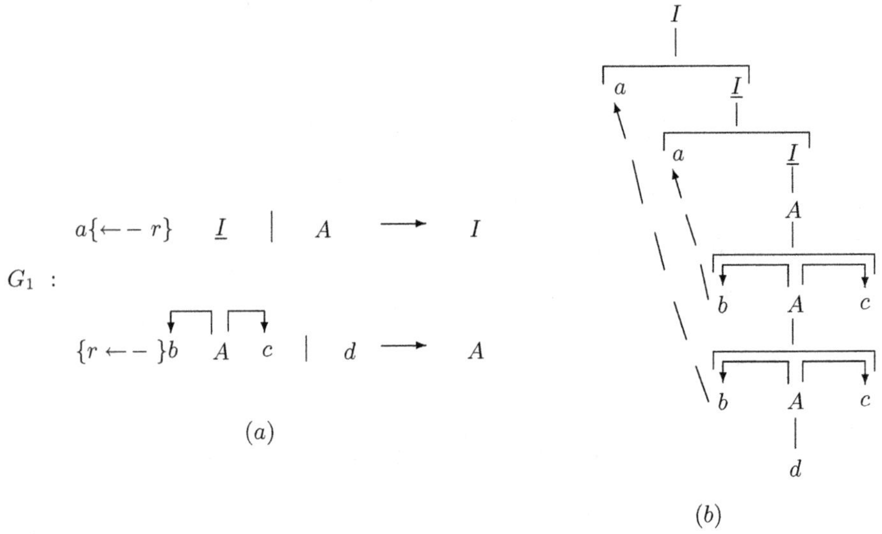

In the first rule, $V(a) = \{-R : r\}$ and $I \in C^{(+)}$ is the unit head component. In the third rule, $V(b) = \{+L : r\}$ and the DV-structure in the left part is the single head component with the root A.

Fig. 7.

We are not aiming at a precise characterization of the class of DTG-languages because this class is too rich for real applications. For example, we find non-semilinear languages in this family : the DT-grammar G_2 in Fig. 8 (a) determines

---

[7] Modification and ordering rules are simulated by rules $\pi \rightarrow A$, where π is a D-tree on Bx or xB with the root in B.

the language $\{w(n) \mid w(n) = a^{2^n}, n \geq 0\}$. The D-tree determined by G_2 on the string $w(3)$ is shown in Fig. 8 (b), and its reduction diagram is given in Fig. 8(c).

Our main interest is to provide for DT-grammars a polynomial time parsing algorithm. The evident problem which arises when applying to DT-grammars Earley type bottom-up algorithms is that, given a string $x \in W^+$, the algorithm can find a reduction ρ of some structure π on x (i.e. $x = w(\pi)$) which is not a D-tree, whereas some D-tree might be available through backtracking (exponentially long in the worst case). So we are looking for "local" (i.e. expressed in grammar rules) sufficient conditions of saturability and cyclelessness of reduced DV-structures.

Definition 9 *Let G be a DT-grammar. For a reduction ρ of a terminal structure, its* defect *is defined as* $\sigma(\rho) = max\{|\sum_{\rho'} \pi'| \mid \rho'$ *is a subreduction of* $\rho\}$. *G has* bounded *(*unbounded*)* defect *if there is some (there is no) constant q which bounds the defect of all its reductions. The minimal constant q having this property (if any) is the* defect *of G (denoted $\sigma(G)$).*

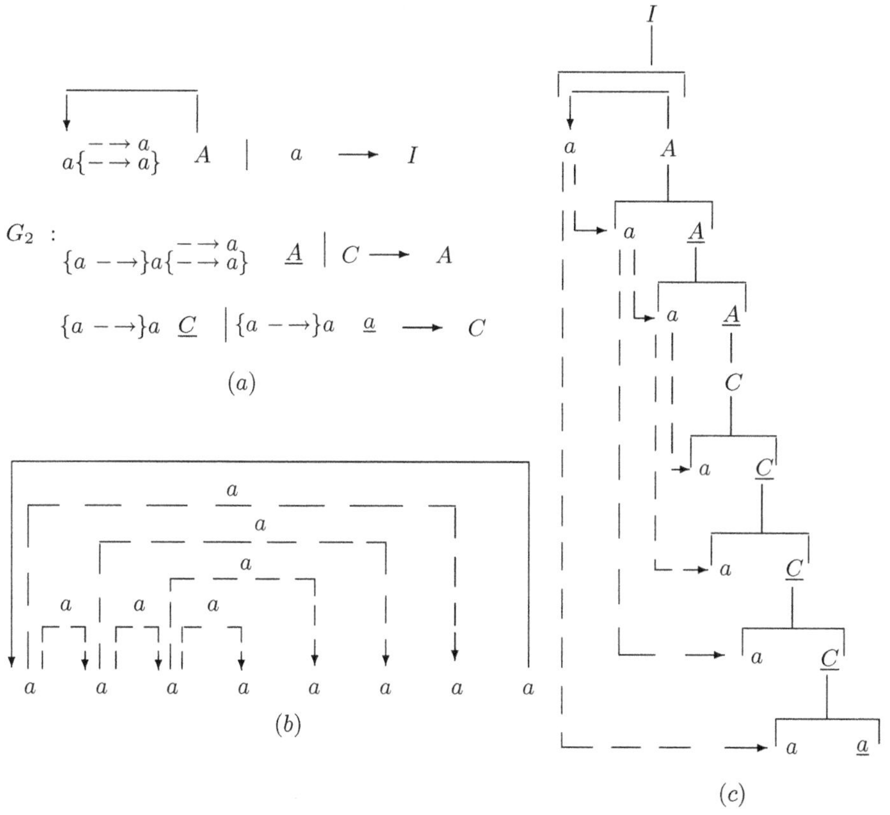

Fig. 8.

It is easy to see that in grammars G_1 in Fig. 7 and G_2 in Fig. 8 the size of integral valency of subreductions grows unlimited (cf. the integral valency of subreductions to type C in DT-grammar G_2). Meanwhile, in grammar G_3 in Fig. 9, the integral valency of all subreductions is either one-element, or empty. So $\sigma(G_3) = 1$. The bounded defect property is of course not local, but as we will see, the grammars can be compiled into equivalent grammars with local control of defect bounded by a constant.

As it concerns local cycles check, we can point out another property of DT-grammars which turns out to be helpful.

Definition 10 *A reduction* $\pi \vdash^{\rho} A$ *is* locally cycle-free (lc-free), *if for any its subreduction* ρ', *and its projection* π', $MS^1(\pi')$ *is cycle-free. A DT-grammar* G *is* lc-free *if any reduction in* G *is lc-free.*

This property is sufficient for a reducible structure to be cycle-free.

Lemma 7 *For any lc-free reduction* $\pi \vdash^{\rho} A$, $MS^1(\pi)$ *is cycle-free.*

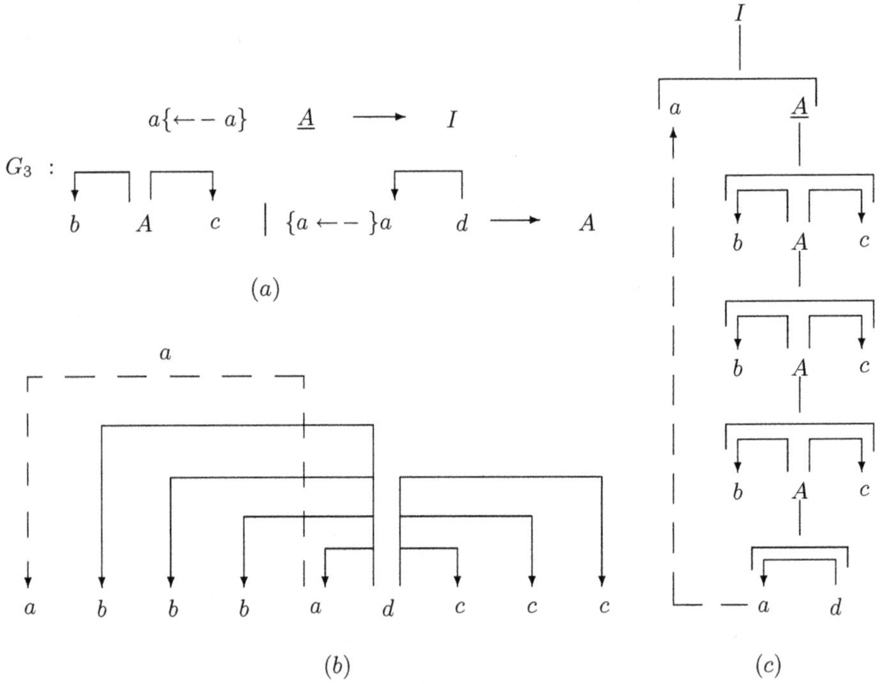

Fig. 9.

All DT-grammars, which appear in our examples, are lc-free. The next theorem shows that lc-free DT-grammars of bounded defect are compiled into cf-grammars which simulate reducibility of D-trees by their rules.

Theorem 1 *For any lc-free DT-grammar* G *of bounded defect there is a weakly equivalent cf-grammar* G_{cf}.

Proof. In order to simplify notation in this proof, we presume that in nonterminal rules $\pi \to A$, $w(\pi)$ has no terminals. Let $\sigma(G) = q$. The cf-grammar G_{cf} is constructed as follows. It has the same terminals as G, the set of nonterminals of the form $A[V]$, where V is a list of valencies of bounded size $|V| \le q$, the axiom $I[\emptyset]$, and the rules of the form :

$A[\sum\limits_{FA} \pi] \to w(\pi)$, where $r = (\pi \to A)$ is a terminal rule of G, and

$A[V_0] \to A_1[V_1]...A_k[V_k]$,

where for some rule $r = (\pi \to A)$ of G, $w(\pi) = A_1...A_k$, and $V_0, V_1, ..., V_k$ are valency lists of bounded size: $|V_i| \le q, 0 \le i \le k$, such that:

(1) $V_0 = \sum\limits_{FA} \bar{\pi}$, where $\bar{\pi} = \pi[A_1\backslash\bar{A}_1, ..., A_k\backslash\bar{A}_k]$, with valency set assignments $V(\bar{A}_i) = V_i, 1 \le i \le k$, and

(2) $MS^1(\bar{\pi})$ is cycle-free.

The weak equivalence $L(G_{cf}) = L(G)$ follows by Lemmas 2, 7 from the assertion :

Claim. *For $x \in W^+$, there is a derivation $A[V_0] \Rightarrow^*_{G_{cf}} x$ iff there is a reduction $\pi_0 \vdash^\rho A$ such that $x = w(\pi_0)$ and $V_0 = \sum\limits_{\rho} \pi_0$.* □

An important consequence of Theorem 1 is that lc-free bounded defect DT-grammars have a $O(n^3)$ parsing algorithm.

Corollary 1 *For each lc-free DT-grammar G of bounded defect there is a parsing algorithm for $L(G)$ in time $O(n^3)$.*

Proof. We follow the construction of Theorem 1, and transform G into a strongly equivalent lc-free DT-grammar G^q with defect $q = \sigma(G)$ and with nonterminals keeping integral valencies. In the place of the cf-rule $A[V_0] \to A_1[V_1]...A_t[V_t]$ constructed from a rule $\pi \to A$ of G, we will have in G^q the rule $\pi[A_1\backslash A_1[V_1], ..., A_k\backslash A_k[V_k]] \to A[V_0]$. We apply to G^q the Earley algorithm in charter form (a charter being a DV-structure). □

Remark. The size of G^q is $v^{k(q+1)}$ times greater than that of G, where v is the number of valencies and k is the maximal length of left parts of rules. So theoretically, the constant factor in the $O(n^3)$ time bound is great. In practice, it shouldn't be as awful, because the majority of valencies combinations in the rules can be filtered out while the compilation, and those which are relevant are few (cf. http://bobo.link.cs.cmu.edu/index.html/ where this kind of precompilation is made for link grammars [19]).

Lc-free bounded defect DT-grammars are stronger than LDT-grammars. The DT-language of the grammar G_3 in Fig. 9 models constructions of the type : *"Who do you think Mary thinks John thinks ... Ann thinks Peter loves?"* This DT-language cannot be determined by LDT-grammars, whereas, it can be determined by a DT-grammar with a single long dependency.

Theorem 2 *No LDT-grammar is strongly equivalent to G_3.*

4 Conclusion

The lc-free DT-grammars of bounded defect are essentially simpler to parse as compared with non-projective D-grammars with lifting control [2,8,11]. Their weak equivalence to cf-grammars shouldn't be interpreted as a disappointing factor. Really essential is their *strong generative capacity*. We conjecture that in many languages the defect through nesting is bounded by a small constant (at most 2 or 3). If this is true, the bounded defect DT-grammars are strong enough to treat the majority of discontinuous constructions.

Acknowledgments

We wish to thank N. Pertsov and an anonymous reviewer for constructive criticism and comments which helped us to fix inconsistencies in the preliminary version of this paper.

References

1. Y. Bar-Hillel, H. Gaifman, and E. Shamir. On categorial and phrase structure grammars. *Bull. Res. Council Israel*, 9F:1–16, 1960.
2. N. Bröker. Separating surface order and syntactic relations in a dependency grammar. In *Proc. COLING-ACL*, pages 174–180, Montreal, 1998.
3. A.Ja. Dikovsky and L.S. Modina. Dependencies on the other side of the curtain. *Traitement Automatique des Langues (TAL)*, 41(1):79–111, 2000.
4. H. Gaifman. Dependency systems and phrase structure systems. Report p-2315, RAND Corp. Santa Monica (CA), 1961. Published in: Information and Control, 1965, v. 8, n. 3, pp. 304-337.
5. M. Hepple. A dependency-based approach to bounded & unbounded movement. In T. Becker and H.-U. Krieger, editors, *Proc. of the 5th Meeting on Math. and Language*, 1997.
6. R.A. Hudson. *Word Grammar*. Basil Blackwell, Oxford-New York, 1984.
7. A.K. Joshi, L.S. Levy, and M. Takahashi. Tree adjunct grammars. *Journ. of Comput. and Syst. Sci.*, 10(1):136–163, 1975.
8. S. Kahane, A. Nasr, and O. Rambow. Pseudo-projectivity : A polynomially parsable non-projective dependency grammar. In *Proc. COLING-ACL*, pages 646–652, Montreal, 1998.
9. A. Lecomte. Proof nets and dependencies. In *Proc. of COLING-92*, pages 394–401, Nantes, 1992.
10. V. Lombardo and L. Lesmo. An earley-type recognizer for dependency grammar. In *Proc. 16th COLING*, pages 723–728, 1996.
11. V. Lombardo and L. Lesmo. Formal aspects and parsing issues of dependency theory. In *Proc. COLING-ACL*, pages 787–793, Montreal, 1998.
12. I. Mel'čuk. *Dependency Syntax*. SUNY Press, Albany, NY, 1988.
13. L.S. Modina. On Some Formal Grammars Generating Dependency Trees. In *Proc. of the MFCS'75, Lecture Notes in Computer Science*, number 32, pages 326–329, 1975.
14. M. Moortgat. La grammaire catégorielle généralisée : le calcul de lambek-gentzen. In Ph. Miller and Th. Torris, editors, *Structure of languages and its mathematical aspects*, pages 127–182. Hermes, Paris, 1990.
15. M. Moortgat and R. Oehrle. Adjacency, dependency and order. In *Proc. of Ninth Amsterdam Colloquium*, 1994.

16. A. Nasr. A formalism and a parser for lexicalized dependency grammars. In *Proc. Int. Workshop on Parsing Technology*, pages 186–195, Prague, 1995.
17. P. Neuhaus and N. Bröker. The Complexity of Recognition of Linguistically Adequate Dependency Grammars. In *Proc. of 35th ACL Annual Meeting and 8th Conf. of the ECACL*, pages 337–343, 1997.
18. Jane J. Robinson. Dependency structures and transformational rules. *Language*, 46(2):259–285, 1970.
19. D. D. Sleator and D. Temperly. Parsing English with a Link Grammar. In *Proc. IWPT'93*, pages 277–291, 1993.
20. E. Stabler. Derivational minimalism. In Ch. Retoré, editor, *Logical Aspects of Computational Linguistics*, number 1328 in LNAI, pages 68–95, Nancy, 1996. Springer Verlag.

Appendix

Proof of Lemma 1. (1) In order to add a long dependency $l = \left(n_1 \;\; \overset{r}{--\!>} \;\; n_2\right)$ to π, the node n_2 must be negative. By point ($v2$) of Definition 3, this excludes the existence of another dependency (local or long) entering n_2.

(2) As a consequence of (1), n_2 can only be the root of a negative component β of π. So if n_1 also belongs to β, then a cycle appears in this component. Suppose that n_1 does not belong to β and α is a component of π which contains it. Let us verify that in this case π_1 is a DV-structure. First of all, let us remark that introduction of l into π cannot augment valency sets, which means that point (v1) of Definition 3 is satisfied in π_1. By definition of saturation, after that l was added, the negative valency it saturates is subtracted from $V(n_2)$ so by point (v1), n_2 becomes positive in π_1. This means that point (v2) of Definition 3 is also true in π_1. Suppose that α is positive in π. Then it is the head component of π, and it is changed. Indeed, adding l makes $\alpha \cup \beta$ a tree, hence a new component of π_1. Negative valencies are never introduced by saturation, therefore this component is positive. So it is a new (and single) head component of π_1. Negative components different from β rest intact. So points (v3) of Definition 3 is also true, and π_1 is a DV-structure in this case. Now suppose that α is also negative. The subgraph $\alpha \cup \beta$ becomes a tree in π_1. Its root is that of α. So it rests negative, and $\alpha \cup \beta$ becomes a new negative component of π_1. Other negative components rest intact. If there was a positive head component in π, then it also rest intact, and single positive component in π_1. So in this case too point (v3) of Definition 3 is satisfied, and π_1 is a DV-structure. □.

Proof of Lemma 2. (1) The only-if part being trivial, let us prove the if-part. By assumption, π is a terminal DV-structure. So it is a union of components $\alpha_0, \alpha_1, ..., \alpha_t$, each component being a tree. One of these components, e.g., α_0 is the head. By point (v3) of Definition 3, all the other components are negative. As we have already remarked in the proof of the Lemma 1, a unique negative valency in each component α_i, $1 \leq i \leq t$, is that of its root. Suppose that $MS^1(\pi)$ is cycle-free. Then by Lemma 1, it is a DV-structure. The condition $\sum_{FA} \pi = \emptyset$ means that all valencies are saturated in $MS^1(\pi)$. So $MS^1(\pi)$ is the union of non-intersecting subtrees $\alpha_0, \alpha_1, ..., \alpha_t$, expanded by arrows in a way that the root of each subtree (maybe besides α_0) is entered by a new arrow, and no two arrows (old or new) enter the same node. Let us consider the graph $c(MS^1(\pi))$, with the nodes $\alpha_0, \alpha_1, ..., \alpha_t$, in which an arrow goes from α_i

to α_j, if there is an arrow in $MS^1(\pi)$ from a node of α_i to the root of α_j. Clearly, $MS^1(\pi)$ is a D-tree iff $c(MS^1(\pi))$ is a tree. We have already seen that $c(MS^1(\pi))$ is cycle-free and that no two its arrows enter the same node. It rests for us to prove that it is connected. Suppose the contrary. Let us consider a maximal connected subgraph of $c(MS^1(\pi))$, which doesn't contain α_0, if it is positive. In this subgraph, for each node there is an arrow entering it. So this subgraph contains a cycle, which contradicts the premise.

Point (2) is an immediate consequence of the uniqueness of the maximal FA-saturation of a terminal DV-structure. □

Proof of Lemma 3. The composition is never made in a terminal node. This means that point (v1) of Definition 3 is satisfied in π, if it is defined. In order to verify (v2), we should check only one node : the new node n, which replaces A in π_0. Suppose that a dependency entered A in π_0. Then A is a positive nonterminal. If composition is defined, then π_1 is a positive DV-structure. There are two cases. First is that the root of π_1 is a positive nonterminal B. Then $n = B$ is a positive node of π. Second is that the root of π_1 is a terminal b with positive $V_{\pi_1}(b)$. Then $n = b$ and $V_{\pi_1}(b) = V_{\pi(n)}$. So in both cases, point (v2) of Definition 3 is satisfied in π. In order to verify point (v3), let us consider a non-head component α of π. If α is a non-head component of π_1, or it is a non-head component of π_0, which is not affected by composition, then it is either a non-head component of π. Suppose that α is the result of composing the head component π_{11} of π_1 into a component β of π_0 in A. The fact that α is a non-head component of π means that β was a non-head component of π_0. Therefore, β was negative. If A is not the root of β, then the root is not affected by composition and rests negative. So is α in this case. If A is the root of β, then it is a negative nonterminal. So if π is defined, then both π_1 and π_{11} are negative, and therefore, the root of π_{11}. Another two cases arise. First is that the root of π_{11} is a negative nonterminal B. Then B becomes the root of α. Second is that the root of π_{11} is a terminal b with negative $V_{\pi_1}(b)$. Then b becomes the root of α, and $V_{\pi_1}(b) = V_{\pi(b)}$. In both cases, α is negative. So point (v3) of Definition 3 is also satisfied in π, and it is a DV-structure.

This reasoning also proves point (2). □

Proof of Lemma 4. In fact, it suffice to prove the following assertion :

Claim. *If there is a long dependency* $l = \left(n \overset{r}{- - >} n'\right)$ *which is first available in* $\pi_0[A\backslash MS^1(\pi_1)]$, *then the first available long dependency in* $\pi_0[A\backslash MS^1(\pi_2)]$ *exists and saturates exactly the same valencies as* l.

Then the Lemma will result by the evident induction on the number of FA-saturation steps needed to obtain $MS^1(\pi_0[A\backslash MS^1(\pi_1)])$ from $\pi_0[A\backslash MS^1(\pi_1)]$. Now, suppose that l is the first available long dependency in $\pi_0[A\backslash MS^1(\pi_1)]$, and that n belongs to π_1, n' belongs to π_0, and l saturates a valency v' by a valency v. This means that v' is a negative valency, $v' \in V_{\pi_0}(n')$, $v \in V_{MS^1(\pi_1)}(n)$, and so $v \in \sum\limits_{FA} \pi_1 = \sum\limits_{FA} \pi_2$. Thus in DV-structure $MS^1(\pi_2)$, there is a node m, which has the same positive valency $v \in V_{MS^1(\pi_2)}(m)$, and which is not saturated inside $MS^1(\pi_2)$. Let us remark that the integral valencies $\sum\limits_{FA} \pi_1$, $\sum\limits_{FA} \pi_2$ coincide as lists (i.e. together with the order of valencies as it is defined in Definition 4). So if there were some other positive valency in $MS^1(\pi_2)$ in some its node m_1 preceding m and saturating a negative valency in π_0, then some corresponding node with this property would also be in $MS^1(\pi_1)$.

Therefore, l would not be the first available. This means that the long dependency $l' = \left(n \ \stackrel{r}{- - >}\ m\right)$ is first available in $\pi_0[A \backslash MS^1(\pi_2)]$ and it also saturates v' by v.

A similar reasoning applies in the other cases: when n belongs to π_0 and n' belongs to π_1 or when both n and n' belong to π_0. □

Proof of Lemma 6. Let us call "old" the dependencies in $MS^1(\pi_1), ..., MS^1(\pi_k)$, and "new" those long dependencies in $MS^1(\pi)$, which are not old. $MS^1(\pi_1), ..., MS^1(\pi_k)$ being cycle-free and $MS^1(\pi)$ having a cycle, there is at least one new dependency $l = \left(n_1 \ \stackrel{r}{- - >}\ n_2\right))$ in $MS^1(\pi)$, which belongs to the cycle but not to the components $MS^1(\pi_1), ..., MS^1(\pi_k)$. Without loss of generality, we can presume that this dependency is the first available in π. Suppose that l saturates valency $v_2 = -O : r$ by valency $v_1 = +\bar{O} : r$. Let us consider the case, where there are some components $MS^1(\pi_{i_1})$, $MS^1(\pi_{i_2})$ of π, which contain respectively the nodes n_1 and n_2, other cases being similar. By the choice of l, $i_1 \neq i_2$, $v_1 \in \sum_{FA} \pi_{i_1}$ and $v_2 \in \sum_{FA} \pi_{i_2}$. By definition of projection, we have $v_1 \in V_{\hat{\pi}}(\bar{A}_{i_1})$ and $v_2 \in V_{\hat{\pi}}(\bar{A}_{i_2})$. Let us show that there is a long dependency $l' = \left(\bar{A}_{i_1} \ \stackrel{r}{- - >}\ \bar{A}_{i_2}\right)$ in $MS^1(\hat{\pi})$, which saturates v_2 by v_1. Since l is first available in π, v_1 is the first non saturated positive valency in π. Moreover, by definition of the composition of DV-structures, it is also the first positive valency in $\sum_{FA} \pi_{i_1}$. So it is also first in $\hat{\pi}$ and in $V_{\hat{\pi}}(\bar{A}_{i_1})$. v_2 belonging to $V_{\hat{\pi}}(\bar{A}_{i_2})$, this means that a long dependency $l' = \left(\bar{A}_{i_1} \ \stackrel{r}{- - >}\ \bar{A}_j\right)$ goes from $\bar{A}_{i_1}$ in the direction of $\bar{A}_{i_2}$, but not further then $\bar{A}_{i_2}$. It also cannot be closer to $\bar{A}_{i_1}$ than $\bar{A}_{i_2}$, because in this case n_2 should belong to some component $MS^1(\pi_j)$, which is closer to $MS^1(\pi_{i_1})$ than $MS^1(\pi_{i_2})$. Therefore, $j = i_2$. In this manner, we show that for each new long dependency in $MS^1(\pi)$, which belongs to the cycle but not to the components $MS^1(\pi_1), ..., MS^1(\pi_k)$, which goes from some $MS^1(\pi_i)$ and enters some $MS^1(\pi_j)$, there is a long dependency in $MS^1(\hat{\pi})$ which goes from $\bar{A}_i$ and enters $\bar{A}_j$. This proves that there is a cycle in $MS^1(\hat{\pi})$. □

Proof of Lemma 7. Suppose that $MS^1(\pi')$ has a cycle for some subreduction $\pi' \vdash^{\rho'} A'$ of ρ with $rr(\rho') = 1$ (clearly, this cycle would be present in $MS^1(\pi)$ too). Then $\rho' = r$ and $r = (\pi' \to A')$ is a rule of G. In this case, π' is the projection of ρ' and the presence of a cycle in $MS^1(\pi')$ contradicts the premise of Lemma. This means that if $MS^1(\pi)$ has a cycle, then there is a subreduction $\pi' \vdash^{\rho'} A'$ of ρ such that $rr(\rho') > 1$, $\rho' = (\rho_1 ... \rho_m; r)$, $r = (\pi_0 \to B)$ is a rule of G with nonterminals $B_1, ..., B_m$ in π_0, $\pi_i \vdash^{\rho_i} B_i$ and $MS^1(\pi_i)$ being cycle-free for all $1 \leq i \leq m$, whereas $MS^1(\pi')$ has a cycle. However in this case, by Lemma 6, the projection $\hat{\pi}' = \pi_0\{B_1[\sum_{FA} \pi_1], ..., B_m[\sum_{FA} \pi_m]\}$ of ρ' produces a cycle in $MS^1(\hat{\pi}')$, which again contradicts the premise of Lemma. □

Proof of the Claim in Theorem 1.
(**Only-if-part**). We prove it by induction on the height of the derivation tree.

If the derivation $A[V_0] \Rightarrow^*_{G_{cf}} x$ has a tree of height 1, then it is a one-step derivation with the rule $A[V_0] \to x$ applied. This rule is constructed from a terminal rule $r = (\pi \to A)$ of G. So for $\pi_0 = MS^1(\pi)$, $\pi_0 \vdash^r A$, $x = w(\pi_0)$, and $V_0 = \sum_{FA} \pi_0 = \sum_r \pi_0$.

Suppose that the derivation $A[V_0] \Rightarrow^*_{G_{cf}} x$ has a tree T of height $h > 1$. Then the rule applied at the first step is not terminal. So it has the form $A[V_0] \rightarrow A_1[V_1]...A_k[V_k]$. This means that T can be decomposed into the minimal tree corresponding to the application of this rule to A and k trees of derivations $A_1[V_1] \Rightarrow^*_{G_{cf}} x_1, ..., A_k[V_k] \Rightarrow^*_{G_{cf}} x_k$, where $x = x_1...x_k$. These trees are of heights lesser than h. Hence, by induction hypothesis, there are reductions $\pi_i \vdash^{\rho_i} A_i$ such that $x_i = w(\pi_i)$ and $V_i = \sum\limits_{\rho_i} \pi_i$, $1 \leq i \leq k$. Now let us consider the rule $r = (\pi \rightarrow A)$ of G, from which the rule $A[V_0] \rightarrow A_1[V_1]...A_k[V_k]$ was constructed. By point (1) of construction, $V_0 = \sum\limits_{FA} \bar{\pi}$, where $\bar{\pi} = \pi[A_1\backslash \bar{A}_1, ..., A_k\backslash \bar{A}_k]$, with valency set assignments $V(\bar{A}_i) = V_i, 1 \leq i \leq k$. On the other hand, by the induction hypothesis, $V_i = \sum\limits_{\rho_i} \pi_i$, $1 \leq i \leq k$. By Lemma 5, $V_0 = \sum\limits_{FA} \bar{\pi} = \sum\limits_{FA} \pi_0$, where $\pi_0 = MS^1(\pi[A_1\backslash \pi_1, ..., A_k\backslash \pi_k])$. We see that $\rho = (\rho_1...\rho_k; r)$ realizes a reduction $\pi_0 \vdash^\rho A$, $\bar{\pi}$ is the projection of this reduction, and $V_0 = \sum\limits_{\rho} \pi_0$. It only remains to remark that by definition of the composition, $w(\pi_0) = x$.

(**If-part**). We prove it by induction on $rr(\rho)$.
If $rr(\rho) = 1$, then ρ is a reduction by a terminal rule $r = (\pi \rightarrow A)$ of G. Since $\sigma(G) = q$, to this rule corresponds in G_{cf} the rule $A[\sum\limits_{FA} \pi] \rightarrow w(\pi)$. This rule gives the needed one-step derivation $A[V_0] \Rightarrow^*_{G_{cf}} x$ for $V_0 = \sum\limits_{FA} \pi$ and $x = w(\pi)$.

Suppose that $\pi_0 \vdash^\rho A$, $rr(\rho) = j > 1$, $V_0 = \sum\limits_{\rho} \pi_0$, and the if-part of the Claim is proven for the reductions of ranks lesser than j. This means that there is a rule $r = (\pi \rightarrow A)$ in G such that $w(\pi) = A_1...A_k$, $\rho = (\rho_1...\rho_k; r)$, and subreductions $\pi_i \vdash^{\rho_i} A_i$, of ranks $rr(\rho_i) < j$, $1 \leq i \leq k$, such that $\pi_0 = MS^1(\pi[A_1\backslash \pi_1, ..., A_k\backslash \pi_k])$. By Lemma 5, the projection $\bar{\pi} = \pi\{A_1[\sum\limits_{\rho_1} \pi_1], ..., A_k[\sum\limits_{\rho_k} \pi_k]\}$ of ρ satisfies the equation $V_0 = \sum\limits_{FA} \bar{\pi}$. Besides this, $|V_0| \leq \sigma(G) = q$. Next, by induction hypothesis, for each $i, 1 \leq i \leq k$, and for $V_i = \sum\limits_{\rho_i} \pi_i$, there is a derivation $A_i[V_i] \Rightarrow^*_{G_{cf}} x_i$, where $x_i = w(\pi_i)$. Hence, $w(\pi) = w(\pi_1)...w(\pi_k) = x$. Now, G being lc-free, $MS^1(\bar{\pi})$ is cycle-free. So the rule r satisfies the conditions (1),(2) in the construction of G_{cf}. Therefore, G_{cf} has the rule $A[V_0] \rightarrow A_1[V_1]...A_k[V_k]$ constructed from r. This rule can be used in the derivation
$A[V_0] \Rightarrow^*_{G_{cf}} A_1[V_1]...A_k[V_k] \Rightarrow^*_{G_{cf}} x_1 A_2[V_2]...A_k[V_k] \Rightarrow^*_{G_{cf}} x_1...x_k = x$. □

Proof of Theorem 2. Suppose that there is an LDT-grammar G such that $D(G) = D(G_3)$. Let T be the tree of some derivation $I \Rightarrow^*_G \pi$ with terminal π. Let N_1 and N_2 be some nonterminal nodes of T such that N_2 is a descendent of N_1. This means that the complete subtree $T(N_2)$ of T with the root N_2 is a complete subtree of $T(N_1)$ and $w(T(N_1)) = \omega_1 w(T(N_2))\omega_2$ for some terminal strings ω_1, ω_2 (called respectively *left* and *right wings* of N_1, N_2). The pair of nodes N_1, N_2 is *iterable*, if the nodes have the same nonterminal label B. Clearly, the length of the longest terminal string which does not contain an occurrence of a (left or right) wing of an iterable pair is bounded by $\beta(G) = c(r-1)2^{(|C|+1)log\ r}$, where r is the maximal length of left hand sides of rules of G. So if we consider a DV-structure π_G such that $w(\pi_G) = ab^{\beta(G)+1}adc^{\beta(G)+1}$, we can find in any its derivation tree T an iterable pair N_1, N_2, whose nonempty left or right terminal wing ω_1 is a substring of $b^{\beta(G)+1}$. If this wing were right, replacing

$T(N_1)$ by $T(N_2)$ we would obtain a DV-structure of a string of the form $ab^i adc^{\beta(G)+1}$, for some $i < \beta(G) + 1$. So ω_1 is a left wing of the iterable pair. The same reasoning shows that the corresponding right wing ω_2 cannot be empty and is a substring of $c^{\beta(G)+1}$. Therefore, in the path from N_2 to d there exists a nonterminal node N' such that a and d both belong to $w(T(N'))$. Let N_3 be the last such node in the path and B be its (nonterminal) label. Since G is a local DT-grammar, π_G is a D-tree in which all dependencies are local. So in particular, in a rule $\pi_1 \to B$ applied in N_3, $w(\pi_1) = \alpha_1 A \alpha_2 D \alpha_3$, where A is a predecessor of the inner occurrence of a in $w(\pi_G)$ (or a itself) and D is a predecessor of the occurrence of d in $w(\pi_G)$ (or d itself). Since d is the root of π_G, there is a local dependency in π_1 from D to A. Moreover, if $A = a$, then in the same π_1 there is an occurrence of a predecessor A_0 of the outermost left occurrence of a in $w(\pi_G)$ (or this outermost left occurrence of a itself) and the dependency from A to A_0. If $A \neq a$, then in the path from A to the inner a there is the first node N_4 labelled by a nonterminal A_1 such that in a rule $\pi_2 \to A_1$ applied in N_4, $w(\pi_2) = \gamma_1 A_l \gamma_2 A_r \gamma_3$, where A_l is a predecessor of the outermost left occurrence of a in $w(\pi_G)$ (or this occurrence of a itself) and A_r is a predecessor of the inner occurrence of a in $w(\pi_G)$ (or this occurrence of a itself) and the dependency from A_r to A_l. In both cases we see that a predecessor of the outermost left occurrence of a in $w(\pi_G)$ is a descendent of N_2 and the more so of N_1. Meanwhile, the outermost left occurrence of a in $w(\pi_G)$ precedes the left wing ω_1 and hence cannot be a descendent of N_1. A contradiction. □

On Mixing Deduction and Substitution in Lambek Categorial Grammars

Annie Foret

IRISA and University of Rennes1
Campus de Beaulieu
35042 Rennes Cedex, France.
foret@irisa.fr

Abstract. Recently, learning algorithms in Gold's model [Gol67] have been proposed for some particular classes of classical categorial grammars [Kan98]. We are interested here in learning Lambek categorial grammars.
In general grammatical inference uses unification and substitution. In the context of Lambek categorial grammars it seems appropriate to incorporate an operation on types based both on deduction (Lambek derivation) and on substitution instead of standard substitution and standard unification.
The purpose of this paper is to investigate such operations defined both in terms of deduction and substitution in categorial grammars and to study a modified unification that may serve as a basis for learning in this framework. We consider some variants of definition : in particular we show that deduction and substitution do not permute. We then consider a modified unification, here called $\|=$ -unification :we give a criterion for the existence and construction of $\|=$ -unifiers in terms of group issues.

1 Introduction

Categorial grammars have been studied in the domain of natural language processing, these grammars are lexicalized grammars that assign types (or categories) to the lexicon. We focus here on Lambek categorial grammars [Lam58] which are closely connected to linear logic introduced by Girard [Gir95]. Classical (AB) grammars have some limitations in modeling behaviours, for example they lack transitivity rules (such as to derive type A / C from A / B and B / C) which are enabled in Lambek calculus.

Learning (in the sense of Gold [Gol67]) in our context is a symbolic issue that may be described as follows. Let $\mathcal{G}$ be a class of grammars, that we wish to learn from examples. The issue is to define an algorithm, that when applied to a finite set of sentences, yields a grammar in the class that generates the examples; the algorithm is also required to converge. Formally, let $\mathcal{L}(G)$ denote the language associated with grammar G, and let V be a given alphabet, a learning algorithm is a function ϕ from finite sets of words in V^* to $\mathcal{G}$, such that for $G \in \mathcal{G}$ with $\mathcal{L}(G) = (e_i)_{i \in N}$ there exists $n_0 \in N$ such that $\forall n > n_0$ $\phi(\{e_1, \ldots, e_n\}) \in \mathcal{G}$ with $\mathcal{L}(\phi(\{e_1, \ldots, e_n\})) = \mathcal{L}(G)$.

P. de Groote, G. Morrill, C. Retoré (Eds.): LACL 2001, LNAI 2099, pp. 158–174, 2001.

One good reason to use categorial grammars in a learning perspective is that they are fully lexicalized : the rules are already known, only types assigned to words have to be derived from examples. Essential known results on this subject may be found in [Kan98]. The learning technique avoids to add a new type each time there is a new use of a word in an example, but applies a unification algorithm instead. One important case is when we limit the number of types per word for example to only one type.

Our aim is to explore learning mechanisms for Lambek calculus, taking for instance parenthesized sentences as structured examples. In such a context, it seems appropriate to use not only unification but also deduction in the learning process. Whereas standard unification is used in existing works [BP90, Kan98, Nic99, Bon00] if we incorporate deduction into unification, we become able to unify such types as $u \setminus v$ and u' / v' using deduction rules such as $x_1 \setminus (x_2 / x_3) \vdash (x_1 \setminus x_2) / x_3$ that hold in Lambek calculus. Also a word with respective types x and $y' / (x' \setminus y')$ inferred from two different grammars will simply receive type x when combining the two grammars, using the type-raising rule $x \vdash y / (x \setminus y)$.

This paper focuses on such a modified unification and relation on types : we investigate some properties, some variants, and we give a characterization of unifiability in this modified sense ; our characterization is expressed in terms of group issues.

The paper is organized as follows. Section 2 addresses background definition and known results. Section 3 investigates the preorder $\models\!\!\!\!|\;$ on types mixing deduction and substitution (it is the basis of the modified unification, here called $||\!=$ -unification). It also outlines our method on examples. Section 4 establishes a characterization of $||\!=$ -unifiability, in terms of groups. This result is obtained using a theorem on conjoinability by Pentus [Pen93a]. Section 5 addresses variants of Lambek calculus. Section 6 concludes.

2 Background

2.1 Typing Examples and Features

In what follows, we illustrate certain aspects of a (simplified) type assignment, using linguistic examples from [Lam58].

Primitive types. To describe the syntactic types assigned to words, we begin by introducing two primitive types : S the type of sentences and N the type of names including proper names like *John* or *Mary* and also names such as *milk*,...

Compound expressions may also receive type N, for example "poor John" and "fresh milk".

Compound types. We also introduce compound types : in general an expression of type x / y followed by an expression of type y produces an expression of type x, similarly an expression of type $y \setminus x$ preceded by an expression of type y produces an expression of type x.

In compound expressions such as "poor John", the adjective *poor* is assigned a compound type $N \ / \ N$. An intransitive verb such as *works* in "John works" is assigned $N \ \backslash \ S$. A transitive verb such as *hates* is assigned $(N \ \backslash \ S) \ / \ N$.

The effect of grouping. Some sentences admit different groupings, for example "John (hates Mary)" and "(John hates) Mary".

Correspondingly, some words like transitive verbs may be assigned different types : *hates* receives $(N \backslash S) / N$ or alternatively $N \backslash (S / N)$ in the above sentences.

Pronouns and type-raising. In examples such as "he works", or "he hates him" *he*[1] receives type $(S / (N \backslash S))$ and *him* receives type $((S / N) \backslash S)$. However an expression of type N should also receive the types of these pronouns, which is achieved by derivation with the so-called type-raising rule in Lambek categorial grammars.

2.2 Categorial Grammars

In this section, we introduce formal definitions concerning categorial grammars. The interested reader may also consult [Cas88, Ret00, Bus97, Moo96, Ret96, Pen93b] for an introduction or for further details.

Let Σ be a fixed alphabet.

Types. *Types* are constructed from *primitive types* and two binary connectives $/$ and $\backslash$. In some versions, we consider a third binary connective $\otimes$ for product.We let Pr and Tp denote the set of primitive types and the set of types, respectively. Pr contains a *distinguished type*, written S, also called the *principal type* ; we assume that $Pr = Pr_c \cup Var$, where Pr_c is a set of *constants* with $S \in Pr_c$ and Var is a set of *variables* (variables are different from constants).

Notation. Letters A, B, $A_1 \ldots$ or t, t', t_1, $\ldots$ range over types.

We then associate to each symbol in the alphabet a finite number of types as follows.

Classical categorial grammar. A *classical categorial grammar* over Σ is a finite relation G between Σ and Tp. If $< c, A > \in G$, we say that G *assigns* A to c, and we write $G \ : c \mapsto A$.

Derivation $\vdash_{AB}$ on types without $\otimes$. The relation $\vdash_{AB}$ is the smallest relation $\vdash$ between Tp^+ and Tp, such that :

- For all $A \in Tp : A \vdash A$
- For all $\Gamma, \Delta \in Tp^+$ and for all $A, B \in Tp$:
  - if $\Gamma \vdash A$ and $\Delta \vdash A \backslash B$ then $\Gamma, \Delta \vdash B$ (Backward application)
  - if $\Gamma \vdash B / A$ and $\Delta \vdash A$ then $\Gamma, \Delta \vdash B$ (Forward application)

We now give a formulation of Lambek calculus including product consisting in introduction rules on the left and on the right of a sequent. For Lambek calculus without product, one simply drops the rules for $\otimes$.

Lambek Derivation $\vdash_L$. The relation $\vdash_L$ is the smallest relation $\vdash$ between Tp^+ and Tp, such that :

---

[1] pronouns such as *he* cannot always replace nouns : in "poor John hates milk", *he* cannot replace *John*, nor *milk*

- For all $A \in Tp : A \vdash A$
- For all $\Gamma \in Tp^+, \Delta, \Delta' \in Tp^*$ and for all $A, B \in Tp$:
  - if $A, \Gamma \vdash B$ then $\Gamma \vdash A \setminus B$ ($\setminus right$)
  - if $\Gamma, A \vdash B$ then $\Gamma \vdash B / A$ ($/right$)
  - if $\Gamma \vdash A$ and $\Delta, B, \Delta' \vdash C$ then $\Delta, \Gamma, A \setminus B, \Delta' \vdash C$ ($\setminus left$)
  - if $\Gamma \vdash A$ and $\Delta, B, \Delta' \vdash C$ then $\Delta, B / A, \Gamma, \Delta' \vdash C$ ($/left$)
  - if $\Delta, A, B, \Delta' \vdash C$ then $\Delta, (A \otimes B), \Delta' \vdash C$ ($\otimes$-left)
  - if $\Gamma \vdash A$ and $\Gamma' \vdash B$ then $\Gamma, \Gamma' \vdash (A \otimes B)$ ($\otimes$-right)

Note the non-empty left hand-side requirement for sequents, expressed by $\Gamma \in Tp^+$. When we replace Tp^+ by Tp^* in the definition above, we get another version of Lambek calculus, without this non-empty left hand-side feature, which we shall refer to as $L_\emptyset$ with derivation relation $\vdash_{L_\emptyset}$.

The cut rule holds for both $\vdash_{AB}$ and $\vdash_L$:

$$if\ \Gamma \vdash A\ and\ \Delta, A, \Delta' \vdash B\ then\ \Delta, \Gamma, \Delta' \vdash B\ (cut)$$

Language. Let G be a classical categorial grammar over Σ. G *generates* a string $c_1 \ldots c_n \in \Sigma^+$ iff there are types $A_1, \ldots, A_n \in Tp$ such that :

$$G\ : c_i \mapsto A_i\ (1 \leq i \leq n)\ \text{ and }\ A_1, \ldots, A_n \vdash_{AB} S$$

The *language of* G, is the set of strings generated by G and is written $L(G)$.

We define similarly $L_L(G)$ by replacing $\vdash_{AB}$ with $\vdash_L$ in the definition of $L(G)$.

Example 1 *Let $\Sigma_1 = \{John, Mary, likes\}$ and let $Pr = \{S, N\}$ for sentences and nouns respectively.*

Let $G_1 = \{John \mapsto N,\ Mary \mapsto N,\ likes \mapsto N \setminus (S / N)\}$

We get ($John\ likes\ Mary \in L(G_1)$) since ($N,\ N \setminus (S / N),\ N \vdash_{AB} S$) (using $N \vdash N$ and $N \setminus (S / N) \vdash N \setminus (S / N)$ we get by backward application : $N, N \setminus (S / N) \vdash S / N$; then by forward application and $N \vdash N$, we get the result).

Rigid and k-valued grammars. Categorial grammars that assign at most k types to each symbol in the alphabet are called *k-valued grammars*; 1-valued grammars are also called *rigid* grammars.

In previous example G_1 is a rigid (or 1-valued) grammar.

2.3 Unification and Grammatical Inference

Substitution and unification play a special role in grammatical inference. In this section we consider some related definitions. We shall adapt the notion of unification in section 4.

Substitutions. A substitution σ is a function from variables in Var to types in Tp which is extended from types to types by :

$\sigma(p) = p$ for $p \in Pr_c$ (with $\sigma(S) = S$)
$\sigma(A \setminus B) = \sigma(A) \setminus \sigma(B)$ $\sigma(B \,/\, A) = \sigma(B) \,/\, \sigma(A)$
$\sigma(B \otimes A) = \sigma(B) \otimes \sigma(A)$ [2]

The following principle (hereafter called the *replacement principle*) holds for both $\vdash_{AB}$ and $\vdash_L$: if $A_1, \ldots, A_n \vdash B$ then $\sigma(A_1), \ldots, \sigma(A_n) \vdash \sigma(B)$

Substitutions extended to grammars. Given a substitution σ, and a grammar G, $\sigma(G)$ denotes the grammar obtained by applying σ in the type assignments, that is : $\sigma(G) = \{< c, \sigma(A) >; < c, A > \in G\}$.

Preorders based on substitutions. Let us write $\theta\sigma$ the composition of substitutions σ with θ : $\forall x : \theta\sigma(x) = \theta(\sigma(x))$. Substitution allows to define several preorders (reflexive and transitive) as follows :

- $\preceq$ on types defined by $A \preceq B$ iff $\exists \sigma : \sigma(A) = B$; B is said an *instance* of A, or also A is said more general than B.

- $\preceq$ on substitutions defined by $\sigma \preceq \theta$ iff $\forall A \in Tp : \sigma(A) \preceq \theta(A)$; this yields $\sigma \preceq \theta$ iff $\exists \rho : \rho\sigma = \theta$; σ is said to be *more general* than θ.

- $\sqsubseteq$ on grammars as follows : $G_1 \sqsubseteq G_2$ iff $\exists \sigma : \sigma(G_1) \subseteq G_2$ [3] where we write $G_1 \subseteq G_2$ whenever G_2 contains all type assignments of G_1.

It is easy to see that if $G_1 \sqsubseteq G_2$ then $L(G_1) \subseteq L(G_2)$.

Unification. Two types A, B (or more generally a set of types $\mathcal{A}$) are said *unifiable* whenever there exists a substitution σ such that $\sigma(A) = \sigma(B)$ (resp. $\sigma(A) = \sigma(B)$ for all $A, B \in \mathcal{A}$); σ is then said a unifier of A and B (resp. of $\mathcal{A}$). Let $U(A, B)$ (or $U(\mathcal{A})$) denote the set of unifiers of A,B (or $\mathcal{A}$). A *principal (or most general) unifier* of A and B (or $\mathcal{A}$) is a unifier σ, such that $\forall \theta \in U(A, B)$ *(resp.* $U(\mathcal{A})$) : $\sigma \preceq \theta$.

The usual unification problem is as follows : for two given types, to indicate if these types are unifiable and when they are unifiable, to provide a principal unifier. One important property is that when two types are unifiable, they admit a principal unifier that is unique modulo variable renaming.

Unification extended to (rigid) categorial AB-grammars and least upper bounds for grammars. A substitution σ is said to unify a family $\mathcal{F}$ of sets of types, if σ unifies each set in the family. A *principal unifier* σ of $\mathcal{F}$ is a unifier of $\mathcal{F}$ such that forall unifier θ of $\mathcal{F} : \sigma \preceq \theta$.

Let us fix *mgu* a function that computes a principal unifier (undefined if there is none) for each set of types (or family of sets of types).

Let G_1 and G_2 be rigid grammars with no common variables. We consider the family $\mathcal{F}$ of the sets $\mathcal{A}_c$ for each c in the alphabet of G_1 or G_2 : $\mathcal{A}_c = \{A; < c, A > \in G_1 \; or \; < c, A > \in G_2\}$. We let $G_1 \sqcup G_2 = mgu(\mathcal{F})(G_1 \cup G_2)$.

This operation computes the least upper bound of rigid grammars (with respect to $\sqsubseteq$); with an added top element it leads to lattice properties of particular interest for the convergence of the learning algorithm.

---

[2] for a calculus including $\otimes$

[3] this is a simplified version : Kanazawa adds a faithfullness condition such that if two types assigned to the same symbol in G_1 are distinct they are kept distinct by σ which has no impact in the rigid case.

2.4 Group Models and Conjoinability in Lambek Calculus

In next sections we shall use the *free group interpretation* and some related results that we recall below : this interpretation is not complete for Lambek Calculus but as shown by Pentus, it is complete for an equivalence $\sim$ introduced in [Lam58] that also coincides with conjoinability.

Free group interpretation. Let FG denote the free group with generators Pr, operation . and with neutral element Λ. We associate with each formula A an element in FG written $[[A]]$ as follows :
$[[p]] = p$ for p atomic
$[[A_1 \setminus A_2]] = [[A_1]]^{-1}.[[A_2]]$
$[[A_1 \,/\, A_2]] = [[A_1]].[[A_2]]^{-1}$
$[[A_1 \otimes A_2]] = [[A_1]].[[A_2]]$
We extend the notation to non-empty sequents by :
$[[A_1, A_2, \ldots, A_n]] = [[A_1]].[[A_2]]. \;\ldots\; .[[A_n]]$
The following known property states that such groups are models :

$$\text{if } \Gamma \vdash_L A \text{ then } [[\Gamma]] =_{FG} [[A]]$$

Conjoinability. The *join-equivalence*, written $\sim$, is defined by :

$$t \sim t' \text{ iff } \exists t_1, ..., t_n : t = t_1, t' = t_n, ((t_i \vdash t_{i+1} \text{ or } t_{i+1} \vdash t_i) \text{ for } i < n))$$

Types $t_1, t_2, ...t_n$ are said *conjoinable* whenever there exists a type t such that : $t_i \vdash t$ (for $i \leq n$). In this case t is called a join for $t_1, t_2, ...t_n$.

The following result is due to Lambek[Lam58].

Proposition 1 (Diamond property) *Let t_1 and t_2 be two types. The following assertions are equivalent.*
(i) t_1 and t_2 are conjoinable ($\exists t : t_1 \vdash t$ and $t_2 \vdash t$)
(ii)($\exists t' : t' \vdash t_1$ and $t' \vdash t_2$)

Proof. We follow the version of Pentus [Pen93a]
- if $t_i \vdash t$, for i=1,2, we verify that $t' \vdash t_i$, for i=1,2, where :

$$t' = (t_1 \,/\, t) \otimes t \otimes (t \setminus t_2)$$

- if $t' \vdash t_i$, for i=1,2, we verify that $t_i \vdash t$, for i=1,2, where :

$$t = (t' \,/\, t_1) \setminus t' \,/\, (t_2 \setminus t')$$

Proposition 2 *Let t_1 and t_2 be two types. The assertion $t_1 \sim t_2$ is also equivalent to (i) and (ii) of the diamond property above.*

It can be checked by an easy induction on the number of intermediates for $\sim$.

The above proposition combined with the following completeness result of Pentus is of particular interest for the investigations in this article.

Theorem 1 (Characterization of $\sim$ by groups). *For any types t and t' : $t \sim t'$ iff $[[t]] =_{FG} [[t']]$*

Sketch of proof : to show that if the interpretations are equal in FG then the classes for $\sim$ are equal, one constructs a group on equivalence classes $[t]$ for $\sim$ by :

$[t_1].[t_2] = [t_1 \otimes t_2]$
$[t]^{-1} = [t \setminus t / t]$
$\Lambda = [t \setminus t] = [t' / t']$

and one considers a morphism h from FG to this group on classes extending $h([[p]]) = [p]$ for which $h([[t]]) = [t]$ is satisfied. Therefore if $[[t]] =_{FG} [[t']]$ then $h([[t]]) = h([[t']])$ that is $[t] = [t']$ ie $t \sim t'$.

3 Mixing Deduction and Substitution : A Preorder on Types

In Lambek calculus, from a learning point of view, we are interested in the following relation on types :

Definition 1 *The relation $\|=$ on types is defined by*

$$t_1 \|= t_2 \text{ iff } \exists\sigma : t_1 \vdash_L \sigma(t_2)$$

where t_1, t_2 are types (formulas in L) and σ is a substitution.

Notation. As is usual we consider S as a distinguished type not modifiable. In general $x, x_1, \ldots, y, y_1, \ldots, u, v, w, \ldots$ will denote atomic variables.

Preorder properties of $\|=$ on types. This relation is clearly reflexive (taking the identity-substitution for $\|=$, and an axiom for $\vdash_L$), and transitive (from the replacement principle and the transitivity of $\vdash_L$).

We now illustrate this relation on selected examples.

Example 2 (Unifying distinct operators) *When we consider a word of type u / v and of type $(u' \setminus v')$ according to two respective grammars G_1 and G_2, we cannot unify these two types in the usual sense, but they can be unified in some broader sense using type $t' = (x_1 \setminus x_2) / x_3 \vdash x_1 \setminus (x_2 / x_3)$ as follows :*

$$\begin{cases} (x_1 \setminus x_2) / x_3 \|= (u / v) \text{ with } \sigma_1(u) = x_1 \setminus x_2; \sigma_1(v) = x_3 \\ (x_1 \setminus x_2) / x_3 \|= (u' \setminus v') \text{ with } \sigma_1(u') = x_1; \sigma_1(v') = (x_2 / x_3) \end{cases}$$

The same holds for $t'' = x_1 \setminus (x_2 / x_3)$ instead of t'.

Example 3 (An example with type-raising) *We also get :*

$$x_1 \|= u \setminus v$$

this can be shown using $\sigma_2(u) = y / x_1; \sigma_2(v) = y$, since $x_1 \vdash (y / x_1) \setminus y$.

Example 4 (Non unifiable types) *Types $u \, / \, u$ and S admit no common type t such that both $t \, \|= u \, / \, u$ and $t \, \|= S$; this fact will be formally justified later.*

Another example is given by $S \, / \, S$ and S, that are invariant by substitution, in such a case, it amounts to check that $t \vdash_L S \, / \, S$ and $t \vdash_L S$ is not possible : this can be performed by means of free group models in which $S \, / \, S$ and S would be in the same class.

3.1   Some Basic Properties of $\|=$ on Types

We introduce the equivalence on Tp induced by $\|=$, written $\|=\|$ as follows :

$$t_1 \, \|=\| \, t_2 \ \text{iff} \ t_1 \, \|= t_2 \ \text{and} \ t_2 \, \|= t_1$$

Upper bounds. Clearly any variable x is an upper bound : by considering for each t a substitution σ such that $\sigma(x) = t$ we get :$\forall t \in Tp : t \, \|= x$. In particular any subset of Tp has an upper bound for $\|=$. Obviously all upper bounds of Tp are $\|=\|$ -equivalent.

Lower bounds. There is no similar situation for lower bounds : some couples of types (t_1, t_2) do not admit any type t' such that both $t' \, \|= t_1$ and $t' \, \|= t_2$. This fact has been stated in example 4. In particular, Tp has no lower bound for $\|=$.

Partial relation. Some couples of types (t_1, t_2) are not comparable by $\|=$: for example $S \, / \, S$ and S are not.

Infinite chains. We can construct infinite chains either increasing or decreasing with respect to both $\vdash_L$ and $\|=$. Repeatedly using type-raising we get :

$$y_0 \vdash_L (y_1 \, / \, y_0) \setminus y_1 \vdash_L (y_2 \, / \, ((y_1 \, / \, y_0) \setminus y_1)) \setminus y_2 \vdash_L \ldots \vdash_L (y_n \, / \, \ldots) \setminus y_n \vdash_L \ldots$$

$$\ldots \vdash_L \ldots S \, / \, ((y_n \, / \, \ldots) \setminus y_n) \ldots \vdash_L S \, / \, ((y_1 \, / \, y_0) \setminus y_1) \vdash_L S \, / \, y_0$$

Observe that in each particular chain above, all types are $\|=\|$ -equivalent.

3.2   Investigating Variants : Do Substitution and Deduction Permute?

The operation $\|=$ uses at the same time substitution and deduction, it is natural to wonder whether these two operations permute.

We examine below different formulations and answer each time negatively : substitution and deduction do not permute.

We consider relations R_1 , R_1' , R_2 , R_2' on types t, t' as follows :

R_1 : $t \, \|= t'$ ie $\exists \sigma'$: $t \vdash_L \sigma'(t')$

R_1' : $\exists t'' \exists \sigma''$: $t = \sigma''(t'')$ and $t'' \vdash_L t'$

R_2 : $\exists \sigma$: $\sigma(t) \vdash_L t'$

R_2' : $\exists t'' \exists \sigma''$: $t \vdash_L t''$ and $\sigma''(t'') = t'$

Note that R_1 is $\|=$; R_2 and R_1' handle substitution on the left, while R_2' handles substitution on the right; R_1 (resp. R_2) can be compared especially to R_1' (resp. R_2').

Proposition 3 *Among R_1 , R_2 , R'_1 , R'_2 no two relations are equivalent.*

Proof. We show that :
(1) R'_1 implies R_1 , but (1') the converse does not hold;
(2) R_1 and R_2 are not equivalent (none implies the other).
(3) R'_2 implies R_2 , but (3') the converse does not hold;
(4) R'_1 does not imply R'_2 .
From which we infer that no two relations among R_1 , R_2 , R'_1 , R'_2 are equivalent. The main step is (1') and (3'), the other cases are rather immediate.

1 If R'_1 then from the replacement principle applied to $t'' \vdash_L t' : \sigma''(t'') \vdash_L \sigma''(t')$ with $t = \sigma''(t')$ which gives R_1 , using $\sigma' = \sigma''$.

1' Let us consider t, t' as follows where x_1, x_2, x_3, u, v are distinct variables :

$$\begin{cases} t = (x_1 \setminus x_2) \,/\, x_3 \\ t' = u \setminus v \\ \text{with } \sigma'(u) = x_1; \sigma'(v) = x_2 \,/\, x_3 \end{cases}$$

For such t, t', R_1 holds since $((x_1 \setminus x_2) \,/\, x_3) \vdash_L (x_1 \setminus (x_2 \,/\, x_3))$.

We now show that R'_1 does not hold for these types t, t'. Suppose on the contrary that : $\exists t'' \exists \sigma''$: $t = \sigma''(t'')$ and $t'' \vdash_L t'$; according to the shape of $t = (x_1 \setminus x_2) \,/\, x_3 = \sigma''(t'')$, no more than 3 cases are possible for t'' : v_1 or $v_1 \,/\, v_2$ or $(v_1 \setminus v_2) \,/\, v_3$, where all v_i are atomic variables; we can verify using models [4] that each case is in contradiction with $t'' \vdash_L t'$ where $t' = u \setminus v$, with u,v, atomic

2 To compare R_2 and R_1 is easy : take $(t, t') = (S, x)$ then $(t', t) = (S, x)$.

3 If R'_2 then by the replacement principle applied to $t \vdash_L t'' : \sigma''(t) \vdash_L \sigma''(t'')$ where $t' = \sigma''(t'')$ which yields R_2 , taking $\sigma = \sigma''$.

3' This case is similar to (1'), take $t' = (x_1 \setminus x_2) \,/\, x_3$ and $t = u \setminus v$ and $\sigma(u) = x_1; \sigma(v) = x_2 \,/\, x_3$: (t,t') satisfies R_2 since $(x_1 \setminus (x_2 \,/\, x_3)) \vdash_L ((x_1 \setminus x_2) \,/\, x_3)$
To show that it does not verify R'_2 , suppose the contrary : $\exists t'' \exists \sigma''$: $t \vdash_L t''$ *and* $\sigma''(t'') = t'$; according to the shape of $t' = \sigma''(t'')$, we get three shapes for t'' :
v_1 or $v_1 \,/\, v_2$ or $(v_1 \setminus v_2) \,/\, v_3$, (using groups) each one contradicts $t \vdash_L t''$ where $t = u \setminus v$

4 This case of R'_1 compared to R'_2 is easy : take $(t, t') = (S, x)$ ■

3.3 Do Variants Using Equations Yield the Same Relation ?

We now consider equations between type-formulas that are derivable one from the other (in L), such as :

$$(x_1 \setminus (x_2 \,/\, x_3)) = ((x_1 \setminus x_2) \,/\, x_3)$$

---

[4] using a free group interpretation is sufficient here : $[[v_1]] \neq_{FG} [[u]]^{-1}.[[v]]$
$[[v_1]].[[v_2]]^{-1} \neq_{FG} [[u]]^{-1}.[[v]]$
$[[v_1]]^{-1}.[[v_2]].[[v_3]]^{-1} \neq_{FG} [[u]]^{-1}.[[v]]$

One may wish to refine the definition of $\|\!=$ to take into account a set E of such equations in several manners. We discuss such variants below.

We define three variants : modulo E on the left as $\|\!=_g$; modulo E on the right after substitution as $\|\!=_d$; modulo E on the right after substitution as $\|\!=_{ds}$:

$$t_1 \|\!=_g t_2 \text{ iff } \exists\sigma\exists t'_1 =_E t_1 : t'_1 \vdash_L \sigma(t_2) \quad \text{(class of } t_1 \text{ instead of } t_1)$$
$$t_1 \|\!=_d t_2 \text{ iff } \exists\sigma\exists t'_2 =_E t_2 : t_1 \vdash_L \sigma(t'_2) \quad \text{(class of } t_2 \text{ instead of } t_2)$$
$$t_1 \|\!=_{ds} t_2 \text{ iff } \exists\sigma\exists t'_2 =_E \sigma(t_2) : t_1 \vdash_L t'_2 \quad \text{(class of } \sigma(t_2) \text{ instead of } \sigma(t_2))$$

The following is easy.

Proposition 4 *The relations* $\|\!=_g$, $\|\!=_d$, $\|\!=_{ds}$ *are all equal to* $\|\!=$.

In other words, derivable equations are already treated by $\|\!=$.

4 $\|\!=$ -Unifiability : Main Criterion

In this section we use free groups and give a main criterion that characterizes the existence and construction of unifiers with respect to $\|\!=$. We first recall standard definitions on unification modulo a set of equations.

Unification in (modulo) an equational theory. For any set E of equations, let $=_E$ denote the equivalence generated by E. We say that a set of terms $\mathcal{A}$ is unifiable modulo E (or E-unifiable) whenever there exists a substitution σ (then called E-unifier), such that for all terms $t, t' \in \mathcal{A} : \sigma(t) =_E \sigma(t')$. Unification has been studied for many equational theories, in particular in connection with rewriting. We recall that free groups (in the abelian case, and also in the non abelian case) admit a finite presentation by equations, that produces a canonical rewriting system; let G denote such a set of equations for non abelian groups.

4.1 Some Definitions

Let us adapt the standard definitions of unification to deal with deduction.

Definition 2 *Two types* A, B *are said* $\|\!=$ -unifiable *whenever (i) there exists a type* t *and a substitution* σ *such that* $t \vdash \sigma(A)$ *and* $t \vdash \sigma(B)$; σ *is then said a* $\|\!=$ -unifier *of* A *and* B *and* t *is a* $\|\!=$ -unificand *of* A *and* B.
These definitions are extended to sets of types in the usual way.

Two remarks :

1. If σ is a (standard) unifier of types A and B (ie $\sigma(A) = \sigma(B)$) then σ also is a $\|\!=$ -unifier of A and B (taking $\sigma(A)$ as left-hand side).
2. When A and B have no common variables, this definition (i) is equivalent to (ii) the existence of a type t such that both $t \|\!= A$ and $t \|\!= B$.
The case without shared variable is precisely the interesting one for the unification step in a learning process such as the RG-algorithm in [Kan98].

4.2 A Criterion for $\|\!=$ -Unifiability

We now relate the two notions of $\|\!=$ -unification and G-unification.

Notation. Letters A, B ... range over types and a, b ... range over groups.

Definition 3 (Translation of substitution)

1. *Let σ denote a substitution on types in Tp, we define its translation written σ_G as the substitution (on FG) defined by : $\sigma_G\ (p) = [[\,\sigma\ (p)]]$ for p atomic.*
2. *We define Φ from FG to Tp by :*
   $\Phi\ (\Lambda) = S \setminus S$
   $\Phi\ (p) = p$ *for* $p \neq \Lambda$ *atomic*
   $\Phi\ (a.b) = \Phi\ (a) \otimes \Phi\ (b)$
   $\Phi\ (a^{-1}) = (S \setminus S)\ /\ \Phi\ (a)$.
   Let θ denote a substitution on FG (group). We then write θ_L the substitution defined by : $\theta_L\ (p) = \Phi\ (\,\theta\ (p))$ (for all p atomic).

Lemma 1 (Translation condition) *Let σ denote a substitution on types in Tp and θ denote a substitution on FG (group) :*
if $\theta\ (p) = [[\,\sigma\ (p)]]$ for all p atomic then $\forall A \in Tp:\ \theta\ ([[A]]) = [[\,\sigma\ (A)]]$

Proof. By easy structural induction on $A \in Tp$, using the definition of $[[]]$ and of substitutions.

Lemma 2 (From $\|\!=$ -unifiers to G-unifiers) *A substitution σ on types is a $\|\!=$ -unifier of A and B iff its translation σ_G is a G-unifier of $[[A]]$ and $[[B]]$.*

Proof. By lemma 1 and the definition of σ_G , we get $\sigma_G\ ([[A]]) = [[\,\sigma\ (A)]]$ and $\sigma_G\ ([[B]]) = [[\,\sigma\ (B)]]$.
By the conjoinability characterization we get that σ is a $\|\!=$ -unifier of types A and B iff $[[\,\sigma\ (A)]] =_{FG} [[\,\sigma\ (B)]]$ therefore iff $\sigma_G\ ([[A]]) =_{FG} \sigma_G\ ([[B]])$ that is iff σ_G is a G-unifier of $[[A]]$ and $[[B]]$ ■

Lemma 3 (From groups to types) $[[\,\Phi\ (a)]] =_{FG} a$ *for all a in FG.*

Proof. By easy structural induction on a ■

Lemma 4 (From G-unifiers to $\|\!=$ -unifiers) *Let θ denote a G-unifier of types $[[A]]$ and $[[B]]$ then*

1. *any substitution σ on Tp such that : $\theta\ (p) = [[\,\sigma\ (p)]]$ (for all p atomic) is a $\|\!=$ -unifier of A and B ;*
2. *the substitution θ_L defined by : $\theta_L\ (p) = \Phi\ (\,\theta\ (p)))$ (for all p atomic), is one such $\|\!=$ -unifier of A and B.*

Proof. 1. Suppose : $\theta\ (p) = [[\,\sigma\ (p)]]$ (for all p atomic)
we get from lemma 1: $[[\,\sigma\ (A)]] = \theta\ ([[A]])$ and $[[\,\sigma\ (B)]] = \theta\ ([[B]])$
By hypothesis : $\theta\ ([[A]]) =_{FG} \theta\ ([[B]])$
therefore : $[[\,\sigma\ (A)]] = [[\,\sigma\ (B)]]$, which asserts from the conjoinability results that σ is a $\|\!=$ -unifier of A and B.

2. Suppose : $\theta_L\ (p) = \Phi\ (\ \theta\ (p)))$ (for all p atomic),
   by lemma 3 we get : $[[\ \theta_L\ (p)]] = [[\ \Phi\ (\ \theta\ (p)]] = \theta\ (p)$ (for all p atomic) ■

We now get our main proposition as a corollary of these lemmas.

Proposition 5 (Characterizing $\|=$ -unifiablity and $\|=$ -unifiers) *Let A and B be two types in Tp*

1. *A and B are $\|=$ -unifiable iff there images $[[A]]$ and $[B]]$ are G-unifiable.*
2. *σ is a $\|=$ -unifier of types A and B iff its translation σ_G is a G-unifier of $[[A]]$ and $[[B]]$, (where σ_G is defined by : $\sigma_G\ (p) = [[\ \sigma\ (p)]]$ for p atomic) ; conversely any G-unifier of $[[A]]$ and $[[B]]$ is the translation of a $\|=$ -unifier of types A and B.*

We also extend this property to sets of types instead of two types.

Proof. This property is a corollary of the joinability results recalled in section 2 and previous lemmas ■

Note. When this is clear from context, we may use the same notation for a $\|=$ -unifier and a corresponding G-unifier.

One may thus benefit from existing results for groups such as [Mak82] (corrections in [Mak84]), [Gut00] and the existence of a canonical rewrite system (for general references, see [CK00, Sie87] and in particular [Che86] for groups). A canonical rewriting system for free groups with neutral element 1 is :

$$\begin{cases} x.1 \rightarrow x & 1.x \rightarrow x & (x.y).z \rightarrow x.(y.z) \\ x.x^{-1} \rightarrow 1 & x^{-1}.x \rightarrow 1 & (x.y)^{-1} \rightarrow y^{-1}.x^{-1} \\ x.(x^{-1}.y) \rightarrow y & x^{-1}.(x.y) \rightarrow y & (x^{-1})^{-1} \rightarrow x \\ 1^{-1} \rightarrow 1 & & \end{cases}$$

In the particular case when types A and B are without variables, one only needs to check whether the two normal forms compiled by the rewriting system coincide.

4.3 Some $\|=$ -Unifiability Examples and Remarks

We now consider particular cases of $\|=$ -unifiability and not $\|=$ -unifiability justified by the above criterion.

In particular, we are now able to justify the case of example 4 as follows.

Example 5 *Types $u\ /\ u$ and S are not $\|=$ -unifiable since*

$$[[\sigma_1(u\ /\ u)]] =_{FG} [[\sigma_1(u)]].[[\sigma_1(u)]]^{-1} =_{FG} \Lambda \neq_{FG} [[S]]$$

Similarly $u\ /\ u$ and $(v\ /\ v)\ /\ S$ are not $\|=$ -unifiable

Example 6 *One more example is given by* $((u \,/\, v) \setminus w)$ *and* $(u' \,/\, (v' \setminus w'))$. *When calculating the relative group-images, we find that they are joinable if* $u' = v, v' = w, w' = u$ *; on the other hand they are* $\|=$ *-unifiable, for example by type-raising we get* $v \vdash ((u \,/\, v) \setminus u)$ *and* $v \vdash (u \,/\, (v \setminus u))$

A general fact. If t_1 and t_2 have no constant then they are $\|=$ -unifiable. One simple way to $\|=$ -unify them is :
(1) to rename by σ_1 all variables of t_1 with only one, say x_1, and rename by σ_2 all variables of t_2 with only one, say x_2;
(2) then to compute the respective normal forms (by means of a canonical rewriting system) of $\sigma_1(t_1)$ and $\sigma_2(t_2)$; for any integer n, let x_1^n denote Λ if $n = 0$, or $\underbrace{x_1.x_1....x_1}_{ntimes}$ if $n > 0$ or else $\underbrace{x_1^{-1}.x_1^{-1}....x_1^{-1}}_{-ntimes}$; it is easy to see that for $\sigma_1(t_1)$ we get some $x_1^{n_1}$ as normal form (since other combinations of x_1, x_1^{-1} and Λ would be reducible) and similarly some $x_2^{n_2}$ for $\sigma_2(t_2)$
(3) we conclude using $x^{n_1 * n_2}$ and $\sigma(x_1) = x^{n_2}$ and $\sigma(x_2) = x^{n_1}$ such that : $\sigma(\sigma_1(t_1)) =_{FG} \sigma(\sigma_2(t_2))$.

A note on $\|=$ **-unifying a set vs pairs.** Whereas a finite set of types has a join iff the types are pairwise conjoinable [Pen93a], (where we can limit the pairs by transitivity) $\|=$ -unifying a set does not reduce to such a pairwise $\|=$ -unifiability as shown by the following example : $\{S, S \,/\, S, u \,/\, v\}$ is such that both $S \|= u \,/\, v$, $S \|= S$, and both $S \,/\, S \|= u \,/\, v$, $S \,/\, S \|= S \,/\, S$, but the pair S and $S \,/\, S$ is not $\|=$ -unifiable as seen previously, and the whole set is not.

In this respect, conjoinability and $\|=$ -unifiability are related (through unification), but enjoy different behaviour properties.

4.4 Investigating a Preorder on Substitutions

When considering $\preceq$ on substitutions, we observe from examples below that there is not always a unique substitution $\|=$ -unifying a set of types.

Example 7 *We have already seen in example 2 that* $\mathcal{A} = \{(u \,/\, v); (u' \setminus v')\}$ *is* $\|=$ *-unifiable using in particular* $t' = (x_1 \setminus x_2) \,/\, x_3$ *such that :*

$$t' \|= (u \,/\, v) \qquad t' \|= (u' \setminus v') \qquad t' \|= x_1 \setminus (x_2 \,/\, x_3)$$

with $\sigma_1(u) = x_1 \setminus x_2; \sigma_1(v) = x_3; \sigma_1(u') = x_1; \sigma_1(v') = (x_2 \,/\, x_3)$.

But there is also a possibility [5] *involving type-raising as in example 3 :*

$$\begin{cases} x \|= (u \,/\, v) \ \ with \ \ \sigma_0(u) = y; \sigma_0(v) = x \setminus y \\ x \|= (u' \setminus v') \ \ with \ \ \sigma_0(u') = y \,/\, x; \sigma_0(v') = y \end{cases}$$

[5] In terms of group models, we look for substitutions such that : $[[\sigma_1(u \,/\, v)]] = [[\sigma_2(u' \setminus v')]]$ ie $[[\sigma_1(u)]].[[\sigma_1(v)]]^{-1} = [[\sigma_2(u')]]^{-1}.[[\sigma_2(v')]]$

One observes on this example no clear relationship between the two substitutions σ_0 and σ_1. Nevertheless, the two types involved as $\|\!=$ -unificand x and $(x_1 \setminus x_2) / x_3$ are $\|\!=\!\|$ -equivalent : note that $x \vdash (x_1 \setminus ((x_1 \otimes x) \otimes x_3)) / x_3$.

Example 8 *We consider* $\mathcal{A} = \{(u / v); (S \setminus v')\}$ *:* $\mathcal{A}$ *is* $\|\!=$ *-unifiable using types* S *or* x *on the left and type-raising on the right. But there are other possibilities*[6] *involving type-raising as in example 3 :*

$$\begin{cases} x \|\!= (u / v) \ \textit{with} \ \sigma_0(u) = S \setminus x; \sigma_0(v) = S \\ x \|\!= (S \setminus v') \ \textit{with} \ \sigma_0(v') = x / S \end{cases}$$

We do not detail more observations on the structure of $\|\!=$ -unifiers here. It should be undertaken through groups that characterize $\|\!=$ as shown previously.

4.5 Connection to Learning (Rigid) Lambek Grammars

The underlying idea is to start from given sentences (possibly structured) as the learning examples, to perform some type assignment on these sentences similar to algorithm RG [Kan98] and to apply $\|\!=$ -unification instead of standard unification to the grammars that appear at this stage.

We now illustrate this point with some features and examples.

Language inclusion. Recall that if $G_1 \sqsubseteq G_2$ (i.e. $\exists \sigma : \sigma(G_1) \subseteq G_2$) then $L(G_1) \subseteq L(G_2)$. We get a similar property for $\|\!=$ -unification as follows.

Let G_k $(k = 1, 2)$ be rigid grammars described by : $G_k = \{c_1 \mapsto A_{1,k},\ c_2 \mapsto A_{2,k},\ \ldots\}$. Suppose that G_1 and G_2 have no common variables occurring in types (after renaming in G_2 if necessary). Let G_0 denote a rigid grammar described by : $\{c_1 \mapsto A_{1,0},\ c_2 \mapsto A_{1,0},\ \ldots\}$ such that $\exists \sigma\ : A_{1,0} \vdash \sigma(A_{1,k}),\ A_{2,0} \vdash \sigma(A_{2,k}),\ \ldots$ (for $k = 1, 2$). Note that σ is a $\|\!=$ -unifier of $\{A_{1,1},\ A_{1,2}\}$ and a $\|\!=$ -unifier of $\{A_{2,1},\ A_{2,2}\}$ ...

It is easy to see that $L_L(G_0) \subseteq L_L(G_k)$ (for $k = 1, 2$).

The above property justifies the replacement of the union of grammars G_1 and G_2 with G_0 in the learning process.

Example 9 (Example 1 revisited) *We consider sentence* $(John\, likes\, Mary)$ *with two distinct groupings :* $(John\ (likes\ Mary))$ *and* $((John\ likes)\ Mary)$.

Suppose that after some type computation, we get the following grammars :
$G_1 = \{John \mapsto x_1,\ Mary \mapsto x_2,\ likes \mapsto (x_1 \setminus S) / x_2\}$ *and*
$G_2 = \{John \mapsto x_3,\ Mary \mapsto x_4,\ likes \mapsto x_3 \setminus (S / x_4)\}$

Standard unification fails to produce a rigid grammar since the types for "likes" are not unifiable. However $\|\!=$ *-unification succeeds since the types for "likes" are* $\|\!=$ *-unifiable. In this particular example, we may replace the union of* G_1 *and* G_2 *by* G_1 *(or by* G_2*).*

Also recall that a standard unifier is a particular case of $\|\!=$ -unifier. $\|\!=$ -unification can be seen as a generalization that seems appropriate to incorporate in such learning process.

---

6 we look for σ such that : $[[\sigma(u / v)]] = [[\sigma(S \setminus v')]]$ ie $[[\sigma(u)]].[[\sigma(v)]]^{-1} = [[\sigma(S)]]^{-1}.[[\sigma(v')]]$

5 Variants of Lambek Calculus

The same definition $\|\!=$ may be undertaken in various calculi.

Allowing empty left hand-side. The first variant to consider is when we drop the non-empty left hand-side requirement. In such a case, there is no significant change, since the characterization of $\sim$ by groups also holds [Pen93a]. More precisely, on the one hand he shows that $t \sim t'$ is equivalent in the two cases with or without the non-empty left hand-side requirement and equivalent to $[[t]] =_{FG} [[t']]$; on the other hand when we drop the non-empty left hand-side requirement it is easy to do the same construction as in the Diamond property.

This shows that a set is $\|\!=$ -unifiable in one system iff it is $\|\!=$ -unifiable in the other, and the $\|\!=$ -unifiers are the same .

Note that however the $\|\!=$ -unificands need not be the same in the two systems as shown in next example.

Example 10 *The disadvantage of the empty sequence usually called upon is to allow incorrect derivations such as : "A very book : NP" that can be typed as follows with the empty sequence but not without it*

$$NP \,/\, N, (N \,/\, N) \,/\, (N \,/\, N), N \vdash_{L\emptyset} NP$$

If we consider the pair $\{(NP \,/\, N) \otimes ((N \,/\, N) \,/\, (N \,/\, N)) \otimes N, NP\}$ *we get,* $(NP \,/\, N) \otimes ((N \,/\, N) \,/\, (N \,/\, N)) \otimes N \|\!= NP$ *if we allow the empty sequence (in* $L_\emptyset$*), but not without it (in L). However this pair gets also* $\|\!=$ *-unified, in L by another left hand-side :*

$$\begin{cases} (NP \,/\, N) \otimes (N \,/\, N) \otimes N \|\!= NP \\ (NP \,/\, N) \otimes (N \,/\, N) \otimes N \|\!= (NP \,/\, N) \otimes ((N \,/\, N) \,/\, (N \,/\, N)) \otimes N \end{cases}$$

Allowing permutations.

We now focus on the permutative calculus. Pentus has also proved a similar joinability equivalence using free abelian groups instead of groups. Therefore, we get a similar characterization for $\|\!=$ -unifiability using unification in abelian groups. We may thus benefit from unification algorithms and rewriting systems[7] that are available in the corresponding theory.

6 Conclusion and Future Works

We have investigated a relation mixing deduction and substitution, in particular we have given a characterization in terms of groups.

[7] A canonical rewriting system modulo the associativity-commutativity of . for free abelian groups with neutral element 1

$$\begin{cases} x.1 & \to x & 1^{-1} & \to 1 \\ x.x^{-1} & \to 1 & (x^{-1})^{-1} & \to x \\ x.(y^{-1}.y) & \to x & (x.y)^{-1} & \to x^{-1}.y^{-1} \end{cases}$$

Such a relation is intended to serve as a basis for learning Lambek categorial grammars, following the work of [Kan98]. Such learning algorithms is the aim of further studies.

We have focused here on associative Lambek calculus. One may also consider variants such as non-associative calculus; following the work of Pentus, we should examine similar joinability criterion in an algebraic way and use unification procedure and rewriting systems in the corresponding theory when available.

Ackowledgments : Thanks to J. Nicolas, C. Retoré who originated this work, to R. Bonato, Y. Le Nir for useful discussions and to the anonymous referees for helpful comments.

References

[Bon00] Roberto Bonato. *A Study On Learnability for Rigid Lambek Grammars.* Italian laurea degree master thesis and irisa research report, to appear, 2000.

[BP90] Wojciech Buszkowski and Gerald Penn. Categorial grammars determined from linguistic data by unification. *Studia Logica*, 49:431–454, 1990.

[Bus97] W. Buszkowski. Mathematical linguistics and proof theory. In van Benthem and ter Meulen [vBtM97], chapter 12, pages 683–736.

[Cas88] Claudia Casadio. Semantic categories and the development of categorial grammars. In R. Oehrle, E. Bach, and D. Wheeler, editors, *Categorial Grammars and Natural Language Structures*, pages 95–124. Reidel, Dordrecht, 1988.

[Che86] Philippe Le Chenadec. *Canonical Forms in Finitely Presented Algebras.* Pitman, 1986.

[CK00] Claude and Hélène Kirchner. *Rewriting Solving Proving.* http://www.loria.fr/˜ vigneron/RewritingHP/, 2000.

[Gir95] Jean-Yves Girard. Linear logic: its syntax and semantics. In Jean-Yves Girard, Yves Lafont, and Laurent Regnier, editors, *Advances in Linear Logic*, volume 222 of *London Mathematical Society Lecture Notes*, pages 1–42. Cambridge University Press, 1995.

[Gol67] E.M. Gold. Language identification in the limit. *Information and control*, 10:447–474, 1967.

[Gut00] Claudio Gutiérrez. Satisfiability of equations in free groups is in PSPACE. *STOC'2000*, 2000.

[Kan98] Makoto Kanazawa. *Learnable classes of categorial grammars.* Studies in Logic, Language and Information. FoLLI & CSLI, 1998. distributed by Cambridge University Press.

[Lam58] Joachim Lambek. The mathematics of sentence structure. *American mathematical monthly*, 65:154–169, 1958.

[Mak82] G.S. Makanin. Equations in a free group. *Izvestia NA SSSR 46(1982), 1199-1273 ; English translation in Math USSR Izvestiya, 21 (1983), 483-546.*, 1982.

[Mak84] G.S. Makanin. Decidability of the universal and positive theories of a free group. *Izvestia NA SSSR 48(1984), 735-749 ; English translation in Math USSR Izvestiya, 25 (1985), 75-88.*, 1984.

[Moo96] Michael Moortgat. Categorial type logic. In van Benthem and ter Meulen [vBtM97], chapter 2, pages 93–177.

[Nic99] Jacques Nicolas. Grammatical inference as unification. Rapport de Recherche RR-3632, INRIA, 1999. http://www.inria.fr/RRRT/publications-eng.html.

[Pen93a] M. Pentus. The conjoinability relation in Lambek calculus and linear logic. ILLC Prepublication Series ML–93–03, Institute for Logic, Language and Computation, University of Amsterdam, 1993.

[Pen93b] Mati Pentus. Lambek grammars are context-free. In *Logic in Computer Science*. IEEE Computer Society Press, 1993.

[Ret96] Christian Retoré. Calcul de Lambek et logique linéaire. *Traitement Automatique des Langues*, 37(2):39–70, 1996.

[Ret00] Christian Retoré. Systèmes déductifs et traitement des langues:un panorama des grammaires catégorielles. Technical Report RR-3917 2000, INRIA, Rennes, France, 2000. A revised version to appear in Traitement automatique du langage naturel, TSI.

[Sie87] J.H. Siekmann. Unification theory. In B. Du Boulay, D. Hogg, and L. Steels, editors, *Advances in Artificial Intelligence — II*, pages 365–400. North-Holland, 1987.

[vBtM97] J. van Benthem and A. ter Meulen, editors. *Handbook of Logic and Language*. North-Holland Elsevier, Amsterdam, 1997.

A Framework for the Hyperintensional Semantics of Natural Language with Two Implementations

Chris Fox and Shalom Lappin*

Dept. of Computer Science, King's College London
The Strand, London WC2R 2LS, United Kingdom
{foxcj,lappin}@dcs.kcl.ac.uk

Abstract. In this paper we present a framework for constructing hyperintensional semantics for natural language. On this approach, the axiom of extensionality is discarded from the axiom base of a logic. Weaker conditions are specified for the connection between equivalence and identity which prevent the reduction of the former relation to the latter. In addition, by axiomatising an intensional number theory we can provide an internal account of proportional cardinality quantifiers, like *most*. We use a (pre-)lattice defined in terms of a (pre-)order that models the entailment relation. Possible worlds/situations/indices are then prime filters of propositions in the (pre-)lattice. Truth in a world/situation is then reducible to membership of a prime filter. We show how this approach can be implemented within (i) an intensional higher-order type theory, and (ii) first-order property theory.

1 Introduction

It has frequently been noted that the characterization of intensions as functions from possible worlds to extensions, as in [21], yields a semantics which is not sufficiently fine grained. Specifically, logically equivalent expressions are co-intensional and so intersubstitutable in all contexts, including the complements of propositional attitude predicates. This view of intensions defines them extensionally in set theoretic terms, and it has been dominant in formal semantics at least since Carnap [5].

* We are grateful to Tom Maibaum and Carl Pollard for invaluable help and advice in developing the semantic approach proposed here. Much of the the second author's research relies heavily on earlier joint work with Pollard, and we are grateful to him for helpful comments on an earlier draft of this paper. We would also like to thank Nissim Francez, Dov Gabbay, Jonathan Ginzburg, Howard Gregory, Jim Lambek, Andrew Pitts, Phil Scott and three anonymous referees for useful discussion of many of the ideas presented in this paper. Of course we bear sole responsibility for the shortcomings of our proposals. The second author's research is funded by grant number AN2687/APN 9387 from the Arts and Humanities Research Board of the United Kingdom.

P. de Groote, G. Morrill, C. Retoré (Eds.): LACL 2001, LNAI 2099, pp. 175–192, 2001.

An alternative view, which (following Lappin and Pollard [17]) we refer to as *hyperintensionalism*, posits propositions as independent intensional entities, and takes truth to be a relation between a proposition and a non-intensional entity. In the past twenty years a variety of hyperintensionalist theories have been proposed, including Thomason [28], situation semantics [3, 2, 25], Landman [16], property theory [6, 29, 32], [22], and Lappin and Pollard [17]. With the exception of Turner [32] these theories have focused on developing a model theory in which logical equivalence does not entail synonymy.

We depart from this tradition by taking an axiomatic approach to hyperintensionalism and assigning model theory a secondary role in our account. We define a class of models that provide a minimal model theory in which our logics are sound and which support counter-examples to the axiom of extensionality.

In section 2 we specify an intensional higher-order type theory in which the axioms of extensionality are replaced by weaker conditions on the relation between identity and equivalence. We introduce an equivalence (weak identity) predicate that can hold between any two expressions of the same type and use it to construct an intensional number theory. This theory permits us to add meaning postulates that characterize certain proportional cardinality quantifiers, like *most*, which have, until now, avoided an axiomatic treatment.

In section 3 we show how our axiomatic version of hyperintensionalism can be implemented in a first-order property theory where properties and other intensional entities are elements of a single multi-sorted domain. It is possible to mimic the higher-order type system of section 2 in this theory by defining appropriate sorting predicates for the domain. It is also possible to characterize S5 modalities in a straightforward way within this theory.

Section 4 gives an algebraic reduction of possible worlds (situations, indices) to prime filters in a (pre-)lattice of propositions.[1] This framework permits us to reduce truth in a hyperintensional semantics to membership in a prime filter of propositions in the (pre-)lattice. An appropriate (pre-)lattice can be constructed for the intensional higher-order type theory of section 2 and a full lattice for the first-order property theory of section 3.

Finally in section 5 we compare our account to other views of hyperintensionalism that have been proposed in the recent literature.

2 An Intensional Higher-Order Type Theory

2.1 The Proof Theory

We define the set of types in our intensional higher-order type theory IHTT as follows.

Basic Types

1. e (individuals)
2. Π (propositions)

[1] This idea is due to Carl Pollard, and it is presented in [17]

Exponential Types

If A, B are types, then A^B is a type.

This is the type system of Church [7], which is equivalent to Ty2 of Gallin [13] without s (possible worlds) as a basic type. For each type A there is (i) a denumerable set of non-logical constants of type A and (ii) a denumerable set of variables of type A. We define the set E_A of expressions of type A as follows.

1. Every variable of type A is in E_A.
2. Every constant of type A is in E_A.
3. If $\alpha \in E_A$ and u is a variable in E_B, then $\lambda u \alpha \in E_{A^B}$.
4. If $\alpha \in E_{B^A}$ and $\beta \in E_A$, then $\alpha(\beta) \in E_B$.
5. If $\alpha, \beta \in E_A$, then $\alpha = \beta \in E_\Pi$.
6. if $\alpha, \beta \in E_A$, then $\alpha \cong \beta \in E_\Pi$.
7. $\top$ and $\bot \in E_\Pi$.
8. If $\phi, \psi \in E_\Pi$, then so are
   (a) $\neg\phi$
   (b) $\phi \vee \psi$
   (c) $\phi \wedge \psi$
   (d) $\phi \rightarrow \psi$
   (e) $\phi \leftrightarrow \psi$
9. If $\phi \in E_\Pi$ and u is a variable in E_A, then $\forall u\phi$ and $\exists u\phi \in E_\Pi$.

We adopt the following axioms, based, in part, on the higher-order intuitionistic type theory presented by Lambek and Scott [15, Part II, Chapter 1].[2]

(IHTT1) $p \vdash \top$
(IHTT2) $\bot \vdash p$
(IHTT3) $\vdash \neg p \leftrightarrow p \rightarrow \bot$
(IHTT4) $r \vdash p \wedge q$ iff $r \vdash p$ and $r \vdash q$
(IHTT5) $p \vee q \vdash r$ iff $p \vdash r$ or $q \vdash r$
(IHTT6) $p \vdash q \rightarrow r$ iff $p \wedge q \vdash r$
(IHTT7) $p \vdash \forall x_{\in B} \phi_{\in \Pi^B}$ iff $p \vdash \phi$
(IHTT8) $\phi(a) \vdash \exists x_{\in B}\phi(x)$ (where $\phi \in \Pi^B$, and a is a constant in B)
(IHTT9) $\vdash \lambda u \phi(v) \cong \phi^{u/v}$ (where u is a variable in A, $v \in$ A, $\phi \in B^A$, and v is not bound when substituted for u in ϕ)
(IHTT10) $\vdash \forall s, t_{\in \Pi}(s \cong t \leftrightarrow (s \leftrightarrow t))$
(IHTT11) $\vdash \forall \phi, \psi_{\in B^A}(\forall u_{\in A}(\phi(u) \cong \psi(u)) \rightarrow \phi \cong \psi)$ [3]
(IHTT12) $\vdash \forall u, v_{\in A} \forall \phi_{\in B^A}(u = v \rightarrow \phi(u) \cong \phi(v))$
(IHTT13) $\vdash \forall t_{\in \Pi}(t \vee \neg t)$

[2] we are grateful to Carl Pollard for proposing the strategy of constructing an intensional higher order type system by starting with the Lambek-Scott system and discarding the axiom of extensionality, and for helpful suggestions on how to specify the relation between $=$ and $\cong$.

[3] As Carl Pollard points out to us, axiom (11) together with axiom (10) entail that $\cong$ is extensional, and hence is an equivalence relation for propositions and predicates. We assume the axioms which specify that $=$ (logical identity) is an equivalence relation.

Axioms (IHTT1)–(IHTT12) yield a higher-order intuitionistic logic. We can obtain a classical Boolean system by adding axiom (IHTT13).

The relation $\cong$ corresponds to extensional equivalence of entities of the same type.[4] It follows from axiom (IHTT12) that logical identity implies equivalence. However, as the converse (the axiom of extensionality) does not hold, any two entities of the same type can be equivalent but not identical. Therefore, two expressions can be logically equivalent but not co-intensional. Specifically, it is possible for two propositions to be provably equivalent but distinct. Axiom (IHTT9) ensures that two sides of a lambda conversion are logically equivalent, but it does not entail that they are identical.

2.2 A Class of Possible Models

A model for IHTT is an ordered quintuple $\langle D, S, L, I, F\rangle$, where D is a family of non-empty sets such that each D_A is the set of possible denotations for expressions of type A, S and L are non-empty sets and $L \subset S$. I is a function from the expressions of IHTT to S such that if α is a non-logical constant, then $I(\alpha) \in L$; otherwise, $I(\alpha) \in S - L$. F is a function from L to members of D. If α is a non-logical constant in A, then $F(I(\alpha)) \in D_A$. If α is a non-logical contant in A^B, then $F(I(\alpha)) \in (D_A)^{D_B}$. $D_\Pi = \{t, f\}$. If v is a variable in A, then $I(v) = v$.[5] I assigns intensions to the expressions of IHTT, and F assigns denotations to the non-logical constants. A valuation g is a function from the variables of IHTT to members of D such that for each variable $v_{\in A} g(v) \in D_A$.

1. If $\alpha_{\in A}$ is a non-logical constant, then $\|\alpha\|^{M,g} = F(I(\alpha))$.
2. If $\alpha_{\in A}$ is a variable, then $\|\alpha\|^{M,g} = g(\alpha)$.
3. $\|\alpha_{\in B^A}(\beta_{\in A})\|^{M,g} = \|\alpha\|^{M,g}(\|\beta\|^{M,g})$.
4. If α is in A and u is a variable in B, then $\|\lambda u\alpha\|^{M,g}$ is a function $h \in (D_B)^D_A$ such that for any $a \in D_A, h(a) = \|\alpha\|^{M,g(u/a)}$.
5. $\|\neg\phi_{\in\Pi}\|^{M,g} = t$ iff $\|\phi\|^{M,g} = f$.
6. $\|\phi_{\in\Pi} \wedge \psi_{\in\Pi}\|^{M,g} = t$ iff $\|\phi\|^{M,g} = \|\psi\|^{M,g} = t$.
7. $\|\phi_{\in\Pi} \vee \psi_{\in\Pi}\|^{M,g} = t$ iff $\|\phi\|^{M,g} = t$ or $\|\psi\|^{M,g} = t$.
8. $\|\phi_{\in\Pi} \rightarrow \psi_{\in\Pi}\|^{M,g} = t$ iff $\|\phi\|^{M,g} = f$ or $\|\psi\|^{M,g} = t$.
9. $\|\phi_{\in\Pi} \leftrightarrow \psi_{\in\Pi}\|^{M,g} = t$ iff $\|\phi\|^{M,g} = \|\psi\|^{M,g}$.
10. $\|\alpha_{\in A} \cong \beta_{\in A}\|^{M,g} = t$ iff $\|\alpha\|^{M,g} = \|\beta\|^{M,g}$.
11. $\|\alpha_{\in A} = \beta_{\in A}\|^{M,g} = t$ iff $I(\alpha) = I(\beta)$.
12. $\|\forall u_{\in A}\phi_{\in\Pi}\|^{M,g} = t$ iff for all $a \in D_A$ $\|\phi\|^{M,g(u/a)} = t$.
13. $\|\exists u_{\in A}\phi_{\in\Pi}\|^{M,g} = t$ iff for some $a \in D_A$ $\|\phi\|^{M,g(u/a)} = t$.

---

[4] Within the framework of program specification theory, Maibaum [19] discusses the use of a weak non-logical equality predicate to express the equivalence/congruence of possibly distinct expressions within a theory.

[5] It follows that if u, v are distinct variables free in $\phi(u)$ and $\phi(v)$, respectively, then $I(\phi(u)) \neq I(\phi(v))$. However, it is possible to restrict I in order to obtain intensional identity under alphabetic variance of bound variables. This involves imposing the constraint that if α' and α differ only in the names of the bound variables, then $I(\alpha) = I(\alpha')$.

14. $\phi_{\in \Pi}$ is true in M (false in M) iff $\|\phi\|^{M,G} = t(f)$ for all g.
15. $\phi_{\in \Pi}$ is logically true (false) iff ϕ is true (false) in every M.
16. $\phi_{\in \Pi} \models \psi_{\in \Pi}$ iff for every M such that ϕ is true in M, ψ is true in M.

The axioms (IHTT1)–(IHTT13) hold in models which satisfy these conditions. Notice that while $\alpha \cong \beta$ is true (relative to M, g) iff the denotations of α and β are the same, $\alpha = \beta$ is true iff I assigns α and β the same value. For a model M $I(\alpha) = I(\beta)$ implies that $\|\alpha\|^{M,g} = \|\beta\|^{M,g}$, for all g, but the converse implication does not hold. Therefore, it is possible for $\|\alpha \cong \beta\|^{M,g}$ to be true for all M, g, but for there to be at least one M and one g such that $\|\alpha = \beta\|^{M,g}$ is false. This would be the case, for example, if α and β were logically equivalent but distinct sentences in IHTT, and in at least one M, I is a function from the closed expressions of IHTT to their Gödel numbers.

2.3 Hyperintensional Number Theory and Proportional Cardinality Quantifiers

We add a new basic type N to our type system.[6] By substituting $\cong$ for $=$ in the Peano axioms, we can construct a hyperintensional number theory within IHTT.

(IHTT14) $\vdash \neg \exists u_{\in N}(succ(u) \cong 0)$
(IHTT15) $\vdash \forall u, v_{\in N}(succ(u) \cong succ(v) \leftrightarrow u \cong v)$
(IHTT16) $\vdash \forall \alpha_{\in \Pi^N}(\alpha(0) \wedge \forall u_{\in N}((\alpha(u) \rightarrow \alpha(succ(u))) \rightarrow \forall v_{\in N}\alpha(v))$

The basic arithmetical operations are defined in the usual way, but with $\cong$ substituted for $=$. In this theory it is possible for distinct representations of a number to be equivalent but not identical. Therefore. $7 + 2 \cong 9$, but it not necessarily the case that $7 + 2 = 9$.

We can specify the relation $<$ by means of the following axiom.

(IHTT17) $\vdash \forall u, v_{\in N}(u < v \leftrightarrow \exists w_{\in N}(\neg(w \cong 0) \wedge u + w \cong v))$

Let P be a property term in Π^A. We characterize the cardinality of P, $|P|$, by the following axioms.

(IHTT18) $\vdash \neg \exists u_{\in A} P(u) \rightarrow |P| \cong 0$
(IHTT19) $\vdash P(u) \rightarrow (\neg P^{-u}(u) \wedge \forall v \in A((\neg(u \cong v) \wedge P(v)) \rightarrow P^{-u}(v)))$
(IHTT20) $\vdash P(u) \rightarrow |P| \cong |P^{-u}| + succ(0)$

Take *most* to be a generalized quantifier of type $\Pi^{(\Pi^A)^{(\Pi^A)}}$. We give the interpretation of *most* by the following axiom.

(IHTT21) $\vdash \forall P, Q_{\in \Pi^A}(most(P)(Q)) \leftrightarrow |\lambda u[P(u) \wedge Q(u)]| > |\lambda u[P(u) \wedge \neg Q(u)|$

[6] We are grateful to Tom Maibaum for suggesting this approach to the internal representation of generalized quantifiers involving cardinality relations

3 A Property-Theoretic Approach

The version of Property Theory presented here is Turner's weak first-order axiomatisation of Aczel's Frege Structures [30, 31, 32, 1]. Rather than avoiding the logical paradoxes of self-application through strong typing, here self-application is permitted, but the theory is deliberately too weak to allow the axioms of truth to apply to pathological cases of self application. Natural language types can be reintroduced as first-order sorts [30, 31, 32].

The methodology of adopting weak axioms to avoid category mistakes can be extended to cases of infelicitous references that arise with both non-denoting definites and anaphora [9, 11, 10, 12, 8].

Here we sketch two extensions to the theory. In the first, we introduce possible worlds to allow for a treatment of doxastic modality. This helps to highlight the distinction between intensionality and modality. In the second extension, we indicate how the theory can be strengthened to give a theory internal analysis of proportional cardinality quantifiers, similar to the one given in section 2.3 but without leaving an essentially first-order regime.

3.1 Basic Property Theory

A highly intensional theory of propositions and truth will allow distinct propositions to be (necessarily) true together. One such theory is Turner's axiomatisation of a Frege Structure [31, 1]; one of a family of theories known as Property Theory. It is a first-order theory with weak typing and consists of a language of terms, in which intensional propositions, properties and relations are represented, and a language of well formed formulæ, in which the (extensional) truth conditions of propositions can be expressed. To avoid a logical paradox, only some terms correspond to propositions, and hence have truth conditions.

In this version of first-order Property Theory, the language of terms is that of the untyped λ-calculus. This gives us a ready-made notion of predication—that of function application[7]—as well as providing the expressivity required for a compositional theory of natural language semantics.

(PT1) $t ::= c \mid x \mid \lambda x(t) \mid t(t) \mid l$ (The language of the untyped λ-calculus—individual constants, variables, abstractions, and applications of terms—together with logical constants.)

(PT2) $l ::= \hat{\wedge} \mid \hat{\vee} \mid \hat{\neg} \mid \hat{\rightarrow} \mid \hat{\forall} \mid \hat{\exists} \mid \hat{=}$ (The logical constants, corresponding with conjunction, disjunction, negation, universal quantification, existential quantification and equality.)

The language of terms is governed by the usual axioms for the untyped λ-calculus, namely those for α and β reduction. These define the equality of terms.

(λ1) $\lambda x(t) = \lambda y(t[y/x])$ if y not free in t. (α-reduction.)
(λ2) $(\lambda x(t))t' = t[t'/x]$ (β-reduction.)

---

[7] Note that there are cases where it is arguably inappropriate to equate predication with function application [4].

The truth conditions of those terms corresponding to propositions can be obtained in the first-order language of well formed formulæ (wff).

(PT3) $\varphi ::= t = t \mid \mathsf{Prop}(t) \mid \mathsf{True}(t) \mid \varphi \wedge \varphi \mid \varphi \vee \varphi \mid \varphi \rightarrow \varphi \mid \neg\varphi \mid \forall x(\varphi) \mid \exists x(\varphi)$ (The language of wff consists of statements of equality between terms, assertions that a term is a proposition, and that a term is a true proposition, together with the usual logical connectives.)

The predicate Prop is used to restrict the axioms of True to terms of the appropriate category. In particular, we cannot consider the truth conditions of terms that correspond with paradoxical statements.

The predicate Prop is governed by the following axioms.

(P1) $(\mathsf{Prop}(s) \wedge \mathsf{Prop}(t)) \rightarrow \mathsf{Prop}(s \hat{\wedge} t)$
(P2) $(\mathsf{Prop}(s) \wedge \mathsf{Prop}(t)) \rightarrow \mathsf{Prop}(s \hat{\vee} t)$
(P3) $\mathsf{Prop}(t) \rightarrow \mathsf{Prop}(\hat{\neg} t)$
(P4) $(\mathsf{Prop}(s) \wedge (\mathsf{True}(s) \rightarrow \mathsf{Prop}(t))) \rightarrow \mathsf{Prop}(s \hat{\rightarrow} t)$
(P5) $\forall x(\mathsf{Prop}(t)) \rightarrow \mathsf{Prop}(\hat{\forall} x(t))$
(P6) $\forall x(\mathsf{Prop}(t)) \rightarrow \mathsf{Prop}(\hat{\exists} x(t))$
(P7) $\mathsf{Prop}(s \hat{=} t)$

It only remains to have axioms for a theory of truth. In a theory without possible worlds, the following is sufficient.

(T1) $(\mathsf{Prop}(s) \wedge \mathsf{Prop}(t)) \rightarrow (\mathsf{True}(s \hat{\wedge} t) \leftrightarrow (\mathsf{True}(s) \wedge \mathsf{True}(t)))$
(T2) $(\mathsf{Prop}(s) \wedge \mathsf{Prop}(t)) \rightarrow (\mathsf{True}(s \hat{\vee} t) \leftrightarrow (\mathsf{True}(s) \vee \mathsf{True}(t)))$
(T3) $\mathsf{Prop}(t) \rightarrow (\mathsf{True}(\hat{\neg} t) \leftrightarrow \neg\mathsf{True}(t))$
(T4) $(\mathsf{Prop}(s) \wedge (\mathsf{True}(s) \rightarrow \mathsf{Prop}(t))) \rightarrow (\mathsf{True}(s \hat{\rightarrow} t) \leftrightarrow (\mathsf{True}(s) \rightarrow \mathsf{True}(t)))$
(T5) $\forall x(\mathsf{Prop}(t)) \rightarrow (\mathsf{True}(\hat{\forall} x(t)) \leftrightarrow \forall x(\mathsf{True}(t)))$
(T6) $\forall x(\mathsf{Prop}(t)) \rightarrow (\mathsf{True}(\hat{\exists} x(t)) \leftrightarrow \exists x(\mathsf{True}(t)))$
(T7) $\mathsf{True}(s \hat{=} t) \leftrightarrow (s = t)$
(T8) $\mathsf{True}(p) \rightarrow \mathsf{Prop}(p)$

We can define a notion of property, Pty.

(PT4) $\mathsf{Pty}(t) =_{\mathsf{def}} \forall x(\mathsf{Prop}(t(x)))$ (Properties are those terms that form a proposition with any term.)

Functional types can be defined in the language of wff.

(PT5) $(Q \Longrightarrow R)(t) =_{\mathsf{def}} \forall x(Q(x) \rightarrow R(tx))$

A type of the form $\langle a, b \rangle$ in Montague's **IL** would be written as $(a \Longrightarrow b)$. However, unlike in **IL**, a term can belong to more than one type.

If we are interested in characterising possible worlds in this intensional theory of propositions, one way of proceeding is to formulate a notion of truth with respect to an information state corresponding to a possible world. We shall try and see how much of the theory can be internally defined, where internal definability (of predicates) is characterised as follows:

(PT6) A predicate P is *internally definable* iff there exists a property p, in the language of terms, such that $\forall x(P(x) \leftrightarrow \mathsf{True}(px))$ [31, 1].

Not all predicates are internally definable. In particular, we cannot introduce properties corresponding to Prop, True without obtaining a paradox [31, 1]. We shall see how much this restricts our ability to internally define a theory of possible worlds in a Frege Structure. In effect, if all the relevant notions were internally definable, then possible worlds would be a conservative extension of a Frege Structure. In other words, a Frege Structure would then already give us what we want, and the theory of possible worlds would be mere syntactic sugar.

In order to provide a familiar notation, a Fregean notion of set and set membership can be defined:

(PT7) $\{x \mid t\} =_{\mathsf{def}} \lambda x(t)$ (A *Fregean set* is sugar for a λ-abstract.)
(PT8) $(t \in s) =_{\mathsf{def}} \mathsf{True}(s(t))$ (Set membership is sugar for asserting that a property holds of a term.)

As we can see, the language of wff is strictly first-order. Using the untyped λ-calculus for the language of terms means that there might be some complexity in determining the equality of terms, but this is really no different from any other first-order theory: the standard way of classifying the formal power of a logic makes no claim about the complexity of determining the truth of atomic propositions.

There are many other approaches to intensionality that incorporate, or at least mimic two notions of equality. One that has been used in the context of linguistics is a semantics based on Martin-Löf's Type Theory (MLTT) [20, 27, 23, 24]. This is essentially constructive in nature, unlike the classical Property Theory presented here. One weakness of pure MLTT in relation to the semantics of natural language is that intensionality collapses in the case of false propositions. Its strength lies in the analysis of the dynamics of language. Because MLTT can be embedded in a Frege Structure [26], this approach to dynamics can be exploited and adapted in various ways within Property Theory [10, 8].

3.2 Property-Theoretic Number Theory, and Proportional Cardinality Quantifiers

As the language of terms of PT is the λ-calculus, the most straightforward way of incorporating numbers into the theory might appear to be to adopt the appropriate the standard untyped λ-calculus definitions for $succ, pred, zero$. There are problems in doing so: the notion of identity in the theory is that of the λ-calculus; terms that are λ-equivalent are indistinguishable, yet we do not necessarily wish to force terms to be identical if they happen to have the same arithmetic evaluation.[8]

[8] These are similar to the arguments against using the λ-internal definitions for truth, false and the logical connectives for the interpretation of the intensional connectives of PT.

Instead, to the language of terms we add $succ, pred, add, mult, 0$ (for the successor, predecessor, addition and multiplication of terms representing natural numbers, and zero, respectively). And to the language of wff, we add Zero, for testing if a term is 0, $=_\eta$ for equality of numeric terms, and Num, a new category corresponding with the natural numbers. So now our language of terms is as follows:

$$t ::= x \mid c \mid tt \mid \lambda x.t \mid \hat{\wedge} \mid \hat{\vee} \mid \hat{\rightarrow} \mid \hat{\neg} \mid \hat{\forall} \mid \hat{\exists} \mid \hat{=} \mid succ \mid pred \mid add \mid mult \mid 0$$

And the language of wff is:

$$\varphi ::= t = t \mid \varphi \wedge \varphi \mid \varphi \vee \varphi \mid \varphi \rightarrow \varphi \mid \neg\varphi \mid \forall x\varphi \mid \exists x\varphi \mid \mathsf{Zero} \mid =_\eta \mid \mathsf{Num}$$

Num has the following closure axioms (axiom schema):

(NPT1) $\mathsf{Num}(0) \wedge \forall y(\mathsf{Num}(y) \rightarrow \mathsf{Num}(succ(y)))$
(NPT2) $(\phi[0] \wedge \forall y(\mathsf{Num}(y) \wedge \phi[y] \rightarrow \phi[succ(y)])) \rightarrow \forall x(\mathsf{Num}(x) \rightarrow \phi[x])$

These give the basic closure axiom on 0 and its successors, together with the weak induction axiom scheme. Now we introduce axioms corresponding to the usual basic formulation of Peano arithmetic:

(NPT3) $\neg\exists x(\mathsf{Num}(x) \wedge succ(x) =_\eta 0)$
(NPT4) $\mathsf{Num}(x) \wedge \mathsf{Num}(y) \rightarrow (succ(x) =_\eta succ(y) \leftrightarrow x =_\eta y)$
(NPT5) $\mathsf{Zero}(0)$
(NPT6) $\mathsf{Num}(x) \rightarrow \neg\mathsf{Zero}(succ(x))$
(NPT7) $\mathsf{Num}(x) \rightarrow pred(succ(x)) =_\eta x$

Here, we not introduce an explicit term for $\perp$, and instead have axioms that are deliberately too weak to derive anything in cases where $\perp$ would otherwise arise.

The operations of addition, multiplication and equality can also be axiomatised:

(NPT8) $\mathsf{Num}(x) \rightarrow add(x)(0) =_\eta x$
(NPT9) $\mathsf{Num}(x) \wedge \mathsf{Num}(y) \rightarrow add(x)(succ(y)) =_\eta succ(add(x)(y))$
(NPT10) $\mathsf{Num}(x) \rightarrow mult(x)(0) =_\eta x$
(NPT11) $\mathsf{Num}(x) \wedge \mathsf{Num}(y) \rightarrow mult(x)(succ(y)) =_\eta add(mult(x)(y))(x)$
(NPT12) $\mathsf{Num}(y) \rightarrow (0 =_\eta y \leftrightarrow \mathsf{Zero}(y))$
(NPT13) $\mathsf{Num}(x) \rightarrow (x =_\eta 0 \leftrightarrow \mathsf{Zero}(x))$

We can define the notion of $<$:

(NPT14) $x < y =_{\mathsf{def}} \mathsf{Num}(x) \wedge \mathsf{Num}(y) \wedge \exists z(\mathsf{Num}(z) \wedge \neg\mathsf{Zero}(z) \wedge add(x)(z) =_\eta y)$

Equivalently, we can axiomatise it as follows:

1. $\mathsf{Num}(y) \rightarrow 0 < y$
2. $\mathsf{Num}(x) \rightarrow x \not< 0$
3. $\mathsf{Num}(x) \wedge \mathsf{Num}(y) \rightarrow (succ(x) < succ(y) \leftrightarrow x < y)$

We can internalise the natural number type and its relations. To the language of terms we add $\eta, \zeta, \hat{=}_\eta$ corresponding with $\mathsf{Num}, \mathsf{Zero}, =_\eta$.

(N$_{\mathsf{PT}}$15) $\mathsf{Prop}(\eta t)$
(N$_{\mathsf{PT}}$16) $\mathsf{True}(\eta t) \leftrightarrow \mathsf{Num}(t)$
(N$_{\mathsf{PT}}$17) $\mathsf{Num}(t) \rightarrow \mathsf{Prop}(\zeta(t))$
(N$_{\mathsf{PT}}$18) $\mathsf{Num}(t) \wedge \mathsf{Num}(s) \rightarrow \mathsf{Prop}(t \hat{=}_\eta s)$
(N$_{\mathsf{PT}}$19) $\mathsf{Num}(t) \rightarrow (\mathsf{True}(\zeta(t)) \leftrightarrow \mathsf{Zero}(t))$
(N$_{\mathsf{PT}}$20) $\mathsf{Num}(t) \wedge \mathsf{Num}(s) \rightarrow (\mathsf{True}(t \hat{=}_\eta s) \leftrightarrow t =_\eta s)$

The term $\hat{<}$ can be defined by:

(N$_{\mathsf{PT}}$21) $x \hat{<} y =_{\mathsf{def}} \eta x \hat{\wedge} \eta y \hat{\wedge} \hat{\exists} z (\eta z \hat{\wedge} \hat{\neg} \zeta(z) \hat{\wedge} add(x)(z) \hat{=}_\eta y)$

"Most" in PT$_n$ The treatment of cardinality and *most* in PT is parallel to the accounts given in IHTT. Cardinality of properties can be given by:

(N$_{\mathsf{PT}}$23) $\mathsf{Pty}(p) \wedge \neg \exists x \mathsf{True}(px) \rightarrow |p| =_\eta 0$
(N$_{\mathsf{PT}}$24) $\mathsf{Pty}(p) \wedge \mathsf{True}(px) \rightarrow |p| =_\eta add(|p - \{x\}|)(succ(0))$

where $|\cdot|$ is a new term, and $-, \{\cdot\}$ are defined in the usual Property-theoretic manner.

Now we can axiomatise *most* by way of the following:

$$\mathsf{Pty}(p) \wedge \mathsf{Pty}(q) \rightarrow \mathsf{Prop}(most(p)(q))$$
$$\mathsf{Pty}(p) \wedge \mathsf{Pty}(q) \rightarrow \mathsf{True}(most(p)(q)) \leftrightarrow |\{x : px \hat{\wedge} \hat{\neg} qx\}| < |\{x : px \hat{\wedge} qx\}|$$

However, give our internalisation of the natural numbers, "most" can be made definitional:

$$most(p)(q) =_{\mathsf{def}} |\{x : px \hat{\wedge} \hat{\neg} qx\}| \hat{<} |\{x : px \hat{\wedge} qx\}|$$

This theory is substantially theorem equivalent with the IHTT version of intensional arithmetic.

3.3 Possible Worlds with Intentional Propositions

We can take information states to be sets of propositions.[9] We will use the terms $\mathfrak{w}, \mathfrak{u}, \mathfrak{v}, \ldots$ to denote information states. We can define the family of information states to be W. We will add W to the language of wff. The terms $\mathfrak{w}, \mathfrak{u}, \mathfrak{v}, \ldots$ are constants which correspond with prime filters over propositions.

We can now axiomatise a theory of truth with respect to information states, or prime filters over propositions. We will write $\mathsf{W}(\mathfrak{w})$ when $\mathfrak{w}$ is an information state corresponding to a possible world, and $p \in \mathfrak{w}$ when the proposition p holds in the information state $\mathfrak{w}$.

[9] In section 4 we formulate the reduction of possible worlds to set of propositions algebraically, where the sets of propositions are prime filters on the lattice of propositions generated by the logic of PT. For IHTT we require a pre-lattice with a pre-order rather than a lattice.

(PW1) $(\mathsf{W}(\mathfrak{w}) \wedge \mathsf{Prop}(p)) \rightarrow \mathsf{Prop}(\mathfrak{w}(p)))$
(PW2) $(\mathsf{W}(\mathfrak{w}) \wedge \mathsf{Prop}(p) \wedge \mathsf{Prop}(q)) \rightarrow ((p \hat{\wedge} q) \in \mathfrak{w} \leftrightarrow (p \in \mathfrak{w} \wedge q \in \mathfrak{w}))$
(PW3) $\mathsf{W}(\mathfrak{w}) \rightarrow ((p \hat{\vee} q) \in \mathfrak{w} \leftrightarrow (p \in \mathfrak{w} \vee q \in \mathfrak{w}))$
(PW4) $\mathsf{W}(\mathfrak{w}) \rightarrow ((p \hat{\rightarrow} q) \in \mathfrak{w} \leftrightarrow (p \in \mathfrak{w} \rightarrow q \in \mathfrak{w}))$
(PW5) $(\mathsf{W}(\mathfrak{w}) \wedge \mathsf{Prop}(p)) \rightarrow ((\hat{\neg} p) \in \mathfrak{w} \leftrightarrow \neg(p \in \mathfrak{w}))$
(PW6) $(\mathsf{W}(\mathfrak{w}) \wedge \mathsf{Prop}(p) \wedge (p \in \mathfrak{w} \rightarrow \mathsf{Prop}(q))) \rightarrow ((p \hat{\rightarrow} q) \in \mathfrak{w} \leftrightarrow (p \in \mathfrak{w} \rightarrow q \in \mathfrak{w}))$
(PW7) $(\mathsf{W}(\mathfrak{w}) \wedge \forall x(\mathsf{Prop}(p))) \rightarrow ((\hat{\forall} x(p)) \in \mathfrak{w} \leftrightarrow \forall x(p \in \mathfrak{w}))$
(PW8) $\mathsf{W}(\mathfrak{w}) \rightarrow ((\hat{\exists} x(p)) \in \mathfrak{w} \leftrightarrow \exists x(p \in \mathfrak{w}))$

The axiom (PW1) is concerned with the felicity of propositions when $\mathfrak{w}$ is used as a proposition. Essentially it encapsulates a typing constraint that we are only concerned with whether or not a proposition is in the prime filter $\mathfrak{w}$. The remaining axioms give $\mathfrak{w}$ the properties of a prime filter.

In effect, each $\mathfrak{w}$ in W is a different theory. We have generalised the axioms of truth in Property Theory so that we have a whole family of truth predicates where before there was just one. These axioms ensure that each state $\mathfrak{w}$ is exhaustive (there is no proposition p such that neither p nor $\hat{\neg} p$ is in $\mathfrak{w}$).

To the language of terms we can add $\mathfrak{W}$, a theory internal analogy of $\mathfrak{w}$:

(PW9) $\mathsf{Pty}(\mathfrak{W})$
(PW10) $\mathsf{True}(\mathfrak{W}(\mathfrak{w})) \leftrightarrow \mathsf{W}(\mathfrak{w})$

Internalised Modal Operators We are now in a position to define modal operators for necessity and possibility. We would like to have the following truth conditions follow from the definition of $\Box$ and $\Diamond$:

$$\mathsf{Prop}(p) \rightarrow (\mathsf{True}(\Box p) \leftrightarrow \forall \mathfrak{w}(\mathsf{W}(\mathfrak{w}) \rightarrow p \in \mathfrak{w}))$$
$$\mathsf{Prop}(p) \rightarrow (\mathsf{True}(\Diamond p) \leftrightarrow \exists \mathfrak{w}(\mathsf{W}(\mathfrak{w}) \wedge p \in \mathfrak{w}))$$

This can be achieved by the following definitions:

(PW11) $\Box p =_{\mathsf{def}} \hat{\forall} \mathfrak{w}(\mathfrak{W}(\mathfrak{w}) \hat{\rightarrow} \mathfrak{w}(p))$
(PW12) $\Diamond p =_{\mathsf{def}} \hat{\exists} \mathfrak{w}(\mathfrak{W}(\mathfrak{w}) \hat{\wedge} \mathfrak{w}(p))$

These definitions naturally allow us to show that $\mathsf{Prop}(\Box p)$ and $\mathsf{Prop}(\Diamond p)$ and that $\mathsf{True}(\Box p) \leftrightarrow \mathsf{True}(\hat{\neg} \Diamond \hat{\neg} p)$ when p is a proposition.

If we had adopted the weaker axioms for $\mathfrak{W}$ above—where $\mathfrak{W}(\mathfrak{w})$ is a proposition only when $\mathfrak{w}$ is of the appropriate category—then we would not be able to prove $\mathsf{Prop}(\Box p)$ and $\mathsf{Prop}(\Diamond p)$. As with $\mathcal{E}(p)$, additional axioms would be required and $\Box, \Diamond$ would no longer be definitional. This is why we adopted the stronger axiomatisation.

The following axiom gives us something akin to necessitation (if $\vdash A$ then $\vdash \Box A$):

(PW13) $\mathsf{Prop}(p) \rightarrow (\mathsf{True}(p) \rightarrow \forall \mathfrak{w}(\mathsf{W}(\mathfrak{w}) \rightarrow p \in \mathfrak{w}))$

Taken together, these axioms give us an **S5** modality.

The theory can be modelled by extending a Frege Structure with a class of terms that correspond with subsets of the class of propositions and supersets of the class of true propositions.

Comments The axioms and definitions above lead to a semantic theory that combines the benefits of fine-grained intensionality, weak typing and first-order power with a treatment of possible worlds. This allows propositional attitudes to be analysed with the intensionality provided by a Frege Structure, with the appealing possible worlds' treatment of the **S5** metaphysical modalities. In this theory, as in the case of logically equivalent propositions in IHTT, propositions are not equated if they hold in the same sets of possible worlds. In addition, possible worlds are not equated if they contain the same sets of propositions.

If we are just interested in the modalities themselves, there may be more appropriate means of adding them to a theory with fine grained intensionality [31]. There may also be philosophical motivations for having modalities in the language of well formed formulæ (unlike in this account, where they reside exclusively within the language of terms). This would allow us to express the following:

$$\Box\mathsf{Prop}(p) \rightarrow (\mathsf{True}(\Box p) \leftrightarrow \Box\mathsf{True}(p))$$

and the full rule of necessitation:

$$\text{If } \vdash A \text{ then } \vdash \Box A$$

Such a move seems to be required if we are interested in anything other than **S5** modality.

In this paper, we have only presented an explicit formalisation of modalities in the case of Property Theory, and not IHTT. In the latter case, we could proceed by taking IHTT to be our non-modal base logic, and then build on this base logics in which each logic can refer to the prime filters of the previous level. We will explore this approach in future work.

4 Possible Worlds as Prime Filters of Propositions

The propositions (members of the type Π) of the IHTT described in 2 define a bounded distributive prelattice. The axioms (IHTT1)–(IHTT13) yield a Heyting prelattice $L = \langle A, \wedge, \vee, \rightarrow, \top, \bot, \rangle$, while (IHTT1)–(IHTT14) generate a Boolean prelattice $L = \langle A, \wedge, \vee, \neg, \top, \bot, \rangle$, with $A =$ the set of elements of Π. The preorder $\leq$ of each prelattice models an entailment relation that does not satisfy antisymmetry. Therefore, for any proposition p in the prelattice, $\{s : p \leq s \& s \leq p\}$ is an equivalence class whose elements are not necessarily identical.

We can define a pre-lattice for PT corresponding to that given for IHTT in section 2.1, axioms (IHTT1)–(IHTT13), modulo difference in the required typing constraints, where basic propositions are of the form $\mathsf{True}(p)$, and where $a \cong b$ is equivalent to $\mathsf{True}(a) \leftrightarrow \mathsf{True}(b)$ in the case where a, b are propositions, and $\forall x(\mathsf{True}(ax) \leftrightarrow \mathsf{True}(bx))$ in the case where a, b are properties.[10] Alternatively, if we define $\cong$ to be PT's λ-equality ($=$), and weaken axiom (11) from a

[10] Note that if we take the notion of λ-equality to be basic, then $\top, \bot$ can be defined by $a = a$ and $a \neq a$ respectively.

biconditional to a conditional[11] then we can define a proof-theoretic lattice. A similar move might be possible in IHTT if we take $\cong$ to be the basic equivalence relation.

Following a suggestion from Carl Pollard (presented in [17]) we define an *index* as a prime filter of propositions in the (pre-)lattice generated by IHTT or PT. A prime filter is closed under meet and the (pre-)order relation, contains $p \vee q$ only if it contains p or q, includes $\top$, and excludes $\bot$. Therefore, an index provides a consistent theory closed under entailment. If a prime filter is maximal (i.e. is an ultrafilter), then it partitions the (pre-)lattice into the propositions that it contains and those in the ideal which is its dual. Such an ultrafilter corresponds to a possible world. If the prime filter is non-maximal, then it corresponds to a possible situation which is a proper part of a world. The indices of Heyting (pre-)lattices can be non-maximal situations of this kind, while those of Boolean (pre-)lattices are worlds.

We take a proposition p to be *true at an index* i iff $p \in i$. A logically true (false) proposition is an element of every (no) index defined by the prelattice. Logically equivalent propositions are elements of all and only the same indices of the prelattice. We can introduce meaning postulates on non-logical constants (like axiom (IHTT21) for *most*) to restrict the set of indices to a proper subset of indices that sustain the intended interpretations of these constants. As we have observed in both IHTT and PT, logically equivalent propositions need not be identical. Therefore, they are not intersubstitutable in all contexts, specifically in the complements of verbs of propositional attitude.

By characterizing indices algebraically as prime filters of propositions in (pre-)lattices we are able to dispense with possible worlds and situations as basic elements of our semantic theory. We also characterise truth of a proposition in a world or situation to membership of a prime filter. The fact that we distinguish between identity and equivalence permits us to distinguish between logically equivalent expressions in our semantic representation language.

5 Comparison with Other Hyperintensionalist Approaches

5.1 Intentional Logic

Thomason [28] proposes a higher-order Intentional Logic in which a type p of propositions is added to e (individuals) and t (truth-values) in the set of basic types. The classical truth functions, quantifiers, and identity relation are defined as functions from types τ (in the case of the truth-functions, $\tau = t$ or $\langle t, t\rangle$) into t. A parallel set of intentional connectives, quantifiers, and identity relation are defined as functions from types τ to p. An extensional operator $^{\cup}\langle p, t\rangle$ denotes a homomorphism from D_p to 2 (the bounded distributive lattice containing only

[11] That is, if we adopt the axiom $\vdash \forall st(\mathsf{Prop}(s) \wedge \mathsf{Prop}(t) \rightarrow (s = t \rightarrow \mathsf{True}(s) \leftrightarrow \mathsf{True}(t)))$.

1 and 0 ($\top$ and $\bot$). The set of homomorphisms which can provide the interpretation of the extensional operator is constrained by meaning postulates like the following (where $\wedge y$ is the extensional universal quantifier, $\cap y$ is the intentional universal quantifier, $\neg$ is extensional negation, $\sim$ is intentional negation, $\wedge$ is extensional conjunction, $\cap$ is intentional conjunction, $=$ is extensional identity, and $\approx$ is intentional identity).

(1) a. $\wedge y^p({}^{\cup}\!\sim y = \neg{}^{\cup}y)$
b. $\wedge y^p z^p({}^{\cup}(y \cup z) ={}^{\cup} y \wedge{}^{\cup} z)$
c. ${}^{\cup}\cap x^{\tau}\phi = \wedge x^{\tau}{}^{\cup}\phi$
d. ${}^{\cup}(\alpha \approx \beta) = (\alpha = \beta)$

(2) $\wedge x^e({}^{\cup}\mathit{groundhog}'_{\langle e,p\rangle}(x) = \mathit{woodchuck}'_{\langle e,p\rangle}(x))$

This last axiom (2) requires that for any individual a, the truth-value of ${}^{\cup}\mathit{groundhog}'(a)$ is identical to that of ${}^{\cup}\mathit{woodchuck}'(a)$. It does not require that $\mathit{groundhog}'(a)$ and $\mathit{woodchuck}'(a)$ be identical propositions, and so it is compatible with (3).

(3) $\wedge x^e\neg(\mathit{groundhog}'(x) = \mathit{woodchuck}'(x))$

The main problem with Thomason's proposal is that he does not specify the algebraic structure of the domain of propositions D_p or the entailment relation which holds among its elements. The connection between intentional identity and intentional bi-implication is not specified, and so the interpretation of these relations is crucially underdetermined.[12]

Consider the theorem (4) (a proof is presented in [14, p.14]), which has (5) as a corollary.

(4) For any a, b in a distributive lattice L such that $a \not\leq b$ there is a homomorphism $h : L \to 2$ in which $h(a) \neq h(b)$.

(5) For any a, b in a distributive lattice L, if every homomorphism $h : L \to 2$ is such that $h(a) = h(b)$, then $a = b$.

If D_p is a bounded distributive lattice, then Thomason must allow the set of homomorphisms from D_p to 2 that provide possible intepretations of the extensional operator ${}^{\cup}\langle p, t\rangle$ to contain mappings from D_p to 2 which do not respect the meaning postulates that he imposes upon the operator. Such homomorphisms will specify impossible worlds which distinguish between non-identical propositions that the meaning postulates require to be identical in truth-value in the subset of homomorphisms corresponding to the intended interpretations of the elements of D_p.

Alternatively, Thomason could characterize D_p as a prelattice whose preorder is not anti-symmetrical. The fact that he does not provide a proof theory for his

[12] These problems were pointed out by Carl Pollard and discussed in [18].

domain of propositions that specifies an entailment relation leaves these central issues unsettled. Therefore, it is not clear precisely how Thomsason's Intentional Logic permits us to distinguish between logically equivalent expressions.

By contrast, in our framework the proof theory defines a relation between generalized equivalence and identity in which the former does not reduce to the latter. We do not require impossible worlds, as we model the entailment relation of the logic in such a way that logically equivalent propositions remain (possibly) distinct.

5.2 Data Semantics

Landman [16] uses a distributive De Morgan lattice L to to model a first-order language. He identifies *facts* as elementary (non-negated) elements of L. Propositions are constructed by applying the operations of L to facts. According to Landman, if a and b are distinct facts in L, $p = a \vee \neg a$ and $q = b \vee \neg b$, then $p \neq q$ beacuse p and q are generated from different facts.

It is not clear how Landman can sustain this distinction between logically equivalent propositions. If L is a bounded distributive lattice, then all logically true propositions reduce to $\top$, and all logically false propositions are identical to $\bot$ by virtue of the antisymmetry of the partial order relation of the lattice. In general, for any proposition p in a distributive lattice, all propositions that are logically equivalent to p are identical to p.

5.3 Infon Algebras

Barwise and Etchemendy [2] propose an infon algebra as the framework for developing the model theory of situation semantics. An infon algebra $\mathrm{I} = \langle Sit, I, \Rightarrow, \models \rangle$ where Sit is a non-empty set of situations, I is a non-empty set of infons, $\langle I, \Rightarrow \rangle$ is a bounded distributive lattice, and $\models$ is a relation on $Sit\ x\ I$ that satisfies the following conditions.

(6) a. If $s \models \sigma$ and $\sigma \Rightarrow \tau$, then $s \models \tau$.
b. $\neg(s \models 0)$ and $s \models 1$.
c. If Σ is a finite set of infons, then $s \models \wedge\Sigma$ iff for each $\sigma \in \Sigma, s \models \sigma$.
d. If Σ is a finite set of infons, then $s \models \vee\Sigma$ iff for some $\sigma \in \Sigma, s \models \sigma$.

The conditions that 6 imposes on the $\models$ relation require that the set of infons which a situation supports is a prime filter.

Supports : $I \rightarrow Pow(Sit)$ is a homomorphism from the set of infons to the power set of situations such that for each $\sigma \in I$, $Supports(\sigma) = \{s \in Sit : s \models \sigma\}$. Consider the following generalization of Johnstone's theorem 4.

(7) Let L be a bounded distributive lattice. For any a, b in a distributive lattice A, if every homomorphism h: A $\rightarrow$ L is such that $h(a) = h(b)$, then $a = b$.
Proof: It follows from 4 that for any a, b in a distributive lattice A such that $a \not\leq b$ there is a homomorphism g: A $\rightarrow$ 2 in which $g(a) = 1$ and

$g(b) = 0$. 2 can be embedded in any bounded distributive lattice L by the homomorphism f: 2 $\rightarrow$ L which is such that $f(1) = 1$ and $f(0) = 0$. Let h: A $\rightarrow$ L $= f \circ g$. Then for any a, b in a distributive lattice A such that $a \not\leq b$, there is homomorphism $h : A \rightarrow$ L in which $h(a) \neq h(b)$. The theorem follows.

The power set of situations is a bounded distributive lattice. Therefore, if for all homomorphisms $h : I \rightarrow Pow(Sit)$ that are permitted instances of *Supports* two infons $\sigma, \tau \in I$ are such that $h(\sigma) = h(\tau)$, then $\sigma = \tau$. But then in order to distinguish between two infons σ and τ which are logically equivalent or equivalent by virtue of meaning postulates it is necessary to posit homomorphisms from I to $Pow(Sit)$ in which $h(\sigma) \neq h(\tau)$. These homomorphisms correspond to impossible situations (impossible partial worlds).

5.4 Situations as Partial Models

Muskens [22] uses a many-valued logic to defined indices as partial models rather than complete worlds. Indices correspond to situations, and they are partially ordered by (distinct types of) containment relations. A partial model M is the indexed union of a set of indices, where each index in the set is an indexed partial model M_i.

Let Γ, Δ be sets of propositions. Δ *strongly follows* from Γ iff in every intended model M (a model that satisfies a given set of axioms), the partial intersection of values of the elements of Γ is included in the partial union of the values of the elements of Δ. For two propositions p, q, q *weakly follows* from p iff for every intended model M, in each M_i of M that satisfies a specified set of meaning postulates, the value of p in M_i is (partially) included in the the value of q at M_i.

Substitution of propositional arguments in predicates denoting relations of propositional attitude is restricted to cases of strong mutual entailment. (8)a and (8)b weakly entail each other.

(8) a. $groundhog'(c)$
b. $woodchuck'(c)$

They are equivalent only in the partial models that satisfy the meaning postulate in 9).

(9) $\lambda i[\forall x(groundhog'(x, i) = woodchuck'(x, i))]$

As (8)a and (8)b are weakly synonymous they are not intersubstitutable in belief contexts.

Muskens' distinction between weak and strong entailment effectively invokes impossible (partial) worlds to distinguish between equivalent propositions.

6 Conclusion

We have presented an axiomatic approach to constructing a hyperintensional semantics for natural language. On this approach we discard the axiom of extensionality and introduce a generalized equivalence (weak identity) relation that does not reduce to strict (logical) identity. We can model the entailment relation of our logic with a bounded distributive (pre-)lattice in which the (pre-)order does not satisfy antisymmetry. We define indices algebraically as prime filters of propositions in the (pre-)lattice, and we reduce truth at an index to membership of such a prime filter. By adding a hyperintensional number theory to our logic we also provide an internal axiomatic treatment of generalized quantifiers like *most* that specify relations among the cardinalities of properties. We have shown how it is possible to implement this approach within both an intensional higher-order type theory and many-sorted first-order Property Theory. Unlike alternative hyperintensionalist models that have been proposed, we can distinguish among equivalent propositions without resorting to impossible worlds to sustain the distinction.

In future work we will extend our axiomatic framework to provide a logic of propositional attitudes, specifically belief. We will also develop a refined characterization of modality that permits us to encode modal logics other than S5. We intend to fully integrate the account of modality given here for PT into our proposed algebraic reduction of possible worlds/situations and to develop a parallel account for IHTT. We hope to implement these hyperintensional treatments of propositional attitudes and modality within a theorem proving module for a computational semantic system.

References

[1] P. Aczel. Frege structures and the notions of proposition, truth and set. In Barwise, Keisler, and Keenan, editors, *The Kleene Symposium*, North Holland Studies in Logic, pages 31–39. North Holland, 1980.

[2] J Barwise and J. Etchemendy. Information, infons, and inference. In R. Cooper, K. Mukai, and J. Perry, editors, *Situation Theory and Its Applications*, volume 1, pages 33–78. CSLI, Stanford, CA, 1990.

[3] J. Barwise and J. Perry. *Situations and Attitudes.* MIT Press (Bradford Books), Cambridge, MA, 1983.

[4] G. Bealer. On the identification of properties and propositional functions. *Linguistics and Philosophy*, 12:1–14, 1989.

[5] R. Carnap. *Meaning and Necessity.* University of Chicago Press, Chicago, 1947.

[6] G. Chierchia and R. Turner. Semantics and property theory. *Linguistics and Philosophy*, 11:261–302, 1988.

[7] A. Church. A foundation for the simple theory of types. *Journal of Symbolic Logic*, 5:56–68, 1940.

[8] Chris Fox. *The Ontology of Language.* CSLI Lecture Notes. CSLI, Stanford, 2000.

[9] C.J. Fox. *Plurals and Mass Terms in Property Theory.* PhD thesis, University of Essex, Colchester, U.K., 1993.

[10] C.J. Fox. Discourse representation, type theory and property theory. In H. Bunt, R. Muskens, and G. Rentier, editors, *Proceedings of the International Workshop on Computational Semantics*, pages 71–80, ITK, Tilburg, 1994.
[11] C.J. Fox. Existence presuppositions and category mistakes. *Acta Linguistica Hungarica*, 42(3/4), 1994. Originally presented at the Fifth Hungarian Symposium in Logic and Language, Noszvaj.
[12] C.J. Fox. Plurals and mass terms in property theory. In F. Hamm and E. Hinrichs, editors, *Plurality and Quanitfication*, number 69 in Studies in Linguistics and Philosophy, pages 113–175. Kluwer Academic Press, Dordrecht, 1998.
[13] D. Gallin. *Intensional and Higher-Order Modal Logic.* North-Holland, Amsterdam, 1975.
[14] P.T. Johnstone. *Stone Spaces.* Cambridge University Press, Cambridge, 1982.
[15] J. Lambek and P. Scott. *An Introduction to Higher Order Categorial Logic.* Cambridge University Press, Cambridge, 1986.
[16] F. Landman. Pegs and alecs. In *Towards a Theory of Information. The Status of Partial Objects in Semantics*, Groningen-Amsterdam Studies in Semantics, pages 97–136. Foris, Dordrecht, 1986.
[17] S. Lappin and C. Pollard. A hyperintensional theory of natural language interpretation without indices or situations. ms., King's College, London and Ohio State University, 1999.
[18] S. Lappin and C. Pollard. Strategies for hyperintensional semantics. ms., King's College, London and Ohio State University, 2000.
[19] T. Maibaum. Conservative extensions, interpretations between theories and all that! In M. Bidoit and M. M. Dauchet, editors, *TAPSOFT '97: Theory and Practice of Software Development*, pages 40–66, Berlin and New York, 1997. Springer.
[20] P. Martin-Löf. *Studies in Proof Theory (Lecture Notes).* Bibliopolis, Napoli, 1984.
[21] R. Montague. *Formal Philosophy: Selected Papers of Richard Montague.* Yale University Press, New Haven/London, 1974. Edited with an introduction by R.H. Thomason.
[22] R. Muskens. *Meaning and Partiality.* CSLI and FOLLI, Stanford, CA, 1995.
[23] A. Ranta. Intuitionistic categorial grammar. *Linguistics and Philosophy*, 14:203–239, 1991.
[24] A. Ranta. *Type Theoretic Grammar.* Oxford University Press, 1994.
[25] J. Seligman and L. Moss. Situation theory. In J. van Bentham and A. ter Meulen, editors, *Handbook of Logic and Language.* Elsvier, North Holland, Amsterdam, 1997.
[26] J.M. Smith. An interpretation of Martin-Löf's Type Theory in a type-free theory of propositions. *Journal of Symbolic Logic*, 49, 1984.
[27] G. Sundholm. Constructive generalised quantifiers. *Synthese*, 79:1–12, 1989.
[28] R. Thomason. A modeltheory for propositional attitudes. *Linguistics and Philosophy*, 4:47–70, 1980.
[29] R. Turner. A theory of properties. *Journal of Symbolic Logic*, 52(2):455–472, June 1987.
[30] R. Turner. Properties, propositions, and semantic theory. In *Proceedings of Formal Semantics and Computational Linguistics*, Switzerland, 1988.
[31] R. Turner. *Truth and Modality for Knowledge Representation.* Pitman, 1990.
[32] R. Turner. Properties, propositions and semantic theory. In M. Rosner and R. Johnson, editors, *Computational Linguistics and Formal Semantics*, Studies in Natural Language Processing, pages 159–180. Cambridge University Press, Cambridge, 1992.

A Characterization of Minimalist Languages

Henk Harkema

University of California, Los Angeles, CA 90095, USA
harkema@ucla.edu

Abstract. In this paper we will fix the position of Minimalist Grammars as defined in Stabler (1997) in the hierarchy of formal languages. Michaelis (1998) has shown that the set of languages generated by Minimalist Grammars is a subset of the set of languages generated by Multiple Context-Free Grammars (Seki et al., 1991). In this paper we will present a proof showing the reverse. We thus conclude that Minimalist Grammars are weakly equivalent to Multiple Context-Free Grammars.

1 Introduction

One influential and recent development in the theory of transformational syntax is Chomsky's Minimalist Program (Chomsky, 1995). The grammars developed in this approach are derivational and feature-driven: phrases are derived by applying transformational operations to lexical items and intermediate structures, and the applicability of the transformational operations is determined by the syntactic features of the structures involved. The Minimalist Grammars presented in Stabler (1997), henceforth MGs, are simple formal grammars that are based on the minimalist approach to linguistic theory. With regard to the generative power of MGs, Michaelis (1998) has shown that the set of languages generated by Minimalist Grammars falls within the set of languages generated by Multiple-Context Free Grammars, henceforth MCFGs (Seki et al., 1991).

In this paper we will show how to construct an MG for an arbitrary MCFG such that both grammars define the same language. The MGs that we will use in this paper do not allow for head-movement or covert phrasal movement, and so are simpler than the ones defined in Stabler (1997) and used in Michaelis (1998). Let ML be the set of languages definable by 'full' MGs, ML^- the set of languages definable by MGs without head-movement and covert phrasal movement, and MCFL the set of languages definable by MCFGs. Michaelis (1998) has shown that ML $\subseteq$ MCFL. Obviously, $ML^- \subseteq ML$. The result presented in this paper implies that MCFL $\subseteq ML^-$. Hence, we conclude that MCFL = ML.[1] Then it follows immediately from earlier results that MGs are weakly equivalent to Linear Context-Free Rewriting Systems (Vijay-Shanker et al., 1987), Multi-Component Tree-Adjoining Grammars (Weir, 1988), and Simple Positive Range

[1] Michaelis (2001) independently established the equivalent claim that MGs and Linear Context-Free Rewriting Systems (Vijay-Shanker et al., 1987) define the same class of string languages.

P. de Groote, G. Morrill, C. Retoré (Eds.): LACL 2001, LNAI 2099, pp. 193–211, 2001.

Concatenation Grammars (Boullier, 1998). The result reported in this paper also implies that $ML^- = ML$, that is, head-movement and covert phrasal movement do not increase the generative power of MGs (see Stabler (2001) for a linguistic perspective).

The paper is structured as follows. We will first provide the definitions for MGs and MCFGs, then describe and illustrate the encoding of a given MCFG into an MG, and finally prove that the MG thus obtained defines the same language as the original MCFG.

2 Minimalist Grammars

In this section we will give a definition of MGs as introduced by Stabler (1997), but without head-movement and covert phrasal movement.[2]

Definition 1. *A tree over a feature set F is a quintuple $\tau = (N_\tau, \lhd_\tau, \prec_\tau, <_\tau, Label_\tau)$ which meets the following three conditions:*

1. *Triple $(N_\tau, \lhd_\tau, \prec_\tau)$ is a finite, binary ordered tree: N_τ is a non-empty set of nodes, $\lhd_\tau \subseteq N_\tau \times N_\tau$ denotes the relation of immediate dominance; $\prec_\tau \subseteq N_\tau \times N_\tau$ denotes the relation of immediate precedence.*
2. *$<_\tau \subseteq N_\tau \times N_\tau$ denotes the relation of immediate projection: for any two nodes $\nu_1, \nu_2 \in N_\tau$ which are sisters in τ, either ν_1 projects over ν_2, $\nu_1 <_\tau \nu_2$, or ν_2 projects over ν_1, $\nu_2 <_\tau \nu_1$.*
3. *$Label_\tau$ is a function from N_τ to F^*, assigning to each leaf of τ a finite sequence of features from F.*

Let $\tau = (N_\tau, \lhd_\tau, \prec_\tau, <_\tau, Label_\tau)$ be tree over a feature set F. Tree τ is a simple tree if it consists of just one node, otherwise it is a complex tree. If τ is a complex tree, then there are proper subtrees τ_0 and τ_1 of τ such that $\tau = [_<\tau_0, \tau_1]$ or $\tau = [_>\tau_0, \tau_1]$, where $[_<\tau_0, \tau_1]$ denotes a tree whose root immediately dominates subtrees τ_0 and τ_1 and in which the root of τ_0 immediately projects over and precedes the root of τ_1, and $[_>\tau_0, \tau_1]$ denotes a tree whose root immediately dominates subtrees τ_0 and τ_1 and in which the root of τ_0 immediately precedes the root of τ_1 and the root of τ_1 immediately projects over τ_0.

If τ is a simple tree, then its head is the single node making up τ. If τ is a complex tree $[_<\tau_0, \tau_1]$, then the head of τ is the head of τ_0; if τ is a complex tree $[_>\tau_0, \tau_1]$, then the head of τ is the head of τ_1. Tree τ is a projection of node $\nu \in N_\tau$, if, and only if, τ is a tree whose head is ν.

A subtree τ_0 of τ is maximal if it is τ or if the smallest subtree of τ properly including τ_0 has a head other than the head of τ_0. A proper subtree τ_0 of τ is a specifier of the head of τ if τ_0 is a maximal subtree, and the smallest subtree of τ properly including τ_0 is a projection of the head of τ, and the head of τ_0 precedes the head of τ. A proper subtree τ_0 of τ is a complement of the head of

[2] See Stabler and Keenan (2000) for a formulation of MGs with overt phrasal movement only in terms of chains (tuples of strings) rather than trees.

τ if τ_0 is a maximal subtree, and the smallest subtree of τ properly including τ_0 is a projection of the head of τ, and the head of τ precedes the head of τ_0.

Tree τ is said to have a feature $\mathtt{f} \in \mathrm{F}$ if the first feature of the sequence that labels the head of τ is $\mathtt{f}$.

Definition 2. *A Minimalist Grammar G is a quadruple $G = (V, Cat, Lex, \mathcal{F})$, which satisfies the following four conditions.*

1. *$V = P \cup I$ is a finite set of non-syntactic features, consisting of a set of phonetic features P and a set of semantic features I.*
2. *$Cat = base \cup select \cup licensors \cup licensees$ is a finite set of syntactic features, such that for each feature $\mathtt{x} \in base$ there is a feature $\mathtt{=x} \in select$, and for each feature $\mathtt{+y} \in licensors$ there is a feature $\mathtt{-y} \in licensees$. The set base minimally contains the distinguished category feature $\mathtt{c}$.*
3. *Lex is a finite set of trees over $V \cup Cat$ such that for each $\tau = (N_\tau, \lhd_\tau, \prec_\tau, <_\tau, Label_\tau) \in Lex$, the function $Label_\tau$ assigns a string from $Cat^* P^* I^*$ to each leaf of τ.*
4. *The set $\mathcal{F}$ consists of the structure building functions merge and move, which are defined as follows:*
   - *(a) A pair of trees (τ, υ) is in the domain of merge if τ has feature $\mathtt{=x} \in select$ and υ has feature $\mathtt{x} \in base$. Then,*

     $$merge(\tau, \upsilon) = [_< \tau', \upsilon'] \text{ if } \tau \text{ is simple, and}$$
     $$merge(\tau, \upsilon) = [_> \upsilon', \tau'] \text{ if } \tau \text{ is complex,}$$

     where τ' is like τ except that feature $\mathtt{=x}$ is deleted, and υ' is like υ except that feature $\mathtt{x}$ is deleted.
   - *(b) A tree τ is in the domain of move if τ has feature $\mathtt{+y} \in licensors$ and τ has exactly one maximal subtree τ_0 that has feature $\mathtt{-y} \in licensees$. Then,*

     $$move(\tau) = [_> \tau_0', \tau'],$$

     where τ_0' is like τ_0 except that feature $\mathtt{-y}$ is deleted, and τ' is like τ except that feature $\mathtt{+y}$ is deleted and subtree τ_0 is replaced by a single node without any features.

Let G = (V, Cat, Lex, $\mathcal{F}$) be an MG. Then $\mathrm{CL}(G) = \bigcup_{k \in \mathbb{N}} \mathrm{CL}^k(G)$ is the closure of the lexicon under the structure building functions in $\mathcal{F}$, where $\mathrm{CL}^k(G)$, $k \in \mathbb{N}$ are inductively defined by:

1. $\mathrm{CL}^0(G) = \mathrm{Lex}$
2. $\mathrm{CL}^{k+1}(G) = \mathrm{CL}^k(G) \cup \{merge(\tau, \upsilon) \mid (\tau, \upsilon) \in \mathrm{Dom}(merge) \cap (\mathrm{CL}^k(G) \times \mathrm{CL}^k(G))\} \cup \{move(\tau) \mid \tau \in \mathrm{Dom}(move) \cap \mathrm{CL}^k(G)\}$,

where Dom(*merge*) and Dom(*move*) are the domains of the functions *merge*, *move* $\in \mathcal{F}$. Let τ be a tree in CL(G). Tree τ is a tree of category $\mathtt{a}$ if the head of τ does not contain any syntactic features except for the feature $\mathtt{a} \in base$. Tree τ is a complete tree if it is a tree of category $\mathtt{c}$ and no node other than the head of τ contains any syntactic features. The yield $\mathrm{Y}(\tau)$ of τ is the concatenation of the phonetic features in the labels of the leaves of τ, ordered by precedence. The language derivable by G consists of the yields of the complete trees in CL(G): L(G)={Y(τ) | $\tau \in$ CL(G), τ is complete}.

An example of an MG can be found in section 6.

3 Multiple Context-Free Grammars

In this section we will define the class of MCFGs. An MCFG is a Generalized Context-Free Grammar which satisfies some additional conditions. In section 3.1 we will provide a definition of Generalized Context-Free Grammars. The conditions on MCFGs are discussed in section 3.2. In section 3.3, we will describe a normal form for MCFGs that will be used in this paper.

3.1 Generalized Context-Free Grammars

Generalized Context-Free Grammars are introduced in Pollard (1984). We will follow the definition found in Michaelis (1998).

Definition 3. *A Generalized Context-Free Grammar is a quintuple G = (N, O, F, R, S) for which the following five conditions hold:*

1. *N is a finite, non-empty set of non-terminal symbols.*
2. *O is a set of finite tuples of finite strings over a finite, non-empty set of terminal symbols* Σ, $\Sigma \cap N = \emptyset$: $O \subseteq \bigcup_{n \in \mathbb{N}^+} (\Sigma^*)^n$.
3. *F is a finite set of partial functions from finite products of O to O:* $F \subseteq \bigcup_{n \in \mathbb{N}}$ F_n*, where* F_n *is the set of partial functions from* O^n *to O.*
4. *R is a finite set of rewriting rules:* $R \subseteq \bigcup_{n \in \mathbb{N}} ((F_n \cap F) \times N^{n+1})$.
5. $S \in N$ *is the distinguished start symbol.*

Let G = (N, O, F, R, S) be a Generalized Context-Free Grammar. A rule $r = (g, \mathrm{A}, \mathrm{B}_1, \ldots, \mathrm{B}_n) \in (\mathrm{F}_n \cap \mathrm{F}) \times \mathrm{N}^{n+1}$ of this grammar is usually written as $\mathrm{A} \rightarrow g[\mathrm{B}_1, \ldots, \mathrm{B}_n]$ if $n > 0$, and $\mathrm{A} \rightarrow g$ if $n = 0$. A rule for which $n > 0$ will be called a non-terminating rule; a rule for which $n = 0$ will be called a terminating rule. Note that F_0 is the set of constants in O. Hence, for a terminating rule $\mathrm{A} \rightarrow g$, $g \in \mathrm{O}$.

For any non-terminal symbol $\mathrm{A} \in \mathrm{N}$ and $k \in \mathbb{N}$, the set $\mathrm{L}_G^k(\mathrm{A}) \subseteq \mathrm{O}$ is defined recursively as follows:

1. If R contains a terminating rule $\mathrm{A} \rightarrow g$, then $g \in \mathrm{L}_G^0(\mathrm{A})$.
2. If $\theta \in \mathrm{L}_G^k(\mathrm{A})$, then $\theta \in \mathrm{L}_G^{k+1}(\mathrm{A})$.
3. If R contains a non-terminating rule $\mathrm{A} \rightarrow g[\mathrm{B}_1, \ldots, \mathrm{B}_n]$ and $\theta_i \in \mathrm{L}_G^k(\mathrm{B}_i)$, $1 \le i \le n$, and $g(\theta_1, \ldots, \theta_n)$ is defined, then $g(\theta_1, \ldots, \theta_n) \in \mathrm{L}_G^{k+1}(\mathrm{A})$.

If $\theta \in \mathrm{L}_G^k(\mathrm{A})$ for some $k \in \mathbb{N}$, then θ is called an A-phrase in G. The language derivable from A in G is the set $\mathrm{L}_G(\mathrm{A})$ of all A-phrases in G: $\mathrm{L}_G(\mathrm{A}) = \bigcup_{k \in \mathbb{N}} \mathrm{L}_G^k(\mathrm{A})$. The language L(G) generated by G is the set of all S-phrases in G: $\mathrm{L(G)} = \mathrm{L}_G(\mathrm{S})$.

3.2 m-Multiple Context-Free Grammars

The following definition of an m-MCFG is based on definitions provided in Seki et al. (1991) and Michaelis (1998).

Definition 4. *For any $m \in \mathbb{N}^+$, an m-Multiple Context-Free Grammar is a Generalized Context-Free Grammar G = (N, O, F, R, S) which satisfies the following four conditions:*

1. *The dimension of the tuples in O is bounded: $O = \bigcup_{i=1}^{m} (\Sigma^*)^i$.*
2. *For function $g \in F$, let $n(g) \in \mathbb{N}$ be the number of arguments of g, i.e., $g \in F_{n(g)}$. For any function $g \in F$, the following 3 conditions hold:*
   (a) *The dimension of the result of g and the dimensions of the arguments of g are fixed, that is, there are numbers $r(g) \in \mathbb{N}$, $d_i(g) \in \mathbb{N}$, $1 \leq i \leq n(g)$, such that g is a function from $(\Sigma^*)^{d_1(g)} \times \ldots \times (\Sigma^*)^{d_{n(g)}(g)}$ to $(\Sigma^*)^{r(g)}$.*
   (b) *The effect of g is fixed in the following sense. Let $X = \{x_{ij} \mid 1 \leq i \leq n(g), 1 \leq j \leq d_i(g)\}$ be a set of pairwise distinct variables, and define $x_i = (x_{i1}, \ldots, x_{id_i(g)})$, $1 \leq i \leq n(g)$. Let g^h be the hth component of g, $1 \leq h \leq r(g)$, that is, $g(\theta) = (g^1(\theta), \ldots, g^{r(g)}(\theta))$ for any $\theta = (\theta_1, \ldots, \theta_{n(g)}) \in (\Sigma^*)^{d_1(g)} \times \ldots \times (\Sigma^*)^{d_{n(g)}(g)}$. Then for each component g^h, there is a fixed number $l_h(g) \in \mathbb{N}$ such that g^h is represented by the following concatenation of constant strings in Σ^* and variables in X:*
   $$g^h(x_1, \ldots, x_{n(g)}) = \alpha_{h0} z_{h1} \alpha_{h1} z_{h2} \ldots z_{hl_h(g)} \alpha_{hl_h(g)},$$
   where $\alpha_{hl} \in \Sigma^*$, $0 \leq l \leq l_h(g)$, and $z_{hl} \in X$, $1 \leq l \leq l_h(g)$.
   (c) *For each pair (i, j), $1 \leq i \leq n(g)$, $1 \leq j \leq d_i(g)$, there is at most one h, $1 \leq h \leq r(g)$, and at most one l, $1 \leq l \leq l_h(g)$, such that variable z_{hl} in the representation of component g^h of g is the variable $x_{ij} \in X$.*
3. *The dimension of any non-terminal symbol $A \in N$ is fixed, that is, for every non-terminal symbol $A \in N$ there is a number $d(A) \in \mathbb{N}$ such that for any rule $A \to g[B_1, \ldots, B_{n(g)}]$ in R, $r(g) = d(A)$ and $d_i(g) = d(B_i)$, $1 \leq i \leq n(g)$.*
4. *The dimension of the distinguished start symbol is 1: d(S) = 1.*

Condition 2.(c) is referred to as the anti-copying condition, because it prevents any variable $x_{ij} \in$ X from occurring more than once in the whole of the representations of the components that define a function g.

Example 1. The 2-MCFG G = ({H, S}, $\bigcup_{i=1}^{2} (\{1, 2, 3, 4\}^*)^i$, {g, f}, {H → ($\epsilon$, ϵ), H → g[H], S → f[H]}, S), where $g[(x_{11}, x_{12})] = (1x_{11}2, 3x_{12}4)$ and $f[(x_{11}, x_{12})] = (x_{11}x_{12})$, generates the language $\{1^n2^n3^n4^n \mid n \geq 0\}$.

3.3 Normal Form for Multiple Context-Free Grammars

The MCFGs used in the proof of equivalence are assumed to be in a particular form. This section defines this normal form and shows that any MCFG can be given in this form. The components of any function $g \in$ F of the m-MCFG G in lemma 1 are assumed to be represented as in definition 4, part 2.(b).

Lemma 1. *For any m-MCFG G = (N, O, F, R, S) there is an m-MCFG G′ = (N′, O′, F′, R′, S′) which is weakly equivalent to G and which satisfies the following four conditions:*

(a) For any non-terminal symbol $A \in N'$ which appears in the left-hand side of some terminating rule in R′, $d(A) = 1$.
(b) Any $g \in F'$, $n(g) > 0$, satisfies the non-erasure condition: for each pair (i, j), $1 \le i \le n(g)$, $1 \le j \le d_i(g)$, there is at least one h, $1 \le h \le r(g)$, and at least one l, $1 \le l \le l_h(g)$, such that variable z_{hl} in the representation of component g^h of g is the variable $x_{ij} \in X$.
(c) Any $g \in F'$, $n(g) > 0$, is free of syncategorematically introduced symbols: for all pairs (h, l), $1 \le h \le r(g)$, $0 \le l \le l_h(g)$, the constant string $\alpha_{hl} \in \Sigma^*$ in the representation of component g^h of g is the empty string.
(d) Grammar G′ is doublet-free: there is no non-terminating rule $r \in R'$ such that there is a non-terminal symbol $T \in N'$ which occurs more than once among the non-terminal symbols in the right-hand side of r.

Proof. The proof of lemma 2.2 in Seki et al. (1991) shows how to construct, for any m-MCFG G = (N, O, F, R, S), another m-MCFG G′ = (N′, O′, F′, R′, S′) satisfying conditions (a), (b), and (c), and such that L(G) = L(G′).

Possible doublets in G′ are removed by replacing a non-terminating rule $r \in$ R′ containing a doublet, i.e., r = A $\rightarrow g[\mathrm{B}_1, \ldots, \mathrm{B}_{n(g)}]$ such that $\mathrm{B}_i = \mathrm{B}_j =$ T $\in$ N′, $1 \le i < j \le \mathrm{n}(g)$, with a rule r' = A $\rightarrow g[\mathrm{B}_1, \ldots, \mathrm{B}_{j-1}, \mathrm{B}'_j, \mathrm{B}_{j+1}, \ldots, \mathrm{B}_{n(g)}]$, where B'_j is a fresh non-terminal symbol, and adding the rule $r'' = \mathrm{B}'_j \rightarrow id_{d(B_j)}[\mathrm{B}_j]$, where $id_{d(B_j)}$ is the identity function with one argument of dimension $\mathrm{d}(\mathrm{B}_j)$. Let H be the resulting grammar: H = (N′ $\cup$ $\{\mathrm{B}'_j\}$, O′, F′ $\cup$ $\{id_{d(B_j)}\}$, (R′ $\cup$ $\{r', r''\}$) - $\{r\}$, S′). H contains one doublet less than G′ and does not violate conditions (a), (b), or (c). For every derivation of a U-phrase θ in G′ involving rule r, U $\in$ N′, there is a derivation of a U-phrase θ in H using rules r' and r'', and vice versa. Derivations not depending on rule r or rules r' and r'' are valid derivations in both G′ and H. Hence, $\mathrm{L}_{G'}(\mathrm{U}) = \mathrm{L}_H(\mathrm{U})$, U $\in$ N′. Then, in particular, L(G′) = $\mathrm{L}_{G'}(\mathrm{S}')$ = $\mathrm{L}_H(\mathrm{S}')$ = L(H). Repeated replacements and additions of rules will eventually produce an m-MCFG G″ = (N″, O′, F″, R″, S′) for which L(G″) = L(G′) = L(G), and which satisfies conditions (a), (b), (c), and (d). □

Example 2. The 2-MCFG G = ({A, B, C, D, E, F, H, S}, $\bigcup_{i=1}^{2}$ ({a, b, c, d}*)^i, $\{g, f, h\}$, {A $\rightarrow$ 1, B $\rightarrow$ 2, C $\rightarrow$ 3, D $\rightarrow$ 4, E $\rightarrow \epsilon$, F $\rightarrow \epsilon$, H $\rightarrow h$[E, F], H $\rightarrow g$[A, B, C, D, H], S $\rightarrow f$[H]}, S), where $h[(x_{11}), (x_{21})] = (x_{11}, x_{21})$, $g[(x_{11}), (x_{21}), (x_{31}), (x_{41}), (x_{51}, x_{52})] = (x_{11}x_{51}x_{21}, x_{31}x_{52}x_{41})$, and $f[(x_{11}, x_{12})] = (x_{11}x_{12})$, is a grammar in normal form which generates the language $\{1^n2^n3^n4^n \mid n \ge 0\}$.

4 Construction of Minimalist Grammar

This section shows how to construct an MG G′ = (V, Cat, Lex, $\mathcal{F}$) for a given m-MCFG G = (N, O, F, R, S) in normal form such that L(G) = L(G′). The general idea behind the construction of G′ is that for any non-terminal symbol A ∈ N and A-phrase $(p_1, \ldots, p_{d(A)})$, the items in Lex allow for a derivation of a tree that has d(A) specifiers, the yields of which are the components p_i, $1 \leq i \leq$ d(A), and a head labeled with feature a ∈ *base* identifying non-terminal symbol A. Each specifier has a feature $-a_t \in$ *licensees*, $1 \leq t \leq$ d(A), so that the specifiers can be moved to form strings that correspond to the values produced by the functions in F.

4.1 Non-syntactic Features

There is no need for G′ to have semantic features: I = ∅. The set of phonetic features will correspond to the set of terminal symbols of G: P = Σ for O ⊆ $\bigcup_{i=1}^{m} (\Sigma^*)^i$. Hence, regarding the non-syntactic features of G′, V = P ∪ I = Σ.

4.2 Syntactic Features

The set of syntactic features Cat is the union of the sets *base*, *select*, *licensees*, and *licensors*, the contents of which are defined as follows. For every non-terminal symbol A ∈ N, there is a feature a ∈ *base*, a feature =a ∈ *select*, and features $+a_t \in$ *licensors*, and features $-a_t \in$ *licensees*, $1 \leq t \leq$ d(A). These features are said to correspond to non-terminal symbol A. The features corresponding to non-terminal symbol S are c ∈ *base*, =c ∈ *select*, $+c_1 \in$ *licensors*, and $-c_1 \in$ *licensees*.[3]

Let $R_e = \langle r_1, \ldots, r_{|R|} \rangle$ be an enumeration of the rules in R. For every non-terminating rule r_s = A → $g[B_1, \ldots, B_{n(g)}]$ in R_e, there are features $a_t^s \in$ *base*, $=a_t^s \in$ *select*, $1 \leq t \leq$ d(A)+1 = r(g)+1, and features $+a_t^s \in$ *licensors*, $-a_t^s \in$ *licensees*, $1 \leq t \leq$ d(A) = r(g). These features are said to correspond to rule r_s. The features corresponding to a non-terminating rule r_s = S → $g[B_1, \ldots, B_{n(g)}]$ are c_1^s, $c_2^s \in$ *base*, $=c_1^s$, $=c_2^s \in$ *select*, and features $+c_1^s \in$ *licensors*, $-c_1^s \in$ *licensees*.

4.3 Structure Building Functions

The structure building functions in $\mathcal{F}$ are prescribed by definition 2: $\mathcal{F}$ = {*merge*, *move*}.

4.4 Lexicon

The contents of Lex are specified as follows. Let $R_e = \langle r_1, \ldots, r_{|R|} \rangle$ be an enumeration of the rules in R. For a terminating rule r_s = A → g in R_e, A ≠ S, the following lexical item is associated with r_s:[4]

[3] By definition 4, d(S) = 1.

[4] In a tree, ∅ represents the empty label. Each internal node of a tree will be labeled '<' or '>', indicating which of the two immediate daughters projects over the other.

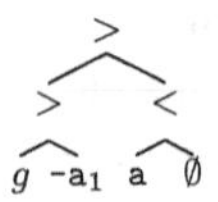

For a terminating rule $r_s = \mathrm{S} \rightarrow g$ in R_e, the following two lexical items will be associated with rule r:

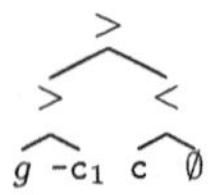

and

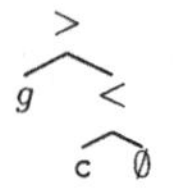

Next, consider a non-terminating rule $r_s = \mathrm{A} \rightarrow g[\mathrm{B}_1, \ldots, \mathrm{B}_{n(g)}]$ in R_e,[5] and assume that the components of g are represented by $g^h(x_1, \ldots, x_{n(g)}) = z_{h1} \ldots z_{hl_h(g)}$, $z_{hl} \in \mathrm{X} = \{x_{ij} \mid 1 \leq i \leq \mathrm{n}(g),\ 1 \leq j \leq \mathrm{d}_i(g)\}$, $x_i = (x_{i1}, \ldots, x_{id_i(g)})$, $1 \leq i \leq \mathrm{n}(g)$, $1 \leq h \leq \mathrm{r}(g)$, $1 \leq l \leq \mathrm{l}_h(\mathrm{g})$, according to definition 4 and lemma 1. Define the set $\mathrm{F}^+_{r_s} = \{\texttt{+b}_{ij} \mid 1 \leq i \leq \mathrm{n}(g),\ 1 \leq j \leq \mathrm{d}(\mathrm{B}_i)\}$.[6] If $\mathrm{A} \neq \mathrm{S}$, then the complex of lexical items associated with rule r_s consists of the following $\mathrm{r}(g)+2$ lexical items:

$$\texttt{=a}^s_1\ \texttt{+a}^s_{r(g)} \ldots \texttt{+a}^s_1\ \texttt{a},$$

and

$$\texttt{=a}^s_{h+1}\ f_{hl_h(g)} \ldots f_{h1}\ \texttt{a}^s_h\ \texttt{-a}^s_h\ \texttt{-a}_h,$$

$1 \leq h \leq \mathrm{r}(g)$, where feature $f_{hl} \in \mathrm{F}^+_{r_s}$ is feature $\texttt{+b}_{ij}$ if, and only if, variable $z_{hl} \in \mathrm{X}$ is variable x_{ij}, $1 \leq l \leq \mathrm{l}_h(g)$, and

$$\texttt{=b}_1 \ldots \texttt{=b}_{n(g)}\ \texttt{a}^s_{r(g)+1}.$$

If $\mathrm{A} = \mathrm{S}$, then non-terminating rule $r_s = \mathrm{S} \rightarrow g[\mathrm{B}_1, \ldots, \mathrm{B}_{n(g)}]$ in R_e is associated with the following complex of $2 \cdot \mathrm{r}(g)+2$ lexical items:[7]

$$\texttt{=c}^s_1\ \texttt{+c}^s_1\ \texttt{c},$$

and

---

[5] The feature in *base* corresponding to non-terminal symbol B_i is written $\texttt{b}_i$, $1 \leq i \leq \mathrm{n}(g)$. Thus the licensor features and licensee features corresponding to B_i will have two subscripts: $\texttt{+b}_{it}$, $\texttt{-b}_{it}$, $1 \leq t \leq \mathrm{d}(\mathrm{B}_i)$.

[6] By definition 4, $\mathrm{d}_i(g) = \mathrm{d}(\mathrm{B}_i)$, $1 \leq i \leq \mathrm{n}(g)$.

[7] By definition 4, if $\mathrm{A} = \mathrm{S}$, then $\mathrm{r}(g) = \mathrm{d}(\mathrm{S}) = 1$.

$$\texttt{=c}_2^s \ f_{1l_1(g)} \cdots f_{11} \ \texttt{c}_1^s \ \texttt{-c}_1^s \ \texttt{-c}_1,$$
$$\texttt{=c}_2^s \ f_{1l_1(g)} \cdots f_{11} \ \texttt{c}_1^s \ \texttt{-c}_1^s,$$

where feature $f_{1l} \in \mathrm{F}^+_{r_s}$ is feature $\texttt{+b}_{ij}$ if, and only if, variable $z_{1l} \in \mathrm{X}$ is variable x_{ij}, $1 \leq l \leq \mathrm{l}_1(g)$, and

$$\texttt{=b}_1 \ldots \texttt{=b}_{n(g)} \ \texttt{c}_2^s.$$

Note that in the lexical items for a non-terminating rule all features f_{hl} are defined for $1 \leq h \leq \mathrm{r}(g)$, $1 \leq l \leq \mathrm{l}_h(g)$: for any particular choice of h there will be a component g^h, whose definition will contain a z_{hl} for any legitimate choice of l.

For every rule r_s in R_e, Lex will contain the lexical items associated with it. Since the number of rules in R is finite and $\mathrm{r}(g)$ is bounded for any $g \in \mathrm{F}$, the number of items in Lex will be finite. Furthermore, since $\mathrm{l}_h(g)$ and $\mathrm{n}(g)$ are also bounded for any $g \in \mathrm{F}$, all items in Lex will consist of finite sequences of syntactic features.

5 Correspondence

Given an m-MCFG G = (N, O, F, R, S) and an MG G′ = (V, Cat, Lex, $\mathcal{F}$) constructed as per the instructions in section 4, we will distinguish a set of non-terminal trees in CL(G′) and define a relationship between these trees and pairs (A, p) ∈ N × O where p is an A-phrase.

Definition 5. *A tree $\tau \in CL(G')$ is a non-terminal tree if, and only if, the following three conditions are met:*

1. *The head of τ is labeled with a single syntactic feature* a *∈ base corresponding to some non-terminal symbol $A \in N$, and does not have any phonetic features.*
2. *Tree τ has k specifiers, $k > 0$. For each specifier τ_i^σ of τ, $1 \leq i \leq k$, the following holds:*
   (a) *The head of τ_i^σ is labeled with the single syntactic feature* $\texttt{-a}_i$ *∈ licensees corresponding to the same $A \in N$ as the syntactic feature labeling the head of τ, and does not have any phonetic features.*
   (b) *In τ_i^σ, no node other than the head is labeled with any syntactic features.*
   (c) *Specifier τ_i^σ precedes specifiers τ_j^σ, $1 < i < j \leq k$.*
3. *The complement τ^c of τ does not contain any nodes labeled with syntactic features or phonetic features.*

Definition 6. *A non-terminal tree $\tau \in CL(G')$ corresponds to a pair $(A, p) \in N \times O$ for which $p = (p_1, \ldots, p_{d(A)}) \in L_G(A)$, if, and only if, the following conditions are met:*

1. *The head of τ is labeled with the feature* a *∈ base corresponding to A.*
2. *Tree τ has $d(A)$ specifiers. For each specifier τ_i^σ of τ, $1 \leq i \leq d(A)$, the following holds: the yield of τ_i^σ is p_i.*

6 Illustration of Proof of Equivalence

The proof that an m-MCFG G = (N, O, F, R, S) and an MG G′ = (V, Cat, Lex, $\mathcal{F}$) constructed according to the instructions section 4 are weakly equivalent involves showing that for every pair (A, p) ∈ N × O such that p is an A-phrase, there is a non-terminal tree $\tau \in$ CL(G′) corresponding to (A, p), and that for every non-terminal tree $\tau \in$ CL(G′), there is a pair (A, p) ∈ N × O, p an A-phrase, to which τ corresponds (propositions 1 and 2 in section 7). In this section we will illustrate these claims by means of a concrete example.

Example 3. Let G = ({A, B, C, D, E, F, H, S}, $\bigcup_{i=1}^{2}$ ({a, b, c, d}*)^i, {g, f, h}, {A → 1, B → 2, C → 3, D → 4, E → ϵ, F → ϵ, H → h[E, F], H → g[A, B, C, D, H], S → f[H]}, S), where $h[(x_{11}), (x_{21})] = (x_{11}, x_{21})$, $g[(x_{11}), (x_{21}), (x_{31}), (x_{41}), (x_{51}, x_{52})] = (x_{11}x_{51}x_{21}, x_{31}x_{52}x_{41})$, and $f[(x_{11}, x_{12})] = (x_{11}x_{12})$, be the grammar from example 2, which generates the language $\{1^n2^n3^n4^n \mid n \geq 0\}$, and let R_e an enumeration of the rules following the order given in the definition of G. Obviously, (1) ∈ L_G(A), (2) ∈ L_G(B), (3) ∈ L_G(C), (4) ∈ L_G(D), and (12, 34) ∈ L_G(H). Hence, by rule r_7 = H → g[A, B, C, D, H], g[(1), (2), (3), (4), (12, 34)] = (1122, 3344) ∈ L_G(H).

1.
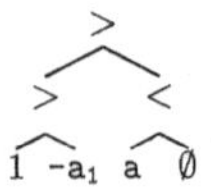

2.
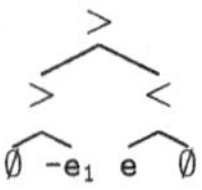

3.
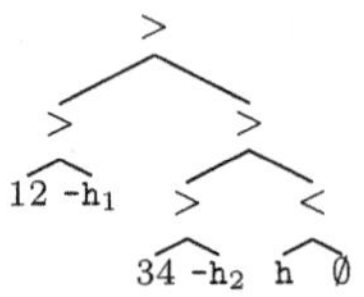

4.
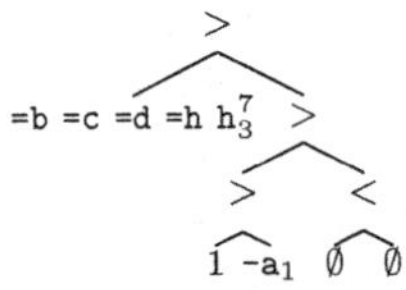

We will now specify MG G′ = (Cat, V, Lex, $\mathcal{F}$) for G by giving the contents of Lex. For terminating rule r_0, Lex will contain the tree given in 1. Lex will include similar trees for rules r_1, r_2, and r_3. For terminating rule r_4, Lex will contain the tree given in 2. There is a similar tree in Lex for rule r_5.

For non-terminating rule r_6, Lex will contain the following lexical items:

5. $=h^6_1\ +h^6_2\ +h^6_1\ h$
6. $=h^6_2\ +e_1\ h^6_1\ -h^6_1\ -h_1$
7. $=h^6_3\ +f_1\ h^6_2\ -h^6_2\ -h_2$
8. $=e\ =f\ h^6_3$

For non-terminating rule r_7, Lex will contain the following lexical items:

9. $=h^7_1\ +h^7_2\ +h^7_1\ h$
10. $=h^7_2\ +b_1\ +h_1\ +a_1\ h^7_1\ -h^7_1\ -h_1$
11. $=h^7_3\ +d_1\ +h_2\ +c_1\ h^7_2\ -h^7_2\ -h_2$
12. $=a\ =b\ =c\ =d\ =h\ h^7_3$

For non-terminating rule r_8, Lex will contain the following lexical items:

13. $=c^8_1\ +c^8_1\ c$
14. $=c^8_2\ +h_2\ +h_1\ c^8_1\ -c^8_1\ -c_1$
15. $=c^8_2\ +h_2\ +h_1\ c^8_1\ -c^8_1$
16. $=h\ c^8_3$

It follows from proposition 1 that CL(G′) will contain non-terminal trees corresponding to the pairs (A, (1)), (B, (2)), (C, (3)), (D, (4)), and (H, (12, 34)). The first four trees are elements of Lex; the tree corresponding to (H,

(12, 34)) is the derived tree in 3.[8] We will now show how the non-terminal tree corresponding to the pair (H, (1122, 3344)) is derived from these smaller non-terminal trees and the lexical items in 9 through 12.

17.

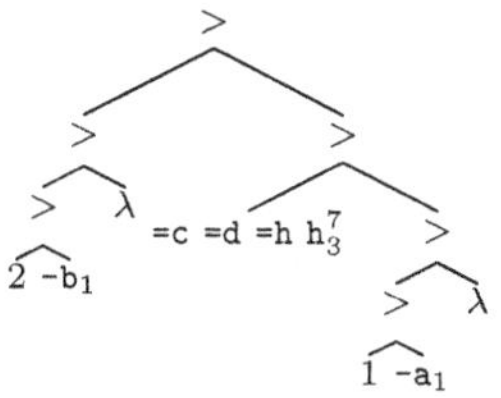

18.

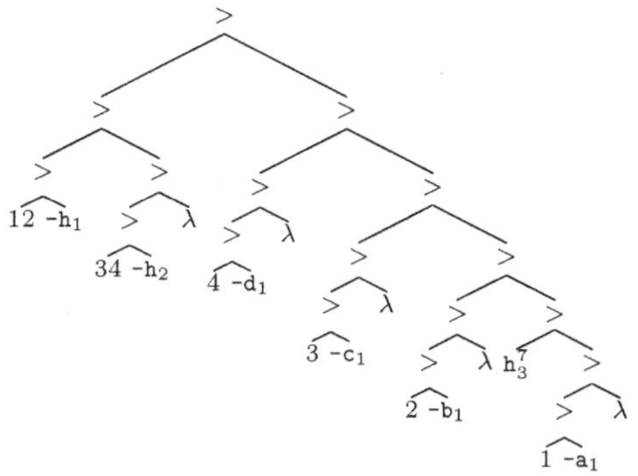

First, item =a =b =c =d =h h$_3^7$ will merge with tree 1, because the former has a feature =a $\in$ *select* and the latter has a feature a $\in$ *base*. The result is the tree in 4. The derivation will continue with merging tree 4 and the lexical item with head b corresponding to the pair (B, (2)). Since tree 4 is a complex tree, the item it merges with will be attached as a specifier, yielding the tree in 17.[9]

19.

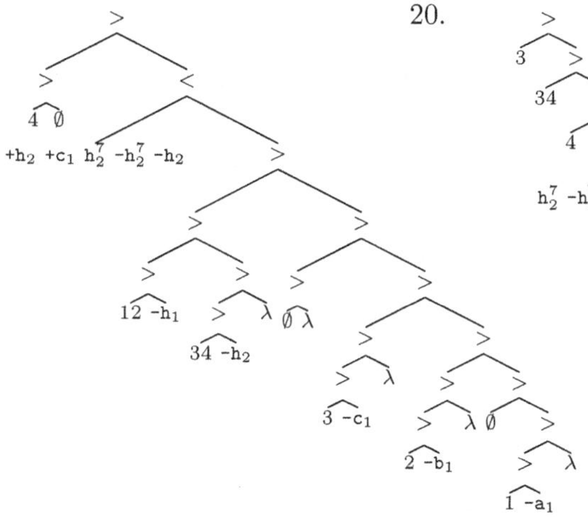

20.

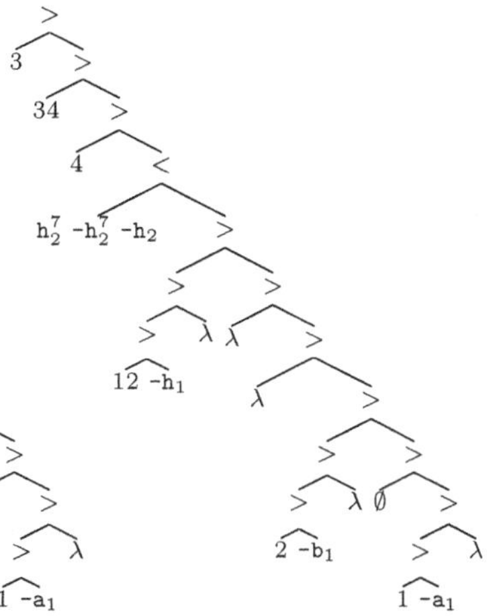

The applications of *merge* triggered by the features =c, =d, and =h occurring in the head of tree 17 will eventually produce the tree in 18. This tree contains the arguments (1), (2), (3), (4), (12, 34) to which g will be applied to obtain the value (1122, 3344) $\in$ $L_G(H)$.

[8] The specifiers of the specifiers of this tree contain nodes with empty labels that are irrelevant and hence not shown.

[9] In order to keep the trees manageable size-wise, λ is used to abbreviate a complex subtree whose leaves are all labeled $\emptyset$.

Next, item $\mathtt{=h}_3^7\ \mathtt{+d}_1\ \mathtt{+h}_2\ \mathtt{+c}_1\ \mathtt{h}_2^7\ \mathtt{-h}_2^7\ \mathtt{-h}_2$ will select tree 18. The resulting tree is $[_<\mathtt{+d}_1\ \mathtt{+h}_2\ \mathtt{+c}_1\ \mathtt{h}_2^7\ \mathtt{-h}_2^7\ \mathtt{-h}_2, \tau]$, where τ is like tree 18, except that the feature $\mathtt{h}_3^7$ is deleted. The left-most feature of the head of $[_<\mathtt{+d}_1\ \mathtt{+h}_2\ \mathtt{+c}_1\ \mathtt{h}_2^7\ \mathtt{-h}_2^7\ \mathtt{-h}_2, \tau]$ is $\mathtt{+d}_1 \in$ *licensors*. Subtree τ contains one, and only one node whose left-most feature is $\mathtt{-d}_1 \in$ *licensees*. This pair of features triggers an application of *move*. The tree in 19 is the result.

After two more applications of *move* involving the features $\mathtt{+h}_2$ and $\mathtt{+c}_1$, the tree in 20 is obtained.[10] The three *move* operations have created a sequence of specifiers whose yields correspond to the value of the second component of $g[(1), (2), (3), (4), (12, 34)] = (1122, 3344)$.

21.

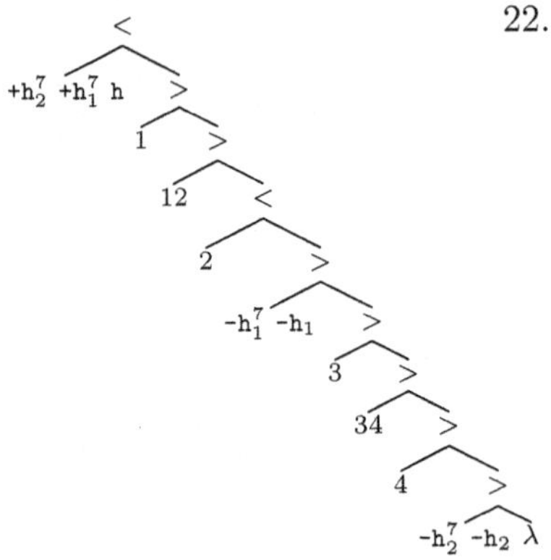

22.

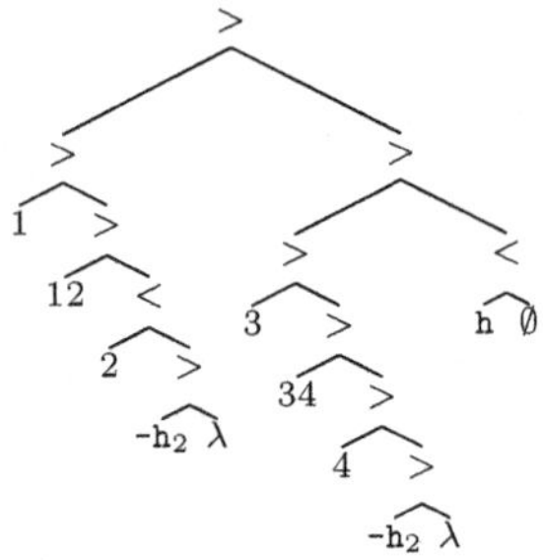

The tree in 20 will be selected by item $\mathtt{=h}_2^7\ \mathtt{+b}_1\ \mathtt{+h}_1\ \mathtt{+a}_1\ \mathtt{h}_1^7\ \mathtt{-h}_1^7\ \mathtt{-h}_1$, which will take care of assembling the string corresponding to the first component of $g[(1), (2), (3), (4), (12, 34)]$. The tree resulting from these *merge* and *move* actions will then be selected by item $\mathtt{=h}_1^7\ \mathtt{+h}_2^7\ \mathtt{+h}_1^7\ \mathtt{h}$, as in 21.

Finally, two applications of *move* triggered by the features $\mathtt{+h}_2^7$, $\mathtt{-h}_2^7$ and $\mathtt{+h}_1^7$, $\mathtt{-h}_1^7$ in tree 21 will produce the non-terminal tree in 22. This tree is a non-terminal tree corresponding to the pair (H, (1122, 3344)).

7 Proof of Equivalence

Let G = (N, O, F, R, S) be an m-MCFG in normal form, R_e an enumeration of R, and G′ = (V, Cat, Lex, $\mathcal{F}$) an MG constructed as specified in section 4. In section 7.2 we will show that L(G) = L(G′). First, we will prove several properties of G′.

7.1 Properties of G′

Consider a non-terminating rule $r_s = \mathrm{A} \rightarrow g[\mathrm{B}_1, \ldots, \mathrm{B}_{n(g)}]$ in R_e and the lexical items associated with rule r_s. Assume that the components of g are represented

[10] To save space, wo-node subtrees of the form $[_<x, \emptyset]$ and $[_>x, \emptyset]$, $x \in \mathrm{Cat}^*\mathrm{P}^*\mathrm{I}^*$, are simply written as x.

as in section 4.4, and let $X = \{x_{ij} \mid 1 \leq i \leq n(g), 1 \leq j \leq d_i(g)\}$ and $F^+_{r_s} = \{\texttt{+b}_{ij} \mid 1 \leq i \leq n(g), 1 \leq j \leq d(B_i)\}$ as in section 4.4.

Theorem 1. *For every feature* $\texttt{+b}_{ij} \in F^+_{r_s}$*, there is at least one pair* (h, l)*,* $1 \leq h \leq r(g)$*,* $1 \leq l \leq l_h(g)$*, such that feature* f_{hl} *is* $\texttt{+b}_{ij}$*.*

Proof. Pick an arbitrary feature $\texttt{+b}_{ij} \in F^+_{r_s}$. Because of the existence of rule r_s in R_e, $d_k(g) = d(B_k)$, $1 \leq k \leq n(g)$. Therefore, there is a variable $x_{ij} \in X$. It follows from the non-erasure condition (lemma 1, part (b)) that there must be a variable z_{hl}, $1 \leq h \leq r(g)$, $1 \leq l \leq l_h(g)$, which is identical to the variable x_{ij}. Then, by the definition of the lexical items associated with rule r_s, feature f_{hl} will be the feature $\texttt{+b}_{ij}$. □

Theorem 2. *For every feature* $\texttt{+b}_{ij} \in F^+_{r_s}$*, there is at most one pair* (h, l)*,* $1 \leq h \leq r(g)$*,* $1 \leq l \leq l_h(g)$*, such that feature* f_{hl} *is* $\texttt{+b}_{ij}$*.*

Proof. Suppose that there are pairs (h, l) and (p, q), $(h, l) \neq (p, q)$, such that features f_{hl} and f_{pq} are the same feature $\texttt{+b}_{ij} \in F^+_{r_s}$, $1 \leq h \leq r(g)$, $1 \leq l \leq l_h(g)$, $1 \leq p \leq r(g)$, $1 \leq q \leq l_p(g)$. Then, by the way the items in Lex are defined, there are variables z_{hl} and z_{pq} in the representation of the components of g, such that both z_{hl} and z_{pq} are the same variable $x_{ij} \in X$. This, however, is ruled out by the anti-copying condition (definition 4, part 2.(c)). □

Theorem 3. *If* $\beta_1, \ldots, \beta_{n(g)}$ *are non-terminal trees in* $CL(G')$ *that have features* $\texttt{b}_1, \ldots, \texttt{b}_{n(g)}$ *respectively, then the projection of lexical item* $\texttt{=a}^s_1\ \texttt{+a}^s_{r(g)} \ldots \texttt{+a}^s_1\ \texttt{a}$*, using lexical items* $\texttt{=a}^s_{h+1}\ f_{hl_h(g)} \cdots f_{h1}\ \texttt{a}^s_h\ \texttt{-a}^s_h\ \texttt{-a}_h$*,* $1 \leq h \leq r(g)$*,* $\texttt{=b}_1 \ldots \texttt{=b}_{n(g)}\ \texttt{a}^s_{r(g)+1}$*, and trees* $\beta_1, \ldots, \beta_{n(g)}$*, is a non-terminal tree of category* $\texttt{a}$*.*

Proof. Item $\texttt{=b}_1 \ldots \texttt{=b}_{n(g)}\ \texttt{a}^s_{r(g)+1}$ will select the trees $\beta_1, \ldots, \beta_{n(g)}$. Because the trees β_i, $1 \leq i \leq n(g)$, are non-terminal trees, the resulting tree ψ will have $\sum_{i=1}^{n(g)} d(B_i)$ licensee features. Thanks to lemma 1, part (d), these features are all different. Consequently, the derivation will not crash because ψ will have more than one maximal subtree that has some feature $\texttt{-y} \in$ *licensees*, cf. definition 2, part 4.(b). Let $F^-_{r_s} = \{\texttt{-b}_{ij} \mid 1 \leq i \leq n(g), 1 \leq j \leq d(B_k)\}$ be the set of all licensee features occurring in the trees β_i, $1 \leq i \leq n(g)$.

For $1 \leq h \leq r(g)$, each item $\texttt{=a}^s_{h+1}\ f_{hl_h(g)} \cdots f_{h1}\ \texttt{a}^s_h\ \texttt{-a}^s_h\ \texttt{-a}_h$ will select the tree projected by its successor, $\texttt{=a}^s_{h+2}\ f_{h+1l_{h+1}(g)} \cdots f_{h+11}\ \texttt{a}^s_{h+1}\ \texttt{-a}^s_{h+1}\ \texttt{-a}_{h+1}$. The last item selected in this chain will select ψ. For these *merge* operations to succeed, all features $f_{hl_h(g)} \cdots f_{h1}$ in all items $\texttt{=a}^s_{h+1}\ f_{hl_h(g)} \cdots f_{h1}\ \texttt{a}^s_h\ \texttt{-a}^s_h\ \texttt{-a}_h$, $1 \leq h \leq r(g)$, should be deleted by an application of *move*. Hence, for each licensor feature f_{hl}, $1 \leq h \leq r(g)$, $1 \leq l < l_h(g)$, there has to be a matching licensee feature in $F^-_{r_s}$. Pick an arbitrary pair (h, l), $1 \leq h \leq r(g)$, $1 \leq l < l_h(g)$ and assume f_{hl} is the feature $\texttt{+b}_{ij} \in F^+_{r_s}$. It follows immediately from the definition of the set $F^-_{r_s}$ that there is a matching licensee feature $\texttt{-b}_{ij} \in F^-_{r_s}$. By theorem 2, there is no other feature f_{pq}, $1 \leq p \leq r(g)$, $1 \leq q \leq l_p(g)$, $(h, l) \neq (p, q)$, such that f_{pq} also is feature $\texttt{+b}_{ij}$. Therefore, feature $\texttt{-b}_{ij} \in \mathrm{F}^-_{r_s}$ will be available to check and delete feature f_{hl}.

Let ϕ be the tree projected from item $\texttt{=a}^s_2\ f_{1l_1(g)} \cdots f_{11}\ \texttt{a}^s_1\ \texttt{-a}^s_1\ \texttt{-a}_1$ through the *merge* and *move* operations described above. The head of ϕ is labeled $\texttt{a}^s_1\ \texttt{-a}^s_1\ \texttt{-a}_1$. The only other syntactic features present in ϕ will be sequences $\texttt{-a}^s_h\ \texttt{-a}_h$, $2 \leq h \leq \mathrm{r}(g)$, from projecting the items $\texttt{=a}^s_{h+1}\ f_{hl_h(g)} \cdots f_{h1}\ \texttt{a}^s_h\ \texttt{-a}^s_h\ \texttt{-a}_h$, $2 \leq h \leq \mathrm{r}(g)$. All other features of these items have been deleted during the derivation of ϕ, and so have all the features of item $\texttt{=b}_1 \ldots \texttt{=b}_{n(g)}\ \texttt{a}^s_{r(g)+1}$, and all the features contributed by the trees β_i, $1 \leq i \leq \mathrm{n}(g)$, selected by this item: pick an arbitrary licensee feature $\texttt{-b}_{ij} \in \mathrm{F}^-_{r_s}$. It follows immediately from the definition of the set $\mathrm{F}^+_{r_s}$ that there is a matching licensor feature $\texttt{+b}_{ij} \in \mathrm{F}^+_{r_s}$. Then, by theorem 1, there will be a pair (h, l), $1 \leq h \leq \mathrm{r}(g)$, $1 \leq l \leq \mathrm{l}_h(\mathrm{g})$, such that feature f_{hl} is $\texttt{+b}_{ij}$. Since feature $\texttt{-b}_{ij}$ does not occur more than once in the set of trees β_i, $1 \leq i \leq \mathrm{n}(g)$, feature $f_{hl} \in \mathrm{F}^+_{r_s}$ will be available to check and delete feature $\texttt{-b}_{ij}$.

Item $\texttt{=a}^s_1\ \texttt{+a}^i_{r(g)} \cdots\ \texttt{+a}^s_1\ \texttt{a}$ will select ϕ. The head of the resulting tree υ is labeled $\texttt{+a}^i_{r(g)} \cdots\ \texttt{+a}^s_1\ \texttt{a}$. The complement of υ will contain sequences of syntactic features $\texttt{-a}^i_h\ \texttt{-a}_h$, $1 \leq h \leq \mathrm{r}(g)$, and no other syntactic features. Hence, *move* will apply $\mathrm{r}(g)$ times to υ to derive another tree τ. It is easy to check that τ meets the conditions on non-terminal trees given in definition 5. □

Theorem 4. *If $\beta_1, \ldots, \beta_{n(g)}$ are non-terminal trees in CL(G′) that have features* $\texttt{b}_1, \ldots, \texttt{b}_{n(g)}$ *respectively, then the projection of lexical item* $\texttt{=c}^s_1\ \texttt{+c}^s_1\ \texttt{c}$, *using lexical items* $\texttt{=c}^s_2\ f_{1l_h(g)} \cdots f_{11}\ \texttt{c}^s_1\ \texttt{-c}^s_1$, $\texttt{=b}_1 \ldots \texttt{=b}_{n(g)}\ \texttt{c}^s_2$, *and trees* $\beta_1, \ldots, \beta_{n(g)}$, *is a complete tree of category* $\texttt{c}$ *in CL(G′).*

Proof. The proof is similar to the proof of theorem 3 for $\texttt{a} = \texttt{c}$; it uses lexical item $\texttt{=c}^s_2\ f_{1l_h(g)} \cdots f_{11}\ \texttt{c}^s_1\ \texttt{-c}^s_1$ rather than lexical item $\texttt{=c}^s_2\ f_{1l_h(g)} \cdots f_{11}\ \texttt{c}^s_1\ \texttt{-c}^s_1\ \texttt{-c}_1$. □

Theorem 5. *If $\beta_1, \ldots, \beta_{n(g)}$ are non-terminal trees and complete trees in CL(G′) that have features* $\texttt{b}_1, \ldots, \texttt{b}_{n(g)}$ *respectively, and at least one of these trees is a complete tree, then no tree of category* $\texttt{a}$ *can be projected from lexical item* $\texttt{=a}^i_1\ \texttt{+a}^i_{r(g)} \ldots \texttt{+a}^i_1\ \texttt{a}$, *using lexical items* $\texttt{=a}^i_{h+1}\ f_{hl_h(g)} \cdots f_{h1}\ \texttt{a}^i_h\ \texttt{-a}^i_h\ \texttt{-a}_h$, $1 \leq h \leq r(g)$, $\texttt{=b}_1 \ldots \texttt{=b}_{n(g)}\ \texttt{a}^i_{r(g)+1}$, *and trees* $\beta_1, \ldots, \beta_{n(g)}$.

Proof. Assume tree β_k is a complete tree, $1 \leq \mathrm{k} \leq \mathrm{n}(g)$. By theorem 1, there is a licensor feature f_{hl}, $1 \leq h \leq \mathrm{r}(g)$, $1 \leq \mathrm{l} \leq l_h(g)$, such that f_{hl} is feature $\texttt{+b}_{kj}$, $1 \leq j \leq \mathrm{d}(\mathrm{B}_k)$. However, tree β_k, being a complete tree, does not contain a matching licensee feature $\texttt{-b}_{kj}$. None of the other trees $\beta_1, \ldots, \beta_{n(g)}$ contains a matching feature either, because they are complete trees, or, if they are non-terminal trees, they will have different sets of licensee features as a result of lemma 1, part (d). Hence feature f_{hl} cannot be checked and deleted and the derivation cannot be completed. □

Theorem 6. *If $\beta_1, \ldots, \beta_{n(g)}$ are trees in CL(G′) that have features* $\mathtt{b}_1, \ldots, \mathtt{b}_{n(g)}$ *respectively, and tree β_i is a complete tree, $1 \leq i \leq n(g)$, and the other trees are either non-terminal trees or complete trees, then no tree of category* c *can be projected from lexical item* $\mathtt{=c}_1^s\ \mathtt{+c}_1^s\ \mathtt{c}$, *using lexical items* $\mathtt{=c}_2^s\ f_{1l_h(g)} \cdots f_{11}\ \mathtt{c}_1^s\ \mathtt{-c}_1^s$, $\mathtt{=b}_1 \ldots \mathtt{=b}_{n(g)}\ \mathtt{c}_2^s$, *and trees $\beta_1, \ldots, \beta_{n(g)}$.*

Proof. The proof is analogous to the proof of theorem 5. □

Theorem 7. *If a tree $\tau \in CL(G')$ has a feature* $\mathtt{a} \in$ *base, then τ is a non-terminal tree or a complete tree of category* a.

Proof. The proof is by induction over k in $\mathrm{CL}^k(\mathrm{G}')$. For $\tau \in \mathrm{CL}^0(\mathrm{G}') = \mathrm{Lex}$, the claim follows immediately from the definition of Lex. Let τ be an arbitrary tree in $\mathrm{CL}^k(\mathrm{G}')$, $k > 0$. If $\tau \in \mathrm{CL}^{k-1}(\mathrm{G}')$, the claim follows from the induction hypothesis. If $\tau \notin \mathrm{CL}^{k-1}(\mathrm{G}')$, then τ is a projection of an item $\mathtt{=a}_1^s\ \mathtt{+a}_{r(g)}^s \cdots \mathtt{a}_1^s\ \mathtt{a}$ in Lex, $1 \leq s \leq |\mathrm{R}|$, involving lexical items $\mathtt{=a}_{h+1}^s\ f_{hl_h(g)} \cdots f_{h1}\ \mathtt{a}_h^s\ \mathtt{-a}_h^s\ \mathtt{-a}_h$, $1 \leq h \leq \mathrm{r}(g)$, and $\mathtt{=b}_1 \ldots \mathtt{=b}_{n(g)}\ \mathtt{a}_{r(g)+1}^s$, or involving items $\mathtt{=c}_2^s\ f_{1l_h(g)} \cdots f_{11}\ \mathtt{c}_1^s\ \mathtt{-c}_1^s$, and $\mathtt{=b}_1 \ldots \mathtt{=b}_{n(g)}\ \mathtt{c}_2^s$. In the first case, assume that $\beta_1, \ldots, \beta_{n(g)}$ are the trees selected by item $\mathtt{=b}_1 \ldots \mathtt{=b}_{n(g)}\ \mathtt{a}_{r(g)+1}^s$. These trees will have features $\mathtt{b}_1 \ldots \mathtt{b}_{n(g)}$ respectively. Since the trees $\beta_1, \ldots, \beta_{n(g)}$ are closer to the lexicon than τ, the induction hypothesis applies: each tree β_i, $1 \leq i \leq \mathrm{n}(g)$, is either a non-terminal tree, or a complete tree. However, by theorem 5, none of the trees $\beta_1, \ldots, \beta_{n(g)}$ can be a complete tree. Hence, they must be non-terminal trees, whence, by theorem 3, tree τ is a non-terminal tree, too. If the projection involves item $\mathtt{=c}_2^s\ f_{1l_h(g)} \cdots f_{11}\ \mathtt{c}_1^s\ \mathtt{-c}_1^s$, tree τ is a complete tree. The argument is similar to the first case, and depends on theorems 6 and 4. □

Theorem 8. *There is a non-terminal tree $\tau \in CL^k(G')$ whose head is labeled with feature* $\mathtt{c} \in$ *base if, and only if, there is a complete tree $\tau' \in CL^k(G')$ which is like τ except for the feature* $\mathtt{-c}_1$.

Proof. This follows from the co-existence in Lex of the items $[_>[_>g,\ \mathtt{-c}_1],\ [_<\mathtt{c},\ \emptyset]]$ and $[_>g,\ [_<\mathtt{c},\ \emptyset]]$ for any terminating rule $\mathrm{S} \rightarrow g$ in R, and the items $\mathtt{=c}_2^i\ f_{1l_1(g)} \cdots f_{11}\ \mathtt{c}_1^i\ \mathtt{-c}_1^i\ \mathtt{-c}_1$ and $\mathtt{=c}_2^i\ f_{1l_1(g)} \cdots f_{11}\ \mathtt{c}_1^i\ \mathtt{-c}_1^i$ for any non-terminating rule $r_s = \mathrm{S} \rightarrow g[\mathrm{B}_1, \ldots, \mathrm{B}_{n(g)}]$ in R. □

7.2 Equivalence

Proposition 1. *For every pair $(A, p) \in N \times O$ such that $p \in L_G(A)$, there is a non-terminal tree $\tau \in CL(G')$ which corresponds to (A, p).*

Proof. We will show by induction on $k \in \mathbb{N}$ that the following claim holds for all $\mathrm{A} \in \mathrm{N}$: if $p \in \mathrm{L}_G^k(\mathrm{A})$, then there is a non-terminal tree $\tau \in \mathrm{CL}(\mathrm{G}')$ such that τ corresponds to the pair (A, p). If $k = 0$, then $p \in \mathrm{L}_G^0(\mathrm{A})$. Hence, R contains a terminating rule $\mathrm{A} \rightarrow p$. Then, by the construction of Lex, there is an item

$[_>[_>p, \texttt{-a}_1], [_<\texttt{a}, \emptyset]]$ in Lex. This is a non-terminal tree which corresponds to the pair (A, p).

For the induction step, pick an arbitrary pair (A, p) such that $p \in \mathrm{L}_G^k(\mathrm{A})$, $k > 0$. If $p \in \mathrm{L}_G^{k-1}(\mathrm{A})$, the claim follows from the induction hypothesis. If $p \notin \mathrm{L}_G^{k-1}(\mathrm{A})$, then there is a non-terminating rule $r_s = \mathrm{A} \to g[\mathrm{B}_1, \ldots, \mathrm{B}_{n(g)}]$ in R_e, such that $\theta_i = (\theta_{i1}, \ldots, \theta_{id(B_i)}) \in \mathrm{L}_G^{k-1}(\mathrm{B}_i)$, $1 \leq i \leq \mathrm{n}(g)$, and $p = g(\theta_1, \ldots, \theta_{n(g)})$. Since $\theta_i \in \mathrm{L}_G^{k-1}(\mathrm{B}_i)$, the induction hypothesis applies: for every pair (B_i, θ_i) there is a non-terminal tree $\beta_i \in \mathrm{CL}(\mathrm{G}')$ such that β_i corresponds to (B_i, θ_i), $1 \leq i \leq \mathrm{n}(g)$.

Because R includes rule r_s, Lex contains the items $\texttt{=a}_1^s\ \texttt{+a}_{r(g)}^s \ldots \texttt{+a}_1^s\ \texttt{a}$, $\texttt{=a}_{h+1}^s\ f_{hl_h(g)} \ldots f_{h1}\ \texttt{a}_h^s\ \texttt{-a}_h^s\ \texttt{-a}_h$, $1 \leq h \leq \mathrm{r}(g)$, and $\texttt{=b}_1 \ldots \texttt{=b}_{n(g)}\ \texttt{a}_{r(g)+1}^s$. It follows from theorem 3 that the projection of item $\texttt{=a}_1^s\ \texttt{+a}_{r(g)}^s \ldots \texttt{+a}_1^s\ \texttt{a}$, using the other items and the trees β_i, $1 \leq i \leq \mathrm{n}(g)$, is a non-terminal tree. Let τ be this tree.

The head of τ is labeled a, which corresponds to A. Since R contains the rule r_s, $\mathrm{r}(g) = \mathrm{d}(\mathrm{A})$. Hence, τ, being a projection of $\texttt{=a}_1^s\ \texttt{+a}_{r(g)}^s \ldots \texttt{+a}_1^s\ \texttt{a}$, has d(A) specifiers. Consider an arbitrary specifier τ_h^σ of τ, $1 \leq h \leq \mathrm{d}(\mathrm{A})$. This specifier is the result of an application of *move* triggered by the licensor feature $\texttt{+a}_h^s$ and the matching licensee feature $\texttt{-a}_h^s$ in item $\texttt{=a}_{h+1}^s\ f_{hl_h(g)} \ldots f_{h1}\ \texttt{a}_h^s\ \texttt{-a}_h^s\ \texttt{-a}_h$. Thus, specifier τ_h^σ is a projection of this item. Specifier τ_h^σ does not contain the complement selected by the feature $\texttt{=a}_{h+1}^s$, because this complement has moved to become specifier τ_{h+1}^σ before specifier τ_h^σ was created. Deleting features $f_{hl_h(g)} \ldots f_{h1}$ has equipped specifier τ_h^σ with $\mathrm{l}_h(g)$ specifiers of its own.

Let τ_{hl}^σ be the specifier of τ_h^σ created by the application of *move* triggered by the licensor feature f_{hl}, $1 \leq l \leq \mathrm{l}_h(g)$. Assume that in the representation of the hth component of g, variable z_{hl} is the variable $x_{ij} \in \mathrm{X}$. Then, by the way the contents of Lex are defined, feature f_{hl} is the licensor feature $\texttt{+b}_{ij}$. The matching licensee feature $\texttt{-b}_{ij}$ is found in tree β_i, whose head is labeled $\texttt{b}_i$. Thus, the yield of specifier τ_{hl}^σ is the yield of the maximal projection in tree β_i of the node labeled $\texttt{-b}_{ij}$, that is, specifier β_{ij}^σ of β_i. By the induction hypothesis, $\mathrm{Y}(\beta_i) = \theta_{i1} \ldots \theta_{id(B_i)}$, whence $\mathrm{Y}(\tau_{hl}^\sigma) = \theta_{ij}$.

To determine the value of the function g applied to the arguments ($\theta_1, \ldots, \theta_{n(g)}$), any occurrence of a variable x_{pq} in the representation of the components of g will be replaced by the value θ_{pq}, $1 \leq p \leq \mathrm{n}(g)$, $1 \leq q \leq \mathrm{d}_i(g) = \mathrm{d}(\mathrm{B}_i)$. Let ρ be this set of replacements.[11] Since by assumption the particular variable z_{hl} is the variable x_{ij}, it follows that $z_{hl}/\theta_{ij} \in \rho$. Hence, $\mathrm{Y}(\tau_{hl}^\sigma) = \theta_{ij} = z_{hl}[\rho]$. Because l is arbitrary and $\mathrm{Y}(\tau_h^\sigma) = \mathrm{Y}(\tau_{h1}^\sigma) \ldots \mathrm{Y}(\tau_{hl_h(g)}^\sigma)$, it follows that $\mathrm{Y}(\tau_h^\sigma) = (z_{h1} \ldots z_{hl_h(g)})[\rho]$. Now $(z_{h1} \ldots z_{hl_h(g)})[\rho]$ is the value of g^h applied to the arguments ($\theta_1, \ldots, \theta_{n(g)}$). Hence, $\mathrm{Y}(\tau_h^\sigma) = g^h(\theta_1, \ldots, \theta_{n(g)})$. Because h is arbitrary and $p = g(\theta_1, \ldots, \theta_{n(g)}) = (g^1(\theta_1, \ldots, \theta_{n(g)}), \ldots, g^{r(g)}(\theta_1, \ldots, \theta_{n(g)}))$, it follows that $\mathrm{Y}(\tau_i^\sigma) = p_i$, $1 \leq i \leq \mathrm{d}(\mathrm{A}) = \mathrm{r}(g)$. Thus τ corresponds to (A, p). □

[11] A replacement will be notated as a pair x/y; $z[\{x/y\}] = y$ if $z = x$, $z[\{x/y\}] = z$ otherwise.

Proposition 2. *For every non-terminal tree $\tau \in CL(G')$, there is a pair (A, p), $p \in L_G(A)$, such that τ corresponds to (A, p).*

Proof. We will show by induction on $k \in \mathbb{N}$ that the following claim holds: if $\tau \in \mathrm{CL}^k(\mathrm{G}')$, τ a non-terminal tree, then there is a pair (A, p), $p \in \mathrm{L}_G(\mathrm{A})$, such that τ corresponds to (A, p). For $k = 0$, $\mathrm{CL}^k(\mathrm{G}') = \mathrm{Lex}$. It follows from the construction of Lex that any non-terminal tree $\tau \in$ Lex is of the form $[_>[_>p, \texttt{-a}_1], [_<\texttt{a}, \emptyset]]$. The presence of τ in Lex implies that R contains the terminating rule $\mathrm{A} \to p$. Hence, $p \in \mathrm{L}_G(\mathrm{A})$, and τ corresponds to the pair (A, p).

For the induction step, pick an arbitrary non-terminal tree $\tau \in \mathrm{CL}^k(\mathrm{G}')$, $k > 0$, with a head labeled a and yield $s = s_1 \ldots s_m$, s_i being the yield of specifier τ_i^σ of τ, $1 \le i \le m$. If $\tau \in \mathrm{CL}^{k-1}(\mathrm{G}')$, the claim follows from the induction hypothesis. If $\tau \notin \mathrm{CL}^{k-1}(\mathrm{G}')$, then τ is a projection of an item $\texttt{=a}_1^s$ $\texttt{+a}_{r(g)}^s \ldots \texttt{a}_1^s$ a in Lex, $1 \le s \le |\mathrm{R}|$. Hence, R contains a non-terminating rule $r_s = \mathrm{A} \to g[\mathrm{B}_1, \ldots, \mathrm{B}_{n(g)}]$. The derivation of τ also involves the items $\texttt{=a}_{h+1}^s$ $f_{hl_h(g)} \cdots f_{h1}$ $\texttt{a}_h^s$ $\texttt{-a}_h^s$ $\texttt{-a}_h$, $1 \le h \le \mathrm{r}(g)$, and $\texttt{=b}_1 \ldots \texttt{=b}_{n(g)}$ $\texttt{a}_{r(g)+1}^s$. Assume $\beta_1, \ldots, \beta_{n(g)}$ are the trees selected by $\texttt{=b}_1 \ldots \texttt{=b}_{n(g)}$ $\texttt{a}_{r(g)+1}^s$. By theorems 3, 5 and 7, these trees are non-terminal trees. Since $\beta_1, \ldots, \beta_{n(g)}$ are closer to the lexicon than τ, the induction hypothesis applies: for each tree β_i there is a pair (B_i, p_i), $p_i = (p_{i1}, \ldots, p_{id(B_i)}) \in \mathrm{L}_G(\mathrm{B}_i)$ such that β_i corresponds to (B_i, p_i), $1 \le i \le \mathrm{n}(g)$. Hence, $p_i = (\mathrm{Y}(\beta_{i1}^\sigma), \ldots, \mathrm{Y}(\beta_{id(B_i)}^\sigma))$, $1 \le i \le \mathrm{n}(g)$. Because of rule r_s, $g(p_1, \ldots, p_{n(g)}) \in \mathrm{L}_G(\mathrm{A})$.

Since τ is a projection of item $\texttt{=a}_1^s$ $\texttt{+a}_{r(g)}^s \ldots \texttt{+a}_1^s$ a and R contains rule r_s, $m = \mathrm{r}(g) = \mathrm{d}(\mathrm{A})$, that is, τ has d(A) specifiers. An arbitrary specifier τ_h^σ of τ, $1 \le h \le \mathrm{r}(g)$, is the result of an application of *move* triggered by the licensor feature $\texttt{+a}_h^s$ and the matching licensee feature $\texttt{-a}_h^s$ in item $\texttt{=a}_{h+1}^s$ $f_{hl_h(g)} \cdots f_{h1}$ $\texttt{a}_h^s$ $\texttt{-a}_h^s$ $\texttt{-a}_h$. Thus, specifier τ_h^σ is a projection of this item. Specifier τ_h^σ does not contain the complement selected by the feature $\texttt{=a}_{h+1}^s$, because this complement has moved to become specifier τ_{h+1}^σ before specifier τ_h^σ was created. Deleting features $f_{hl_h(g)} \cdots f_{h1}$ has equipped specifier τ_h^σ with $\mathrm{l}_h(g)$ specifiers of its own. Let τ_{hl}^σ denote the specifier of τ_h^σ arising from the *move* operation triggered by the licensee feature f_{hl}, $1 \le l \le \mathrm{l}_h(g)$. By assumption, $\mathrm{Y}(\tau_h^\sigma) = s_h$. Since no phonetic features are found outside specifiers and τ_h^σ has an empty complement, $\mathrm{Y}(\tau_h^\sigma) = s_h = s_{h1} \ldots s_{hl_h(g)}$, where $\mathrm{Y}(\tau_{hl}^\sigma) = s_{hl}$, $1 \le l \le \mathrm{l}_h(g)$. Assume that the licensor feature f_{hl} involved in the creation of specifier τ_{hl}^σ is the feature $\texttt{+b}_{ij} \in \mathrm{F}_{r_s}^+$. Hence, the matching licensee feature $\texttt{-b}_{ij}$ is found in tree β_i, the head of which is labeled $\texttt{b}_i$. Then the yield of the maximal projection in β_i of the node labeled $\texttt{-b}_{ij}$ is identical to the yield of specifier τ_{hl}^σ. By assumption, $\mathrm{Y}(\tau_{hl}^\sigma) = s_{hl}$, whence $\mathrm{Y}(\beta_{ij}^\sigma) = s_{hl}$.

To determine the value of the function g applied to the arguments $(p_1, \ldots, p_{n(g)})$, any occurrence of a variable x_{pq} in the representation of the components of g will be replaced by the value $p_{pq} = \mathrm{Y}(\beta_{pq}^\sigma)$, $1 \le p \le \mathrm{n}(g)$, $1 \le q \le \mathrm{d}_i(g) = \mathrm{d}(\mathrm{B}_i)$. Let ρ be this set of replacements. Since by assumption the particular feature f_{hl} is the feature $\texttt{+b}_{ij}$, it follows from the specification of Lex that the variable z_{hl} is the variable x_{ij}. Hence, ρ contains the replacement $z_{hl}/\mathrm{Y}(\beta_{ij}^\sigma)$. Since $\mathrm{Y}(\beta_{ij}^\sigma) = s_{hl}$, this replacement is identical to the replacement z_{hl}/s_{hl}.

Since l is arbitrary, $g^h(p_1, \ldots, p_{n(g)}) = z_{h1} \ldots z_{hl_h(g)}[\rho] = s_{h1} \ldots s_{hl_h(g)}$. Since h is arbitrary, $g(p_1, \ldots, p_{n(g)}) = (g^1(p_1, \ldots, p_{n(g)}), \ldots, g^{r(g)}(p_1, \ldots, p_{n(g)})) = (s_{11} \ldots s_{1l_1(g)}, \ldots, s_{r(g)1} \ldots s_{r(g)l_{r(g)}(g)}) = (\mathrm{Y}(\tau_1^\sigma), \ldots, \mathrm{Y}(\tau_{r(g)}^\sigma)) \in \mathrm{L}_G(\mathrm{A})$. Hence, τ corresponds to $(\mathrm{A}, (\mathrm{Y}(\tau_1^\sigma), \ldots, \mathrm{Y}(\tau_{r(g)}^\sigma)))$. □

Corollary 1. *$L(G) = L(G')$.*

Proof. Assume $p \in \mathrm{L}(\mathrm{G}')$. Then there is a complete tree $\tau \in \mathrm{CL}(\mathrm{G}')$ with yield p. Since τ is a complete tree, its head is labeled $\mathtt{c}$. By theorem 8, there is a non-terminal tree $\tau' \in \mathrm{CL}(\mathrm{G}')$ which is like τ, but has a licensee feature $\mathtt{-c}_1$. It follows from proposition 2 that there is a pair $(\mathrm{A}, p) \in \mathrm{N} \times \mathrm{O}$ such that $p \in \mathrm{L}_G(\mathrm{A})$ and τ' corresponds to (A, p). Since the head of τ' is labeled $\mathtt{c}$, $\mathrm{A} = \mathrm{S}$. Hence, $p \in \mathrm{L}(\mathrm{G})$.

Assume $p \in \mathrm{L}(\mathrm{G})$. Then there is a pair $(\mathrm{S}, p) \in \mathrm{N} \times \mathrm{O}$ and $p \in \mathrm{L}_G(\mathrm{S})$. It follows from proposition 1 that there is a non-terminal tree $\tau \in \mathrm{CL}(\mathrm{G}')$ which corresponds to the pair (S, p). Hence, the head of τ is labeled $\mathtt{c}$ and $\mathrm{Y}(\tau) = p$.[12] By theorem 8, there is a complete tree $\tau' \in \mathrm{CL}(\mathrm{G}')$ which is like τ, but lacks the licensee feature $\mathtt{-c}_1$. Since τ' is a complete tree, $\mathrm{Y}(\tau') = \mathrm{Y}(\tau) = p \in \mathrm{L}(\mathrm{G}')$. □

8 Conclusion

In this paper we have shown how to construct a Minimalist Grammar G′ for an arbitrary Multiple-Context Free Grammar G such that the language generated by G′ is identical to the language generated by G. It follows that the set of languages generated by Multiple-Context Free Grammars is a subset of the set of languages generated by Minimalist Grammars. Michaelis (1998) has shown that the reverse inclusion also holds. We thus conclude that Minimalist Grammars and Multiple-Context Free Grammars are weakly equivalent. The result presented in this paper also implies that head movement and covert phrasal movement do not increase the generative power of a Minimalist Grammar.

References

P. Boullier, 1998. Proposal for a Natural Language Processing Syntactic Backbone. *Research Report N° 3342*, NRIA-Rocquencourt, `http://www.inria.fr/RRRT/RR-3342.html`.

N. Chomsky, 1995. *The Minimalist Program.* MIT Press

J. Michaelis, 1998. Derivational Minimalism is Mildly Context-Sensitive. In: *Logical Aspects of Computational Linguistics*, Grenoble.

J. Michaelis, 2001. Transforming Linear Context-Free Rewriting Systems into Minimalist Grammars. In: *this volume.*

C.J. Pollard, 1984. Generalized Phrase Structure Grammars, Head Grammars, and Natural Language. Ph.D. thesis, Stanford University.

[12] By definition 4, d(S) = 1, so τ has only one specifier.

H. Seki, T. Matsumura, M. Fujii, and T. Kasami, 1991. On Multiple Context-Free Grammars. In: *Theoretical Computer Science*, 88.

E.P. Stabler, 1997. Derivational Minimalism. In: *Logical Aspects of Computational Linguistics*, Lecture Notes in Artificial Intelligence, 1328, C. Retoré (ed.).

E.P. Stabler, 2001. Recognizing Head Movement. In: *this volume.*

E.P. Stabler and E.L. Keenan, 2000. Structural Similarity. In: *Algebraic Methods in Language Processing*, A. Nijholt, G. Scollo, T. Rus, and D. Heylen (eds.). University of Iowa.

K. Vijay-Shanker, D.J. Weir, and A.K. Joshi, 1987. Descriptions Produced by Various Grammatical Formalisms, In: *ACL Proceedings 25.*

D.J. Weir, 1988. *Characterizing Mildly Context-Sensitive Grammar Formalisms.* Ph.D. thesis, University of Pennsylvania.

Part of Speech Tagging from a Logical Point of View

Torbjörn Lager[1] and Joakim Nivre[2]

[1] Uppsala University, Department of Linguistics,
Torbjorn.Lager@ling.uu.se
[2] Växjö University, School of Mathematics and Systems Engineering,
Joakim.Nivre@msi.vxu.se

Abstract. This paper presents logical reconstructions of four different methods for part of speech tagging: Finite State Intersection Grammar, HMM tagging, Brill tagging, and Constraint Grammar. Each reconstruction consists of a first-order logical theory and an inference relation that can be applied to the theory, in conjunction with a description of data, in order to solve the tagging problem. The reconstructed methods are compared along a number of dimensions including ontology, expressive power, mode of reasoning, uncertainty, underspecification, and robustness. It is argued that logical reconstruction of NLP methods in general can lead to a deeper understanding of the knowledge and reasoning involved, and of the ways in which different methods are related.

1 Introduction

Comparing different methods for solving a particular problem is a necessary and natural part of the development of any field of science or engineering. So also in the field of NLP, where, for example, newly proposed methods for part of speech tagging are compared to already existing ones.

Unfortunately, within the field of NLP, the use of different mathematical frameworks, or idiosyncratic formalisms and notations, tends to make such activities hard. It has led to a situation where different solutions to a problem are usually compared only on the level of performance, rather than on the level of knowledge representation and inference, and where attempts to combine different methods often fail to take advantage of their respective strengths.

In an attempt to find a remedy for this situation, we want to explore ways to reconstruct different NLP methods within a single framework. We choose to work with first order predicate logic (FOPL), often considered the *lingua franca* of knowledge representation. In this paper, we reconstruct four methods for part of speech tagging: Finite State Intersection Grammar, HMM tagging, Brill tagging, and Constraint Grammar.

The common framework will allow us to compare these four tagging methods with respect to issues such as the following: What kind of inference engines are these part of speech taggers? What kind of reasoning do they perform? What

P. de Groote, G. Morrill, C. Retoré (Eds.): LACL 2001, LNAI 2099, pp. 212–227, 2001.

kind of knowledge do they exploit and how can the required knowledge be represented in first-order predicate logic? In this way, we hope to contribute to a better understanding of these particular methods and, thereby, also to demonstrate the usefulness of the methodology of logical reconstruction in general. (Further motivation for this kind of study can be found in section 2.3 below.)

2 Background

2.1 Reconstruction of Part of Speech Tagging

What does it mean to reconstruct a tagging method as a logical theory? For each method M, the reconstruction consists of two parts:

1. Specifying a FOPL theory T_M, representing the knowledge that the method uses in order to tag a sequence of words.
2. Specifying an inference relation I_M, such that the use of the inference relation for the representation will yield a solution to the tagging problem.

In addition, we need some way of representing sequences of words and their analyses. Let *yield*(s) denote the description of a sequence of words s, in the form of a set (or, equivalently, a conjunction) of ground, atomic sentences. For example, *yield*("the can smells") is:

word(1, the). word(2, can). word(3, smells).

Let *analysis*(s) denote the assignment of parts of speech to positions in s, again in the form of a set of ground, atomic sentences. For example, we assume that *analysis*("the can smells") is:

pos(1, dt). pos(2, nn). pos(3, vb).

Throughout the paper, we will use the simple example of tagging the string *the can smells*, which has the advantage of not requiring too much space. We will assume that the correct analysis is the one given above.

Finally, we note that, even if we adopt FOPL as our common framework, some of our reconstructions will only make use of a subset of the full system (e.g. Horn clause logic). We will also apply different inference strategies for different theories. However, this does not alter the fact that the methods are reconstructed within the same framework, although it may say something about the expressive power or inference mechanisms required for reconstructing different methods.

2.2 Ontology

A commitment to FOPL does not carry with it a commitment to a particular ontology. Before we continue, we therefore need to say something about our conceptualization of the objects, properties and relations in our domain. For each of the methods we will talk about three kinds of things:

1. Positions in a text (represented by integers)
2. Word forms
3. Part of speech tags

We have tried to be as uniform as possible here, and the only variation is that for one of the methods – the CG approach – we will also talk about sets of part of speech tags. Furthermore, for one of the methods – the HMM approach – we also need to refer to probabilities (represented as real numbers in the interval $[0, 1]$). Thus, positions, word forms, tags, sets of tags, and probabilities, are the individuals in our ontology; they will be values of variables and arguments of predicates in our theories.

As for properties and relations, all theories will include the predicates *word* and *pos* introduced in section 2.1, as well as the ordinary operations of arithmetic (notably $+$ and $-$). Additional properties and relations will differ from one theory to the other. In fact, the comparison will show that there is an interesting tradeoff between expressive power, ontological assumptions, and the kind of properties and relations distinguished, where abundance in one domain can make up for austerity in others.

2.3 Why Logical Reconstruction?

There are several reasons for wanting to logically reconstruct a method M (or a number of methods M_1 to M_n) for solving a particular NLP problem:

- It allows us – even forces us – to clarify and make more precise a formulation of a method which is vague and open to interpretation. And even if the original formulation of M is simple and clear enough, looking at it from another angle may bring new insights. In any case, it may advance our understanding of M, its strengths and weaknesses.
- It may facilitate the comparison of two different methods M_i and M_j for solving the same problem, especially on the level of knowledge representation and inference.
- It may facilitate the combination of two different methods M_i and M_j in a way that leads to a better overall solution to the problem at hand.
- It may put us in a position to find novel implementation techniques for M. In particular, T_M in combination with a theorem prover implementing I_M may turn out to be a perfectly practical implementation of M.
- It allows us to regard standard implementation techniques of M as special purpose inference engines for the kind of representations that T_M exemplifies.
- By factoring out the knowledge component T_M from a method M, we may be able to find interesting novel uses for T_M which M was not designed for in the first place.
- It may allow us to come up with better ideas for interfacing components dealing with different NLP tasks. For example, in the case of part of speech taggers, it may help us to discover new ways to interface a tagger with a lexicon, or a tagger with a parser.

- It may give us more to say about the acquisition of knowledge for a particular method M. For example, expressing the knowledge in a logical framework may enable us to use inductive logic programming methods.

In the sequel, we will return to these points as they become relevant in the discussion of different methods for part of speech tagging.

3 Part of Speech Tagging Reconstructed

3.1 Part of Speech Tagging as Deduction I

In Finite-State Intersection Grammar (Koskenniemi 1990), sequences of words, rules, and analyses are all represented as finite-state automata (FSAs). Applying the rules to a tagged sequence of word means intersecting the automaton representing the tagged sequence with the automata representing the rules. Each path through the resulting FSA represents a possible analysis of the word sequence.

The particular kind of logic that will be used to reconstruct this method has clauses of the following form:

$$a_1; \ldots; a_k \leftarrow b_1, \ldots, b_n$$

That is, the consequent of a clause may consist of a disjunction of atomic formulas.[1] Explicit negative information can be given as follows:

$$\leftarrow b_1, \ldots, b_n$$

A collection of such clauses forms a disjunctive theory. This logic has the expressive power of full first order predicate logic.

It is well-known that every model of a logic program can be represented by a set of ground atomic formulas. Furthermore, a model M is a minimal model of a theory T if there exists no other model of T which is included (in the set-theoretic sense) in M. Whereas a theory in the language of pure Prolog always has exactly one unique minimal model, a disjunctive theory in general does not (see, e.g., Fernández and Minker 1992).

The (disjunctive) minimal model state of a theory T is the set of positive ground disjunctions all of whose minimal models satisfy T. Thus it provides a single, and often a very compact, representation of a set of minimal models. The minimal model state follows deductively from the set of constraints in union with the goal/query:

$$T \cup g \vdash mms$$

An interesting special case is:

$$T \cup g \vdash \bot$$

This means that $T \cup g$ is inconsistent, and thus has no model.

[1] For reasons we need not touch upon here, clauses must be range-restricted, which means that all variables occurring in a clause must occur in at least one of the body atoms $b_1, \ldots, b_n$.

Theorem provers have been built – so called model generation theorem provers – which given a set of sentences in a disjunctive logic are able to generate (representations of) the corresponding set of minimal models or the corresponding minimal model state. One example is DisLog (Seipel and Thöne 1994).

In Lager (1998), it was proposed that the essence of the knowledge available to a FSIG tagger is captured by a disjunctive theory, such as the following:

pos(P, dt) ← word(P, the).
pos(P, nn) ; pos(P,vb) ← word(P, can).
pos(P, nn) ; pos(P,vb) ← word(P, smells).

← pos(P1, dt), P2 is P1+1, pos(P2, vb).
← pos(P1, nn), P2 is P1+1, pos(P2, nn).

Tagging consists in trying to find a minimal model state corresponding to a non-empty set of minimal models for the grammar in union with *yield*(*s*).

$$T \cup \mathit{yield}(s) \vdash \mathit{analysis}(s)$$

The parts of speech of the individual words can be read off from the minimal model state. In this framework, part of speech tagging can fail, and this happens when

$$T \cup \mathit{yield}(s) \vdash \bot$$

i.e., when the constraints in union with the description of the input has no model. In Finite-State Intersection Grammar, this corresponds to an FSA with just one non-final start state with no outgoing transitions.

Tagging may also fail to eliminate all ambiguity, in which case the minimal model state will contain disjunctive formulas. For example, the theory

pos(P, pn) ; pos(P, dt) ← word(P, what).
pos(P, nn) ; pos(P, vb) ← word(P, question).

← pos(P1, dt), P2 is P1+1, pos(P2, vb).

word(1, what). word(2, question).

has three minimal models. The corresponding unique minimal model state is

pos(1, dt) ; pos(1, pn).	word(1, what).
pos(2, vb) ; pos(2, nn).	word(2, question).
pos(1, pn) ; pos(2, nn).	

In Finite-State Intersection Grammar, this corresponds to a determinized and minimized FSA with three paths leading from the start state to the final state, one path for each analysis.

This way of axiomatizing part of speech tagging has the same properties as Finite State Intersection Grammar in terms of uniformity of representations, order independence, (lack of) robustness, and 'packing' of analysis results. In a way, it is also the simplest and most natural way of using logic to capture the fundamental flow of information in part of speech tagging, and – as we shall see – an interesting point of departure for comparisons with other approaches.

3.2 Part of Speech Tagging as Probabilistic Abduction

In a typical Hidden Markov Model (HMM) for part of speech tagging there are states (representing parts of speech or sequences thereof), transitions between states, and symbols (words) emitted by the states. There are two kinds of probabilities associated with a HMM: transition probabilities, i.e. the probability of a transition from one state to another, and output probabilities, i.e. the probability of a certain state emitting a certain word. An HMM tagger tries to find the sequence of state transitions most likely to have generated the input sequence of words.

The key idea here is that if we conceive of the sequence of words as an observation and the sequence of state transitions as a possible explanation for the observation, then HMM tagging has a very abductive flavor. Consequently, HMM tagging will be formalized using the framework of Probabilistic Horn Abduction, which is a simple framework for knowledge representation in Horn-clause logic (Poole 1993a), and for using a special purpose inference engine to reason with it (Poole 1993b). The system is capable of selecting the most probable abductive explanation among the competing ones. The following brief description of the framework closely follows Poole (1993a), to which the reader is referred for further information.

A definite clause is of the form

$$a \leftarrow b_1, \ldots, b_n$$

where a and each b_i are atomic symbols. A disjoint declaration is of the form

$$\text{disjoint}([h_1 : p_1, \ldots, h_n : p_n]).$$

where each h_i is atomic, and each p_i is a real number $0 \leq p_i \leq 1$ such that $\sum_i p_i = 1$. Any variable appearing in one h_i must appear in all of the h_i (i.e., all the h_i share the same variables). The h_i are referred to as possible hypotheses.

A probabilistic Horn abduction theory is a collection of definite clauses and disjoint declarations such that if a ground atom h is an instance of a possible hypothesis in one disjoint declaration, then it is not an instance of another hypothesis in any of the disjoint declarations, nor is it an instance of the head of any clause.

If g is a closed formula describing an observation, an explanation of g from a probabilistic Horn abduction theory is a set of hypotheses $H = \{h_1, \ldots, h_n\}$, where each h_i is a ground instance of a possible hypothesis. Each explanation H is associated with a probability $P(H)$. In fact, all of the probabilistic calculations in the system reduce to finding the probabilities of explanations. More precisely, the probability of an explanation H is computed by multiplying the probabilities of the hypotheses generated, as follows:

$$P(H) = P(h_1, \ldots, h_n) = \prod_{i=1}^{n} P(h_i)$$

In terms of probability theory, this amounts to the assumption that all the hypotheses in an explanation are mutually independent.

The probabilistic model of an HMM tagger is represented by clauses of the following form (where the first set of clauses describes relations between states and symbols, while the second set defines state transitions):

word(P, the) ← pos(P, dt), etc(P, the, dt).
word(P, can) ← pos(P, vb), etc(P, can, vb).
word(P, smells) ← pos(P, vb), etc(P, smells, vb).
word(P, can) ← pos(P, nn), etc(P, can, nn).
word(P, smells) ← pos(P, nn), etc(P, smells, nn).

pos(P, dt) ← P1 is P-1, pos(P1, start), etc(P1, dt, start).
pos(P, vb) ← P1 is P-1, pos(P1, dt), etc(P1, vb, dt).
pos(P, nn) ← P1 is P-1, pos(P1, dt), etc(P1, nn, dt).
pos(P, vb) ← P1 is P-1, pos(P1, vb), etc(P1, vb, vb).
pos(P, vb) ← P1 is P-1, pos(P1, nn), etc(P1, vb, nn).

The *etc* goals can be thought of as encoding the extra conditions, the satisfaction of which guarantees the truth of the conclusion. These goals can never be proven deductively but only assumed with a certain probability. The probabilities are defined by disjoint declarations of the following kind:

disjoint([etc(P, the, dt):1.00]).
disjoint([etc(P, can, nn):0.70, etc(P, smells, nn):0.30]).
disjoint([etc(P, can, vb):0.90, etc(P, smells, vb):0.10]).

disjoint([etc(P, dt, start):1.00]).
disjoint([etc(P, vb, dt):0.01, etc(P, nn, dt:0.99)]).
disjoint([etc(P, vb, nn):0.80, etc(P, nn, nn):0.20]).
disjoint([etc(P, vb, vb):0.20, etc(P, nn, vb):0.80]).

The first set of disjoint declarations defines the output probabilities of the corresponding HMM, while the second set defines transition probabilities.

Given a theory of this form, part of speech tagging consists in trying to abductively prove the goal *yield*(*s*), i.e. trying to find a set of hypotheses *analysis*(*s*) such that:

$$T \cup \mathit{analysis}(s) \vdash \mathit{yield}(s)$$

$$P(\mathit{analysis}(s)) = P(h_1, \ldots, h_n) = \max_{h_1,\ldots,h_n} \prod_{i=1}^{n} = P(h_i)$$

The part of speech tags corresponding to the yield can be read off from the abductive explanation.

Often, logically reconstructing a problem solving method may allow us to implement it in a cleaner way, and sometimes even more efficiently. This has happened before, witness research in automatic planning, where high performance deduction systems are able to outperform special purpose planning systems. In the case of our reconstruction of a statistical part of speech tagger however, it appears that it would make little sense to use a general theorem-prover – and an abductive one at that – for a task for which another very elegant and efficient procedure – the Viterbi algorithm (Viterbi 1967) – is known.

In this case, it is perhaps more interesting to take the opposite perspective, and instead regard the Viterbi algorithm as an algorithm for abduction. As such, it is able to perform a best-first search for the most probable set of hypotheses consistent with the observations, and it is able to do this very efficiently – in time proportional to the length of the word sequence. Actually, we would like to suggest that since the kind of HMM part of speech tagger described in this paper is commonly regarded as the canonical part of speech tagger (Charniak 1997) then tagging as probabilistic abduction has already been used for tagging millions and millions of words from running texts.

Before concluding this section, we will take up one other issue discussed in section 2.3, namely the claim that reconstructing different theories in one formal framework may enable us to see more clearly how they can be combined in a principled way. For example, the reconstructions so far have shown that the knowledge exploited by the HMM approach and the FSIG approach, albeit formalized differently, can nevertheless be related, and that it should therefore be possible to combine the two methods. Let us briefly consider how this could be done.

A simple way of combining an HMM-like and an FSIG-like tagger is by adding a set C of integrity constraints to the HMM framework, explicitly expressed as FOPL clauses. (Adding integrity constraints to an abductive framework is a common strategy for reducing the number of possible explanations.) Presumably, we would like to have clauses in C expressing the kind of knowledge that an HMM cannot (easily) capture, e.g. constraints such as "a sentence must contain a finite verb".

The inference procedure to go with this is once again abduction, but of a slightly more general form than before. Part of speech tagging consists in trying to find a set of hypotheses *analysis*(s) such that:

$$T \cup \mathit{analysis}(s) \vdash \mathit{yield}(s)$$

$$T \cup C \cup \mathit{analysis}(s) \not\vdash \bot$$

$$P(\mathit{analysis}(s)) = P(h_1, \ldots, h_n) = \max_{h_1, \ldots, h_n} \prod_{i=1}^{n} P(h_i)$$

Here, C will effectively constrain *analysis*(s). Just as before, the result can be read off from the abductive explanation.

The combined system can be implemented as follows. At compile time, build automata corresponding to the constraints in C and compute their intersection. At runtime, build an automaton representing the result of performing lexical lookup of each word in the input sequence of words. (At the same time, mark each part of speech link with its lexical probability.) Intersect this automaton with the automaton representing C. The resulting automaton represents the set of minimal models of the constraints in union with the description of the input sequence of words. Finally, use the Viterbi algorithm to compute the most probable path through the automaton.[2]

3.3 Part of Speech Tagging as Deduction II

Brill tagging (Brill 1995) consists in assigning default initial tags to each word (usually the most frequent tag for that word), and then applying, in a sequence, replacement rules such as the following:

replace tag *vb* with *nn* if the previous tag is *dt*
replace tag *nn* with *vb* if the previous tag is *nn*

The secret behind the effectiveness of a Brill tagger is that rules that are very effective in the sense that they correct a lot of errors, but also are responsible for introducing new ones, are placed early in the sequence. Rules later in the sequence are not as effective, but they tend to correct some of the errors made by rules earlier in the sequence.[3]

As shown in Lager (1999), a Horn clause theory enhanced with negation can be used to represent the knowledge available to a Brill tagger:[4]

pos(P, T) ← pos3(P, T).

pos3(P, vb) ← pos2(P, nn), P1 is P-1, pos2(P1, nn).
pos3(P, T) ← pos2(P, T), P1 is P-1, ¬ pos2(P1, nn).

pos2(P, nn) ← pos1(P, vb), P1 is P-1, pos1(P1, dt).
pos2(P, T) ← pos1(P, T), P1 is P-1, ¬ pos1(P1, dt).

pos1(P, dt) ← word(P, the).
pos1(P, vb) ← word(P, can).
pos1(P, nn) ← word(P, smells).

The idea is that for each rule in the above sequence of rules a new predicate pos_i is introduced, where the number i indicates where in the sequence the rule belongs. Semantically, pos_i relates a position to a part of speech, and the formulas define this predicate in terms of the predicate pos_{i-1} plus a number

[2] In the same way as our original reconstruction of the FSIG tagger in section 3.1, this tagger will not be robust, since the set of minimal models may turn out to be empty. However, in the combined system we can always fall back on ordinary HMM tagging and apply the Viterbi algorithm to the original input in case this should happen.

[3] The Transformation-Based Learning algorithm is responsible for placing the rules in this order.

[4] To simulate classical negation, we can for example rely on Negation as Failure (NAF). However, note that whereas NAF can be regarded as a non-monotonic reasoning operator by means of which default reasoning can be implemented, it is not used in this way here. The reasoning performed here is pure classical deduction. Furthermore, since there is no recursion through negation, the logic program still has a unique minimal model.

of other predicates. Each pos_i corresponding to a replacement rule is defined by two clauses – one stating the conditions under which a part of speech tag is replaced with another part of speech tag, the other one stating the conditions under which the old tag is kept.

The purpose of this scheme is to simulate, in pure logic, the effect of composing a number of contextual replacement rules. Order is important, in that a rule in the sequence is applied to the output of rules earlier in the sequence and feed rules later in the sequence.

The analysis in this case is entailed by the theory in conjunction with the description of the input sequence of words:

$$T \cup \mathit{yield}(s) \vdash \mathit{analysis}(s)$$

In fact, Brill tagging can be modeled by performing an ordinary Prolog style constructive proof of the goal statement *pos*(P, T) (for all positions P in *s*) from the theory. This provides values for goal variables, which constitute the output of the tagging process.

This is tagging as deduction, and what is more, it is highly practical. In Lager (2000) it was shown that by converting a sequence of 280 Brill tagging rules into this format,[5] applying conventional memoing techniques in order to avoid unnecessary recomputations, and running the whole thing in Prolog, one can build a part of speech tagger capable of tagging a decent 350 words per second on a 166MHz PC. This serves to illustrate one of the points made earlier: The logical reconstruction of an NLP method may result in novel and interesting implementation techniques.

It was also shown that the resulting program can be used, not only for identifying the parts of speech of particular words, but also for searching for words having a particular parts-of-speech. It all hinges on the mode in which we choose to call the predicate. This illustrates yet another point from section 2.3, namely that the very same theory can be used in different ways, for different purposes.

3.4 Part of Speech Tagging as Deduction III

In a Constraint Grammar (CG) tagger (Karlsson *et al* 1995), a lexical lookup module assigns sets of alternative tags to occurrences of words, disregarding context. A rule application module then removes tags from such sets, on the basis of what appears in the local context, using rules such as these:

remove tag *vb* if the previous tag is *dt*
remove tag *nn* if the previous tag is *nn*

However, in order to guarantee that each word token is left with at least one tag, the rule application module adheres to the following principle: "Don't remove the last remaining tag."

[5] Actually, Prolog's if-then-else was used instead of negation as failure, but this amounts to the same thing.

A CG tagger can be made to almost never remove the correct, intended tag from a word, which leads to a high recall. However, it is also characteristic of a CG tagger that it does not always resolve all ambiguity introduced in the lexical lookup process, and this means that the precision of such a tagger may be low.

Just like Brill tagging, CG tagging can be construed as the application of an ordered sequence of contextually triggered rules, and thus the approach to axiomatization used in the previous section can be used again:

pos(P, T) ← pos3(P, T).

pos3(P, T) ← pos2(P, T0), diff(T0, [nn], T), T ≠ [ ], P1 is P-1, pos2(P1, [nn]).
pos3(P, T) ← pos2(P, T), (singleton(T) ; P1 is P-1, ¬ pos2(P1, [nn])).

pos2(P, T) ← pos1(P, T0), diff(T0, [vb], T), T ≠ [ ], P1 is P-1, pos1(P1, [dt]).
pos2(P, T) ← pos1(P, T), (singleton(T) ; P1 is P-1, ¬ pos1(P1, [dt])).

pos1(P, [dt]) ← word(P, the).
pos1(P, [nn,vb]) ← word(P, can).
pos1(P, [nn,vb]) ← word(P, smells).

Here, *diff* is a predicate that implements set difference. The "don't remove the last tag" principle is implemented by checking that the result of applying *diff* is different from the empty set before removing any tag, and by allowing any singleton to be left intact regardless of its environment.

Just as with the Brill tagger, we are interested in what is entailed by the theory in conjunction with the description of the input sequence of words:

$$T \cup \mathit{yield}(s) \vdash \mathit{analysis}(s)$$

And here too, simple Prolog style deduction is sufficient. For our simple example, we are able to prove *pos*(1, [dt]), *pos*(2, [nn]), and *pos*(3, [vb]), but nothing more.

In a Constraint Grammar we find other kinds of rules as well. For example, consider the following (sub-)sequence:

select tag *jj* if the word is *high* and the next tag is *nn*
remove tag *vb* if the word is *table*
remove tag *wbs*

The first rule removes all tags except *jj* if the given conditions are satisfied. Assuming that the lexical lookup module assigns the set [*nn*,*vb*] to the word *table*, the second rule removes the *vb* tag again unless some rule earlier in the sequence has already removed the *nn* tag. The third rule unconditionally removes the *wbs* tag unless it is the last remaining tag, something which is a sensible thing to do if *wbs* is a very uncommon tag. The order dependence between rules is very evident here, but all of these rules can be logically reconstructed along the lines given above.

Also, the right-hand sides of CG rules may consist of very complex logical conditions looking very far into the left and/or right context of the word to be disambiguated. This means that very difficult disambiguation tasks, which may be beyond the reach of other methods, can be solved in the CG framework by writing very specific rules.

Although reconstructing Constraint Grammar in this way amounts to a claim that CG tagging is in certain respects similar to Brill tagging, there are important differences as well. For example, a CG tagger cannot, once a tag is removed from a set of tags, rely on rules later in the sequence to add it back in again. Therefore, we will have to be very certain about each rule, since if it makes errors a drop in recall will result. Our experience from writing disambiguation rules in the CG style tells us that it is fairly straightforward to write such rules. The downside, of course, is that thousands of rules are needed and that coding them by hand is tedious and time consuming. Reconstructing CG in logic may help us find a way to learn them automatically from tagged corpora.

Whereas the reconstruction of Brill tagging is very faithful to the original, the Constraint Grammar reconstruction may be less so. We feel we have given a reasonable logical interpretation of the essence of Constraint Grammar, but at the same time we admit that the originators perhaps would not agree. On the other hand, this only illustrates yet another one of our points. Logical reconstruction serves to make the formulation of a method more precise, and less open to interpretation. (This of course is just the usual argument for wanting to formalize something.)

4 Discussion

Having reconstructed four different methods of part-of-speech tagging, we first note that whereas all four taggers start from the same formula – from a description of a sequence of words – the HMM tagger solves the tagging problem using abductive reasoning, while the three other taggers perform deduction. We have captured the difference as follows:

$$T \cup \mathit{analysis}(s) \vdash \mathit{yield}(s)$$

$$T \cup \mathit{yield}(s) \vdash \mathit{analysis}(s)$$

The representation of knowledge that each of the described approaches requires is determined by how it is, so to speak, driven by the mode of reasoning. Let us consider, for example, the representation of lexical knowledge, i.e., knowledge of the relation between words and their parts of speech, and let us begin by contrasting the FSIG tagger with the HMM tagger.

Since an FSIG tagger is driven by deduction, it is natural to represent the association between words and tags in a way which supports inference from words to tags, thus:

pos(P, vb) ; pos(P, nn) ← word(P, can).

Since the statistical tagger, on the other hand, is driven by abduction, the natural form of representation is one which supports inference from tags to words:

word(P, can) $\leftarrow$ pos(P, vb), etc(P, can, vb).
word(P, can) $\leftarrow$ pos(P, nn), etc(P, can, nn).

A moment of reflection reveals that some of what we know about the association between words and parts of speech can be expressed in the form of equivalences such as the following:

word(P, can) $\leftrightarrow$ (pos(P, vb), etc(P, can, vb)) ; (pos(P, nn), etc(P, can, nn)).

The FSIG representation follows logically from this equivalence, and so does the HMM representation. But they capture different parts, where neither follows logically from the other. Thus, in this respect, FSIG tagging and HMM tagging may be said to exploit the same kind of knowledge, but to represent it in different (but not incompatible) ways.

At first sight, the lexical representations of the Brill tagger looks similar to those of the FSIG tagger, since they support reasoning from words to tags:

pos1(P, vb) $\leftarrow$ word(P, can).

It is important to note, though, that the predicate pos_1 appearing in the head of this clause is not the same as the predicate *pos* appearing in the HMM and FSIG representations (as well as in the final analysis). Thus, the formula above is not a statement about a word and its actual part(s) of speech; it is a statement about a word and its default part of speech. Taken as a statement of the former kind it would simply be false.

This points to a crucial difference between the representation of lexical knowledge in HMM and FSIG, on the one hand, and Brill tagging, on the other. Whereas the former two theories contain statements which purport to be true about words and their actual parts of speech, and which may therefore be evaluated in the absence of any other knowledge (e.g., knowledge about constraints on possible sequences of parts of speech), the latter theory is only meaningful in relation to another theory somehow relating default tags to actual tags and can therefore not be evaluated in isolation.

In Constraint Grammar, finally, lexical rules also support reasoning from words to tags. In contrast to the Brill tagger, but in accordance with the FSIG tagger, the CG lexical rules also say something which purports to be true about words and their parts of speech, although this time expressed in terms of sets of tags, rather than using disjunction.

We can see in these different representations four different ways to handle the uncertainty that pervades knowledge about language. The FSIG approach uses disjunction to represent ambiguity in the relation between words and tags. By contrast, the HMM approach uses a weak logical formalism in which virtually every statement about relations between words and tags would be too strong, if it were not for the probabilities that can be associated with them.

The Brill tagging approach is similar to the HMM approach in that it avoids the use of disjunction and formulates statements that prima facie are too strong. But these statements are not taken to be probabilistic in nature. Instead, they are taken to express defaults, that can be overridden by other parts of the theory.

Finally, although the CG approach is similar to the Brill approach in certain ways, it does not handle uncertainty in the same way. Rather, it relies on its different ontology – a world containing sets of tags – in such a way that the uncertainty that possibly remains after we have applied a sequence of rules is captured, not by disjunctions as in FSIG, but by sets that contain more than one tag. Thus, this is an example of how a richer ontology can compensate for lack of expressive power in the formalism.

However, using this simple strategy, the CG approach cannot cope with all the uncertainty that the FSIG approach can cope with. For example, consider again the phrase *what question*, where *what* can be either a determiner or a pronoun, and where *question* can be either a noun or a verb. Given a constraint that rules out determiner followed by verb, there still remains three alternatives ($dt+nn$, $pn+nn$, and $pn+vb$). This poses no problem for the FSIG approach (cf. section 3.1), but the CG approach cannot even represent it, since removing a tag from either word leaves us with only two remaining alternatives.

It is well known that "the expressive power of FOPL determines not so much what can be said, but what can be left unsaid" (Levesque and Brachman 1985). This is exactly the reason why disjunction and negation are used in the FSIG approach: the linguistic knowledge is uncertain and disjunction and negation are two of the instruments provided by FOPL for representing uncertain knowledge.

However, it can be argued that disjunction and negation are blunt instruments, which cannot cope with all subtleties involved in reasoning under uncertainty and thus that we need probability theory as well. That is why probability theory is used in the HMM approach, while the Brill tagging approach uses its fairly weak expressive power to formulate layers of defaults, exceptions to defaults, exceptions to exceptions to defaults, etc.

On the other hand, in the context of sufficient additional information, sound conclusions can perhaps be drawn that (occasionally) lead us to the only possible analyses, not just the most probable ones, and here we have another approach to coping with uncertainty: Just throw more knowledge at it, and it may go away! The moral implicit in this strategy is: "Don't guess if you know." (Tapanainen and Voutilainen 1994). This is the strategy used in both FSIG and CG, while the representations used in HMM tagging and Brill tagging seems to be less amenable to such an approach.

However, the unmitigated use of this strategy is not without drawbacks either. Both FSIG and CG may fail to resolve all ambiguities in the input, in cases where the information available is insufficient, and FSIG may even fail to produce an analysis at all because all the alternatives are eliminated (a pitfall that CG avoids through the "don't remove the last tag" principle). By contrast, both HMM and Brill always assign one and only one tag to each word.

We summarize our comparison in Table 1, where we contrast our reconstructions of the four methods along the dimensions of ontology, expressive power, mode of reasoning, uncertainty, underspecification, and robustness.

Table 1. Comparison, on the level of representation and inference, between four methods for part of speech tagging.

	FSIG	HMM	BRILL	CG
Ontology: What kind of entities does the tagger reason over?	positions words tags	positions words tags probabilities	positions words tags	positions words sets of tags
Expressive means: What do we need in the language in order to simulate the method?	disjunctive logic with negation	Horn clause logic	Horn clause logic with negation in antecedent	Horn clause logic with negation in antecedent
Mode of reasoning	deductive	abductive	deductive	deductive
How does the method deal with uncertainty?	disjunction negation	probabilities	default reasoning	sets of tags
Underspecification: Does the final analysis represent remaining ambiguity?	yes (disjunction)	no	no	yes (sets of tags)
Robustness: Does the method always produce an analysis?	no	yes	yes	yes

5 Conclusion

In this paper, we have presented logical reconstructions of four different methods for part of speech tagging: Finite State Intersection Grammar, HMM tagging, Brill tagging, and Constraint Grammar. Each reconstruction consists of a first-order logical theory and an inference relation that can be applied to the theory, in conjunction with a description of data, in order to solve the tagging problem. We hope to have provided a "proof of concept" for the methodology of logical reconstruction, in particular by showing how the reconstructed methods can be compared along a number of dimensions including ontology, expressive power, mode of reasoning, uncertainty, underspecification, and robustness, but also, by way of small examples, how the methodology of logical reconstruction may allow us to discover more fruitful ways of combining methods, to explore novel implementation techniques, and more generally, to increase our understanding of the issues involved when knowledge about language is applied to language in use.

References

[1995]Brill, E. (1995) Transformation-Based Error-Driven Learning and Natural Language Processing: A Case Study in Part of Speech Tagging. *Computational Linguistics* 21, 543–565.

[1997]Charniak, E. (1997) Statistical Techniques for Natural Language Parsing. *AI Magazine* 18(4), 33–44.

[1992]Fernández, J. A. and Minker, J. (1992) Disjunctive Deductive Databases. In *Proceedings of the Logic Programming and Automated Reasoning Conference.*

[1995]Karlsson, F., Voutilainen, A., Heikkilä, J., Anttila, A. (eds) (1995) *Constraint Grammar: A Language-Independent System for Parsing Unrestricted Text.* Mouton de Gruyter.

[1990]Koskenniemi, K. (1990) Finite-State Parsing and Disambiguation. In *Proceedings of COLING'90*, Helsinki, Finland.

[1998]Lager, T. (1998) Logic for Part of Speech Tagging and Shallow Parsing. In *Proceedings of NODALIDA'98*, Copenhagen, Denmark.

[1999]Lager, T. (1999) The μ-TBL System: Logic Programming Tools for Transformation-Based Learning. In *Proceedings of CoNLL'99*, Bergen, Norway.

[2000]Lager, T. (2000) A Logic Programming Approach to Word Expert Engineering. In *Proceedings of ACIDCA 2000: Workshop on Corpora and Natural Language Processing*, Monastir, Tunisia.

[1985]Levesque, H. and Brachman, R. (1985) A Fundamental Tradeoff in Knowledge Representation and Reasoning. In Brachman, R. and Reiter, H. (eds) *Readings in Knowledge Representation.* Morgan Kaufman.

[1993a]Poole, D. (1993a) Probabilistic Horn Abduction and Bayesian Networks. *Artificial Intelligence* 64(1), 81–129.

[1993b]Poole, D. (1993b) Logic Programming, Abduction and Probability: A Top-Down Anytime Algorithm for Computing Prior and Posterior Probabilities. *New Generation Computing*, 11(3-4), 377–400.

[1994]Seipel, D. and Thöne, H. (1994) DisLog – A System for Reasoning in Disjunctive Deductive Databases. In *Proceedings of the International Workshop on the Deductive Approach to Information Systems and Databases 1994 (DAISD'94).*

[1994]Tapanainen, P. and Voutilainen, A. (1994) Tagging Accurately – Don't Guess If You Know. In *Proceedings of the Fourth Conference on Applied Natural Language Processing*, Stuttgart, Germany.

[1967]Viterbi, A. J. (1967) Error Bounds for Convolutional Codes and an Asymptotically Optimal Algorithm. *IEEE Transactions on Information Theory* IT-13(2), 260–269.

Transforming Linear Context–Free Rewriting Systems into Minimalist Grammars*

Jens Michaelis

Universität Potsdam, Institut für Linguistik,
PF 601553, 14415 Potsdam, Germany
michael@ling.uni-potsdam.de

Abstract. The type of a minimalist grammar (MG) as introduced by Stabler [11,12] provides an attempt of a rigorous algebraic formalization of the new perspectives adopted within the linguistic framework of transformational grammar due to the change from GB–theory to minimalism. Michaelis [6] has shown that MGs constitute a subclass of mildly context–sensitive grammars in the sense that for each MG there is a weakly equivalent linear context–free rewriting system (LCFRS). However, it has been left open in [6], whether the respective classes of string languages derivable by MGs and LCFRSs coincide. This paper completes the picture by showing that MGs in the sense of [11] and LCFRSs give in fact rise to the same class of derivable string languages.

1 Introduction

The type of a minimalist grammar (MG) as introduced in [11,12] provides an attempt of a rigorous algebraic formalization of the new perspectives adopted within the linguistic framework of transformational grammar due to the change from GB–theory to minimalism. As shown in [6], MGs expose a subclass of mildly context–sensitive grammars in the sense that for each MG there is a weakly equivalent linear context–free rewriting system (LCFRS). More recently, in [1] it has been pointed out how the method to convert an MG into a weakly equivalent LCFRS can be employed to define a agenda–driven, chart–based recognizer for minimalist languages solving the recognition problem as to a given MG and an input string in deterministic polynomial time. Nevertheless, it has been left open until now, whether the respective classes of string languages derivable by MGs and LCFRSs coincide. This paper completes the picture by proving each LCFRS to necessarily generate a string language which indeed is also an MG–definable string language. Hence, one of the interesting outcomes is that MGs, beside LCFRSs, join to a series of formalism classes—among which there is e.g. the class of *multicomponent tree adjoining grammars (MCTAGs)* (cf. [16])—all generating

* This work has been carried out funded by DFG–grant STA 519/1-1. I especially wish to thank Kai–Uwe Kühnberger and Ed Stabler for inspiring discussions.

P. de Groote, G. Morrill, C. Retoré (Eds.): LACL 2001, LNAI 2099, pp. 228–244, 2001.

the same class of string languages, which is known to be a *substitution–closed full AFL*. Furthermore, another consequence, type specific of the MG–formalism, arises from our particular construction of a weakly equivalent MG for a given LCFRS. The crucial point implied is that each MG can be transformed into a weakly equivalent MG that does not employ any kind of head movement or covert phrasal movement. This does not only prove a quite simpler formal setting for MGs to have the same weak generative capacity as the original one, but this also chimes in with current developments within the linguistic framework.

2 Linear Context–Free Rewriting Systems

The class of *linear context–free rewriting systems (LCFRSs)* [15,16] constitutes a proper subclass of the class of *multiple context–free grammars (MCFGs)* [10] where in terms of derivable string languages both classes have identical generative power. MCFGs in their turn expose a special subtype of *generalized context–free grammars (GCFGs)* as introduced in [8].

Definition 2.1 ([8]). A five–tuple $G = \langle N, O, F, R, S\rangle$ for which (G1)–(G5) hold is called a *generalized context–free grammar (GCFG).*

(G1) N is a finite non–empty set of *nonterminal symbols.*
(G2) O is a set of *(linguistic) objects.*
(G3) F is a finite subset of $\bigcup_{n\in\mathbb{N}} F_n\setminus\{\emptyset\}$, where F_n is the set of partial functions from $\langle O\rangle^n$ into O, i.e. $F_0\setminus\{\emptyset\}$ is the set of all constants in O.[1]
(G4) $R \subseteq \bigcup_{n\in\mathbb{N}}(F\cap F_n)\times N^{n+1}$ is a finite set of *(rewriting) rules.*[2]
(G5) $S\in N$ is the distinguished *start symbol.*

A rule $r = \langle f, A_0A_1\cdots A_n\rangle \in (F\cap F_n)\times N^{n+1}$ for some $n\in\mathbb{N}$ is generally written $A_0 \to f(A_1,\dots,A_n)$, and also just $A_0\to f()$ in case $n = 0$. If the latter, i.e. $f()\in O$, then r is *terminating*, otherwise r is *nonterminating.* For each $A\in N$ and each $k\in\mathbb{N}$ the set $L^k_G(A)\subseteq O$ is given recursively in the following sense:

(L1) $\theta\in L^0_G(A)$ for each terminating rule $A\to\theta\in R$.
(L2) $\theta\in L^{k+1}_G(A)$, if $\theta\in L^k_G(A)$, or if there is a rule $A\to f(A_1,\dots,A_n)\in R$ and there are $\theta_i\in L^k_G(A_i)$ for $1\le i\le n$ such that $\langle\theta_1,\dots,\theta_n\rangle\in Dom(f)$ and $f(\theta_1,\dots,\theta_n)=\theta$.[3]

[1] $\mathbb{N}$ denotes the set of all non–negative integers. For $n\in\mathbb{N}$ and any sets $M_1,\dots,M_n$, $\prod_{i=1}^n M_i$ is the set of all n–tuples $\langle m_1,\cdots,m_n\rangle$ with i–th component $m_i\in M_i$, where $\prod_{i=1}^0 M_i=\{\emptyset\}$, $\prod_{i=1}^1 M_i = M_1$, and $\prod_{i=1}^j M_i=\prod_{i=1}^{j-1}M_i\times M_j$ for $1<j\le n$. We write $\langle M\rangle^n$ instead of $\prod_{i=1}^n M_i$ if for some set M, $M_i=M$ for $1\le i\le n$.
[2] For any set M and $n\in\mathbb{N}$, M^{n+1} is the set of all finite strings in M of length $n+1$. M^* is the Kleene closure of M, including ϵ, the empty string. M_ϵ is the set $M\cup\{\epsilon\}$.
[3] For each partial function g from some set M_1 into some set M_2, $Dom(g)$ denotes the domain of g, i.e. the set of all $x\in M_1$ for which $g(x)$ is defined.

We say A *derives* θ *(in G)* if $\theta \in L_G^k(A)$ for some $A \in N$ and $k \in \mathbb{N}$. In this case θ is called an *A–phrase (in G)*. For each $A \in N$ the *language derivable from A (by G)* is the set $L_G(A)$ of all A–phrases (in G), i.e. $L_G(A) = \bigcup_{k \in \mathbb{N}} L_G^k(A)$. The set $L_G(S)$, also denoted by $L(G)$, is the *language derivable by G*.

Definition 2.2. An GCFG G_1 and G_2 are *weakly equivalent* if $L(G_1) = L(G_2)$.

Definition 2.3 ([10]). For $m \in \mathbb{N} \setminus \{0\}$ an *m–multiple context-free grammar (m–MCFG)* is a GCFG $G = \langle N, O_\Sigma, F, R, S\rangle$ which satisfies (M1)–(M4).

(M1) $O_\Sigma = \bigcup_{i=1}^m \langle \Sigma^* \rangle^i$ for some finite non–empty set Σ of *terminal symbols* with $\Sigma \cap N = \emptyset$. Hence O_Σ, the set of objects, is the set of all non–empty, finite tuples of finite strings in Σ such that each tuple has at most m components.

(M2) For each $f \in F$ let $n(f) \in \mathbb{N}$ be the *rank of f*, the number of components of an argument of f, i.e. $f \subseteq \langle O_\Sigma\rangle^{n(f)} \times O_\Sigma$. Then for each $f \in F$ there exists a number $\varphi(f) \in \mathbb{N} \setminus \{0\}$, called the *fan-out of f*, and there are numbers $d_i(f) \in \mathbb{N} \setminus \{0\}$ for $1 \leq i \leq n(f)$ such that f is a (total) function from $\prod_{i=1}^{n(f)} \langle \Sigma^* \rangle^{d_i(f)}$ into $\langle \Sigma^* \rangle^{\varphi(f)}$ for which (f1) and, in addition, the *anti-copying condition* (f2) hold.

(f1) Define $I_{Dom(f)}$ by $\{\langle i,j\rangle \in \mathbb{N} \times \mathbb{N} \,|\, 1 \leq i \leq n(f), 1 \leq j \leq d_i(f)\}$ and take $X_f = \{x_{ij} \,|\, \langle i,j\rangle \in I_{Dom(f)}\}$ to be a set of pairwise distinct variables. For $1 \leq i \leq n(f)$ let $x_i = \langle x_{i1}, \ldots, x_{id_i(f)}\rangle$. For $1 \leq h \leq \varphi(f)$ let f_h be the h–th component of f, i.e. the function f_h from $\prod_{i=1}^{n(f)} \langle \Sigma^* \rangle^{d_i(f)}$ into Σ^* such that $f(\theta) = \langle f_1(\theta), \ldots, f_{\varphi(f)}(\theta)\rangle$ for all $\theta \in \prod_{i=1}^{n(f)} \langle \Sigma^* \rangle^{d_i(f)}$. Then, for each $1 \leq h \leq \varphi(f)$ there is an $l_h(f) \in \mathbb{N}$ such that f_h can be represented by

$$(\mathrm{c}_{f_h}) \quad f_h(x_1, \ldots, x_{n(f)}) = \zeta(f_{h0})\, z(f_{h1})\, \zeta(f_{h1}) \cdots z(f_{hl_h(f)})\, \zeta(f_{hl_h(f)})$$

with $\zeta(f_{hl}) \in \Sigma^*$ for $0 \leq l \leq l_h(f)$ and $z(f_{hl}) \in X_f$ for $1 \leq l \leq l_h(f)$.

(f2) Define $I_{Range(f)}$ by $\{\langle h,l\rangle \in \mathbb{N} \times \mathbb{N} \mid 1 \leq h \leq \varphi(f), 1 \leq l \leq l_h(f)\}$ and let g_f denote the binary relation on $I_{Dom(f)} \times I_{Range(f)}$ such that $\langle\langle i,j\rangle, \langle h,l\rangle\rangle \in g_f$ iff $x_{ij} = z(f_{hl})$. Then g_f is a partial function from $I_{Dom(f)}$ into $I_{Range(f)}$,[4] i.e. there is at most one occurrence of each $x_{ij} \in X_f$ within all righthand sides of (c_{f_1})–$(\mathrm{c}_{f_{\varphi(f)}})$.

(M3) There is a function d_G from N to $\mathbb{N}$ such that, if $A_0 \to f(A_1, \ldots, A_n) \in R$ for some $n \in \mathbb{N}$ then $\varphi(f) = d_G(A_0)$ and $d_i(f) = d_G(A_i)$ for $1 \leq i \leq n$, where $\varphi(f)$ and $d_i(f)$ for $1 \leq i \leq n$ are as in (M2).

(M4) $d_G(S) = 1$ for the start symbol $S \in N$.

[4] Note that this implies that g_f is an injective, but not necessarily total, function from $I_{Dom(f)}$ onto $I_{Range(f)}$.

The *rank of G*, denoted by *rank*(G), is defined as $\max\{rank(f) \mid f \in F\}$. Note that $L(G) \subseteq \Sigma^*$ by (M4). In case that $m = 1$ and that each $f \in F \setminus F_0$ is the concatenation function from $(\Sigma^*)^{n+1}$ to Σ^* for some $n \in \mathbb{N}$, G is a context–free grammar (CFG) and $L(G)$ a context–free language (CFL) in the usual sense.

Definition 2.4. Each $L \subseteq \Sigma^*$ for some set Σ such that there is an m–MCFG G with $L = L(G)$ is an *m–multiple context-free language (m–MCFL)*.

Definition 2.5 ([15]). For $m \in \mathbb{N} \setminus \{0\}$ an m–MCFG $G = \langle N, O_\Sigma, F, R, S\rangle$ according to Definition 2.3 is called an *m–linear context-free rewriting system (m–LCFRS)* if for each $f \in F$ the *non-erasure condition* (f3) holds in addition to (f1) and (f2).

(f3) The function g_f from (f2) is total, i.e. each $x_{ij} \in X_f$ has to appear in one of the righthand sides of (c_{f_1})–$(c_{f_{\varphi(f)}})$.

Definition 2.6. Each $L \subseteq \Sigma^*$ for some set Σ such that there is an m–LCFRS G with $L = L(G)$ is an *m–linear context-free rewriting language (m–LCFRL)*.

For each $m \in \mathbb{N} \setminus \{0\}$, a given m–MCFG, m–MCFL, m–LCFRS, or m–LCFRL is likewise referred to simply as an *MCFG*, *MCFL*, *LCFRS*, or *LCFRL*, respectively.

The class of all MCFGs and the class of all LCFRSs are essentially the same. The latter was first described in [15] and has been studied in some detail in [16].[5] The MCFG–definition technically generalizes the LCFRS–definition by omitting the non–erasure condition (f3). But this bears no consequences as to matters of weak generative capacity as is fixed by Lemma 2.2 in [10]. Looking at the construction that Seki et al. [10] propose in order to end up with a weakly equivalent LCFRS for a given MCFG, it becomes clear that the following holds:

Corollary 2.7. *For each m–MCFG* $G = \langle N, O_\Sigma, F, R, S\rangle$ *with* $m \in \mathbb{N} \setminus \{0\}$ *there exists a weakly equivalent m–LCFRS* $G' = \langle N', O_\Sigma, F', R', S'\rangle$ *such that* $rank(G') \leq rank(G)$.

Combining this result with Theorem 11 in [9] we get

Corollary 2.8. *For every MCFG G there is an LCFRS G′ with* $rank(G') \leq 2$ *deriving the same language as G.*

---

[5] In particular, Weir [16] carefully develops the leading idea to come up with the definition of LCFRSs: the specific aim of the LCFRS–formalism is to provide a perspective under which several types of grammar formalisms, that all can be restated (in terms of weak equivalence) as specific GCFG–types dealing with more or less distinct types of objects, become directly comparable. This is achieved by taking the functions of the respective GCFGs to be simply function symbols rather than concrete operators applying to corresponding (tuples of) objects. Then, these function symbols are interpreted as *unique yield functions* which map the derived objects to tuples of terminal strings.

3 Minimalist Grammars

Throughout this section we let $\neg Syn$ and Syn be a set of *non–syntactic features* and a set of *syntactic features*, respectively, according to (F1)–(F3).

(F1) $\neg Syn$ is a finite set partitioned into a set *Phon* of *phonetic features* and a set *Sem* of *semantic features.*

(F2) *Syn* is a finite set disjoint from $\neg Syn$ and partitioned into a set *Base* of *(basic) categories*, a set *Select* of *selectors*, a set *Licensees* of *licensees* and a set *Licensors* of *licensors.* For each $x \in Base$, usually typeset as `x`, the existence of three pairwise distinct elements in *Select*, respectively denoted by `=x`, `=X` and `X=`, is possible. For each $x \in Licensees$, usually depicted in the form `-x`, the existence of two distinct elements in *Licensors*, denoted by `+x` and `+X`, is possible. Selectors and licensors of the form `=X`, `X=` or `+X` are said to be *strong*, those of the form `=x` or `+x` are said to be *weak.*

(F3) `c` is a distinguished element from *Base*, the *completeness category.*

We take *Feat* to be the set defined by $\neg Syn \cup Syn$.

Definition 3.1. A *tree domain* is a non–empty set $N_\tau \subseteq \mathbb{N}^*$ which is *prefix closed* and *left closed*, i.e. for all $\chi \in \mathbb{N}^*$ and $i \in \mathbb{N}$ it holds that $\chi \in N_\tau$ if $\chi\chi' \in N_\tau$ for some $\chi' \in \mathbb{N}^*$, and $\chi i \in N_\tau$ if $\chi j \in N_\tau$ for some $j \in \mathbb{N}$ with $i < j$.

Definition 3.2. A five–tuple $\tau = \langle N_\tau, \triangleleft_\tau^*, \prec_\tau, <_\tau, label_\tau \rangle$ fulfilling (E1)–(E4) is called an *expression (over Feat).*

(E1) $\langle N_\tau, \triangleleft_\tau^*, \prec_\tau \rangle$ is a finite, binary (ordered) tree defined in the usual sense, where N_τ is the finite, non–empty set of *nodes*, and where $\triangleleft_\tau^*$ and $\prec_\tau$ are the binary relations of *dominance* and *precedence* on N_τ, respectively. Thus, $\triangleleft_\tau^*$ is the reflexive–transitive closure of $\triangleleft_\tau \subseteq N_\tau \times N_\tau$, the relation of *immediate dominance*, and each non–leaf in $\langle N_\tau, \triangleleft_\tau^*, \prec_\tau \rangle$ has exactly two children.[6]

(E2) $<_\tau \subseteq N_\tau \times N_\tau$ is the asymmetric relation of *(immediate) projection (in τ)* that holds for any two siblings in $\langle N_\tau, \triangleleft_\tau^*, \prec_\tau \rangle$, i.e. each node different from the root either *(immediately) projects* over its sibling or vice versa.

(E3) $label_\tau$ is the *leaf–labeling function (of τ)* which assigns an element from $Syn^* Phon^* Sem^*$ to each leaf of $\langle N_\tau, \triangleleft_\tau^*, \prec_\tau \rangle$, i.e. each leaf–label is a finite sequence of features from *Feat.*

(E4) $\langle N_\tau, \triangleleft_\tau^*, \prec_\tau \rangle$ is a subtree of some natural tree domain interpretation.[7]

The set of all expressions over *Feat* is denoted by *Exp*(*Feat*).

---

[6] Up to an isomorphism $\langle N_\tau, \triangleleft_\tau^*, \prec_\tau \rangle$ is the *natural (tree) interpretation* of some tree domain. In other words, up to an isomorphism N_τ is a tree domain such that for all $\chi, \psi \in N_\upsilon$ it holds that $\chi \triangleleft_\tau \psi$ iff $\psi = \chi i$ for some $i \in \mathbb{N}$, and $\chi \prec_\tau \psi$ iff $\chi = \omega i \chi'$ and $\psi = \omega j \psi'$ for some $\omega, \chi', \psi' \in \mathbb{N}^*$ and $i, j \in \mathbb{N}$ with $i < j$.

[7] That is, there is some tree domain N_υ with $N_\tau \subseteq N_\upsilon$ such that, as to the natural tree interpretation $\langle N_\upsilon, \triangleleft_\upsilon^*, \prec_\upsilon \rangle$ of N_υ, the root r_τ of $\langle N_\tau, \triangleleft_\tau^*, \prec_\tau \rangle$ meets the condition that for each $x \in N_\upsilon$ it holds that $x \in N_\tau$ iff $r_\tau \triangleleft_\upsilon^* x$. Moreover it holds that $\triangleleft_\upsilon^* = \triangleleft_\tau^* \restriction_{N_\upsilon \times N_\upsilon}$ and $\prec_\upsilon = \prec_\tau \restriction_{N_\upsilon \times N_\upsilon}$.

Let $\tau = \langle N_\tau, \triangleleft_\tau^*, \prec_\tau, <_\tau, label_\tau \rangle \in Exp(Feat)$.

For each $x \in N_\tau$, the *head of* x *(in* τ*)*, denoted by $head_\tau(x)$, is the (unique) leaf of τ such that $x \triangleleft_\tau^* head_\tau(x)$, and such that each $y \in N_\tau$ on the path from x to $head_\tau(x)$ with $y \neq x$ projects over its sibling. The *head of* τ is the head of τ's root. τ is said to be a *head* (or *simple*) if N_τ consists of exactly one node, otherwise τ is said to be a *non–head* (or *complex*).

A *subexpression of* τ is a five–tuple $\upsilon = \langle N_\upsilon, \triangleleft_\upsilon^*, \prec_\upsilon, <_\upsilon, label_\upsilon \rangle$ such that $\langle N_\upsilon, \triangleleft_\upsilon^*, \prec_\upsilon \rangle$ is a subtree of $\langle N_\tau, \triangleleft_\tau^*, \prec_\tau \rangle$, and such that $<_\upsilon = <_\tau \restriction_{N_\upsilon \times N_\upsilon}$ and $label_\upsilon = label_\tau \restriction_{N_\upsilon}$. Thus, υ is an expression over *Feat*. The set of all subexpressions of τ is denoted by $Subexp(\tau)$.

An expression $\upsilon \in Subexp(\tau)$ is a *maximal projection (in* τ*)* if υ's root is a node $x \in N_\tau$ such that x is the root of τ, or such that $sibling_\tau(x) <_\tau x$.[8] Thus, the number of maximal projections in τ and the number of leaves of τ coincide, and two maximal projections in τ are identical in case they share the same head. We take $MaxProj(\tau)$ to be the set of all maximal projections in τ. Note that for each subexpression $\upsilon \in MaxProj(\tau)$ it holds that $MaxProj(\upsilon) \subseteq MaxProj(\tau)$.

$comp_\tau \subseteq MaxProj(\tau) \times MaxProj(\tau)$ is the binary relation such that for all $\upsilon, \phi \in MaxProj(\tau)$ it holds that $\upsilon \; comp_\tau \; \phi$ iff $head_\tau(r_\upsilon) <_\tau r_\phi$, where r_υ and r_ϕ are the roots of υ and ϕ, respectively. If $\upsilon \; comp_\tau \; \phi$ for some $\upsilon, \phi \in MaxProj(\tau)$ then ϕ is a *complement of* υ *(in* τ*)*. $comp_\tau^+$ is the transitive closure of $comp_\tau$. $Comp^+(\tau)$ is the set $\{\upsilon \mid \tau \; comp_\tau^+ \; \upsilon\}$.

$spec_\tau \subseteq MaxProj(\tau) \times MaxProj(\tau)$ is the binary relation such that for all $\upsilon, \phi \in MaxProj(\tau)$ it holds that $\upsilon \; spec_\tau \; \phi$ iff $r_\phi = sibling_\tau(x)$ for some $x \in N_\tau$ with $r_\upsilon \triangleleft_\tau^+ x \triangleleft_\tau^+ head_\tau(r_\phi)$, where r_υ and r_ϕ are the roots of υ and ϕ, respectively. If $\upsilon \; spec_\tau \; \phi$ for some $\upsilon, \phi \in MaxProj(\tau)$ then ϕ is a *specifier of* υ *(in* τ*)*. $spec_\tau^*$ is the reflexive–transitive closure of $spec_\tau$. $Spec(\tau)$ and $Spec^*(\tau)$ are the sets $\{\upsilon \mid \tau \; spec_\tau \; \upsilon\}$ and $\{\upsilon \mid \tau \; spec_\tau^* \; \upsilon\}$, respectively.

An $\upsilon \in MaxProj(\tau)$ is said to *have feature* f or, likewise, to *be with feature* f if for some $f \in Feat$ the label assigned to the head of υ by $label_\tau$ is non–empty and starts with an instance of f.

τ is *complete* if its head–label is in $\{\mathsf{c}\}Phon^*Sem^*$ and each other of its leaf–labels is in $Phon^*Sem^*$. Hence, a complete expression over *Feat* is an expression that has category c, and this instance of c is the only instance of a syntactic feature within all leaf–labels.

The *yield of* τ, denoted by $Y(\tau)$, is defined as the string which results from concatenating in "left–to–right–manner" the labels assigned to the leaves of $\langle N_\tau, \triangleleft_\tau^*, \prec_\tau \rangle$ via $label_\tau$. The *phonetic yield (of* τ*)*, denoted by $Y_{Phon}(\tau)$, is the string which results from $Y(\tau)$ by replacing all instances of non–phonetic features in $Y(\tau)$ with the empty string.

An expression $\upsilon = \langle N_\upsilon, \triangleleft_\upsilon^*, \prec_\upsilon, <_\upsilon, label_\upsilon \rangle \in Feat(Exp)$ is *(labeling preserving) isomorphic to* τ if there exists a bijective function i from N_τ onto N_υ such that $x \triangleleft_\tau y$ iff $i(x) \triangleleft_\upsilon i(y)$, $x \prec_\tau y$ iff $i(x) \prec_\upsilon i(y)$, and $x <_\tau y$ iff $i(x) <_\upsilon i(y)$ for all $x, y \in N_\tau$, and such that $label_\tau(x) = label_\upsilon(i(x))$ for all $x \in N_\tau$. This function i is an *isomorphism (from* τ *to* υ*)*.

[8] $sibling_\tau(x)$ denotes the (unique) sibling of a given $x \in N_\tau$ different to τ's root

Definition 3.3. For each given $\tau = \langle N_\tau, \triangleleft^*_\tau, \prec_\tau, <_\tau, label_\tau \rangle \in Exp(Feat)$ with $N_\tau = r_\tau N_\upsilon$ for some $r_\tau \in \mathbb{N}^*$ and some tree domain N_υ, and for each given $r \in \mathbb{N}^*$, the *expression shifting τ to r*, denoted by $(\tau)_r$, is the expression $\langle N_{\tau(r)}, \triangleleft^*_{\tau(r)}, \prec_{\tau(r)}, <_{\tau(r)}, label_{\tau(r)} \rangle \in Exp(Feat)$ with $N_{\tau(r)} = rN_\upsilon$ such that the function $i_{\tau(r)}$ from N_τ onto $N_{\tau(r)}$ with $i_{\tau(r)}(r_\tau x) = rx$ for all $x \in N_\upsilon$ constitutes an isomorphism from τ to $(\tau)_r$.[9]

Introducing a related notational convention, we assume υ and ϕ to be expressions over *Feat*, and consider the expressions $(\upsilon)_0$ and $(\phi)_1$ shifting υ to 0 and ϕ to 1, respectively. We write $[_<\upsilon, \phi]$ (respectively, $[_>\upsilon, \phi]$) in order to refer to the complex expression $\chi = \langle N_\chi, \triangleleft^*_\chi, \prec_\chi, <_\chi, label_\chi \rangle$ over *Feat* with root ϵ such that $(\upsilon)_0$ and $(\phi)_1$ are the two subexpressions of χ which roots are immediately dominated by ϵ, and such that $0 <_\chi 1$ (respectively, $1 <_\chi 0$).

We next introduce a type of MGs strongly in line with the definition given in [11]. But different to there, we do so by demanding all selection features of an MG to be weak, and all licensor features to be strong. In this sense, we only define a subtype of MGs as introduced in [11]. For this subtype there is no need to explicitly define what is meant by *(overt) head movement* or *covert (phrasal) movement*, respectively, since there are no features which potentially trigger these kinds of movement (cf. [11]). Moreover, this subtype will be sufficient to prove the class of LCFRSs to be weakly embeddable into the class of MGs.

Definition 3.4. A five–tuple $G = \langle \neg Syn, Syn, Lex, \Omega, \mathtt{c} \rangle$ that obeys (N0)–(N2) is called a *minimalist grammar (MG)*.

(N0) All syntactic features from *Select* are weak, while all syntactic features from *Licensors* are strong.

(N1) *Lex* is a *lexicon (over Feat)*, i.e. a finite subset of $Exp(Feat)$ such that for each $\tau = \langle N_\tau, \triangleleft^*_\tau, \prec_\tau, <_\tau, label_\tau \rangle \in Lex$ the set of nodes, N_τ, is a tree domain and the leaf–labeling function, $label_\tau$, maps each leaf of τ onto an element from $Select^* \, Licensors_\epsilon \, Select^* \, Base_\epsilon \, Licensees^* \, Phon^* \, Sem^*$.

(N2) The set Ω consists of the structure building functions *merge* and *move* defined w.r.t. $\neg Syn \cup Syn$ as in (me) and (mo) below, respectively.

(me) The operator *merge* is as a partial mapping from $Exp(Feat) \times Exp(Feat)$ into $Exp(Feat)$. A pair $\langle \upsilon, \phi \rangle$ of some expressions υ and ϕ over *Feat* belongs to $Dom(merge)$ if for some $\mathtt{x} \in Base$ conditions (i) and (ii) are fulfilled.

(i) υ has selector $^=\mathtt{x}$, and

(ii) ϕ has category $\mathtt{x}$.

Thus, there are $\kappa_\upsilon, \kappa_\phi \in Syn^*$ $\nu_\upsilon, \nu_\phi \in Phon^* Sem^*$ such that $^=\mathtt{x}\kappa_\upsilon\nu_\upsilon$ and $\mathtt{x}\kappa_\phi\nu_\phi$ are the head–labels of υ and ϕ, respectively. The value of $\langle \upsilon, \phi \rangle$ under *merge* is subject to two distinct subcases.

---

[9] Hence, $\langle N_{\tau(\epsilon)}, \triangleleft^*_{\tau(\epsilon)}, \prec_{\tau(\epsilon)} \rangle$ is identical to the natural tree interpretation of the tree domain N_υ. Note that by (E4), for every $\tau = \langle N_\tau, \triangleleft^*_\tau, \prec_\tau, <_\tau, label_\tau \rangle \in Exp(Feat)$ there do exist an $r_\tau \in \mathbb{N}^*$ and a tree domain N_υ with $N_\tau = r_\tau N_\upsilon$.

(me.1) $merge(\upsilon, \phi) = [_<\upsilon', \phi']$ if υ is simple,

where υ' and ϕ' are the expressions resulting from υ and ϕ, respectively, by replacing the head–labels: the head–label of υ becomes $\kappa_\upsilon \nu_\upsilon$ in υ', that of ϕ becomes $\kappa_\phi \nu_\phi$ in ϕ'. Hence, υ' and ϕ' respectively result from υ and ϕ just by deleting the instance of the feature that the corresponding head–label starts with.

(me.2) $merge(\upsilon, \phi) = [_>\phi', \upsilon']$ if υ is complex,

where υ' and ϕ' are defined the same way as in (me.1).

(mo) The operator *move* is a partial mapping from *Exp*(*Feat*) into *Exp*(*Feat*). An $\upsilon \in Exp(Feat)$ belongs to *Dom*(*move*) if for some $\texttt{-x} \in Licensees$ conditions (i) and (ii) are true.

(i) υ has licensor feature $\texttt{+X}$, and

(ii) there is exactly one maximal projection ϕ in υ that has feature $\texttt{-x}$.

Thus, there are $\kappa_\upsilon, \kappa_\phi \in Syn^*$, $\nu_\upsilon, \nu_\phi \in Phon^* Sem^*$ such that $\texttt{+X}\kappa_\upsilon \nu_\upsilon$ and $\texttt{-x}\kappa_\phi \nu_\phi$ are the head–labels of υ and ϕ, respectively. The outcome of the application of *move* to υ is defined as

$$move(\upsilon) = [_>\phi', \upsilon'],$$

where the expression υ' results from υ by canceling the instance of $\texttt{+X}$ the head–label of υ starts with, while the subtree ϕ is replaced by a single node labeled ϵ. ϕ' is the expression arising from ϕ just by deleting the instance of $\texttt{-x}$ that the head–label of ϕ starts with.

For each MG $G = \langle \neg Syn, Syn, Lex, \Omega, \texttt{c} \rangle$ the *closure of Lex (under the functions in Ω)*, briefly referred to as the *closure of G* and denoted by *CL*(*G*), is defined as $\bigcup_{k \in \mathbb{N}} CL^k(G)$, a countable union of subsets of *Exp*(*Feat*), where for $k \in \mathbb{N}$ the sets $CL^k(G)$ are inductively given by

(C1) $CL^0(G) = Lex$

(C2) $CL^{k+1}(G) = CL^k(G)$
$\cup \{merge(\upsilon, \phi) \mid \langle \upsilon, \phi \rangle \in Dom(merge) \cap CL^k(G) \times CL^k(G)\}$
$\cup \{move(\upsilon) \mid \upsilon \in Dom(move) \cap CL^k(G)\}$

Recall that the functions *merge* and *move* are structure building by strict feature consumption. Thus, since $CL^0(G) = Lex$, each application of *merge* or *move* deriving some $\tau \in CL(G)$ can be seen as "purely lexically driven."

Every $\tau \in CL(G)$ is an *expression of G*. The *(string) language derivable by G* is the set $\{Y_{Phon}(\tau) \mid \tau \in CL(G)$ such that τ is complete$\}$, denoted by *L*(*G*).

Definition 3.5. Each $L \subseteq Phon^*$ for some set *Phon* such that there is an MG *G* with $L = L(G)$ is called a *minimalist language (ML)*.

Just in order to complete the picture in terms of a formal definition we give

Definition 3.6. An MG *G* and an MCFG *G'* are *weakly equivalent* if they derive the same (string) language, i.e. if $L(G) = L(G')$.

4 MCFLs as MLs

In this section we take $G = \langle N, O_\Sigma, F, R, S\rangle$ to be an arbitrary, but fixed m–MCFG for some $m \in \mathbb{N} \setminus \{0\}$. In order to prepare the construction of a weakly equivalent MG we start by considering the functions from F of the MCFG G in some more detail.

Let $f \in F$. We first choose non–negative integers $n(f)$, $1 \leq \varphi(f) \leq m$ and $1 \leq d_i(f) \leq m$ for $1 \leq i \leq n(f)$, existing according to (M2) such that

$$f \text{ is a (total) function from } \textstyle\prod_{i=1}^{n(f)} \langle \Sigma^* \rangle^{d_i(f)} \text{ into } \langle \Sigma^* \rangle^{\varphi(f)}.$$

Next we define

$$I_{Dom(f)} = \{\langle i, j\rangle \,|\, 1 \leq i \leq n(f), 1 \leq j \leq d_i(f)\},$$

we let $X_f = \{x_{ij} \,|\, \langle i,j\rangle \in I_{Dom(f)}\}$ be a set of pairwise distinct variables, and we set $x_i = \langle x_{i1}, \ldots, x_{id_i(f)}\rangle$ for $1 \leq i \leq n(f)$. Then, for $1 \leq h \leq \varphi(f)$ we take f_h to be the h–th component of f, i.e. $f(\theta) = \langle f_1(\theta), \ldots, f_{\varphi(f)}(\theta)\rangle$ for all $\theta \in \prod_{i=1}^{n(f)} \langle \Sigma^* \rangle^{d_i(f)}$, and we fix $l_h(f) \in \mathbb{N}$, $\zeta(f_{hl}) \in \Sigma^*$ for $0 \leq l \leq l_h(f)$, and $z(f_{hl}) \in X_f$ for $1 \leq l \leq l_h(f)$, existing by (f1), such that f_h is represented by

$$f_h(x_1, \ldots, x_{n(f)}) = \zeta(f_{h0})\, z(f_{h1})\, \zeta(f_{h1}) \,\cdots\, z(f_{hl_h(f)})\, \zeta(f_{hl_h(f)}) \,.$$

Proceeding for each $f \in F$ we let

$$I_{Range(f)} = \{\langle h, l\rangle \,|\, 1 \leq h \leq \varphi(f), 1 \leq l \leq l_h(f)\} \,,$$

and we take g_f to be the injective partial function from $I_{Dom(f)}$ onto $I_{Range(f)}$ which exists according to (f2) such that

$$g_f(i,j) = \langle h, l\rangle \text{ iff } x_{ij} = z(f_{hl}) \text{ for each } \langle i,j\rangle \in Dom(g_f).$$

Sticking to a further notational convention introduced in Section 2, we take

$$d_G \text{ to denote the function from } N \text{ into } \mathbb{N}$$

existing due to (M3) and (M4). Thus $1 \leq d_G(A) \leq m$ for $A \in N$, where $d_G(S) = 1$.

We now define an MG $G_{\text{MG}} = \langle \neg Syn, Syn, Lex, \Omega, \mathsf{c}\rangle$ according to (N0)–(N2) and prove it to be weakly equivalent to the MCFG G afterwards. To do so successfully, we assume w.l.o.g. G to be an LCFRS with $rank(G) = 2$, what is possible according to Corollary 2.8.

Let us start with a motivation of the concrete construction we suggest below. For that, we consider some $r = A \to f(A_1, \ldots, A_{n(f)}) \in R$ and let $p_h \in L_G(A_h)$ for $1 \leq h \leq n(f)$. Thus we have $p = f(p_1, \ldots, p_{n(f)}) \in L_G(A) \subseteq \langle \Sigma^* \rangle^{d_G(A)}$. Our aim is to define G_{MG} such that we are able to derive an expression $\tau \in CL(G_{\text{MG}})$ from existing expressions $\upsilon_1, \ldots, \upsilon_{n(f)} \in CL(G_{\text{MG}})$, thereby successively "calculating" the $\varphi(f)$–tuple p in $n(f) + 3\varphi(f) + \sum_{h=1}^{\varphi(f)} 2l_h(f)$ steps. Recall that we have $d_G(A) = \varphi(f)$. Each υ_i for some $1 \leq i \leq n(f)$ will be related to A_i

and p_i, and the resulting expression τ to A and p in a specific way (cf. Definition 4.1). Roughly speaking, as for τ, for each $1 \leq h \leq d_G(A)$ there will be some $\tau_h \in \mathit{MaxProj}(\tau)$ provided with a particular licensee instance. Up to those proper subtrees of τ_h which are themselves maximal projections with some licensee feature, the component p_h will be the phonetic yield of τ_h.

••• First we let $\mathit{Phon} = \Sigma$ and $\mathit{Sem} = \emptyset$.

••• Defining the sets *Licensees* and *Licensors*, for $1 \leq h \leq m$ and $0 \leq n \leq 2$ we take $\texttt{-l}_{\langle h,\, n\rangle}$ to be a licensee and $\texttt{+L}_{\langle h,\, n\rangle}$ to be a corresponding strong licensor such that *Licensees* and *Licensors* both are sets of cardinality $3m$.

••• In order to define the sets *Base* and *Select*, for each $A \in N$ we introduce new, pairwise distinct basic categories $\texttt{a}_{\langle h,\, n\rangle}$ as well as corresponding weak selection features of the form $\texttt{=a}_{\langle h,\, n\rangle}$ with $1 \leq h \leq d_G(A)$ and $1 \leq n \leq 2$.

Furthermore, for each $A \rightarrow f(A_1, \ldots, A_{n(f)}) \in R$ we introduce new, pairwise distinct basic categories $\texttt{a}_{\langle f,\, \varphi(f)+1,\, 0\rangle}$ and $\texttt{a}_{\langle f,\, h,\, l\rangle}$ as well as corresponding weak selection features of the form $\texttt{=a}_{\langle f,\, \varphi(f)+1,\, 0\rangle}$ and $\texttt{=a}_{\langle f,\, h,\, l\rangle}$, where $1 \leq h \leq \varphi(f)$ and $0 \leq l \leq l_h(f)$. Recall that $\varphi(f) = d_G(A)$ by choice of d_G.

Finally, we let $\texttt{c} \in \mathit{Base}$ be the completeness category and assume it to be different from every other element in *Base*.

••• Next we define the set *Lex*, the lexicon over $\neg\mathit{Syn} \cup \mathit{Syn}$. While doing so, we identify each lexical item with its (unique) head-label, taking such an item to be a simple expression with root ϵ. First of all we define one entry which is the only one that will allow "to finally derive" a complete expression of G_{MG}.

$$\alpha_{\texttt{c}} \;=\; \texttt{=s}_{\langle 1,\, 1\rangle}\; \texttt{+L}_{\langle 1,\, 1\rangle}\; \texttt{c}\,,$$

where $\texttt{s}_{\langle 1,\, 1\rangle} \in \mathit{Base}$ is the corresponding category arising from $S \in N$, the start symbol in G. The form of all other entries in *Lex* depends on the production rules belonging to R. Since G is of rank 2, we distinguish three cases.

<u>*Case 1*</u>. $A \rightarrow f(B, C) \in R$ for some A, B, $C \in N$ and $f \in F$. In this case $\varphi(f) = d_G(A)$, $n(f) = 2$, $d_1(f) = d_G(B)$ and $d_2(f) = d_G(C)$. Then, the following element belongs to *Lex*:

$$\alpha_{\langle A,\, f,\, B,\, C\rangle} \;=\; \texttt{=c}_{\langle 1,\, 2\rangle}\; \texttt{=b}_{\langle 1,\, 1\rangle}\; \texttt{a}_{\langle f,\, \varphi(f)+1,\, 0\rangle}$$

<u>*Case 2*</u>. $A \rightarrow f(B)$ for some $A, B \in N$ and $f \in F$. In this case $\varphi(f) = d_G(A)$, $n(f) = 1$ and $d_1(f) = d_G(B)$. Then, as an element of *Lex* we take

$$\alpha_{\langle A,\, f,\, B,\, -\rangle} \;=\; \texttt{=b}_{\langle 1,\, 1\rangle}\; \texttt{a}_{\langle f,\, \varphi(f)+1,\, 0\rangle}$$

<u>*Case 3*</u>. $A \rightarrow f()$ for some $A \in N$ and $f \in F$. In this case $\varphi(f) = d_G(A)$ and $n(f) = 0$. Since f is a constant in $\langle \Sigma^* \rangle^{\varphi(f)}$, we have $l_h(f) = 0$ for each $1 \leq h \leq \varphi(f)$, i.e. $f() = \langle \zeta(f_{10}), \ldots, \zeta(f_{\varphi(f)0}) \rangle$. The following entry is in *Lex*:

$$\alpha_{\langle A,\, f,\, -,\, -\rangle} \;=\; \texttt{a}_{\langle f,\, \varphi(f)+1,\, 0\rangle}$$

Moreover, in all three cases for each $1 \leq h \leq \varphi(f)$ further entries are added to *Lex* depending on whether $l_h(f) = 0$ or not.

For each $1 \leq h \leq \varphi(f)$ with $l_h(f) = 0$ we just add

$$\alpha_{\langle A,\, f,\, h,\, 0\rangle} \;=\; {}^{=}\mathtt{a}_{\langle f,\, h+1,\, 0\rangle}\; \mathtt{a}_{\langle f,\, h,\, 0\rangle}\; \mathtt{-l}_{\langle h,\, 0\rangle}\; \zeta(f_{h0})\,.$$

For each $1 \leq h \leq \varphi(f)$ with $l_h(f) > 0$ we add

$$\alpha_{\langle A,\, f,\, h,\, 0\rangle} \;=\; {}^{=}\mathtt{a}_{\langle f,\, h,\, 1\rangle}\; \mathtt{a}_{\langle f,\, h,\, 0\rangle}\; \mathtt{-l}_{\langle h,\, 0\rangle}\; \zeta(f_{h0})\;, \text{ and}$$

$$\alpha_{\langle A,\, f,\, h,\, l_h(f)\rangle} \;=\; {}^{=}\mathtt{a}_{\langle f,\, h+1,\, 0\rangle}\; \mathtt{+L}_{\langle j,\, i\rangle}\; \mathtt{a}_{\langle f,\, h,\, l_h(f)\rangle}\; \zeta(f_{hl_h(f)})\;,$$
$$\text{where } 1 \leq i \leq n(f) \text{ and } 1 \leq j \leq d_i(f) \text{ with } z(f_{hl_h(f)}) = x_{ij}.$$

For each $1 \leq h \leq \varphi(f)$ and for each $1 \leq l < l_h(f)$ we add

$$\alpha_{\langle A,\, f,\, h,\, l\rangle} \;=\; {}^{=}\mathtt{a}_{\langle f,\, h,\, l+1\rangle}\; \mathtt{+L}_{\langle j,\, i\rangle}\, \mathtt{a}_{\langle f,\, h,\, l\rangle}\; \zeta(f_{hl})\;,$$
$$\text{where } 1 \leq i \leq n(f) \text{ and } 1 \leq j \leq d_i(f) \text{ with } z(f_{hl}) = x_{ij}.$$

Finally, in all three cases for $1 \leq n \leq 2$ we take as an element of *Lex*

$$\alpha_{\langle A,\, \varphi(f),\, n\rangle} \;=\; {}^{=}\mathtt{a}_{\langle f,\, 1,\, 0\rangle}\; \mathtt{+L}_{\langle \varphi(f),\, 0\rangle}\; \mathtt{a}_{\langle \varphi(f),\, n\rangle}\mathtt{-l}_{\langle \varphi(f),\, n\rangle}\;,$$

and for $1 \leq h < \varphi(f)$ we take

$$\alpha_{\langle A,\, h,\, n\rangle} \;=\; {}^{=}\mathtt{a}_{\langle h+1,\, n\rangle}\; \mathtt{+L}_{\langle h,\, 0\rangle}\; \mathtt{a}_{\langle h,\, n\rangle}\; \mathtt{-l}_{\langle h,\, n\rangle}\;.$$

Definition 4.1. For every given $A \in N$, $p = \langle \pi_1, \ldots, \pi_{d_G(A)} \rangle$ with $\pi_i \in \Sigma^*$ for $1 \leq i \leq d_G(A)$, and $1 \leq n \leq 2$ an expression $\tau \in CL(G_{\text{MG}})$ is said to *correspond to* the triple $\langle A, p, n\rangle$ if (Z1)–(Z4) are fulfilled, where $\tau_{\langle 1,n\rangle} = \tau$.

(Z1) The head–label of τ is of the form $\mathtt{a}_{\langle 1,\, n\rangle}\; \mathtt{-l}_{\langle 1,\, n\rangle}\; \pi_{\langle 1,\, n\rangle}$ for some $\pi_{\langle 1,\, n\rangle} \in \Sigma^*$.

(Z2) For each $2 \leq h \leq d_G(A)$ there is exactly one $\tau_{\langle h,\, n\rangle} \in \mathit{Comp}^+(\tau)$ which head–label is of the form $\mathtt{-l}_{\langle h,\, n\rangle}\; \pi_{\langle h,\, n\rangle}$ for some $\pi_{\langle h,\, n\rangle} \in \Sigma^*$.

(Z3) For each $1 \leq h \leq d_G(A)$ it holds that

$$\{\upsilon \in \mathit{MaxProj}(\tau_{\langle h,\, n\rangle}) \setminus \{\tau_{\langle h,\, n\rangle}\} \,|\, \upsilon \text{ has some licensee feature}\}$$
$$= \{\tau_{\langle i,\, n\rangle} \,|\, h < i \leq d_G(A)\},$$

i.e. for each $1 \leq h < d_G(A)$ the subexpression $\tau_{\langle h+1,\, n\rangle}$ is the unique maximal maximal projection in $\tau_{\langle h,\, n\rangle}$ that has some licensee feature.

(Z4) For each $1 \leq h \leq d_G(A)$ the string π_h is the phonetic yield of $\upsilon_{\langle h,\, n\rangle}$. Here we have $\upsilon_{\langle d_G(A),\, n\rangle} = \tau_{\langle d_G(A),\, n\rangle}$, and for $1 \leq h < d_G(A)$ the expression $\upsilon_{\langle h,\, n\rangle}$ results from $\tau_{\langle h,\, n\rangle}$ by replacing the subtree $\tau_{\langle h+1,\, n\rangle}$ with a single node labeled ϵ.

Proposition 4.2. *Let $\tau \in CL(G_{MG})$ such that τ has category feature $\mathsf{a}_{\langle 1,\, n\rangle}$ for some $A \in N$ and $1 \leq n \leq 2$. Then there is some $p \in L_G(A)$ such that τ corresponds to $\langle A, p, n\rangle$.*

Proof (sketch). In order to avoid the trivial case we assume that there is some expression $\tau \in CL(G_{\text{MG}})$ such that τ has category $\mathsf{a}_{\langle 1,\, n\rangle}$ for some $A \in N$ and $1 \leq n \leq 2$. Then there is a smallest $K \in \mathbb{N}$ for which $CL^K(G_{\text{MG}})$ includes such a τ. According to the definition of *Lex* we have $K > 0$. The proof follows from an induction on $k \in \mathbb{N}$ with $k + 1 \geq K$.

For some $k \in \mathbb{N}$ with $k + 1 \geq K$ consider some arbitrary, but fixed expression $\tau \in CL^{k+1}(G_{\text{MG}}) \setminus CL^k(G_{\text{MG}})$ such that τ has category $\mathsf{a}_{\langle 1,\, n\rangle}$ for some $A \in N$ and $1 \leq n \leq 2$. Taking into account the definition of *Lex* it turns out that the procedure to derive τ as an expression of G_{MG} is deterministic in the following sense: there are some $r = A \rightarrow f(A_1, \ldots, A_{n(f)}) \in R$, some $k_0 \in \mathbb{N}$ with $k_0 = k + 1 - 3\varphi(f) - \sum_{h=1}^{\varphi(f)} 2l_h(f)$ and some $\chi_0 \in CL^{k_0}(G_{\text{MG}})$ such that χ_0 serves to derive τ in G_{MG}. χ_0 has category feature $\mathsf{a}_{\langle f,\, \varphi(f)+1,\, 0\rangle}$ and is of one of three forms depending on r:

<u>*Case 1*</u>. There is some $r = A \rightarrow f(B, C) \in R$, and there are $\upsilon, \phi \in CL^{k_0}(G_{\text{MG}})$ such that υ and ϕ have category feature $\mathsf{b}_{\langle 1,\, 1\rangle}$ and $\mathsf{c}_{\langle 1,\, 2\rangle}$, respectively, and

$$\chi_0 = \mathit{merge}(\upsilon, \mathit{merge}(\alpha_{\langle A,\, f,\, B,\, C\rangle}, \phi)).$$

By induction hypothesis there are some $p_B \in L_G(B)$ and $p_C \in L_G(C)$ such that υ and ϕ correspond to $\langle B, p_B, 1\rangle$ and $\langle C, p_C, 2\rangle$, respectively. In this case we define $p \in L_G(A)$ by $p = f(p_B, p_C)$.

<u>*Case 2*</u>. There are some $r = A \rightarrow f(B) \in R$ and $\upsilon \in CL^{k_0}(G_{\text{MG}})$ such that υ has category feature $\mathsf{b}_{\langle 1,\, 1\rangle}$, and such that

$$\chi_0 = \mathit{merge}(\alpha_{\langle A,\, f,\, B,\, -\rangle}, \upsilon).$$

By induction hypothesis there is some $p_B \in L_G(B)$ such that υ corresponds to $\langle B, p_B, 1\rangle$. Let $p = f(p_B) \in L_G(A)$.

<u>*Case 3*</u>. There is some $r = A \rightarrow f() \in R$ and χ_0 is a lexical item,

$$\chi_0 = \alpha_{\langle A,\, f,\, -,\, -\rangle}.$$

In this case we simply let $p = f() \in L_G(A)$.

Note that, if $k + 1 = K$ (constituting the base case of our induction) then χ_0 is necessarily of the last form by choice of K. In any case, it turns out that the given $\tau \in CL^{k+1}(G_{\text{MG}}) \setminus CL^k(G_{\text{MG}})$ corresponds to $\langle A, p, n\rangle$. The single derivation steps to end up with τ starting from χ_0 are explicitly given by the following procedure.

Procedure (derive τ from χ_0).

For $0 \leq h < \varphi(f)$

$$\psi_{\langle h+1,\,0\rangle} = \chi_h$$

for $0 \leq l < l_{\varphi(f)-h}(f)$

$$\boxed{\text{step } 2l+1+h+\textstyle\sum_{h'=0}^{h-1} 2l_{\varphi(f)-h'}(f)}$$

$$\psi_{\langle h+1,\,2l+1\rangle} = \mathit{merge}(\alpha_{\langle A,\,f,\,\varphi(f)-h,\,l_{\varphi(f)-h}(f)-l\rangle}, \psi_{\langle h+1,\,2l\rangle})$$

$$\boxed{\text{step } 2l+2+h+\textstyle\sum_{h'=0}^{h-1} 2l_{\varphi(f)-h'}(f)}$$

$$\psi_{\langle h+1,\,2l+2\rangle} = \mathit{move}(\psi_{\langle h+1,\,2l+1\rangle})$$

[checks licensee $\texttt{-l}_{\langle j,\,i\rangle}$
with $g_f(i,j) = \langle \varphi(f)-h, l_{\varphi(f)-h}(f)-l\rangle$]

$$\boxed{\text{step } h+1+\textstyle\sum_{h'=0}^{h} 2l_{\varphi(f)-h'}(f)}$$

$$\chi_{h+1} = \mathit{merge}(\alpha_{\langle A,\,f,\,\varphi(f)-h,\,0\rangle}, \psi_{\langle h+1,\,2l_{\varphi(f)-h}(f)\rangle})$$

For $0 \leq h < \varphi(f)$

$$\boxed{\text{step } 2h+1+\varphi(f)+\textstyle\sum_{h'=1}^{\varphi(f)} 2l_{h'}(f)}$$

$$\chi_{\varphi(f)+2h+1} = \mathit{merge}(\alpha_{\langle A,\,\varphi(f)-h,\,n\rangle}, \chi_{\varphi(f)+2h})$$

$$\boxed{\text{step } 2h+2+\varphi(f)+\textstyle\sum_{h'=1}^{\varphi(f)} 2l_{h'}(f)}$$

$$\chi_{\varphi(f)+2h+2} = \mathit{move}(\chi_{\varphi(f)+2h+1})$$

[checks licensee $\texttt{-l}_{\langle \varphi(f)-h,\,0\rangle}$]

$$\tau = \chi_{3\varphi(f)}$$

An embedded induction on $0 \leq h < \varphi(f)$ and $0 \leq l < l_{\varphi(f)-h}(f)$ yields that τ indeed corresponds to $\langle A, p, n\rangle$, which shows that the proposition is true. The reader is encouraged to verify the details. One crucial point that we like to stress here concerns Case 1 and 2: since G is an LCFRS, the injective function g_f from $I_{Dom(f)}$ onto $I_{Ran(f)}$ is total, i.e. g_f is bijective. This guarantees that each instance of a licensee feature appearing within the yield of χ_0 gets checked off by some derivation step $2l+2+h+\sum_{h'=0}^{h-1} 2l_{\varphi(f)-h'}(f)$ with $0 \leq h < \varphi(f)$ and $0 \leq l \leq l_{\varphi(f)-h}(f)$. □

At this point it seems to be suitable to emphasize the reason for a specific peculiarity intrinsic to G_{MG} by definition of *Lex*: assume $\tau \in CL(G_{\text{MG}})$ to have category feature $\mathtt{a}_{\langle 1,\, n\rangle}$ for some $A \in N$ and $1 \leq n \leq 2$. Consider the derivation process from appropriate $\chi_0 \in CL(G_{\mathrm{MG}})$ to τ as given above, showing that τ corresponds to $\langle A, p, n, \rangle$ according to Definition 4.1 for the respective $p \in L_G(A)$. The question that might arise is, why, by virtual means of G_{MG}, each component p_{h+1} of p for some $0 \leq h < d_G(A)$ is first related to some maximal projection that has licensee $\mathtt{-l}_{\langle h+1,\, 0\rangle}$ and not directly to some maximal projection that has licensee $\mathtt{-l}_{\langle h+1,\, n\rangle}$. The answer is straightforward: the corresponding instance of $\mathtt{-l}_{\langle h+1,\, n\rangle}$ becomes potentially subject to the move–operator exactly after the expression $\chi_{d_G(A)-h}$ has been selected by a lexical head under an application of *merge*. To put it differently, the resulting expression χ contains a maximal projection $\chi'_{d_G(A)-h}$ that has licensee $\mathtt{-l}_{\langle h,\, 0\rangle}$. Namely, $\chi'_{d_G(A)-h}$ is the complement of χ, i.e. the right co–constituent of the head of χ. If we now look at the representations of the components of the involved function $f \in F$ by means of variables and constants from Σ^*, we see that it is possible that the variable x_{nh} occurs within such a representation of some component $f_{h'}$ of f with $1 \leq h' < h$. This means that we have to be aware of the fact that, beside $\chi'_{d_G(A)-h}$, χ may include a further maximal projection $\chi''_{d_G(A)-h}$ that has licensee $\mathtt{-l}_{\langle h,\, n\rangle}$. If $\chi'_{d_G(A)-h}$ and $\chi''_{d_G(A)-h}$ had the same licensee, we would never be able to check off one of both respective instances due to the definition of *move*. Therefore, a derivation of a complete expression of G would unavoidably be blocked.

Proposition 4.3. *Let $A \in N$, $p \in \langle \Sigma^* \rangle^{d_G(A)}$ and $1 \leq n \leq 2$. If $p \in L_G(A)$ then there is some $\tau \in CL(G_{MG})$ such that τ corresponds to $\langle A, p, n\rangle$.*

Proof (sketch). Once more an induction will do the job to prove the proposition. Let $A \in N$, $p \in \langle \Sigma^* \rangle^{d_G(A)}$ and $1 \leq n \leq 2$. Assume that $p \in L_G(A)$. Then, w.l.o.g. we are concerned with one of three possible cases.

Case 1. There is some $r = A \rightarrow f(B, C) \in R$, and for some $k \in \mathbb{N}$ there are some $p_B \in L^k_G(B)$ and $p_C \in L^k_G(C)$ such that $p = f(p_B, p_C) \in L^{k+1}_G(A) \setminus L^k_G(A)$. By hypothesis on k there exist some $\upsilon, \phi \in CL(G_{\mathrm{MG}})$ such that υ and ϕ correspond to $\langle B, p_B, 1\rangle$ and $\langle C, p_C, 2\rangle$, respectively. Therefore, we can define $\chi_0 \in CL(G_{\mathrm{MG}})$ by

$$\chi_0 = merge(\upsilon, merge(\alpha_{\langle A,\, f,\, B,\, C\rangle}, \phi).$$

Case 2. There is some $r = A \rightarrow f(B, C) \in R$, and for some $k \in \mathbb{N}$ there is some $p_B \in L^k_G(B)$ such that $p = f(p_B) \in L^{k+1}_G(A) \setminus L^k_G(A)$. Here, by induction hypothesis we can choose some $\upsilon \in CL(G_{\mathrm{MG}})$ such that υ corresponds to $\langle B, p_B, 1\rangle$. Then we define $\chi_0 \in CL(G_{\mathrm{MG}})$ by

$$\chi_0 = merge(\alpha_{\langle A,\, f,\, B,\, -\rangle}, \upsilon).$$

Case 3. There is some $r = A \rightarrow f() \in R$ such that $p = f() \in L^0_G(A)$. In this case we take χ_0 to be a particular lexical item. We set

$$\chi_0 = \alpha_{\langle A,\, f,\, -,\, -\rangle}.$$

In all three cases the respective derivation procedure from the proof of the last proposition shows that χ_0 serves to derive a $\tau \in CL(G_{\mathrm{MG}})$ that has the demanded properties. □

Corollary 4.4. *$\pi \in L(G)$ iff $\pi \in L(G_{MG})$ for each $\pi \in \Sigma^*$.*

Proof. First suppose that $\tau \in CL(G_{\mathrm{MG}})$ is complete such that $\pi \in \Sigma^*$ is the phonetic yield of τ. Then, due to the definition of *Lex*, there is some expression $\tau' \in CL(G_{\mathrm{MG}})$ which has category $\mathtt{s}_{\langle 1,1\rangle}$ such that $\tau = move(merge(\alpha_{\mathtt{C}}, \tau'))$. By Proposition 4.2 there is some $p' \in L_G(S) = L(G)$ such that τ' corresponds to $\langle S, p', 1\rangle$. Because $d_G(S) = 1$, this implies that p' is not only the phonetic yield of τ', but also the phonetic yield of the specifier of τ. Since the phonetic yield of $\alpha_{\mathtt{C}}$ is empty, we conclude that $p' = \pi$.

Now assume that $\pi \in L(G) = L_G(S)$ for some $\pi \in \Sigma^*$. By Proposition 4.3 there is some $\tau' \in CL(G_{\mathrm{MG}})$ such that τ' corresponds to $\langle S, \pi, 1\rangle$. Then, because $d_G(S) = 1$, π is the phonetic yield of τ'. Moreover, $\tau = move(merge(\alpha_{\mathtt{C}}, \tau'))$ is defined and complete, and π is the phonetic yield of τ. □

5 Conclusion

We have shown that each LCFRS can be transformed into a weakly equivalent MG as defined in [11]. As shown in [6], the converse holds, as well. Hence, combining these results crucially implies that MGs fit in within a series of different formal grammar types, each of which constituting a class of generating devices that have the same weak generative power as LCFRSs, respectively MCFGs.[10] The presented result, therefore, also provides an answer to several questions as to the properties of MLs that have been left open so far, and that can be subsumed under a more general question: does the class of MG–definable string languages constitute an *abstract family of languages (AFL)*? The answer to this question is now known to be positive; even a stronger property is true for this language class, since it is provably a *substitution–closed full AFL* (cf. [10]).

Taking into account our specific construction of a weakly equivalent MG for a given LCFRS, we have moreover shown that each MG in the sense of [11] can be converted into a weakly equivalent one which does not employ any kind of head movement or covert phrasal movement.[11] In fact, it is this subtype of MGs which Harkema's recognizer [1] for MLs is actually defined for. But maybe even more crucially, this implication could be considered to provide some technical support to Stabler's proposal of a revised type of an MG given in [13], which, in particular, completely dispense with those two types of movement motivated by recent linguistic work which heads in exactly this direction (see e.g. [3], [4], [5]). The same holds as to the type of a *strict MG (SMG)*, also introduced in [13] keeping closely to some further suggestions in [4], which likewise banishes any

[10] For a list of some of such classes of generating devices, beside MCTAGs, see e.g. [9].
[11] This is still true, if we additionally allow *affix hopping* to take place within an MG in the way suggested in [14].

kind of head movement or covert phrasal movement from the list of possibilities to "displace material" by means of the structure building functions of an MG. Furthermore, each lexical item of an MG of revised type as well as an SMG is by definition a simple expression, i.e. a head, and in case of an SMG the label of such a head is an element from $Select_{\epsilon}(Select \cup Licensors)_{\epsilon} Base\, Licensees^{*} \neg Syn^{*}$. This latter property is also common to the MG G_{MG} as it results according to our construction in Section 4 from a given LCFRS G, i.e. the constructed MG G_{MG} being weakly equivalent to the LCFRS G. Thus, the creation of *multiple specifiers* is avoided during the derivation of an expression of G_{MG}. To put it differently, whenever, for some $\tau \in CL(G_{\mathrm{MG}})$ and some $\upsilon \in MaxProj(\tau)$, we have $Spec(\upsilon) \neq \emptyset$, $Spec(\upsilon)$ is a singleton set. Indeed, this specific property constitutes one of the main differences to the construction of a weakly equivalent MG for a given LCFRS as it is independently developed in [2]. Although quite similar in some other aspects, within Harkema's construction the use of multiple specifiers is rather a constitutive element.[12]

The last remarks should, certainly, be treated with some care: as demonstrated in [7], thereby confirming the corresponding conjecture in [13], the revised MG–type and the SMG–type introduced in [13] give rise to the same class of derivable string languages. This is an immediate consequence of the fact that both types are provably weakly equivalent to one and the same particular subtype of LCFRSs, respectively MCFGs. However, as to our knowledge, it is an open problem whether this LCFRS–subtype in its turn is weakly equivalent to the class of all LCFRSs, and thus to the class of MGs in the sense of [11]. Note that, deviating from the definition in [11], the revised MG–type as well as the SMG–type does not only dispense with any kind of head movement and covert phrasal movement, but also some additional restriction is imposed on the move–operator as to which maximal projection may move overtly.[13] Therefore, neither our method to convert a given LCFRS into a weakly equivalent MG in the sense of [11], nor the method of Harkema does necessarily yield, at the same time, a weakly equivalent MG or, likewise, SMG in the sense of [13]; and there is no straightforward adaption of either of both methods in order to achieve this.

[12] Another significant difference between our approach and the one of Harkema is given by the fact that within our resulting, weakly equivalent MG no maximal projection moves more than one time in order to check its licensee features, i.e. the (non–trivial) chains created by applications of the move–operator are all simple.

[13] As to an MG of revised type, an $\upsilon \in Exp(\neg Syn \cup Syn)$ belongs to the domain of the move–operator only if, in addition to condition (i) and (ii) of (mo), it holds that there is some $\chi \in Comp^{+}(\upsilon)$ with $\phi = \chi$ or $\phi \in Spec(\chi)$ for the unique maximal projection ϕ that has licensee `-x`. As to an SMG, an $\upsilon \in Exp(\neg Syn \cup Syn)$ belongs to the domain of the move–operator only if, in addition to condition (i) and (ii) of (mo), it holds that there is a $\chi \in Comp^{+}(\upsilon)$ with $\phi \in Spec^{*}(\chi)$ for the unique maximal projection ϕ that has licensee `-x`, and applying the move–operator to υ, it is the constituent χ that is raised into the specifier position.

References

1. Henk Harkema. A recognizer for minimalist grammars. In *Proceedings of the Sixth International Workshop on Parsing Technologies (IWPT 2000)*, Trento, pages 111–122, 2000.
2. Henk Harkema. A characterization of minimalist languages, 2001. This volume.
3. Richard S. Kayne. Overt vs. covert movement. *Syntax*, 1:128–191, 1998.
4. Hilda Koopman and Anna Szabolcsi. *Verbal Complexes*. MIT Press, Cambridge, MA, 2000.
5. Anoop Mahajan. Eliminating head movement. In *GLOW Newsletter #44*, pages 44–45, 2000. Abstract of the talk held at *the 23rd Generative Linguistics in the Old World Conference (GLOW 2000)*, Vitoria–Gasteiz/Bilbao.
6. Jens Michaelis. Derivational minimalism is mildy context–sensitive. In M. Moortgat, editor, *Logical Aspects of Computational Linguistics (LACL '98)*, Lecture Notes in Artificial Intelligence Vol. 2014. Springer, Berlin, Heidelberg, to appear. Also available at `http://www.ling.uni-potsdam.de/~michael/papers.html`.
7. Jens Michaelis. On formal properties of minimalist grammars. Potsdam University, Potsdam, in preperation.
8. Carl J. Pollard. *Generalized Phrase Structure Grammars, Head Grammars, and Natural Language*. PhD thesis, Stanford University, Stanford, CA, 1984.
9. Owen Rambow and Giorgio Satta. Independent parallelism in finite copying parallel rewriting systems. *Theoretical Computer Science*, 223:87–120, 1999.
10. Hiroyuki Seki, Takashi Matsumura, Mamoru Fujii, and Tadao Kasami. On multiple context–free grammars. *Theoretical Computer Science*, 88:191–229, 1991.
11. Edward P. Stabler. Derivational minimalism. In C. Retoré, editor, *Logical Aspects of Computational Linguistics (LACL '96)*, Lecture Notes in Artificial Intelligence Vol. 1328, pages 68–95. Springer, Berlin, Heidelberg, 1997.
12. Edward P. Stabler. Acquiring languages with movement. *Syntax*, 1:72–97, 1998.
13. Edward P. Stabler. Remnant movement and complexity. In G. Bouma, G.–J. M. Kruijff, E. Hinrichs, and R. T. Oehrle, editors, *Constraints and Resources in Natural Language Syntax and Semantics*, pages 299–326. CSLI Publications, Stanford, CA, 1999.
14. Edward P. Stabler. Recognizing head movement, 2001. This volume.
15. K. Vijay–Shanker, David J. Weir, and Aravind K. Joshi. Characterizing structural descriptions produced by various grammatical formalisms. In *25th Annual Meeting of the Association for Computational Linguistics (ACL '87)*, Stanford, CA, pages 104–111. ACL, 1987.
16. David J. Weir. *Characterizing Mildly Context–Sensitive Grammar Formalisms*. PhD thesis, University of Pennsylvania, Philadelphia, PA, 1988.

Recognizing Head Movement

Edward P. Stabler

University of California,
Los Angeles CA 90095-1543, USA,
stabler@ucla.edu
http://www.linguistics.ucla.edu/people/stabler/

Abstract. Previous studies have provided logical representations and efficient recognition algorithms for a simple kind of "minimalist grammars." This paper extends these grammars with head movement ("incorporation") and affix hopping. The grammars are presented as lexicons together with CKY-like reduction rules, so an efficient CKY-like recognition method is immediately given, and logical perspectives are briefly considered.

Michaelis (1998) showed how the derivations of a simple kind of minimalist grammar (MG) (Stabler, 1997) correspond to derivations of exactly the same strings in a multiple context free grammar (MCFG) (Seki et al., 1991). MGs build structures by *merging* pairs of expressions, and simplifying single expressions by *moving* a subexpression in them. The basic idea behind the correspondence with MCFGs can be traced back to Pollard (1984) who noticed, in effect, that when a constituent is going to move, we should not regard its yield as included in the yield of the expression that contains it. Instead, the expression from which something will move is better regarded has having multiple yields, multiple components – the "moving" components have not yet reached their final positions. In a completed derivation, the component strings of all the categories are eventually ordered to yield a sentence. This conception behind the Michaelis result relies on the fact that for any MG, there is a fixed finite bound on the number of categories and rules, and on the number of components that any constituent will have.

These recent results led to efficient parsing methods (Stabler, 1999; Harkema, 2000), to connections with multimodal logics (Cornell, 1999; Vermaat, 1999; Lecomte and Retoré, 1999), and to a succinct reformulation of MGs (Stabler and Keenan, 2000) in which the multiple components of expressions are explicit. The parsing methods, the logics, and the succinct reformulation were provided for MGs with only overt, phrasal movement (as explained below). This paper extends these results with two kinds of head movement, providing an efficient parsing method and some preliminary observations about bringing this work into a logical perspective like that proposed by (Lecomte and Retoré, 1999). And for illustration, in the course of the paper, we present small example grammars for (G1) subject-auxiliary inversion and (G3) affix-hopping in English, and (G2) object clitics in French.

P. de Groote, G. Morrill, C. Retoré (Eds.): LACL 2001, LNAI 2099, pp. 245–260, 2001.

1 Minimalist Grammars with Phrasal Movement

We begin from the succinct presentation of MGs introduced in (Stabler and Keenan, 2000). We will define a set of linguistic expressions which are built from a nonempty set of pronounced elements Σ, a two-element set of types $T = \{::, :\}$, and a set of features F (where the sets Σ, T, F are pairwise disjoint). F is partitioned into four sets, given by a nonempty set of basic features $B \subset F$ and three functions with domain C and disjoint ranges: **base** $B = \{v, n, np, case, wh, \ldots\}$, **selectors** $S = \{\texttt{=}f \mid f \in B\}$, **licensees** $M = \{-f \mid f \in B\}$, **licensors** $N = \{+f \mid f \in B\}$. So the set of features $F = B \cup S \cup M \cup N$.

Let the set of **chains** $C = \Sigma^* T F^*$. We use the types $T = \{::, :\}$ to distinguish lexical chains from derived chains, where :: is the lexical type, so the set of **lexical chains** $LC = \Sigma^* :: F^*$. The set of **expressions** $E = C^+$, the set of nonempty sequences of chains. When an expression has more than one chain, we will separate the chains with commas to enhance readability. A **lexicon** Lex is a finite set of lexical chains. And finally, a **minimalist grammar** G is just a lexicon, $G = Lex$.

For any minimalist grammar $G = Lex$, the **language** $L(G)$ is the closure of Lex under the fixed set of structure building functions $\mathcal{F} = \{merge, move\}$, where these functions are defined below. And for any $\texttt{f} \in B$, the strings of category $\texttt{f}$, $S_{\texttt{f}}(G) = \{s \mid s \cdot \texttt{f} \in L(G) \text{ for some } \cdot \in T\}$.

$merge : (E \times E) \to E$ is the union of the following 3 functions, for $s, t \in \Sigma^*$, for $\cdot \in \{:, ::\}$, for $f \in B$, $\gamma \in F^*$, $\delta \in F^+$, and for chains $\alpha_1, \ldots, \alpha_k, \iota_1, \ldots, \iota_l$ $(0 \leq k, l)$

$$\frac{s :: \texttt{=}f\gamma \qquad t \cdot f, \alpha_1, \ldots, \alpha_k}{st : \gamma, \alpha_1, \ldots, \alpha_k} \text{ r1}$$

$$\frac{s : \texttt{=}f\gamma, \alpha_1, \ldots, \alpha_k \qquad t \cdot f, \iota_1, \ldots, \iota_l}{ts : \gamma, \alpha_1, \ldots, \alpha_k, \iota_1, \ldots, \iota_l} \text{ r2}$$

$$\frac{s \cdot \texttt{=}f\gamma, \alpha_1, \ldots, \alpha_k \qquad t \cdot f\delta, \iota_1, \ldots, \iota_l}{s : \gamma, t : \delta, \alpha_1, \ldots, \alpha_k, \iota_1, \ldots, \iota_l} \text{ r3}$$

Here st is the concatenation of strings s, t. And note that since the domains of r1, r2, and r3 are disjoint, their union is a function.

$move : E \to E$ is the union of the following 2 functions, for $s, t \in \Sigma^*$, $f \in B$, $\gamma \in F^*$, $\delta \in F^+$, and for chains $\alpha_1, \ldots, \alpha_k, \iota_1, \ldots, \iota_l$ $(0 \leq k, l)$ satisfying the following condition: (SMC) none of $\alpha_1, \ldots, \alpha_{i-1}, \alpha_{i+1}, \ldots, \alpha_k$ has $-f$ as its first feature.

$$\frac{s : +f\gamma, \alpha_1, \ldots, \alpha_{i-1}, t : -f, \alpha_{i+1}, \ldots, \alpha_k}{ts : \gamma, \alpha_1, \ldots, \alpha_{i-1}, \alpha_{i+1}, \ldots, \alpha_k}\ \text{m1}$$

$$\frac{s : +f\gamma, \alpha_1, \ldots, \alpha_{i-1}, t : -f\delta, \alpha_{i+1}, \ldots, \alpha_k}{s : \gamma, \alpha_1, \ldots, \alpha_{i-1}, t : \delta, \alpha_{i+1}, \ldots, \alpha_k}\ \text{m2}$$

Notice that the domains of m1 and m2 are disjoint, so their union is a function. The (SMC) restriction on the domain of *move* is a simple version of the "shortest move condition" (Chomsky, 1995).

1.1 G0: Wh-Movement in a Simple SOV Language

A simple approach to wh-movement allows us to derive simple sentences and wh-questions like the following, in an artificial Subject-Object-Verb language with no verbal inflections:

(1) the king the pie eat
(2) which pie the king eat

Linguists have proposed that not only is the question formed by moving the wh determiner phrase (DP) [which pie] from object position to the front, but in all clauses the pronounced DPs move to case positions, where transitive verbs assign case to their objects ("Burzio's generalization"). So then the clauses above get depictions rather like this, indicating movements by leaving coindexed "traces" (t) behind:

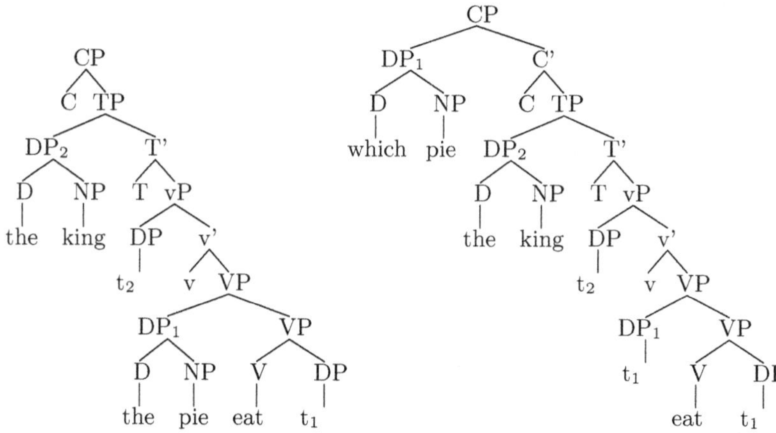

As indicated by coindexing, in the tree on the left, there are two movements, while the tree on the right has three movements because [which pie] moves twice: once to a case position, and then to the front, wh-question position. The sequences of coindexed constituents are sometimes called "chains."

These expressions can be defined by an MG with the following 10 lexical items (writing ϵ for the empty string, and using **k** for the abstract "case" feature):

ϵ:: =T C	ϵ:: =T +wh C
ϵ:: =v +k T	ϵ:: =V =D v
eat:: =D +k V	laugh:: V
the:: =N D -k	which:: =N D -k -wh
king:: N	pie:: N

With this grammar, we can derive strings of category C as follows, where in these trees the leaves are lexical items, a node with two daughters represents the result of *merge*, and a node with one daughter represents the result of a *move*.

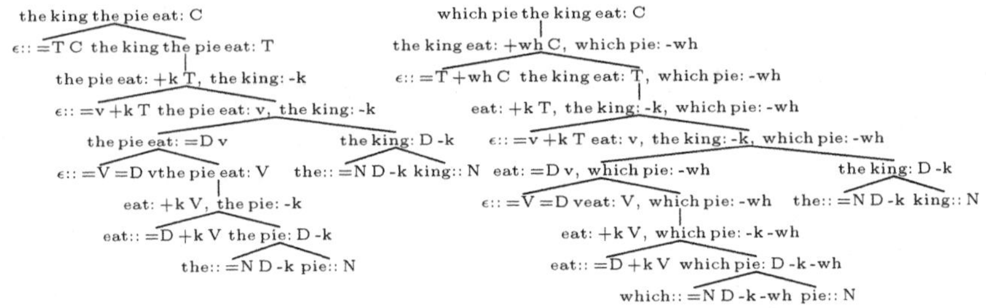

Since *merge* is binary and *move* is unary, it is easy to see that the tree on the left has two movements, while the one on the right has three. A full discussion of the correspondence between the linguists' conception of derivations and the one formally defined here is beyond the scope of this paper, but the correspondence is very close (Stabler, 1999).

2 Incorporation

Many linguists believe that in addition to phrasal movement of the sort discussed above, there is "head movement", which moves not the whole phrase but just the "head". In the simplest, "canonical" examples, a head X of a phrase XP moves to adjoin to the left or right of the head Y that selects XP. Left-adjoining X to Y is often depicted this way:

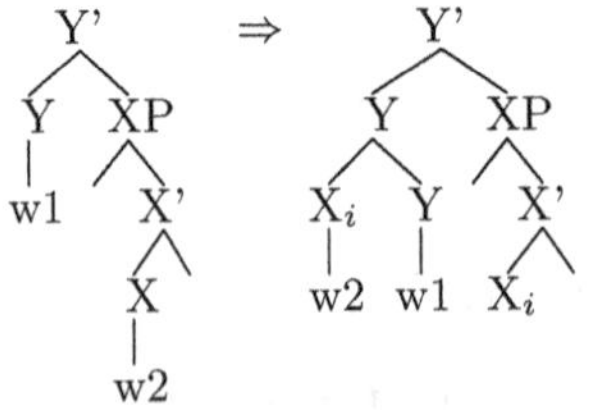

For example, questions with inversion of subject and inflected verb may be formed by moving the T head to C (sometimes called T-to-C or I-to-C movement); verbs may get their inflections by V-to-T movement; particles may get associated with verbs by P-to-V movement; objects may incorporate into the verb with N-to-V movement, and there may also be v-to-V movement.

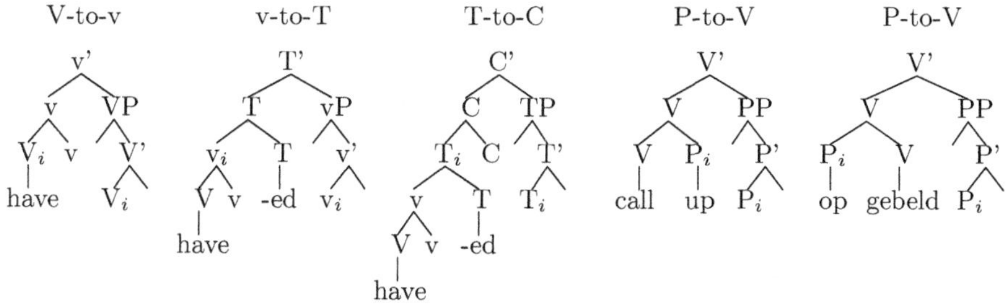

As indicated by these examples of v-to-T and T-to-C movement, heads can be complex. And notice that the P-to-V movement is right-adjoining in the English [call up] but left-adjoining in the Dutch [opgebeld] (Koopman 1993, 1994). Similarly (though not shown here) when a verb incorporates a noun, it is usually attached on the left, but sometimes on the right (Baker, 1996, 32).

The MGs defined above can be extended to allow these sorts of movements. Since they involve the configuration of selection, we follow the suggestion in Stabler (1997) that they be regarded as part of the *merge* operation. Remembering the essential insight from Pollard and Michaelis, mentioned on the first page, the key thing is to keep the phonetic contents of any movable head in a separate component. A head X is not movable after its phrase XP has been merged, so we only need to distinguish the head components of phrases until they have been merged. So rather than expressions of the form:

$$\mathtt{s}_1 \cdot \mathtt{Features}_1,\ \mathtt{s}_2 \cdot \mathtt{Features}_2, \ldots, \mathtt{s}_k \cdot \mathtt{Features}_k,$$

we will use expressions in which the string part $\mathtt{s}_1$ of the first chain is split into three (possibly empty) pieces `s(pecifier)`, `h(head)`, `c(omplement)`:

$$\mathtt{s,h,c} \cdot \mathtt{Features}_1,\ \mathtt{s}_2 \cdot \mathtt{Features}_2, \ldots, \mathtt{s}_k \cdot \mathtt{Features}_k.$$

So **lexical chains** now have a triple of strings, but only the head can be non-empty: $LC = \epsilon, \Sigma^*, \epsilon :: F^*$. As before, a **lexicon** is a finite set of lexical chains.

Head movement will be triggered by a specialization of the selecting feature. The feature =>V will indicate that the head of the selected VP is to be adjoined on the left; and V<= will indicate that the head of the selected VP is to be adjoined on the right. The former set of features is thus extended by adding these two new functions on the base categories B: **right-incorporators** $R = \{f\texttt{<=} \mid f \in B\}$, and **left-incorporators** $L = \{\texttt{=>}f \mid f \in B\}$. So now the set of syntactic features $F = B \cup S \cup M \cup N \cup R \cup L$. The new work of placing heads properly is done by the *merge* function, so the earlier functions r1 and r3 each break into 3 cases. Define *merge* as the union of the following 7 functions:

$$\frac{\epsilon, s, \epsilon :: \texttt{=}f\gamma \qquad t_s, t_h, t_c \cdot f, \alpha_1, \ldots, \alpha_k}{\epsilon, s, t_s t_h t_c : \gamma, \alpha_1, \ldots, \alpha_k}\ \text{r1'}$$

$$\frac{\epsilon, s, \epsilon :: f\texttt{<=}\gamma \qquad t_s, t_h, t_c \cdot f, \alpha_1, \ldots, \alpha_k}{\epsilon, s t_h, t_s t_c : \gamma, \alpha_1, \ldots, \alpha_k}\ \text{r1right}$$

$$\frac{\epsilon, s, \epsilon :: \texttt{=>}f\gamma \qquad t_s, t_h, t_c \cdot f, \alpha_1, \ldots, \alpha_k}{\epsilon, t_h s, t_s t_c : \gamma, \alpha_1, \ldots, \alpha_k}\ \text{r1left}$$

$$\frac{s_s, s_h, s_c : \texttt{=}f\gamma, \alpha_1, \ldots, \alpha_k \qquad t_s, t_h, t_c \cdot f, \iota_1, \ldots, \iota_l}{t_s t_h t_c s_s, s_h, s_c : \gamma, \alpha_1, \ldots, \alpha_k, \iota_1, \ldots, \iota_l} \text{r2'}$$

$$\frac{s_s, s_h, s_c \cdot \texttt{=}f\gamma, \alpha_1, \ldots, \alpha_k \qquad t_s, t_h, t_c \cdot f\delta, \iota_1, \ldots, \iota_l}{s_s, s_h, s_c : \gamma, t_s t_h t_c : \delta, \alpha_1, \ldots, \alpha_k, \iota_1, \ldots, \iota_l} \text{r3'}$$

$$\frac{s_s, s_h, s_c :: f\texttt{<=}\gamma, \alpha_1, \ldots, \alpha_k \qquad t_s, t_h, t_c \cdot f\delta, \iota_1, \ldots, \iota_l}{s_s, s_h t_h, s_c : \gamma, t_s t_c : \delta, \alpha_1, \ldots, \alpha_k, \iota_1, \ldots, \iota_l} \text{r3right}$$

$$\frac{s_s, s_h, s_c :: \texttt{=>}f\gamma, \alpha_1, \ldots, \alpha_k \qquad t_s, t_h, t_c \cdot f\delta, \iota_1, \ldots, \iota_l}{s_s, t_h s_h, s_c : \gamma, t_s t_c : \delta, \alpha_1, \ldots, \alpha_k, \iota_1, \ldots, \iota_l} \text{r3left}$$

And *move* changes only trivially. It is the union of the following functions:

$$\frac{s_s, s_h, s_c : +f\gamma, \alpha_1, \ldots, \alpha_{i-1}, t : -f, \alpha_{i+1}, \ldots, \alpha_k}{t s_s, s_h, s_c : \gamma, \alpha_1, \ldots, \alpha_{i-1}, \alpha_{i+1}, \ldots, \alpha_k} \text{m1'}$$

$$\frac{s_s, s_h, s_c : +f\gamma, \alpha_1, \ldots, \alpha_{i-1}, t : -f\delta, \alpha_{i+1}, \ldots, \alpha_k}{s_s, s_h, s_c : \gamma, \alpha_1, \ldots, \alpha_{i-1}, t : \delta, \alpha_{i+1}, \ldots, \alpha_k} \text{m2'}$$

As before, for any grammar $G = Lex$, the language $L(G)$ is the closure of Lex under the fixed set of structure building functions $\mathcal{F} = \{merge, move\}$. And for any $\texttt{f} \in B$, the strings of category $\texttt{f}$, $S_{\texttt{f}}(G) = \{s_s s_h s_c | \; s_s, s_h, s_c \cdot \texttt{f} \in L(G)$ for some $\cdot \in T\}$.

2.1 G1: Subject-Auxiliary Inversion in English

Introductions to transformational syntax like (Fromkin, 2000, §5) often present a simplified account of English auxiliaries and question formation that can now be represented with a lexicon like the following (writing $\texttt{s}_h\texttt{::}$ Fs for each ($\texttt{s}_s\texttt{,s}_h\texttt{,s}_c\texttt{::}$ Fs)$\in Lex$, since $\texttt{s}_s$ and $\texttt{s}_c$ are always empty in the lexicon):[1]

ε:: =T C	ε:: =>T C	ε:: =>T +wh C	
-s:: =>Modal +k T	-s:: =>Have +k T	-s:: =>Be +k T	-s:: =v +k T
will:: =Have Modal	will:: =Be Modal	will:: =v Modal	
have:: =Been Have	have:: $=\text{v}_{en}$ Have		
be:: $=\text{v}_{ing}$ Be	been:: $=\text{v}_{ing}$ Been		
ε:: =>V =D v	-en:: =>V =D v_{en}	-ing:: =>V =D v_{ing}	
eat:: =D +k V	laugh:: V		
the:: =N D -k	which:: =N D -k -wh		
king:: N	pie:: N		

[1] I follow the linguistic convention of punctuating a string like -s to indicate that it is an affix. This dash that occurs next to a string should not be confused with the dash that occurs next to syntactic features like -wh.

With this grammar we have derivations like the following

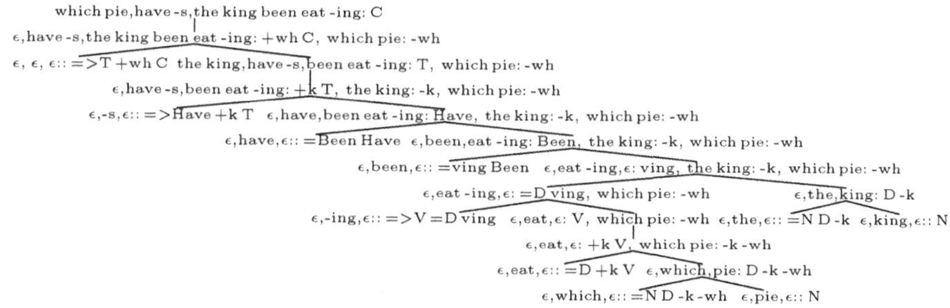

The behavior of this grammar is English-like on a range of constructions:

(3) will -s the king laugh
(4) the king be -s laugh -ing
(5) which king have -s eat -en the pie
(6) the king will -s have been eat -ing the pie

We also derive

(7) -s the king laugh

which will be discussed in §4.

2.2 G2: A Simple Approach to French Clitics

(Sportiche, 1998) reviews some of the difficulties in providing an account of French clitics. Following Kayne (1989), Zwicky (1985) and many others, he points out that they act like heads attached to a verb when, for example, they move with the verb in "complex inversion" (just as the verb and inflection move together in English questions, in the previous section):

(8) Jean [l'aurait]$_i$-il t_i connu?
John him-would-have-he known

'Would John have known him?'

But clitics are also related to argument positions, and these need not be adjacent to the verb:

(9) Il lui$_i$ donnera le chapeau t_i
He to-him will-give the hat

'He will give him the hat'

A clitic can be associated with the argument position of a verb other than the one it is attached to:

(10) Jean la$_i$ veut manger t$_i$
John it wants to-eat

'John wants to eat it'

And finally, a verb can be associated with multiple clitics:

(11) Il le$_j$ lui$_i$ donnera t$_j$ t$_i$
he it to-him will-give

'he will give it to him'

However, there is a limit on the number of clitics that can be associated with a verb in French. They are limited to at most one from each of the following sets, and at most one from the third and fifth sets together (Sportiche, 1998, 247):

Nom	Neg	Refl12	Acc3	Dat3	Loc	Gen
{il}	{ne}	{me,te,se,nous}	{le,la,les}	{lui,leur}	{y}	{en}

One way to get the proper order of these clitics that is considered by (Sportiche, 1995, 266ff) involves assuming that over V there is a projection for each of these sets. Then a Dat3 head can select V to form [lui V] by (right adjoining) head movement, which in turn can be selected by Acc3 to form [le lui V], and so on. And the association with argument positions can be accomplished by moving not the clitics themselves, but phrases ("operators," phonetically empty), so that the argument positions are properly "bound" by the clitics. If the binding of arguments by clitics in the 3rd and 5th set is accomplished by the same movement feature +F, then the (SMC) will prevent both from occurring at once, as desired. This approach is captured by a grammar like the following:

ϵ::=T C				
ϵ::=Refl12 +k T	ϵ::=Acc3 +k T	ϵ::=Dat3 +k T	ϵ::=v +k T	
se::=Acc3 +F Refl12	se::=Dat3 +F Refl12	se::=v +F Refl12		
le::=Dat3 +G Acc3	le::=v +G Acc3			
lui::=v +F Dat3				
ϵ::vacc<= =D v	ϵ::vdat<= =D +k vacc	ϵ::V<= =p vdat	montrera::V	
ϵ::P<= p	a::=D +k P	ϵ::p -F		
Jean::D -k	Marie::D -k	le::=N D -k	ϵ::D -k -F	ϵ::D -k -G
roi::N	livre::N			

With this grammar, we have derivations like the following, with the more conventional transformational depiction on the right. Notice that an element has moved from the lower P specifier of the vdatP argument of the verb to the Dat3P clitic phrase:

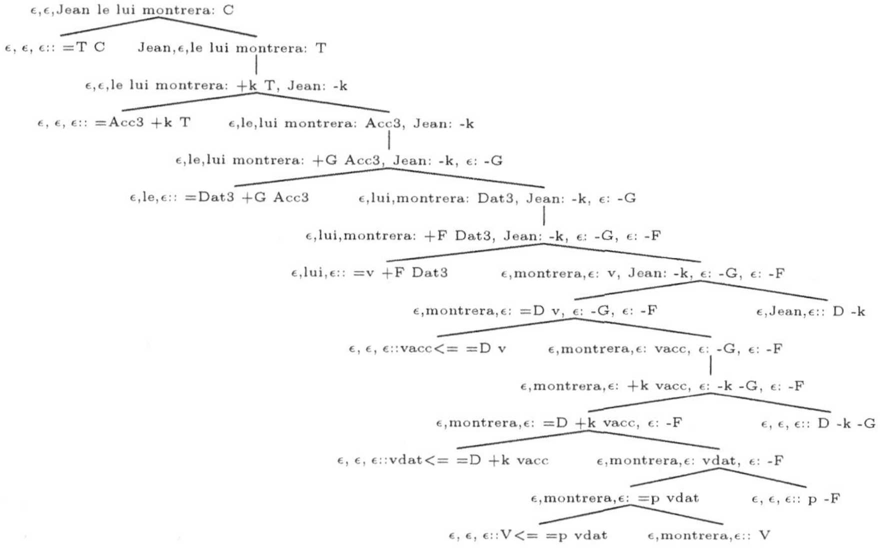

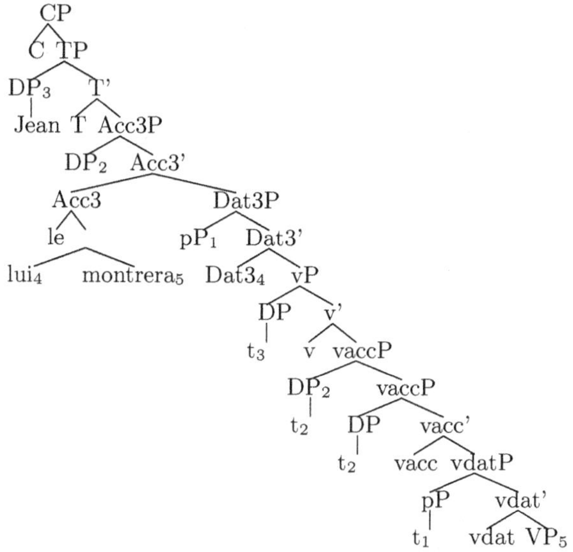

The reader can check that with this grammar we also have, as desired:

(12) Jean montrera le livre à Marie
(13) Jean se montrera à Marie
(14) *Jean se lui montrera

The proper semantics for these constructions must be left to another paper, but see (Sportiche, 1998) for an informal discussion of what is intended.

This simple syntax of clitic constructions leaves out agreement and many other important phenomena, but many of the more sophisticated recent proposals similarly mix phrasal and head movement. Agreement is carefully considered in (Sportiche, 1998), and interesting accounts of stylistic inversion and subject clitic inversion in French are provided in (Kayne and Pollock, 1999; Pollock et al., 1999; Poletto and Pollock, 1999). It appears that all these fall easily in the scope of the mechanisms proposed here.

3 Affix Hopping

The grammar of §2.1 does not derive the simple tensed clause: *the king eat -s the pie.* The problem is that if we simply allow the verb *eat* to pick up this inflection by head movement to T, as the auxiliary verbs do, then we will mistakenly also derive **eat -s the king the pie.* Since Chomsky (1957), one common proposal is that when there is no auxiliary verb, the inflection can lower to the main verb. This lowering is sometimes called "affix hopping." In the present context, it is interesting to notice that once the head of unmerged phrases is distinguished for head movement, no further components are required for affix hopping.

We can formalize this idea in our grammars as follows. We introduce two new kinds of features $\texttt{<=}f$ and $f\texttt{=>}$ (for any $f \in B$), and we add the following additional cases to definition of *merge*:

$$\frac{\epsilon, s, \epsilon :: f\texttt{=>}\gamma \qquad t_s, t_h, t_c \cdot f, \alpha_1, \ldots, \alpha_k}{\epsilon, \epsilon, t_s t_h s t_c : \gamma, \alpha_1, \ldots, \alpha_k} \text{ r1hopright}$$

$$\frac{\epsilon, s, \epsilon :: \texttt{<=}f\gamma \qquad t_s, t_h, t_c \cdot f, \alpha_1, \ldots, \alpha_k}{\epsilon, \epsilon, t_s s t_h t_c : \gamma, \alpha_1, \ldots, \alpha_k} \text{ r1hopleft}$$

$$\frac{\epsilon, s, \epsilon :: f\texttt{=>}\gamma, \alpha_1, \ldots, \alpha_k \qquad t_s, t_h, t_c \cdot f\delta, \iota_1, \ldots, \iota_l}{\epsilon, \epsilon, \epsilon : \gamma, t_s t_h s t_c : \delta, \alpha_1, \ldots, \alpha_k, \iota_1, \ldots, \iota_l} \text{ r3hopright}$$

$$\frac{\epsilon, s, \epsilon :: \texttt{<=}f\gamma, \alpha_1, \ldots, \alpha_k \qquad t_s, t_h, t_c \cdot f\delta, \iota_1, \ldots, \iota_l}{\epsilon, \epsilon, \epsilon : \gamma, t_s s t_h t_c : \delta, \alpha_1, \ldots, \alpha_k, \iota_1, \ldots, \iota_l} \text{ r3hopleft}$$

This formulation of affix-hopping as a sort of string-inverse of head movement has the consequence that an affix can only "hop" to the head of a selected phrase, not to the head of the head selected by a selected phrase. That is, affix hopping can only take place in the configuration of selection.[2] It is now a simple matter to obtain a grammar G2 that gets simple inflected clauses.

[2] (Sportiche, 1998, 382) points out that the proposal in (Chomsky, 1993) for avoiding affix hopping also has the consequence that affixes on main verbs in English can only occur in the configuration where head movement would also have been possible.

3.1 G3: Affix Hopping in English

We elaborate grammar G1 by adding a single lexical item:

```
-s:: v=> +k T
```

It is left as an exercise for the reader to verify that the set of strings of category C now allows main verbs to be inflected but not fronted, as desired:

(15) the king eat -s the pie
(16) *eat -s the king the pie

This kind of account of English clause structure commonly adds one more ingredient: do-support. Introductory texts sometimes propose that *do* can be attached to any stranded affix, perhaps by a process that is not part of the syntax proper. We accordingly take it up in the next section.

4 Recognition

4.1 From Input to Syntactic Atoms

Phonological and morphological analysis of an acoustic input will commonly yield more than one possible analysis of the input to be parsed. Sometimes it is assumed that the set of possible analyses can be represented with a regular grammar or finite state machine. We will adopt that idea here, implementing a simple kind of "morphological analysis" with a finite state transducer.

For any set S, let $S^\epsilon = (S \cup \{\epsilon\})$. Then as usual, a **finite state machine**(FSM) $A = \langle Q, \Sigma, \delta, I, F\rangle$ where Q is a finite set of states ($\neq \emptyset$); Σ_1 is a finite set of input symbols ($\neq \emptyset$); $\delta \subseteq Q \times \Sigma^\epsilon \times Q$, $I \subseteq Q$, the initial states; $F \subseteq Q$, the final states. Intuitively, a **finite transducer** is an acceptor where the transitions between states are labeled by pairs. Formally, we let the pairs come from different alphabets: $T = \langle Q, \Sigma_1, \Sigma_2, \delta, I, F\rangle$ where Q is a finite set of states ($\neq \emptyset$); Σ_1 is a finite set of input symbols ($\neq \emptyset$); Σ_2 is a finite set of output symbols ($\neq \emptyset$); $\delta \subseteq Q \times \Sigma_1^\epsilon \times \Sigma_2^\epsilon \times Q$, $I \subseteq Q$, the initial states; $F \subseteq Q$, the final states. And as usual, we assume that for any state q and any transition function δ, $\langle q, \epsilon, \epsilon, q\rangle \in \delta$.

For any transducers $T = \langle Q, \Sigma_1, \Sigma_2, \delta_1, I, F\rangle$ and $T' = \langle Q', \Sigma_1', \Sigma_2', \delta_2, I', F'\rangle$, define the **composition** $T \circ T' = \langle Q \times Q', \Sigma_1, \Sigma_2', \delta, I \times I', F \times F'\rangle$ where $\delta = \{\langle\langle q_i, q_i'\rangle, a, b, \langle q_j, q_j'\rangle\rangle |$ for some $c \in (\Sigma_2^\epsilon \cap \Sigma_1'^\epsilon)$, $\langle q_i, a, c, q_j\rangle \in \delta_1$ and $\langle q_i', c, b, q_j'\rangle \in \delta_2\}$ (Kaplan and Kay, 1994, for example). And finally, for any transducer $T = \langle Q, \Sigma_1, \Sigma_2, \delta, I, F\rangle$ let its **second projection** $2(T)$ be the FSM $A = \langle Q, \Sigma_1, \delta', I, F\rangle$, where $\delta' = \{\langle q_i, a, q_j\rangle |$ for some $b \in \Sigma_2^\epsilon$, $\langle q_i, a, b, q_j\rangle \in \delta\}$.

Now for any input $s \in V^*$ where $s = w_1 w_2 \ldots w_n$ for some $n \geq 0$, let *string*(s) be the transducer $\langle\{0, 1, \ldots, n\}, \Sigma, \Sigma, \delta_0, \{0\}, \{n\}\rangle$, where $\delta = \{\langle i - 1, w_i, w_i, i\rangle | \; 0 \leq i\}$. A (finite state) **morphology** is a transducer $M = \langle Q, V, \Sigma, \delta, I, F\rangle$ such that for any $s \in V^*$, $2(string(s) \circ M)$ represents the sequences of syntactic atoms to be parsed with a grammar whose vocabulary is Σ. For any morphology M, let the function $input_M$ from V^* to Σ^* be such that for any $s \in V^*$, $input(s) = 2(string(s) \circ M)$.

4.2 M0: A Simple Morphology for G3

Let $M0$ be the 4-state transducer $\langle\{A,B,C,D\},V,\Sigma,\delta,\{A\},\{A\}\rangle$ where δ is the set containing the following 4-tuples:

⟨A,the,the,A⟩	⟨A,has,have,B⟩	⟨A,eaten,eat,C⟩	⟨A,eating,eat,D⟩
⟨A,king,king,A⟩	⟨A,is,be,B⟩	⟨A,laughed,laugh,C⟩	⟨A,laughing,laugh,D⟩
⟨A,pie,pie,A⟩	⟨A,eats,eat,B⟩	⟨C,ϵ,-en,A⟩	⟨D,ϵ,-ing,A⟩
⟨A,which,which,A⟩	⟨A,laughs,laugh,B⟩		
⟨A,eat,eat,A⟩	⟨A,will,will,B⟩		
⟨A,laugh,laugh,A⟩	⟨B,ϵ,-s,A⟩		
⟨A,does,-s,A⟩			

With this morphology, $input_{M0}$(`the king has eaten`) is the FSM depicted below, a machine that accepts only `the king have -s eat -en`:

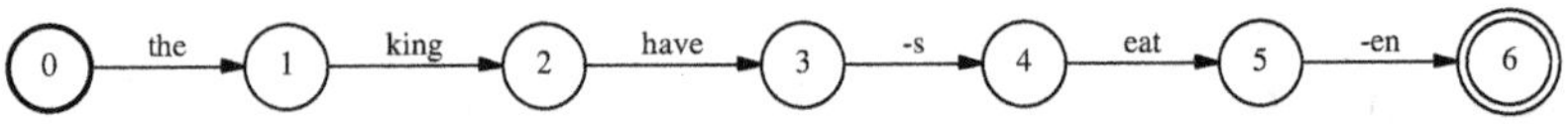

Notice that the last triple in the left column above provides a simple kind of do-support, so that $input_{M0}$(`what does the king eat`) is the FSM that accepts only: `what -s the king eat`. This is like example (7) from §2.1, and we see here the beginning of one of the traditional accounts of this construction.

These values of $input_{M0}$ have just one successful path, but this is not required. Obviously, more complex morphologies (and phonologies) can be represented by FSMs (Ellison, 1994; Eisner, 1997).

4.3 From Syntactic Atoms to Phrase Structures

The input to syntactic analysis is a finite state machine $input(s) = \langle Q,V,\Sigma,\delta,I,F\rangle$. The analysis is computed by closing the set δ under the *move* and *merge*, where these functions are given exactly as above, except that each string t is represented by a pair of states that is connected by a path in $2(input(s))$ that is labeled by t. So for example, the definition of *move* given in §2 above includes the case r1', which, now representing strings as pairs of states, is the function which for any states $w,x,y_0,y,z_0,z_1,z_2,z \in Q$, any any $\cdot \in \{:,::\}$, any $f \in B$, $\gamma \in F^*$, and any chains $\alpha_1,\ldots,\alpha_k$ $(0 \leq k,l)$ maps arguments to values as follows:

$$\frac{(x,x),(y_0,y),(w,w) :: \texttt{=}f\gamma \qquad (z_0,z_1),(z_1,z_2),(z_2,z)\cdot f,\alpha_1,\ldots,\alpha_k}{(x,x),(y_0,y),(z_0,z) : \gamma,\alpha_1,\ldots,\alpha_k}\ \text{r1'}$$

Treating all the other cases similarly, this closure can be computed with the semi-naive closure algorithm implemented by "chart parsers" like the one in (Shieber et al., 1993).[3]

Harkema (2000) shows that the complexity of this recognition algorithm, when restricted to phrasal movement, is $\mathcal{O}(n^{4k+4})$ where $n = |Q|$ and k is the number of different licensee features that occur in lexical items of the grammar.

[3] An implementation is available from the author.

Adding two new components to the head component of each chain increases the maximum number of items just as adding 2 new licensees would, and the recognition procedure is otherwise unchanged in its essentials, so the bound remains polynomial.

5 Logical Perspectives

One of the appeals of type-logical approaches to language is their connection to semantics. The structure building function *merge* corresponds to function application, and this part of the grammar captures basic predicate-argument relations. Phrasal movement has rather complex and subtle effects on scope relations, but head movement does not. Head movement appears to be a semantically empty rearrangement of phonetic material, something that can be handled by "structural rules" (Vermaat, 1999; Moortgat, 1996; Morrill, 1994), or in the labels of a labeled type-logical deduction. The approaches of (Lecomte and Retoré, 1999; Lecomte, 2001), based on a partially commutative linear logic, come especially close to those presented here, because string manipulation is relegated to the labels, and the effect of (SMC) is captured transparently with a restriction on derivations. Let's briefly consider how that approach might be elaborated to capture deductions like those explored here.

The basic idea of Lecomte and Retoré is to keep the logical analysis simple and close to the linguists' conception: all the deductive steps are elimination rules; these steps must be taken in a prescribed order; and the string label calculation is separately stated. In this framework, it appears that two modes of application may suffice: one that is order-sensitive, and one that is not. In the grammars proposed here, we still have only two elimination steps: move and merge, but the string labels are now tuples of strings, and the way the string labels are calculated depends on the particular sub-case of merge or move being applied. The prospects for developing a rigorous logical perspective along these lines look promising, and the hope is that by factoring the theory into these components, the basic type logic can remain much simpler than would otherwise be possible.

6 Conclusions and Assessments

The "transformational" tradition in syntax encompasses many diverse theoretical proposals, and rather wide-ranging empirical research. Formal tools can provide useful insights into this work, making the basic ideas more accessible to other frameworks. A great effort and years of critical assessment have gone into theories that involve both head- and phrasal-movement, and this paper makes just a beginning toward a clearer and simpler formal conception of this work, following the pioneering studies of (Michaelis, 1998; Harkema, 2000). Some researchers think that the role of head movement should be reduced or eliminated (Koopman and Szabolcsi, 2000; Mahajan, 2000), but very many linguists are unconvinced, and so the mechanisms explored in this paper remain of interest. Many other proposals in the recent "minimalist" tradition remain to be carefully explored, including the various proposals about "asymmetric" feature checking (Chomsky, 1995; Collins, 1997, for example), and proposals about trans-derivational "economy" or "optimality" (Pesetsky, 1989; Sportiche, 1998; Chomsky, 1995; Chomsky, 1999; Bresnan, 2000; Legendre, 2000).

It is clear that all of the MG extensions proposed here can be implemented in MCFGs. That is, the Michaelis (1998) result can be extended to all of them. Recently, Harkema (2001) has provided the converse to that result: all languages defined by MCFGs can be defined (and in a very similar way) by MGs. These results then have the perhaps surprising consequence that none of the elaborations proposed here change the definable languages. The languages defined by MCFGs, MGs, MGs with head movement, and by MGs with head movement and affix hopping, are all exactly the same. Obviously, then, the linguistic motivation for these elaborations then cannot come from differences in the definable languages. What does it come from? A full discussion is beyond the scope of this paper, but clearly it has something to do with the simplicity and elegance of the definition.

References

Mark Baker. 1996. *The Polysynthesis Parameter.* Oxford University Press, NY.

Joan Bresnan. 2000. Optimal syntax. In *Optimality Theory: Phonology, Syntax and Acquisition.* Oxford University Press, Oxford.

Noam Chomsky. 1957. *Syntactic Structures.* Mouton, The Hague.

Noam Chomsky. 1993. A minimalist program for linguistic theory. In Kenneth Hale and Samuel Jay Keyser, editors, *The View from Building 20.* MIT Press, Cambridge, Massachusetts.

Noam Chomsky. 1995. *The Minimalist Program.* MIT Press, Cambridge, Massachusetts.

Noam Chomsky. 1999. Derivation by phase. MIT. Forthcoming.

Chris Collins. 1997. *Local Economy.* MIT Press, Cambridge, Massachusetts.

Thomas L. Cornell. 1999. Lambek calculus for transformational grammar. In *Proceedings of the Workshop on Resource Logics and Minimalist Grammars, ESSLLI'99*, Utrecht.

Jason Eisner. 1997. Efficient generation in Primitive Optimality Theory. In *Proceedings of the 35th Annual Meeting of the Association for Computational Linguistics.*

Mark T. Ellison. 1994. Phonological derivation in optimality theory. In *Procs. 15th Int. Conf. on Computational Linguistics*, pages 1007–1013. (Also available at the Edinburgh Computational Phonology Archive).

Victoria Fromkin, editor. 2000. *Linguistics: An Introduction to Linguistic Theory.* Basil Blackwell, Oxford.

Henk Harkema. 2000. A recognizer for minimalist grammars. In *Sixth International Workshop on Parsing Technologies, IWPT'2000.*

Henk Harkema. 2001. A characterization of minimalist languages. In *Proceedings, Logical Aspects of Computational Linguistics, LACL'01*, Port-aux-Rocs, Le Croisic, France.

Ronald Kaplan and Martin Kay. 1994. Regular models of phonological rule systems. *Computational Linguistics*, 20:331–378.

Richard Kayne and Jean-Yves Pollock. 1999. New thoughts on stylistic inversion. Manuscript, New York University and CNRS, Lyon.

Richard Kayne. 1989. Null subjects and clitic climbing. In O. Jaeggli and K. Safir, editors, *The Null Subject Parameter*. Kluwer, Dordrecht.

Hilda Koopman and Anna Szabolcsi. 2000. *Verbal Complexes*. MIT Press, Cambridge, Massachusetts.

Hilda Koopman. 1993. The structure of Dutch PPs. UCLA manuscript.

Hilda Koopman. 1994. Licensing heads. In David Lightfoot and Norbert Hornstein, editors, *Verb Movement*, pages 261–296. Cambridge University Press, NY.

Alain Lecomte and Christian Retoré. 1999. Towards a minimal logic for minimalist grammars. In *Proceedings, Formal Grammar'99*, Utrecht.

Alain Lecomte. 2001. Rebuilding MP on a logical ground. In *Journal of Language and Computation*.

Geraldine Legendre. 2000. An introduction to optimality theory in syntax. In Geraldine Legendre, Jane Grimshaw, and Sten Vikner, editors, *Optimality-theoretic Syntax*. MIT Press, Cambridge, Massachusetts.

Anoop Mahajan. 2000. Eliminating head movement. In *The 23rd Generative Linguistics in the Old World Colloquium, GLOW '2000*.

Jens Michaelis. 1998. Derivational minimalism is mildly context-sensitive. In *Proceedings, Logical Aspects of Computational Linguistics, LACL'98*, Grenoble. Available at `http://www.ling.uni-potsdam.de/~michael/papers.html`.

Michael Moortgat. 1996. Categorial type logics. In Johan van Benthem and Alice ter Meulen, editors, *Handbook of Logic and Language*. Elsevier, Amsterdam.

Glyn V. Morrill. 1994. *Type-logical Grammar: Categorial Logic of Signs*. Kluwer, Dordrecht.

David Pesetsky. 1989. Language-particular processes and the earliness principle. In *GLOW '89*. Manuscript available at `http://www.mit.edu/afs/athena.mit.edu/org/l/linguistics/www/pesetsky.home.html`.

Cecilia Poletto and Jean-Yves Pollock. 1999. On the left periphery of Romance wh-questions. University of Padua, Université de Picardia à Amiens.

Carl Pollard. 1984. *Generalized phrase structure grammars, head grammars and natural language*. Ph.D. thesis, Standford University.

Jean-Yves Pollock, Nicola Munaro, and Cecilia Poletto. 1999. Eppur si muove! In *A Celebration*. MIT Press, Cambridge, Massachusetts. Available at `http://mitpress.mit.edu/chomskydisc/polleto.html`.

Hiroyuki Seki, Takashi Matsumura, Mamoru Fujii, and Tadao Kasami. 1991. On multiple context-free grammars. *Theoretical Computer Science*, 88:191–229.

Stuart M. Shieber, Yves Schabes, and Fernando C. N. Pereira. 1993. Principles and implementation of deductive parsing. Technical Report CRCT TR-11-94, Computer Science Department, Harvard University, Cambridge, Massachusetts. Available at `http://arXiv.org/`.

Dominique Sportiche. 1995. Sketch of a reductionist approach to syntactic variation and dependencies. In Hector Campos and Paula Kempchinsky, editors, *Evolution and Revolution in Linguistic Theory*. Georgetown University Press, Washington. Reprinted in Dominique Sportiche, *Partitions and Atoms of Clause Structure: Subjects, agreement, case and clitics*. NY: Routledge.

Dominique Sportiche. 1998. *Partitions and Atoms of Clause Structure : Subjects, Agreement, Case and Clitics*. Routledge, NY.

Edward P. Stabler and Edward L. Keenan. 2000. Structural similarity. In A. Nijholt, G. Scollo, T. Rus, and D. Heylen, editors, *Algebraic Methods in Language Processing, AMiLP 2000*, University of Iowa. Revised version forthcoming in *Theoretical Computer Science*.

Edward P. Stabler. 1997. Derivational minimalism. In Christian Retoré, editor, *Logical Aspects of Computational Linguistics*, pages 68–95. Springer-Verlag (Lecture Notes in Computer Science 1328), NY.

Edward P. Stabler. 1999. Minimalist grammars and recognition. In *Linguistic form and its computation*, Bad Teinach, Germany. Presented at the Final Workshop of SFB340, October 1999. Publication forthcoming.

Willemijn Vermaat. 1999. The minimalist *move* operation in a deductive perspective. In *Proceedings of the Workshop on Resource Logics and Minimalist Grammars, ESSLLI'99*, Utrecht.

Arnold Zwicky. 1985. Clitics and particles. *Language*, 61:283–305.

Combinators for Paraconsistent Attitudes

Jørgen Villadsen

Informatics and Mathematical Modelling
Technical University of Denmark
Richard Petersens Plads, Building 321
DK-2800 Kongens Lyngby, Denmark
jv@imm.dtu.dk

Abstract. In order to analyse the semantics of natural language sentences a translation into a partial type logic using lexical and logical combinators is presented. The sentences cover a fragment of English with propositional attitudes like knowledge, belief and assertion. A combinator is a closed term of the lambda calculus possibly containing lexical and/or logical constants. Such combinators seem promising from both a cognitive and computational point of view. There is approximately one lexical combinator for each word, but just eleven logical combinators for the present fragment. The partiality is only used for embedded sentences expressing propositional attitudes, thereby allowing for inconsistency without explosion (also called paraconsistency), and is based on a few key equalities for the connectives giving four truth values (truth, falsehood, and undefinedness with negative and positive polarity; only the first truth value is designated, i.e. yields the logical truths).

1 Introduction

In the last decades there has been much interest in paraconsistent logics, viz. logics that, as opposed to classical or intuitionistic logic, allow for inconsistency without explosion [4]. We provide a paraconsistent logical semantics of propositional attitudes of knowledge, belief, assertion etc. expressed in a natural language fragment described in section 1.1. The problem of paraconsistency and relevance is discussed in section 1.2 and our use of combinators [5] is illustrated in section 1.3. Section 1.4 is an overview of the subsequent sections.

1.1 Propositional Attitudes in Natural Language

We consider propositional attitudes of the form 'π α that ϕ' where π is an agent, α is the attitude and ϕ is the embedded sentence [17,6,9]. Propositional attitudes can be nested:

Gloria knows that John believes that Victoria smiles (*)

We return to the semantics of (*) in section 1.3 (it should be noted that the sentence does not end with a full-stop; this will make a difference later).

P. de Groote, G. Morrill, C. Retoré (Eds.): LACL 2001, LNAI 2099, pp. 261–278, 2001.

We consider the following fragment of natural language:

Propositional attitudes	know believe assert ...
Intransitive verbs	cheat smile ...
Transitive verbs	cheat love ...
Common nouns	man woman ...
Proper nouns	John Nick ...
Adjectives	popular quick ...
Copula	be
Negation and coordination	not / and / or
Quantification	a / every
Relativization	that
Reflexivization	himself / herself

Although we only consider present tense and singular nouns the following rather artificial paragraph illustrates the coverage:

> John knows that it is not the case that Gloria loves everyone that Nick asserts that Victoria loves. John does not love himself and cheats everyone that cheats. Nick is a quick and popular thief and John or a man that helps John is quick.

The semantics of the natural language sentences can be tested when used in correct, respectively incorrect, arguments:

$$\frac{\text{John believes that Victoria smiles and dances.}}{\text{John believes that Victoria smiles.}} \quad \surd$$

$$\frac{\text{John believes that Victoria smiles.}}{\text{John believes that Victoria smiles and dances.}} \quad \div$$

Let K, B and A be the modal operators for knowledge, belief and assertion, respectively. The main principles are given by the following schemas (we say more about logical omniscience in section 1.2):

$$\text{Omniscience} \quad \frac{K\phi \quad \phi \Rightarrow \psi}{K\psi} \surd \qquad \frac{B\phi \quad \phi \Rightarrow \psi}{B\psi} \surd \qquad \frac{A\phi \quad \phi \Rightarrow \psi}{A\psi} \surd$$

$$\text{Opaqueness} \quad \frac{\phi}{K\phi} \div \qquad \frac{\phi}{B\phi} \div \qquad \frac{\phi}{A\phi} \div$$

$$\text{Only knowledge factive} \quad \frac{K\phi}{\phi} \surd \qquad \frac{B\phi}{\phi} \div \qquad \frac{A\phi}{\phi} \div$$

$$\text{Only knowledge and belief introspective} \quad \frac{K\phi}{KK\phi} \surd \qquad \frac{B\phi}{BB\phi} \surd \qquad \frac{A\phi}{AA\phi} \div$$

$$\text{Knowledge yields belief} \quad \frac{K\phi}{B\phi} \surd \qquad \text{Assertion not always honest} \quad \frac{A\phi}{BK\phi} \div$$

1.2 Paraconsistency and Relevance

Even an observer employing classical logic must handle inconsistencies in other agents attitudes. Let us look at assertion. We want:

$$\text{Paraconsistency} \quad \frac{A(\phi \wedge \neg\phi)}{A\psi} \div \qquad \text{Relevance} \quad \frac{A\phi}{A(\phi \wedge (\psi \vee \neg\psi))} \div$$

Hence the agent asserting the inconsistency, either explicitly like above or implicitly from multiple sources, cannot be logically omniscient according to classical logic, but must employ a non-classical paraconsistent logic. We even want:

$$\text{Strong Paraconsistency / Relevance} \quad \frac{A(\phi \wedge \neg\phi)}{A(\psi \vee \neg\psi)} \div \qquad \frac{}{A(\psi \vee \neg\psi)} \div$$

In section 2 we develop a new approach to paraconsistency (and relevance).

1.3 Lexical and Logical Combinators

The translation is based on a categorial grammar, with a multi-dimensional type theory as model theory and a sequent calculus as proof theory [18,19,8,30,36]. The sentence (*) from section 1.1 has the following translation into a paraconsistent type logic:

Gloria know John believe Victoria smile

$\rightsquigarrow$ **know**$\star$ $\lambda\star$(**believe**$\star$ $\lambda\star$(**smile**$\star$ **Victoria**$\star$) **John**$\star$) **Gloria**$\star$

$\rightsquigarrow \mathbf{P}\ \lambda i(K\star Gi)\ \lambda\star(\mathbf{P}\ \lambda i(B\star Ji)\ \lambda\star(S\star V))$

$\rightsquigarrow \forall i(K\star Gj \Rightarrow \forall j(BiJj \Rightarrow SjV))$

We start with a string, that is, a sequence of so-called tokens, obtained from the sentence (*) in a very simple way. For instance, the word order is not changed.

The first formula contains lexical combinators and a single variable $\star$ ranging over so-called situations (or indices [10]). The variable $\star$ is always hung on to the preceding term. The tokens and the combinators are in one-to-one correspondence. Besides the definition of the combinators the key issue is the structure of the formula derived from the categorial grammar. As a pleasant property we have that sentences embedded in propositional attitudes are translated independently of the embedding.

The second formula contains logical combinators and auxiliary variables i and j ranging over situations (like $\star$). Names do not depend on the situation. Only eleven logical combinators are introduced. For instance, the preservation combinator $\mathbf{P} \equiv \lambda pq\forall i(pi \Rightarrow qi)$ mirrors logical implication. Systematic definitions link the lexical and logical combinators, for instance **Gloria** $\equiv \lambda\star G$, **John** $\equiv \lambda\star J$, **Victoria** $\equiv \lambda\star V$, **know** $\equiv \lambda\star px(\mathbf{P}\lambda i(K\star xi)p)$, **believe** $\equiv \lambda\star px(\mathbf{P}\lambda i(B\star xi)p)$, and **smile** $\equiv \lambda\star x(S\star x)$ (the last combinator is equal to S, but we prefer the expanded form).

The third formula shows the final formula for the sentence. The variable $\star$ is still free since we are not dealing with an argument.

1.4 Overview of Subsequent Sections

The underlying paraconsistent type logic is explained in section 2. Section 3 defines the lexicon, the combinators and a few postulates mainly in order to characterize the propositional attitudes. Section 4 briefly describes an axiomatization of the categorial grammar and develops various sample derivations. Finally section 5 comprises the conclusions.

2 A Paraconsistent Type Logic

We describe the propositional part in section 2.1 and return to the paraconsistent type logic in section 2.2.

2.1 Propositional Logic

In [21] a logical semantics of propositional attitudes is presented where classical logic is replaced by a partial logic, that is, a logic with "undefined" truth values. We think that although this semantics makes the correct predictions for the present fragment, it does it for the wrong reasons and for more complicated fragments of natural language it might not work, since it is based on a special implication connective such that we do not have $\phi \hookrightarrow \phi$ for all formulas ϕ. The symbol $\hookrightarrow$ is not defined explicitly in [21], but we discuss its definition and truth table at the end of this subsection.

We propose a different partial logic such that $\phi \Rightarrow \phi$ and based on a few key equalities. Classical logic has two truth values, namely **T** and **F** (truth and falsehood). The designated truth value **T** with symbol $\top$ yields the logical truths.

The semantic clauses and the common definition $\top \equiv \neg\bot$ work for classical logic and also for our partial logic (basic semantic clause omitted):

$$[\![\phi = \psi]\!] = \begin{cases} \mathbf{T} \text{ if } [\![\phi]\!] = [\![\psi]\!] \\ \mathbf{F} \text{ otherwise} \end{cases}$$

$$[\![\neg\phi]\!] = \begin{cases} \mathbf{T} & \text{if } [\![\phi]\!] = \mathbf{F} \\ \mathbf{F} & \text{if } [\![\phi]\!] = \mathbf{T} \\ [\![\phi]\!] & \text{otherwise} \end{cases} \qquad \begin{aligned} \top &= \neg\bot \\ \bot &= \neg\top \end{aligned}$$

$$[\![\phi \wedge \psi]\!] = \begin{cases} [\![\phi]\!] \text{ if } [\![\phi]\!] = [\![\psi]\!] \\ [\![\psi]\!] \text{ if } [\![\phi]\!] = \mathbf{T} \\ [\![\phi]\!] \text{ if } [\![\psi]\!] = \mathbf{T} \\ \mathbf{F} \quad \text{otherwise} \end{cases} \qquad \begin{aligned} \phi &= \phi \wedge \phi \\ \psi &= \top \wedge \psi \\ \phi &= \phi \wedge \top \end{aligned}$$

$$[\![\phi \Leftrightarrow \psi]\!] = \begin{cases} \mathbf{T} & \text{if } [\![\phi]\!] = [\![\psi]\!] \\ [\![\psi]\!] & \text{if } [\![\phi]\!] = \mathbf{T} \\ [\![\phi]\!] & \text{if } [\![\psi]\!] = \mathbf{T} \\ [\![\neg\psi]\!] & \text{if } [\![\phi]\!] = \mathbf{F} \\ [\![\neg\phi]\!] & \text{if } [\![\psi]\!] = \mathbf{F} \\ \mathbf{F} & \text{otherwise} \end{cases} \qquad \begin{aligned} \top &= \phi \Leftrightarrow \phi \\ \psi &= \top \Leftrightarrow \psi \\ \phi &= \phi \Leftrightarrow \top \\ \neg\psi &= \bot \Leftrightarrow \psi \\ \neg\phi &= \phi \Leftrightarrow \bot \end{aligned}$$

In the semantic clauses several cases may apply if and only if they agree on the truth value result. Note that the double negation law $\phi = \neg\neg\phi$ holds. We make the following definitions:

$$\phi \vee \psi \equiv \neg(\neg\phi \wedge \neg\psi) \qquad \phi \Rightarrow \psi \equiv \phi \Leftrightarrow (\phi \wedge \psi)$$

$$\phi \rightarrow \psi \equiv \neg\phi \vee \psi \qquad \phi \leftrightarrow \psi \equiv (\phi \rightarrow \psi) \wedge (\psi \rightarrow \phi)$$

We now consider additional truth values. First we add just $[\![\dagger]\!] = \mathbf{N}$ for the "undefined" truth value. We do not have $\phi \vee \neg\phi$, hence not $\phi \rightarrow \phi$, but $\phi \Rightarrow \phi$ of course. Unfortunately we also have $(\phi \wedge \neg\phi) \Rightarrow (\psi \vee \neg\psi)$ (try with the truth values **T**, **F** and **N**). The reason is that in a sense there is not only a single "undefined" truth value, but a unique one for each basic formula. However, only two "undefined" truth values are ever needed, corresponding to the left and right hand side of the implication (in other words, the negative and positive occurrences suggest undefinedness with negative and positive polarity). Hence we add $[\![\ddagger]\!] = \mathbf{P}$ for the alternative "undefined" truth value. We then define $\bot \equiv \dagger \wedge \ddagger$ as seen from the truth tables:

=	T	F	N	P
T	**T**	**F**	**F**	**F**
F	**F**	**T**	**F**	**F**
N	**F**	**F**	**T**	**F**
P	**F**	**F**	**F**	**T**

∧	T	F	N	P
T	**T**	**F**	**N**	**P**
F	**F**	**F**	**F**	**F**
N	**N**	**F**	**N**	**F**
P	**P**	**F**	**F**	**P**

∨	T	F	N	P
T	**T**	**T**	**T**	**T**
F	**T**	**F**	**N**	**P**
N	**T**	**N**	**N**	**T**
P	**T**	**P**	**T**	**P**

¬	
T	**F**
F	**T**
N	**N**
P	**P**

→	T	F	N	P
T	**T**	**F**	**N**	**P**
F	**T**	**T**	**T**	**T**
N	**T**	**N**	**N**	**T**
P	**T**	**P**	**T**	**P**

↔	T	F	N	P
T	**T**	**F**	**N**	**P**
F	**F**	**T**	**N**	**P**
N	**N**	**N**	**N**	**T**
P	**P**	**P**	**T**	**P**

⇒	T	F	N	P
T	**T**	**F**	**N**	**P**
F	**T**	**T**	**T**	**T**
N	**T**	**N**	**T**	**N**
P	**T**	**P**	**P**	**T**

⇔	T	F	N	P
T	**T**	**F**	**N**	**P**
F	**F**	**T**	**N**	**P**
N	**N**	**N**	**T**	**F**
P	**P**	**P**	**F**	**T**

Our partial logic is a relevant logic [1] and differs from other four-valued logics based on bilattices [7,16,15,3,29] where the third value means "neither true nor false" and the fourth value means "both true and false" (so **P** is replaced by a new designated truth value **B**). See also [22].

We now return to the definition of $\hookrightarrow$ as implicitly used in [21, page 80] where $T\phi$ is taken to mean 'ϕ is true' (note that we do not have $\phi \hookrightarrow \phi$ for all formulas ϕ, because although the formula $\ddagger \hookrightarrow \ddagger$ holds, the formula $\dagger \hookrightarrow \dagger$ does not hold and it would not be reasonable to take **N** as a designated truth value):

$$T\phi \equiv (\phi = \top) \vee (\phi = \ddagger) \qquad \phi \hookrightarrow \psi \equiv \phi \rightarrow T\psi$$

↪	T	F	N	P
T	**T**	**F**	**F**	**T**
F	**T**	**T**	**T**	**T**
N	**T**	**N**	**N**	**T**
P	**T**	**P**	**P**	**T**

↠	T	F	N	P
T	**T**	**F**	**F**	**F**
F	**T**	**T**	**T**	**T**
N	**T**	**F**	**T**	**F**
P	**T**	**F**	**F**	**T**

We have also shown the truth table for the implication based on equality corresponding to entailment in [21, page 80] (note that we have $\phi \twoheadrightarrow \phi$ for all formulas ϕ):

$$\phi \twoheadrightarrow \psi \;\equiv\; \phi = (\phi \wedge \psi)$$

2.2 Type Logic

We now present a type logic [2] with the same propositional part as above. It is similar to the m-sorted n-valued functional type logic TY_m^n with single designated truth value developed in [21] ($m \geq 1$ and $n \in \{2,3,4\}$), but with a different implication connective, as explained in section 2.1.

The set of types and terms (for each type τ) is:

$$\mathcal{T} \equiv \mathcal{T}\mathcal{T} \mid K$$

$$\mathcal{L}_\tau \equiv \mathcal{L}_{\sigma\tau}\mathcal{L}_\sigma \mid \lambda x_\rho \mathcal{L}_\kappa \mid K_\tau \mid x_\tau$$

Here K ranges over type constants, K_τ and x_τ range over term constants and variables of type τ, respectively, and $\tau, \sigma, \rho, \kappa \in \mathcal{T}$ and such that $\tau = \rho\kappa$.

We often write $\tau_1 \ldots \tau_m \sigma$ instead of the type $\tau_1(\ldots(\tau_m\sigma))$ and $\alpha\beta_1 \ldots \beta_n$ instead of the term $((\alpha\beta_1)\ldots)\beta_n$.

A universe U is an indexed set of type universes $U_\tau \neq \emptyset$ such that $U_{\alpha\beta} \subseteq U_\beta^{U_\alpha}$. The universe is full if $\subseteq$ is replaced by $=$.

A basic interpretation function F on a universe U is a function $F\colon \bigcup K_\tau \to \bigcup U_\tau$ such that $FK_\tau \in U_\tau$. Analogously, an assignment function a on a universe U is a function $a\colon \bigcup x_\tau \to \bigcup U_\tau$ such that $ax_\tau \in U_\tau$.

A model $M \equiv \langle U, F \rangle$ consists of a basic interpretation function F on a universe U such that for all assignment functions a on the universe U the interpretation function $[\![\cdot]\!]^{M,a}\colon \bigcup \mathcal{L}_\tau \to \bigcup U_\tau$ has $[\![\alpha_\tau]\!]^{M,a} \in U_\tau$ for all terms $\alpha_\tau \in \mathcal{L}$, where (we use the lambda calculus in the meta-language as well):

$$\begin{aligned}
[\![K]\!] &= FK \\
[\![x]\!] &= ax \\
[\![\lambda x_\rho \alpha_\kappa]\!] &= \lambda u [\![\alpha]\!]^{a[x \mapsto u]} \\
[\![\alpha_{\sigma\tau}\beta_\sigma]\!] &= [\![\alpha]\!]\,[\![\beta]\!]
\end{aligned}$$

For clarity we omit some types and parameters.

What we call just a model is also known as a general model, and a full model is then a standard model. An arbitrary basic interpretation function on a universe is sometimes considered a very general model.

We add a type constant o as the type of truth values. We call terms of type o formulas. We often write $\langle \alpha \ldots \beta \rangle$ instead of $\alpha \ldots \beta o$ (and hence $\langle\rangle$ instead of o). Besides this type constant we often add other type constants.

Instead of a classical model with two truth values in U_o we consider a partial logic with the following four truth values:

$+-$	Inclusion of verity & Exclusion of falsity
$-+$	Exclusion of verity & Inclusion of falsity
$--$	Exclusion of verity & Exclusion of falsity
$++$	Inclusion of verity & Inclusion of falsity

Note how the first character takes care of the inclusion/exclusion of verity and the second character takes care of the inclusion/exclusion of falsity.

The names of the four truth values are just suggestive; it is the formal properties that are essential, of course. In particular $--$ and $++$ are not direct opposite, but to be seen as undefinedness with negative and positive polarity.

We also need a special notation in order to address the inclusion/exclusion of verity/falsity separately:

$+\cdot$	Inclusion of verity (falsity not addressed)
$-\cdot$	Exclusion of verity (falsity not addressed)
$\cdot+$	Inclusion of falsity (verity not addressed)
$\cdot-$	Exclusion of falsity (verity not addressed)

We extend $\mathcal{L}_o$ with the following basic formulas and interpretations (ϕ and ψ are formulas and x has type ρ):

$$[\![\dagger]\!] = --$$

$$[\![\ddagger]\!] = ++$$

$$[\![\alpha = \beta]\!] = \left\{ \begin{matrix} +\cdot \\ \cdot+ \end{matrix} \right\} \quad \text{iff} \quad \left\{ \begin{matrix} [\![\alpha]\!] = [\![\beta]\!] \\ [\![\alpha]\!] \neq [\![\beta]\!] \end{matrix} \right\}$$

$$[\![\neg\phi]\!] = \left\{ \begin{matrix} +\cdot \\ \cdot+ \end{matrix} \right\} \quad \text{iff} \quad \left\{ \begin{matrix} [\![\phi]\!] = \cdot+ \\ [\![\phi]\!] = +\cdot \end{matrix} \right\}$$

$$[\![\phi \wedge \psi]\!] = \left\{ \begin{matrix} +\cdot \\ \cdot+ \end{matrix} \right\} \quad \text{iff} \quad \left\{ \begin{matrix} [\![\phi]\!] = +\cdot \text{ and } [\![\psi]\!] = +\cdot \\ [\![\phi]\!] = \cdot+ \text{ or } [\![\psi]\!] = \cdot+ \end{matrix} \right\}$$

$$[\![\forall x\phi]\!] = \left\{ \begin{matrix} +\cdot \\ \cdot+ \end{matrix} \right\} \quad \text{iff} \quad \left\{ \begin{matrix} [\![\phi]\!]^{a[x\mapsto u]} = +\cdot \text{ for all } u \in U_\rho \\ [\![\phi]\!]^{a[x\mapsto u]} = \cdot+ \text{ for some } u \in U_\rho \end{matrix} \right\}$$

As usual we have $\exists x\phi \equiv \neg\forall x\neg\phi$. Observe that we have $=$ on all types.

A closed formula ϕ is valid iff $[\![\phi]\!]^M = +-$ for all models M (for open formulas all assignments functions a must be considered in addition to the models M).

For formulas the truth tables are identical to the propositional part of section 2.1 when $\mathbf{T} = +-$, $\mathbf{F} = -+$, $\mathbf{N} = --$ and $\mathbf{P} = ++$. Furthermore [21] provides a sequent calculus for the partial type logic that is complete for general models and shows that it is expressively adequate, hence $\Leftrightarrow$ is definable (and of course $\Rightarrow$ is to be used instead of $\hookrightarrow$ and $\twoheadrightarrow$). We can therefore view the partial type logic as an extension of the propositional logic from section 2.1 and it is paraconsistent in the sense that for instance the formula $(\phi \wedge \neg\phi) \Rightarrow (\psi \vee \neg\psi)$ is invalid.

3 Definition of Combinators

We first briefly describe the categorial grammar and define the lexicon in section 3.1. We define the logical combinators in section 3.2, the lexical combinators in section 3.3, and a few postulates and abbreviations in section 3.4.

3.1 Lexicon

The categorial grammar is not essential to the approach here. The categorization below has left-looking and right-looking constructors $\backslash$ and $/$, a scope constructor $\|$ which lets the second part span over the first part and a modal constructor $\_$ which captures the point of reference. The last two construct are often written $\Uparrow$ and $\Box$ [19]. We prefer our notation since the rules for the scope constructor $\|$ are a kind of combination of the rules for the constructors $/$ and $\backslash$, and we only have a single modal constructor $\_$ which is never deeply nested and does not contribute to syntax (see [34] for details). An axiomatization is provided in section 4.1.

The top category is $\bullet$ for arguments. Basic categories are D (discourse), S (sentence), N (proper noun - name) and G (common noun - group).

John Nick Gloria Victoria : $\underline{N}$

run dance smile : $\underline{N\backslash S}$

find love cheat help : $\underline{(N\backslash S)/N}$

cheat help : $\underline{N\backslash S}$

man woman thief unicorn : $\underline{G}$

popular quick : $\underline{G/G}$

assert believe know : $\underline{(N\backslash S)/\underline{S}}$

be : $\underline{(N\backslash S)/N}$

be : $\underline{(N\backslash S)/(G/G)}$

someone everyone : $\underline{\underline{N}\|S}$

a every : $\underline{(\underline{N}\|S)/G}$

that : $\underline{(G\backslash G)/(\underline{N}\backslash S)}$ $\underline{(G\backslash G)/(S/\underline{N})}$

and or : $\underline{S\backslash(S/S)}$

and or : $\underline{(N\backslash S)\backslash((N\backslash S)/(N\backslash S))}$ $\underline{(G/G)\backslash((G/G)/(G/G))}$

or : $\underline{(S/(N\backslash S))\backslash((S/(N\backslash S))/(S/(N\backslash S)))}$

not : $\underline{(N\backslash S)/(N\backslash S)}$

nix : $\underline{S/S}$

self : $\underline{N\|(N\backslash S)}$

stop : $\underline{\underline{S}\backslash D}$

ok : $\underline{D}$

also : $\underline{D\backslash(D/D)}$

so : $\underline{D}\backslash(\bullet/\underline{D})$

A discourse is a succession of sentences and an argument consists of two discourses which are the premises and the conclusions, respectively. Some tokens live in several categories and are listed on separate lines if the corresponding lexical combinators differ (see section 3.3).

3.2 Logical Combinators

We add the types ϵ of entities (agents) and ι of indices (situations). The variable $\star$ is a special variable of type ι. We use the following type conventions for variables:

$a\ b\ c$	$\langle\rangle$	$p\ q$	$\langle\iota\rangle$
$d\ e$	$\langle\langle\epsilon\rangle\rangle$	$r\ s$	$\langle\epsilon\epsilon\rangle$
$f\ g\ h$	$\langle\langle\epsilon\rangle\epsilon\rangle$	$t\ u$	$\langle\epsilon\rangle$
$i\ j\ k\ l$	ι	$v\ w$	$\langle\iota\epsilon\rangle$
$m\ n$	$\langle\langle\iota\epsilon\rangle\rangle$	$x\ y\ z$	ϵ

We introduce auxiliary constants E of type $\langle\iota\epsilon\rangle$ and I of type $\langle\iota\rangle$ such that Ii ensures integrity and Eix existence at index i for entity x. Both I and E are forced to be classical by the postulates, see section 3.4.

We define the following logical combinators:

$\mathbf{Q} \equiv \lambda xy(x = y)$		Equality
$\mathbf{N} \equiv \lambda a(\neg a)$		Negation
$\mathbf{C} \equiv \lambda ab(a \wedge b)$		Conjunction
$\mathbf{D} \equiv \lambda ab(a \vee b)$		Disjunction
$\mathbf{E} \equiv \lambda it\exists x(Eix \wedge tx)$		Existentiality
$\mathbf{U} \equiv \lambda it\forall x(Eix \Rightarrow tx)$		Universality
$\mathbf{O} \equiv \lambda itu\exists x(Eix \wedge (tx \wedge ux))$		Overlap
$\mathbf{I} \equiv \lambda itu\forall x(Eix \Rightarrow (tx \Rightarrow ux))$		Inclusion
$\mathbf{T} \equiv \lambda i(Ii)$		Triviality
$\mathbf{F} \equiv \lambda ip(Ii \wedge pi)$		Filtration
$\mathbf{P} \equiv \lambda pq\forall i(pi \Rightarrow qi)$		Preservation

The overlap combinator takes two sets and test for a common entity that exists at the pertinent index (analogously for the inclusion combinator). The triviality combinator is used in case of missing premises or missing conclusions in an argument, and filtration is used for full-stops; both ensure the integrity at the pertinent index. The preservation combinator tests for inclusion of indices and is used between the premises and the conclusions in an argument as well as for propositional attitudes.

3.3 Lexical Combinators

There is at least one lexical combinator for each token in the lexicon given in section 3.1, for example the combinator **John** for the token John, **be** and **be'** for be etc. Tokens and combinators are always spelled exactly the same way except for the mark ′ (possibly repeated) at the end.

In order to display the lexicon more compactly we introduce two so-called place-holders ("holes") for combinators and constants, respectively. $\bigcirc$ is place-holder for logical combinators (if any) and $\circ$ is place-holder for (ordinary and predicate) constant (if any); the combinators and constants to be inserted are shown after the separator | for the following lexical combinators:

$$\textbf{John}\;\;\textbf{Nick}\;\;\textbf{Gloria}\;\;\textbf{Victoria} \equiv \lambda\star\circ \mid J\;\; N\;\; G\;\; V$$
$$\textbf{run}\;\;\textbf{dance}\;\;\textbf{smile} \equiv \lambda\star x(\circ\star x) \mid R\;\; D\;\; S$$
$$\textbf{find}\;\;\textbf{love}\;\;\textbf{cheat}\;\;\textbf{help} \equiv \lambda\star yx(\circ\star xy) \mid F\;\; L\;\; C\;\; H$$
$$\textbf{cheat'}\;\;\textbf{help'} \equiv \lambda\star x(\bigcirc\star\lambda y(\circ\star xy)) \mid \mathbf{E} \mid C\;\; H$$
$$\textbf{man}\;\;\textbf{woman}\;\;\textbf{thief}\;\;\textbf{unicorn} \equiv \lambda\star x(\circ\star x) \mid M\;\; W\;\; T\;\; U$$
$$\textbf{popular}\;\;\textbf{quick} \equiv \lambda\star tx(\bigcirc(\circ\star x)(tx)) \mid \mathbf{C} \mid P\;\; Q$$
$$\textbf{assert}\;\;\textbf{believe}\;\;\textbf{know} \equiv \lambda\star px(\bigcirc\lambda i(\circ\star xi)p) \mid \mathbf{P} \mid A\;\; B\;\; K$$
$$\textbf{be} \equiv \lambda\star yx(\bigcirc xy) \mid \mathbf{Q}$$
$$\textbf{be'} \equiv \lambda\star fx(f\lambda y(\bigcirc xy)x) \mid \mathbf{Q}$$
$$\textbf{someone}\;\;\textbf{everyone} \equiv \lambda\star m(\bigcirc\star\lambda x(m\lambda ix)) \mid \mathbf{E}\;\; \mathbf{U}$$
$$\textbf{a}\;\;\textbf{every} \equiv \lambda\star tm(\bigcirc\star t\lambda x(m\lambda ix)) \mid \mathbf{O}\;\; \mathbf{I}$$
$$\textbf{that} \equiv \lambda\star mtx(\bigcirc(tx)(m\lambda ix)) \mid \mathbf{C}$$
$$\textbf{and}\;\;\textbf{or} \equiv \lambda\star ab(\bigcirc ab) \mid \mathbf{C}\;\; \mathbf{D}$$
$$\textbf{and'}\;\;\textbf{or'} \equiv \lambda\star tux(\bigcirc(tx)(ux)) \mid \mathbf{C}\;\; \mathbf{D}$$
$$\textbf{or''} \equiv \lambda\star det(\bigcirc(dt)(et)) \mid \mathbf{D}$$
$$\textbf{not} \equiv \lambda\star tx(\bigcirc(tx)) \mid \mathbf{N}$$
$$\textbf{nix} \equiv \lambda\star a(\bigcirc a) \mid \mathbf{N} \qquad \textbf{ok} \equiv \lambda\star(\bigcirc\star) \mid \mathbf{T}$$
$$\textbf{self} \equiv \lambda\star rx(rxx) \qquad \textbf{also} \equiv \lambda\star ab(\bigcirc ab) \mid \mathbf{C}$$
$$\textbf{stop} \equiv \lambda\star p(\bigcirc\star p) \mid \mathbf{F} \qquad \textbf{so} \equiv \lambda pq(\bigcirc pq) \mid \mathbf{P}$$

We do not have to list the types of constants since either the type of a constant is ϵ or the type can be determined by the types of its arguments.

We have made the following choices. Proper nouns do not depend on the index (neither do copula, relativization, coordination, negation or reflexivization). Intransitive verbs have existential commitment with respect to the corresponding transitive verbs, if present. Adjectives have conjunctive commitment (ditto for relativization). Propositional attitudes have preservative commitment.

It does not seem worthwhile to eliminate the remaining repetitions in the display of the lexicon and the corresponding combinators.

3.4 Postulates and Abbreviations

We need the following postulates. The auxiliary constant E for existence is classical and entities exist for all indices:

$$\forall i \forall x (Eix = \top \vee Eix = \bot) \qquad \forall i \exists x (Eix)$$

Existence for all non-auxiliary constants $\mathcal{K}$ of type ϵ and $\langle \iota \underbrace{\epsilon \dots \epsilon}_{n \text{ times}} \rangle$:

$$\forall i (Ei\mathcal{K}) \qquad \forall i \forall x_1 \dots x_n (\mathcal{K}ix_1 \dots x_n \Rightarrow (Eix_1 \wedge \dots \wedge Eix_n))$$

The auxiliary constant I for integrity is introduced (and becomes classical):

$$\forall i (Ii \Leftrightarrow (\forall x_1 \dots x_n (\mathcal{K}ix_1 \dots x_n = \top \vee \mathcal{K}ix_1 \dots x_n = \bot) \wedge \dots))$$

Here $\mathcal{K}$ ranges over all non-auxiliary constants of type $\langle \iota \underbrace{\epsilon \dots \epsilon}_{n \text{ times}} \rangle$.

Knowledge is factual and yields belief:

$$\forall i \forall x (Kixi = \top) \qquad \forall ij \forall x (Kixj \Rightarrow Bixj)$$

Positive introspection for knowledge and belief (not for assertion):

$$\forall ijk \forall x (((Kixj \wedge Kjxk) \Rightarrow Kixk) \wedge ((Bixj \wedge Bjxk) \Rightarrow Bixk))$$

Finally we use the following abbreviations (similar for $\exists$):

$$\forall x \in i\, \phi \equiv \forall x (Exi \Rightarrow \phi) \qquad \forall \hat{\imath} \phi[\hat{\imath}] \equiv \forall i (Ii \Rightarrow \phi[i]) \quad (i \text{ is a fresh variable})$$

4 Derivations

Section 4.1 provides an axiomatization of the categorial grammar and a sample derivation is provided in section 4.2. Sections 4.3 and 4.4 deal with ambiguities and section 4.5 gives illustrations of paraconsistency.

4.1 Axiomatization

The categorial grammar is based on a multi-dimensional type theory. We present an axiomatization in the form of a sequent calculus where the first dimension (syntax) is implicit and the second dimension (semantics) is explicit [19,34]. We use the following conventions:

$x \;\; y \;\; z$	Variable
$A \;\; B \;\; C$	Type
$\alpha \;\; \beta \;\; \gamma$	Term (or formula for type $\bullet$)
$\Delta \;\; \Gamma \;\; \Theta \;\; \Phi \;\; \Psi$	Configuration, viz. declarations $x_1 : A_1 \dots x_n : A_n$

A sequent $\Delta \succ \alpha : A$ is read 'Δ yields α in A'. An underlined configuration $\underline{\Gamma}$ means that all types in Γ must be underlined (but not all sub-types).

$$\Delta[\Gamma] \succ \beta[x \mapsto \alpha] : B \qquad \text{Cut}$$
$$\Gamma \succ \alpha : A$$
$$\Delta[x : A] \succ \beta : B$$

$$x : A \succ x : A \qquad =$$

$$\Delta[\Gamma \;\; z : B\backslash A] \succ \gamma[x \mapsto (z\ \beta)] : C \qquad \backslash\text{L}$$
$$\Gamma \succ \beta : B$$
$$\Delta[x : A] \succ \gamma : C$$

$$\Gamma \succ \lambda y \alpha : B\backslash A \qquad \backslash\text{R}$$
$$y : B \;\; \Gamma \succ \alpha : A$$

$$\Delta[z : A/B \;\; \Gamma] \succ \gamma[x \mapsto (z\ \beta)] : C \qquad /\text{L}$$
$$\Gamma \succ \beta : B$$
$$\Delta[x : A] \succ \gamma : C$$

$$\Gamma \succ \lambda y \alpha : A/B \qquad /\text{R}$$
$$\Gamma \;\; y : B \succ \alpha : A$$

$$\Gamma[z : \underline{A}] \succ \beta[x \mapsto (z\ \star)] : B \qquad \underline{\text{L}}$$
$$\Gamma[x : A] \succ \beta : B$$

$$\underline{\Gamma} \succ \lambda \star \alpha : \underline{A} \qquad \underline{\text{R}}$$
$$\underline{\Gamma} \succ \alpha : A$$

$$\Delta[\Gamma[z : A \| B]] \succ \gamma[y \mapsto (z\ \lambda x \beta)] : C \qquad \|\text{L}$$
$$\Gamma[x : A] \succ \beta : B$$
$$\Delta[y : B] \succ \gamma : C$$

$$\Gamma \succ \lambda z (z\ \alpha) : A \| B \qquad z \notin \Gamma \qquad \|\text{R}$$
$$\Gamma \succ \alpha : A$$

$$\Delta \succ \alpha' : A \qquad \alpha \leadsto_{\lambda} \alpha' \qquad \lambda$$
$$\Delta \succ \alpha : A$$

The implicit syntactic dimension means that the antecedents form a sequence rather than a set and that the syntactic component for the succedent is the concatenation of the strings for the antecedents. All rules work unrestricted on the semantic component from the premises to the conclusion.

We use $\rightsquigarrow_\lambda$ for λ-conversion using the α-, β- and η-rules. Only the right rule of λ is possible, since only variables and not expressions in general are allowed on the left side of the sequent symbol.

The rule /R is to be understood as follows: if we prove that (the syntactic components for the types in) Γ with (the syntactic component for the type) B to the right yield (the syntactic component for the type) A, then we conclude that (the syntactic component...) Γ (alone) yields (...) A/B; furthermore if the variable y represents (the semantic component for the type) B and the term α represents (the semantic component for the type) A, then the λ-abstraction $\lambda y \alpha$ represents (...) A/B (we do not care about the semantic components for the types in Γ since these are being taken care of in α).

In the same manner the rule /L is to be understood as follows: if we prove that Γ yields B and also prove that Δ with A inserted yields C, then we conclude that Δ with A/B and Γ (in that order) inserted (at the same spot as in the premise) yields C; furthermore if the term β represents B and the term γ represents C (under the assumption that the variable x represents A), then γ with the application $(z\ \beta)$ substituted for all free occurrences of the variable x represents C (under the assumption that the variable z represents A/B).

The rule $\|$R is rather special since the type B in the conclusion does not occur in the premise (as the type A does). Apparently no pair of left- and right-rules for the type constructor $\|$ gives a complete sequent calculus; instead we could define $A\|B \equiv (B \uparrow A) \downarrow B$, where $\uparrow$ and $\downarrow$ are new primitive type constructors called wrap and infix [19, page 151].

4.2 A Sample Derivation

We consider the following (incorrect) argument:

$$\frac{}{\text{John believes that Victoria smiles.}} \quad \div$$

We only show the derivation for a sentence of the form 'John believes that...' of category S. The corresponding string is $\mathsf{John\ believe}\ \Theta$ (for some meta-variable Θ of category $\underline{S}$).

We first obtain a derivation for the syntactic component, and then the semantic component using numbers as place-holders becomes **believe**$\star$ $\lambda\star\theta$ **John**$\star$ with the lexical combinators **believe** and **John** inserted (for some meta-variable θ corresponding to the meta-variable Θ mentioned above).

$$\underline{N}\ \ \underline{(N\backslash S)/S}\ \ \underline{\Theta} \succ S \qquad \underline{\mathrm{L}}$$

$$N\ \ \underline{(N\backslash S)/\underline{S}}\ \ \underline{\Theta} \succ S \qquad \underline{\mathrm{L}}$$

$$N\ \ (N\backslash S)/\underline{S}\ \ \underline{\Theta} \succ S \qquad /\mathrm{L}$$

$$\underline{\Theta} \succ \underline{S} \qquad \underline{\mathrm{R}}$$

$$\underline{\Theta} \succ S$$

$$N\ \ N\backslash S \succ S \qquad \backslash\mathrm{L}$$

$$N \succ N \qquad =$$

$$S \succ S \qquad =$$

$$1\ \ 3\ \ \Theta \succ 3\star\ \lambda\star\theta\ 1\star \qquad \underline{\mathrm{L}}$$

$$2\ \ 3\ \ \Theta \succ 3\star\ \lambda\star\theta\ 2 \qquad \underline{\mathrm{L}}$$

$$2\ \ 1\ \ \Theta \succ 1\ \lambda\star\theta\ 2 \qquad /\mathrm{L}$$

$$\Theta \succ \lambda\star\theta \qquad \underline{\mathrm{R}}$$

$$\Theta \succ \theta$$

$$2\ \ 3 \succ 3\ 2 \qquad \backslash\mathrm{L}$$

$$2 \succ 2 \qquad =$$

$$1 \succ 1 \qquad =$$

The numbers are automatically introduced in a bottom-up manner.

The derivation can be extended to the argument of top category • and the validity can be assessed using the lexical combinators, the logical combinators, or the expanded formulas with/without abbreviations as shown below; from both a cognitive and computational point of view the combinator "levels" seem promising as a kind of natural logic, cf. [24,25,26,35]. We have found that our combinators are quite easy to work with manually and we are looking into various computer implementations, for example in the theorem prover Isabelle [23].

ok so John believe Victoria smile stop

$\rightsquigarrow$ **so ok** $\lambda\star($**stop**$\star\ \lambda\star($**believe**$\star\ \lambda\star($**smile**$\star$ **Victoria**$\star)$ **John**$\star))$

$\rightsquigarrow \mathbf{P}\ \lambda\star(\mathbf{T}\star)\ \lambda\star(\mathbf{F}\star\ \lambda\star(\mathbf{P}\ \lambda i(B\star Ji)\ \lambda\star(S\star V)))$

$\rightsquigarrow \forall i(Ii \Rightarrow Ii \wedge \forall j(BiJj \Rightarrow SjV))$

$\rightsquigarrow \forall\hat{\imath}(\forall j(B\hat{\imath}Jj \Rightarrow SjV))$ Invalid closed formula!

4.3 Quantification Scope Ambiguity

The sentence 'every man loves a woman' has a well-known ambiguity:

every man love a woman

$\rightsquigarrow$ **every**$\star$ **man**$\star$ $\lambda v($**a**$\star$ **woman**$\star$ $\lambda w($**love** $w\star$ $v\star))$

$\rightsquigarrow \mathbf{I}\star\ \lambda x(M\star x)\ \lambda x(\mathbf{O}\star\ \lambda y(W\star y)\ \lambda y(L\star xy))$

$\rightsquigarrow \forall x(E\star x \Rightarrow (M\star x \Rightarrow \exists y(E\star y \wedge (W\star y \wedge L\star xy))))$

$\rightsquigarrow \forall x \in \star(M\star x \Rightarrow \exists y \in \star(W\star y \wedge L\star xy))$

&...

$\rightsquigarrow$ **a**$\star$ **woman**$\star$ $\lambda w($**every**$\star$ **man**$\star$ $\lambda v($**love** $w\star$ $v\star))$

$\rightsquigarrow \mathbf{O}\star\ \lambda y(W\star y)\ \lambda y(\mathbf{I}\star\ \lambda x(M\star x)\ \lambda x(L\star xy))$

$\rightsquigarrow \exists y(E\star y \wedge (W\star x \wedge \forall x(E\star x \Rightarrow (M\star x \Rightarrow L\star xy))))$

$\rightsquigarrow \exists y \in \star(W\star y \wedge \forall x \in \star(M\star x \Rightarrow L\star xy))$

4.4 De Dicto / De Re Ambiguity

The sentence 'Nick believes that a thief runs' also has a well-known ambiguity:

Nick believe a thief run

$\rightsquigarrow$ **believe**$\star$ $\lambda\star($**a**$\star$ **thief**$\star$ $\lambda v($**run**$\star$ $v\star))$ **Nick**$\star$

$\rightsquigarrow \mathbf{P}\ \lambda i(B\star Ni)\ \lambda\star(\mathbf{O}\star\ \lambda x(T\star x)\ \lambda x(R\star x))$

$\rightsquigarrow \forall i(B\star Ni \Rightarrow \exists x(Eix \wedge (Tix \wedge Rix)))$

$\rightsquigarrow \forall i(B\star Ni \Rightarrow \exists x \in i(Tix \wedge Rix))$

&...

$\rightsquigarrow$ **a**$\star$ **thief**$\star$ $\lambda v($**believe**$\star$ $\lambda\star($**run**$\star$ $v\star)$ **Nick**$\star)$

$\rightsquigarrow \mathbf{O}\star\ \lambda x(T\star x)\ \lambda x(\mathbf{P}\ \lambda i(B\star Ni)\ \lambda\star(R\star x))$

$\rightsquigarrow \exists x(E\star x \wedge (T\star x \wedge \forall i(B\star Ni \Rightarrow Rix)))$

$\rightsquigarrow \exists x \in \star(T\star x \wedge \forall i(B\star Ni \Rightarrow Rix))$

4.5 Paraconsistency and Relevance Examples

The arguments 1, 2 and 3 test the logic outside the propositional attitudes — this is a classical logic. The arguments 4, 5 and 6 show that the logic inside the propositional attitudes behaves reasonable, while arguments 7, 8 and 9 show the robustness of the logic inside the propositional attitudes against contradictions and logical omniscience — this is a non-classical logic.

[1]

$$\frac{\text{Gloria runs.}\qquad \text{Gloria smiles.}}{\text{Gloria runs and smiles.}}\quad \surd$$

2

$$\frac{}{\text{Victoria dances or does not dance.}} \quad \surd$$

3

$$\frac{\text{Gloria runs and does not run.}}{\text{Everyone dances.}} \quad \surd$$

4

$$\frac{\text{John believes that Gloria runs.}}{\text{John believes that someone runs.}} \quad \surd$$

5

$$\frac{\text{John believes that Gloria runs.} \quad \text{John believes that Gloria smiles.}}{\text{John believes that Gloria runs and smiles.}} \quad \surd$$

6

$$\frac{\text{John believes that Gloria runs and smiles.}}{\text{John believes that Gloria runs.}} \quad \surd$$

7

$$\frac{}{\text{John believes that Victoria dances or does not dance.}} \quad \div$$

8

$$\frac{\text{John believes that Gloria runs.}}{\text{John believes that Victoria dances or does not dance and Gloria runs.}} \quad \div$$

9

$$\frac{\text{John believes that Gloria runs and does not run.}}{\text{John believes that Victoria dances or does not dance.}} \quad \div$$

The derivations for these examples and numerous other can be found in [34]. Argument 9 above corresponds to the following string and combinator formulas:

John believe Gloria run and not run stop
so John believe Victoria dance or not dance stop

so
$\lambda\star(\mathbf{stop}\star\ \lambda\star(\mathbf{believe}\star\ \lambda\star(\mathbf{and'}\star\ \mathbf{run}\star\ (\mathbf{not}\star\ \mathbf{run}\star)\ \mathbf{Gloria}\star)\ \mathbf{John}\star))$
$\lambda\star(\mathbf{stop}\star\ \lambda\star(\mathbf{believe}\star\ \lambda\star(\mathbf{or'}\star\ \mathbf{dance}\star\ (\mathbf{not}\star\ \mathbf{dance}\star)\ \mathbf{Victoria}\star)\ \mathbf{John}\star))$

P
$\lambda\star(\mathbf{F}\star\ \lambda\star(\mathbf{P}\ \lambda i(B\star Ji)\ \lambda\star(\mathbf{C}\ (R\star G)\ (\mathbf{N}\ (R\star G)))))$
$\lambda\star(\mathbf{F}\star\ \lambda\star(\mathbf{P}\ \lambda i(B\star Ji)\ \lambda\star(\mathbf{D}\ (D\star V)\ (\mathbf{N}\ (D\star V)))))$

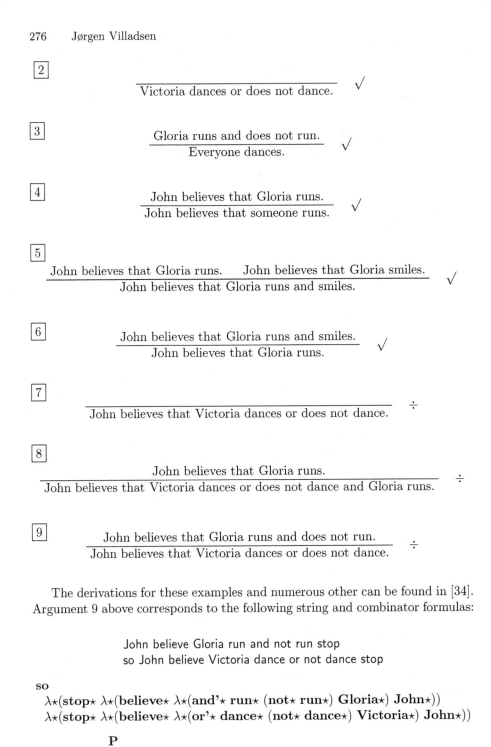

5 Conclusions

A robust treatment of propositional attitudes in natural language is critical for many AI applications. We have shown how to obtain a paraconsistent and relevant logic for the attitudes of agents while retaining classical logic for the observer. The solution uses a new partial logic based on a few key equalities for the connectives, notably $=$, $\neg$, $\wedge$ and $\Leftrightarrow$, as first described in [36]. We plan to investigate the partial logic and its embedding in classical higher-order logic.

Our use of combinators is inspired by work in natural logic [24,25,26,35] and differs from previous uses in computer science, mathematical logic and natural language semantics [11,12,13,27,28] who do not address the intensionality of propositional attitudes (but see [31]). We simply map the sentence 'Victoria knows that John loves himself' to **know**$\star$ $\lambda\star$(**self**$\star$ **love**$\star$ **John**$\star$) **Victoria**$\star$ and we use the same logical combinator for the lexical combinator **know** as for arguments as such with multiple premises and conclusions, and moreover we use pure combinators like **self**, that is, combinators without constants.

For the present fragment of natural language the logical semantics is essentially first-order, with two sorts, entities (agents) and indices (situations). But higher-order facilities are built-in. It would be interesting to extend our combinatory approach with anaphora, tense and/or plurality along the lines of [20,32,33,14], possibly extending the categorial grammar as well [18,19,8].

Acknowledgements

I would like to thank Jørgen Fischer Nilsson for guidance. Nikolaj Oldager and the anonymous referees also offered valuable comments.

References

1. A.R. Anderson and N. D. Belnap Jr. *Entailment: The Logic of Relevance and Necessity.* Princeton University Press, 1975.
2. P. B. Andrews. *An Introduction to Mathematical Logic and Type Theory: To Truth through Proof.* Academic Press, 1986.
3. O. Arieli and A. Avron. Bilattices and paraconsistency. In *Frontiers in Paraconsistent Logic*, pages 11–28. Research Studies Press, 2000.
4. R. Audi, editor. *The Cambridge Dictionary of Philosophy.* Cambridge University Press, 1995.
5. H. P. Barendregt. *The Lambda Calculus, Its Syntax and Semantics.* North-Holland, revised edition, 1984.
6. J. Barwise and J. Perry. *Situations and Attitudes.* MIT Press, 1983.
7. N. D. Belnap Jr. A useful four-valued logic. In *Modern Uses of Multiple-Valued Logic*, pages 8–37. D. Reidel, 1977.
8. B. Carpenter. *Type-Logical Semantics.* MIT Press, 1997.
9. G. Chierchia and S. McConnell-Ginet. *Meaning and Grammar: An Introduction to Semantics.* MIT Press, 2nd edition, 2000.
10. M. J. Cresswell. *Entities and Indices.* Kluwer Academic Publishers, 1990.

11. P.-L. Curien. *Categorical Combinators, Sequential Algorithms and Functional Programming.* Pitman, 1986.
12. H. B. Curry, R. Feys, and W. Craig. *Combinatory Logic I.* North-Holland, 1958.
13. H. B. Curry, J. R. Hindley, and J. P. Seldin. *Combinatory Logic II.* North-Holland, 1972.
14. J. Dölling. Ontological domains, semantic sorts and systematic ambiguity. *International Journal of Human-Computer Studies*, 43:785–807, 1995.
15. M. Fitting. Bilattices and the theory of truth. *Journal of Philosophical Logic*, 18:225–256, 1989.
16. M. Ginsberg. Multivalued logics: A uniform approach to inference in artificial intelligence. *Computer Intelligence*, 4:265–316, 1988.
17. R. Montague. The proper treatment of quantification in ordinary English. In *Approaches to Natural Language*, pages 221–242. D. Reidel, 1973.
18. M. Moortgat. *Categorial Investigations: Logical and Linguistic Aspects of the Lambek Calculus.* Foris Publications, 1988.
19. G. Morrill. *Type Logical Grammar.* Kluwer Academic Publishers, 1994.
20. R. Muskens. Anaphora and the logic of change. In *Logics in AI: European Workshop JELIA*, pages 412–427. Springer, LNCS 478, 1991.
21. R. Muskens. *Meaning and Partiality.* CSLI Publications, 1995.
22. R. Muskens. On partiality and paraconsistent logics. *Notre Dame Journal of Formal Logic.* To appear.
23. L. C. Paulson. *Isabelle: A Generic Theorem Prover.* Springer, LNCS 828, 1994.
24. W. C. Purdy. A logic for natural language. *Notre Dame Journal of Formal Logic*, 32:409–425, 1991.
25. W. C. Purdy. Surface reasoning. *Notre Dame Journal of Formal Logic*, 33:13–36, 1992.
26. V. Sánchez. *Studies on Natural Logic and Categorial Grammar.* PhD thesis, University of Amsterdam, 1991.
27. P. Simons. Combinators and categorial grammar. *Notre Dame Journal of Formal Logic*, 30:242–261, 1989.
28. M. Steedman. Combinators and grammars. In *Categorial Grammars and Natural Language Structures*, pages 417–442. D. Reidel, 1988.
29. E. Thijsse. *Partial Logic and Knowledge Representation.* PhD thesis, Tilburg University, 1992.
30. J. van Benthem. *Language in Action: Categories, Lambdas and Dynamic Logic.* North-Holland, 1991.
31. J. Villadsen. Combinatory categorial grammar for intensional fragment of natural language. In *Scandinavian Conference on Artificial Intelligence*, pages 328–339. IOS Press, 1991.
32. J. Villadsen. Anaphora and intensionality in classical logic. In *Nordic Computational Linguistics Conference*, pages 165–175. Norwegian Computing Centre for the Humanities, 1992.
33. J. Villadsen. Information states as first class citizens. In *Annual Meeting of the Association for Computational Linguistics*, pages 303–305. 1992.
34. J. Villadsen. *Nabla: A Linguistic System based on Multi-dimensional Type Theory.* PhD thesis, Technical University of Denmark, 1995.
35. J. Villadsen. Using lexical and logical combinators in natural language semantics. *Consciousness Research Abstracts*, pages 51–52, 1997.
36. J. Villadsen. Meaning and partiality revised. In *Scandinavian Conference on Artificial Intelligence*, pages 163–164. IOS Press, 2001.

Combining Syntax and Pragmatic Knowledge for the Understanding of Spontaneous Spoken Sentences

Jeanne Villaneau[1], Jean-Yves Antoine[1], and Olivier Ridoux[2]

[1] VALORIA, Université de Bretagne Sud, Lorient-Vannes,
{Jeanne.Berthelemy, Jean-Yves.Antoine}@univ-ubs.fr
[2] IRISA, Campus Universitaire de Beaulieu, 35042 RENNES cedex,
Olivier.Ridoux@irisa.fr

Abstract. In Human-Computer dialogue, spoken language understanding systems use mainly selective methods and are limited to very specific domains. On the contrary we present in this paper a speech understanding system which achieves a more detailed analysis of spoken recognized utterances.

The semantic representation of a sentence is a logic formula. Semantic and pragmatic considerations shape the formula. The analysis itself is split into two phases based on different principles. The first phase is almost exclusively syntactic. It corresponds to a segmentation into chunks whose meaning is obtained by composing λ-terms to build elementary formulas. In the second phase, the chunks are interpreted and then composed, mainly through coordination. These compositions are mainly based on pragmatic contraints provided most of the time by the context of the application.

We give here an account of the results obtained from a first series of tests. We also discuss the use of the same ideas for applications in well defined semantic domains such as database processing.

1 Introduction

During the last decade, spoken man-machine dialogue has known significant improvements that should lead shortly to the development of real use systems. Most of present researches in spoken man-machine communication address an unique kind of tasks, which is accessing an information systems. In such application domains, the dialogue system aims at finding in a specific data-base some information in response to a user's request. As an illustration, in ATIS (Air Transport Information Systems) dialogue systems the database contains flight timetables, etc, and the spoken dialogue systems is able to recognize and understand the spoken request of the user (speech recognition and speech understanding module in figure 1). The understanding module provides the dialogue manager with a semantic representation of the spoken utterance. This last component aims at managing the dialogue with the user and the interface with the database (e.g., SQL query).

P. de Groote, G. Morrill, C. Retoré (Eds.): LACL 2001, LNAI 2099, pp. 279–295, 2001.

The progress of the last few years in automatic speech recognition causes an increasing interest in the improvement of the other components of spoken dialogue systems. This paper presents precisely a speech understanding system which aims at achieving a refined, but robust, analysis of spontaneous spoken utterances.

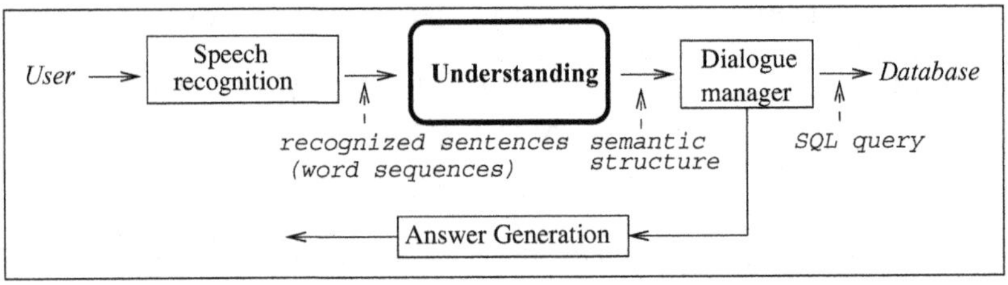

Fig. 1. Spoken Dialogue System

The sentences studied are the word sequences that have been identified by the speech recognizer. These sequences do not include prosodic information (intonation, pauses...). Likewise there is no signs of ponctuation. As we know, spoken language fails to respect definite syntactic rules. The unexpected structural elements such as repetitions, hesitations and speech repairs [BBMB90] make detailed syntactic analysis for these sentences impossible. Even so, present standard systems are giving satisfactory results in some specific domains that correspond to very restricted tasks: they are using selective methods where comprehension is limited to the selection of word strings or keywords to be inserted in predefinite semantic frames [Sen92, MAJ99]. For example, the ATIS (Air Travel Information Services) system of the LIMSI (Laboratoire d'Informatique pour la Mécanique et les Sciences de l'Ingénieur, Computing Lab for Mechanical Engineering Sciences) aims at recognizing five types of queries: flights, fares, stops, aircrafts and booking [Min96]. Now the scalability of these approaches into domains of larger semantic scopes or for less definite tasks is unknown [Hir98].

On the contrary, this paper presents an approach based on a richer linguistic analysis, with methods which are hybrid between natural language processing and spoken language processing (the application studied is touristic information and the considered language is spoken French). The semantic scope of this application domain remains relatively limited. Nevertheless the range of the addressed tasks is much wider than for standard information systems. The first outcomes of the system are satisfying enough to raise the problems of its limits and of its applicability to other applications.

2 Problems and Principles

Our speech understanding system is working on word sequences which are provided by a speech recognizer. The analysis aims at providing to the dialogue manager a semantic representation of the sentence. It tries to identify and to interpret all the elements in the sentence that are helpful for the database query and the dialogue control. Therefore, some components of the sentence may be missing from the final representation. Thus, the expression *"j'ai la grippe" ("I have the flu")* does not appear in the pragmatical representation of the following sentence:

J'ai la grippe pouvez-vous m'indiquer la pharmacie la plus proche?

(I have the flu can you tell me where is the nearest pharmacy?)

Spontaneous speech presents numerous unexpected structures which do not respect any definite syntactic rules. A complete syntactic analysis is difficult if not impossible. Nevertheless, these sentences have some essential properties. For instance, in French the reparandum of repetitions or self-corrections always involve the beginning of the altered phrase [BBMB90]:

près de près du euh près de la Tour Eiffel

(near near the er, near the Eiffel Tower).

Moreover, in French, while the order between the phrases is relatively flexible, word order variations inside a phrase are very uncommon: for example, there is no reverse order between the preposition, the article and the noun in a noun-phrase. Thus, spoken french phrases present some useful structural regularities. We thus have decided to base the first phase of our system on a segmentation of the sentence into chunks [Abn91] which should be defined as non-recursive phrases. This shallow parsing relies mainly on syntactic considerations which garantees its genericity in terms of task independance. The analysis consists in the association of adjoining words by means of a categorial grammar. Every association of words (i.e. chunk) corresponds to a concept of the task.

In a second stage, the identified chunks are interpreted in terms of objects of the task and their properties. A pragmatic-based analysis is then achieved which aims at linking these elements according to:

- the context of the application (knowledge on the task universe)
- the context of the dialogue

A first step identifies links between the different objects, and a second step provides the semantic structure of the sentence: the outcome is the final formula (cf. Figure 2). In summary, the first phase is syntactic, while the second phase is driven by pragmatics.

For the semantic representation of the sentence, we have chosen logical formulas built by composing λ-terms. This semantic knowledge representation is sometimes said to be heavy, likely to get more complex formula than the sentence itself [Sow00]. However it is a flexible, generic and exhaustive representation. Again, the restricted nature of the task allows to choose a rather simple logical formalism which is described in the following section.

3 Semantic Representation

The analysis produces a first-order logic formula according to Montague formalism [Mon74] where the objects have the noun-phrase function. In general, the type of the formula is a pair *(sentence_nature object)*. For example, when the sentence is a query, the form of the output formula is *(question object)*.

In this section, we present the object representation first and then the representation of the sentence nature.

3.1 Object Representation

The types *object* and *properties* are primitive types. The name of the type (*properties* → *object*) is *label*; it is an object constructor.

The name of the special property that corresponds to the absence of properties is *any* (identity). The property *name* is an example of property constructor of the type (*string* → *properties*). So *(hotel (name "Caumartin"))* refers to the *"hotel Caumartin"*.

Constructors like *and* and *or* are defined in order to represent the logical coordinations of the properties. Other constructors allow type conversion. For instance, a *with* constructor is defined for the conversion (*object* → *properties*): *"un cinéma qui passe des films en VO"* (*"a cinema showing films in the original version"*) refers to *(cinema (with (films (of_type "VO"))))*.

3.2 Sentence Nature Representation

Information Request: The formalism is aimed at producing a pragmatical formula. For instance, when the sentence is recognised as an information query, the logical formula expresses the nature of the expected answer. Three kinds of answers should be distinguished in our application domain (tourism information):

1. The expected answer can be *extensive* (*open* query): list of the objects that are suited to a lot of required conditions. The corresponding question is *search_q*.
   Est-ce qu'il y a des hôtels deux étoiles pas trop trop loin du Louvre ?
   (Are there two-star hotels not far from the Louvre?)

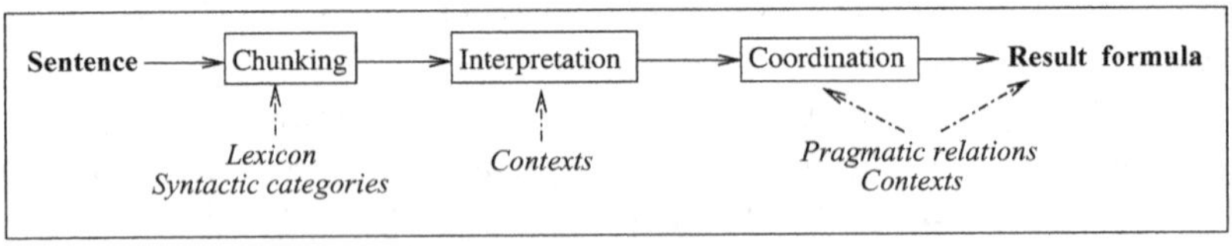

Fig. 2. The Different Steps in the Analysis

Sentence nature		Expected answer
search_q		list of objects
(info_q	*nature_info_q*)	property or list of properties
	how_many)	numeral
	where)	address - location
	when)	hours - dates
	...	...
(yes_no_q *property*)		yes/no
thanks		no answer
demand_q		confirmation of change in the database
(inform_of *nature_info*)		no answer

Fig. 3. Requests and Informations

(search_q (hotel (and (with (star (quantity 2)))
(near (museum (name "Le Louvre"))))))
It is possible to impose varied additionnal conditions on the reply like quantifications:
Je voudrais l'hôtel le moins cher
(I would like the least expensive hotel)
(search_q (hotel (least expensive))) ,
Quelle est la pharmacie la plus proche ?
(What is the nearest pharmacy?)
(search_q (pharmacy (least far))) , etc.

2. The query can be an information query on a given object or a set of given objects. The *info_q* question corresponds to this generic quest. In some cases, it is possible to specify the nature of the expected reply. For example, the expected reply to the following sentence is an integer (question *(info_q how_many)*):
Combien il a d'étoiles le Caumartin ?
(How many stars has the Caumartin?)
((info_q how_many) (star (of hotel (name "Caumartin"))))
3. The expected answer can be simply of *yes_no* type (*closes* query) like in the sentences:
L'hotel Caumartin c'est bien un trois étoiles ?
(The Caumartin hotel is a two-star hotel isn't it?)
(yes_no_q (with (star (quantity 2))) (hotel (name "Caumartin")))

Information Sentences: Some sentences are just giving informations. On their own they are not a query from the speaker. However, their understanding is essential for an efficient management of the dialogue.

1. They can express the end of the dialogue:
Bien merci pour tous ces renseignements et au revoir
(Thank you for the information and good bye)
thanks .

2. They can include an information that is changing the context of the dialogue.
   J'ai réservé un billet par téléphone
   (I have booked a ticket on the phone)
   (inform_of (booking (of (ticket any)))) .
3. Some sentences are essential because they act as an order for a change in the database itself (*demand_q*):
   Bon finalement je réserve une chambre double pour ce soir dans cet hotel
   (Ok all right I reserve a double room in this hotel)
   (demand_q (reservation (of (room (and (of_type "double")
   (of (hotel contextual *)))))))*

Multi-sentences: Some word sequences correspond to a juxtaposition or to a coordination of two or three sentences.

1. Some sentences can express more than one query:
   Où est l'hotel Caumartin et quels sont ses tarifs?
   (Where is the Caumartin hotel and which are its prices?
   (then ((info_q where) (hotel (name "Caumartin")))
   ((info_q gen) (price (of (hotel (name "Caumartin"))))))
2. A not uncommon case is a two-part sentence: first, an informative part followed by a real request. There, the first part of the sentence constitutes the context of the dialogue of the following part.
   J'ai réservé un billet par téléphone où puis-je le retirer ?
   (I have reserved a ticket by telephone where can I collect it?)
   ((info_q where) (collection (of (ticket any))))

4 The Different Steps in the Analysis

We will detail the behaviour of our system through the study of an example of analysis that concerns the following sentence :

Est-ce que vous pourriez m'indiquer un euh un hotel pres de la gare pas trop trop cher.

(could you find me a er an hotel near the station not too expensive)

Standard selective approaches will represent this sentence by a semantic frame which should look like the following one :

```
[ question = [ list
               object = [hotel
                         localisation =  [ distance = near
                                           object = station ]
                         price = moderate
                        ]
             ]
]
```

This representation will be used by the dialogue manager in order to provide the database with a corresponding SQL query. Likewise, our system aims at building at least such a restricted representation. Besides, it handles a more detailed analysis than standard selective methods, which suggests his usefulness for more complex tasks or for a more refined dialogue control. In accordance with the previous section, the representation of this sentence in our system is:

(search_q (hotel (and (near (station (name "St Lazare")))
(with_price "moderate"))))

The following sections describe how this representation is built by the system.

4.1 Chunk Parsing

Sentence	Lexicalization	End of Phase 1
est-ce	(quest_wd "yes_no")	(quest_wd "yes_no")
que vous pourriez	(req_wd "neutral")	(req_wd "neutral")
m indiquer	(req_wd "query")	(req_wd "query")
un	(article λx.(indef sing x)) (numeral 1)	
euh	hesitation	
un hotel	(article λx.(indef sing x)) (numeral 1) (nn_obj hotel eq_any)	(indef sing (nn_obj hotel eq_any))
près	(adj proche)	(adj near)
de la gare	(prep λx.(deprep x)) (article λx.(def sing x)) (nn_obj station eq_any)	(deprep (def sing (nn_obj station eq_any)))
pas trop trop cher	(adjr λx.(adj (no x))) (coordination "no") (verbl λx. (verb (not x))) (adjr λx.(adj x)) (adjr λx.(adj x)) (adj expensive)	(adj (no expensive))

Fig. 4. Lexicalisation and Chunking

In a first phase, a categorial grammar is used to segment the sentence into several chunks. The considered application is targeted towards the access to a data-base. The queries to the data-base are themselves formal sentences, even if this boils down to SQL queries. So, the problem is to find in a spontaneous spoken sentence hints to form a formal query. Because of the noise such sentences contain, not every part of them will serve in forming a formal query. However, the experience shows that unexpected constructions do not occur everywhere: e.g., simple noun-phrases can be considered as generated by a formal grammar.

A lexicalised formalism seems the most appropriate since one does not know where unexpected constructions are. One is reduced to collate consecutive words in as large chunks as possible, according to the meaning of individual words.

Obviously, the use of other kinds of lexicalised formalisms — such as Tree Adjoining Grammars [Jos87] as well as dependency [Cov90] or link grammars [ST91] for this phase is perfectly conceivable. For instance, shallow parsing has already been investigated with a TAG-based approach (supertags [Sri97]). Theoretical results on the formal equivalence of lexicalized formalisms [JVSW89] suggests nevertheless that categorial grammars [Ste98, Moo97] are also an interesting candidate for this chunking phase.

Standard application domains of spoken man-machine communication involve a vocabulary from around five thousand to ten thousand words on the whole. During the parsing, the out-of-vocabulary words leaves a mark; word positions are therefore kept by the system, although these out-of-vocabulary words will not be considered further by the system. A list of *lexical equivalents* corresponds to the different definitions of every lexem that is recognized as belonging to the vocabulary of the application. These lexical equivalents are represented as λ-terms. According to the principles of categorial grammars, two sorts of categories are distinguished: basic categories and complex (or functor) categories. Thus, for instance, the word "pas" has three definitions in our application: the first one is related to the basic category *coordination* which is often a mark of speech repair (see below 5.1). The second one is the functor category *adj/adj*. It corresponds to right composition with an adjective to produce an other adjective. The third one is the functor category *verb\verb* to express a negative verb phrase. In our system, these three definitions are given with the list:

[(coordination "no"), (adjr λx.(adj (no x))), (verbl λx. (verb (not x)))]

Definitions are composed until there is no more possible compositions. These compositions come first: if two sequences have several categories among which only a part can be composed, then only these categories are retained, the others that can not be composed are eliminated. Note that all possible combinations are kept. For example, the phrase *"des magasins"* give two combinations: one is *(indef plur (nn_obj store eq_any)) ("some stores")*, the others are *(ab [*or *deprep] def plur (nn_obj store eq_any)) ("from [*or *of] the stores")*

This first phase ends with the elimination of unused articles, prepositions, adverbs, numerals, etc. Lastly, the system only retains the significant chunks of the sentence (cf. Figure 4).

4.2 Interpretation and Coordination

The identified chunks are then interpreted and this interpretation process produces a classification of these chunks into three basic classes: objects, properties, and terms that are used for the determination of the nature of the sentence. These terms correspond to request-words and question-words (see below). For example, adjectives may be interpreted as properties of some objects that are specified in a given list (cf. Figure 5).

The understanding of most of the spoken utterances requires the consideration of the dialogue context. To interpret some expressions like *"par ici"* (*"here"*), *"à cette heure-ci"* (*"now"*), place context and time context are needed. In the example sentence, the interpretation of *"la gare"* (*"the station"*) is:

(eqobj (obj station (name "St Lazare")))

given that the place context is the Paris railway station Saint-Lazare. To understand a lot of sentences it is necessary to use the context of the dialogue. The dialogue manager is monitoring the dialogue; however, to understand some elliptical sentences without resorting to the dialogue manager, the system uses a reduced dialogue history including the objects in the context and the nature of the previous sentences. Thus the interpretation of the syntactic equivalent of the words *"cet hôtel" ("this hotel")* is the hotel of the contextual object system provided this latter exists.

After interpretation, the properties are specifically studied; the definition of a property contains the list of objects labels to which this property can be applied. This list is replaced by self-intersection with the list of labels of the sentence objects and of the contextual objects. For the most obvious cases, the properties are directly linked with the object. This is for instance the case when the property follows directly the object in the sentence. Thus, the two properties *(with_price "moderate")* and *(near (station (name "St Lazare")))* are linked with the object *hotel* in our example.

In a final phase, consecutive objects or properties are compared in order to detect possible coordinations (see Figure 7). This operation is not only essential for the analysis of coordinations, but also for detecting spontaneous structures such as repetitions, repairs or self-corrections (see Section 5.1).

Before Phase 2	After Interpretation
(quest_wd "yes_no")	(quest_wd "yes_no")
(req_wd "neutral")	(req_wd "neutral")
(req_wd "query")	(req_wd "query")
(indef sing (nn_obj hotel eq_any))	(eqobj (obj hotel any) noprep)
(adj (no expensive))	(eqprop [hotel,...] (with_price "moderate"))
(adj near)	(eqprop [hotel,...] (lprop near))
(deprep (def sing (nn_obj station eq_any)))	(eqobj (obj station (name "St Lazare")) de)

Fig. 5. Phase 2 - Interpretation Step

The *request words (req_wd)* and the *question words (quest_wd)* are in the class of the lexical equivalents that allow to study the nature of the sentence. For example, *(quest_wd "yes_no")* is the lexical equivalent for the lexem *"est-ce"*; *(req_wd "neutral"), (req_wd "search"), (req_wd "info_yes_no")* are the lexical equivalents for *"voudrais", "cherche", "savoir si" ("would like to", "search-*

ing","to know if") respectively. Partial orders are defined on the sets of the question words and of the request words respectively, to compose these lexical equivalents. When two request words or two question words are comparable, the most precise of the two is retained alone (the lowest words in Figure 6).

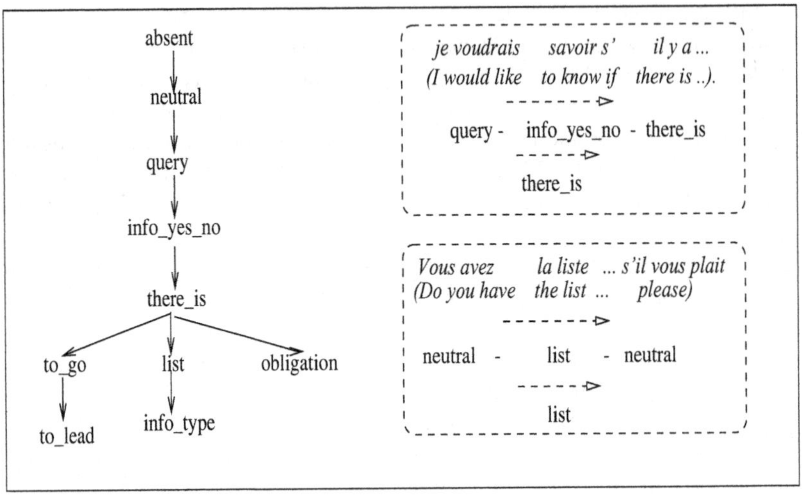

Fig. 6. Partial Order on the Request Words

After Interpretation	After Coordination
(quest_wd "yes_no")	(quest_wd "yes_no")
(req_wd "neutral") (req_wd "query")	(req_wd "query")
(eqobj (obj hotel any) noprep) (eqprop [hotel,...] (with_price "moderate")) (eqprop [hotel,...] (lprop near)) (eqobj (obj station (name "St Lazare")) de)	(eqobj (obj hotel (and (with_price "moderate") (near (obj station (name "St Lazare"))))) noprep)

Fig. 7. Phase 2 - Coordination Step

In order to achieve compositions between the objects, pragmatical relations are defined on the task universe objects.

4.3 Semantic Context and Object Strings

A part of the pragmatical knowledge of the system is obtained by unfolding the running dialogue and so is mainly independant of the application.

Another part of the pragmatical knowledge is related to the context of the application and especially to the objects of the task universe. These various objects entertain relations of interdependencies. In our application, the objects with the label *room* or *star* are for instance classified as *sub_object* for the object with the label *hotel*. The specific object *Caumartin* is an instance of the *hotel* object. A representation closely related to the conceptual graphs [Sow84, Sow00] is used for the representation of these semantic relations (cf. Figure 8). They are carried out by simple binary relations.

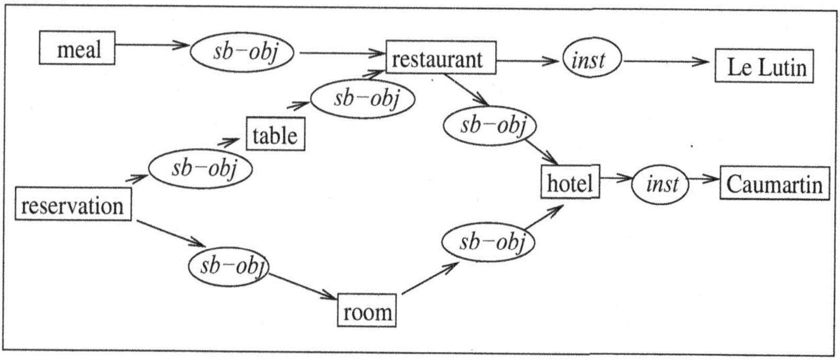

Fig. 8. A Sample of the Relations between the Objects

Considering these relations, the system tries to compose the different objects of the sentence. We define the concept of *object strings* to represent these compositions.

A *single object string* is a sequence of objects that is completely ordered by the *sub_object* relation. The *kind* of the string is the label of the most specific object (leftmost in Figure 8). A *compound object string* is an object string which is connected and partially ordered by the *sub_object* relation. Quite often there are coordinations between two objects of a string which are not comparable. The *kind* of this string is well-defined only if there is a unique most generic object (see Figure 9).

Lastly, semantic compatibility between the questions and the kind of the objects also belongs to the pragmatical knowledge: as an illustration, it is possible to apply the questions *search_q* and *info_q* to a generic hotel whereas it is not possible on the contrary to apply the question *search_q* to a definite hotel.

4.4 Accordance between the Requests and the Object Strings

A comparison of the object strings and of the request and question words of the sentence is performed in order to complete the semantic representation of the sentence.

- In the simplest case, the object system is a string with a well defined kind (as define above cf. section 4.3) and the nature of the sentence is precise and semantically compatible with this kind.
  Est-ce que vous avez la liste des films qui passent au Gaumont Opera?
  (Do you have the list of the films shown in Gaumont Opera?)
  (search_q (films (of (cinema (name "Gaumont Opera")))))
  With a compound string, the formula is obtained by means of coordination of two request formulas.
  Pouvez-vous m'indiquer les tarifs d'une chambre double d'un deux étoiles et d'un trois etoiles?
  (Can you give to me the prices for a double room in a two-star hotel and in a three-star hotel?)
  (then (search_q (price (of (hotel (with (stars (quantity 2)))))))
  (search_q (price (of (hotel (with (stars (quantity 3))))))))

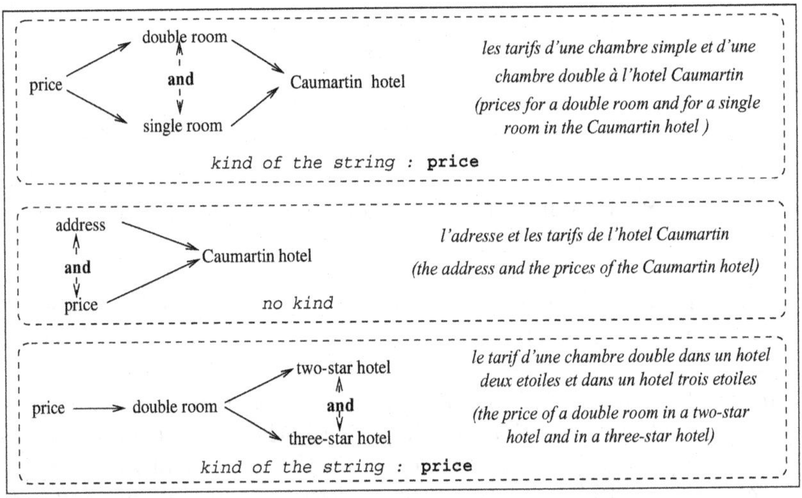

Fig. 9. Samples of Compound Objects and their Kinds

Final Formula:
(search_q (hotel (and (with_price "moderate")
(near (station (name "St Lazare"))))))

Fig. 10. Final Formula for the Example

- In many sentences, because of the vagueness of the request words and of the question words, the study of the object string is necessary for determining the nature of the request. Consider for instance the two following sentences:
  - *Est-ce qu'il y a des hôtels deux étoiles pas trop trop loin du Louvre?*
    (Are there two-star hotels not far from the Louvre?)
    (search_q (hotel (near (musee (name "Louvre")))))
  - *Est-ce qu'il y a des réductions pour les étudiants au Louvre?*
    (Are there reductions for students in the Louvre?)
    (yes_no_q (reduction (of_type "students")) (musee (nom "Louvre")))

  In the first sentence, the object string is a generic object and the appropriate request is *search_q*. In the second sentence, the appropriate request is *yes_no_q* because the object string comes within a specific object.
  In the example sentence, the object string is a generic object. With the question word "*yes_no*" and the request word "*query*", the appropriate request is *search_q*.
- In some cases, there is no request words and question words:
  - Thanking formula: there is in the sentence at least one polite remark and there is no new (i.e., absent from the context of the dialogue) object or property.
  - Informative sentence:
    Je vais aller au Louvre finalement (I am going to the Louvre after all).
    ((inform_of (intention "to go")) (museum (name "Louvre")))
    No reply is expected from the user but the museum Le Louvre becomes a contextual object.
    Je vais prendre une réservation dans cet hotel (I am going to book in this hotel) .
    (demand_q (reservation (of (hotel (name "...")))))
    The user is waiting for his reservation to be recorded: the database has to change.

5 Speech Repairs, Ellipses, and Multi-sentences

This section details the behaviour of the system on some specific phenomena such as unexpected spoken construcions as well as multi-sentences.

5.1 Speech Repairs

The system deals with hesitations and repairs of spoken language at several levels of the analysis. However, the principle used is always the same. It has been shown that most of repairs can be considered efficiently as a particular kind of coordination [Ant96], since the alteration presents the same syntactic or semantic function as the reparandum [HA99]. In the following two examples, the objects are coordinated in the first sentence and compared in the second:

Je voudrais aller au Louvre non pardon à la Tour Eiffel (I would like to go to the Louvre no I mean to the Eiffel Tower).

Je voudrais aller au musée au musée du Louvre (I would like to go to the museum, er the museum the Louvre).

5.2 Incomplete Sentences

The property of the system to return partial analysis is essential: besides the use of ellipses, the sentences submitted to the system should also correspond to incomplete sentence structures. Incomplete sentences are therefore very frequent in spoken man-machine dialogue. The ability of the system to provide the dialogue manager with partial analysis allows the latter to question the user.

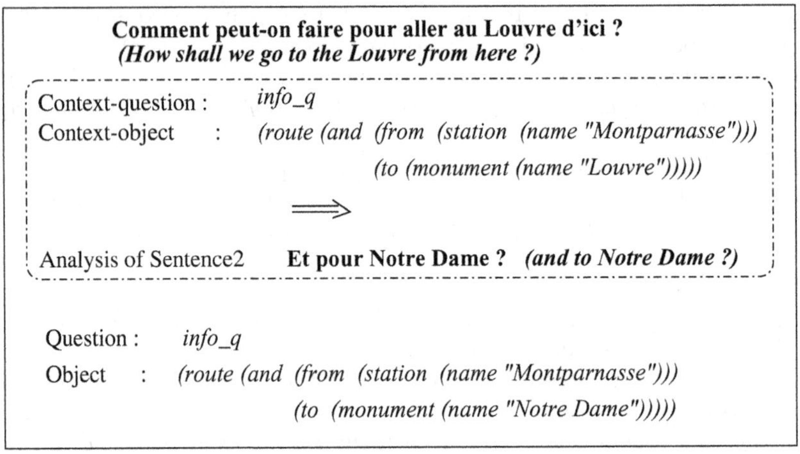

Fig. 11. Using the Context of the Dialogue

- One should note that some simple ellipses should be resolved directly by the speech understanding component. For instance, the expression *"un deux étoiles" ("a two-star")* is recognized as an abbreviation of *"un hotel deux étoiles" ("a two-star hotel")*.
- Other ellipses are refering to the context of the dialogue (cf. Figure 11). Thus, the sentence *"et pour Notre-Dame"* does not include words to express the nature of the sentence. The system attempts to understand this sentence as an addition or a change in the previous request. The preposition *"pour"* suggests a change in the destination.
- When the system fails to relate a property, an object or a question with the context of the dialogue, it provides the dialogue manager with an incomplete formula where void constructors are used. For example, the formula returned for the sentence *"c'est pour deux personnes"* (*"it's for two people"*) is: *(nulreq (nullabel (nbpeople 2)))*

5.3 Multi-sequences

The system should fail in the analysis because of the presence of different incompatible components (different kinds of object strings or several strings of objects). In such cases, it tries to divide the sentence in two or more successive sentences. Then the objects of the first part of the sentence are contextual objects for the other parts. Some coordination words may serve as guides to divide the sentence but this is not always the case. The following sentence expresses two queries. The first one contains the context object of the following:

Quelle est la station de metro la plus proche et comment on fait pour y aller?
(What is the nearest metro station and how to get there?)

```
(then (search_q (station
          (and (of metro)
               (maxi (near (station (name "Saint Lazare")))))))
      (info_q (route
               (to (station
                    (and (of metro)
                         (maxi (near (station (name "Saint Lazare")))))))
```

6 Results and Conclusion

The implementation of prototypes of this system has been made with λProlog, a logic programming language whose terms are simply-typed λ-terms with $\alpha-$, $\beta-$, and η-equivalences [MN86, BBR99]. The composition of the λ-terms and their β-reduction are thus an integral part of the language[1]. The direct availability of λ-terms composition is a bonus for implementing the proposed system. Moreover, λProlog offers a rich management of a context, including the use of intuitionistic implication in goals, which is directly used in our prototypes for managing the dialogue context.

A first prototype of the system [Vil00] has been evaluated on a test corpus made of two hundred and fifty sentences. This evaluation campaign has been achieved in a quantitative predictive framework using the DCR methodology [ASC+00]. This evaluation has focused on the correctness of the semantic representations. The system has achieved an interesting error rate of 10.5 per cent. Most of the observed system errors correspond to speech repairs[2]. This first prototype did not include the analysis of speech repairs completely as described in Section 5.1. A second prototype includes this improvement and behaves much better; about fifty per cent of these error cases are now correctly handled by the system.

The analysis strategy with two main successive phases is a way to solve efficiently a part of the problems raised by unexpected structural elements of the spoken language. Besides, it seems relevant to establish the object system of

---

[1] The version of λProlog used is Prolog/MALI, implemented at IRISA - Rennes - France.

[2] For more details on the mistakes see [ASC+00].

the sentence as the basis of the semantic context of the application in order to compose the different objects and their properties.

The composition of the objects is only limited by semantic constraints; this flexibility exceeds the possibilities given by predefinite frames in the selective approaches. Thus, this refined analysis is able to process correctly most of informative sentences, by opposition with standard selective approaches.

Although the order relations defined on the *question words* and on the *request words* constitute a satisfying approach in most cases, this method presents however some weaknesses (which we intend to improve in the future). Among other things, the system struggles sometimes to analyse properly the sentences where the query is following or preceding an unclear information. For example, the following sentence is not properly understand:

J'ai réservé une chambre par téléphone à l'hôtel Caumartin vous pouvez m'indiquer le metro pour y aller

(I have booked a room in the Caumartin hotel by phone can you tell me the metro to get there)

Considering that our system is largely based on pragmatical knowledge, one may fear that a context widening should produce ambiguities difficult to elude without an increase of the syntactic analysis. So it seems that the method is rather well adapted to applications in specific domains. Database queries and management are such applications.

Although we have conceived the system we present in this paper to allow the understanding of spoken language, with all its specificities such as the unexpected contructions, we think that a similar system can be used for the understanding of a language with less structural variability too. Because it is not possible to take into account in a formal grammar all the constructions of a language, the constructions left out become unexpected. If one wants a system of understanding that will not reject the sentences which include these unexpected structures, this system has to know how to compose fragments of sentences, using semantic knowledge. A variant of our system where the grammatical capacity is not limited to simple noun-phrases could be used in this new context.

References

[Abn91] S. Abney. Parsing with chunks. In C. Tenny R. Berwick, S. Abney, editor, *Principle-Based Parsing.* Kluwer Academic Publishers, 1991.

[Ant96] J-Y. Antoine. Parsing spoken language without syntax. In *COLING'96*, pages 47–52, Copenhagen, Danmark, 1996.

[ASC+00] J-Y. Antoine, J. Siroux, J. Caelen, J. Villaneau, J. Goulian, and M. Ahafhaf. Obtaining predictive results with an objective evaluation of spoken dialogue systems: Experiments with the DCR assessment paradigm. In *LREC'2000, Athènes*, 2000.

[BBMB90] C. Blanche-Benveniste and K. Van Den Eynde M. Bilger, C. Rouget. *Le Français parlé ; études grammaticales.* CNRS éditions, 1990.

[BBR99] C. Belleannée, P. Brisset, and O. Ridoux. A pragmatic reconstruction of λProlog. *J. Logic Programming*, 41(1):67–102, 1999.

[Cov90] M.A. Covington. A dependency parser for variable-word-order languages. In *Artificial Intelligence Programs*. University of Georgia, USA, 1990.

[HA99] P.A. Heeman and J.F. Allen. Speech repairs, intentional phrases and discourse markers: modeling speakers' utterances in spoken dialogue. *Computational Linguistics*, 25(4):527–573, 1999.

[Hir98] L. Hirschman. Language understanding evaluations: lessons learned from MUC and ATIS. In *LREC'98*, pages 117–122, Granada, Spain, 1998.

[Jos87] A. Joshi. Introduction to tree adjoining grammars. In *The Mathematics of Language*. J. Benjamins, Amsterdam, The Netherlands, a. manaster ramer edition, 1987.

[JVSW89] A. Joshi, K. Vijay-Shanker, and D. Weir. The convergence of middly context-sensitive formalisms. In *Fundamentals in Natural Language Processing*. MIT Press, p. sells, s. shieber, t. wasow edition, 1989.

[MAJ99] W. Minker, A.Waibel, and J.Mariani. *Stochastically Based Semantic Analysis*. Kluwer, Amsterdam, The Netherlands, 1999.

[Min96] W. Minker. Compréhension dans le domaine ATIS. In *Actes 21ièmes Journées d'Étude sur la parole, JEP'96*, pages 417–420, Avignon, France, 1996. JEP'96.

[MN86] D.A. Miller and G. Nadathur. Some uses of higher-order logic in computational linguistics. In 24th *Annual Meeting of the Association for Computational Linguistics*, pages 247–255, 1986.

[Mon74] R. Montague. *Formal Philosophy*. Yale University Press, New Haven, USA, 1974.

[Moo97] M. Moorgat. Categorial type logics. In Elsevier Science B.V., editor, *Handbook of Logic and Language*, pages 93–177. J. van Benthem and A. ter Meulen, 1997.

[Sen92] S. Sennef. Tina: a natural language system for spoken language applications. *Computational Linguistics*, 18:61–86, 1992.

[Sow84] J. F. Sowa. *Conceptual Structures: Information Processing in Mind and Machine*. Addison-Wesley, Reading, MA, 1984.

[Sow00] J.F. Sowa. *Knowledge Representation*. Brooks/Cole Thomson Learning, USA, 2000.

[Sri97] B. Srinivas. Performance evaluation of supertagging for partial parsing. In *5th International Workshop on Parsing Technologies Philadelphia, PA*, 1997.

[ST91] D. Sleator and D. Temperley. Parsing english with a link grammar. Research report cmu-cs-91-196, School of Computer Science, USA, 1991.

[Ste98] M. Steedman. *The MIT Encyclopedia of Cognitive Sciences*. MIT Press, Cambridge MA, 1998.

[Vil00] J. Villaneau. Un système basé sur les types logiques pour la compréhension de la parole. In *TALN 2000*, pages 529–534, Lausanne, 2000. EPFL and Université de Genève.

Atomicity of Some Categorially Polyvalent Modifiers

R. Zuber

Laboratoire de Linguistique Formelle
CNRS and Universite Paris 7
rz@ccr.jussieu.fr

Abstract. Some arguments are given to show that the particle *only*, considered as a categorially polyvalent modifier, denotes atoms of the corresponding denotational Boolean algebras. This fact explains its relatively constant meaning in all expressions with various categories in which it can occur. Some other consequences of this fact are discussed.

1 Introduction

It is by now well-established that the use of algebraic methods in the analysis of various domains of natural languages can lead to progress in our understanding of the complex phenomenon which is natural language. In the domain of semantics the application of simple algebraic notions has allowed us to make some generalisations, explain many apparent differences and discover or understand many similarities. One can say, for instance, that progress was made in our understanding of noun phrases when it was realized that that there are diverse and numerous linguistic structures which share important algebraic properties with expressions denoting quantifiers known from logic. Thus the class of quantifier denoting expressions could be extended and studied with the logico-algebraic tools of the generalized quantifiers theory (Barwise and Cooper 1981, Keenan and Moss 1985, Keenan and Stavi 1986, Keenan 1996, Keenan and Westerstahl 1997). Another result of such an application of algebraic tools to the study of natural languages, which appears simple from the algebraic point of view but which is conceptually far reaching, concerns the existence of expressions which are categorially polyvalent: these are (functional) expressions which can in some systematic way can be considered as having multiple categories since they can apply to argument expressions of various categories to form expressions of different categories. What is important, however, is the fact that these categorially polyvalent expressions exhibit a degree of constancy of meaning under all their category assignments. The best known examples of such categorially polyvalent expressions are expressions denoting Boolean connectives (operations). For instance the conjunction *and* in English, as is also the case with the corresponding conjunction in many other languages, can be used to conjoin naturally noun phrases, common noun phrases, verb phrases, adjectival phrases, adverbs, and even nominal determiners or prepositions. Furthermore, all such conjunctions,

P. de Groote, G. Morrill, C. Retoré (Eds.): LACL 2001, LNAI 2099, pp. 296–310, 2001.

when relating expressions of various categories, have in some sense the same meaning and it is possible in particular to construct with them logically equivalent sentences in which the same lexical material but different conjoined syntactic categories are used. This meaning constancy can easily be accounted for if one considers that the conjonction *and* corresponds to (denotes) the meet operation in the denotational Boolean algebras in which the expressions conjoined denote. Concrete and precise proposals in this sense are by now well-known (Gazdar 1980, Keenan and Faltz 1985).

One can easily see that many other connectives, Boolean and non-Boolean, including the one-place connective expressing negation and "non-standard" binary connectives like exclusive disjunction, are also categorially polyvalent and can be treated in a similar way.

A somewhat different categorial polyvalency is related to non-objectual domains of quantification. In this case some lexical items ressemble roughly expressions denoting quantifiers because they also involve quantification but the domain of quantification may change systematically. The item *mostly*, obviously related to *most*, is an example of such categorially polyvalent quantifiers: according to the type of its argument it involves different domains of quantification.

The existence of these and of many other types of categorially polyvalent expressions was one of the motivations for an extension of categorial grammars (Keenan and Timberlake 1988). The purpose of this paper is to discuss some specific categorially polyvalent modifiers. Modifiers are functional expressions which when applied to an argument-expression of a given category give as result a complex expression of the same category. The modifier I will essentially consider is the modifier *only* and, to a lesser degree, a related modifier, *also*. I will suggest that the constancy of the meaning of *only*, when it modifies expressions of various categories, should be related to the fact that it always denotes an atomic function (an atom) of the corresponding denotational algebra in which the modifiers of the appropriate category denote: if *only* is of category C/C then it denotes an atom of the algebra in which expressions of the category C/C denote. In addition, and this fact is logically related to the preceding one, the complex modifier-modified expression, i.e. the expression resulting from the application of *only* to an argument (of category C) denotes an atom of the algebra in which expressions of category C denote.

2 Formal Preliminaries and Notations

The theoretical tools which will be used in what follows are those of Boolean semantics as developed by Keenan (Keenan 1983, Keenan and Faltz 1985), including a simple version of a categorial grammar. To every expression of English (or a suitable fragment) is associated at least one grammatical category. Grammatical categories are of two types: basic categories, among which is the category S of sentences, and derived, or functional categories. Functional categories are of the form B/A: it is a category of an expression which when applied (by functional composition) to an expression of category A holds a (complex) expression of category B. For semantic interpretation we assume that with every category C is associated its denotational type D_C, or denotational algebra D_C, which is a set of possible denotations of expressions of category C. The denotational type D_S for sentences is the algebra $\{O, 1\}$. From the empirical point of view denotational types D_C form atomic (and complete) Boolean algebras, at least for major categories C. The partial order in these denotational algebras is interpreted as a generalized entailment. Thus it is meaningful to say that an entailment holds between two NPs, between two nominal determiners, between two VPs, etc.

Although usually elements of $D_{B/A}$ are functions from D_A to D_B and Boolean operations on them are defined pointwise (it is possible since D_B is a Boolean algebra), as we will see, there are various, linguistically motivated, restrictions on such functions. Consequently the notation $D_{B/A}$ does not generally indicate the set of all functions from D_A to D_B and will be completed by the indication of the constraint on functions.
As indicated above, denotational algebras D_C are atomic. The atomicity of $D_{B/A}$ is inheritated, so to speak, from the atomicity of D_B. In the simplest case when there are no constraints on functions from D_A on D_B, atoms of $D_{B/A}$ are determined by atoms of D_B in the following way:

Prop 1: For any $a \in D_A$, and for any $\alpha \in AT(D_B)$, the function $f_{a,\alpha} \in D_{B/A}$ defined as $f_{a,\alpha}(x) = \alpha$ if $x = a$, and O_{D_B} otherwise, is an atom of $D_{B/A}$. Furthermore, every element of $D_{B/A}$ contains an atom of this form.

Proof: Obviously $f_{a,\alpha} \neq 0_{D_{B/A}}$. Suppose that there is some $g \in D_{B/A}$ such that $g \leq f_{a,\alpha}$. This means that for any $x \in D_A$, $g(x) \leq f_{a,\alpha}(x)$. So for any $x \neq a$, $g(x) = f_{a,\alpha}(x) = 0_{D_{B/A}}$. If $x = a$ then either $g(x) = 0_{D_B}$ and thus $g = 0_{D_{B/A}}$ or $g(x) = \alpha$ and thus $g = f_{a,\alpha}$. Consequently $f_{a,\alpha}$ is an atom.
To show the second part, suppose that $0_{D_{B/A}} \neq g \in D_{B/A}$. So there is an $x_0 \in D_A$ such that $g(x_0) \neq 0_{D_B}$. But since D_B is atomic there is $\alpha \in D_B$ such that $\alpha \leq g(x_0)$. One can easily check now that the atom $f_{x_0,\alpha}$ is contained in g.

Let us use this proposition to determine atoms of the denotational algebra of expressions of category NP. Expressions of this category denote functions from properties onto truth values. So their denotations are elements of D_{NP} which are sets of sets. According to the above result, for any property P, the function f_P defined as $f_P(X) = 1$ if $X = P$ and $f_P(X) = O$ if $X \neq P$ is an atom of D_{NP}. Since such functions can be considered as characteristic functions of sets, atoms of D_{NP} are singletons which contain a set as their unique element.

Let us analyse now some denotations of functional expressions corresponding to functions satisfying some specific conditions. Consider first (unary) nominal determiners, i.e. expressions of category NP/CN. Denotations of nominal determiners are members of D_{Det} and are those functions from properties into a set of properties which satisfy the property $CONS$ of conservativity which is considered as a language universal. By definition $F \in CONS$ iff for all properties X,Y and Z, if $X \cap Y = X \cap Z$ then $F(X)(Y) = F(X)(Z)$.

There are two important sub-algebras of the algebra D_{Det} of conservative functions: the algebra of intersective functions, INT, and the algebra of co-intersective functions, $CO - INT$ (Keenan 1993). By definition $F \in INT$, iff for all properties X, Y, Z and W, if $X \cap Y = Z \cap W$ then $F(X)(Y)$ is true iff $F(Z)(W)$ is true. Similarly, $F \in CO - INT$ iff for all properties X, Y, Z and W, if $X - Y = Z - W$ then $F(X)(Y)$ is true iff $F(Z)(W)$ is true. Both sets INT and $CO - INT$ form atomic (and complete) Boolean algebras with the Boolean operations defined pointwise. Atoms of INT are functions at_P, where P is a property, such that $at_P(X)(Y)$ is true iff $X \cap Y = P$. Similarly atoms of $CO - INT$ are functions at_P such that $at_P(X)(Y)$ is true iff $X - Y = P$.

The INT algebra has an important sub-algebra $CARD$ of (intersective) cardinal determiners: they are denotations of, roughly speaking, various numerals. By definition, $f \in CARD$ iff for all properties X, Y, Z and W, if $card(X \cap Y) = card(Z \cap W)$ then $F(X)(Y)$ is true iff $F(Z)(W)$ is true. Atoms of $CARD$ are the functions f_α, where α is a cardinal, such that $f_\alpha(X)(Y)$ is true iff $card(X \cap Y) = \alpha$. From this definition it follows that any cardinal determines an atom of $CARD$.
It is easy to show that INT and $CO - INT$ are isomorphic to D_{NP}. Indeed (cf. Keenan 1993) the function g defined on elements of INT as $g(F(X)(Y)) = F(E)(Y)$, where E is the universe of discourse, establishes the isomorphism between INT and D_{NP}.

There is another way, in addition to algebras of functions from a set to an algebra, to form a new Boolean algebra from a given Boolean algebra. Roughly speaking, given a Boolean algebra B, it is possible to form from it another Boolean algebra by taking two elements $\alpha, \beta \in B$ such that $\alpha \leq \beta$ and taking as elements of the new algebra all elements x such that $\alpha \leq x \leq \beta$. Then by considering α as zero and β as unit element and relativizing the operation of complement appropriately, we obtain a new Boolean algebra (in which not all operations are defined pointwise). I will consider two particular cases of this general possibility, the case of restrictive algebras, when $\alpha = 0_B$ and $\beta \neq 1_B$, and the second case, the case of contextual algebras when $\alpha \neq 0_B$.

The restricting algebras I will consider are denotational algebras for modifiers. A modifier is a functional expression of category C/C for various choices of C. Now, given the algebra $D_{C/C}$ of all functions from D_C onto D_C we will consider a restrictive algebra in which the restricting element β equals the identity function id_c. Thus we consider the set $RESTR(C)$ of functions called *restrictive functions*, $f_c \in D_{C/C}$, satisfying the condition $f_c \leq id_c$, or equivalently, the set of functions satisfying the condition $f_c(x) \leq x$, for any $x \in D_C$. Then we have the following property:

Prop 2: Let B be a Boolean algebra. Then the set of functions f from B onto B satisfying the condition $f(x) \leq x$ forms a Boolean algebra R_B with the Boolean operations of meet and join defined pointwise: $0_{R_B} = 0_B$, $1_{R_B} = id_B$, $f'(x) = x \cap (f(x))'$

The atomicity of R_B is defined as follows (Keenan 1983):

Prop 3: If B is atomic so is R_B. For all $b \in B$ and all atoms α of B such that $\alpha \leq b$, functions $f_{b,\alpha}$ defined by $f_{b,\alpha}(x) = \alpha$ if $x = b$ and $f_{b,\alpha}(x) = O_B$ if $x \neq b$ are the atoms

There is an important sub-class $ABS(B)$ of restrictive functions (relative to a given Boolean algebra B): these are the so-called *absolute functions*. By definition $f \in ABS(B)$ iff for any $x \in B$, we have $f(x) = x \cap f(1_B)$. One can show (Keenan 1983) the following property:

Prop 4: $ABS(B)$ is a sub-algebra of R_B

One observes (cf. Keenan and Faltz 1985, pp.146) that atoms of R_B do not belong to $ABS(B)$. The following property indicates the atoms of $ABS(B)$:

Prop 5: If B is atomic so is $ABS(B)$. For all atoms α of B, functions f_α, defined by $f_\alpha(x) = \alpha$ if $\alpha \subseteq x$ and $f_\alpha(x) = O_B$ otherwise, are the atoms of $ABS(B)$

The following proposition expresses a fact which is important, although easy to prove, concerning the relationship between an algebra B and the algebra $ABS(B)$:

Prop 6: B and $ABS(B)$ are isomorphic. The mapping h which for any $a \in B$ associates the function f, defined as $h(a) = f(x) = x \cap a$ is the isomorphism.

Of course it is possible to impose other restrictions on functions denoted by modifiers. In particular a restriction dual to restrictiveness gives rise to negative restrictive and absolute algebras. Let B be a Boolean algebra and f a function from B onto B. We will say (Zuber 1997b) that f is negatively restrictive, noted $f \in NR_B$, iff for all $x \in B$ we have $f(x) \leq x'$. The set NB_R forms a Boolean algebra with the complement defined as $f'(x) = x' \cap (f(x))'$ and the unit element being the complement of the identity function: $f(x) = x'$. Similarly we can define the set $NABS(B)$ of absolute negative functions (from B onto B). By definition $f \in NABS(B)$ iff for all $x \in B$ we have $f(x) = x' \cap f(0_B)$. $NABS(B)$ is a sub-algebra of NB_R and if B is atomic then NB_R and $NABS(B)$ are atomic (Zuber 1997b).

It is interesting to note that atomic functions corresponding to possible denotations of modifiers, i.e. atoms of the agebra $D_{C/C}$, for any C, are either restrictive or negatively restrictive functions. More precisely we prove:

Prop 7: Let α be an atom of $D_{C/C}$ for C arbitrary. Then α is a restrictive function or a negatively restrictive function

Proof: Let id_C be the identity function (from D_C onto D_C): for any $x \in D_C$, $id_C(x) = x$. So $id_C \in D_{C/C}$. Given an arbitrary element of an (atomic) algebra and an atom of this algebra it is always the case that the atom is included in this element or in its complement. Since α is an atom it is either included in (dominated by) id_C or included in the complement of id_C. In the first case α is a restrictive function and in the second case it is a negatively restrictive function.

Finally let me give some details of contextual algebras. Let B be a Boolean algebra and a a non-zero element of B. Then the set $CONT(B, a) = \{x \in B : a \leq x\}$ is a Boolean algebra, where the the unit element and the meet and join operations are as in B, the zero element is a itself and the complement operation c is defined by $c(x) = a \cup x'$. (the complement operation "$'$" on the right refers to the complement operation in B). $CONT(B, a)$ is called the contextual algebra (of B) generated by a. Atoms of contextual algebras are indicated by the following property:

Prop. 8 If B is atomic, so is $CONT(B, a)$, for any $a \in B$. For all atoms α of B such that $\neg(\alpha \leq a)$, elements $\alpha \cup a$ are atoms of $CONT(B, a)$.

We also have algebras $CONREST(B : a, b)$ which are both contextual and restrictive. By definition, $CONREST(B : a, b) = \{x : x \in B, a \leq x \leq b\}$. Complement operation c in such algebras is defined as: $c(x) = a \cup (x' \cap b)$. Atoms are given by:

Prop 9: For all α, atoms of B such that $\neg(\alpha \leq a)$ and $\alpha \leq b$, elements $\alpha \cup a$ are atoms of $CONREST(B : a, b)$.

To conclude this section, notice that atoms of functions denoted by functional expressions of category C/D are always determined by, or are "indexed" by, the atoms of the denotational algebra of the resulting expression of category C. Atoms of restrictive algebras are even double indexed. In some cases atoms are determined by a property: in the case of algebras D_{NP}, INT and $CO-INT$ with any property P one can associate atoms of these algebras determined by P and with any atom of these algebras one can associate a property. In all cases the first index (of the atom) is determined by (the denotation of) the argument expression.

3 *Only* and Atomicity

Our aim is now to show that *only*, treated as a modifier, denotes atoms of the denotational algebra of restrictive functions relative to the algebra of the denotations of arguments of *only*. And this is true for arguments of *only* having various grammatical categories. In what follows I will not be concerned with all major categories expressions of which can contain *only*. I will limit my description to the two basic categories: the category of NPs and the category of VPs. Since all other categories are functionally related to one of these two, their description in many cases will be straightforward.

There is nothing linguistically peculiar in the fact that some expressions can systematically denote atoms of a denotational algebra. One of the best known examples of this phenomenon, although the details still need to be formally worked out, is exhibited by the superlative constructions. Indeed, the superlative "operation", whether expressed morphologically, or lexically, can be considered as an operation on adjectival phrases giving atomic expressions as result, i.e. expressions denoting atoms. This is because common nouns with superlative adjectival phrases express atomic properties: *the highest mountain* denotes an atomic property.

Formally clearer examples of atomic expressions are furnished by the so-called exclusion determiners. It has been noticed (cf. Keenan 1993) that many determiners found in exclusion phrases denote atoms of INT or $CO-INT$. For instance let the common noun *student* denote the property S, the verb phrase *danced* denote the property D, the proper name *Leo* denote the (atomic) property $\{L\}$ and the conjunction *Leo and Naomi* denote the set $\{L,N\}$. Consider now the following sentences:

(1a) No student except Leo and Naomi danced
(1b) Every student except Leo danced

Sentence (1a) is true iff $S \cap D = \{L,N\}$ and (1b) is true iff $S-D=\{L\}$. So, given the definitions of atoms of INT and of $CO-INT$, both these sentences contain "atomic" determiners which denote atoms of INT and $CO-INT$ respectively. Cardinal determiners offer even clearer example of atomic expressions. Thus the cardinal determiner like *No... except n* denotes the atom of $CARD$ determined by the cardinal n.

It is interesting to note (cf. Zuber 1997a) that numeral determiners (with or without exceptions) and more generally exclusion determiners, which are in general syntactically complex, can be analysed as a result of an application of a modifier corresponding to *No... except* or *Every... except* applying to a linguistic material (proper nouns, conjonctions of proper nouns or numerals) which is a remnant of an ellipsis of a determiner. Then semantically such a modifier denotes a restrictive function which has as argument an intersective (or co-intersective) function. The result of application of this function to its argument is an atom in the intersective (co-intersective) algebra. As we will see *only* behaves in the same way: it "choses" an atom of the argument and this atom is in general determined by a particular expression. To see this consider again (1a). This sentence is equivalent to (1c):

(1c) No student except all students who are Leo or Naomi, danced

Let $P=\{L,N\}$. The complement of *except* in (1c) denotes a quantifier having as memebers sets Y which satisfy the condition $P=\{L,N\} \subseteq (S \cap Y)$.

This quantifier corresponds to the value at $X = P$ of the intersective function $f_P(X)(Y) = 1$ iff $P \subseteq (X \cap Y)$. This intersective function, considered as an element of INT, is modified by the restrictive function denoted by the expression *No ... except* and as a result of this modification we obtain the atom $at_P(X)(Y) = 1$ iff $P = X \cap Y$. Thus the modifier *No... except* denotes a restrictive function which applies to intersective functions determined by a property and "chooses" the atom determined by the same property.

The above examples differ from the case of *only* by the fact that in principle the atomic functional expressions involved in them are not categorially polyvalent; they cannot apply to two expressions of different categories. They are interesting, however, since at least some of them can be used to test some empirical claims. For indeed, given the properties of an atom, two different atoms are always incompatible: their intersection is empty. So if two atomic expressions have a common semantic content (denotation), in fact they denote the same atom. For instance one observes that the expressions *No (X) except n* and *Only n (X)* are semantically equivalent (for any expression X denoting a property). But, since, as we have seen, the first, considered as a functional expression (over common nouns) denotes an atom, (an atom of $CARD$ determined by the cardinal n) the second should also denote an atom.

It is useful to begin the analysis by recalling some relevant data. Let us consider the following examples:

(2) Only Leo danced on weekdays with Lea in the garden
(3) Leo only danced on weekdays with Lea in the garden
(4) Leo danced only on weekdays with Lea in the garden
(5) Leo danced on weekdays only with Lea in the garden
(6) Leo danced on weekdays with Lea only in the garden
(7) Leo danced on weekdays with Lea in the garden

Although there are many other possibilities one can see in these examples that *only* can apply syntactically to (i.e. combine according to the rule of functional composition) an NP, as in (2), an intransitive verb or a verb phrase, as in (3), an adverb, as in (4), and different prepositional phrases, as in (5) and (6). Furthermore in each of these cases *only* should be considered as a modifier since the category of the expression obtained by such an application is the same as the category of expression to which *only* applies. These facts indicate that syntactically *only* is a categorially polyvalent modifier.

It is important to notice that *only* cannot combine freely with all NPs. The following examples are not grammatical, unless *only* has in its scope a common noun, the argument of the determiner:

(8) * Only most/all/none of students danced

The second observation related to examples (2) to (7) concerns some semantic facts. One notices that phrases modified by *only* entail the argument to which *only* applies: *only Leo* entails *Leo*, *only danced* entails *danced*, *only in the garden* entails *in the garden*, etc. For this reason in particular all sentences (2) to (6) entail sentence (7). This means that *only* should be interpreted by a restrictive function.

Another semantic observation I will use is that *only* denotes a kind of increasingly monotonic function: when its argument is increased by a disjunction then it behaves like an increasingly monotonic function (see, however, Atlas 1996). For instance (2) entails (9) and (3) - with *only* modifying the VP- entails (10):

(9) Only Leo or Bill danced yesterday with Lea in the garden
(10) Leo only (danced or sang) with Lea in the garden

This observation and the fact that all elements of an atomic algebra are joins of atoms it dominates, leads to the following generalisation: *only A* entails *only (A or B)*. This generalisation suggests that *only* denotes an absolute function since restrictive non-absolute functions need not be monotone.

In the next step we have to show that when the category of *only* is chosen among its possible categories and fixed as, say, C/C then it denotes an atom in the $D_{C/C}$ algebra. Let us consider the case when $C = NP$, i.e. the case when *only* is a NP modifier. The clearest situation is when the NP in question is a proper name PrN. Then it is easy to see that *Only PrN* denotes an atom of D_{NP}. It is enough to observe that the function which establishes the isomorphism between D_{NP} and INT associates with denotations of expressions of the form *only NP* atoms of INT. For instance the denotation of *No (X) except Leo* is associated with the denotation of *No object except Leo* and this last expression is equivalent to *only Leo.* So since the first expression denotes an atom the expression denoting an object to which an atom is sent by an isomorphism is also an atom. Intuitively this is also clear: if property P belongs to the quantifier denoted by *only Leo* then it must be a property expressed by a singleton containing as the only element *Leo* and there is only one such a property.

Notice now that *only* cannot denote an atom of a restrictive algebra. The reason is that *only* "choses" an atom of the element denoted by its argument expression which is also indexed (determined) by this argument expression (or an "index" uniquely associated with the argument expression) and in general it does not "choose" the same atom from an arbitrary argument and from the argument corresponding to the unit element of the denotational algebra. Furthermore, given the property Prop 5, these facts are compatible with *only* denoting an atom of the $ABS(D_{NP})$ algebra.

Before going on to another basic category expressions of which can also be arguments of *only*, let me make some remarks about a specific NPs *only* can modify. In English, as well as in many other languages, there exist naked NPs, i.e. NPs without an overt determiner: these are so-called bare plurals, BP, like *students, teachers*, etc. When *only* applies to a BP one might think that it plays a role of a determiner similar to *most, ten*, etc. Consider now examples in (11):

(11a) Only students danced
(11b) Only students are students who danced
(11c) Students danced

If *only* is a determiner then it does not denote a conservative function, as all other (non vague and extensional) determiners do: (11a) is not equivalent to (11b). In addition one observes that (11a) entails (11c). This suggests that *only* is a modifier. Now, if *only* is a modifier which applies to a BP to give an "ordinary" NP then we are in trouble because then *only BP* does not denote an atom of D_{NP}. Indeed a plausible denotation of an NP of the form *only BP* is indicated in (12):

(12) If BP denotes the property P then *only BP* denotes the set $\{Y : Y \neq \emptyset, Y \subseteq P\}$.

The denotation of *only BP* indicated in (12) is not an atom of D_{NP} since atoms of this algebra are determined by a property and contain exactly one property (set) as element. A way out of this difficulty is to recall that bare plurals are very special noun phrases and in particular they differ from all other NPs with determiners (cf. Carlson 1977). Their behaviour with *only* is also very special (von Fintel 1997). So very likely BPs do not denote quantifiers of type $< 1 >$ as do "ordinary" NPs (neither do they denote properties as is assumed in (12)). Since they behave like other Boolean categories, in particular with respect to basic Boolean operations, it is to be expected that their possible denotations are members of an atomic Boolean algebra different from D_{NP}. But obviously atoms of such an algebra are different from atoms of D_{NP}.

The second basic category modified by *only* that I would like to consider is the case of verb phrases. From the empirical point of view this case is rather special since readings involved in the modification of VPs and their parts are contextually very loaded; often it is not even clear what such modifications mean in isolation. Consider (13):

(13) Leo only danced (in the garden)

This sentence means in some sense that Leo did not do anything else except dance (in the garden) and possibly, someone other than Leo did something else. This is basically a "contrastive" reading. Furthermore, dancing entails (not only pragmatically) many other things: dancing, in its normal reading, entails movement (but movement does not entail dancing) and clearly if Leo danced he also moved. Obviously (11) is compatible with such a situation: it probably says that Leo did not do anything which dancing does not entail. However, strictly speaking, Leo can have also other properties which, although not entailed by dancing, are necessary for Leo to exist. More formally, proper nouns denote ultrafilters and ultrafilters are complete in the sense that for any property P either P of its complement P' belongs to the ultrafilter. Thus if Leo dances then he dances barefoot or not barefoot. So Leo has also properties entailing dancing. Whether such properties are out of the scope of *only* is not clear. Whatever is the exact empirical status of the above examples we see that *only* when applied to a VP particions the set of properties that the subject NP has into two kinds: those properties which entail the property denoted by the VP and those which are entailed by the denotation of the VP.

Notice that an analysis of *only* applied to a VP according to which *only* denotes an (atomic) absolute function should imply that *only* is "permutable" with another modifier denoting an absolute function: if M_1 and M_2 are two absolute functions (over the same algebra) then $M_1(M_2(x))$ is equivalent to $M_2(M_1(x))$. In addition, $M_1(M_2(x))$ and $M_2(M_1(x))$ are both equivalent to $M_1(x) \wedge M_2(x)$ (cf. Keenan and Faltz 1985, p.131). This means for instance that (14a), (14b) and (14c) should come out as logically equivalent:

(14a) Leo ((only danced) in the garden)
(14b) Leo ((danced in the garden) only)
(14c) Leo (danced only) and Leo (danced in the garden)

There is still another, more technical problem, concerning the modification of a VP by *only*. As we have seen, given the the isomorphism between D_{NP} and INT, there is a one-to-one correspondence between properties and atoms of D_{NP}. Thus atoms of D_{NP} can be distinguished by a specific property one can associate with (some) NPs. This is not the case with atoms of D_{VP}. So, if the expression of the form *Only VP* is to denote an atom, we have to determine which atom it is since in general the denotation P of VP has the number equal to $card(P)$ of "indistinguishable" atoms. In some cases a distinction between these atoms is possible by using the denotation of the subject NP. Consider for instance (15a) and (15b), where *only* is supposed to apply to the VP:

(15a) Leo only danced
(15b) Naomi only danced

If we use the simplest way to determine the atoms "chosen" by *only* in the above examples, we are obliged to say that in (15a) the atom $\{L\}$ is chosen and in (15b) the atom $\{N\}$ is chosen. Such a move seems incompatible with compositionality as applied to *only danced.* Moreover, it is not clear how this way of proceeding would account for cases where subject NPs do not denote individuals.

Another difficulty related to compositionality is illustrated by the following examples:

(16a) Leo danced and sang
(16b) Leo ((danced and sang) only)
(16c) Lea danced only but Leo danced and sang

Although (16a) does not en tail (16b), it seems that (16c) entails (16b). In other words the second conjunct in (16c), the sentence after *but* seems to mean (16b) and not (16a).

All the difficulties mentioned above lead inevitably to the conclusion that the effects of the application of *only* to a VP necessitate a specific development. It seems to me that some of them can be solved by the use of contextual or contextual and restrictive algebras. For instance if we use contextual algebra $CONT(D_{VP}, P)$, where P is a "contextually given property, to interpret verb phrases modified by *only* than (15a) is true if the ultrafilter of this algebra generated by the atom $L \cup P$ contains the property D (the denotation of *danced*). Similarly, we could use for this purpose the contextual and restrictive algebra $CONREST(D_{VP} : P, D)$. In this case if (15a) is true, then Leo denotes exactly the set of all properties which "contain" Leo and which are included in D.

4 Preliminary Conclusions

In order to explain the degree of constancy of the meaning of categorially polyvalent *only* it has been argued that complex phrases obtained by the application of *only* to an argument expression denote atoms in the appropriate denotational algebra. Since atoms are defined in terms of the order proper to the algebra and independently of particular properties that elements belonging to the domain of the algebra may have, the constancy of meaning of *only* is thus partly explaned. By the same token an explanation has been given why phrases with *only* have a "quantificational force". Although formally such phrases do not denote quantifiers (except when *only* modifies an NP or possibly a bare plural) their "naive" semantics involves quantification. This can be understand if we suppose that their meaning is determined by their status as atomic elements.

Atomicity induced by *only* can also help us to understand the frequently noted fact that it is difficult to find a case where *only* applies to the whole sentence. There are surely deep reasons for this. However, this problem may be related to the difficulty of the possible status of an atomic proposition. Given, by supposition, the Boolean structure of propositions and their possible denotations, if there were one atomic proposition, there would be infinitely, even uncountably many of them. Furthermore, it is difficult to see what would be an atomic proposition, i.e. a (contingent) proposition not entailed by another (contingent) proposition. This difficulty, if not impossibility, comes from the fact that for any given sentence expressing a contingent proposition, it is always possible to find a conjonction of two contingent sentences one of which will be the given one. Since conjunctions entail each of the conjoints, and since apparently *only* cannot have in its scope unlimited conjunctions, atomic sentences cannot exist.

It was also suggested, although with less argumentation, that *only* itself denotes an atom in the denotational functional algebras of absolute functions in which modifiers denote. Since modifiers denote restrictive (sometimes even absolute) functions this means that *only* picks up an atom of the element denoted by the argument to which *only* applies. Which atom is thus picked is in some cases determined, since atomic functions may be "indexed" by their argument. This is, however, not always the case, for instance this is not the case when *only* applies to a VP, and this can lead to difficulties.

It should be noted that although the analysis concerned the item *only*, in some cases other items have a meaning closer to the one described. For instance in the case of cardinal determiners it is probably not *only* which is analysed but rather *exactly*: the cardinal determiner *exactly n* denotes the atom determiner by the cardinal n in the algebra $CARD$. The item *only* seems to have an additional, possibly pragmatic, content.

More importantly, one might object that I completely avoided talking about other important syntactic and semantic aspects of *only*. Indeed as has often been observed (Bonomi and Casalegno 1993, von Fintel 1997, de May 1996, Rooths 1992, 1996) *only* is focus sensitive. This is deliberate: it seems to me that the formal status remains unclear. If, however, as suggested in part by the work done on this domain, *only* should be considered not as denoting just one place function but possibly a (binary) relation or even two-place function, my proposal is still compatible with such an requirement. Indeed, binary relations can also form atomic Boolean algebras.

The method applied to *only* can also be applied to other categorially polyvalent modifiers. Natural languages display a great variety of focus particles in various aspects similar to *only* (Koenig, 1991). Some of them are logically related to *only*. This is in partiular the case with *also* which is also categorially polyvalent and seems to be just the Boolean complement of *only* (cf. Zuber 1998). There is, however, an assymmetry between *only* and *also* concerning presuppositions they can induce, which needs an explanation. Many categorially polyvalent focus particles, determiners and even interrogative determiners (Zuber 2000b, Zuber, forthcoming) seem to be of the same type. My contention is that many of the so-called scalar particles can be analysed in a similar way.

Notice also that the analysis in this vein can also be carried out on modifiers which possibly denote negatively restrictive functions (cf. Zuber 1997b). Such modifiers may involve intensionality (Keenan and Faltz 1985). In addition the full analysis of *only* should also take into account intensionality. For instance the difference between the following two truths should be related to intensionality:

(17a) Students are students
(17b) Only students are students

As already mentioned the analysis of *only* modifying VPs poses many specific problems. The situation becomes even more complex when an additional *only* modifies some other constituents; sentences like (18) seem to be possible:

(18) Only Leo only danced

This sentence has at least two readings one of them implying that there is not only Leo in the universe. It seems to me that any analysis of *only* should account for such a possibility.

Although I was basically concerned with atomic modification of NPs and VPs, it is clear, given the functional dependence between various categories, that similar methods can be applied to other categories. This is in particular possible with propositional determiners such as *if* or a verbal modifier (quantifier?) such as *when* in order to explain the somewhat mysterious connectives *only if* or *only when* (cf. Zuber 2000a). In this case one has to suppose that *if* is a non-nominal determiner (cf. van Benthem 1984, Lapierre 1996) which can be modified by *only* in the same way as other (nominal) determiners can be modified. It is interesting to notice similarities in the behaviour of *only* in both cases. Thus is has been observed (van Fintel 1997) that the natural interpretation of sentences of the type *only if p, q* necessitates that the first sentential argument, the sentence *p*, be contrasted with another sentence and thus is in the scope of focus. A similar situation obtains in the case of *only* applied to *all*. Consider (19a) and (19b):

(19a) Only if it rains Leo will sleep
(19b) Only all students were dancing

The sentence (19b) is interpretable only if *only* has *students* in its scope, thus inducing a contrast between students and another class expressed by a common noun. This similarity with (19a) is noticeable given the fact that *if* is usually considered as a universal quantifier over, roughly, propositional objects.

Thus we can see that the full analysis of the atomic modification by *only* is related to many important theoretical problems in semantics. We have seen that it may be related to the problem of contextuality, the problem of compositionality, intensionality and, probably most importantly,to the problem of focus-topic partition and topic sensitivity. All these problems are still awaiting a general solution.

References

1. Atlas, J. D. (1996) 'Only' Noun Phrases, Pseudo-Negative Generalized Quantifiers, Negative Polarity Items, and Monotonicity *J. of Semantics*13, pp.265-328
2. Barwise, J. and Cooper, R. (1981) Generalized Quantifiers and Natural Language, *Linguistics and Philosophy* 4, pp.159-219
3. van Benthem, J. (1984) Foundations of Conditional Logic, *J. of Symbolic Logic* 49, pp. 303-4349
4. Bonomi, A. Casalegno, P. (1993) *Only*: Association with Focus in Event Semantics, *Natural Language Semantics* 2:1, pp. 1-46
5. Carlson, G. (1977) A Unified Analysis of the English Bare Plural, *Linguistics and Philosophy* 1:3, pp.413-456
6. von Fintel, Kai (1997) Bare Plurals, Bare Conditionals and *Only*, *Journal of Semantics* 14, pp1-56
7. Gazdar, G. (1980) A Cross-Categorial Semantics for Coordination, *Linguistics and Philosophy* 3:3, pp. 407-410

8. Keenan, E. L. (1983) Boolean Algebra for Linguists, *in* Mordechay, S. (ed.) *UCLA Working Papers in Semantics* pp. 1-75
9. Keenan, E. L. (1993) Natural Language, Sortal Reducibility and Generalized Quantifiers, *Journal of Symbolic logic* 58:1, pp. 314-325.
10. Keenan, E. L. and Faltz, L. M. (1985) *Boolean Semantics for Natural Language*, D. Reidel Publishing Company, Dordrecht.
11. Keenan, E. L. and Moss, L. (1985) Generalized Quantifiers and the Expressive Power of Natural Language, *in* van Benthem, J. and ter Meulen, A. (eds.) *Generalized Quantifiers in Natural Language*, Foris Publications, pp.73-126
12. Keenan, E. L. and Timberlake, A. (1988) Natural Language Motivations for Extending Catagorial Grammar, *in* Oehrle, R. *et al* (eds.) *Catagorial Grammars and Natural Language Structures*, Reidel Publ. Company, pp. 265-295.
13. Keenan , E. L. and Westerstahl, D. (1997) Generalized Quantifiers in Linguistics and Logic, *in* van Benthem, J. and ter Meulen, A. (eds.) *Handbook of Logic and Language*, Elsevier, pp. 837-893.
14. Koenig, E. (1991) *The meaning of Focus Particles: A Comparative Perspective*, Routledge, London
15. Lapierre, S. (1996) Conditionals and Quantifiers, *in* van der Does, J. and van Eijck, J. (eds.) *Quantifiers, Logic, and Language*, CSLI Publications, Stanford, pp. 237-253.
16. Mey, Sjaak de (1996) Generalized Quantifier Theory and the Semantics of Focus, *in* van der Does, J. and van Eijck, J. (eds.) *Quantifiers, Logic, and Language*, CSLI Publications, Stanford, pp. 269-280.
17. Rooth, Mats (1992) A theory of focus interpretation, *Natural Language Semantics* 1, pp.75-116
18. Rooth, Mats (1996) Focus, *in* Lappin, S. (ed.) *Handbook of Contemporary Semantic Theory*, Blackwell, pp.272-297
19. Zuber, R. (1997a) Some algebraic properties of higher order modifiers, *in* Becker, T. and Krieger (eds.) *Proceedings of the Fifth Meeting on Mathematics of Language*, Deutsches Forschungszentrum fur Kunstlische Intelligenz, pp.161-168.
20. Zuber, R. (1997b) On negatively restricting Boolean algebras, *Bulletin of the Section of Logic*, 26-1, pp. 50-54
21. Zuber, R. (1998) On the Semantics of Exclusion and Inclusion Phrases, *in* Lawson, A. (ed.) *SALT8*, Cornell University Press, pp.267-283
22. Zuber, R. (2000a) Exclusion phrases and criticisms of semantic compositionality, in Ikeya, A. and Kawamori, M. (eds.)*Proc. of the 14th Pacific Asia Conference of Language, Information and Computation*, pp.401-412
23. Zuber, R. (2000b) On Inclusive Questions, in Billerey, R. *et al.* (eds.) *WCCFL 19 Proceedings*, Cascadilla Press, pp. 617-630
24. Zuber, R. (forthcoming) Some Spanish Quantifier Modifiers, forthcoming in Gutierrez-Rexach, J. (ed.) *Semantics and Pragmatics of Spanish*

Author Index

Lecture Notes in Artificial Intelligence (LNAI)

Vol. 1866: J. Cussens, A. Frisch (Eds.), Inductive Logic Programming. Proceedings, 2000. X, 265 pages. 2000.

Vol. 1867: B. Ganter, G.W. Mineau (Eds.), Conceptual Structures: Logical, Linguistic, and Computational Issues. Proceedings, 2000. XI, 569 pages. 2000.

Vol. 1881: C. Zhang, V.-W. Soo (Eds.), Design and Applications of Intelligent Agents. Proceedings, 2000. X, 183 pages. 2000.

Vol. 1886: R. Mizoguchi, J. Slaney (Eds.), PRICAI 2000: Topics in Artificial Intelligence. Proceedings, 2000. XX, 835 pages. 2000.

Vol. 1898: E. Blanzieri, L. Portinale (Eds.), Advances in Case-Based Reasoning. Proceedings, 2000. XII, 530 pages. 2000.

Vol. 1889: M. Anderson, P. Cheng, V. Haarslev (Eds.), Theory and Application of Diagrams. Proceedings, 2000. XII, 504 pages. 2000.

Vol. 1891: A.L. Oliveira (Ed.), Grammatical Inference: Algorithms and Applications. Proceedings, 2000. VIII, 313 pages. 2000.

Vol. 1902: P. Sojka, I. Kopeček, K. Pala (Eds.), Text, Speech and Dialogue. Proceedings, 2000. XIII, 463 pages. 2000.

Vol. 1904: S.A. Cerri, D. Dochev (Eds.), Artificial Intelligence: Methodology, Systems, and Applications. Proceedings, 2000. XII, 366 pages. 2000.

Vol. 1910: D.A. Zighed, J. Komorowski, J. Żytkow (Eds.), Principles of Data Mining and Knowledge Discovery. Proceedings, 2000. XV, 701 pages. 2000.

Vol. 1916: F. Dignum, M. Greaves (Eds.), Issues in Agent Communication. X, 351 pages. 2000.

Vol. 1919: M. Ojeda-Aciego, I.P. de Guzman, G. Brewka, L. Moniz Pereira (Eds.), Logics in Artificial Intelligence. Proceedings, 2000. XI, 407 pages. 2000.

Vol. 1925: J. Cussens, S. Džeroski (Eds.), Learning Language in Logic. X, 301 pages 2000.

Vol. 1930: J.A. Campbell, E. Roanes-Lozano (Eds.), Artificial Intelligence and Symbolic Computation. Proceedings, 2000. X, 253 pages. 2001.

Vol. 1932: Z.W. Raś, S. Ohsuga (Eds.), Foundations of Intelligent Systems. Proceedings, 2000. XII, 646 pages.

Vol. 1934: J.S. White (Ed.), Envisioning Machuine Translation in the Information Future. Proceedings, 2000. XV, 254 pages. 2000.

Vol. 1937: R. Dieng, O. Corby (Eds.), Knowledge Engineering and Knowledge Management. Proceedings, 2000. XIII, 457 pages. 2000.

Vol. 1952: M.C. Monard, J. Simão Sichman (Eds.), Advances in Artificial Intelligence. Proceedings, 2000. XV, 498 pages. 2000.

Vol. 1955: M. Parigot, A. Voronkov (Eds.), Logic for Programming and Automated Reasoning. Proceedings, 2000. XIII, 487 pages. 2000.

Vol. 1967: S. Arikawa, S. Morishita (Eds.), Discovery Science. Proceedings, 2000. XII, 332 pages. 2000.

Vol. 1968: H. Arimura, S. Jain, A. Sharma (Eds.), Algorithmic Learning Theory. Proceedings, 2000. XI, 335 pages. 2000.

Vol. 1972: A. Omicini, R. Tolksdorf, F. Zambonelli (Eds.), Engineering Societies in the Agents World. Proceedings, 2000. IX, 143 pages. 2000.

Vol. 1979: S. Moss, P. Davidsson (Eds.), Multi-Agent-Based Simulation. Proceedings, 2000. VIII, 267 pages. 2001.

Vol. 1991: F. Dignum, C. Sierra (Eds.), Agent Mediated Electronic Commerce. VIII, 241 pages. 2001.

Vol. 1994: J. Lind, Iterative Software Engineering for Multiagent Systems. XVII, 286 pages. 2001.

Vol. 2003: F. Dignum, U. Cortés (Eds.), Agent-Mediated Electronic Commerce III. XII, 193 pages. 2001.

Vol. 2007: J.F. Roddick, K. Hornsby (Eds.), Temporal, Spatial, and Spatio-Temporal Data Mining. Proceedings, 2000. VII, 165 pages. 2001.

Vol. 2014: M. Moortgat (Ed.), Logical Aspects of Computational Linguistics. Proceedings, 1998. X, 287 pages. 2001.

Vol. 2019: P. Stone, T. Balch, G. Kraetzschmar (Eds.), RoboCup 2000: Robot Soccer World Cup IV. XVII, 658 pages. 2001.

Vol. 2033: J. Liu, Y. Ye (Eds.), E-Commerce Agents. VI, 347 pages. 2001.

Vol. 2035: D. Cheung, G.J. Williams, Q. Li (Eds.), Advances in Knowledge Discovery and Data Mining – PAKDD 2001. Proceedings, 2001. XVIII, 596 pages. 2001.

Vol. 2039: M. Schumacher, Objective Coordination in Multi-Agent System Engineering. XIV, 149 pages. 2001.

Vol. 2056: E. Stroulia, S. Matwin (Eds.), Advances in Artificial Intelligence. Proceedings, 2001. XII, 366 pages. 2001.

Vol. 2062: A. Nareyek, Constraint-Based Agents. XIV, 178 pages. 2001.

Vol. 2070: L. Monostori, J. Váncza, M. Ali (Eds.), Engineering of Intelligent Systems. Proceedings, 2001. XVIII, 951 pages. 2001.

Vol. 2083: R. Goré, A. Leitsch, T. Nipkow (Eds.), Automated Reasoning. Proceedings, 2001. XV, 708 pages. 2001.

Vol. 2099: P. de Groote, G. Morrill, C. Retoré (Eds.), Logical Aspects of Computational Linguistics. Proceedings, 2001. VIII, 311 pages. 2001.

Lecture Notes in Computer Science

Vol. 2045: B. Pfitzmann (Ed.), Advances in Cryptology – EUROCRYPT 2001. Proceedings, 2001. XII, 545 pages. 2001.

Vol. 2047: R. Dumke, C. Rautenstrauch, A. Schmietendorf, A. Scholz (Eds.), Performance Engineering. XIV, 349 pages. 2001.

Vol. 2048: J. Pauli, Learning Based Robot Vision. IX, 288 pages. 2001.

Vol. 2051: A. Middeldorp (Ed.), Rewriting Techniques and Applications. Proceedings, 2001. XII, 363 pages. 2001.

Vol. 2052: V.I. Gorodetski, V.A. Skormin, L.J. Popyack (Eds.), Information Assurance in Computer Networks. Proceedings, 2001. XIII, 313 pages. 2001.

Vol. 2053: O. Danvy, A. Filinski (Eds.), Programs as Data Objects. Proceedings, 2001. VIII, 279 pages. 2001.

Vol. 2054: A. Condon, G. Rozenberg (Eds.), DNA Computing. Proceedings, 2000. X, 271 pages. 2001.

Vol. 2055: M. Margenstern, Y. Rogozhin (Eds.), Machines, Computations, and Universality. Proceedings, 2001. VIII, 321 pages. 2001.

Vol. 2056: E. Stroulia, S. Matwin (Eds.), Advances in Artificial Intelligence. Proceedings, 2001. XII, 366 pages. 2001. (Subseries LNAI).

Vol. 2057: M. Dwyer (Ed.), Model Checking Software. Proceedings, 2001. X, 313 pages. 2001.

Vol. 2059: C. Arcelli, L.P. Cordella, G. Sanniti di Baja (Eds.), Visual Form 2001. Proceedings, 2001. XIV, 799 pages. 2001.

Vol. 2060: T. Böhme, H. Unger (Eds.), Innovative Internet Computing Systems. Proceedings, 2001. VIII, 183 pages. 2001.

Vol. 2062: A. Nareyek, Constraint-Based Agents. XIV, 178 pages. 2001. (Subseries LNAI).

Vol. 2064: J. Blanck, V. Brattka, P. Hertling (Eds.), Computability and Complexity in Analysis. Proceedings, 2000. VIII, 395 pages. 2001.

Vol. 2065: H. Balsters, B. de Brock, S. Conrad (Eds.), Database Schema Evolution and Meta-Modeling. Proceedings, 2000. X, 245 pages. 2001.

Vol. 2066: O. Gascuel, M.-F. Sagot (Eds.), Computational Biology. Proceedings, 2000. X, 165 pages. 2001.

Vol. 2068: K.R. Dittrich, A. Geppert, M.C. Norrie (Eds.), Advanced Information Systems Engineering. Proceedings, 2001. XII, 484 pages. 2001.

Vol. 2070: L. Monostori, J. Váncza, M. Ali (Eds.), Engineering of Intelligent Systems. Proceedings, 2001. XVIII, 951 pages. 2001. (Subseries LNAI).

Vol. 2071: R. Harper (Ed.), Types in Compilation. Proceedings, 2000. IX, 207 pages. 2001.

Vol. 2072: J. Lindskov Knudsen (Ed.), ECOOP 2001 – Object-Oriented Programming. Proceedings, 2001. XIII, 429 pages. 2001.

Vol. 2073: V.N. Alexandrov, J.J. Dongarra, B.A. Juliano, R.S. Renner, C.J.K. Tan (Eds.), Computational Science – ICCS 2001. Part I. Proceedings, 2001. XXVIII, 1306 pages. 2001.

Vol. 2074: V.N. Alexandrov, J.J. Dongarra, B.A. Juliano, R.S. Renner, C.J.K. Tan (Eds.), Computational Science – ICCS 2001. Part II. Proceedings, 2001. XXVIII, 1076 pages. 2001.

Vol. 2075: J.M. Colom, M. Koutny (Eds.), Applications and Theory of Petri Nets 2001. Proceedings, 2001. XII, 403 pages. 2001.

Vol. 2077: V. Ambriola (Ed.), Software Process Technology. Proceedings, 2001. VIII, 247 pages. 2001.

Vol. 2078: R. Reed, J. Reed (Eds.), SDL 2001: Meeting UML. Proceedings, 2001. XI, 439 pages. 2001.

Vol. 2081: K. Aardal, B. Gerards (Eds.), Integer Programming and Combinatorial Optimization. Proceedings, 2001. XI, 423 pages. 2001.

Vol. 2082: M.F. Insana, R.M. Leahy (Eds.), Information Processing in Medical Imaging. Proceedings, 2001. XVI, 537 pages. 2001.

Vol. 2083: R. Goré, A. Leitsch, T. Nipkow (Eds.), Automated Reasoning. Proceedings, 2001. XV, 708 pages. 2001. (Subseries LNAI).

Vol. 2084: J. Mira, A. Prieto (Eds.), Connectionist Models of Neurons, Learning Processes, and Artificial Intelligence. Proceedings, 2001. Part I. XXVII, 836 pages. 2001.

Vol. 2085: J. Mira, A. Prieto (Eds.), Bio-Inspired Applications of Connectionism. Proceedings, 2001. Part II. XXVII, 848 pages. 2001.

Vol. 2089: A. Amir, G.M. Landau (Eds.), Combinatorial Pattern Matching. Proceedings, 2001. VIII, 273 pages. 2001.

Vol. 2091: J. Bigun, F. Smeraldi (Eds.), Audio- and Video-Based Biometric Person Authentication. Proceedings, 2001. XIII, 374 pages. 2001.

Vol. 2092: L. Wolf, D. Hutchison, R. Steinmetz (Eds.), Quality of Service – IWQoS 2001. Proceedings, 2001. XII, 435 pages. 2001.

Vol. 2096: J. Kittler, F. Roli (Eds.), Multiple Classifier Systems. Proceedings, 2001. XII, 456 pages. 2001.

Vol. 2097: B. Read (Ed.), Advances in Databases. Proceedings, 2001. X, 219 pages. 2001.

Vol. 2099: P. de Groote, G. Morrill, C. Retoré (Eds.), Logical Aspects of Computational Linguistics. Proceedings, 2001. VIII, 311 pages. 2001. (Subseries LNAI).